The Old Testament Story

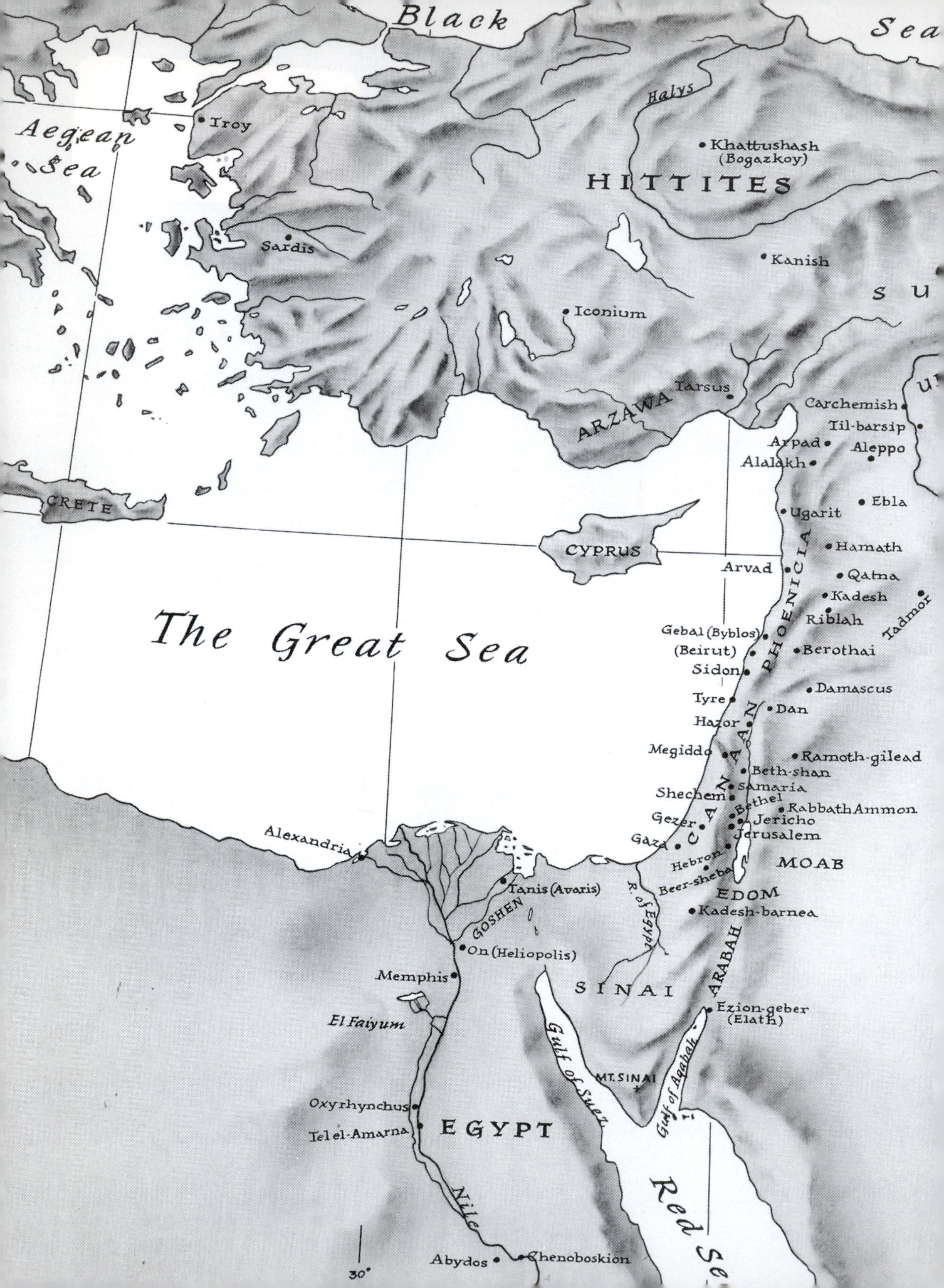

Black
Sea
Aegean
Sea
Troy
Halys
Khattushash
(Bogazkoy)
HITTITES
Sardis
Kanish
S U
Iconium
Tarsus
ARZAWA
Carchemish
Til-barsip
Arpad
Aleppo
Alalakh
CRETE
Ebla
Ugarit
CYPRUS
Hamath
Arvad
Qatna
Kadesh
Tadmor
Riblah
PHOENICIA
Gebal (Byblos)
(Beirut)
Berothai
The Great Sea
Sidon
Damascus
Tyre
Dan
Hazor
Megiddo
Ramoth-gilead
CANAAN
Beth-shan
Samaria
Shechem
Bethel
Rabbath Ammon
Gezer
Jericho
Gaza
Jerusalem
Alexandria
Hebron
MOAB
Beer-sheba
R. of Egypt
Tanis (Avaris)
EDOM
Kadesh-barnea
GOSHEN
On (Heliopolis)
Memphis
SINAI
ARABAH
Ezion-geber
(Elath)
El Faiyum
Gulf of Suez
Gulf of Aqabah
MT. SINAI
Oxyrhynchus
Tel el-Amarna
EGYPT
Nile
Red Se
Abydos
Chenoboskion
30°

THE ANCIENT NEAR EAST

Ninth Edition

The Old Testament Story

John H. Tullock
Professor Emeritus
Belmont University

Revised by

Mark McEntire
Professor of Religion
Belmont University

Prentice Hall
Boston Columbus Indianapolis New York San Francisco Upper Saddle River
Amsterdam Cape Town Dubai London Madrid Milan Munich Paris Montreal Toronto
Delhi Mexico City Sao Paulo Sydney Hong Kong Seoul Singapore Taipei Tokyo

Editorial Director: Craig Campanella
Editor in Chief: Dickson Musslewhite
Publisher: Nancy Roberts
Editorial Project Manager: Nicole Conforti
Editorial Assistant: Nart Varoqua
Director of Marketing: Brandy Dawson
Senior Marketing Manager: Laura Lee Manley
Marketing Assistant: Lisa Kirlick
Senior Managing Editor: Maureen Richardson
Project Manager: Annemarie Franklin
Operations Supervisor: Mary Fischer
Operations Specialist: Christina Amato
Cover Design Manager: Jayne Conte
Cover Art Director/Designer: Bruce Kenselaar
Image Lead, Image Asset Services: Ben Ferrini
Manager, Image Asset Services: Beth Brenzel
Cover Art: © Nimbus/Fotolia
Media Director: Brian Hyland
Digital Media Editor: Rachel Comerford
Full-Service Project Management: Kelly Ricci
Composition: Aptara®, Inc.
Printer/Binder: STP Courier
Cover Printer: STP Courier
Text Font: Minion

Credits and acknowledgments borrowed from other sources and reproduced, with permission, in this textbook appear on appropriate page within text or on page 370.

Library of Congress Cataloging-in-Publication Data

Tullock, John H.
The Old Testament Story/John H. Tullock; revised by Mark McEntire.— 9th ed.
p. cm.
Includes bibliographical references and index.
ISBN-13: 978-0-205-09783-8
ISBN-10: 0-205-09783-9
1. Bible. O.T.—History of Biblical events. 2. Bible. O.T.—History of contemporary events.
3. Bible. O.T.—Introductions. I. McEntire,
Mark Harold, 1960- II. Title.
BS1197.T78 2011
221.9′5—dc22

2010053116

10 9 8 7 6 5 4 3 2 1

Prentice Hall
is an imprint of

PEARSON

www.pearsonhighered.com

ISBN 10: 0-205-09783-9
ISBN 13: 978-0-205-09783-8

Dedication

To Helen the love of my life, faithful fan for over sixty years, whose loving support still makes telling the story a joy.

JT

To my colleagues on the faculty of the School of Religion at Belmont University

MM

CONTENTS

BIBLIOGRAPHICAL ABBREVIATIONS

AB	Anchor Bible
ABD	Anchor Bible Dictionary
ABRL	Anchor Bible Reference Library
ANE	The Ancient Near East
ANET	The Ancient Near East—An Anthology of Texts and Pictures
ARCH	Archaeology
BA	Biblical Archaeologist
BAR	Biblical Archaeology Review
BBC	Broadman Bible Commentary
BR	Bible Review
FOTL	Forms of Old Testament Literature
HER	Hermeneia
IB	Interpreter's Bible
IDB	Interpreter's Dictionary of the Bible
INT	Interpretation
ITC	International Theological Commentary
JBL	Journal of Biblical Literature
JBQ	Jewish Bible Quarterly
JBR	Journal of Bible and Religion
LAI	Library of Ancient Israel
LBC	Layman's Bible Commentary
LXX	The Septuagint (the Greek Version of the Hebrew Bible)
KJV	King James Version of the Bible
MBA	Macmillan Bible Atlas
MCB	Mercer Commentary on the Bible
MDB	Mercer Dictionary of the Bible
NCBC	New Century Bible Commentary
NEA	Near Eastern Archaeology
NIB	New Interpreter's Bible
NICOT	New International Commentary on the Old Testament
NJBC	New Jerome Bible Commentary
NOAB	New Oxford Annotated Bible
NRSV	New Revised Standard Version
OBA	Oxford Bible Atlas
OTL	The Old Testament Library
TEV	Today's English Version, or Good News for Modern Man
WBC	Word Biblical Commentary

MAPS

PREFACE

The purpose of this textbook is to introduce students to the collection of literature from ancient Israel that has, for Christian traditions, become the Old Testament. This task necessitates familiarity with the content of the literature itself, an awareness of the basic framework of the history and culture of the ancient Near East, and insight from the methods of reading ancient texts that have been developed in contemporary scholarship.

WHAT'S NEW TO THIS EDITION?

- Expanded and enhanced study aids for students
- Synthetic literary treatments of each of the prophetic scrolls
- An uninterrupted treatment of the story line of the Israelite monarchy
- Expanded discussion of the influence of African cultures on ancient Israel
- Updated discussion of the influence of Diaspora Judaism on the formation of the canon

The preface to the eighth edition of *The Old Testament Story* made reference to the massive shift that has taken place in the field of biblical studies over the last three decades. This shift has two facets that are closely connected. First, the dominance of a historical framework has given way to a more eclectic field of study in which literary approaches to the text continue to gain prominence. Second, the chorus of voices that take part in academic and ecclesial conversations about the Bible has become much more diverse in terms of gender, ethnicity, geography, and economics. Attention has been given to many of the effects of this shift in all of the new editions of this book during that period. The revisions for the ninth edition, however, necessitate the first major reorientation of material since the book's inception. There are still fifteen chapters, and the first five and last three chapters retain most of their previous structure, but chapters 6 through 12 have been significantly reorganized. The previous editions of this book told the story of the Monarchy, the Exile, and the Restoration in these middle chapters and placed all of the material related to the prophetic books within the framework of this story. In this edition, the discussion of the prophetic books has been extracted and reorganized into its own set of chapters.

I. Developing Connections and Context

Chapter 1 explains what the Old Testament is and where it came from. It also describes some of the ways that people have read these texts and how related areas of study contribute to our understanding. Chapter 2 describes the places, people, and cultures of the ancient Near East, from which the cultural context of the Israelites arose and the place that serves as the setting for the literature of the Old Testament.

II. Following the Essential Story

Chapters 3 through 9 follow the story of Israel from the primeval period through the work of Ezra and Nehemiah. The continuous story told by the books of Genesis through II Kings moves from creation to the Exile, with the development of Israelite monarchy as its high point. The content of these books, sometimes called the "Primary History," will be the focus of these chapters, with an examination of the contents of I and II Chronicles and Ezra-Nehemiah providing another biblical perspective of this story.

III. Prophetic Responses to Israel's Story

Chapters 10 through 12 treat the prophetic literature from a literary-canonical perspective. This reorganization reflects the changes in the ways that this material is most commonly studied today, a shift that has been taking place for more than twenty years and that has now reached a level of accomplishment that needs to be reflected in an introductory textbook. This means that those following the plan of the book will cover the entire narrative of the people of Israel as presented in the Old Testament before examining the final form of the prophetic literature, beginning with the book of Isaiah, as a response to that entire story.

IV. Responses in Stories and Poems

Chapters 13 through 15 examine the parts of the Old Testament that do not fit precisely into one chronological place in Israel's story. Instead, they are artistic responses to the entirety of that story, which often struggle with how to be a faithful Israelite in many different contexts. The focus of Psalms is worship, while Proverbs is concerned with ordinary issues of daily life, and Job and Ecclesiastes struggle with the pain and futility that often result from that activity. Books like Ruth, Jonah, and Esther tell stories of foreigners in Israel and Israelites living in foreign places, as the Old Testament moves away from its geographical center in Jerusalem. There has been a growing recognition that "exile and return" characterized the experience of only a minority of Israelites during the sixth and fifth centuries. Numerically, far more Israelites either stayed in Judah or fled to Egypt than were taken into captivity in Babylon. Thus, we have tried to add emphasis on those other communities and their experience.

Two important milestones should be identified as the ninth edition of *The Old Testament Story* moves toward publication. First, 2011 will mark thirty years of the publication of this textbook. For all of us involved in the project through the years, it is most gratifying that this book still finds a place within the conversation about the Bible and its role in our lives. Second, on a grander scale, this year is the 400th anniversary of the publication of the King James Version of the Bible. The English translation of the Bible used as the primary basis for this textbook is the New Revised Standard Version, a direct descendent in the family of translations initiated by the King James Version. Despite its obvious limitations as a translated text of the Bible, the King James Version is a great example of the twin processes of advancing biblical scholarship at its cutting edge and using the results of that scholarship to make the biblical literature more accessible to readers of all levels of experience. To the readers of this ninth edition of *The Old Testament Story*, welcome to the conversation.

ACKNOWLEDGMENTS

Nine editions and thirty years of use reflect a stunning record of achievement for this textbook. This has only been possible because of the work and support of many people. I will always be grateful to John Tullock and his family for the opportunity they have given me to continue this project. The contributions of Beth Tullock Sizemore and David Tullock have been a great benefit to this edition.

On behalf of John Tullock and myself, I want to thank the staff at Prentice Hall whose dedication and hard work keep this project alive and growing. We are particularly grateful to Nicole Conforti for her careful attention to the vast array of tasks that are involved in creating a new edition. We also wish to thank our colleagues past and present in the School of Religion at Belmont University, where the combined tenures of John and myself now approach fifty years. These great teachers and companions have been and are a constant source of inspiration and life. We also gratefully acknowledge the reviewers of this edition: John Harris, East Texas Baptist University; Jeff Tillman, Wayland Baptist University; Thomas Steele, LaGrange College; and Steven Godby, Broward College–South Campus.

Portions of the Old Testament are quoted many times in this book. In a minority of cases, they are acknowledged as my own translation, from the *King James Version*, or from *The Bible in Today's English Version* (© 1966, 1971, 1976). In all other cases, biblical quotations are taken from *The New Revised Standard Version* (© 1989, by the division of Christian Education of the National Council of Churches in the United States and are used by permission. All rights are reserved).

CHAPTER 1

The Book and Those Who Study It

Timeline

1200 B.C.E.	First mention of Israel on the Merneptah Stele in Egypt
500 B.C.E.	Approximate date for the completion of the final form of the Torah
200 B.C.E.	Approximate date for the beginning of translation of the Hebrew scriptures into Greek
100 C.E.	Approximate date for the closing of the Hebrew canon
400 C.E.	Approximate date of the copying of the Vatican and Alexandrian Codices of the Septuagint
1000 C.E.	Copying of the Leningrad Codex
1450 C.E.	Invention of the printing press by Gutenburg and the production of the first printed Bible
1535 C.E.	First complete English translation of the Bible by Coverdale
1611 C.E.	Completion of the King James Version of the Bible

Chapter Outline

I. The Old Testament: What Is It?
II. How It Began
III. How It Developed
IV. The Work of Scholars
V. Archaeology as a Tool for Understanding
VI. Why Study the Old Testament?

CHAPTER OVERVIEW

This chapter serves as an introduction to the academic study of the Old Testament. The first task is to define *Old Testament,* a task that becomes more difficult when we realize that different religious communities understand and use this collection of literature in different ways. The next step is to describe the process by which the Old Testament came into being, a task that can only be hypothetical at many points because of a lack of evidence. The remainder of the chapter describes how scholars of various types approach the Old Testament, by examining different methods of reading, and how the historical study, including archaeology, is applied to the understanding of the text.

THE OLD TESTAMENT: WHAT IS IT?

Definition

The Old Testament is a set of texts that originated among the people who, at differing times in their history, have been called Hebrews, Israelites, and Jews, and which became their sacred scriptures. The Old Testament is actually a library of books, produced over a period of more than a thousand years (1200–200 B.C.E.).[1] This was the Bible that was known to Jesus, the Apostles, and members of the early Christian church—especially in the period before the fall of Jerusalem to the Romans in 70 C.E., when the church was still viewed as another Jewish sect. After 70 C.E., the collection of Christian writings (which began with some of Paul's letters and the earliest of the Gospels) began to be viewed as sacred. And thus having the status of scripture, Christians began to refer to the Hebrew Bible as the Old Covenant or the Old Testament and their sacred writings as the New Covenant or the New Testament. They took the term *covenant* from the prophet Jeremiah (Jer. 31:31–34).

"Tell me a story" is the frequent plea of a child. It is through stories that we transmit to our children our values, our family traditions, and much of our view of life. So it has always been with humankind, and so it was with ancient Israel. Its stories took many forms: the accounts of the creation of the universe and of people, its legal system, the oracles of its prophets, the songs of its singers, and the wisdom of its sages. All these are part of the Old Testament story.

The Literary Forms That Carry the Story[2]

NARRATIVE. In our culture, we normally expect narrative to be the means of communicating a story. Thus, we are not surprised that much of the Old Testament is made up of narrative material. Readers soon discover, however, that stories that come from a very different time and place follow very different conventions. One of the most striking examples is the lack of descriptive language in these stories. The most important human character in the Old Testament is Moses. He dominates four large books, from Exodus to Deuteronomy, yet there is not a word about his physical appearance. Readers are not told whether he is tall or short, large or small, or has blue eyes or brown. The stories of the Old Testament have a density and economy about them that makes them significantly different from most contemporary written stories. The story of Cain and Abel, in Genesis 4:1–16, is one of the most powerful and influential stories in all of Western culture, yet it is slightly less than 200 words long in Hebrew and was translated to slightly less than 400 English words in the King James Version of the Bible. John Steinbeck's classic novel, *East of Eden,* is in many ways a modern retelling of the Cain and Abel story, and in its most commonly published form is nearly 700 pages long.

The narratives in the Bible often make use of, or are supplemented by, other literary forms such as laws, songs, genealogies, and lists. Yet these forms are woven into the narrative in such a way that they become a vital part of it. Narrative is the principal literary vehicle from Genesis through 2 Kings, in major portions of the prophetic books, including Isaiah, Jeremiah, Ezekiel,

Jonah, and Haggai, and in the less familiar books of the Old Testament, such as 1 and 2 Chronicles, Ezra-Nehemiah, Esther, Daniel, and Ruth.

What is unusual about all this is that narrative was not a common literary device in other surviving literature from the ancient Near East. Outside of legal codes, most of what is known about its gods, goddesses, legendary heroes, and kings is told in poetry. Poetry's primary function is to impart a sense of emotion and praise for its subject, while narrative serves to give the stories a sense of time and place, to flesh out their characters, and to impart a sense of the flow of life to what is being told.

There are at least two stories in the Old Testament that are told twice, once in prose narrative and once in poetry. The first is the crossing of the sea by the Israelites as they were pursued through the wilderness by Pharaoh's army, after their escape from slavery in Egypt. Exodus 14 tells the story in prose, then the Israelites, led by Moses, sing the "Song of the Sea" in Exodus 15, which tells the story again in a different way. The powerful poetry of Judges 5 conveys the sense of celebration for the LORD's delivery of Israel by the hand of Deborah from a powerful enemy. This "Song of Deborah" is preceded by a prose account of the same story in Judges 4.

LEGAL MATERIALS. The Old Testament contains numerous sets of laws, which have been placed into the narrative of the exodus from Egypt and the journey through the wilderness. Closer examination of these laws later will reveal that they seem to come from different times and places, but their placement within a story provides a powerful and dynamic way of preserving and presenting legal material.

POETRY. One would naturally expect Psalms and the Song of Songs to be poetry. What might come as a surprise to those who have not used modern translations of the Bible is that large portions of the books of the prophets are also in poetic form. The line between poetry and prose is not always clear. They are perhaps better understood as two ends of a continuum rather than two distinct categories. The first chapter of the Bible, Genesis 1, is typically understood as prose, and is printed that way, but careful reading of this text reveals that it has many of the qualities of poetry.

WISDOM LITERATURE. Although wisdom literature—Proverbs, Job, Ecclesiastes—is almost entirely in poetic form, it is a special category because of its subject matter. It discusses matters of everyday life in a way that is not closely connected to specific religious traditions and ponders difficult, philosophical questions about suffering and the meaning of existence. In structure, it ranges from extended wisdom poems to one-line proverbs. Except for Chapters 1 through 2 and 42:7–16, Job is an extended poetic drama in the form of a dialogue between Job and his friends, followed by two speeches by God. The book of Ecclesiastes is a mixture of prose and poetry.

The Crucial Event

As it stands now, the Old Testament starts at the beginning of all things—the Creation—but this order is probably not how the story of Israel was first told. Throughout the Old Testament, the one theme that continually appears is the Exodus. This was the supreme event in Israelite history. Israel became a people through this event and those that followed. Thus, it is commemorated in song, in story (Exodus to Deuteronomy), and in numerous references in Psalms (such as 66:6; 68:7–18; 78:11–55; 114; 135:8–12; and 136:10–22), as well as in other places in the Bible. A classic summary of the Exodus story is found in Deuteronomy 26:5–9:

> You shall make this response before the LORD your God: "A wandering Aramean was my ancestor; he went down into Egypt and lived there as an alien, few in number, and there he became a great nation, mighty and populous. When the Egyptians treated us harshly and afflicted us, by imposing hard labor on us, we cried to the LORD, the God

> of our ancestors; the LORD heard our voice and saw our affliction, our toil, and our oppression. The LORD brought us out of Egypt with a mighty hand and an outstretched arm, with a terrifying display of power, and with signs and wonders; and he brought us into this place and gave us this land, a land flowing with milk and honey."

The Exodus event made Israel aware of itself as a people with common experiences that united them. Just as a baby first notices its fingers and toes, leading to the awareness of itself as a person, so Israel became aware of itself as a people. When the "Who am I?" question is answered, there inevitably follows the question, "Where did I come from?" The "Aramean" in Deuteronomy 26:5 is Jacob, whom all Israelites came to understand as their ancestor.

When people begin to ask these kinds of questions, they begin to look at their history. So Israel, in times of literary activity, had historians who gathered together the memories and traditions of the people and began to weave them into a story. In this story, they not only explained their own origins in the Exodus, but also carried that explanation back through the patriarchs to the origin of the human race and even to the universe itself. As the nation grew, the history was expanded and revised, either in written or oral form. Then, when the tragedy of the Babylonian Exile struck and it looked as though not only historical materials, but also the words of the prophets, the wisdom materials, and the songs of the people might be lost, a concerted effort was made to gather together and preserve the literary heritage.

HOW IT BEGAN

How did the Old Testament come to be written? Did someone just suddenly decide, "I'm going to write the Old Testament"? Or was it a more complicated process?

To answer this question with certainty is impossible. A New Testament writer, for whom the Old Testament was the Bible, spoke of how "Holy men of old wrote as they were moved by the Spirit of God" (2 Pet. 1:21). Yet even that statement, setting forth the conviction that God was the initiator of the process that led to the writing, also suggests that the development of the Old Testament was an historical process. The following is a suggested scheme of how the Old Testament may have been developed.

First the Event

Nothing happens without a cause; something must trigger it. The Old Testament grew out of the events and circumstances of the life of the people of Israel. Although the Exodus and related events served as the catalyst for the development of the sacred literature of the Israelites, many events before and after that crucial event contributed to the material resources from which the Old Testament was constructed.

Then the Story—the First Interpretation

First, things happened. The people to whom things happened told others about their experiences. Just as every family has a fund of stories about various relatives, much of the Old Testament is composed of stories that came from the oral tradition of the people who were to be known as Israel. Not all the stories, however, were based on actual events. Some stories, known as **etiologies,** for example, were created to answer "why" questions. Other stories, like Jotham's fable about the trees (Judg. 9:7–15), or Samson's riddle (Judg. 14:14), were told to make a point. Telling the stories over the centuries also had its effects on their nature and their subsequent interpretation. The study of how literary texts are interpreted is called **hermeneutics.**

Then the Reinterpretation

When things happen to us, we interpret them in the light of existing circumstances. Later, however, as we look back, we may view a particular event in an entirely different way than we did when it happened. Time and circumstances may have given us a different insight into its significance for us. For instance, an event once seen as a disaster may later be looked on as something very positive and meaningful for us.

Then the History—the Continuing Interpretation

The Old Testament grew from such hindsight. At some point in the life of Israel as a people, someone, or a number of someones, looked back at the past and concluded that God had been at work in the lives of the people—calling their ancestors out of paganism, making himself known to them, leading them from the Tigris and Euphrates River valleys to Palestine and eventually into Egypt and bondage. But even that bondage, a disaster by most normal standards, was God's way of preserving the Israelites as a people. God raised up a leader, Moses, and prepared him, as the adopted son of the Egyptian princess and as a Midianite shepherd, for the difficult job of leading a band of slaves and a mixed multitude of others into the Sinai desert, there to weld this motley group into a people united in covenant to God.

Furthermore, God led them to a land—a land that had been promised to their ancestors, Abraham, Isaac, and Jacob. After a long and difficult period, the land became theirs. But their troubles were not over. After many years of struggle to achieve some kind of national unity, they finally settled on a monarchy as the kind of government they would have. After a sputtering start under Saul, the storytellers describe a remarkable growth during David's time, when the nation reached its greatest territorial limits, enabling it to withstand any challenge. Solomon gained the fruits of his father's success, enjoying a time of peace and great economic prosperity. Yet, he sowed seeds of discontent that would come to full flower under his son Rehoboam, whose unwise policies resulted in the kingdom's splitting into two separate states.

For two centuries, the two parts of the once proud kingdom of David limped along—sometimes as enemies, sometimes as allies. At times, in their periods of friendship, they combined forces to bring a measure of prosperity to their people. But for most of the time, they were like pawns, toyed with by the great powers of the time—Egypt and Assyria. Finally, in 721 B.C.E., Israel, the Northern Kingdom, was blotted out of existence by the Assyrian giant who destroyed its cities and deported all that was left of its upper classes, replacing them with foreigners who were to intermarry with the poor people left in the land, producing the Samaritans.

Judah, the Southern Kingdom, struggled on for just over a century, but it too fell, this time to Babylonia, the nation that had succeeded Assyria as the terror of the Near East.

As had been the case with Israel, most of the members of Judah's surviving leadership were deported, but different factors were at work that allowed the people to keep their identity. The prophets had warned that such an occurrence was likely if Judah persisted in its wrongdoing. Seemingly, the stability of the government in the south gave the people a greater sense of unity, aiding them in holding together in the time of national disaster. Then, too, the Babylonians seem to have contributed to the situation by settling the people in communities in which they could follow the advice of the prophet Jeremiah and live as normal a life as possible (Jer. 29).

In response to the trauma of the Exile and the threat of annihilation, Jewish scholars began in earnest to collect and shape the literature of the people. Although history writing may have begun earlier, the Exile gave the work a new sense of urgency. Along with the writing of history, poetry was collected, the law was codified, and the words of the great prophets were arranged and preserved. Much of the Old Testament as we now know it took shape during the Exile and immediately afterward.

With the people now convinced of the importance of the preservation of their traditions, the period following the Exile, while not a time of glory, was a time of collection, preservation, and interpretation that reached its climax in the final canonization of the Old Testament early in the Christian era.

HOW IT DEVELOPED

The Process

Did the process of forming the literature of the Old Testament begin during the Exile? The answer most certainly is "No." The development of the Old Testament may be compared to a river and its tributaries. A river does not begin full sized. Rather, it is a combination of dozens of smaller streams that have joined together to form the river. So it was with the Old Testament. Some will be quick to point out that it began with God. Even so, God worked through human agents, and it is the work of these human agents that is being discussed. The common belief that God directly dictated the words of the Bible is called **plenary verbal inspiration.** This view is not assumed here.

The first tiny streams were the oral traditions: the poems of victory, the stories of the ancestors, and the memories of great events that were treasured, gathered, and passed on for many generations. These oral treasures were the means by which families preserved their values and their sense of who they were. Not only did they remember heroes, they remembered villains as well. Both played roles in events the community deemed important. Thus, the people preserved the stories—from exalted stories, such as that of the call of the patriarch Abraham from the paganism of Ur of the Chaldees, to less than exalted stories, such as the account of how Jacob outwitted both his brother Esau and his father, Isaac, to secure the birthright and the blessing. The most frequently told story of all, however, was that of God's marvelous delivery of their ancestors during the flight from Egypt. The storyteller was the teacher and the story was the medium through which he taught.

At shrines in which clans (extended families) gathered for worship, the stories were combined into larger units to form cycles of tradition, each with its own distinctive point of view. Finally, someone conceived the idea, through what religious people call *inspiration*, that the stories of God's dealings with the people needed to be written down or put into a complete story so that they could be preserved.

The Written Story

Exactly when the smaller streams of tradition were combined to form a connected story is a matter of dispute. Scholars of a more conservative bent argue for a date as early as the time of Moses. Others see the smaller streams of tradition continuing either in an oral or a written form until the time of David and Solomon. They say it was during this period that the first attempts were made to write a history of Israel. The process continued until the post-Exilic period and embraces not only the Pentateuch (Genesis through Deuteronomy), or Torah, but also all the major historical books: Joshua through 2 Kings, as well as 1,2 Chronicles, Ezra, and Nehemiah.

According to this view, the stream of tradition that began with the Exodus stories was chosen as the mainstream. To it were added the stories of the *ancestors* (people like Abraham, Sarah, Isaac, Rebekah, Jacob, Leah, and Rachel) and the stories of the Creation. This edition of the history of Israel (characterized by referring to God by the personal name YHWH and designated by scholars by the letter J) was largely composed of materials from the southern part of Israel. It flowed on for a hundred years or so, until it was joined by another stream of materials from the northern part of the country identified by the use of a more general or "family" name for God—*Elohim* (E). These materials started with stories about Abraham, but they became so mingled with the mainstream that it is difficult to determine just how much each contributed to the total volume.

The next tributary was of such volume and force that it became dominant in the historical materials. During the reign of Josiah, king of Judah (640–609 B.C.E.), the *book of the law* was found in the temple when repairs were being made (2 Kings 22:8). Scholars conclude, on the basis of the religious reforms that followed and that seem to be based on the contents of the book of the law, that this book was essentially the book of Deuteronomy. Some argue that Deuteronomy was written less than one hundred years before its discovery. Yet, it is usually agreed that a major part of the materials it contains is from an earlier time.

Like a river whose whole character is changed by the joining of a major tributary, so the character of the presentation of the history of Israel is changed by the reform growing out of the discovery of the Deuteronomic materials (D). Beginning particularly with the book of Judges, Israel's history is interpreted in a distinct fashion. It is viewed as following a cycle: Israel *sins, judgment* comes through the oppression of an enemy, Israel *repents,* God raises up a leader to *deliver* the people from their enemies. To see a clear example of this, read Judges 3:7–11. Less obvious examples are found in the history of the monarchy (1,2 Sam.; 1,2 Kings).

The exile in Babylon (586–538 B.C.E.) and the years following saw a floodtide of materials enter the stream. Because the danger of the extinction of the people brought a new reverence for the sacred traditions and a zeal for preserving the sacred literature, the people established a unifying symbol. *Torah*—now expanded to mean not only the Pentateuch, but also the history and sayings of the great prophets, the wisdom of the sages, and the sacred songs of the people—gave them a sense of unity and purpose that was to enable them to survive many centuries of adversity.

Just as today, when the dangers of losing natural beauty have led to government action to preserve some streams as scenic rivers, so the Jews moved to preserve their most meaningful literature by designating it as sacred. The final contributors to this literary river were the priests of the Exilic and post-Exilic periods. They gave the material its final form (P) through an editorial process and through collecting those books known as the Writings, which include the last edition of the history as found in 1,2 Chronicles, plus Ezra and Nehemiah. All that remained was the climax of the process of canonization sometime prior to 100 C.E. So, as the river finally reaches the ocean, the Hebrew Bible became the possession of the world through the Jewish community and its major offspring, Christianity.

The Final Product: The Canon[3]

The word ***canon*** originally referred to a reed used for measuring, such as a yardstick. When applied to literature, it has come to mean a body of writing that, for religious folk, is held to be sacred because *it contains God's message to the faithful.* The process by which these books achieved that status is thus called *canonization.* For Jews and Christians alike, then, the Old Testament, or the Hebrew Bible, is sacred literature.

THE HEBREW CANON. Although the process of canonization took place over a long period of time, the following approximations are commonly used:

1. 400 B.C.E. The *Torah* (Genesis through Deuteronomy), or Law, achieved sacred status.
2. 200 B.C.E. The *Nebi'im,* or Prophets, became canonical. There was a twofold division of the Prophets:
   a. The Former Prophets—the books of Joshua, Judges, 1,2 Samuel, and 1,2 Kings.
   b. The Latter Prophets—Isaiah, Jeremiah, Ezekiel, and the Twelve, generally known to Christians as the Minor Prophets.

3. 100 C.E. Not later than this date, the *Kethubim*, or Writings, had achieved canonical status. These include Psalms, Job, Proverbs, Ecclesiastes, the Song of Songs, Lamentations, 1,2 Chronicles, Ezra, Nehemiah, Ruth, Esther, and Daniel.

The question might legitimately be asked, "Why were these books included and not others?" That there were others is abundantly clear. The Dead Sea Scrolls alone had manuscripts and fragments of nearly a thousand religious writings, while other Jewish sects developed their own sacred books. Basically, two tests determined what books would be in the Old Testament canon. These primarily were the tests of time and usage. The literature, oral and written, which continued to speak to the believing community over the years, was judged to have the breath of Divine about it. Admittedly, the survival of the community that used the literature also had to be a factor in the development of the canon.

A common assumption is that the rabbis of Jamnia, an academy established by Johanan ben Zakkai after the fall of Jerusalem in 70 C.E., declared the canon closed around 100 C.E. This assumption is increasingly challenged today because it drastically oversimplifies the issue. By that time the vast majority of Hebrew canon had been determined. At most there may have been some remaining disagreement about a few books. The most disputed were probably Song of Songs, Esther, and Ecclesiastes. All three of these books are part of the collection known as the *Megilloth* (Festival Scrolls), which are traditionally read as part of synagogue services on the days of Jewish festivals. The regular use of these books on festival days was likely a major factor in favor of their canonization. Books that just missed the canon likely did so because of the language in which they were written. The Wisdom of Solomon and II Maccabees were likely written originally in Greek. Sirach and I Maccabees were probably first written in Hebrew, but by the first century C.E. the Greek translations of these books had become dominant and the Hebrew versions may have disappeared. Obviously, books that existed only in the Greek language could not be included in the Hebrew canon.

THE GREEK CANON (Septuagint). The Greek translation of the Hebrew Bible, used by the Jewish community of Alexandria in Egypt, differed from the Hebrew canon as to what books should be included in the *Kethubim.* It contained some fifteen extra books or additions to books in the Hebrew canon: 1,2 Esdras; Tobit; Judith; the additions to the Book of Esther; the Wisdom of Solomon; Ecclesiasticus, or the Wisdom of Jesus Son of Sirach; Baruch; the Letter of Jeremiah; the additions to the book of Daniel; the Prayer of Manasseh; and 1,2 Maccabees. Roman Catholic Christians include these within their canon. Various groups of Orthodox Christians accept these and a few additional writings, such as 3,4 Maccabees and Psalm 151, as part of their canon. Some readers within these traditions attempt to chart a middle course between these ways of conceiving the canon by referring to these writings, which are in some canons but not others, as **deuterocanonical**.

The **Septuagint** influenced the great fourth-century scholar Jerome in preparing his Vulgate translation, which became the standard Latin version of the Bible for many centuries. Thus, both Roman Catholic and Eastern Orthodox Bibles include the Apocrypha in their canon. Although other Christians do not consider the books of the Apocrypha canonical, most modern translations include them, because they are studied for their contribution to understanding the history of the period in which they developed.

THE WORK OF SCHOLARS

How do we know that the Old Testament developed in this or any other way? That it exists is ample evidence that it developed somewhere, somehow, and at some time. Because there are no time machines to transport us back through the ages to watch the Bible being written,

Canon List

Hebrew Canon	**Greek Canon/Catholic Old Testament**	**Protestant Old Testament**
24 Books	46 Books	39 Books
Law	Genesis	Genesis
Genesis	Exodus	Exodus
Exodus	Leviticus	Leviticus
Leviticus	Numbers	Numbers
Numbers	Deuteronomy	Deuteronomy
Deuteronomy	Joshua	Joshua
	Judges	Judges
Former Prophets	Ruth	Ruth
Joshua	I Samuel*	I Samuel
Judges	II Samuel	II Samuel
Samuel	I Kings	I Kings
Kings	II Kings	II Kings
	I Chronicles	I Chronicles
Latter Prophets	II Chronicles	II Chronicles
Isaiah	Ezra	Ezra
Jeremiah	Nehemiah	Nehemiah
Ezekiel	Tobit	Esther
The Twelve	Judith	Job
	Esther (plus Greek additions)	Psalms
Writings	I Maccabees	Proverbs
Psalms	II Maccabees	Ecclesiastes
Job	Job	Song of Songs
Proverbs	Psalms	Isaiah
Ruth	Proverbs	Jeremiah
Song of Songs	Ecclesiastes	Lamentations
Ecclesiastes	Song of Songs	Ezekiel
Lamentations	Wisdom of Solomon	Daniel
Esther	Sirach	Hosea
Daniel	Isaiah	Joel
Ezra-Nehemiah	Jeremiah	Amos
Chronicles	Lamentations	Obadiah
	Baruch	Jonah
	Ezekiel	Micah
	Daniel (plus Greek additions)	Nahum
	Hosea	Habakkuk
	Joel	Zephaniah
	Amos	Haggai
	Obadiah	Zechariah
	Jonah	Malachi
	Micah	
	Nahum	
	Habakkuk	
	Zephaniah	
	Haggai	
	Zechariah	
	Malachi	

*The Greek tradition actually refers to the books of I and II Samuel and I and II Kings as I, II, III, and IV Kingdoms.

we must depend upon those who can discover and interpret clues about its beginnings and growth.

But the following questions arise: "Why go to all that trouble?" "Why not just accept it as it is?" Those who ask such questions probably would agree that one needs to understand the Old Testament—or the Bible as a whole, for that matter—as much as possible. Just as we can understand others better if we understand their background, so we can understand the Bible better if we understand its background. If we study the results of their efforts, all types of biblical scholars can contribute to our understanding of the Bible. These include textual specialists or theologians, form critics or archaeologists, literary historians or redaction critics, those who look at particular parts, or those who try to look at the message of the Bible as a whole. We need, then, to describe briefly some (but not all) of the kinds of scholarship that are used to aid us in understanding and interpreting the Bible.

Textual Criticism

First are those scholars whose concern is the biblical text itself. Sometimes called *lower criticism*, the concerns of **textual criticism** are of basic importance to all who study the Bible seriously for any reason, because no one possesses a single original copy of any book of the Bible, either from the Old or the New Testament. The oldest complete copy of any Old Testament book is a manuscript of the book of Isaiah, found among the Dead Sea Scrolls, which dates to about the time of Christ. This means that the original copy of the book of Isaiah was written several hundred years before the Dead Sea Scroll Isaiah was copied. The Dead Sea Scrolls, however, contain less than half of the contents of our Old Testament. The oldest complete copy of the TANAK in Hebrew is a manuscript commonly called the Leningrad **Codex**, which was written around 1000 C.E. Modern versions of the Old Testament are essentially translations of this manuscript. There are two virtually complete manuscripts of the Septuagint, the Greek translation of the Hebrew Bible, that were written in the fourth or fifth century. Modern translators also consult these manuscripts when doing their work.

In addition to the ancient Greek translation in the Septuagint, the **TANAK** was translated into other ancient languages, such as Aramaic and Syriac. Aramaic translations of individual books and collections of books are called *Targums.* No copies of these translations written earlier than the Middle Ages exist. The most significant Syriac translation is called the *Peshitta*, but, again, the oldest existing copies are centuries removed from the actual translation process. Because these Aramaic and Syriac translations contain significant amounts of elaboration and are not represented by reliable early manuscripts, they play a minor role in modern Bible translation. They are most significant as indicators of how early faith communities struggled to understand and use the Bible.

Although the lack of availability of ancient manuscripts of the Bible is a problem, there are more copies of biblical manuscripts than of any other kind of ancient manuscript. There is far more manuscript evidence for the prophets of Israel than there is for Plato and Aristotle. That such a profusion of manuscripts exists creates something of a problem, however, in that they differ in places. Investigating such differences requires the talents of the textual scholar. Through a vast knowledge of the ancient languages, the textual specialist is able to compare the various manuscripts and thus better estimate what the original copies said. It should be pointed out that most of the variations in the text involve only about 5 percent of the total material.

Literary and Historical Studies

In the second place, there are scholars who study the text from the literary and historical standpoint. Although there is a great degree of unanimity about the aims of textual criticism, there is far less agreement about the result or, in some cases, even the need for literary or higher criticism.

Aaron Ben Moses Ben Asher

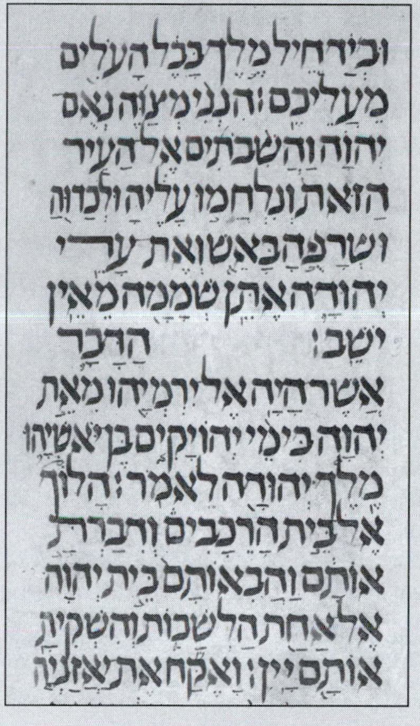

Countless persons over many centuries are responsible for the dedicated and painstaking work that has made it possible for us to have the Old Testament available today. Perhaps nobody is a better representative of these persons than Aaron Ben Moses Ben Asher. Aaron was a member of a famous family of scribes and lived during the tenth century of the Common Era. The members of this family were the most prominent members of a large group of scribes called the *Masoretes,* whose work spans much of the Middle Ages. Before the work of the Masoretes, there was no standard way to write copies of the Hebrew canon with the necessary markings of vowels, accents, and punctuation required for understanding it. Aaron Ben Moses Ben Asher labored all of his life to produce a standardized system for making copies of the text, all of which were handwritten because the printing press would not be invented for another 500 years.

Two codices produced by the Ben Asher family, the Aleppo Codex and the Leningrad Codex, are our best representatives of the Hebrew text that lies behind our Old Testament. The Leningrad Codex is our oldest complete copy of the Hebrew scriptures and modern versions of the Old Testament are, more than anything else, translations of this book. This codex is believed to be a copy of another codex that was written by Aaron Ben Moses Ben Asher himself. We know little else about the life of this man, but if you can find a copy of a Hebrew Bible, imagine sitting at a rough desk by candlelight, with a pen and an ink bottle, making copies of this text for most of your life. On the other hand, we do know that Aaron Ben Moses Ben Asher lived in Teberias, on the beautiful western shore of Lake Genesaret, also known as the Sea of Galilee, so he and his family had a pleasant setting in which to do their important work.

Literary and historical studies are directed toward three basic concerns: source (was there an author or authors?), form (in what form or style was the composition written or spoken?), and history (how did the present book develop?).

The first concern can be illustrated by the question "Who wrote the Pentateuch?" Perhaps no other question in biblical studies has evoked a wider variety of responses than this one.

MOSAIC AUTHORSHIP OF THE PENTATEUCH. Many readers are aware of the idea that Moses wrote the **Pentateuch,** the first five books of the Bible, but they may be unaware of the source of this assumption. A few texts in the Pentateuch (e.g., Exodus 17:14 and Deuteronomy 31:9) refer to Moses writing something, but it is unclear what he was writing. At some point in Israelite tradition, it became common to refer to the books of Genesis through Deuteronomy as "the books of Moses." It is unclear what this phrase originally meant. It could have been an acknowledgment that Moses is the main character throughout most of the Pentateuch. It also became common practice in Israelite tradition to associate written collections with famous figures of the past, for example, the book of Psalms with David, or the Wisdom Literature with Solomon. Mosaic authorship of the

A Text-Critical Problem

I Samuel 13:1 presents a problem for anyone studying the Bible, because manuscripts differ in what they say at this point in the text.

The Standard Hebrew (Masoretic) text says:

> Saul was ________ years old when he began to reign, and he reigned over Israel for two years.

Some Greek (Septuagint) manuscripts omit 13:1 entirely, while others say:

> Saul was thirty years old when he began to reign, and he reigned over Israel two years.

Some Syriac manuscripts say:

> Saul was twenty-one years old when he began to reign, and he reigned over Israel.

This manuscript situation raises numerous difficult questions. Why does the Hebrew text not give Saul's age at the beginning of his reign, and should English translations supply one of the numbers from the other ancient versions? Could all of Saul's reign, as presented in I Samuel, really have taken place in only two years, or has part of the number been omitted? In the Christian Bible, this issue is complicated by the report in Acts 13:21 that Saul reigned for forty years. How should a contemporary version of the Bible present the problems associated with this number?

Pentateuch thus turns out to be a tradition of unknown origin. Because of this, it is difficult to construct rational arguments for or against this idea. The simple observation that this material does not look like something that a single person wrote has led to other questions and proposals about who may have written it and, more importantly, how and why it may have been written.[4]

THE DOCUMENTARY HYPOTHESIS. The Mosaic authorship of the Pentateuch began to be questioned as early as the twelfth century by certain Jewish rabbis. Then, in the 1700s, two individuals, H. B. Witter, a German pastor (d. 1711), and Jean Astruc, a French physician (d. 1753), noticed the alternation of the divine names *Elohim* in Genesis 1 and YHWH *Elohim* in Genesis 2. Others then noticed, among other things, third-person references to Moses; repetitions (Gen. 12, 20, 26; Exod. 20, 24; Deut. 5); and differing names for the same place or person (Mount Sinai and Mount Horeb; Jethro and Reuel).

The resulting process of **source criticism** led to the classical expression of the Documentary, or JEDP Hypothesis, in the late nineteenth century by Julius Wellhausen, a German biblical scholar. It proposed that Israel's history was written in four stages:

- J. A history using YHWH as the principal name for God, written in the time of Solomon or shortly thereafter.
- E. A history using *Elohim* as the principal name for God, written around 750 B.C.E.
- D. A history influenced by the finding of the Book of Deuteronomy during the reign of Josiah (621 B.C.E.). This history is generally dated around 550 B.C.E.
- P. A history written by the priests around 450 B.C.E., adding legal materials related to worship and geneological lists.

In this scheme, P typically represents a writer, or writers, with priestly concerns, who produced their own material and compiled other materials to mold the books of the Pentateuch into something close to their present form. Although this hypothesis possessed tremendous explanatory power, it suffers from a number of weaknesses. Two of these are its exaggerated sense of certainty about a historical framework based on little evidence and its reliance on a developmental view of Israelite religion. In these and other aspects, the Documentary Hypothesis was very much a child of its time in the second half of the nineteenth century and the first half of the twentieth century.

MODIFICATIONS OF WELLHAUSEN'S VIEWS. Another German scholar introduced the first important modification of Wellhausen's views. Instead of emphasizing completed documents, Hermann Gunkel shifted the emphasis to the building blocks of those documents—the oral stories, poems, legal materials, wisdom sayings—that the author(s) used to put the final product together. This is called *form criticism*[5]—the study of the smaller units that make up the larger text. Form critics look for the distinctive types of speech patterns that characterize a certain kind of life situation. For example, a person who has had a lifetime involvement in sports, either as a fan or as a participant, is likely to use figures of speech from sports to describe other aspects of life. So, one might say after failing to achieve a goal, "I struck out!"

Israel's prophets, familiar with the legal activity they saw taking place at the city gate, were fond of using legal language to describe God's judgment of the people. As an illustration of this, read Micah 6:1–8, in which is found an indictment (6:1–2); the case presented against the defendant (6:3–5); the defense (6:6–7); and the verdict (6:8).

A further challenge to Wellhausen came from a group of Scandinavian scholars led by Ivan Engnell. Coming from a culture in which oral literature was a part of the heritage, Engnell and his group challenged Wellhausen on two points: (1) the age of the materials and (2) the nature of the "documents." Wellhausen proposed that each of the "histories" (J, E, D, or P) reflected the time in which it was written, whereas Engnell and his colleagues argued that the basic materials from which J, E, D, and P were developed were much older than the documents themselves, having been a part of the oral tradition of the Israelite people (see the Song of Deborah and Judges 5 as examples). Even the so-called documents could have been passed down in oral form before being recorded in written form. This, in turn, has led to an area of study that attempts to trace the history of these traditions.

REDACTION CRITICISM. Redaction criticism studies how various sources were combined into larger units. Three kinds of sources were used: written, oral, and what might be called *editorial additions.* The redactor was a theologian with a message shaped by the units of material that were selected and by the narrative transitions that were added. An example of this would be the story of David's life (1 Sam. 16 to 1 Kings 2:12 and 1 Chr. 10:1–29:30). Although the Chronicler's history repeats much of the material found in 1 Samuel and 1 Kings, there are important omissions—for example, David's affair with Bathsheba. By the Chronicler's time (the post-Exilic period), David was seen as the ideal king, so much so that the Jews envisioned a new day when a new David, the Messiah, would come to deliver Israel from its enemies. So, the redactor, or editor, saw no good purpose in bringing up David's indiscretion with Bathsheba.

More Recent Trends in Old Testament Studies

A marked shift in emphasis has occurred in Old Testament studies in recent years. There has been a movement away from examining the pieces that make up the literature to examining the finished product. This has taken two forms in particular: (1) studies that examine the text for its literary merit and (2) studies that center on the question of what the finished text had to say to the particular audiences to which it was addressed.

THE BIBLE AS LITERATURE. Differing from earlier works, the Bible as a whole is examined as a work of literary force and authority. It is seen as a work that demonstrates "the remarkable ingenuity of biblical authors" in creating literature that is so entirely credible that it shaped the minds and lives of intelligent men and women for two millennia and more. The text is not only read for its beauty but also for its meaning as a whole.[6] In this textbook, there are introductory paragraphs before each Old Testament book that discuss the literary aspects of that particular book, because most, if not all, of the thirty-nine books in the Protestant Old Testament have a discernible organization as pieces of literature. Before each book is studied, this textbook will attempt to illustrate its structure.

One additional problem concerns the treatment of books that appear in pairs or as part of a larger group. These include the books of Samuel, the books of Kings, the books of Chronicles, Ezra and Nehemiah, and the Book of the Twelve. Each of these groupings appears to have been originally perceived as a single work or scroll. This is why the Hebrew Bible counts only twenty-four books in its contents rather than thirty-nine, even though its contents are identical to those of the Protestant Old Testament. In these cases, the discussion will attempt to give attention to both levels of structure—that of the individual books and that of the scroll containing the whole grouping.

CANONICAL CRITICISM. The Bible shares the aim of those who study it as literature, insofar as it emphasizes the canonized text. But it differs in that it assumes that a given segment in its final form was designed to speak to problems of that time. As one well-known critical scholar recently asked, "Should we not ask what the final author (or authors) of the *book* wanted to tell the reader?"[7] The redactor or editor was much like a student writing a dissertation. A subject is selected, and sources are examined and selected to support the thesis being proposed. Thus, the editors or redactors were theologians who had something to say, who selected the materials from available sources, and, when needed, created materials that supported the point or points that were to be made in the finished product.

THE SOCIOHISTORICAL APPROACH. There is growing interest in how common folk lived. Sources for this approach include physical remains, such as garbage pits and village ruins; written sources, including the biblical texts and texts from similar ancient sources; and comparisons with similar present-day societies. A major problem that this approach has to deal with is this: In comparing Israelite society with other societies, just how similar is the society in question to ancient Israelite society? Furthermore, most archaeological evidence is mute and thus is subject to often conflicting interpretations. Despite these problems, this approach makes valuable contributions to our understanding of Israelite society.[8] In addition to *sociohistorical* approaches that may not differ significantly from other historical ways of studying Old Testament texts, some sociological methods make more deliberate use of data from contemporary societies. For example, observations about the lives of modern exiled people may shed light on texts that are about or were shaped by the Israelite experience of exile, and studies of modern nomadic cultures may help us understand biblical stories, like Genesis 12–36, that present nomadic characters and settings.

DEVELOPERS OF THE FINISHED PRODUCT. Present-day scholars emphasize the role of three major groups in the development of the narrative materials in the Old Testament (Genesis–

Numbers; Deuteronomy–2 Kings; 1,2 Chronicles–Ezra–Nehemiah). First, the priestly redactors are credited with giving Genesis through Numbers its final form, because, apart from Genesis, much of the material is concerned with legal and cultic matters—the areas of special interest to the priest. Second, the Deuteronomistic editors are seen as responsible for Joshua through 2 Kings, with Deuteronomy being the bridge between the Genesis–Numbers narrative and what is commonly called the *Deuteronomic History*. The latter influence may spill over into the narrative portions of Jeremiah. Another group of historians produced an alternative vision of Israel's history from the Creation to the Exile in the books of Chronicles. These historians are sometimes referred to collectively as the Chronicler. The story of Israel after the Exile is continued in the books of Ezra and Nehemiah, which are often linked to Chronicles.

ARCHAEOLOGY AS A TOOL FOR UNDERSTANDING

Archaeology is increasingly in the news. Whether it is the report of the inscriptional reference to the "house of David,"[9] the uncovering of a complete city gate in the ancient Canaanite city of Laish,[10] or the making of popular movies that portray a breed of archaeologist that is as outdated as the horse-drawn carriage, archaeology is a subject that draws attention.

Because *archaeology* is a term that is often misunderstood, certain questions should be examined: "What is archaeology?" "How does the archaeologist know where to dig?" "What digging methods are used?" "What is the value of archaeology?"

Basic Matters

THE PURPOSE OF ARCHAEOLOGY. Contrary to the popular image of an archaeolgist as a fortune hunter, archaeology is a serious scientific discipline dedicated to the search for truth about ancient cultures by studying the material remains of those cultures. Remains may be such simple things as broken pottery, animal bones, seeds, remains of buildings, and, if the archaeologist is fortunate, written materials. Biblical archaeologists in particular are interested in the peoples mentioned in the biblical story, and especially the Israelites. Even here, the archaeologist does not set out to prove the Bible. Instead, the purpose is to shed light on the Bible by trying to understand its peoples and their culture more thoroughly.

THE PRACTICE OF ARCHAEOLOGY. Sites in biblical lands are called **tells**. These are flattopped hills, built up over centuries of construction and destruction on basically the same site. Such sites were limited in number because of the lack of available water sources. The discovery of how to make lime plaster made possible the development of cisterns—cavities dug into the soft rock and then plastered to make them waterproof so that rainwater could be stored in them. This made it possible to build in an area that previously had been inaccessible. The important city of Samaria was one such site.

The tell is divided into squares, each one measuring 5 meters by 5 meters. For two reasons, only selected squares are excavated: (1) the limits of financial resources and manpower and (2) the need to leave areas for later scholars to examine when increased knowledge may lead to a more accurate evaluation of what is found. As the selected squares are excavated, only a few inches of soil are removed at a time. The sides of the square are kept as straight as possible, and adjoining squares are separated by a dirt wall, or *balk*. This is essential in determining the various levels of occupation. Any important finds are photographed, and charts are kept depicting their exact location in the square.

Formerly, the emphasis was on digging such areas as the city gate, because this was the center of governmental functions; the areas in which worship was carried on; and the homes of the city's rulers—palaces and monumental buildings. Present-day archaeologists, while not ignoring these important features of tells, are turning more and more attention to the dwellings of the common people to determine how they lived and the types of societies they had.

One way to accomplish this is through a combination of ethnology (the study of contemporary peoples and their cultures) and archaeology (the study of ancient peoples and their cultures). The contemporary peoples live in traditional societies, using methods that have changed little throughout the centuries. On Cyprus, until the 1950s, grain harvesting used methods like those spoken of in the Bible (Isa. 41:15–16). Ethnoarchaeology "not only provides technological details . . . useful in archaeological interpretations," but also shows how that technology fits "into people's lives and what they thought of it."[11]

THE SKILLS AND TOOLS OF ARCHAEOLOGY. The basic tools of the trade are hand tools, because excavation must be done carefully and systematically. Such small tools as trowels, hand picks, and a variety of brushes are used to carefully expose the finds. Earth that is removed is sifted for smaller items that might escape visual detection. Interpretation of what is found involves many scientific disciplines—physical and cultural anthropologists to study physical changes and social organizations; paleobotanists and paleozoologists to study the remains of ancient plant and animal life, to name but a few.

Various types of electronic gear are increasingly important. The computer is used for recording and analyzing data, while ground-penetrating radar, echo sound, and other such techniques are used for at least two purposes: to determine those areas in which digging would be most fruitful and to detect underground structures, which would prohibit digging altogether or where there is neither time nor resources available to dig.[12]

Such electronic tools are useful especially in area surveys, a major emphasis in present-day archaeological work. In years past, such surveys consisted of examining surface features of tells. Judgments were made on the basis of such features as to the occupants of the tell and when they occupied it. With modern electronic tools, a much wider range of data can be collected, leading to much sounder judgments about the nature of a given site.

DATING WHAT IS FOUND. One of the early techniques for dating was developed by two pioneer archaeologists, Sir Flinders Petrie and William F. Albright. They noticed that pottery found at the same level in different tells over an area had the same basic features. From this, they developed a method of dating, based on the changes in pottery. Epigraphical dating is based on written materials and involves the changing styles of letter formation. Broken pottery was the most convenient material upon which to write, particularly in Israel. Formerly, it was scrubbed to discover writing, but now it has been discovered that simply dipping it in water is the better method.[14] The carbon-14 test can be used on any plant-based samples of surviving materials. For example, both epigraphy and carbon-14 tests were used to date the Dead Sea Scrolls.

THE DEAD SEA SCROLLS. These scrolls are undoubtedly the most famous archaeological discovery of the twentieth century. It began in 1947 when a Bedouin boy found the first manuscripts in a cave near the Dead Sea. When experts recognized their value, a systematic examination was made of other caves in the area, leading to the discovery of a veritable treasure of both biblical and nonbiblical manuscripts. This discovery made available manuscripts or portions

Important Discoveries

The following are a few examples of discoveries that have had an impact on biblical studies:[13]

The Rosetta Stone. This trilingual inscription, discovered in 1801 by an engineer in Napoleon's army, made possible the translation of thousands of previously unreadable Egyptian inscriptions. Although its impact on the interpretation of the Bible is indirect, it nevertheless gave insight into the history of a people who were intimately involved with the Israelites.

The Gilgamesh Epic. In the mid-nineteenth century, Austen Henry Layard, a British explorer, discovered an ancient Assyrian library at Nineveh. Later, while translating the clay tablets, George Adam Smith, a young assistant at the British Museum, came across a flood story that had remarkable parallels to the biblical flood story. Unfortunately, the tablet was broken. Subsequently, Smith returned to the site of the discovery and, within five days of digging, found a tablet containing the rest of the story. This story, whose hero is Utnapishtim, predates the biblical story, suggesting that the biblical storyteller was familiar with it and used materials from it for his own purposes.

The Beni Hasan Mural. This wall painting, found in a large rock-hewn tomb near the village of Beni Hasan, 150 miles north of Cairo, dates to the early nineteenth century B.C.E. The painting portrays a group of Asiatics who have come to Egypt either to trade or to seek mining rights. Where in Asia they originated is unclear, but the picture suggests the types of trading relationships described in the stories of the patriarchs in Genesis.

The Gezer High Place. Discovered by R. A. S. Macalister in 1902, this site has been interpreted as dating from times ranging from 2500 B.C.E. to 1600 B.C.E. It consists of a series of ten upright stone pillars and a large rectangular block of stone with a depression cut into its top. Although the purpose of the basin is something of a mystery, the most likely explanation for the upright stones is that they served as witnesses of some sort of covenant ceremony, like the one described in the story of the confrontation of Jacob and Laban (Gen. 31:43–54; see also Josh. 24:25–27).

The Tel Dan Inscription. The Tel Dan Inscription now consists of three fragments from what was likely a larger stele produced by or for an Aramean or Syrian king in the ninth century B.C.E. The pieces were found in 1993 and 1994 in the excavation of a mound identified with the ancient city of Dan in northern Israel. Most interest in these fragments results from the appearance of the phrase "house of David" on one of them. If this is a reference to the biblical King David, or at least to the royal dynasty in Israel that traced its origins to him, then it is the oldest such reference outside the Bible by several centuries.

of manuscripts of every Old Testament book except two, some of which are 1000 years older than previously known manuscripts. In addition, there are manuscripts from nearly 1000 nonbiblical books.

The Value of Archaeology

A major aim of archaeology is to discover as much as possible about ancient peoples. Ideally, the archaeologist does not set out to prove anything, but tries to let the evidence speak for itself.

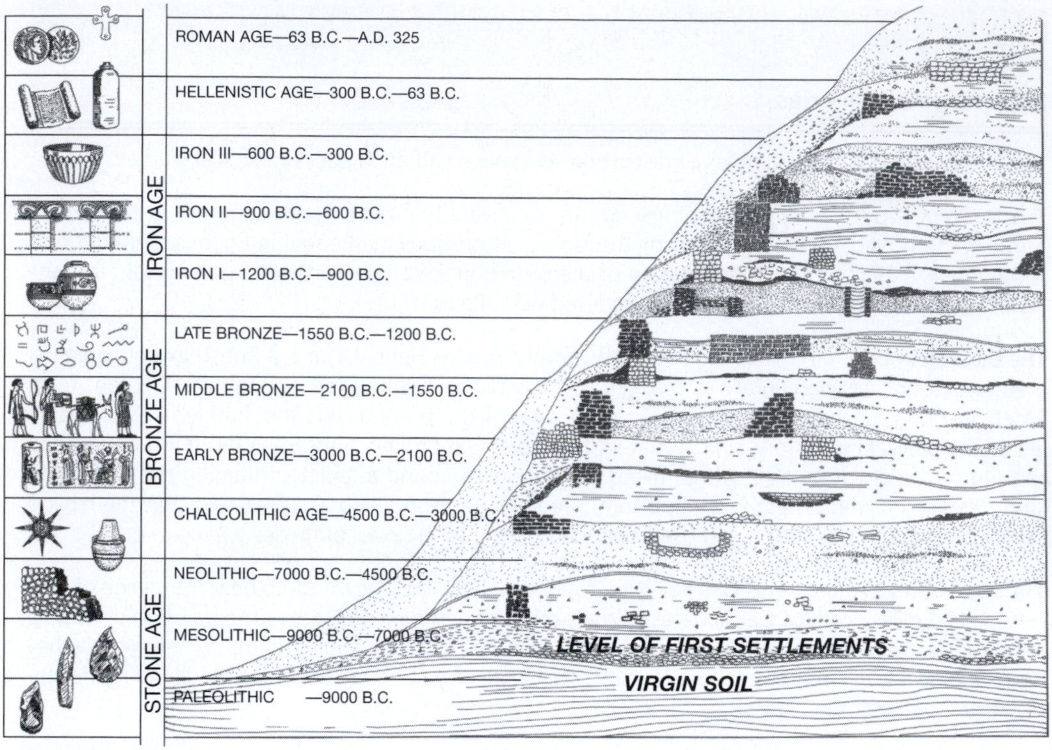

FIGURE 1–1 Cultural and archaeological ages of the past in Palestine. This illustration shows how a tell was built up by layers, over the centuries, as cities were built and destroyed. From *Compass Points for Old Testament Study* by Mark H. Lovelace. © 1972 by Abingdon Press. Used by permission.

Sometimes it speaks for what is described in the Bible, at others it is neutral, and at still others it is contrary to what the Bible describes. If one turns up written materials, the task of interpretation is clarified somewhat. Most of the evidence that is found, however, is mute. That is the reason why often in archaeology, two interpreters will take the same evidence and reach seemingly opposite conclusions.

Despite these limitations, because of the work of archaeologists, we know more about the lives of the peoples of biblical times than we discern from reading the Bible alone. We know the kinds of houses they lived in, their customs, what languages they spoke, the foods they ate, and even how they made out property deeds. More importantly, we are far richer in the manuscript evidence for biblical books, and our ability to understand these texts is far greater, thanks to archaeological discoveries. All in all, archaeology has proven to be a useful tool in biblical interpretation.

WHY STUDY THE OLD TESTAMENT?

People study the Old Testament for a variety of reasons. Many people study it as an aid to understanding our language and culture, because much of our great literature has been influenced by Old Testament themes and figures of speech. Even nonreligious people read such Old Testament books as Job, Proverbs, or Psalms with appreciation for their literary merit.

FIGURE 1–2 The Gezer High Place.

But for devout Jews and Christians alike, there is a sense of the sacred about the Old Testament, or the Hebrew Bible. They view it as inspired literature—inspired on a higher and different level from other great literary works. But even so, there are differences as to how the Bible is inspired. Some hold that every word in the original manuscripts was dictated by God to persons whose only function was to write them down in the idiom of their own time. Others view biblical inspiration as a process in which persons encountered the Divine in their everyday living and wrote down their reaction to that encounter.

Such a view would say that God's power is unlimited and surely includes the power of self-revelation and that inspiration is the human reaction to God's self-revelation. The biblical writers' ability, however, to understand what God was revealing definitely was limited, and that limitation is reflected in what is written about what God has done or is doing in the world. The Old Testament mirrors the strengths and weaknesses of those people whose experiences are portrayed, including their understanding and misunderstanding of the nature of God and of God's will for their lives. For instance, the Christian apostle Paul accepted slavery as part of his world and gave instructions about how slaves were to behave. Today, we do not accept, nor do we believe that God approves of, slavery. What has changed—God's will about slavery or our understanding? The obvious answer is that God has not changed—rather, our understanding of God's will has changed. But even in the realization that a biblical character could misunderstand God's will, we learn one of the great lessons of our faith—that we, too, are prone to error but can still be effective servants of God. This is part of what has been called *progressive revelation.*

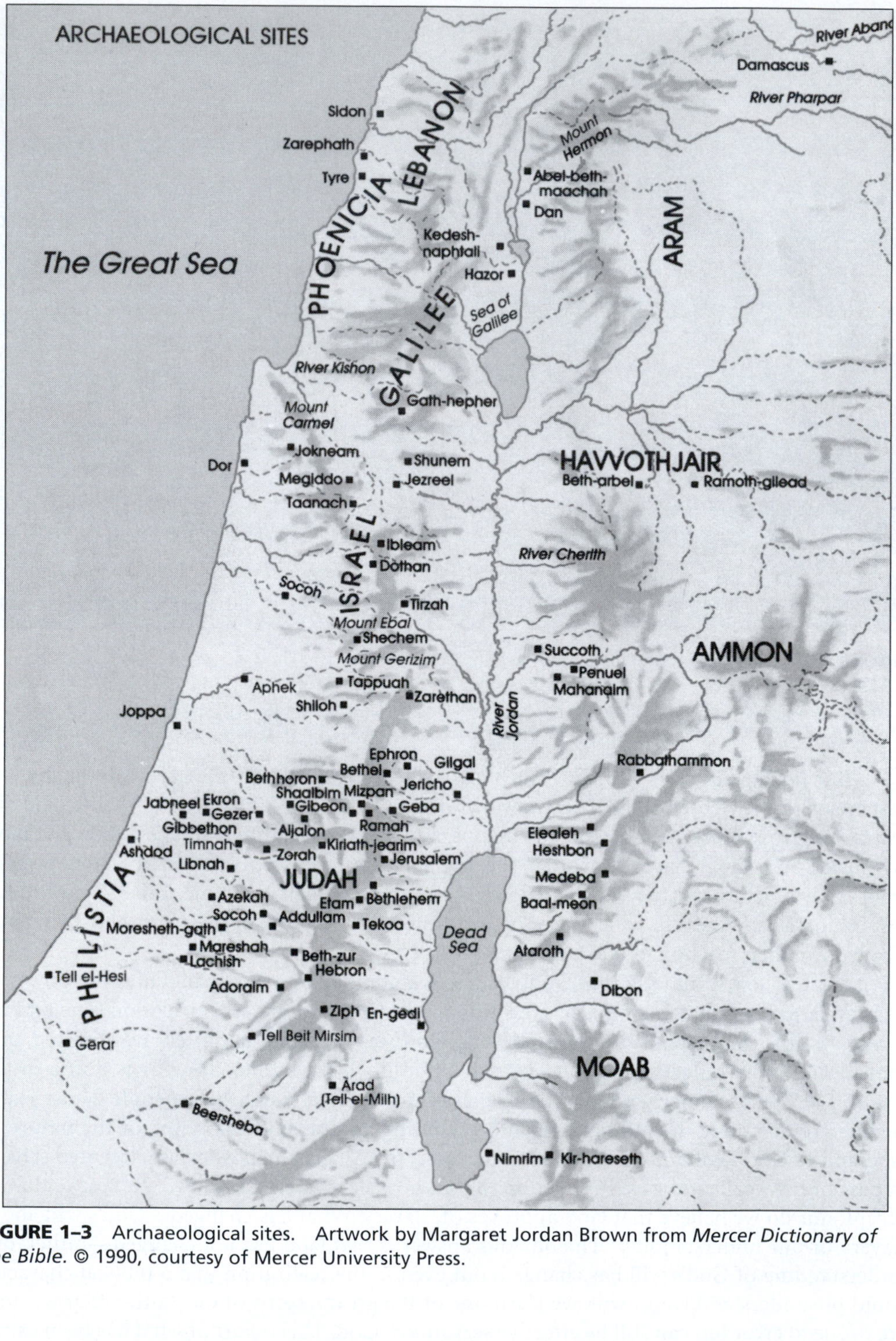

FIGURE 1–3 Archaeological sites. Artwork by Margaret Jordan Brown from *Mercer Dictionary of the Bible*. © 1990, courtesy of Mercer University Press.

Key Terms

Codex, *10*
Hermeneutics, *4*
Pentateuch, *11*
Plenary Verbal Inspiration, *6*
Source Criticism, *12*
TANAK, *10*
Tell, *15*
Canon, *7*
Septuagint, *8*
Textual Criticism, *10*
Etiology, *4*
Deuterocanonical, *8*

Study Questions

1. What is the Old Testament, and how did the term originate?
2. What do the abbreviations B.C.E. and C.E. mean?
3. Why is it unusual that the Old Testament has so much narrative material?
4. Why did the Israelites begin their story with the Exodus?
5. How were the early traditions about Israel developed and passed on from generation to generation?
6. What are etiologies, and what is their purpose?
7. What were the high points of Israel's story beginning with the Exodus and ending with the Babylonian Exile?
8. What is the meaning of the term *TANAK?*
9. How did the Septuagint affect the way various Christian groups view the biblical canon today?
10. What is the basic concern of textual criticism?
11. What are the three major concerns of literary and historical studies of the biblical text?
12. What forms of evidence are cited to argue for the Mosaic authorship of the Pentateuch (Genesis through Deuteronomy)?
13. What major shift in emphasis has taken place in Old Testament studies in recent years?
14. What three groups of redactors or editors have most source-critics identified as being responsible for the final form of the major narrative complexes of the Old Testament?
15. What is the basic purpose of archaeology?
16. How are archaeological dig sites selected?
17. What are some ways in which modern technology is making a contribution to archaeology?
18. What are the strengths and weaknesses in using archaeology in biblical interpretation?
19. Learn at least one important fact about each of the archaeological examples given in this chapter.
20. How does the inspiration of other great literature differ from the inspiration of the Hebrew Bible? Or does it?

Endnotes

1. In keeping with more recent practices, B.C.E., "before the Common Era," and C.E., "Common Era," will be used in this text instead of B.C. and A.D.
2. For this insight, I am indebted to Tamara Cohn Eskenazi, "Torah as Narrative and Narrative as Torah," in *Old Testament Interpretation: Past, Present, and Future—Essays in Honor of Gene M. Tucker.* Edited by James Luther Mays, David L. Petersen, and Kent Harold Richards (Nashville: Abingdon Press, 1995), 14.
3. On the problem of the formation of the canon, see John J. Collins, "Before the Canon: Scriptures in Second Temple Judaism," in James L. Mays et al., *NIB*, I, 225–241. For a look at how the differing order of the Hebrew Bible by Jews and Christians affects the interpretation of various books, see James A. Sanders, "'Spinning' the Bible: How Judaism and Christianity Shape the Canon Differently," *BR*, XIV, 3 (June 1998), 22–29. For a discussion of the development of the Bible as a written work, see William M. Schniedewind, *How the Bible Became a Book: The Textualization of Ancient Israel* (Cambridge: Cambridge University Press, 2004).
4. For a more thorough discussion of issues surrounding Mosaic authorship, see Mark McEntire, *Struggling With God: An Introduction to the Pentateuch* (Macon, GA: Mercer University Press, 2008), 8–11.
5. *Critic* and *criticism* are used here to mean "one who analyzes" or "the analysis of" the materials for the purpose of coming to a better understanding of them. It does not imply a destructive purpose.

6. James L. Crenshaw, "The Bible as Literature," *MDB,* 515–519, is a good survey of this field of study. Two books that use this approach are Robert Alter and Frank Kermode, *Introduction to the Literary Guide to the Bible* (Cambridge, MA: Belknap Press, 1987), and Brian Peckham, *History and Prophecy: The Development of the Late Judean Literary Traditions* (New York: Doubleday, 1993).
7. A major work based on this interest is Rainer Albertz, *A History of Israelite Religion in the Old Testament Period.* Translated by John Bowden (Louisville, KY: Westminster–John Knox Press, 1994), 2 vols.
8. Victor H. Matthews, *Manners and Customs in the Bible: An Illustrated Guide to Daily Life in Bible Times* (Peabody, MA: Hendrickson Publishers, 1988), is a comprehensive work on this aspect of biblical life.
9. "David Found at Dan," *BAR,* 20, 2 (March–April 1994), 26–39.
10. Avraham Biran, "The Discovery of the Middle Bronze Gate at Dan," *BA,* 44, 1 (November 1981), 139–144.
11. John C. Whitaker, "The Ethnoarchaeology of Threshing in Cyprus," *NEA,* 63, 2 (June 2000), 62–63. Both *NEA,* 63, 1 and 2 (March and June 2000), are devoted to articles on ethnoarchaeology.
12. A fascinating example of this is described by Dan Bahat, "Jerusalem Down Under: Tunneling Along Herod's Temple Wall," *BAR,* 21, 6 (November–December 1995), 30–47. See also Thomas E. Levy, "From Camels to Computers: A Short History of Archaeological Method," *BAR,* 21, 4 (July–August 1995), 44–51, 64. Chris Scarre, "High Tech 'Digging,' " *ARCH,* 52, 5 (September–October 1999), 50–56, presents a fascinating look at the use of electronic technology in modern archaeology.
13. James L. Crenshaw, *Education in Ancient Israel: Across the Deadening Silence* (New York: Doubleday, 1998), 39f.
14. For a number of these examples, I am indebted to Michael D. Coogan, "10 Great Finds," *BAR,* 21, 3 (May–June 1995), 36–47.

CHAPTER

2

The Geographical and Historical Settings for the Old Testament Prior to 1200 B.C.E.

Timeline

3000 B.C.E.	Beginning of the **Bronze Age**
2800 B.C.E.	Rise of the Sumerian Empire
2300 B.C.E.	Rise of the Akkadian Empire
1800 B.C.E.	Frequent guess about the time of Abraham and Sarah
1700 B.C.E.	Beginning of the Hyksos period in Egypt and the possible arrival of Joseph in Egypt
1400 B.C.E.	Height of Ugaritic culture
1300 B.C.E.	Rule of Pharaohs Seti and Ramses II in Egypt
1200 B.C.E.	Merneptah Stele mentions Israel at the Beginning of the **Iron Age**

Chapter Outline

I. The Ancient Near East
II. Mesopotamia
III. Asia Minor
IV. Africa
V. Syria-Phoenecia
VI. Palestine

CHAPTER OVERVIEW

Chapter Two draws a historical and cultural map of the geographical area in which the Old Testament story takes place. The discussion moves generally in an arc from east to north to west and then focuses on the area in which Israel is found in more detail. Israel exchanged much with the other cultures identified in this chapter. For example, nearly every type of literature found in the Old Testament has matching material in the documents from these other cultures. By the end of the chapter, a setting for the Old Testament is established, and material is revealed from these other cultures that assists our understanding of the Old Testament.

THE ANCIENT NEAR EAST

In a remarkable photograph taken from the *Gemini XI* spacecraft in 1966, the biblical world from **Egypt** to Mesopotamia is captured in one magnificent view. One is struck by the dry, barren look that characterizes much of this area, called the Near East. And dry it is. Deserts abound—the Arabian Desert is on the east, the desert of the Sinai Peninsula is to the south, and the great Sahara in the north of Africa pushes its way right up to the banks of the Nile River in Egypt. In early times, there was settled life only where there were rivers. These rivers furnished water for drinking and for irrigation, which made possible the development of agriculture. Other regions might have, in the occasional oasis, enough water for nomadic herdsmen, but these oases were so far apart that desert travel was limited until the domestication of the camel. Nomads, until late in the second millenium B.C.E., traveled by ass or by donkey and thus were limited in their range.

The watered areas of the Near East form a roughly crescent-shaped pattern known as the **Fertile Crescent.** This fertile strip of land begins in the east at the Persian Gulf and runs northwestward, taking in the valleys of the Tigris and Euphrates Rivers. North of this region, high mountains form a barrier between the rivers and what we know today as southern Russia. **Mesopotamia**, the name given to this region, literally means "in the midst of, or between, rivers." The mountains continue in the northwest, separating Mesopotamia from Asia Minor and the Mediterranean Sea.

The center of the Fertile Crescent was Syria-Palestine, a narrow band of fertile land caught in a vise between the Arabian Desert and the Mediterranean Sea. All the major roads from Africa to Asia passed through this narrow strip of land, thus making it a prize to be seized by the great powers of the time.

The southern end of the crescent was Egypt, the land of the Nile. Isolated from other major civilizations by deserts and distance, it developed one of the earliest, most powerful civilizations.

MESOPOTAMIA

3000 to 2000 B.C.E.

THE SUMERIANS. These people, named for their major area, **Sumer,** occupied a number of city-states that dominated the lower Mesopotamian region from 3150 to 2350 B.C.E. and again from 2060 to 1950 B.C.E. In this later period, Ur, one of the truly great cities of the ancient world, was dominant. The Sumerians invented the earliest known form of writing (**cuneiform**) and introduced counting by sixties (the method we use to count seconds and minutes). They were conquered by the Elamites.[1]

Gilgamesh

Archaeological expeditions in Mesopotamia in the nineteenth century produced a large collection of ancient texts that tell stories of a great hero named **Gilgamesh.** This epic figure likely has some connection to an actual king of Uruk named Gilgamesh, but the significance of the literary hero far outweighs that of the historical king. The mother of Gilgamesh was a goddess and his father was a human, so he resembles the half-human, half-divine giants described in Genesis 6:1–4.

In the Epic of Gilgamesh, Gilgamesh torments his subjects until they call upon the gods to save them. The gods send a wild man named Enkidu who wrestles with Gilgamesh until they become friends and companions. Together they battle and slay the great Bull of Heaven, but Enkidu dies soon after this great feat. Devastated by the loss of his friend, Gilgamesh wanders the earth. One of his heroic acts during this wandering period involves the killing of a group of lions.

Most startling to readers of the Bible is the story of the flood that took place near the end of the Epic of Gilgamesh. In this flood story, which precedes the biblical story by many centuries, Utnapishtim is the figure who survives the flood on a boat along with his family and animals he has gathered. The gods decide to flood the earth to kill all of the humans because the humans are so noisy that the gods cannot sleep. Utnapishtim receives instructions on how to survive the flood. The biblical story of Noah obviously resembles the flood story in the Epic of Gilgamesh, but the relationship between the two is difficult to determine. The end of the epic sings with sadness about the loss of the glorious hero, and the people give great offerings for his burial.

THE AKKADIANS. The first empire builder was Sargon of Akkad, who interrupted the Sumerian dominance of Mesopotamia in 2350 B.C.E., establishing an empire that would last until 2180 B.C.E. His people, the Akkadians, were Semites, a people from whom the later Israelites came. The Akkadians moved northwest into Mesopotamia from the Arabian Peninsula. Their language and literature continued to dominate Mesopotamia through their heirs, the **Babylonians** and the **Assyrians.** Through archaeology, that language and literature have come to us, furnishing a wealth of knowledge about the religious and cultural life of the region.

2000 to 1500 B.C.E.

THE AMORITES (ARAMEANS). These people, known as *Westerners,* were originally seminomadic tribesmen from Arabia. In the 200 years after 2000 B.C.E., they appeared all over the Fertile Crescent, causing great disruptions. After some time, they settled down, building new towns in northern and western Palestine and establishing two strong states in Mesopotamia around 1800 B.C.E.—Mari, located in the northeast, and Babylonia, in south-central Mesopotamia. Babylonia's most famous king was Hammurabi, best known for his famous law codes. From Mari, we have the Mari Tablets, which shed light on many patriarchal customs.

Like the Akkadians, the Amorites were Semitic people. Their invasion of the Fertile Crescent occurred during the general time of the Hebrew patriarchs Abraham, Isaac, and Jacob.

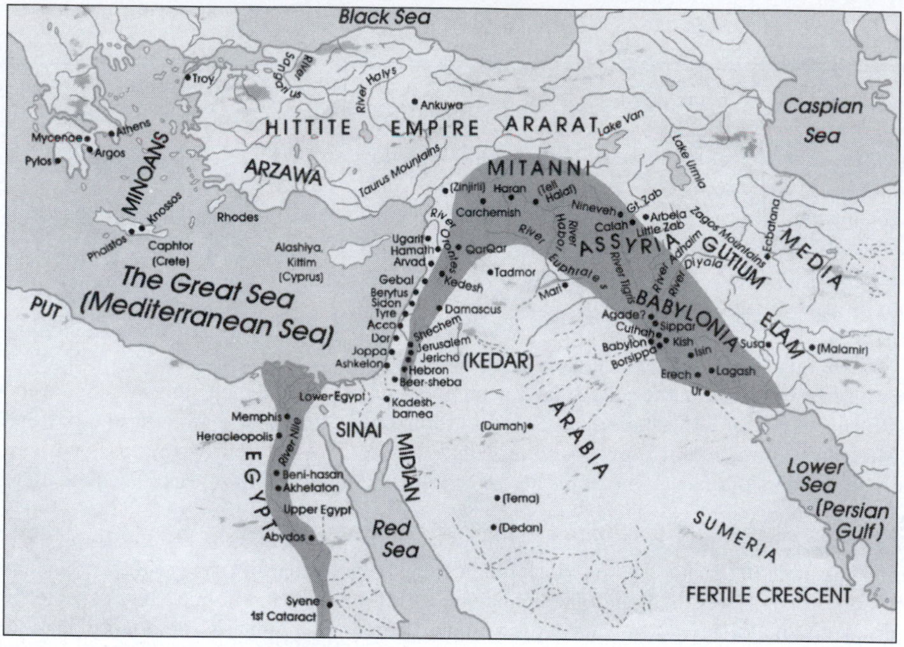

FIGURE 2–1 This map of the ancient Near East illustrates the Fertile Crescent, which extends from the Persian Gulf in the east to Canaan in the west. Artwork by Margaret Jordan Brown. © Mercer University Press.

What has been learned about the Amorites through archaeology fits in well with the descriptions of the lifestyle of the patriarchs.

THE HURRIANS. The Amorite states also passed away, succeeded by the Hurrians, or *Horites* as the Old Testament calls them. They absorbed the Amorite population into a state called *Mitanni*, and they also absorbed much of the Amorite culture. Fortunately, many of their writings were preserved on clay tablets at Nuzi, one of their major cities. The discovery of these tablets has helped clear up many obscure passages in the Old Testament.

1500 to 1000 B.C.E.

ARAMEANS AND HABIRU. Again, as had happened 500 years before, the Fertile Crescent was overrun by seminomads from Arabia. Among them were people referred to as *Apiru* or *Habiru*. Who they were has been the subject of much discussion. They appeared in many roles—as outlaws, as hired soldiers or mercenaries, as slaves, and as seminomadic wanderers. The similarity of their name to the word *Hebrew* makes it tempting to say that they were the Hebrews. However, references to the Habiru come from places all over the Fertile Crescent, so they cannot be one and the same as the Hebrews. *Habiru* refers to a much broader range of people. On the other hand, the Hebrews seem to have belonged to the same class of people. In other words, not all Habiru were Hebrews, but the Hebrews seem to have been Habiru. They were a social class from which the Hebrews came.

ASIA MINOR

THE HITTITES. Although it actually lay outside the bounds of the Fertile Crescent, **Asia Minor** was to play a very influential role in biblical history, especially in the Christian era. For many years, however, it was thought that it had little or no role in Old Testament history. Now we know that central Asia Minor was the center of the Hittite Empire. The **Hittites** are known in the Old Testament as the "sons of Heth." Their capital was Hattusa. They pushed down from Asia around 1400 B.C.E. into what is now known as Lebanon and Syria, having won the area from the Mitanni. Their greatest threat was to the power of Egypt, which controlled Palestine during that time.[2]

AFRICA

3000 to 2000 B.C.E.

THE EGYPTIANS. The part of Egypt comprising the fertile area—a narrow strip of land along the Nile River—looks like a crooked tree with a fan-shaped top representing the Nile Delta. There the river breaks up into many branches before entering the Mediterranean Sea. This delta region was a tempting target for hungry nomads throughout biblical history, because its well-watered lands produced food and pasturage in abundance, while other areas were devastated by drought.

At the same time, Egypt's separation from the rest of the Fertile Crescent by the land bridge of Palestine and the Sinai Desert enabled its civilization to develop with a minimum of interruption from outside forces. This early period, before 2000 B.C.E., was the time of the building of the great pyramids.

2000 to 1000 B.C.E.

THE EGYPTIANS. Genesis 12:10–20 tells the story of Abram (Abraham) taking his family to Egypt. This kind of emigration was common at that time. It also came at the time when the Fertile Crescent was experiencing invasions by the Amorites, the Semitic tribesmen from Arabia.

From 1720 to 1570 B.C.E., Egypt was ruled by the Hyksos, or "foreigners." The Hyksos were among the first to use chariots and cavalry units for warfare. They also built cities with a distinctive kind of protective wall. These walls had a steep slope, or *glacis,* extending from the base of the wall, which made it difficult for aggressors to attack the wall. The Hyksos kingdom included both Egypt and Palestine.

The Hyksos were overthrown by the eighteenth Egyptian dynasty, founded by Ahmose I. In the centuries that followed, the Egyptians dominated Palestine. Their rule there was opposed by the Hurrian (Horite) kingdom of Mitanni, or *Naharin.* Later, the Hittites took control of the Hurrian Empire, but Egypt was still able to control Palestine proper until late in the 1200s B.C.E. Egypt's last great rulers were Seti I (1308–1290 B.C.E.) and Seti II (1290–1224 B.C.E.). These pharoahs are often associated with the Hebrew Exodus from Egypt.

THE CUSHITES. The word **Cush** appears in the Bible for the first time in Genesis 2:13. It is the location of one of the four rivers that flows out of the Garden of Eden. The name of the river, the "Gihon," is a traditional name for the Blue Nile, which is located in the area of Africa known today as Ethiopia and the Sudan. Cush next appears in Genesis 10:6 as one of the sons of Ham, along with Egypt and Put, again indicating an African identity for this place and corresponding group of people. In 10:8, Cush is identified as the father of Nimrod, which creates some confusion, because this "larger-than-life" character is associated with both African and Mesopotamian cities, territories, and people. When the Hebrew Bible was translated into Greek, Cush was regularly rendered as "*Aithiops*," so the Greek translators apparently associated this word automatically with an East African location, related to the area we refer to today as Ethiopia.[3] Cush and the Cushites began to appear in Egyptian records in the early second millennium B.C.E. These terms clearly refer to a territory and group of people to their south, with whom the Egyptians had a long record of interactions.[4]

Cush, as a territory, and the Cushites, as a people group, appear in the Old Testament a total of fifty-four times, and their precise identity remains somewhat ambiguous. This takes place on a personal level, when a dispute arises in Numbers 12 between Moses and his siblings, Miriam and Aaron, over Moses' marriage to a Cushite woman. This woman's name is never provided by the text, leaving her identity uncertain. The named wife of Moses, Zipporah, is identified in Exodus 2 as a Midianite. All of these examples would seem to confirm that the ancient Israelites encountered these people regularly, but that their origin was a mystery to the biblical writers, and that they may have even used this sense of ambiguity and mystery deliberately. The lack of precision with which this term is used and understood in the biblical tradition has led David Tuesday Adamo to argue that the best English translation for these words that denote an area and a people group south and west of Egypt should be "Africa" and "Africans."[5]

SYRIA-PHOENICIA

3000 to 2000 B.C.E.

Syria, bounded on the west by the Mediterranean Sea and on the east by the Arabian Desert, is the northern portion of the land bridge connecting Mesopotamia, Asia Minor, and Egypt. Its southern boundaries during the period of the Israelite kingdoms varied from period to period, but generally were marked by Mount Hermon, whose melting snows furnish water for the major sources of the Jordan River.

Because Syria was part of the corridor connecting the continents, its population varied with each new outbreak of migration and conquest. Until recently, no major civilization was known to have existed in Syria before 2000 B.C.E. Now, however, the discoveries at Ebla in northern Syria have radically changed that assessment. Ebla seems to have flourished in two periods, the first of which was from 2400 to 2250 B.C.E. During this time, it was strong enough to challenge the empire of Sargon of Akkad, who ruled the first great Near Eastern empire. The first period of Ebla's prosperity ended when the city was conquered and burned by the Akkadian ruler Namar-Sin. Ebla flourished again between 2000 and 1600 B.C.E., as is evidenced by the discovery of an elaborate palace complex. It is certain that the eventual decipherment and translation of thousands of tablets found in the Ebla excavations will add much to our knowledge of ancient Syria in the second and third millennia. The initial suggestion, however, that they would have great significance for Old Testament studies now seems to be far less certain.[6]

2000 to 1000 B.C.E.

The southwestern coast of Syria, known in biblical times as *Phoenicia* and *Lebanon*, was one of the major strongholds of the Canaanite populations so frequently mentioned in the Old Testament. Because the area possessed the finest natural harbors on the eastern end of the Mediterranean Sea, coupled with an abundance of fine timber and a lack of agricultural land, its economy was based on the sea. The Phoenicians developed a merchant fleet that became, in effect, the navy and merchant fleet of the Israelite kings David, Solomon, Omri, and Ahab, who

FIGURE 2–2 The Sphinx and the Great Pyramid—symbols of the grandeur of ancient Egypt.
Courtesy of H. Armstrong Roberts.

had trade agreements with the local kings, especially the kings of Tyre. In addition, Israelite building programs used Phoenician architects, craftsmen, and vast quantities of the famous cedars of Lebanon.

Farther north lay the city of Ugarit, a center for Canaanite culture and learning around 1400 B.C.E. Here were discovered the Ras Shamra texts, which, like the Dead Sea Scrolls, opened up new areas of understanding in Old Testament studies. These texts provide us with a direct view of many of the elements of the Canaanite religion that early Israelites might have encountered and that many biblical texts may address.

The most famous of all Syrian cities was, and still is, Damascus, which was already an old city in the time of the patriarchs. Through it passed the traders, wanderers, and armies of the ancient world.

PALESTINE

Its Importance

Possibly no geographical area in the Western world holds a greater fascination for more people than Palestine. For three great religions, it is the Holy Land. Its strategic location made it the object of a continual tug-of-war among the ancient empires. Each one coveted its territory, not because it possessed vast land or rich resources, but simply because anyone going anywhere north or south in the ancient Near East had to cross Palestine to get there. On the west, the barrier was the Mediterranean Sea. Although some small ships sailed its waters, it was not a major means of travel for many centuries. To the east lay the vast reaches of the Arabian Desert, virtually impassable to the donkey-riding traders of early times. The famous ship of the desert, the camel, did not come into common use until after 1000 B.C.E. Thus, all land traffic between Africa, Asia Minor, and Mesopotamia was funneled through Palestine. This area is also referred to as the **Levant**.

Geographical Features

As one moves eastward from the Mediterranean coastal area, four major divisions of the land are evident. First is the *coastal plain* itself. The plain, broader in the southern region, becomes narrower, generally speaking, as one goes north. In the south it is known as the Plain of Philistia after its most famous inhabitants, the **Philistines**. They were a seafaring people who settled there, either after having been repulsed in an attack on Egypt or as mercenaries placed there by the Egyptians after being conquered by them.[7] They had five major cities—Gaza, Ashdod, Ashkelon, Ekron, and Gath. Not until David's time was the area under Israelite control.

The northern border of the Philistine territory was the Yarkon River, one of the few free-flowing streams in Palestine. From the Yarkon north to Mount Carmel was the Plain of Sharon, covered in biblical times by forests. It, too, came under Israelite control rather late.

Mount Carmel, a major landmark jutting out into the Mediterranean, divided the Plain of Sharon from the Plain of Acco, or Acre, a much smaller plain extending northward to the "Ladder of Tyre," where, once again, the mountains meet the sea. This latter feature marked the boundary at times between Israel and its northern neighbors. While David controlled the Plain of Acco, Solomon had to give it up to pay his building debts to Hiram, king of Tyre. The second major division as one moves eastward is the *central hill country.* In the north, the hills of upper Galilee vary in height from 2000 to 3000 feet, whereas lower Galilee (farther south) has hills of 2000 feet or less. Separating the Galilee hills and the Carmel range is the flat triangular Plain of Megiddo. On this plain stood the powerful city of Megiddo, one of the great cities of the ancient Near East.

As one moves southward, the mountains become progressively higher, pierced occasionally by valleys running west to east. This region is known as the *hill country of Ephraim* in much of biblical history. Farther south, it becomes the *hill country of Judah.* This region actually has two parts: (1) the Shephelah, an area of low-lying hills, and (2) the plateau on which Jerusalem is located. Separating the Shephelah and the Judean plateau is a north–south valley that made approaching the plateau from the coastal plain especially difficult. There are basically four approaches: (1) the Valley of Aijalon, which is the easiest and most famous; (2) the Valley of Sorek; (3) the Valley of Azekah; and (4) the Valley of Elah. The last three were more narrow and deep, making major movements, such as by armies, more difficult. In biblical times, if whoever controlled the plateau also controlled the Valley of Aijalon, many of the major defensive problems were solved.[8]

South of Judah, the hill country begins to decrease in altitude. In the south is the Negev, an area of rather flat land, primarily suited for raising sheep and limited agriculture. Beyond the Negev lies the Sinai Desert.

The third division, the *Jordan Rift,* is a deep scar in the earth that stretches from the base of Mount Hermon in the north all the way through Palestine and eventually into East Africa. In

Palestine it is the channel for the Jordan River, the Sea of Galilee (its only large body of fresh water), and the Dead Sea (one of the world's most unusual lakes).

The Jordan, appropriately named the *down-rusher,* is formed from a number of smaller sources—the primary ones being the Snir, the Dan, and the Banias Rivers—that rise near Mount Hermon. In earlier times, the Jordan flowed into Lake Huleh—a swampy area now drained for

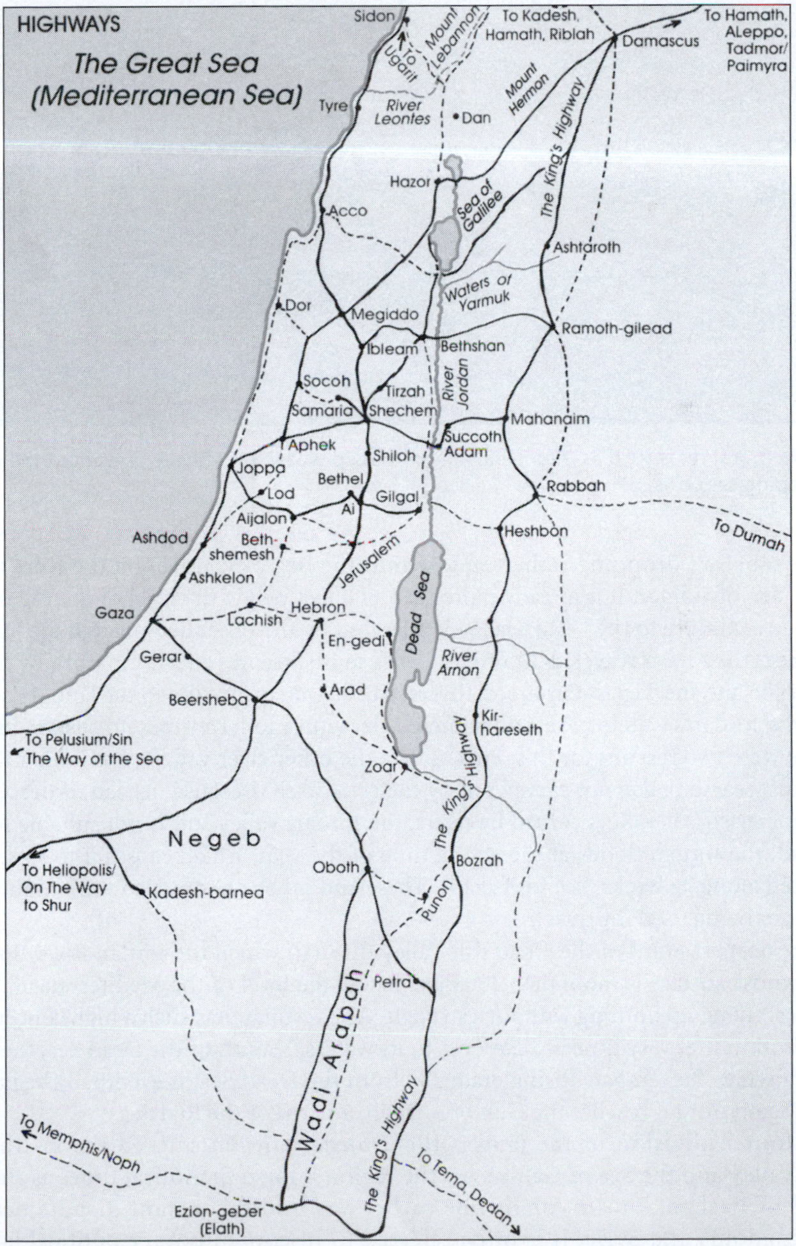

FIGURE 2–3 The highways of Palestine.

FIGURE 2–4 Coral reefs such as these, and a lack of deep water, effectively prevented the Israelites from developing seaports.

agriculture—before dropping rather rapidly into the Sea of Galilee. By the time the Jordan reaches the Sea of Galilee, it is already more than 600 feet below the level of the Mediterranean. From the Sea of Galilee to the Dead Sea is 65 miles, but by the time the waters of the Jordan reach the Dead Sea, they have traveled 135 miles because of the meandering nature of the stream. Unlike the Nile and the Tigris–Euphrates Rivers, whose waters give life to the land through which they pass, the Jordan's waters have contributed little, until modern times, to sustain life along its path. There were two reasons for this. First, unlike the other river valleys, the Jordan River valley was formed by earthquake, not carved out by the river itself. Because instead of deep, rich loam that is characteristic of valleys carved by rivers, the Jordan Valley soil is not suitable for agriculture. Second, the Jordan floods at the wrong time of the year, which causes it to wash away any crops planted along its banks (see Josh. 3:15). These and other reasons also prevent the Jordan or its valley from being used for travel.

At the deepest point of the Great Rift Valley through which the Jordan River flows lies the Dead Sea, whose surface is more than 1300 feet below the level of the Mediterranean. The Dead Sea is a taker, giving up nothing without a struggle. As a result, it has such a high concentration of natural pollution that very little life can exist in its waters.[9] South of the Dead Sea, the Great Rift Valley is known as the *Arabah*. Rising gradually from the Dead Sea, it eventually begins to slope downward again until it reaches the Gulf of Aqabah, an arm of the Red Sea.

The fourth division of the land is the *Transjordan Plateau*. To the north opposite the Huleh Valley and the Sea of Galilee was the region known in biblical times as *Bashan*. The ownership of Bashan, known for its fine cattle, was under constant dispute between the Israelite kingdoms and Syria. It is often referred to in contemporary political language as the *Golan Heights*. The territory known as Gilead in the Bible was on the east side of the

Jordan River, across from the hill country of Ephraim. The Jabbok River, another major tributary of the Jordan, ran through it. It was at one of the fords of the Jabbok that Jacob had his famous wrestling match (Gen. 32:22–32). The hill country of Gilead descends to form a broad plateau area. Traditionally called *Moab,* it bordered the Dead Sea and was ideal sheep country. Its broad, flat plains are broken only by an occasional stream, the chief one being the Arnon River.

The Brook Zered, which enters the Arabah at the southern end of the Dead Sea, was the traditional border between Moab and Edom. The Edomite territory was more rugged and less suited to pastoral or agricultural development than the other parts of Transjordan. This area often went for long periods with no major settlements. Those who did settle there were famous as traders and merchants.

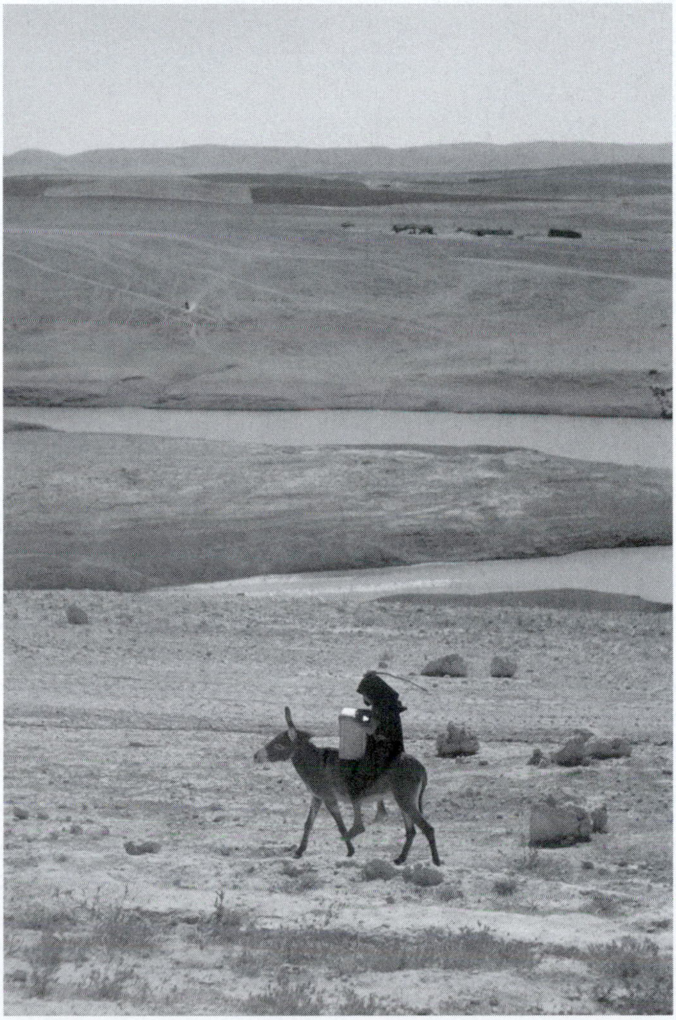

FIGURE 2–5 The Negev, lying between the sown land and the desert, was the home of pastoral groups such as the Amalekites.

FIGURE 2–6 An aerial view of the Jordan River as it follows a serpentine path to the Dead Sea.

Major Roads

The chief value of Palestine to the ancient world powers lay in two major roads that crossed its territory. The more important road was called the *Way of the Philistines* or the *Way of the Sea.* In Roman times, it was called the *Via Maris.*[10] As its name suggests, it followed the seacoast as it ran northeastward from Egypt, passing through the important Philistine cities of Gaza and Ashdod. As it neared the northern boundaries of the Philistine territory, it had to swing eastward toward the foothills to avoid the swamps caused by shifting sands that blocked the Yarkon River. Proceeding northward, it passed through the Carmel range near Megiddo and across the plain, skirting the Sea of Galilee and crossing the Jordan near Hazor, the largest city in ancient Palestine. From there, it continued northeastward through Damascus and on to Mesopotamia.

The desire to control this road was motivated by two things—power and money. The Via Maris was the major invasion route followed by armies from Mesopotamia, Egypt, and Asia Minor. The nation controlling this road beyond its borders could expect greater safety for its empire. Furthermore, the caravans that traveled over it were made to pay for that privilege, thus providing a rich source of revenue for the country that controlled it.

To a lesser degree, the same was true of the major north–south route east of the Jordan River—the King's Highway. Beginning with a major trans-Sinai route from Egypt to Edom, the King's Highway proceeded northward until it, too, came to Damascus. It was this route that Israel followed in part as it came out of the desert to invade Palestine.

Although not of international importance like the Via Maris and the King's Highway, a number of secondary roads were important for travel within the land. Perhaps the most significant

FIGURE 2–7 The King's Highway, a modern road in Jordan, runs along the same path as the ancient road the Bible calls by this name in Numbers 20:17.

of these was the route that ran through the hill country, connecting such strategic points as Shechem, Bethel, Jerusalem, Hebron, and Beersheba. A major cross-country route ran from the Plain of Acre through Megiddo and on to the Jordan River, through the Valley of Jezreel. In the south, routes into the central hill country followed the Valleys of Aijalon and Elah.

Key Terms

Study Questions

1. What is the Fertile Crescent, and why is it so significant to the world of the Old Testament?
2. Explain the significance of the following groups of people: Sumerians, Akkadians, Amorites, Hurrians, Arameans, Habiru, and Hittites.
3. What was the importance of the Nile River for ancient Egypt?
4. Who were the Hyksos? What role might they have played in the early history of Israel?
5. Why was the discovery of Ebla important?
6. Why are Ugarit and the Ras Shamra texts important for Old Testament studies?
7. What are the four major divisions of Palestine from west to east?
8. How did the Shephelah function in biblical times to protect the area of Judah?
9. Why was the Jordan River of little positive importance in Old Testament times?
10. What were the two major north–south roads in ancient Palestine, and why were they so important?

Endnotes

1. William W. Hallo, "Sumerian Literature: Background to the Bible," *BR*, IV, 3 (June 1988), 29.
2. A complete issue of *BA*, 53, 2 and 3, (June–September 1989) is devoted to articles on the Hittites.
3. For a more extensive discussion of these issues, see Robert Houston Smith, "Ethiopia," *ABD*, II, 665–667.
4. See the description of this group and other African groups appearing in the Bible in David Tuesday Adamo, *Africa and Africans in the Old Testament* (San Francisco: Christian Universities Press, 1998).
5. Ibid., 35–37.
6. For a comprehensive summary of the Ebla discoveries, see Robert D. Biggs, "Ebla Tablets," *ABD*, II, 263–270. See also Stephen M. Hooks, "Ebla," *MDB*, 225–227.
7. For opposing points of view on this issue, see Bryant G. Wood, "The Philistines Enter Canaan—Were They Egyptian Lackeys or Invading Conquerors?" *BAR*, XVII (November–December 1991), 44–52. Wood argues that the Philistines were conquerors. See also Itamar Singer, "How Did the Philistines Enter Canaan?" *BAR*, XVIII (November–December 1992), 44–46. Singer argues that they were Egyptian mercenaries.
8. Harold Brodsky, "The Shephelah—Guardian of Judea," *BR*, III (Winter 1987), 48–50.
9. Harold Brodsky, "The Jordan—Symbol of Spiritual Transition," *BR*, VIII (June 1992), 34–43, 52.
10. Barry J. Beitzel, "The *Via Maris* in Literary and Cartographic Sources," *BA*, 54, 2 (June 1991), 64–75, argues that *Via Maris* referred to an east–west road rather than the major north–south coastal road.

CHAPTER 3

Israel Looks at the Beginnings

Timeline

2200 B.C.E.	Beginning of the Middle Bronze Age
2050 B.C.E.	Approximate date of resurgence of the Sumerian Empire
1800 B.C.E.	Frequent guess concerning the time of Abraham and Sarah
1700 B.C.E.	Beginning of the Hyksos period in Egypt, possible arrival of Joseph in Egypt, and approximate date of the production of the Code of Hammurabi
1500 B.C.E.	Beginning of the Late Bronze Age

Chapter Outline

I. The Primeval Complex
II. The Ancestral Complex
III. Genesis in Retrospect

CHAPTER OVERVIEW

The book of Genesis commands greater attention than any other book in the Old Testament, so it deserves its own chapter in this text. As the first book in the canon, it sets the tone for the Bible, establishing many of its characteristic ways of speaking and telling stories. Genesis draws an opening portrait of the creation of the world and then leads the reader from the odd and distant primeval world to the seminomadic Near East of the Israelite ancestors. Genesis will introduce these great ancestors, such as Abraham, Sarah, Hagar, Isaac, Rebekah, Jacob, Rachel, Leah, and Joseph, and will introduce the idea of covenant, which will define the people of Israel. By the end of the book, we will find our way with these ancestors to the land of Egypt, the place where the thrilling events at the beginning of the book of Exodus will take place.

THE PRIMEVAL COMPLEX

Genesis 1–11 is a strange kind of literature. It contains a story with a talking snake and magic fruit. In many of its texts God seems to have human body parts, performs human actions, and interacts with human beings much as another human being might. Heaven and earth appear to be directly connected, so that God and other heavenly beings can move back and forth naturally between these two realms. Genesis 1–11 pays very little attention to geography. Few of its events happen in identifiable places. It also treats time differently, often paying little if any attention to the passage of time and assigning life spans of hundreds of years to its characters. Scholarship has struggled to find an adequate name for Genesis 1–11. The adjective *primeval* seems fitting and is widely used, but the choice of a noun for it to modify is more difficult. Some use the term *history*, but this literature does not look like history as modern readers tend to understand it. The use of *Primeval Narrative* has become quite common, and can be useful, but not all of this material is narrative—there are also poems and lists. We have chosen the term *Primeval Complex*, because it is vague enough to include all of the literary types that appear in this collection and because it points to its diverse nature.

Part of the strangeness of this literature may be attributed to its age and to the way it originated as oral material and was transmitted in oral form for many centuries. The character of this material also performs an important literary function, though. It gives these opening chapters of the Bible a distant, long-ago feel. These stories are not happening in the world that is familiar to us. A literary construct like this allows the book of Genesis to deal with some vital theological issues that would be difficult to address in a literary world that functions like the one in which we live. Perhaps the most important of those theological issues is Creation, which requires speech about a Divine character who is active and visibly present in the world in a way that is different from our experience.

The cultural environment of the ancient Near East produced many different traditions about creation. One of those stories probably originated with the people known as the *Akkadians*, who lived in Mesopotamia in the third millennium B.C.E. This tradition was revised and passed on by the Babylonians, and so it is often called a Babylonian creation story or is simply labeled using the first two words of the text, *Enuma Elish.*

Genesis is a Greek translation of the Hebrew title for this book—*bereshith.* This Hebrew phrase means "in beginning." Genesis not only introduces the Pentateuch, or Torah, but the whole of the Hebrew Bible, or TANAK. TANAK is a word formed by using the first letters of the name for the three divisions of the canon: *T*orah, *N*ebi'im, and *K*ethubim.

Genesis naturally falls into two parts: chapters 1–11, the Creation, the Fall, and the consequences of the Fall; and chapters 12–50, the patriarchs or ancestors of Israel—Abraham, Isaac, Jacob, and Joseph. Whoever was responsible for the final form of this book obviously had access

The Literary Structure of Genesis

Note: A boxed section like this, explaining the literary structure of each of the twenty-four books of the Hebrew canon, will appear near the place where discussion of that particular book begins. The format of a survey textbook like this often places the discussion of a biblical book in multiple places and combines it with discussion of other books. These sections are designed to provide a relatively brief, cohesive description of the overall shape of the biblical books all in one place.

The book of Genesis may appear to be just a sequence of loosely connected stories or a collection of major cycles of stories about people like Abraham, Isaac, and Jacob. Is there a sense of organization to the whole book? Over the past few decades, a general consensus has emerged concerning this aspect of the book of Genesis. The common understanding is that Genesis is deliberately organized around a framework of genealogies. There are ten specific genealogical notices, which begin with the formula *'aleh toledoth*, "these are the generations of. . . ." The genealogies introduced in this way appear in Genesis as follows:

2:4	the heavens and the earth
5:1	Adam
6:9	Noah
10:1	Noah's sons
11:10	Shem
11:27	Terah (the father of Abram/Abraham)
25:12	Ishmael
25:19	Isaac
36:1	Esau (this line about Esau is repeated in 36:9)
37:2	Jacob

This series of genealogies traces the formation of the people of Israel right down to their primary identification as children of Jacob/Israel. The genealogies also serve to send off the other branches of the human family and to differentiate them from Israel. Thus, Genesis becomes a giant ethnography or *people picture* that defines Israel and its place in the world among all of the other groups of people known to them.

The book of Genesis is also typically divided into two distinct halves, although they are not equal in length. The first part consists of Genesis 1:1–11:26 and is often called the *Primeval Narrative*. Because this section contains a great deal of nonnarrative literature, it will be called the *Primeval Complex* in this book. The second half of Genesis, 11:27–50:26, has frequently been called the *Patriarchal Narrative*, but because of its nonnarrative elements and its inclusion of important female characters, it will be called the *Ancestral Complex* in this book. Five of these genealogies listed above are found in the Primeval Complex and five in the Ancestral Complex. This fivefold structure may be related to the fivefold structure of the Torah or Pentateuch. Within each of these sets of five, the middle section is the longest. Within the Ancestral Complex, the first, third, and fifth sections are long. These long sections stand at the beginning of the three major sets of stories about Abraham and Sarah, Jacob and his wives, and Joseph. In each case, the set of stories is about the youngest son of the person named in the genealogical notice.

11:27–25:11—The stories of Abraham (son of Terah) and Sarah

25:19–35:29—The stories of Jacob (son of Isaac), Leah, Rachel, Bilhah, and Zilpah

37:2–50:26—The stories of Joseph (son of Jacob)

The genealogies function as a framework that identifies people groups and summarizes the passage of many generations in very little space. The stories within this genealogical framework provide a close-up view of the people and events in which Israelites ought to be most interested.

These kinds of literary patterns appear to be present at many levels of the book of Genesis, from the whole book down to the internal structure of individual units. What this larger structure demonstrates is that the final composer of the book of Genesis deliberately shaped the book for a number of purposes. Perhaps the most prominent purpose is to answer the question "Who are the people of Israel, and how are they related to all of the other peoples of the world?"

Another feature that holds the book of Genesis together as a cohesive literary work is the phenomenon that may be called *linked stories*. There are several sets of stories that are very much alike. Some of them involve what interpreters call *type scenes*, in which different characters seem to be acting out the same, or a very similar, set of actions. These linked groups of stories include:

Drunken Father and Disrespectful Children (9:18–28, 19:30–38)

Wife–Sister Deception (12:10–20, 20:1–18, 26:1–12)

Endangering the Son (21:8–21, 22:1–19)

Birth of Twins (25:19–28, 38:27–30)

Finding a Wife at the Well (24:1–33, 29:1–14)

Confusion of Siblings (27:1–29, 29:15–30, 48:1–22)

Despite the length of the book of Genesis and the huge diversity of materials it contains, a sense of familiarity is created by the stories so that the reader might often get the sense of having been in this place before. The book of Genesis closes with the death notice of Joseph, a literary unit reminiscent of descriptions of the deaths of Sarah, Abraham, Isaac, Rebekah, and other important characters in other parts of the book.

to a variety of materials—creation stories, genealogical lists, flood stories, sagas, and other popular stories. Priestly concerns are evident in emphases on religious ceremonies, such as covenant making and circumcision (Gen. 17). The primary purpose of the book is theological—that is to say, relating that Israel was brought into being by the LORD God, the Creator of the Universe.

The Israelite Understanding of Creation

The Old Testament is filled with references to Creation. Such is the case of Psalm 104:1b–8, in which God is described as follows:

> You are clothed with honor and majesty,
> wrapped in light as a garment.
> You stretch out the heavens like a tent,
> you set the beams of your chambers on the waters.
> You make the clouds your chariot,
> you ride on the wings of the wind.
> You make the winds your messengers,
> fire and flame your ministers.
> You set the earth on its foundations,
> so it shall never be shaken.

You cover it with the deep as a garment;
 the waters stood above the mountains.
At your rebuke they flee;
 at the sound of your thunder they take flight.
They rose up to the mountains, ran down to the valleys
 to the place that you appointed for them.
You set a boundary that they may not pass,
 so that they might not again cover the earth.

The concepts used by the Psalmist reflect images present in the world of that time. Other Creation texts can be found at Psalm 74, Proverbs, Job 38, and Isaiah.

The influence of Israel's world can best be seen, however, in the Genesis Creation story. Both Genesis 1:1–2:4a and the *Enuma Elish* speak of the watery chaos, covered by darkness, that precedes the work of Creation; they follow something of the same order of Creation—firmament, land, sun and moon, humanity—and in each, the Creator rests after the work is finished. But, as is often true, the agreements in detail are not nearly so significant as the differences. After all, all humans are similar—their differences make them unique.

GENESIS 1:1–2:4A. This account of Creation, the product of centuries of theological reflection, was put into its final form by the priestly theologians of Israel. Well aware of other Creation stories, they expressed the conviction that the God of Israel was the only God and the Creator of the visible universe.[2] In the myths, the gods arose out of the creative process. This was not so for Israel. God did not arise from Creation—God was the Creator! There is no speculation about God's beginning; Israel assumed that God was and always had been. Thus, the emphasis in Israel's Creation story is more on God than on what was created.

"In the beginning, God created the heavens and the earth" (1:1) is a summary statement of all that is to follow. God (called *Elohim*) is *transcendent* (separated from the material universe) and powerful (God speaks and things come into being). There is no struggle to bring order to chaos, but the majestic God calls things into existence. Like the notes of a symphony, certain phrases appear and reappear—for example "and God said," "God called (named)," "God saw that it was good," "God made," "And there was evening, and there was morning."

There seems to be a conscious effort to counter the Near Eastern Creation myths. In contrast to the struggle waged between Marduk and Tiamat, God is in complete control of Creation. The heavenly bodies—the sun, the moon, and the stars (1:14–19), worshipped as gods by Israel's neighbors—are created (1:14). They get their light from God, not from their own powers. Furthermore, the earth, looked upon as the mother goddess by many ancient people, has no power to give life except as God commands (1:21). Finally, humanity, the last act of Creation, is made in God's image and is commissioned by God to be the caretaker of Creation (1:26–27).

For two reasons, the statement "Let *us* make humankind in *our* image and after *our* likeness" (1:26) is one that has drawn much attention (1) because of the personal pronouns *us* and *our* and (2) because of the meaning of the expression *image of God*.

Three possible explanations of the use of the plural pronouns are advanced: (1) Because the word for God (*Elohim*) is a plural form, the use of the plural pronoun is expected. The problem with this explanation is that *Elohim* is used in other places with the singular pronoun. (2) It is simply the equivalent of "Let's do it," as if to say, "I will do it" (Isa. 6:8). (3) God is pictured as a king, addressing a **heavenly court**, or council, expressing to those who serve him what he wants done.[3]

The meaning of the expression *image of God* has caused much ink to be used. That the ancient Hebrews thought of God as having certain physical traits cannot be denied, because

Enuma Elish

This ancient poem describes how the gods were the offspring of Tiamat and Apsu in chaos. Later, there was warfare among the gods and goddesses, caused by the fact that Apsu (the lover of Tiamat) had been killed by Ea. Tiamat vowed to get revenge on Ea. Ea trembled in fear at the possibility of having to face Tiamat, so he turned to Anshar, his father, for advice. It was decided that Marduk, the strong man of the gods, would face Tiamat. As his price for taking on that responsibility, Marduk demanded first place among the gods. Anshar, mortally afraid of Tiamat, agreed.

Taking along the four winds to help him, Marduk went out to meet Tiamat. She came out at him with her mouth open, intending to devour him. That was her fatal mistake. Marduk unleashed the four winds, which entered her mouth, blowing her up like a balloon. Then Marduk took his sword and sliced her into halves like a grapefruit. He used the upper half of her body for the dome of the heavens and the lower half to create the earth. They then killed her latest lover, Kingu, and made human beings out of his blood.[1]

numerous references are made to such traits in the Old Testament. The temptation is to see *image* and *likeness* in these terms, but it surely goes more deeply than a physical image. One aspect of the image seems to lie in the fact that humankind, like God, who is the ruler over all Creation, is given power to rule over the earth. The privilege of naming the animals signifies power over them. Another aspect of the image of God must lie in the fact that humankind is endowed by God with intelligence and the power of creativity.

GENESIS 2:4B–2:25. In reading this version of Israel's Creation story, the first thing to notice is that God is referred to as the "LORD God" (2:4) (Hebrew: *YHWH Elohim*). Some would call this the *Yahwistic* version of Creation, as it uses Israel's personal name for God, *YHWH*. Its simplicity and directness seem to indicate that it is much older than the more highly developed account in 1:1–2:4a. The main interest is the creation of humanity, which is placed first. The creation of the world is already assumed to have taken place.

The patterned kind of story found in 1:1–2:4a is missing in this account. Furthermore, God's creative acts are described in human terms. To say that "the LORD God *formed* man from the dust," "*breathed* into his nostrils the breath of life," "*planted* a garden," and "*took* the man and *put* him in the garden" is to speak in what is called *anthropomorphic language*—that is, to describe God in human terms. God is pictured as acting in human ways as he made human beings, talked with them, and, like a concerned father, disciplined them when they did wrong (Gen. 3).

Just as an exalted view of God in Genesis 1:1–2:4a (which theologians call *transcendence*) is needed, so that God will be reverenced and respected by the worshiper, a more personal view of God (a view that theologians speak of as *immanence*) emphasizes God's nearness to and concern for the worshiper. These two views of God must be kept in proper relationship to each other. If transcendence is overemphasized, God becomes so far removed so as to have little or no interest in humankind. An overly transcendent view makes any personal relationship with the Deity a farce.

On the other hand, an overly humanized Deity can lead to overfamiliarity, with the result that God becomes a "big Daddy" or "the man upstairs." Extreme humanization of God also makes the Deity irrelevant. A balance between the two extremes more nearly represents the biblical view.

The man, created by God from the dust of the earth and given life by the breath of God, is not created for idleness. Instead, he is placed in the garden that the LORD God has "planted" and given the responsibility for its cultivation (2:15). As tenant, he has privileges, but he also has responsibilities. The man, from the first, has his "dos" and "do nots," and the major "do not" is "Do not eat of the tree of the knowledge of good and evil" (2:17). He is given power over the animals, symbolized by the privilege of naming them (2:19–20); but power does not satisfy the basic human need for companionship. So woman is created, and man is complete (2:23). Made for each other, they have nothing to hide (2:25).

The First Family

Genesis 2 ends with a wedding of sorts, so it is possible to see Genesis 3 as the beginning of the story of the first family. However one understands the events in the garden story in Genesis 3, it is plain enough that one of the effects of God's pronouncement of curses is the imposition of a pattern of strained hierarchy on family life in 3:16. This strain is evident in many places: The woman and the man are isolated in their tasks of child rearing and agriculture (3:16–19), the first two children born into this family will have to compete for God's approval (4:1–17), and the generational lines that descend from this family in the genealogies of 4:17–24 and 5:1–31 will continue this competition in a world of limited resources. Of course, this competition is also built into the nature of storytelling. It is not possible to continue to tell the story of everybody, as the human population expands. The narrator must choose to focus attention on some and not others. This narrative necessity runs parallel to the limitations that arise when God chooses some persons as recipients of covenant, blessing, and protection and does not choose others.

TRANSGRESSION (GEN. 3:1–24). The glory of human beings is also their undoing. Created in God's image, their *hubris* (pride or arrogance) moves them to substitute their judgment for that of God. This sense of pride underlies the appeal of the serpent to the woman when he tells her that if she eats the forbidden fruit, she will "be like God, knowing good and evil" (3:5). The ancient storyteller had a marvelous understanding of human nature. His description of the forbidden fruit's appeal to Eve's appetite ("good for food"), to her sense of beauty ("a delight to the eyes"), and to her sense of pride ("the desire to make one wise" 3:6) shows how well he understood the nature of temptation. If he lived today, he probably could make a fortune in advertising.

The woman falls for the serpent's line so quickly that she is hooked before she realizes what is happening. The man, no less gullible than the woman, falls for the same line. Suddenly, they are ashamed of what they see in each other, so they try to cover their nakedness with clothing made of leaves (3:7).

Discovery of disobedience brings God's displeasure. Because humans want to be like God, they have to take responsibility for their action. Now they hide from God, who created humanity and gave them paradise (3:10). As a further result of their disobedience, they are banished from the garden and separated from God. Work becomes a burden, and life loses much of its joy (3:17–20).

The biblical writer here has given his view of humanity's basic problem in relation to God. Adam (humankind) wants to be God, but the Creator cannot and will not yield his unlimited authority to His Creation. Humans have been given as much power as they can handle wisely. To give them more would be disastrous to them, so limits have to be established (3:24).

CAIN AND ABEL (GEN. 4:1–26). No single story has had a greater impact on human consciousness in Western civilization than that of Eve and Adam in the Garden of Eden in Genesis 3,

Cain Murders Abel

The story of what is often understood as the first murder has long fascinated readers. Once Adam and Eve have left the Garden of Eden, Genesis moves quickly to the story of their first two sons. Although most readers make some assumptions, the text offers no reason why Abel's offering is well regarded by God and Cain's is not. Part of the key to this problem is in the literal reading of the text. God "looks upon" Abel's offering but does not "look upon" Cain's. This is most likely the language of blessing, and likely means that Abel was successful and Cain was not. This situation elicits the jealousy that complicates the story in 4:5. The most troubling element of the story is that God speaks to Cain and warns him about the dangers of sin and this "burning" that threatens him, but God does not speak to Abel to warn him about the murderous intentions of Cain.

Abel, whose name means "emptiness" or "breath," is gone from the text as quickly as he appears. His purpose in the story is to be killed. Genesis 4 offers a genealogy for Cain but not for Abel. With no offspring, Abel is not remembered and has no continuing life. It even appears that Abel's would-be genealogy has been absorbed into Cain's when Abel-like names appear in Cain's genealogy in 4:20–21. One of the most striking elements of the story is God's statement in 4:10 that "the blood(s) of your brother cry out to me from the ground." Many centuries later, the Mishnah would contend that the plural form of *blood* in this verse indicates that Cain also murdered all of the potential offspring of Abel, all of whom cry out to God from the ground.

There are many theories about the meaning of this story. Is it about the threat settled agriculture and technology pose to the nomadic, herding way of life? Notice that in Genesis 4:17–26 Cain is a city builder and his offspring includes the first iron worker, Tubal–Cain. Many popular western movies address this same tension between free-range herders and ranchers or between ranchers and "sodbusters." Is the story an attempt to portray farmers as villains who deserve to have their land taken away from them? Others have read the story as a typical example of sibling rivalry, so that Cain is the Bible's version of Romulus, who killed his twin brother, Remus, and founded the city of Rome. The book of Genesis will continue to play with the fascinating dimensions of the relationships between brothers all the way through the book.

but the nearest rival may be the story that immediately follows it in Genesis 4. Cain and Abel have taken on gigantic metaphorical identities in our culture, and this first story of murder in the Bible often functions as a lens through which we view much of the conflict and violence in our world. The story of these two brothers is mysterious and difficult to bring into focus. No overt reason is given for God's failure to "look upon" the offering of Cain. One can only observe that the favoring of Abel matches the consistent preference for younger brothers in Genesis and the identification of Israel with persons who had a seminomadic, sheepherding lifestyle. This latter observation reveals that this conflict is much larger than just competition and jealousy between two brothers. It is a struggle between two ways of life, wandering and settling, which has gone on in virtually all parts of the world from the earliest time about which we know.

God's concern for Cain may be the most surprising element of the story. God speaks to Cain both before and after the murder, and, despite the punishment that falls upon Cain, there seems to be a note of redemption at the end of the story. This redemption appears to take hold in the following genealogy of Cain in 4:17–24, as the first murderer becomes the first city builder and his descendants become the first musicians and metal workers. There is an enormous amount of creativity embodied in this family line that will so soon be forgotten. The redemption that looked so promising comes to an end with the ominous presence of Lamech at the end of this genealogy, who reminds the reader of Cain's identity as a murderer in 4:24.

When Seth is born to Adam and Eve in 4:25, he is declared to be a replacement for Abel, but he really replaces both of his older brothers, as he becomes the son through whom Adam and Eve's family line will continue in Genesis 5.

FROM ADAM TO NOAH (GEN. 5:1–31). The narrator ties the stories of Creation to the story of the Flood by "the list of the descendants of Adam" (Gen. 5). This genealogy rapidly moves the reader from Adam to Noah, like a literary fast-forward mechanism. Note the similarities between the names in this genealogy and those in the Cain genealogy of Genesis 4:17–22. The development of these lists is a complex and mysterious issue that cannot be fully resolved. They now play a significant literary role in the text of Genesis. The long life spans in this genealogy, for example, help create a sense of distance between the world of the reader and the misty world of the primeval past.

Flood Stories and the Flood (Gen. 5:32–9:19)

Flood stories are a part of the traditions of many peoples. The biblical Flood story (which properly begins with the introduction of Noah and his sons in 5:32) shares common features with two accounts of a great flood in Mesopotamia—the Gilgamesh Epic and the Atrahasis Epic.

THE GILGAMESH EPIC. Gilgamesh, the hero, seeks the secret of eternal life. He goes to Utnapishtim, who tells him how the gods tried to destroy humanity with a great flood. Ea, one of the gods, had warned Utnapishtim, who escaped by building an ark. The flood was so great that even the gods themselves thought they were going to be destroyed.

When the waters receded a bit, the ark landed on Mount Nisir. Utnapishtim sent out a dove and a raven to see if the waters had receded sufficiently for him to leave the ark. When the flood was over, he made a sacrifice:

> *The gods smelled the sweet savor,*
> *The gods crowded like flies about the sacrifice.*[4]

THE ATRAHASIS EPIC. This epic, first published in 1922, also comes from the Babylonians. Like the biblical account, it starts with a creation story. The people are so numerous and noisy that the gods decide to destroy them. A number of solutions are tried—plague, drought, famine—but none is satisfactory. Finally, a flood is called for, after which a new kind of world will appear, in which various means will be used to control the population.[5]

THE BIBLICAL FLOOD STORY (GEN. 5:32–9:19). The story of the marriage of the "sons of God" and the "daughters of men" (6:1–4) serves as the background for the biblical account of the Flood because it illustrates the conclusion reached in 6:5:

> *The LORD saw that the wickedness of humankind was great in the earth, and that every inclination of the thoughts of their hearts was only evil continually.*

The reference to the "sons of God" reflects an ancient belief that marriage between divine men and human women produced a race of giants (6:4). Here the older story is given new meaning by serving as an illustration of the depths of human sinfulness that result in the Flood.[6]

That Israel also had at least two different flood traditions can be seen when one separates the passages using LORD from those using *God*.[7] Each series of passages tells a story of the Flood. The two have been blended without regard to duplications.[8]

Numerous attempts have been made to confirm the Flood story through archaeology. None of these attempts has been conclusive, including well-publicized attempts to find the **Ark**.[9] The importance of the Flood story does not depend on the archaeologist, or on anyone else for that matter. The ancient storyteller did not let variations in the traditions he received deter him from his purpose of weaving these materials together to say what he wanted to say about God. For him, the story of Noah is a vehicle to tell about (1) God's judgment on sin, which had so affected Creation; (2) God's concern to preserve what was begun in Creation; and (3) God's reaching out to humankind in covenant.

Unlike the Atrahasis Epic, in which people had become so numerous and noisy that the gods decided to destroy them, Israel's theologians see destruction resulting from corruption that arises from people's abuse of the created order. The covenant brings law and structure to society where such has not existed before. The shedding of blood especially is singled out as taboo.

It seems that, for the priestly theologians, this polluting of the land by the shedding of human blood may well have been the "wickedness" that led to God's desire to start anew.[10]

THE COVENANT (GEN. 9:1–17). Noah represented a new beginning. Like Adam, he was told to "be fruitful and multiply and fill the earth" (9:1, 7), but earth was no longer a paradise where people and beasts lived in harmony—the beasts feared humans, who were made master over them. Humanity, which had shed blood so freely, was now made accountable in a more stringent way for the shedding of blood (9:6).

God made a covenant, or contract, with Noah and his descendants that said that humanity would never again be destroyed by a flood. This covenant, or agreement between parties, was initiated by God, not Noah, and was evidence of divine mercy extended to the survivors of the Flood. The rainbow was given as an everlasting symbol of the contract between the Creator and His creatures (9:8–17).

The Noah narratives end with the story involving a drunken Noah pronouncing a curse upon one of his sons who saw him naked. Somehow the curse fell upon his grandson, Canaan (9:18–27). Curses such as this were believed to have the power to carry out what was threatened. Blessings given at special times of life were believed to have this same power.

Again, the narrator inserted a genealogy (Gen. 10) to introduce a new segment of the story. One purpose was to say something about the geography of the ancient Near East sometime in the period of the second millennium (2000–1000 B.C.E.). A second purpose was to express the author's conviction that the human race was in unity growing out of its descent from Noah. This serves, then, as a background for what follows in Genesis.

The Tower of Babel (Gen. 11:1–9)

Humanity was united not only in language (11:1), but also in its determination to rebel against God. This rebellion took the form of building a tower to reach the heavens, where the challenge to God could be made (11:4). The rebellion was nipped in the bud, however. People lost their ability to communicate with one another when their language, which had bound them together, became a barrier—a babble that began with **Babel**. The ancient Israelites probably saw the great *ziggurats,* or pyramidlike towers, in Babylon, built originally as worship centers for Babylonian deities. From those edifices, they concluded that this had caused God to confuse people by giving them many languages instead of one.

Summary of the Primeval Complex

Genesis 1–11 contains a collection of literature that is unclear in scope and chronology. The genealogies serve to tie this collection together, and there is some coherent sense of a struggle between God's intent for Creation and the behavior of human beings. Another issue that arises multiple times is the struggle between a settled lifestyle and a wandering, nomadic existence. The texts dealing with settled life, including agriculture, technology, and city building appear to view it negatively. This way of life is associated with Cain (4:17–24), Nimrod (10:8–11), and the builders of the Tower of Babel (11:1–9). This final story in the Primeval Complex seems to be God's ultimate judgment on settled life. The people of Babel are scattered against their will. This scattering clears space both on the land and in the text for the emergence of a new set of characters. The family of Abraham and Sarah fit the nomadic, pastoral ideal, and the book of Genesis will narrow its scope to focus on the members of this particular family, the great ancestors of the people of Israel.

THE ANCESTRAL COMPLEX[11]

As the character first known as Abram is introduced in Genesis 11:27, the manner of storytelling changes as distinctly as the content. The remainder of Genesis tells the stories of Israel's great ancestors—Abraham, Sarah, Isaac, Rebekah, Jacob, Leah, Rachel, Bilhah, Zilpah, and Joseph. In this part of Genesis, the flat characters and vague geography of Genesis 1–11 give way to highly developed personalities and a recognizable landscape. Even some of the characters who are sent off, away from the Israelites, such as Hagar and Esau, are more carefully drawn than any of those who appeared in the Primeval Complex. It is reasonable to suppose that the kinds of people, places, and events in this part of Genesis would have been very familiar to the first readers of this book. Traditionally, this part of Genesis is often called the *Story of the Patriarchs.* This designation accurately reflects the dominance of the male characters in the stories, but it ignores the significant presence of the female ancestors. Paying appropriate attention to the female characters, while acknowledging that the text of Genesis is patriarchal in nature, provides a significant challenge for any interpreter.

The Time

There is no universal agreement as to the dating of the time of the ancestors. Yet, the names, customs, and mode of life seem to fit into what is known of the first half of the second millennium B.C.E. They seem to be connected to the rise of Amorite influence in this region. Although there is no absolute proof for these conclusions, evidence seems to point to the probability that these stories are, in the main, authentic memories about real people. Abraham's journey from Ur of the Chaldees (Gen. 12) usually is associated with the movement of the Amorites from Mesopotamia into Palestine in the nineteenth and eighteenth centuries B.C.E.[12]

Joseph, the last of the four major figures in Genesis 12–50, is often associated with the Hyksos rule in Egypt. The Hyksos were foreign rulers of Egypt who conquered the country in the eighteenth century B.C.E. and established a dynasty that ruled for more than 150 years. Like the Hebrews (as the Israelites were first known), the Hyksos had among them many people of Semitic origin. They made extensive use of chariot warfare. They built cities whose fortifications included walls with a steep ramp, or *glacis,* designed to prevent easy approaches to the walls. If Joseph did come in this period, the patriarchs would be dated from about 2000 to 1550 B.C.E.

Their Lifestyle

The picture given of Abraham, Isaac, and Jacob is that of people who habitually moved about. Yet, it was not an aimless wandering; instead, they seem to have followed a yearly cycle based on the availability of pasturage for their flocks. During the dry season, they would move into the empty spaces in the central hill country, where, among other things, they could graze in the cut-over grain fields. There they remained until the rains came. They might even have planted a grain crop on unclaimed land to be harvested when they returned, after the grasses in the Negev had died out. For this reason, they were not **nomads** in the modern sense of the term. Their chief beast of burden was the ass or donkey. Camels were not yet in general use.[13]

In contrast to our limited families of today (consisting of parents or a parent and, on rare occasions, a grandparent or grandparents included), the patriarchs were heads of extended families consisting of wives, children, relatives of varying degrees, and servants—most of whom undoubtedly were slaves. A man's wealth was measured in terms of the number of wives, sons, and cattle he possessed (see Job 1). For all these persons, the patriarch was the chief decision maker. He determined who his sons married and which of his sons would succeed him as patriarch. It was customary for the eldest son to become the patriarch, but it was not always so.

Abraham and Sarah, the First Ancestors

To discover what Abraham and Sarah were like some 4000 years ago is no easy task. Although numerous stories have them as the major characters, they lack many of the ingredients necessary for the writing of history. These narratives, called *sagas,* have real people at the core, but what we can actually learn about the details of their lives is quite limited. No dates are given, and no events that can be confirmed in an independent study are mentioned. No archaeologist has dug up a tablet saying "Abraham slept here." Nevertheless, we do have the biblical stories—stories that at least suggest that behind those stories was a great personality claimed by three great world religions—Judaism, Christianity, and Islam. Our purpose is to learn from the stories as they are.

FROM UR TO EGYPT (GEN. 12). The stories of the ancestors are religious history. Persons, places, and events are secondary to what the LORD is doing through those persons, places, and events. Abraham (called Abram until Gen. 17:5), a native of Ur of the Chaldees in southeastern Mesopotamia (on what is today the Persian Gulf), moved to Haran in northwestern Mesopotamia while he was still in the clan of Terah, his father. There, Terah died and Abraham became the patriarch (11:31–32).

In Haran, life took a new direction. Abraham was called by the LORD to leave the familiar faces of his kinsmen and the well-watered areas of northwestern Mesopotamia to go to a new land that the LORD would show him. It was a promise that carried with it universal meaning. Abraham would receive the blessing of a land, numerous descendants, and divine protection; and through him, all the nations were to be blessed (12:1–3). This promise was repeated with differing emphases a number of times in the Abraham stories (Gen. 12:7; 13:14–17; 15:7–21; 17:1–21).

Although the biblical narratives present Abraham as a man of God, they certainly do not present him as a perfect saint. Driven to Egypt by famine in Palestine, he persuaded his wife to lie about her relationship to him, resulting in her being chosen for the Pharaoh's harem. This action brought a plague upon the Egyptian people. Somehow, when Pharaoh realized what had happened, he sent them away with their belongings. Of course, this story foreshadows the Exodus story in some way, but it also raises some difficult questions. Why did the Egyptian people suffer for Abraham's misbehavior? How did Pharaoh know the cause of the plague? Was Sarai forced into an adulterous relationship because of Abraham's cowardice? This story will be replayed later in the lives of Abram (Abraham) and Sarai (Sarah).

In Genesis 20:1–18, Abraham again told a foreign king, Abimelech of Gerar, that Sarah was his sister. Abimelech was warned by God in a dream, however, before he became involved with Sarah. Because he was obedient to the dream, no illicit relationship developed and the people of Gerar did not suffer from a plague. In addition, we and Abimelech are informed that Sarah is Abraham's half-sister, thus his deception involved a half-truth rather than an outright lie. Notice that this version of the story resolves the questions raised by the earlier story. One last difficulty remains, however. Why does Abraham gain wealth in each of the stories because of his deception? One new problem is raised in this telling of the story. Why is a foreigner portrayed as the one who receives the divine message and responds to it obediently? This story will be played out one more time in the life of Isaac. Stay tuned.

CONFLICT AND COVENANT (GEN. 13–16). Abraham settled in the Negev, the southern region of Judah, between the sown land and the desert region of Sinai. Here, possibly as a caravaneer (i.e., a trader), he gained great wealth in the form of herds of animals. Conflict between his herdsmen and those of his nephew Lot arose, causing a parting of the ways. Lot chose the well-watered valley of the Jordan, while Abraham chose the hill country. Conflict and crisis brought a reaffirmation of the promise from the LORD of numerous descendants and possession of the land (13:14–17).

Another kind of conflict is described in Genesis 14. Abraham appears as no ordinary desert chieftain, but as one who was powerful enough to challenge the rulers of the area. Lot, captured in warfare between a group of kings, was carried off to northern Syria. Abraham, with his personal army of 318 men ("born in his house"), rescued Lot. On his return, Abraham paid tithes to Melchizedek, the king of Salem (later known as Jerusalem). The name used for God was *El Elyon*, "God Most High." His later descendants could point to Abraham's association with Jerusalem when it became David's capital city to validate their claim to it.[14]

Social and physical conflict is followed by mental conflict (15:1–21). No child had blessed the marriage of Abraham and Sarah. Their only heir was a foreign slave, Eliezer of Damascus, whom Abraham adopted as his heir. Such a custom is known from the Nuzi tablets (about 1500 B.C.E.). Abraham agonized about his lack of a son by Sarah, and the LORD reassured him. Then followed a strange ceremony.

A sacrifice was made, but not on the usual altar. Instead, the larger animals were cut in half, the halves being laid on the ground opposite each other. As the sun sank in the west, Abraham went to sleep. The vision came as a dream. The LORD spoke of the Egyptian sojourn. A smoking pot and a flaming torch passed between the split animals, and the covenant was made. The boundaries of the land, essentially as they stood in the time of David, were described to Abraham.

Domestic conflict arose when, in keeping with custom, Sarah gave Abraham her maid Hagar as a secondary wife, or **concubine,** so that Hagar could have a child for her by proxy (16:1–15). Hagar's instant fertility gave her a feeling of superiority over her barren mistress (16:1–4). Hagar then had to flee from the wrath of Sarah. Hagar's son, Ishmael, was said to have been the father of the Ishmaelites, who roamed the southern desert areas of Palestine (16:5–15).

THE COVENANT AND CIRCUMCISION. Here, one finds another view of the covenant. First, another name for God is used. He is *El Shaddai,* "God Almighty" (17:1).[15] Then, Abraham, called Abram to this point, is now called Abraham, "the father of a multitude" (17:4). In addition, *circumcision* (the cutting off of the male foreskin) is described as the symbol of the covenant with God. Sarah (formerly Sarai) also underwent a name change, and assurance was once more given that she would be the mother of Abraham's heir and successor as patriarch. All these elements suggest the emphases one might expect of the priests, causing this to be considered by many as the priestly version of the covenant story.

THE PROMISE OF NEW LIFE AND FOREBODINGS OF DOOM (GEN. 18–19). The promise of a son and heir to Abraham finally moved toward its fulfillment. The patriarch looked out from his tent one day to see three strangers approaching. True to his cultural sense of courtesy, he invited them in and gave them water to wash their dusty, tired feet. He spread for them "a morsel of bread," which in reality was bread, cheese, milk, and meat (18:1–8). In the story of the three strangers, the narrator described a **theophany**—the appearance of the divine to a human being.

The divine visitors had some good news and some bad news. First, they told Abraham that in the spring Sarah would bear a child. This struck Sarah, who was well past the age of childbearing, as somewhat ridiculous. Her giggles, as she hid behind the tent door, reached the ears of the divine messenger, who heard her and gave her a gentle rebuke (18:9–15).

Then came the bad news. Abraham was told of the doom of Sodom and Gomorrah, the licentious cities in the Dead Sea area, where Lot lived. Despite Abraham's plea (18:16–23), judgment fell and only Lot and his two daughters escaped (19:1–23).

The description of the destruction of these cities suggests that an earthquake occurred, which resulted in the sinking of the land. The fire and brimstone were burning gases and sulfur, both common in this region (19:24–29). Geologists have proposed that a massive earthquake "liquified the rocks and the soil the cities were built upon, toppling all the buildings." The site was then covered by the waters of the Dead Sea.[16]

The last picture of Lot is a sad one. Old and drunk, he is debauched by his own daughters (19:30–38). The result of these incestuous unions is the birth of two sons, Moab and Ammon, who bear the names of two of Israel's neighboring enemy nations. Among other things, this story is surely a jab at the characters of these two nations.

ISAAC AND ISHMAEL (GEN. 21). After the second incident involving Sarah and a foreign king (Gen. 20:1–18), the long-expected child, Isaac, was born. Conflict again arose between Sarah (old enough to be her son's great-grandmother) and Hagar (Abraham's slave wife and mother of Ishmael). Jealousy forced Hagar to flee so that Isaac would have preeminence. Here again, the word used to refer to the divine being changes to *Elohim,* "God." In yet another narrative concerning conflict with a local chieftain, Abimelech, the term *El Olam* (the "everlasting God") is introduced. The shifting of terms may indicate that these are parallel traditions, that is, the same story coming from different tribes or clans. This could be especially true of the Sarah–Hagar conflict stories.

THE TEST (GEN. 22). The high point of the Abraham drama was played out on a mountain "in the land of Moriah." Later, according to tradition, Solomon's temple would be built on this site. The passage emphasizes that "God tested Abraham" by commanding that Isaac be offered as a sacrifice to God. Abraham obeys, but at the climactic moment, just as he is about to take his son's life, his attention is drawn to a ram caught in a nearby thicket. The ram serves as the sacrifice instead. In Jewish tradition, this episode is called the Akedah story. ***Akedah*** refers to the "binding" of Isaac.

Three possible interpretations have been offered for this incident. Some see it as a parable, the point of which is that God does not require human sacrifice. That this interpretation has some validity is seen by the fact that human sacrifice never played the important role in the Israelite religion that it did in others. A second interpretation sees Isaac as representing Israel and its relationship to God. The dominant interpretation, however, sees it as enshrining Abraham in the history of religion as the man of faith, revered by three great world religions—Judaism, Christianity, and Islam.[17]

SARAH'S DEATH AND BURIAL (GEN. 23). When Sarah died, a burial place had to be bought. Abraham went to the village elders and engaged in a typical bargaining session, complete with flowery phrases and exaggerated gestures. Finally, a purchase price was named—after the owner offered to "give" the land and the cave of Macpelah to Abraham, and, in the process, obligated Abraham to buy more property than he wanted. Today, the traditional site of the burial at Hebron is a sacred site to both Muslims and Jews.

A WIFE FOR ISAAC (GEN. 24:1–25:18). Before Abraham died, he had to ensure that Isaac had a wife. The custom of the parents choosing a bride for their son is still practiced in some cultures. Abraham sent his trusted servant Eliezer back to Haran to find a wife for Isaac. Here, we are introduced to the wily Laban, the brother of Rebekah, Isaac's future wife. Although the storyteller credits the LORD with pointing out the right girl, Laban was quite willing to give up his sister when he saw the rich gifts Abraham had sent for the bride price (24:53–61).

As in Genesis 1–11, a genealogy is used to summarize and conclude the Abraham story (25:1–18).

Isaac and Rebekah

Of all the patriarchs, Isaac receives the least attention. He is pictured as an introvert—a shy, quiet, meditative person dominated by the stronger personalities around him. Such a person was Rebekah, his wife. The choosing of Rebekah as Isaac's wife and her subsequent domination of her husband receives more attention in the tradition than does Isaac himself (24:15–61; 25:20–24; 26:6–11; 27:5–17).

One of the stories about Isaac is suspiciously like those about Abraham. Like his father, Isaac led the people of Gerar to believe that his wife was his sister (26:6–11). This time, Abimelech discovered the deception not by a divine dream, but when he saw Isaac and Rebekah behaving romantically toward each other. Again, trouble was avoided, and this time Isaac did not receive financial reward for his deception. He was blessed economically by the LORD at a later time (26:12–13). The troubling aspects of the second telling of the story are thus avoided in the third telling. This series of related stories, like others in the Old Testament, probably indicates the incorporation of parallel collections of material into Genesis and other books of the Bible. Notice, however, that in the final form of Genesis, the parallel versions of the story function in sequence to resolve some of the difficulties raised by this tradition. Be sure to pay attention to how the related stories of Jacob tricking people and being tricked are interwoven into the story of his life.

As in the past, the covenant was reaffirmed also with Isaac (26:1–5; 23–25). He did not have to wait as long for an heir as did Abraham, however.

Jacob, the Supplanter

Most of the stories about Jacob are the kinds of stories one prefers to tell about a relative who is long since dead. If he were alive, one would only whisper about his escapades at family gatherings and hope that the neighbors had not found out about the wayward son's latest caper.

JACOB AND ESAU. Jacob was a twin of Esau. Esau was born first, but Jacob's later reputation as a schemer was such that the tradition arose that he had hold of Esau's heel when Esau was born, trying to pull him back so Jacob could come out of the womb first (25:19–26).

Esau was an outdoorsman and a man who lived by impulse. Jacob, on the other hand, was more like his father, but with the cunning of his strong-willed mother. Esau, as the elder of the two sons, was first in line to be the patriarch. In addition to the birthright, one had to secure the blessing of the patriarch as he approached death in order to have the right to succeed him (25:27–28).

The blessing was important because the spoken word, in primitive societies, was viewed as having much more power than it has today. The ancients believed that a blessing or curse carried with it a sort of self-fulfilling power. Neither was given lightly, nor were they taken lightly. The blessing was greatly desired, and the curse was greatly feared.

It was for this reason, then, that Jacob—in trying to get the right to be patriarch himself over the firstborn Esau—had to secure both the birthright and the blessing. He had failed to get out ahead of Esau, but that was not his last attempt to get ahead of him!

BUYING THE BIRTHRIGHT (GEN. 25:29–34). The **birthright** was his first goal. Esau, slave of his appetites, fell into Jacob's trap like a hungry bird. Coming from an exhausting and probably futile hunt, Esau smelled the red bean soup Jacob was cooking. When he asked Jacob for food, Jacob set a high price—Esau's birthright. Esau, listening more to his hunger pangs than to his head, agreed. And so, on a solemn oath, Esau sold Jacob his future for a bowl of bean soup (25:33).

STEALING THE BLESSING (GEN. 27:1–45). But the birthright was not enough. Jacob still had to have Isaac's blessing. On his side, he had a very powerful ally—his mother, Rebekah. Isaac favored Esau, perhaps because he saw in him those characteristics of strength and self-confidence that he lacked and secretly longed to have. Isaac, as the saying goes, enjoyed poor health. Troubled by eye disease (a common malady in the Near East) and other ailments (either real or imagined), he feared that death might overtake him at any time. He decided, therefore, that the time had come to pass on to his older son the responsibility of being patriarch. Calling Esau in, he gave him instructions to prepare for him a dish of wild game and bring it to him. Then he would bless Esau (27:1–4).

As Esau left to hunt game, Rebekah (who overheard the conversation) immediately gave Jacob instructions to kill a young goat and bring it to her. Taking the goat, she made stew, dressed Jacob in Esau's clothes, and put fresh goat skins on Jacob's arms and neck so that he would look hairy, like Esau (27:5–17).

When Jacob went to Isaac, claiming to be Esau, Isaac was suspicious because the voice did not sound right. If it were Esau, he had returned rather quickly. Calling Jacob to him, Isaac felt his now-hairy arms and neck and ate the savory stew. As he kissed Jacob prior to giving the blessing, he smelled his clothes. The voice was Jacob's, but the body odor was Esau's! And so the blind Isaac—deceived by his sense of taste, touch, and smell—blessed the deceiver. Jacob left with a blessing that Isaac could not take back, even though Esau soon came in and Isaac learned the truth of what had been done (27:18–45).

JACOB ON THE RUN (GEN. 27:46–28:22). Rebekah, having overheard Esau's threats to kill Jacob, immediately persuaded Isaac to send Jacob to her brother Laban's house in Haran to escape the wrath of Esau. Taking the road north through the central hill country, Jacob came to a place in the barren, rocky hills north of present-day Jerusalem. Using one of the numerous limestone rocks for a pillow, he tried to get some sleep. In a dream, the LORD appeared to him, saying:

> I am the LORD, the God of Abraham your father and the God of Isaac; the land on which you lie I will give to you and to your offspring; and your offspring will be like the dust of the earth . . . and all the families of the earth shall be blessed in you and in your offspring. (28:13–14)

Jacob was awed by the experience. But even though he set up a memorial stone, he only committed himself to serve the LORD as his God if he returned to his father's house safely (28:18–22).

JACOB AND LABAN: AN AMATEUR VERSUS A PROFESSIONAL (GEN. 29:1–30).[18] On coming to the territory of Laban, Jacob met his cousin Rachel at the well used for watering sheep. One look was all it took! He fell hopelessly in love with Rachel. Laban, being a shrewd man of the world, sized up the situation. Before Jacob knew it, he was committed to working seven years for the privilege of marrying Rachel, because he had no money for the bride price. What seems to have been involved here was a kind of herding contract in which Jacob agreed to work as a herdsman for Laban for seven years in return for the privilege of marrying Rachel.

The seven years passed swiftly, but when Jacob went forward to claim his wage, he received a shocking surprise. Custom decreed that the veiled bride be brought to the groom's tent under the cover of darkness. So Jacob saw his new bride only *after* the honeymoon night was over. His bride was not Rachel! It was her unattractive older sister Leah.

Jacob, with murder in his eyes, was pacified by his new father-in-law with the promise that when the seven-day celebration of his marriage to Leah was over, he could marry Rachel. Of course, after the second wedding to Rachel was over, he had to work an additional seven years to pay for her (29:27–30).

JACOB AND LABAN: THE TABLES TURNED (GEN. 30:1–31:55). The years passed, and Jacob, the father of many children, had learned well his lessons from Laban. Getting Laban to agree to let him have any animal that was not white, Jacob used a mixture of folk medicine (30:37–39) and shrewd observation to cause more of the animals to be born spotted, speckled, or black. While Laban was away, Jacob gathered his family and flocks and left the territory. Laban followed in angry pursuit when he found out what had happened. Before he caught up with Jacob, God appeared to Laban in a dream and told him not to harm Jacob (30:40–31:24).

As a result, when he caught up with Jacob, Laban could only bluster and accuse Jacob of stealing his household idols (31:30). Possession of such symbols gave the possessor claim to the family property.

Rachel, however, not Jacob, had taken the idols. Although her reason is not given, she may have taken them to get back at her father, who had not given her a proper dowry at marriage. A woman's dowry was her social security in her old age. When Laban came searching for them in her tent, she was seated on a camel's saddle in which the idols were hidden. She kept him from finding them by saying she could not rise because "the way of women is upon me" (31:35). In this narrative, there are two new ways of referring to God. In 31:42, God is called the "*God of my father,* the God of Abraham, and the *Fear of Isaac.*"

In parting, a memorial stone was set up and a solemn oath calling on the "God of Abraham and the God of Nahor, the God of their father, [to] judge between us" (31:52–54) was taken. This ceremony, a kind of covenant, was sealed by the oath taking and the sharing of a meal. It was basically a plea to the gods, as guarantors of the covenant, to keep an eye on Jacob and Laban so that they would not cheat each other again (31:25–55)![19]

JACOB AND ESAU: A MAN FACES HIS PAST (GEN. 32:1–33:20). The biblical narrative did not gloss over the weakness of the ancestors. It was not so with Abraham, nor was it so with Jacob, whose sons gave their names to the twelve tribes of Israel. The narrator believes in divine retribution, that is, that evil will be punished. Abraham's lies to the Egyptians concerning Sarah resulted in expulsion from Egypt to face the risk of starvation in the famine conditions of Palestine. Likewise, Jacob's past came back to haunt him.

Traveling down the King's Highway, the major north–south route east of the Jordan, Jacob realized he would soon enter the territory of Esau. First, Jacob sent messengers to Esau to tell him he was coming (32:2–5). When he received word that Esau, with an army of 400, was coming to meet him, he divided his forces and flocks, hoping that an attack on the forward group would give the second group a chance to escape (32:6–8). The prayer of a man facing death and destruction was quite different from the prayer of the brash young man who had stolen his brother's blessing (28:20–22).

Another part of Jacob's strategy was to send an impressive gift to Esau. But even this was not enough to still his fears. We are told of a strange experience in the night when Jacob wrestled with a man (32:13–24). This, in part, suggests a theophany (an appearance of the divine), but it also suggests that Jacob's inner struggle was reaching a climax.[20] From the experience, Jacob derived a new name (Israel), symbolic of a changed man. So that he would remember the experience, he received an injury that caused him to limp (32:25–32).

Jacob was the picture of abject humility when he met Esau. Surprisingly, Esau (now a prosperous desert chieftain) was generous to the brother who had cheated him. They parted, Esau going south to Seir and Jacob going west into the hill country near the ancient city of Shechem (33:1–20).

TROUBLE AT SHECHEM (GEN. 34). In a rare story about a woman, the narrator tells of the rape of Dinah (Jacob and Leah's daughter) and the subsequent vengeance taken by Simeon and Levi, two of Jacob's sons. The story is of interest for two reasons: (1) Levi is mentioned as a secular tribe, indicating that this story is quite old, because in later history, Levi is the priestly tribe. (2) It is believed that this story is included here to indicate why Shechem did not have to be conquered by the Israelites when they came out of Egypt. This would be because some of the Jacob tribes remained near Shechem and did not go to Egypt.[21]

BACK TO BETHEL AND TWO GENEALOGIES (GEN. 35–36). The major stories in which Jacob plays a leading role end with the story of his return to **Bethel**, where he had experienced God's presence some twenty years or more earlier. His wives were instructed to put away foreign gods in preparation for worship (35:2), just as Joshua was to do to the tribes of Israel many years later (Josh. 24). Next, another story of Jacob's name change is associated with worship at Bethel (35:9–15). Finally, there is the account of Rachel's death. The cycle of stories, as is true throughout Genesis, is brought to a close by extended genealogies of Jacob (35:16–29, with the note that Isaac finally died!) and Esau (Gen. 36). Jacob's story is interrupted by the story of Joseph and the beginning of Egyptian bondage.

Joseph: A Wise Israelite Succeeds in Egypt

The story of Joseph takes the form of a novella, or miniature novel. It is as if the storyteller has taken the Joseph traditions and sketched a novel he is going to write. He introduces his hero, Joseph, and the villains, his brothers. Then Joseph goes through a series of reverses and advances,

FIGURE 3–1 "The same night he arose . . . and crossed the ford of the Jabbok" (Gen. 32:22). This site on the Jabbok River is the traditional site of Jacob's nighttime struggles prior to meeting his brother Esau.

climaxing with a suspense-filled scene where Joseph, the prime minister of Egypt, reveals his identity to his brothers, who thought he was long since dead.

The stories concerning Joseph differ in many ways from the stories of the patriarchs. First of all, they have certain of the characteristics of wisdom stories in the Near East: (1) the theme of the stories is that goodness is always rewarded and evil is always punished, which is a major theme of the book of Proverbs; (2) the theme of the oppressed righteous man who overcomes all obstacles and comes out on top, particularly because he possesses the wisdom to interpret dreams, is like that found in the stories concerning Daniel.

A second difference in these stories concerns how God communicates with Joseph. Here there are no divine messengers—no theophanies. Instead, God guides Joseph through the events and circumstances of life.

A third major difference is in the background reflected by the Joseph stories. It is an Egyptian background. The names of the characters, the bestowing of the signet ring and the gold chain as symbols of Joseph's office, and the emphasis on dreams—these and other matters are known from Egyptian records to be characteristic of Egyptian civilization.

Finally, these stories differ in that they are more than a collection of stories. Here, there is a more unified single story, without the repeating of similar stories, as was true in the Abraham–Isaac–Jacob cycle of stories. The only interruption is for the Judah–Tamar story (Gen. 38).

A FANCY COAT AND ANGRY BROTHERS (GEN. 37:1–36). Joseph, the eleventh of Jacob's twelve sons, was his father's favorite. He relished the position, lording it over his older brothers by showing off his fancy clothes and telling them of dreams in which he came out superior to them.

Rough shepherds that they were, they decided to take drastic action to squelch their obnoxious younger brother. Some wanted to kill him, but Reuben prevailed, and they put him into a pit in the dry country instead. Reuben had secretly hoped to rescue him later. Instead, Joseph was sold to a caravan, either to the Ishmaelites (37:25, 27) or Midianites (37:28, 36). (Here is one of the few places that the text shows a blending of traditions.) Eventually, he was sold in Egypt to Potiphar, an officer of the Pharaoh.

JUDAH AND TAMAR (GEN. 38). A rather uncomplimentary story about Joseph's brother Judah interrupts the Joseph narrative. Judah failed to observe the law of custom regarding his obligation to give his widowed daughter-in-law another of his sons as her husband. The purpose of the *law of the levirate* was that the name of a husband who died without a male heir should have his name preserved in the naming of the first son of his widow's second marriage. The second husband was to be his brother or his nearest surviving relative. This arose from the fact that there was no belief in life after death in that time, and one could only continue to exist through his sons. Judah, having failed to give his daughter-in-law a proper husband, was subsequently tricked by Tamar into having a child by her by playing the role of a prostitute. When Judah found out that she was pregnant, he accused her of prostitution, only to find out that he was the one who was guilty of having sexual relations with her. The reason this story is here is not clear, but it does fill in a time gap in the story of Joseph. See the legal discussion of this custom in Deuteronomy 25 and the only other dramatization of it in the book of Ruth.

JOSEPH LOSES ANOTHER CLOAK AND LANDS IN JAIL (GEN. 39:1–20). Years passed, and Joseph was put in charge of Potiphar's business. Mrs. Potiphar tried to seduce the handsome young servant. He refused her advances and, as he ran away, she seized his cloak and yelled, "Rape!" As a result, Joseph landed in jail.

JOSEPH THE PRISONER AND INTERPRETER OF DREAMS (GEN. 39:21–41:56). Joseph, ever the man of responsibility, soon became a trusted prison aide (39:22). When the king's butler and baker, imprisoned because they were in disfavor, had strange dreams, Joseph interpreted them correctly. As predicted, the butler was restored and the baker was hanged. The butler forgot Joseph after promising to reward him (40:1–23).

Then the Pharaoh began to have strange dreams. When all of Pharaoh's wise men failed to interpret them, the butler finally remembered Joseph. Joseph was called before the Pharaoh and interpreted the dreams, predicting that Egypt would have seven years of plenty followed by seven years of famine. The Pharaoh was so impressed by Joseph's wisdom that the former chief prison trusty was made prime minister of Egypt. He was put in charge of the preparations for the great famine (41:1–56).[22]

JOSEPH AND HIS BROTHERS AGAIN (GEN. 42–45). The famine came. Joseph's brothers came to Egypt to buy grain, not realizing that their obnoxious younger brother was now Egypt's chief grain salesman. They did not recognize him (42:8), but Joseph knew them and began a series of tests to find out what sort of characters they now were. First, he accused them of being spies (42:9). Vowing their innocence, they agreed to leave one of their number (Simeon) as a surety until they could return home and bring Benjamin, their younger brother, with them, as Joseph demanded. On the way home, they found all their money in their grain sacks (42:1–38).

When the continuing famine forced the brothers to make a mandatory return trip to Egypt, Joseph's demand that Benjamin be brought aroused strong objections from the aged Jacob. To win his father's reluctant approval for the trip, Judah solemnly vowed to Jacob that Benjamin would be kept safe at the cost of his (Judah's) own life (43:9). When they arrived in Egypt with Benjamin, Simeon was released. Following Simeon's release, the brothers were invited to eat in Joseph's house, with Benjamin receiving special treatment (43:34).

Joseph's testing of the brothers was not at an end, however. He gave orders that when they made their grain purchases, his personal cup was to be hidden in Benjamin's sack. Joseph's soldiers then pursued them and brought them back, and the missing cup was found in Benjamin's sack. Judah, who had played such a prominent role in disposing of Joseph many years before, made a stirring plea for his younger brother, citing the drastic effect the failure of Benjamin's

Lists of the Twelve Sons of Jacob or Twelve Tribes of Israel

The Old Testament presents fifteen lists of tribal names. They vary significantly in order and slightly in the number of tribes included. All of the lists are provided for a purpose within the biblical narrative. Below is a list of the texts where these can be found.

Genesis 29:31–30:24—This text contains the birth accounts of the first eleven sons in chronological order: Reuben, Simeon, Levi, Judah, Dan, Naphtali, Gad, Asher, Issachar, Zebulun, and Joseph. The birth of Benjamin is reported in 35:16–21.

Genesis 35:23–26—The twelve sons are presented within maternal groups: Leah (Reuben, Simeon, Levi, Judah, Issachar, and Zebulun), Rachel (Joseph and Benjamin), Bilhah (Dan and Naphtali), and Zilpah (Gad and Asher).

Genesis 46:8–27

Genesis 49:2–27

Exodus 1:2–4

Numbers 1:6–15—Most of the lists in Numbers omit Levi, because of its priestly status, but they divide Joseph into two tribes, Ephraim and Mannaseh, still producing a total of twelve.

Numbers 1:17–47

Numbers 2

Numbers 7:12–83

Numbers 10

Numbers 13:1–16

Numbers 26:5–51

Numbers 34:16–29

Deuteronomy 27:11–14

Deuteronomy 33:6–29—A poem called the "Blessing of Moses" speaks of the tribes in this order: Reuben, Judah, Levi, Benjamin, Joseph, Zebulun, Issachar, Gad, Dan, Naphtali, Asher. The movement of Benjamin and the omission of Simeon are the most noticeable differences from the initial list in Genesis.

A sixteenth list can be constructed from the land allotment procedure in Joshua 13–22. Like all of the lists above, this one indicates that the negotiation of status and relationships among the tribes was likely a complex, ongoing process in ancient Israel.

return would have on their father (44:18–34). Joseph, now convinced that his brothers had suffered enough, revealed his true identity to them (45:1–4). Rather than blaming them for their mistreatment of him, he interpreted it as the providential work of God, who had sent him to Egypt to preserve them all (45:7).

THE FAMILY IN EGYPT (GEN. 46–50). The brothers returned to Palestine and brought their father to Egypt. His meeting with the Pharaoh involved some verbal sparring to determine who was the elder of the two. Because Jacob was the elder, he had to pronounce a blessing on the Pharaoh (47:7–12). Some see this as evidence that the Egyptian ruler was a Semite, as was Jacob, because a native Egyptian would not seek blessing from a Semite—he would have instead held him in contempt. This would have taken place, then, during the Hyksos rule (1720–1570 B.C.E.), because they were Semites.

Genesis ends with the blessing of Jacob's sons (Gen. 49), the story of Jacob's death and burial, and, finally, Joseph's death, preceded by his request not to be buried in Egypt (Gen. 50).

GENESIS IN RETROSPECT

The Ancestral Complex was composed by later historians from traditions from different times and different places. The many names for God that have been noted, the different versions of the same story, the different emphases in the accounts of the covenant, and the shifting back and forth of certain personal names (Jacob, Israel) all indicate something of the variety of sources that were used. But to concentrate on the differences would be to miss the main purpose the writers had in mind. Like Genesis 1–11, Genesis 12–50 has much to say about God and His divine relationship to the world but more particularly to a people—Israel.

A vast array of literary techniques has served to bring the reader of Genesis from a vague and unfamiliar primeval world to a more certain and recognizable one. Most significant perhaps is the movement from those who walk and talk with God (Eve, Adam, and Enoch) to those who speak directly with God (Abraham, Sarah, and Isaac) to those guided by dreams and intuition (Jacob, Leah, Tamar, and Joseph).[23]

The later Israelites were convinced that they were a people divinely chosen to fulfill God's purpose in the world. That choice was embodied in a particular man, Abraham, and was symbolized by the covenant, a binding contract between God and Abraham that involved Abraham's loyalty to God and God's blessing of Abraham and, through him, his descendants. The covenant was reaffirmed to each succeeding patriarch, but it also demanded their commitment to it. Thus, Jacob had to be purified through long years of subjection to the wiles of Laban and the frightening confrontation with Esau before he could be called Israel, "prince of God." The writers knew that God had to work through imperfect people, because those are the only kind of people available. Through the long years, God was preparing (1) a person, (2) a family, and (3) finally, a people to serve the divine purpose in the world.

Key Terms

Akedah, *50*
Ark, *46*
Babel, *47*
Bethel, *54*
Birthright, *52*
Concubine, *49*
Covenant, *38*
Genealogy, *44*
Haran, *48*
Heavenly Court, *41*
Nomad, *48*
Theophany, *50*

Study Questions

1. What does the statement "The primary purpose of Genesis is theological" mean? Does that exclude other purposes?
2. How does the biblical Creation story differ from other creation stories?
3. Compare the portraits of God in 1:1–2:4a to those in 2:4b–3:25. What do they say about Israel's understanding of God?
4. Identify (a) *Enuma Elish,* (b) Atrahasis Epic, (c) Gilgamesh Epic, (d) covenant, and (e) ziggurat.
5. What is the theological importance of the biblical Flood story?
6. If one assumes that the Tower of Babel is an etiology, what "Why?" questions would it answer?
7. What factors contribute to a dating of the patriarchs in the period from 2000 B.C.E. to 1500 B.C.E.?
8. The patriarchs were heads of extended families or clans. What does this mean?
9. How are the covenant accounts in Genesis 13:14–17, 15:17–21, and 17:1–21 alike, and how do they differ?
10. Many readers have noticed that Genesis 14 looks and sounds quite different from the material surrounding it. What unusual features are present in this chapter?
11. What is the nature of the relationship between Sarah and Hagar?
12. If Abraham were living today and attempted to sacrifice his son, how would you view it? Why should your view be different in the light of his times?
13. What is a theophany? How are theophanies portrayed in the book of Genesis?
14. How did Abraham respond to his prolonged inability to produce an heir with Sarah?
15. How do you account for the similarities between the stories about Sarah and the Pharaoh (Gen. 12:14–20), Sarah and Abimelech (20:1–18), and Rebekah and Abimelech (26:6–11)?
16. In a good Bible dictionary, read about *blessing* and *curse.* What part do these play in the Jacob–Esau stories?
17. Why do you suppose the biblical storyteller glorifies Jacob's deceptive ways?
18. How can one understand Jacob's willingness to work for Laban for such a long time?
19. What result, other than a change of name, came from Jacob's experience at the Jabbok River?
20. How do the stories about Joseph differ from other patriarchal stories?
21. Why is Joseph usually associated with the Hyksos rulers of Egypt?
22. What reason does Genesis 45 give for Joseph's experiences?
23. What literary features distinguish Genesis 12–50 from Genesis 1–11?

Endnotes

1. For all the gory details, see James B. Pritchard, ed., *The Ancient Near East: An Anthology of Texts and Pictures (ANE)* (Princeton, NJ: Princeton University Press, 1958), 30–39.
2. Compare the view of God here with that found in Isaiah 40:12–31.
3. See 1 Kings 22:19–23; Zechariah 3:1–2; and Job 1–2. For a good discussion of this problem, see Bruce Vawter, *On Genesis: New Reading* (Garden City, NY: Doubleday, 1977), 53ff. See also Edward M. Curtis, "Image of God," *ABD,* III, 389–391.
4. Pritchard, *ANE,* 70.
5. Wilford G. Lambert and A. R. Millard, *Atrahasis: The Babylonian Story of the Flood* (New York: Oxford University Press, 1969), is the most recent translation.
6. For an extended discussion of the matter, see Ronald S. Hendel, "When the Sons of God Cavorted with the Daughters of Men," *BR,* III, 2 (Summer 1987), 8–13.
7. God (Priestly version): 6:1–4, 9–22; 7:11–8:5, 13–19. LORD (Yahwist version): 6:5–8; 7:1–10; 8:6–12, 20–22.
8. See Vawter, *On Genesis,* 115, for a list of duplications.
9. For a serious discussion of wood samples for Mount Ararat, see Lloyd R. Bailey, "Wood from Mount 'Ararat': Noah's Ark?" *BA,* 40, 4 (December 1977), 137–146. On the significance of the Flood story, see, by the same author, *Noah: The Person in History and Tradition* (Columbia: University of South Carolina Press, 1989).
10. See Tikva Frymer-Kensky, "The Atrahasis Epic and Its Significance for Our Understanding of Genesis 1–9," *BA,* 40, 4 (December, 1977), 147–155.
11. For two somewhat contradictory, yet related, articles on the background of the patriarchal age, see

Kenneth Kitchen, "The Patriarchal Age: Myth or History?" *BAR*, 21, 2 (March–April, 1995), 48–56, and Ronald Hendel, "Finding Historical Memories," 59, 70–71. For a radically different view, see J. Van Seters, *Abraham in History and Tradition* (New Haven, CT: Yale University Press, 1975).

12. For a contrary view suggesting that Abraham came from Asia Minor, see Cyrus H. Gordon, "Where Is Abraham's Ur?" *BAR*, III, 2 (June 1977), 21–22, 52.

13. For this and other characteristics of patriarchal life, see Victor H. Matthews, *Manners and Customs in the Bible* (Peabody, MA: Henrickson Publishers, 1988), 1–32.

14. For a discussion of the relationship of Genesis to the rest of the Abram cycle, see E. A. Speiser, "Genesis," in *AB*, 1, 105–109.

15. On the meaning of this and other names for God in Genesis, see Ranier Albertz, *A History of Israelite Religion in the Old Testament Period*, I, John Bowden, translator (Louisville, KY: Westminster–John Knox Press, 1994), 29–32.

16. This report on an article by Graham Harris and Anthony Beardow was written by Associated Press reporter Edith M. Lederer, "Geologists Say Quake Destroyed Sodom, Gomorrah," *The Chattanooga News-Free-Press*, December 19, 1995.

17. For the many ways this passage has been interpreted, see Robin M. Jensen, "This Binding or Sacrifice of Isaac—How Jews and Christians See Differently," *BR*, IX, 5 (October 1993), 42–51; and another alternative by Lippman Bodoff, "God Tests Abraham," op cit., 53–56, 62.

18. Martha A. Morrison, "The Jacob and Laban Narratives in Light of Near Eastern Sources," *BA*, 45, 3 (Summer 1983), 155–164, is an excellent article on the Jacob–Laban stories. In addition, Samuel Dresner, "Rachel and Leah: Sibling Rivalry or the Triumph of Piety and Compassion?" *BR*, VI, 2 (April 1990), 6, points out that the names of Leah's sons reflect the desire to be loved by her husband, while the names of Rachel's sons reflect her desire to be a mother.

19. Gordon Tucker, "Jacob's Terrible Burden," *BR*, X, 3 (June 1994), 20–28, argues that Jacob felt that his oath to Laban was the cause of Rachel's premature death, as well as his problems with Joseph and Benjamin.

20. Jack Miles, "Jacob's Wrestling Match: Was It an Angel or Esau?" *BR*, XIV, 5 (October 1998), 22–23, makes an interesting argument that it was Esau with whom Jacob wrestled.

21. Richard Elliott Friedman, *Who Wrote the Bible?* (Upper Saddle River, NJ: Prentice Hall, 1987), 62f., suggests that the story of Dinah was told by the Judahites to embarrass the tribe of Ephraim and that the story of Judah's incestuous relationship with his daughter-in-law Tamar (Genesis 37) was designed to embarrass the tribe of Judah.

22. Nahum M. Sarna, "Exploring Exodus: The Oppression," *BA*, 49, 2 (June 1986), 70, points out that the Joseph stories fit well into what is known as the Hyksos period (1720–1570 B.C.E.). "The Second Intermediate Period in Egyptian history is marked by a strong Semitic presence."

23. See the discussion of this pattern of changing interaction with God in Jack Miles, *God: A Biography* (New York: Vintage Books, 1995), 78–80.

CHAPTER

4

Israel Becomes a People

Exodus and Wilderness

Timeline

1500 B.C.E.	Beginning of the Late Bronze Age
1305 B.C.E.	Beginning of the reign of Pharaoh Seti
1290 B.C.E.	Beginning of the reign of Ramses II
1280 B.C.E.	Possible date of the Exodus from Egypt
1250 B.C.E.	Frequent guess for date of Israelite entrance into the Promised Land
1224 B.C.E.	Mernerptah's invasion of Palestine
1200 B.C.E.	Beginning of the Iron Age

Chapter Outline

I. The Book of Israel's Beginnings
II. Moses: Birth and Wilderness Years
III. Moses: The Struggle with the Pharaoh
IV. The Exodus Event
V. Sinai and the Giving of the Law
VI. After Mount Sinai
VII. Themes in the Pentateuch

CHAPTER OVERVIEW

This chapter covers a vast amount of biblical material: the books of Exodus, Leviticus, Numbers, and Deuteronomy. What holds all of this material together is the gigantic figure of Moses, who is born in Exodus 2 and dies in Deuteronomy 34. The first part of the book of Exodus will tell the story of the departure of the Israelites from Egypt. After this, the forging of the Israelites as a people appears in four movements that alternate in form and content. Exodus 14–18 will tell the initial story of the Israelites in the wilderness, leading up to their arrival at Mount Sinai. A large, diverse collection of legal material then fills the vast majority of Exodus 19 through Numbers 9 (including the entire book of Leviticus). A second collection of wilderness narratives is found in Numbers 10–36, with smaller pieces of legal material within it. Finally, most of the book of Deuteronomy contains legal material presented by Moses to the Israelites in Moab as they wait to enter the Promised Land. Thus, the whole story presents an alternating pattern: wilderness–law–wilderness–law. This pattern highlights the contrast between the threat of death and disorder and the promise of life and order contained in Mosaic law.

The Literary Structure of Exodus

The book of Exodus, because of its varied and composite nature, does not have an easily discernible overall design. Many attempts to determine a structure for the book of Exodus have focused upon place and movement. The book would then fall into sections such as

1:1–12:36	The Israelites in Egypt
12:37–18:27	The Israelites in the Wilderness
19:1–40:30	The Israelites at Sinai

On the other hand, based upon literary form, Exodus falls roughly into two halves: the story of the departure from Egypt (1–18) and the reception of the law at Mount Sinai (19–40). The situation is more complex than either of these simple outlines, though. There is legal material in the first half of the book, and there is narrative material in the second half. The relationship between the book of Exodus and the book of Leviticus, which follows it, also complicates the issue. There is a strong sense of continuity between the second half of Exodus and Leviticus, just as there is continuity between Genesis and the first half of Exodus. Thus, this second book of the Bible tends to get pulled apart from both ends. If there is a sense of unity and literary design to the book, then the feeling of movement and the mixture of literary forms indicate that it should probably be based upon transitions and points of connection. The structure proposed here is less certain and less defined than that proposed earlier for the book of Genesis, but it may point to a way to view the book of Exodus as a whole.

Rather than understanding the beginning of the legal material in Exodus as a break or division, it may be more helpful to view it as a transitional center. The giving of the Ten Commandments in 20:1–21 may function as a pivotal point in the story. Until the end of chapter 19, the people of Israel are moving toward God with Moses in the lead (19:17). The experience of receiving the Ten Commandments convinces the people that they want no part in direct contact with God, but want Moses to act as an intermediary (20:18–21). The stories of the first half of the book of Exodus (slavery, calling of Moses, plagues, wilderness travels) are centered on the Passover legislation, in which Moses receives instructions from God and passes them on to the people (12:1–27). Everything operates according to plan, and God liberates the Israelites. The legal material in the second half of the book is centered on the golden calf episode in chapters 32 to 34. This set of stories illustrates the danger of not following proper procedures. Implements of worship are produced without instructions from Moses, and disaster follows. The two halves of the book thus operate as mirror images of one another and establish a pattern of law and narrative functioning together for the rest of the Torah. The giving of the Ten Commandments is a story about giving and receiving law that works out the way in which it should be done. It turns out that the Exodus story solves a major problem for those in Israel who wished to publish a body of laws. The story operates as an ideal vehicle for presenting the legal material, and it provides its main character, Moses, to be the ideal teacher of the law.

THE BOOK OF ISRAEL'S BEGINNINGS

In the Hebrew Bible, Exodus is called *w'elah sh'mot,* "these are the names," referring to the twelve sons of Jacob. It also has been called "the book of the departure from Egypt," by the LXX, or Septuagint, from which our title *Exodus* is derived.

Exodus begins Israel's story with Moses, his preparation for and elevation to the leadership of his people (by the LORD's hand) and the Exodus (1:1–12:36). It continues with the wilderness experiences (12:37–18:27), and it ends with the giving of the Law at Sinai, including the Covenant Code and the story of the completion of the tabernacle (18:28–40:38).[1]

The Importance of the Exodus Story

What the Fourth of July is to the citizens of the United States, Bastille Day is to the French, and the Magna Carta is to the English, the Exodus was to the Israelites. The Israelite writers have mentioned the Exodus more than any other event in their history. In the book of Psalms, for instance, the Exodus theme is sounded again and again. A good example is Psalm 105. After recounting the plagues, the psalmist says:

> Then he brought Israel out with silver and gold,
>   and there was no one among their tribes who stumbled.
> Egypt was glad when they departed,
>   for the dread of them had fallen upon it.
> He spread a cloud for a covering,
>   and fire to give light by night.
> They asked, and he brought quails,
>   and gave them food from heaven in abundance.
> He opened the rock, and the water gushed out;
>   it flowed through the desert like a river.
> For he remembered his holy promise,
>   and Abraham, his servant.

The Nature of the Exodus and the Exodus Materials

The picture that emerges from a superficial reading of the narrative portions of the books of Exodus and Numbers gives the familiar outline of the Exodus as most people know it—the sojourn in Egypt; the birth and preparation of Moses; the Exodus, with its dramatic delivery of the Israelites at the Red Sea; the wilderness wanderings and the rebellious murmurings of the people; the giving of the Law at Sinai; and the subsequent experiences of the people in the years before the invasion of Palestine.

The picture given, however, is the simplified version of a much more complicated process. None of my own ancestors came to America prior to the American Revolution. Yet, I, like most Americans, speak of our "founding fathers" as if I actually had an ancestor among the early settlers at Jamestown or Plymouth. Likewise, later Israelites, and even present-day Jews, speak as though they are all direct descendants of the people Moses led out of Egypt. Yet, as Joshua 24:14–28 indicates, what became Israel actually was a diverse group, composed of people of a Semitic background as well as non-Semites, including people of the land who never had been in Egypt. This is supported by a careful reading of the book of Exodus, which shows how various sources have been brought together to tell what the LORD had done for Israel. Moses is the major human character in the Exodus narratives, but they are designed not to glorify Moses, but rather to glorify the LORD, the God of Israel. It was the LORD of history and the master of the created order who brought Israel out of Egypt. The narration of the Exodus events was a central theme in the worship of Israel, and no word of praise was too elaborate to describe what the LORD did in bringing Israel from Egyptian slavery.[2]

MOSES: BIRTH AND WILDERNESS YEARS

Changed Times and Changed Circumstances (Exod. 1)

Joseph could not live forever, nor could one expect the Hyksos rulers to dominate Egypt forever. Joseph died, and the Hyksos were overthrown. As native Egyptians regained control of their government, the circumstances of the Hebrews changed. They had been settled in northeastern Egypt, east of the delta, where the Nile broke up into a number of branches, like the fingers on a hand. The area known as Goshen was suitable for the grazing of the sheep and cattle of the tent-dwelling Hebrews.

Over time, the original seventy persons in the family of Jacob prospered and their numbers expanded. This alarmed the rulers of Egypt, who, in typical political exaggeration, said that the people of Israel were "too many and too mighty for us" (1:9). This was their justification for enslaving the Hebrews to build projects at the cities of Pithom and Ramses (1:11). It is not clear how the Pharaoh and the Egyptians thought that enslaving the Israelites would limit their population growth. The failure of such a plan is indicated by two additional attempts to control their population. The first of these plans fails when the midwives, Shiphrah and Puah, refuse to help the Pharaoh by killing all of the Hebrew male children at the time of their birth. The effects of the second plan, commanding the Egyptian people to throw all Hebrew baby boys into the Nile, are never described, but this ploy sets the stage for the dramatic events in the next chapter.

Moses' Early Life[3]

It is a great irony that Moses will eventually rise up and defeat Egypt, for he is "thrown into the Nile," just as the Pharaoh commanded, at the end of the first chapter. It is also the Pharaoh's own daughter who saves Moses. The second chapter of Exodus moves through the life of Moses in rapid fashion. One of the problems it must solve is that of the Egyptian identity Moses has acquired in the story. By the end of this chapter, though, Moses has fled from danger in his own family, traveled through the wilderness, met his wife by a well, become the caretaker of his father-in-law's sheep, and had a son. He has shed the Egyptian identity and begun to look quite a lot like an Israelite, specifically like Jacob.

Moses' future identity as the liberator of Israel is foreshadowed in this chapter by the story in which he kills an Egyptian who is beating a Hebrew slave. This story raises some difficult moral

Miriam

The sister of Moses receives only occasional attention in the Exodus and wilderness stories. When her name is first mentioned in Exodus 15:20, she is not identified as the sister of Moses but rather as the sister of **Aaron**. It is commonly assumed that Miriam is the sister who, in Exodus 2:1–11, makes sure that Moses ends up taken care of by Pharaoh's daughter, but her name is never provided in that story. It is not until a genealogical notice in Numbers 26:59 that **Miriam** is specifically identified by name as the sister of Moses. The Exodus and wilderness narratives provide only occasional glimpses of this character in Exodus 15:20–21. She is portrayed singing in celebration of the defeat of the Egyptians and is described as a "prophet." The words of her brief song have already been absorbed, however, into the longer Song of the Sea, sung by Moses in 15:1–18.

The next time Miriam appears is in the strange story in Numbers 12 in which she and Aaron complain about Moses' marriage to a Cushite woman. It is not clear why they object to this marriage. The claim made by Miriam and Aaron that God had also spoken through them likely confirms the earlier identification of Miriam as a prophet. Nevertheless, God is angered by their opposition to Moses and strikes Miriam with leprosy. Curiously, Aaron is not punished in any way here. Aaron, of course, is the High Priest, and a High Priest with leprosy would be a tremendous problem. Aaron, however, does plead for the life of Miriam. As a result, her leprosy is limited to a seven-day period and her life is spared.

The next mention of Miriam is a brief notice of her death in Leviticus 20:1. Later remembrances of Miriam are split in their view of her. In Deuteronomy 24:9 her leprosy is used as a threat against potential disobedience by the Israelites. In Micah 6:4 she is listed, along with Moses and Aaron, as a leader sent by God to Israel. It seems likely that the role of Miriam may have been significant, but it has been overshadowed in Israelite tradition by the gigantic figure of Moses.

issues regarding Moses, but the person Moses is coming to resemble, Jacob, was also of questionable moral character. It is difficult to miss the significant role that female characters play in making the career of this great liberator possible. He would not have survived were it not for the actions of his mother, who hid him; his sister, who watched over him; and the Pharaoh's daughter, who took him from the water. The sister is not named here, but she will be identified later as Miriam, a woman with whom Moses has a complicated relationship (see Exodus 15 and Numbers 12).[4]

The birth story of Moses invites some comparison with the birth stories of other ancient heroes, particularly an Akkadian king named Sargon, who lived about 1000 years earlier. The legend of Sargon includes a story in which he was saved from danger as an infant by a mother who hid him in a basket in a river. Moses' story is something of a reversal of Sargon's, who was royal offspring endangered by internal conflict and was raised as a commoner after he was rescued from the river.[5]

Exodus 2 ends the way Exodus 1 begins, with the death of a pharaoh. Still, the Israelites are suffering in slavery, but God hears their cries and "remembers his covenant with Abraham, Isaac, and Jacob."

The Call of Moses (Exod. 3:1–4:17)

Moses was not destined to be a sheepherder all his life. His solitary job through the years had given him knowledge of the desert that was to be invaluable in the work of leading the people from Egypt. It was not conscious preparation on Moses' part. Rather, for the storyteller, it was the providence of God working to prepare the man for the work he was to do.

Those years of preparation came to an end on a mountain called Horeb in one tradition (3:1) and Sinai in another (19:11). While pasturing his flocks, Moses suddenly became aware of a bush that was aflame, seemingly without burning up. As he went closer, he became aware of a "presence." Out of this experience came Moses' call to lead the people out of Egypt. This call experience is significant because it was said to be the time when God revealed his personal name to Moses. Of the two major terms used by Israel to speak of God, *Elohim* was what one might call the general or, to use a common analogy, the "family," name for God. It was not only used to refer to the one God, but also might be used to refer to any god or gods (3:1–5).

The name **YHWH** seems to be related to God's statement *'eyeh 'eyeh* (translated I AM WHO I AM in the New Revised Standard Version) in Exodus 3:14. This name, first revealed to Moses on the mountain, was the personal name of God. For example, there might be a large family of Fafoofniks, but only one Fafoofnik with the personal name Abercrombie. Thus, there were many *Elohims,* but only one YHWH.

The proper pronunciation and meaning of the name YHWH is subject to much debate because it ceased to be pronounced sometime after the Babylonian Exile. It is believed, however, that it was pronounced *Yahweh.* In Jewish religious services today, the tetra-grammaton, YHWH, is not pronounced, because to pronounce it wrongly would defile the holiness of God. A substitute word, *Adonai* (translated LORD), is used. This practice of using LORD for YHWH is followed in this textbook. Its meaning is variously interpreted: I AM WHO I AM, I WILL BE WHO I WILL BE, I CAUSE TO BE WHAT IS. Each translation has strong arguments in its favor.

Moses' Objection

When God called Moses, Moses was told that this was the God of the patriarchs (3:6). Moses was awestruck, but he was not so awed that he could not argue, especially when the LORD said, "I will send you to Pharaoh that you may bring my people, the sons of Israel, out of Egypt." Moses immediately began to make excuses: (1) The excuse: "Who am I that I should go?" (3:11); the answer: "You will have the LORD's presence with you, and He will bring the people to this mountain (3:12); (2) the excuse: "Who are you that you are sending me?" (3:13); the answer: "You shall say, 'YHWH {the LORD}, the God of Abraham, of Isaac, and of Jacob has sent me' " (3:14–22); (3) the excuse: "But they will not believe me" (4:1); the answer: "I will give you signs—a rod changed to a snake, a leprous hand healed" (4:2–9); (4) the final excuse: "LORD, I cannot talk!" (4:10); the answer: "I will give you your eloquent brother **Aaron** to be your spokesman" (4:14–17).

On the Road to Egypt (Exod. 4:18–31)

His excuses in tatters by the divine answers, Moses set out for Egypt, with the blessing of Jethro. The story of the return to Egypt contains a strange incident (4:24–26), somewhat like Jacob's wrestling match in Genesis 32. At a lodging place in the wilderness, it is said that the LORD attempted to kill Moses. He was saved when Zipporah, his wife, **circumcised** their son and touched Moses with the bloody foreskin, saying, "Truly, you are a bridegroom of blood to me!" Although the meaning of this ancient story is unclear, it probably indicated that Moses was not properly circumcised. Furthermore, in much of the Old Testament, the LORD is looked upon as the cause of everything. This is reflected in the saying of the prophet Amos: "Can disaster befall the city, unless the LORD has done it?" (Amos 3:8). The idea of an evil force in the world outside of God's control that caused bad things to happen did not come into prominence until the post-Exilic period of Israel's history. The Hebrews did believe in demons, but the demons were under divine control. This may reflect the idea of a demonic attack on Moses. Why it is included here is uncertain.[6]

Aaron, hearing that Moses was returning to Egypt, met him on the way. Moses briefed him on what they were to do. As soon as the brothers arrived in Egypt, Aaron, in turn, told the Hebrews what was to happen.

MOSES: THE STRUGGLE WITH THE PHARAOH

The Struggle Begins: Moses and Aaron before the Pharaoh (Exod. 5:1–6:1)

The task before Moses and Aaron was not an easy one. As an excuse to get the people out of Egypt, they asked the Pharaoh to let the people take a three-day journey into the wilderness to worship. The Pharaoh's reaction was an outright rejection of the request and an increase in the workload on the Hebrews (5:1–9). They, in turn, vented their anger on Moses and Aaron, calling down the LORD's judgment upon them (5:20–21). Moses complained to the LORD, who assured him that there would soon be action.[7]

Moses' Call, the Covenant, and a Genealogy (Exod. 6:2–7:7)

Ancient covenants were of at least two types: (1) The *suzerainty treaty* was an agreement or contract between a superior party and an inferior party. The superior party (in this case, God) set forth the terms of the agreement, because he had the power to do so. The superior party could obligate himself only if he chose to do so; the inferior party had no choice. Divine mercy and honor obligated God to meet the terms set forth. (2) The *parity treaty* was an agreement between equals in which both parties contributed to the agreement and both bore equal obligations to see that it was preserved.[8]

Another version of the call of Moses is given here, with a strong emphasis on the suzerainty covenant made with the patriarchs.

Abraham, Isaac, and Jacob knew God as *El Shaddai* (God Almighty) and not as YHWH (the LORD) (6:2–3). The people were to be reminded of the earlier covenant to assure them that God would (1) deliver them from Egypt, (2) make them God's people, (3) be their God, and (4) give them their own land. As usual, when Moses told the people, they ignored him. When he complained to God, he was told to keep telling them (6:9–13).

This priestly version of the call of Moses and Aaron includes a genealogy to establish their credentials. Perhaps of greater significance here is the statement in 7:1 concerning Aaron's role in relation to Moses. In the account of Moses' call in 3:1–4:17, Moses had complained of his speech problems. Here, Moses voices the same complaint (6:30) and is told, "See, I have made you like God to Pharaoh, and your brother Aaron shall be your prophet" (7:1). This word *prophet* was the same term used to describe the great prophets of Israel. Just as Aaron spoke for Moses, the prophets spoke for God.

The Plagues (Exod. 7:8–11:10)

The stage was set for the struggle to free the Hebrews. It was not just a struggle between human powers; rather, it was a struggle between the LORD and the gods of Egypt in the person of their earthly representative, the divine Pharaoh. Because the gods of Egypt were associated with the Nile, Moses chose to challenge them on their home court, so to speak.

After an opening round in which the Egyptian magicians duplicated the actions of Moses and Aaron (the use of serpent magic, the reddening of the Nile, and the **plague** of the frogs), the Egyptian magicians surrendered, saying, "This is the finger of God" (8:19). From that point on, the plagues increased in intensity until the climax was reached with the death of the Egyptian firstborn and the escape from Egypt.

The number of plagues varies according to the source. Psalms 78:43–51 lists eight plagues, a number believed to be based on an old epic source (or J, according to the Documentary Hypothesis) and emphasizes the role of Moses in Exodus. Psalm 105:27–36 seemingly is based on the priestly tradition that magnifies Aaron's role. The book of Exodus shows evidence of both traditions.[9]

The plagues were evidence for later Israel that the LORD had been at work on their behalf, using divine power over nature to convince the Pharaoh that he must free them from bondage. Israel's later retelling of the events did not have as its primary purpose recording history for twentieth-century readers, but rather "as a celebration of God's great victory whereby he is glorified and acknowledged as sole sovereign and power."[10] This is not to deny that the accounts of the plagues grew out of actual events, but rather that Israel was more concerned about praising God than it was about writing history.

THE PLAGUES AS MIRACLE. *Miracle* is a term often used in religious circles. A rather common element in many definitions of *miracle* is that it is something that cannot be explained by ordinary means. A believer in God would say that it is evidence of God's power. But any definition of the miraculous that requires that the happening must not be explainable in human terms means that, once it can be explained, it will no longer be a miracle. Our great-great-grandfathers would say that television is a miracle, but to us it is a common, everyday fact of life. We do not look at it as a miracle. One's inability to explain an event, therefore, is not a reliable standard for judging whether or not it is miraculous.

All definitions of *miracle* start with the basic idea that it is a religious interpretation of an event. If this is true, then whether an event is miraculous depends, to a certain extent, on the person who views that event. It has been illustrated in this fashion: A bear was chasing a man through Yellowstone Park. The man ran across the site of the Old Faithful geyser, which erupts every sixty minutes or so. The bear, close behind, crossed the geyser the split second it erupted, throwing him high into the air and killing him. To the onlookers, it was a spectacular event; to the man, it was a miracle; to the bear, it was a catastrophe.[11]

To develop a workable definition of *miracle*, it is necessary to examine the Israelite view of God's relationship to the world. According to the Creation story in Genesis 1–2, the world was created through God's power. It is God's world, and He is active in it, bringing both judgment (as in the case of Sodom and Gomorrah) and blessing (the promise to Abraham). Nothing happens in the world except as God wills it to happen. To the Israelites, there was no such thing as a natural event. God was in everything—whether it was a storm, a drought, or a baby's birth. In short, the biblical writers—especially the Old Testament writers—did not make the distinction between natural and supernatural that we make.

The biblical writers used miracles to "call attention to something else which was going on that was even more important than the miracle." For example, the importance of the burning bush (Exodus 3:2–5) was that it directed Moses' attention to God rather than to the bush itself.[12]

In this light, the plagues were viewed by the Israelites as the activity of God because God is active in everything. Two things characterized them as miraculous for Israel: (1) Moses predicted them, and (2) their timing was right for Israel's needs. Had these same events happened at a different time or under different circumstances, Israel might well have interpreted them in an entirely different light. A miracle, then, could be defined as any event that, when seen through the eyes of faith, strengthens the faith of the believer.

THE PHARAOH'S COMPROMISE OFFER AND THE EIGHTH AND NINTH PLAGUES (EXOD. 10:1–11:10). The Pharaoh's advisers urged him to give in to the demands of Moses and Aaron, but the proud ruler did not want to admit complete defeat. Calling the Hebrew leaders in, he offered a series of compromises. He asked Moses who was to go. Moses replied that all of their families and flocks had to go. The Pharaoh offered his first compromise: "Go, but take only the men."

The LORD's reply through Moses was a plague of locusts. These insects, a variety of grasshopper, have been a plague of Africa and the Eastern countries throughout recorded history. Their devastation is chillingly described by the prophet Joel (1:4, 7, 10):

> What the cutting locust left,
> the swarming locust has eaten.
> What the swarming locust left,
> the hopping locust has eaten.
> What the hopping locust left,
> the destroying locust has eaten.
> It (the locust) has laid waste my vines,
> and splintered my fig trees;
> it has stripped off their bark and thrown it down;
> their branches have turned white.
> The fields are devastated,
> the ground mourns;
> for the grain is destroyed,
> the wine dries up,
> the oil fails.

The locusts were blown into the land by a strong east wind, the dread *sirocco,* which blew in from the Sinai Desert. Another wind, called a "strong sea breeze" by the Hebrew text and thus a north wind in Egypt, caused the plague to be lifted when Moses prayed (10:18–20). But when the pressure let up, the Pharaoh was back to his old ways.

The ninth plague (10:21–29), "a darkness that can be felt" (10:21), was in some ways the most disturbing of all. The probable cause was the blinding sandstorms that come with the March winds from the Sahara. The darkness blotted out the sun, or Amun Re, the chief deity among the Egyptian gods. Amun Re's daily march across the heavens was the greatest constant in Egyptian life and as such was a symbol of life itself. For the LORD to prevent Amun Re from rising for three days was a clear demonstration that the LORD was more powerful than Amun Re.

Because the pharaohs also were thought to be divine, the statement "the LORD hardened Pharaoh's heart" also had a religious connotation. One of the three words translated as *hardened* (*kaved,* 10:1) literally means "to make heavy." The Egyptian notion of the final judgment was that one's heart was weighed on a balance with a feather as a counterweight. If one's heart was pure, there was a balance and the person gained eternal life. If, however, one's heart outweighed the feather, the person was devoured by the goddess Amenit. To say that the Pharaoh had a hard (heavy) heart meant that he was no deity. Instead, he was no more than an ordinary mortal whose heavy heart would lead to his destruction at the hands of the LORD of all creation.[13]

The Plagues as Attack Against Egyptian Deities

Plague	Deity or Deities Against Whom the Plague Was Directed
1. Nile turned to blood	Khnum—creator of water and life; or Hapi—the Nile God; or Osiris—the Nile was his bloodstream
2. Frogs	Heket—goddess of childbirth, whose symbol was the frog
3. Lice	No known deity
4. Flies	No known deity
5. Pestilence in cattle	Hathor—mother and sky goddess, whose symbol was the cow; or Apis—the bull god
6. Boils	No known deity
7. Hail	Seth—god of wind and storms
8. Locusts	Isis—goddess of life; or Min—goddess of fertility and vegetation
9. Darkness	The sun deities, Amun-Re, Atum, or Horus
10. Death of the firstborn	Osiris—judge of the dead and patron deity of the Pharaoh

Pharaoh summoned Moses and Aaron to deal with them again. This time he offered to let them take their families, but they had to leave their herds. Moses quickly rejected any compromise: "Not a hoof shall be left behind," he declared (10:24–25). After all, one could not have a sacrifice without a victim. With that rejection, Moses was ordered from the presence of the Pharaoh.

THE FINAL PLAGUE: THE DEATH OF THE FIRSTBORN (EXOD. 11:1–10, 12:29–32). Although timing was the significant factor in the first nine plagues, causing them to be wonders in the eyes of the Hebrews, both the timing and the selective nature of the tenth plague made it the climactic event for Israel. The firstborn son was the most important child, especially from a practical standpoint. This was illustrated by Jacob's devious actions designed to secure the rights of the firstborn for himself. To lose the firstborn was (and still is) a devastating psychological blow to a family, and was even more so in ancient days if the firstborn was a son. For the firstborn son of the Pharaoh, who considered himself to be divine, this would be the crowning blow in the struggle between the LORD and the gods of Egypt.

THE MEANING OF THE PLAGUES. How are the plagues to be interpreted? A basic assumption is that whatever one's understanding of what actually happened and how it happened, for Israel the plagues were a manifestation of the power of God, the mighty act that the LORD had done in Egypt (Exod. 14:31). Beyond that basic assumption, two interpretations have been proposed: (1) that they were attacks against the deities of Egypt (Num. 33:4) and (2) that they were meant to teach Israel that the God of Creation was the God who had delivered them from Egypt. The latter interpretation is suggested by the Sabbath commandment as found in Deuteronomy 5:15.

This way of interpreting the plagues views them as a reversal of Creation intended to make Israel aware of God's power. He who had brought order out of chaos in Creation had now turned the orderly life of Egypt back to chaos. The climactic act was the drowning of the Egyptian army in the waters of chaos at the Red Sea.[14]

FIGURE 4–1 "The Pharaoh said to (Moses), 'Get away from me . . . do not see my face again'" (Exod. 10:28). This statue is a representation of Ramses II, believed to be the Pharaoh of the Exodus.

THE EXODUS EVENT

Passover and Departure

Exodus 12–13 tell the story of the Israelite departure from Egypt and are dominated by the *Passover* tradition. Instructions for both the immediate Passover event, which will protect the Israelites from the effect of the final plague, and the perpetual observation of Passover, which will provide for a remembrance of the event, are given by God to Moses and Aaron in 12:1–21. Moses then passes on a much briefer set of instructions to the Israelite elders in 12:1–27, and the Israelite performance of the ritual is reported very briefly in 12:28. After telling the story of the departure from Egypt, the narrator returns, in 12:43–13:16, to instructions about the observation of Passover, interwoven with instructions for the consecration of the Israelite firstborn, those whose lives were spared by the first observance of **Passover**. The escape from Egypt and Passover become inseparable ideas, and the remainder of the Old Testament will continue to link them together.

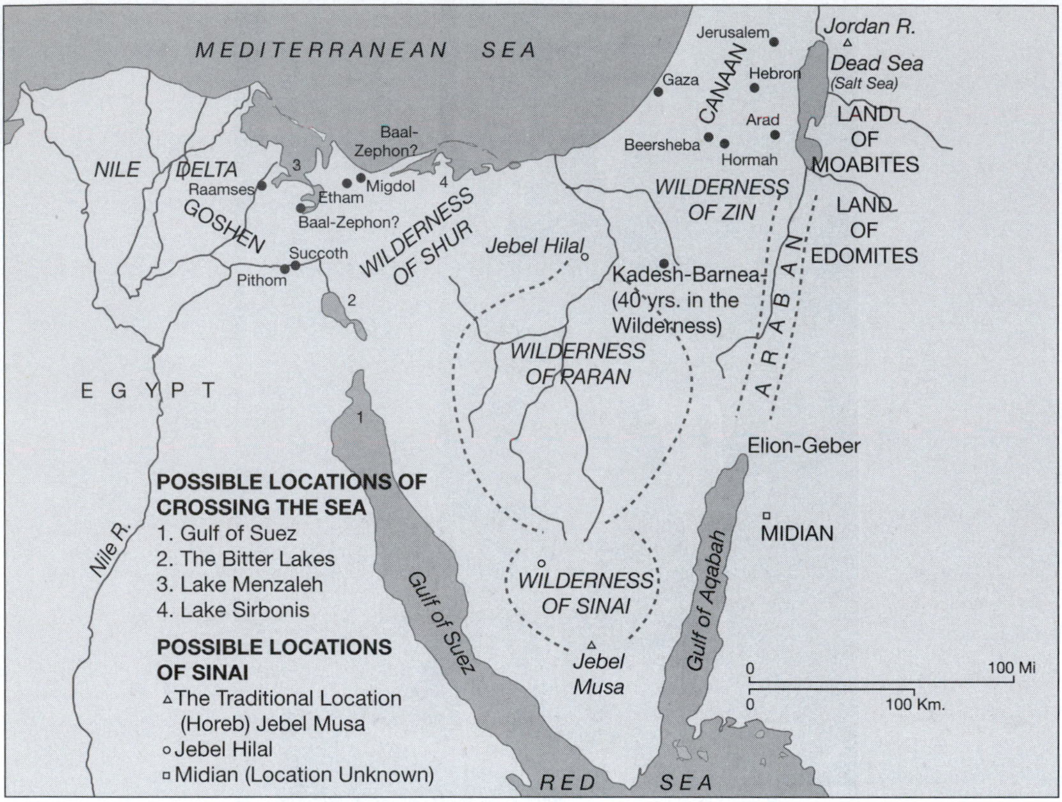

FIGURE 4–2 The Exodus and Sinai.

The Initial Wilderness Period

CONFRONTATION AT THE RED SEA (EXOD. 14–15:21). Exodus 14 and 15:1–21 provide a rare opportunity within the Old Testament. These two passages provide a narrative account of the crossing of the Red Sea, followed by a poem that sings about the same event. The only other instance like this occurs in Judges 4–5, which provide a narrative and a poetic account of an Israelite battle. The narrative account in Exodus 14 provides more of the background for the story, reporting Pharaoh's change of heart about letting the Israelites go. It also frames the event as the first in a series of *complaint* stories, in which the Israelites face hardship and accuse Moses of having led them into the wilderness to die. The familiar parts of the story are also present, including the parting of the water, the Israelites crossing the sea on dry land, and the drowning of the Egyptian army. The song in Exodus 15 includes these familiar components, using significantly different language, and adds a celebration of the effect this great event will have on the occupants of the Promised Land, whom the Israelites will have to face in future battles. The opening line in the Song of the Sea (15:1–18) is revealed in 15:20–21 to be taken from a briefer Song of Miriam, sung by Moses' sister.

TROUBLE ON THE WAY (EXOD. 15:22–17:7). The Sinai Desert very quickly put to the test the leadership skills of Moses. Egypt, even with its slavery, did provide at least a minimum of food and plenty of water to drink. In contrast, the Sinai made Egypt look like the Garden of Eden. First, the stagnant pools of water the Israelites found at Marah caused complaint. Moses threw the bark or leaves of a desert shrub into the water to make it drinkable (15:22–26). Soon they found an oasis at Elim that had plenty of fresh water (15:27).

The next complaint was about food. The supplies they brought from Egypt began to run low, and the complaints increased (16:1–12). Again the LORD, through nature, met the needs of the people with (1) manna and (2) quail. Manna was the secretion of a tiny scale insect, still eaten today by the Bedouin. Quail, similar to the American bird, often fall exhausted in the northern Sinai after migratory flights over the Mediterranean. They can be captured easily by hand during this time (16:13–36).

Water again became a problem. Moses' experience as a desert sheepherder once more stood him in good stead, for he found a water-bearing rock that satisfied the thirst of the people (17:1–7).

THE AMALEKITE RAID (EXOD. 17:8–16). An even greater danger lay ahead. At Rephedim, the people were attacked by the Amalekites, a fierce tribe of desert dwellers. The task of leading the people to battle was given to Joshua, the son of Nun, who one day would become the leader. While Moses held up his rod, the battle favored the Israelites; but when his arms fell down, the tide of the battle changed. The effect of the rod was psychological, because it reminded the people how the LORD had defeated the Pharaoh, who was much more powerful than the Amalekites (17:8–16). The Israelites won the battle, and Moses found a general.

A FATHER-IN-LAW'S ADVICE (EXOD. 18:17–27). The people came at last to Sinai. Soon afterward, Moses' family—accompanied by his father-in-law, Jethro—joined him there. It did not take the older man long to see that Moses was overworking himself, trying to do everything for the people. Calling Moses aside, Jethro advised him to set up a system whereby the people would be divided into groups of 10, 50, 100, and 1000. A leader would be responsible for handling all problems that arose in his group. If he could not handle them, he would consult the leader of the larger unit of which his smaller group was a part. That way, only the most pressing problems would reach Moses. This allowed Moses to devote his time to the more important work of interceding with God for the people and teaching them God's laws (18:17–27).

This tradition of the influence of Jethro on Moses may be evidence of other influences. Some have suggested that even the personal name for God (YHWH) may have originated with Jethro's clan. At present, however, there is no conclusive proof of that.

The Exodus and History

The relationship between the events recorded in the book of Exodus and a contemporary understanding of *history* has been a subject of intense debate. The question could be posed this way: If someone wished to write a complete history of the world, which was as objective as possible, in what way would the events of the Exodus be included? These events could not be entirely ignored, because there is no dispute that a group of people called the Israelites formed themselves into a small nation that eventually had a massive impact on Western civilization, and this set of stories in the book of Exodus played an essential role in that group's understanding of itself and its place in the world. The difficulty arises when examining the events themselves, because there is no direct evidence outside of the Bible that any of this occurred, and the events as described seem highly unlikely. The huge array of questions may be organized under the categories of Who?, When?, and Where?

Perhaps the center of the problem is the traditional understanding of the number of people involved. Exodus 12:37 reports that about 600,000 adult men left Egypt and took part in the

Exodus. A number of this magnitude is also confirmed by the census reports in Numbers 1. Multiplying this number conservatively, to include women and children, would produce a total number of at least 2 million people. We live in a world with a population exceeding 6 billion people, in which perhaps 200 metropolitan areas have populations at least this large, so this may not immediately strike the modern reader as too large a number. Common estimates of the population of the entire world at the time these events would have occurred, however, are 50 million or less. This would mean that the Exodus included 4 or 5 percent of the world's entire population. Add to this the logistical problems of moving such a massive number of people through the wilderness for an extended period of time and this traditional number begins to appear far beyond the realm of possibility. Even many of the scenes in the biblical story—for example, Moses gathering the entire group for a proclamation of the Sabbath regulations in Exodus 35:1–2—cannot be imagined with such a large group. Some interpreters have used the identification of two midwives in Exodus 1:15 to estimate the size of the Israelite population in Egypt. How large a population could two midwives reasonably serve? Even if they both delivered one baby every day, this would only suffice for a population in the tens of thousands, but such calculations ignore many problems. These two midwives could have had responsibilities besides delivering Hebrew children, so the population could have been smaller than this. There could have been many more midwives, but the story only names two of them for the sake of economy or some other reason; thus, the population could have been larger. The incidental naming of two midwives in this kind of narrative is simply not the kind of datum that can be reliably used to make judgments about the size of an ancient population. Perhaps the simplest solution involves the observation that the Bible has a tendency to magnify numbers by adding zeroes. For example, II Chronicles 7:4–5 reports that at the dedication of the temple in Jerusalem, Solomon sacrificed 142,000 animals, an impossibly large number. Whatever may have happened, it certainly involved a significantly smaller number of people than the traditional 2 million, but would a smaller number really make the events less significant or even less miraculous?

There is no direct evidence, outside the Bible, of Israelites living and working as slaves in Egypt during the second millennium B.C.E., but this is one place where some indirect evidence does exist. There are various kinds of evidence among Egyptian records and artifacts that persons like the family of Jacob traveled to Egypt to escape famines and that slaves were used in Egypt to perform various tasks related to construction.[15] Of course, this only proves that a story like the one found in Exodus is plausible, not that this one happened as recorded.

This situation regarding the "Who?" of the Exodus leads to the attempt to place a possible date on such events. Again, evidence outside the Bible is of limited help and the Bible itself provides little assistance, because all of its chronology is only relative, even if taken literally. The Bible, for example, offers two different lengths of time for the period of bondage in Egypt, 400 years in Genesis 15:13 and 430 years in Exodus 12:40, but it has no way of providing a fixed date for the beginning or end of this period. I Kings does attach the Exodus to another event by claiming that Solomon began building the temple 480 years after the Israelites left Egypt. Still, it is not possible to fix an absolute date on any part of Solomon's reign, and 480, which is 12×40, looks suspiciously like a symbolic number rather than a precise arithmetic value. Egyptian records do not help much, because the Bible does not name any of the Pharaohs involved in the Exodus story. The traditional assumption has been that the Pharaoh of the Exodus story was named Ramses, because that is the name of one of the cities named in Exodus 1:11. There was more than one Pharaoh with this name in Egypt, but the most common assumption is that the Pharaoh in the Exodus story was Ramses II, who ruled Egypt in the thirteenth century. Although such a date seems reasonable within the biblical chronology, this guess is still based upon numerous speculations.

The final category of questions involves locations. According to the biblical narrative, the Israelites left Egypt, traveled in the wilderness for forty years, and made significant stops at many places, including the Red Sea (or "Sea of Reeds"), **Mount Sinai**, and Kadesh–Barnea. One would think that such locations would have held great importance in Israelite tradition, but they have been largely forgotten, if they were ever known for certain. The location of Mount Sinai is probably the most significant example. Determining its location is linked to the attempt to determine the route the Israelites might have taken through the wilderness from Egypt to Canaan. Several possible locations for Mount Sinai have been proposed. The most prominent is a mountain in the southern Sinai Peninsula called Jebel Musa. Christian tradition, including the building of a prominent monastery there, connects this site with the Mount Sinai of the biblical story, but such an identification presents at least two major problems. First, the location near the southern tip of the peninsula puts this mountain far away from any reasonable path from Egypt to Canaan. Second, many readers understand the description of the conditions on Mount Sinai in Exodus 19 as volcanic activity, and Jebel Musa was not volcanic during the period of time when the Exodus could have happened. Another possible location for Sinai is a mountain called Jebel Halal in the northern Sinai Peninsula. The location makes more sense, but this is not a very imposing mountain, and it would also not have been volcanic. The nearest volcanic mountain would have been in Midian, a region that Exodus 2–3 associates with Moses, but the location is far to the east of a reasonable route to Canaan, and Israelite tradition has not identified this location with Mount Sinai. Again, this is a category of questions that modern historians cannot answer.

The events of the Exodus are beyond the investigative powers of modern historians for two reasons. First, the kind of evidence that historians typically use to reconstruct past events is too sparse to aid such an attempt in this case. Second, the story itself claims much of its own content to be a miracle, a category that lies outside the boundaries of historical investigation. This part of the biblical text is a good place to observe that questions of faith and literary genre can become seriously entangled. What kind of literature is the book of Exodus? For many modern readers of the Bible, the only kind of literature that can be true is that which reports past events precisely as they happened. For the Bible to be true, a proposition that these readers accept on faith, this story must have happened just as the Bible records it. For other readers, the truth of the story may lie in the impact that it had in unifying the people of ancient Israel around a common tradition. The genre of the book of Exodus may be something other than what we would call history in a modern sense, so how it relates to actual events in the past is of little importance. These readers would contend that God can inspire various kinds of literature and that nobody insists on a literal, historical reading of all the material in a book like Psalms. Both of these positions of faith hold the text to be sacred, although "true" in very different ways. To those for whom the Bible is not a sacred text, the book of Exodus might look very much like the kind of legendary material that many cultures construct to explain their identity and origins; thus, it may be of sociological, anthropological, or literary interest, but neither of historical nor religious value. This is an issue individual readers must decide for themselves, and it involves assumptions about how faith relates to the development of literature that cannot be adequately tested.

SINAI AND THE GIVING OF THE LAW

Israel's Initial Encounter with God at Sinai (Exod. 19–24)

Moses finally achieved one of his major goals: He brought the people to Sinai. It was there that the constitution of the Israelite people was made and ratified. Through Moses, the people were told, "If you will obey my voice and keep my covenant, you shall be a treasured possession out of all peoples." If they met the conditions, they were to be a "priestly kingdom and a holy nation" (19:5–6). To be a holy people meant to be a people set apart for special service for the LORD, as holiness carries with it the idea of separation.

When he came down from the mountain, Moses called the leaders of the people and told them the conditions of the covenant. They agreed to do as the LORD commanded (19:7–8). Then instructions were given for the all-important covenant-making ceremony. Elaborate preparations relating to cleanliness and sexual abstinence had to be made (19:10–11, 14–15). Boundaries were established around the holy mountain so that the people would not come too close. The ancient belief in the power and awesomeness of the Holy was evidenced by the threats of death by stoning to anyone who violated the boundaries around the sacred mountain (19:12–13).

On the great day came thunder and lightning from the cloud-shrouded mountain, accompanied by the loud blast of the *shophar,* a trumpet made of ram's horn. Descriptions of the appearance of God (theophany) in the setting of the thunderstorm are common in the Old Testament (Judg. 5:4–5; Ps. 18:8–15; 29:3–9). The summons came for Moses to go up the mountain. At the LORD's command, Moses then descended and brought Aaron back up the mountain with him (19:16–25).

THE TEN WORDS (EXOD. 20:1–17; SEE ALSO DEUT. 5:6–21). As they now stand, the Ten Commandments (known as the *Ten Words* in Judaism) are expanded from the earliest form, which is believed to have consisted of ten concise statements:

1. You shall have no other gods (*elohim*) before me.
2. You shall not make for yourself a graven image.
3. You shall not take the name of the LORD your God in vain.
4. Remember the Sabbath day and keep it holy.

FIGURE 4–3 "On the third new moon after the Israelites had gone out of . . . Egypt . . . they came into the wilderness of Sinai" (Exod. 19:1). Jebel Musa, the traditional site of Mount Sinai, is located in this range of mountains.

5. Honor your father and your mother.
6. You shall not murder.
7. You shall not commit adultery.
8. You shall not steal.
9. You shall not bear false witness against your neighbor.
10. You shall not covet.

As evidence that the Commandments in their longer form represent an expansion, one needs to compare the version found in Deuteronomy 5:6–21 and, more particularly, the Fourth, Fifth, and Tenth Commandments, with the version in Exodus. The Fifth Commandment says:

Exodus 20:12	*Deuteronomy 5:16*
Honor your father and your mother, so that your days may be long in land that the LORD your God is giving you.	Honor your father and your mother, *as the* LORD *your God commanded you,* that your days may be long *and that it may go well with you* in the land that the LORD your God is giving you.

A more important difference is to be found in the Tenth Commandment:

Exodus 20:17	*Deuteronomy 5:21*
You shall not covet your neighbor's house; you shall not covet your neighbor's wife, or male or female slave, or ox, or donkey or anything that belongs to your neighbor.	Neither shall you covet your neighbor's *wife,* Neither shall you desire your neighbor's *house* or *field,* or male or female slave, or ox, or donkey, or anything that belongs to your neighbor.

These differences suggest a changing view of the Commandments in their applications to specific situations. The Tenth Commandment, in particular, reflects either a change in the status of women or, possibly, a difference in their status (in a later time) from one section of the country to another.

For Israel, the Ten Commandments were the Constitution, the laying down of the basic principles from which a legal system would develop. A common way of looking at the Commandments sees them as reflecting the two poles of Israel's existence as a people. (1) Commandments 1 to 4 are concerned with Israel's relationship to God: absolute loyalty, imageless worship, reverence for the Name (YHWH), and regular worship. (2) Commandments 5 to 10 deal with the Israelites' relationship to the social order: family solidarity, reverence for life, respect for property, truthfulness in speech, and a proper attitude toward others and their property. No other set of moral principles has been so influential in Western legal systems.

ABSOLUTE LAW AND CASE LAW. The Ten Commandments were also unique in their form. They are stated as absolutes; that is, they allow for no contradictions. This kind of law is known as **apodictic law** and rarely was found in the ancient Near East outside of the Israelite law codes. A second type of law is **casuistic law**, or case law. It, too, was found in Israel but also was common in other law codes. Case law stated a condition and told what the penalty was if the condition existed.

THE TEN COMMANDMENTS AND COVENANT CEREMONIES. When the covenant ceremony in which Israel accepted the obligations of the Ten Commandments as the basic law of its existence is compared with covenant ceremonies of other peoples, some interesting parallels appear. Among the Hittites, a fourteenth-century B.C.E. people from Asia Minor, there were suzerainty treaties (covenants involving a stronger and a weaker party) that had six major elements: (1) a prologue identifying the maker of the covenant; (2) a historical record stating why the suzerain or LORD had a right to make the covenant; (3) the conditions of the covenant; (4) the requirement for the preservation and the periodic public reading of the text; (5) a list of the gods who were witnesses to the covenant; and (6) curses and blessings on those who kept and those who neglected the covenant.[16]

THE COVENANT AND ISRAELITE LIFE. Two covenants competed for Israel's attention during its history—the Sinai covenant and the Davidic covenant. The latter covenant would not come into existence for another three centuries. Although there might not be universal agreement on what happened at Sinai, most would attest that something of supreme importance for Israel as a people did happen by the persistence of the covenant idea in Israelite life. Israel became the people of the LORD through divine grace, and the LORD became its God—Ruler, Patriarch, Savior, and Judge.

Exodus 20:2	
Prologue	"I am the LORD your God."
Historical record:	"who brought you up out of the land of Egypt, out of the house of bondage."
Exodus 20:3–17	
Stipulations:	The Ten Commandments
Exodus 24:4, 7	
Preservation and public readings:	"And Moses wrote down all the words of the Lord. . . . Then he took the book of the covenant, and read it in the hearing of the people; and they said, 'All that the Lord has spoken we will do, and we will be obedient.' "
List of gods as witnesses:	These obviously would not appear in light of the First Commandment.
Blessings and curses:	These do not appear in connection with the Ten Commandments, but Deuteronomy 27:11–26 preserves a cursing ceremony, which may have originated in a covenant-renewal festival during which each generation accepted the obligations of the Ten Commandments and the laws that grew out of them.

The covenant was kept alive by a reenactment of the covenant ceremony, at times in a systematic fashion, at other times sporadically. Joshua 24 is an example of what must have happened in such ceremonies. Nehemiah 8 describes the revival of such a ceremony after what appears to have been a long period when no such reenactment had taken place. Perhaps a major stumbling block for the Sinai covenant was that it was supplanted by the Davidic covenant during the period of David's monarchy. Although the two covenants were of a different nature—David's covenant having to do with the continuation of his line on the throne of the kingdom, whereas the Sinai covenant was of a more moral and ethical nature—David's covenant offered a kind of security that did not make moral demands on the people and thus was more readily accepted. Another problem was the assimilation of a large non-Israelite population into the kingdom as the result of David's conquests. Consequently, a large part of the population neither knew nor cared about Sinai. The Ten Commandments' demand for absolute loyalty to the LORD and the expectation that every Israelite would treat every other follower of the LORD as a family member were lost in the vast changes that took place during that time. An additional factor was the change in Israel's economic circumstances. Society became more stratified with the passing years, with more and more power being concentrated in the hands of fewer and fewer people. As a result, the old family ideal fell by the wayside.

Yet, in spite of the difficulties it faced over the years, the Sinai covenant would not die, but continued to come alive at opportune times in Israel's history. Some even see it as the glue that held Israel together.[17]

The Principles Made Practical: The Law Codes

Just as the United States Constitution was the beginning of America's legal system, the Ten Commandments were the beginning of law for Israel. The principles took the form of laws. These laws are found in three major codes, or groups, in the Old Testament: the Covenant Code (Exod. 20:22–23:33), the Deuteronomic Code (Deut. 5:1–28:68), and the Priestly Code (principally in the book of Leviticus but with some laws in Exodus and Numbers). The narratives present the laws as if all of them were given directly to Moses, but closer examination reveals that they developed over a long period of time. Moses was the lawgiver in the sense that the basic principles from which all the laws of Israel were to come were given through him.

THE COVENANT CODE (EXOD. 20:22–23:33). The **Covenant Code** probably was the oldest Israelite code but not the oldest Near Eastern code. There were a number of older Near Eastern codes, the best known being the Code of Hammurabi, which dates from the nineteenth century B.C.E. There are laws from Hammurabi's Code that are very similar to laws in Israelite codes. Compare, for example, the laws concerning dangerous oxen:

Hammurabi's Code	*Covenant Code*
If a seignior's ox was a gorer and . . . [it was] . . . made . . . known to him that it was a gorer, but he did not pad its horns (or) tie up his ox, and it gored to death a member of the aristocracy, he shall give one-half mina of silver.[18]	If the ox has been accustomed to gore in the past, and the owner has been warned but has not restrained it, and it kills a man or a woman, the ox shall be stoned, and its owner shall be put to death. If a ransom is imposed on the owner then the owner shall pay whatever is imposed for the redemption of the victim's life (Exod. 12:29–30).

The Covenant Code contains laws designed for a society in which agriculture was the major means of earning a living—a condition that did not exist for Israel until it entered the land of Canaan. The Code also contains laws that are classed as civil or criminal laws, but religion was such a basic part of the Israeli lifestyle that religious offenses were subject to criminal penalties. A brief summary of the contents is as follows:

20:22–23	A repetition of the commandment concerning idols
20:24–26	A demand for only earthen altars or altars of uncut stones, in contrast to the elaborate altars of the Canaanites
21:1–11	Regulations concerning slaves, both male and female

21:12–32	Crimes against fellow Israelites and their penalties
21:33–22:17	Laws governing property
22:18–23:9	Miscellaneous laws, many of which relate to the treatment of the weak and defenseless—that is, (1) the treatment of strangers, widows, and orphans (22:21–24); (2) the lending of money to the poor (22:25–27); and (3) another warning against oppressing the weak (23:9)
23:10–19	The sabbatical year, the sabbath, and the three major feasts
23:20–33	A promise of success in the conquest if the law is faithfully kept

THE PRIESTLY CODE. Unlike the Covenant Code and the Deuteronomic Code, the Priestly Code is much more complex and scattered. For this reason, only some outstanding sections of this Code will be mentioned. Although it follows the Covenant Code in the biblical order, it actually came later than either of the other codes, probably reaching its final form sometime during or immediately after the Babylonian Exile. Like the other two codes, it is composed of a mixture of earlier and later laws. A major difference, though, is that the Priestly Code is concerned primarily with proper worship. For example, in Exodus 25–31, a detailed description of (1) the Ark and (2) the **Tabernacle** is given. The Ark (described in Exodus 25) was a rather elaborate wooden box carried on two long staves or poles that passed through rings on the corners of the box. It was approximately 45 inches long, 27 inches wide, and 27 inches high, overlaid with gold and with a **mercy seat** on top and winged figures on either end. The seat represented the throne of God, and as such, symbolized the presence of God among the people. It was thought to be effective especially when carried with the people as they fought their enemies.

The Tabernacle (Exod. 26–27) was a tent of skins in which the Ark was kept. The tent was surrounded by a fence of skins that formed a sort of courtyard. Inside the tent were two rooms. The larger room was the Holy Place. Its furnishings were (1) a table for the "bread of the Presence" (25:23–30), which was one of the sacrificial offerings; (2) a seven-branched lamp called the *menorah* (25:31–40); and (3) the altar for burning incense (3:1–10). The priests entered the Holy Place daily in carrying out their duties.

The smaller room, separated from the Holy Place by a curtain, was the Most Holy Place or Holy of Holies. Here, the Ark of the Covenant was kept. Only the High Priest could enter the Holy of Holies, and that happened on only one day in the year: *Yom Kippur,* the Day of Atonement. His activity on that day was for the purpose of securing forgiveness of the people's sins.[19]

Much attention is devoted in the Priestly Code to the priests and their activities. An example of this is Exodus 28:1–29:46, which provides a description of the priestly garments and the ordination of Aaron and his sons. Leviticus 6:1–9:24 discusses the function of the priest in sacrifices and then turns again to the dedication of Aaron and his sons to the priesthood.

These examples should serve to emphasize the important role the priest played in ancient Israel. In the patriarchal days, the patriarch himself functioned as the priest. When Israel became a distinct people, the priesthood became a separate group of men whose sole job was to function as priests. The descriptions found in the law codes may well reflect a later, more developed priestly establishment, but there can be little doubt that the priesthood played a role in Israelite life in the wilderness.

The power of the priest lay in the belief that he controlled access to God. He was the expert in communicating with the awesome Deity who brought Israel out of Egypt. The power controlled by the priest carried with it the temptation to corruption; but the continued existence and positive influence of Israelite religion over many centuries must be credited, in part, to the integrity of many of the priests.

The Literary Structure of Leviticus

There is no denying that, for most modern readers, Leviticus is a dull and tedious book to read. Sensitivity to literary development in the book can hardly transform it into a page turner, but it is important to ask whether Leviticus is more than just a listing of laws.

There is general agreement concerning certain structural features of this book. Chapter 16, which concerns the Day of Atonement, stands out in the center of Leviticus. The material immediately following this, Chapters 17–26, is almost universally understood as a cohesive body of law known as the Holiness Code. This body of law attempts to define and regulate for the people of Israel what makes them holy, what distinguishes or separates them from those who are not holy. The material in the first fifteen chapters is primarily concerned with the lives and duties of priests. The recognition of these broad generalities and the transitional character of Chapter 16 leads to a way of reading and perceiving the whole book of Leviticus.

Leviticus 1–7 provides careful instructions concerning aspects of the institution of sacrifice. This is the primary duty of the priests. Chapters 8–10 develop the process of ordination, both in general, legal terms and in the more specific narrative about Aaron and his sons. Chapters 10–15 then address other duties of priests in relation to various aspects of the lives of the people of Israel. Attention is already turning here from the priesthood itself to the interaction of priests and other Israelites. The Day of Atonement ceremony in Leviticus 16 specifically delineates the ritual for atoning for the sins of the priesthood and then for all the people. This second act of atonement points to the **Holiness Code** and its discussion of purity for all Israelites. The Holiness Code makes little distinction between priest and nonpriest. All people are expected to be holy.

The book of Leviticus is set within the larger context of the Torah, with the Israelites encamped at the foot of Mount Sinai. It propounds an understanding of holiness that flows from God to Moses to the priests to the people. The literary structure of the book and its changing modes of address match this understanding of the dynamic nature of holiness.

One of the main functions of the priest was to carry out the sacrifices described in the laws. Because most of the people were illiterate, sacrifice was a visual aid to worship. Its effectiveness as an aid to worship depended, in large measure, upon how it was viewed. Three basic views of sacrifice prevailed in ancient societies: (1) that sacrifice was made to appease an angry deity—in short, to bribe him; (2) that sacrifice was an act of communion whereby the worshiper had fellowship with the deity; (3) that sacrifice was a gift to the deity as an act of praise. The sacrifice of an animal was regarded as substituting for the life of a human being, but it had a deeper meaning than mere substitution.

> What then, did it mean when an Israelite had sinned and brought a sacrifice to be offered at the altar? Basic to any understanding of this question is the conception of one's relatedness to all that he had, including family and possessions. One's land and possessions were bound up with his life because they were the means of sustaining life. Naboth's reluctance to surrender his land to Ahab, even for a fair price, is a vivid illustration of this feeling of oneness that the Israelite had for land and possessions (1 Kings 21:3). It is also illustrated by the destruction of Achan, his family, and all of his possessions, because he had sinned (Joshua 7:25). All that he had was contaminated by his sin because it was thought of as being a part of him. When one brought

an animal to sacrifice it, it was his possession and therefore was a part of himself. He laid his hands on its head to symbolize his identity (oneness) with it (Leviticus 1:4). When its blood was shed in the ritual, the life that was given was symbolically his own. It was not a substitute; it was the offerer giving of himself.[20]

The major kinds of sacrifice are described in Leviticus 1:1–6:7.[21] (1) The whole **burnt offering** was the major daily sacrifice and had as its purpose making the people right with God, that is, atoning for sin (1:1–17). (2) Cereal offerings were peace offerings, expressing thanks for the produce of the land (2:1–16). (3) In contrast to the whole burnt offering was the peace offering. The animal was slain, its blood was thrown against the altar, the fat and internal organs were burned, and the meat was eaten by the priests and the worshipers in an act of communion (3:1–17). (4) The sin offering for "anyone [who] sins unwittingly" was a whole burnt offering (4:1–5:13). (5) The guilt offering involved not only a sacrifice, but also an act of restoring any loss that had resulted from sin (5:14–6:7).

HOLIDAYS AND HOLY DAYS (LEV. 23:1–44). (1) Passover—Unleavened Bread, which came in March or April, was to celebrate the Exodus events. (2) The Feast of Weeks celebrated the grain harvest and came fifty days after Passover, which is why it is called Pentecost (Greek for *fiftieth*) in the New Testament (Acts 2:1). (3). The Feast of Booths (Tabernacles) came in the early fall and celebrated the fruit harvest. (4) The most solemn day of the year was the Day of Atonement, when the High Priest entered the Holy of Holies in the Tabernacle to make atonement for the sins of the people (Lev. 16:1–34).

THE HOLINESS CODE (LEV. 17–26). Mention needs to be made of one other major section of the Priestly Code. Chapters 17–26 of Leviticus constitutes a major section containing many ancient traditions grouped around the theme of Israel's need to be a holy people, set apart and dedicated to the service of God. Chapter 19, in particular, highlights the idea of holiness as embodied in the famous line "You shall love your neighbor as yourself" (19:18).

THE DEUTERONOMIC CODE. The Deuteronomic Code, found in the Book of Deuteronomy, was first discovered during the reign of Josiah in Judah in 621 B.C.E., many centuries after the Exodus. But, like the Covenant Code and the Priestly Code that came after it, it contained many ancient laws, as well as laws brought into being much nearer to the time of its discovery. It, too, had a version of the Ten Commandments (5:6–27). As its title, *Deuteronomy* ("second law"), suggests, it was a restatement of the law—in short, a sort of updating, or modernizing, of the law to fit a changed situation. For this reason, old laws still usable were kept, while new laws, suitable for new conditions that had arisen, were added. It may be summarized as follows:

5:1–11:32	The Ten Commandments and exhortations to keep them
12:1–32	The command to have all worship in one central sanctuary
13:1–18	The awfulness of idolatry
14:1–15:23	Regulations for a holy people: warnings against pagan customs, regulations about clean and unclean animals, the law of the tithe, the sabbatical year as related to debts and slavery of Hebrews, offering of firstborn animals

16:1–17	The major festivals: Passover—Unleavened Bread; Festival of Weeks (Pentecost in the New Testament) or grain harvest festival; and Festival of Booths or Tabernacles, which celebrated the fruit harvest
16:18–17:20	Rules for the administration of justice
18:1–22	How to worship God in a proper manner
19:1–21	Legal problems: manslaughter, property fraud, proper evidence for determining guilt in a crime
20:1–20	How to conduct a holy war
21:1–23:14	Various laws concerning unsolved murder, treatment of captive women, disrespect for parental authority, rules for hanging a man, responsibilities for a man's lost property, a woman's use of a man's clothes, protection of bird life, building codes, the mixing of unlike things, relations between the sexes, relations to outcasts and other people, proper sanitary procedures
23:15–25:19	Humanitarian and religious laws: runaway slaves, cult prostitutes, taking of interest on loans, making vows to God, respect for property, divorce procedures, the newly married, taking security for debts, stealing, rules for the leper, extending credit, relation to the poor and needy, individual responsibility, the sojourner and the widow, law of punishment, just payment for services, law of the Levirate marriage, dirty fighting, false weights and measures, relations with the Amalekites
26:1–19, 28:1–68	Rules for worship: the service of first fruits, the tithing ceremony, a plea to observe the law and the consequences for failing to do so

The Ten Commandments and the Codes

By taking one of the Commandments and showing how it was used in the codes, perhaps one can see the differences that the passage of time brought in the interpretation of the Commandments. The Sixth Commandment is "You shall not murder." See how the three codes treat this Commandment in the following comparison:

***Covenant Code* (*Exod. 21:12–14*)**	***Deuteronomic Code* (*Deut. 19:4–6; 11–13*)**	***Priestly Code* (*Num. 35:11–12; 16–25a*)**
Whoever strikes a person mortally shall be put to death. If it was not premeditated, but came about by an act of God,	Now this is the case of a homicide . . . who might flee there and live, that is, someone who has killed another person unintentionally when the two had not been	Then you shall select cities . . . of refuge for you, so that a slayer who kills a person without intent may flee there. The cities shall be for you a refuge from the avenger, so that the slayer, may not die

then I will appoint for you a place to which the killer may flee. But if someone willfully attacks and kills another by treachery, you shall take the killer from my altar for execution.

at enmity before: Suppose someone goes into the forest with another to cut wood, and when one swings the ax to cut down a tree, the head slips from the handle and strikes the other person, who then dies; the killer may flee to one of these cities and live. But if the distance is too great, the avenger of blood . . . might pursue and overtake and put the killer to death, although the death sentence was not deserved, since the two had not been at enmity before. . . .

But if someone at enmity with another lies in wait and attacks and takes the life of that person, and flees into one of these cities, then the elders of the killer's city shall send to have the culprit taken from there and handed over to the avenger of blood to be put to death. Show no pity; you shall purge the guilt of innocent blood from Israel, so that it may go well with you.

until there is a trial before the congregation.

But anyone who strikes another with an iron object, and death ensues, is a murderer; the murderer shall be put to death. Or anyone who strikes another with a stone in hand that could cause death, and death ensues, is a murderer; the murderer shall be put to death. Or anyone who strikes another with a weapon of wood in hand that could cause death, and death ensues, is a murderer; the murderer shall be put to death. The avenger of blood is the one who shall put the murderer to death; when they meet, the avenger of blood shall execute the sentence. Likewise, if someone pushes another from hatred, or hurls something at another, lying in wait, and death ensues, or in enmity strikes another with the hand, and death ensues, then the one who struck the blow shall be put to death; that person is a murderer; the avenger of blood shall put the murderer to death when they meet.

But if someone pushes another suddenly without enmity, or hurls any object without lying in wait, or, while handling a stone that could cause death, unintentionally drops it on another and death ensues, though they were not enemies, and no harm was intended, then the congregation shall judge between the slayer and the avenger of blood, in accordance with these ordinances; and the congregation shall rescue the slayer from the avenger of blood.

The Golden Calf Incident (Exod. 32)

The people's commitment to the covenant did not erase their proneness to rebellion. When Moses delayed coming down from the mountain, they assumed that the worst had happened and demanded that Aaron make images for them to serve as gods. Aaron did as they requested, trying still to point them to the LORD (32:1–6). This incident reflects a theme common throughout Israel's history—that is, the temptation to dilute the religion of the God of Sinai with the popular religions of the time. Moses' magnificent prayer of intercession following the LORD's threat to destroy the rebels revealed the depth of the man's commitment to his people (32:7–14). That love for the people did not keep him from a wrathful explosion when he came down from the mountain and found the people dancing around a **golden calf**. In a fit of temper, he threw down the tablets on which the Commandments were written, literally breaking the Ten Commandments! The calf, probably a gold-covered wooden frame, was destroyed (32:15–20).

The Literary Structure of Numbers

The fourth book of the Bible is traditionally called *In the Wilderness* in the Hebrew Bible. The Greek title, *arithmoi,* provides the basis for the commonly used English title, Numbers. Careful consideration of these two titles may provide a key to the book's literary design. Twice in the book of Numbers, Moses is ordered to conduct a **census** of the people of Israel, to "number" them. The first census is in Numbers 1 and the second is in Numbers 26. The two numberings take place while the Israelites are in the wilderness, and they perform a combined purpose.

The book of Numbers opens with the Israelites still encamped at Mount Sinai. The first census identifies all of the adults who were present at that time. In Numbers 10 the Israelites finally set out from this place, where they have been since Exodus 19. The two census reports thus surround a very significant event in Israel's history. The departure from Sinai is followed by a collection of stories about Israel's adventures in the wilderness. The collection of wilderness stories in Numbers 10–25 is a much larger reflection of the similar collection of stories in Exodus 14–18. Together these two collections form what is often called the *murmuring tradition* because of the murmuring, or complaining, of the Israelites during their journey.

The second census confirms that all of the adults counted in the first census, except for Joshua and Caleb (26:65), are dead. With the disobedient generation gone, the Israelites are ready to move on toward the Promised Land. This second census, like the first, is followed immediately by a section of legislation and then a travel narrative. This provides the book of Numbers with a parallel structure, which is set up by the census reports. These two parallel sections are Chapters 1–25 and 26–36. The end of the book of Numbers, which reports the arrival of the Israelites on the plains of Moab, prepares the way for the book of Deuteronomy that follows.

It is obvious that the book of Numbers, like many other books of the Bible, is composed of a large number of originally independent stories, traditions, and documents. A careful survey of its structure, however, reveals that these components have not simply been thrown together, but have been artistically woven together into a literary work that has a sense of unity and purpose surpassing the sum of its parts.

Moses then turned to Aaron, whose excuse sounded as pathetic as that of a small boy caught with his hand in the cookie jar. There followed a violent purge of the rebels led by the Levites. Moses again interceded for the people and received the command to be on the road toward the Promised Land again (32:21–35). The covenant was renewed, and the promise was repeated (34:1–16).

AFTER MOUNT SINAI

On the Road to Kadesh–Barnea (Num. 10:11–12:16)

Following the report of a census (Num 1:1–4:9)—giving the book its name, based on the Latin *numeri* (Hebrew *bemidbar,* "in the wilderness")—another section of the Priestly Code (5:1–6:27) and narratives concerning the Tabernacle, the account of the journey resumes.[22] A song that was sung on the march is preserved in 10:35–36:

> Arise, O LORD, and let your enemies be scattered,
> and your foes flee before you. . . .
> Return, O LORD of the ten thousand thousands of Israel.

But the songs did not muffle the complaints, whether they were about food (11:4–35) or Aaron and Miriam's complaint about Moses' Cushite wife. It seems that even Moses had to deal with racial prejudice.

Spying Out the Land (Num. 13:1–33)

A second major time of decision had arrived. The march had brought the people to the southern reaches of the Negev, Palestine's southernmost habitable region. This was the most logical place from which to launch an invasion of the land.

Choosing twelve men (a representative from each tribe), Moses sent them north into the hill country to estimate the chances of a successful invasion (13:1–24). The returning spies gave a glowing report of the richness of the land, especially when compared with the barren territory through which they had come. But for ten of the men, the minuses in the form of walled cities far outweighed the pluses. In view of the disadvantages, they gave a majority report that counseled against an invasion (13:28–29, 32–33). Caleb and Joshua gave a strong minority report recommending an invasion (13:30–31).

The Invasion Nobody Believed Would Succeed—and It Didn't (Num 14:1–45)

Rebellion flared once again, coming almost to the stoning of Moses and Aaron by the people (14:1–10a). Moses, in turn, had to plead with the LORD to keep the people from being destroyed, appealing to the LORD's sense of honor (14:10b–19). The rebellion condemned that generation to the wilderness, except Caleb and Joshua (14:20–38).

A plague convinced the people that an invasion was imperative, although Moses warned that it was doomed to failure. He was right; the Israelites suffered defeat at the hands of the Amalekites and Canaanites (14:39–45). Some Israelites probably stayed in the northern Negev, however, joining forces with the Joshua-led group some forty years later when it invaded from east of the Jordan. After this failure, Kadesh–Barnea became the base of operations for the main body of Israelites for the next generation.

The Kadesh Years and More Priestly Laws (Num. 15–19:22)

The Israelite storyteller gave little attention to what happened in the years at Kadesh–Barnea. Chapter 15 contains laws concerning offerings and an incident about a man who violated the Sabbath law on work (15:1–41). The major headline was the rebellion led by a quartet of men named Korah, Dathan, Abiram, and On (16:1–19). Their subsequent punishment, as well as that of their whole families, illustrates the concept of *corporate responsibility*, a commonly held view in biblical times. It held that a man's actions affected his whole family, either for good or ill. They shared his guilt and his glory (16:20–50).

There follows another section of the Priestly Code that deals with priestly stories and duties, as well as the ritual for purifying a person made unclean by contact with a corpse (17:1–13).

Bound for the Promised Land (Num. 20:1–21:9)

The passage of time brought the passing of the older generation, including Miriam and Aaron. Miriam died before Israel left Kadesh–Barnea (20:1). Time did not lessen the rebelliousness of the people, however. As they moved away from the oasis at Kadesh–Barnea to continue their movement toward the land promised to them, lack of water—an ever-present problem when they were on the move (see Exodus 15)—brought still another crisis. Moses, commanded by the LORD to speak to a rock to find water, seems to have struck it in anger, bringing the LORD's judgment that Moses, too, would die on the trail and would never enter Canaan (20:2–13).

Trouble came not only from within, but also from external forces. Failing in attempts to invade Canaan from the south, Moses then proposed to cross the Arabah, the continuation of the great Rift Valley south of the Dead Sea, and to follow the King's Highway north through the territories of Edom and Moab. Contacting the king of Edom, Moses promised to pass through the land peaceably, paying for any water used. The Edomites refused passage, however, and threatened to attack Israel (20:14–21).

Aaron died and was buried on Mount Hor. This left only Moses of the first-generation leaders (20:22–29). Eventually, the people set out in the direction of the Gulf of Aqabah (called the Red Sea) in an attempt to circumvent Edom. They encountered numerous poisonous snakes on the way. Moses was instructed to make a bronze serpent and to make people look at it to be healed when they were bitten (21:4–9). In this same general area in a Midianite archaeological site, a bronze snake was found. This suggests that such a technique was used among the Midianites in the case of a snakebite. Furthermore, it is evidence of a possible ancient relationship between Israel and Midian.[23]

The Moabites and Balaam (Num. 21:10–24:25)

Unable to circumvent Edom, the Israelites turned north along the Arabah, coming at last to the southern end of the Dead Sea. Passing through the valley of the Brook Zered, which served as the border between Edom and Moab, they finally reached the major caravan road, the King's Highway (21:10–20). Not wanting trouble with the Moabites, Moses asked permission to pass through the territory peaceably. When the king refused, Israel attacked, took control of much of the Moabite kingdom, and even took some Ammonite territory north of Moab (21:21–35).

At this point, the prophet Balaam entered. He was one of those characters about whom the Israelites spoke for many generations. As a matter of fact, not only did the Israelites talk about

FIGURE 4–4 Exodus 15:27 reports the arrival of the Israelites at an oasis called Elim. This photograph shows a modern oasis in the Sinai region of Egypt.

this famous prophet, but others did also. We now know of Balaam apart from the biblical text through inscriptions that have been found in Transjordan. That this is the same prophet spoken of in Numbers 22–24 is shown by the fact that he is identified in these inscriptions as "Balaam, the son of Beor" (cf. Num. 22:5). The inscriptions also speak of him receiving his oracles at night, as in Numbers 22:8, 19f. Unlike in the Bible, however, he is further described as "seer of the gods," who speak to him at night. This would indicate that he was by no means an Israelite prophet or a follower of YHWH (the LORD). There is mention also of goddesses, another idea foreign to Israelite religion. As in the biblical account, he is pictured as one who pronounces curses.[24] It is in light of these texts, then, that the Balaam stories in Numbers will be examined.

Desperate for a way to stop the marauding Israelites, Moab's King Balak sent for the famous Balaam, a Mesopotamian holy man. Balak wanted Balaam to curse the Israelites so that they could not defeat his armies (22:1–6). Taking money with them, Balak's messengers came to Balaam, who told them he would give them an answer in the morning. The next morning, Balaam told the messengers that the LORD would not let him go (22:7–14). After reporting to Balak, the messengers came back with a much larger sum of money. This time Balaam agreed to go, under the instructions to do as God told him (22:15–21).

At this point, the text seems to contradict itself. After saying that Balaam went on God's command (22:20), it says that God was angry with him for going (22:22). It must be remembered that God was believed to cause everything. Thus, for Him to cause a person to commit an action and then be angry with him for doing it was not viewed as an inconsistency on God's part. If we were telling the story, we probably would say that the large sum of money offered to Balaam was what changed his mind. This resulted in God's being angry with him for going with the Moabites.

Then follows the most famous part of the story. Saddling his donkey, Balaam set out for Moab. On the way, strange things began to happen. The donkey, seeing things that Balaam did not see, ran off the road and crushed Balaam's foot against a stone wall. Finally, the donkey lay down in the road. Balaam, who had been beating the donkey for its seeming stubbornness, suddenly heard the donkey speak up in its own defense (22:22–30). To top it off, the LORD spoke out in defense of the donkey, telling Balaam that he had been trying to get his attention through the donkey. Balaam was told that he was to go with the Moabites (22:31–35). Did anyone else hear what the donkey and God said to Balaam? The text is silent on this point.

When Balaam came to the Moabites, he made preparations to carry out the request of Balak. But, try as he might, each time he started to pronounce a curse, a blessing was pronounced on Israel. Needless to say, Balak was most unhappy. He soon sent Balaam back the way he came (22:36–24:25).

Trouble at Peor (Num. 25:1–18)

While the Israelites were in Moabite territory, they encountered the worship of fertility gods. These were nature deities believed to have the power to make the crops grow. This type of worship, which was to be a major problem for Israel throughout much of the pre-Exilic period, involved so-called holy women, who played the role of goddesses in sacred prostitution. The Israelite men were attracted to the worship, so much so that one man brought a Moabite prostitute into the camp. An epidemic, probably a venereal disease, broke out in the camp. Again, radical action was taken; Moses ordered the execution of anyone who had patronized the fertility cult. In this way, the disease was checked.

Miscellaneous Materials (Num. 26–36)

The latter part of the book of Numbers contains a variety of materials: a census (26:1–65); an incident concerning the inheritance of property by women (27:1–11); the appointment of Joshua as Moses' successor (17:12–23); rules concerning offerings for the major holidays—the Sabbath, the New Moon, Passover—Unleavened Bread, the Feast of Weeks or Grain Harvest, the New Year's Festival, the Day of Atonement, and the Feast of Booths or Fruit Harvest (28:1–29:40); the law of vows (30:1–6); holy war against Midian (31:1–54); the story of assigning territory east of the Jordan to the tribes of Reuben, Gad, and Manasseh (32:1–42); a summary of the journey from Egypt to Moab (33:1–56); a discussion of the territorial boundaries of the people in Canaan (34:1–29); a discussion of the Levitical cities and the cities of refuge (35:1–34); and finally, a discussion of a married woman's inheritance (36:1–13).

Two things are important here: holy war (Num. 31), which will be dealt with later, and the route of the march, described in Numbers 33. Some archaeologists argue that the cities mentioned—Iyyim, Dibon, Almon-Diblathaim, and Abel-Shittim—did not exist when the Exodus is thought to have taken place. Yet, Egyptian temple lists from this period cite most of them as existing cities in the same order that Numbers lists them.[25]

Deuteronomy's Contribution to the Wilderness Story

The name *Deuteronomy* comes from the Greek name of the book and means "the second law." The Hebrew title means "These are the words," based on the first verse of the book. The word *Deuteronomy* is very descriptive of the contents of this book, because 1:1–4:49 is a summary statement of the wilderness wanderings of Israel, presented in the form of an address to the people on the plains of Moab.[26]

The second major section (5:1–26:19: 28:1–68) has already been discussed in the section on the law codes. Two major themes in this section deserve more lengthy comment: (1) the command for a single place for worship and (2) the concept of *holy war.*

The command to have a single place of worship is found in 12:5, 11, 18, 26. In its original time and context, it probably referred to either Shiloh or Shechem. Both seem to have served as the major worship center at one time or another. When the essentials of what is known today as Deuteronomy were discovered, or rediscovered, in the time of King Josiah (621 B.C.E.), the references to a single place of worship were taken to mean Jerusalem. By this time, Jerusalem was the capital of all that remained of the Israelite kingdoms. Even more important was that the Temple was located there and was controlled by a powerful and influential priesthood.

The second important theme was the holy war. The Hebrew word is *cherem,* sometimes translated as "the ban." The key passage is Deuteronomy 20:16–18:

> But as for the towns of the peoples the LORD your God is giving you as an inheritance, you must not let anything that breathes remain alive. You shall annihilate them—the Hittites and the Amorites, the Canaanites and the Perizzites, the Hivites and the Jebusites—just as the LORD your God has commanded, so that they may not teach you to do all the abhorrent things to do for their gods, and you thus sin against the LORD your God.

The justification for such an action is found in 20:18, which says, in effect, that the people of the land were like an infection in the body. It must be gotten rid of, even though the solution is a radical one. Similarly, today the amputation of a limb is viewed as a radical solution to a physical ailment. Yet, at times, it is the only solution to the problem.

But the question arises, "How does one justify such actions?" The simple answer is that there is no way it can be justified. The best one can do is to understand that the Israelites practiced holy war in a time when many nations did so. They justified their actions in the same manner as those who slaughter their neighbors in religious and ethnic wars do today. We can only try to understand why it was the way it was without giving our approval.[27]

Deuteronomy's Place in the Canon

It has long been recognized that Deuteronomy stands at a crucial juncture in the canon. Although tradition has numbered it with Genesis through Numbers as part of the Torah or Pentateuch, it also has marked affinities with the books that follow it—Joshua, Judges, 1 and 2 Samuel, 1 and 2 Kings. Because themes from Deuteronomy play a prominent role in these latter books, scholars call it the *Deuteronomistic History.* At the same time, Deuteronomy recapitulates Exodus through Numbers and answers questions about the fate of Moses. Thus, it serves as a bridge between the Pentateuch and the books that follow it.

The Old Passes—the New Comes (Deut. 29:1–34:12)

Like other Pentateuchal materials, Deuteronomy has a strong emphasis on the covenant. The description of a covenant ceremony in Moab is found in 29:1–29. This was part of the third major section of Deuteronomy and is followed by an exhortation that could be titled *The Two Ways* (30:1–20). In it, the people were given the choice of blessing or curse, depending on whether they chose the good way of obedience to the LORD or the way of disobedience.

After Deuteronomy's version of the choosing of Moses' successor (31:1–8), there is a command to have a ceremony of covenant renewal every seven years at the time of the Feast of Booths (31:9–29). Much debate has taken place among Old Testament scholars about whether this ceremony

The Literary Structure of Deuteronomy

Because Deuteronomy is a more obviously self-contained work of literature, its literary structure has received more attention than that of other books around it. The book is presented as a sequence of words or sermons of Moses, which he spoke to the Israelites while they were encamped on the plains of Moab. Four introductory phrases mark off the major sections of the book:

1:1	These are the words that Moses spoke to all Israel . . .
4:44	This is the law that Moses set before the Israelites.
29:1	These are the words of the covenant that the LORD commanded Moses to make . . .
32:1	This is the blessing with which Moses, the man of God, blessed the Israelites . . .

The first section is largely Moses' recounting of the days in the wilderness after leaving Horeb/Sinai. Together with the brief narrative of Moses' death in Deuteronomy 34, this section forms a narrative framework for the rest of the book. The long second section is filled with legal material, much of which appears to be a reformulation of that found in earlier parts of the Torah. It is this section that provides the book with its Greek and subsequent English name, which means "second" (*deutero-*) "law" (*nomos*). The third and fourth sections begin the move toward the death of Moses. In the third section a covenant is enacted, based upon the law laid out in the second section. In the fourth section, Moses speaks his final words to the Israelites in blessing and song.

Deuteronomy is, therefore, a true book of Moses. It highlights his career as leader, lawgiver, and man of God on Israel's behalf, and it brings his life to a close on the top of Mount Nebo. Deuteronomy begins with Moses' recollection of the departure from one mountain, Sinai/Horeb, and ends with his final departure from another. His final gaze upon the Promised Land in 34:1–3 points forward to the remainder of Israel's story and brings the Torah to a fitting close.

Several aspects of the book of Deuteronomy help it to function as an introduction to the books that follow it. Joshua, Judges, Samuel, and Kings are often referred to by scholars as the Deuteronomistic History. Themes that emerge in Deuteronomy, such as land, holy war, blessing and curse, and God's decision to make God's name dwell in a specific place (Jerusalem), are worked out in great detail in these books that follow the Pentateuch.

in early Israel was like the New Year's festival celebrated by the Babylonians. There is little direct evidence for such a festival in Israel; therefore, drawing a definite conclusion from parallels is not possible. The important point is that such a ceremony of covenant renewal was designed to make the covenant meaningful for each generation.

Deuteronomy concludes with two songs: (1) a song not unlike those found in the book of Psalms, seemingly used in celebrations of the Exodus events (32:1–43), and (2) a deathbed blessing similar to the blessing of Jacob in Genesis 49 (33:1–29).

Moses, the servant of the LORD, saw the land of promise; but he died on Mount Nebo. The final words of the book of Deuteronomy serve as his epitaph:

> Never since has there arisen a prophet in Israel like Moses, whom the LORD knew face to face. He was unequaled for all the signs and wonders that the LORD sent him to perform in the land of Egypt, against Pharaoh and all his servants and his entire land, and for all the mighty deeds and all the terrifying displays of power that Moses performed in the sight of all Israel.

THEMES IN THE PENTATEUCH

Even if one grants that the Pentateuch has been developed from many sources over several hundred years, two questions remain: "What is the ruling purpose behind its final form?" and "What major themes are used to enunciate this purpose?"

As for the first question, the obvious answer is that the Pentatuech gave Israel an explanation for its existence as a people. The themes used to enunciate this purpose include the following:

1. The LORD is Creator of the heavens and the earth, including humankind, to whom He has given lordship over the earth both to use and to preserve.
2. Humankind violated the LORD's trust by rebellion and thus sinned, provoking the LORD's judgment.
3. Israel's connection to the LORD, creation, humankind, and sin was through the patriarchs.
4. The LORD made a covenant with Abraham, the first patriarch, that demanded loyalty to the LORD on Abraham's part. The LORD, in turn, promised that Abraham's descendants would become a people who would receive a land if they kept the covenant.
5. The material from Exodus through Deuteronomy describes the fulfillment of the first part of the promise—the creation of a people and how their story is intertwined with the Law.
6. The Pentateuch ends with the anticipation of the fulfillment of the second part of the covenant—the giving of the land.

Key Terms

Aaron, *65*
Apodictic Law, *77*
Burnt Offering, *83*
Casuistic Law, *77*
Census, *85*
Circumcision, *66*
Covenant Code, *79*
Golden Calf, *85*
Holiness Code, *82*
Mercy Seat, *80*
Miriam, *66*
Mount Sinai, *75*
Passover, *71*
Plague, *68*
Tabernacle/Tent of Meeting, *80*
YHWH, *66*

Study Questions

1. What major events in Israel's story are described in the book of Exodus?
2. What forms of evidence are cited for dating the Exodus to the 1300–1200 B.C.E. time period?
3. From the perspective of the book of Exodus, what was the LORD's role in the events it portrays?
4. How did Moses' life experiences, up to and including his call on Mount Horeb, prepare him for his leadership role?
5. What meanings might the name YHWH have?
6. Compare Aaron's role as described in Exodus 4:10–31 to that in 6:2–7:7. What differences, if any, do you detect? How can they be explained?
7. What is the distinction between a suzerainty treaty or covenant and a parity treaty or covenant?
8. Define *miracle* and describe the function of the miraculous.
9. What are some of the natural phenomena that seem to correspond to the descriptions of the plagues in Exodus?
10. In what two ways did the ninth plague strike at the Pharaoh's power?
11. What are two ways to interpret the plagues?
12. Although they are now associated with the Exodus, what were the probable origins of the festivals of Passover and Unleavened Bread?
13. What problems are presented by the claim that at least 2 million people were involved in the Exodus?
14. Where are the four possible places for the crossing of the Red Sea?

15. Where was Sinai?
16. What is the relationship between the Song of Moses (Exodus 15: 1–18) and the Song of Miriam (15:21)?
17. How did Jethro assist Moses?
18. Explain the relationship between apodictic and casuistic law.
19. Look up *covenant* in a Bible dictionary and determine its role in Israelite religion.
20. What are the characteristics of the three major law codes in the Pentateuch, and how are they related to the Ten Commandments?
21. Why is Moses called the *lawgiver?*
22. What seems to have been the intent of sacrifice in early Israel, and how did that intent change over the years?
23. Why did Israel fail in its attempt to invade Canaan from the south?
24. What extrabiblical evidence is there for the prophet Balaam?
25. How do the Balaam stories illustrate the ancient belief in the power of the spoken word?
26. How is one to understand Deuteronomy's humanitarian strain in light of the instructions for holy war?
27. Why is Deuteronomy's place in the canon unique?
28. What are the major themes of the Pentateuch?
29. Define *Elohim, El Shaddai, Amalakites, prophet, Yam Suph,* and *Yom Kippur.*

Endnotes

1. For a succinct introduction to Exodus, see John I. Durham, "Exodus," in *MCB,* 127–129.
2. Although some who would minimize the historical value of the biblical narratives concerning the Exodus and the conquest of the land are able to marshal some convincing arguments for a different scenario of the formation of Israel as a people, their greatest weakness in every case is how to account for the development of the worship of Yahweh as the God of Israel, whatever Israel's roots. Someone or something had to be responsible, and the personality of Moses and the events described in Exodus are much better than whatever alternatives have been proposed to this point.
3. For an excellent work on the life of Moses, see Dewey Beegle, *Moses, the Servant of Yahweh* (Grand Rapids, MI: Wm. B. Eerdmans, 1972).
4. Tikva Frymer-Kensky, "Forgotten Heroines of the Exodus: The Exclusion of Women from Moses' Vision," *BR,* XIII, 6 (December 1997), 38–44, points out how the patriarchal system obscured the important roles women played in important events of biblical history.
5. J. B. Pritchard, ed., *ANET* (Princeton, NJ: Princeton University Press, 1969), 85.
6. See Durham, "Exodus," *MCB,* 135, for a "reasonable guess" as to the meaning of this incident.
7. On conditions during the oppression, see Nahum Sarna, "Exploring Exodus: The Oppression," *BA,* 49, 2 (June 1986), 69–79. See also Hershel Shanks, "An Ancient Israelite House in Egypt?" *BAR,* 19, 4 (July–August 1993), 44–45.
8. On covenants, see John H. Hayes, "Covenant," *MCB,* 178–181; George E. Mendenhall and Gary A. Herion, "Covenant," *ABD,* I, 1179–1202.
9. See Bernhard W. Anderson, *Understanding the Old Testament,* 4th ed. (Englewood Cliffs, NJ: Prentice Hall, 1986), 70, for a chart comparing the different traditions.
10. L. Mihelic and G. Ernest Wright, "Plagues in Exodus," *IDB,* III, 822. Also see Karen B. Joines, "Plagues," *MDB,* 692.
11. From Chester Warren Quimby, "Straight from the Classroom," *JBR,* XXI, 1 (1953), 62.
12. I am indebted to David Noel Freedman, "Did God Play a Dirty Trick on Jonah at the End?" *BR,* VI, 4 (August 1990), 27, for this insight.
13. On the Egyptian background of this material, see John E. Currid, "Why Did God Harden Pharaoh's Heart?" *BR,* XI, 6 (December 1993), 46–51, esp. 49–50.
14. This is based on Ziony Zevit, "Three Ways to Look at the Plagues," *BR,* VI, 3 (June 1990), 16–23, 42.
15. James K. Hoffmeier, *Israel in Egypt: The Evidence for the Authenticity of the Exodus Tradition* (New York: Oxford University Press, 1999), 112–115.
16. Mendenhall and Herion, "Covenant," *ABD,* 1, 1179–1194.
17. Walter Eichrodt, *Theology of the Old Testament,* 2 vols., trans. J. A. Baker (Louisville, KY: Westminster—John Knox Press, 1961, 1967), sees the covenant as the dominant idea in Israel's history.
18. Pritchard, *ANET,* 165.
19. Some have argued that the Tabernacle is an invention of the Exilic times, but see Kenneth Kitchen,

"The Desert Tabernacle: Pure Fiction or Plausible Account?" *BR,* XVII, 6 (December 2000), 14–21, and Michael H. Homan, "The Divine Warrior in His Tent: A Military Model for Yahweh's Tabernacle," *BR,* XVIII, 6 (December 2000), 22–23, 55, both of whom argue that there were similar structures in Egypt in the second millennium that could have served as models for the Tabernacle.

20. John H. Tullock, *Blood-Vengeance Among the Israelites in the Light of Its Near Eastern Background* (Ann Arbor, MI: University Microfilms, 1966), 165.

21. On the nature of Leviticus, "the priestly book," (LXX), or *wayylqra'* "and he called," (Hebrew Bible), see W. H. Bellinger, Jr., "Leviticus, Book of," *MDB,* 511f.

22. See Claude Mariottini, "Numbers, Book of," *MDB,* 621.

23. Suzanne Singer, "From These Hills," *BAR,* IV (June 1978), 16–27.

24. Andrew Lemaire, "Fragments of the Book of Balaam Found at Deir Alla," *BAR,* XI, 5 (September–October 1985), 26–39. See also Jacob Hoftijzer, "The Prophet Balaam in a 6th Century Aramaic Inscription," *BA,* 39, 1 (March 1976), 11–17. Lemaire would date the texts to the eighth century B.C.E.

25. For a fuller discussion, see Charles R. Krahmalkov, "Exodus Itinerary Confirmed by Egyptian Evidence," *BAR,* XX, 5 (September–October 1994), 54–62.

26. John H. Tullock, "Deuteronomy," *MCB,* 201.

27. See extensive discussions of this issue in Millard C. Lind, *Yahweh Is a Warrior: The Theology of Warfare in Ancient Israel* (Scottsdale, PA: Herald Press, 1980), Susan Niditch, *War in the Hebrew Bible: A Study in the Ethics of Violence* (New York: Oxford University Press, 1993), and Gerhard von Rad, *Holy War in Ancient Israel,* trans. Marva J. Dawn and John H. Yoder (Grand Rapids, MI: Wm. B. Eerdmans, 1991). This final work was published in German in 1958.

CHAPTER

5

Israel Gains a Home

Joshua and Judges

Timeline

1250 B.C.E.	Frequent guess for Israelite entrance into the Promised Land
1200 B.C.E.	Beginning of the Iron Age and the first reference to Israel on the Merneptah Stele
1100 B.C.E.	Philistine settlement in Palestine
1020 B.C.E.	Frequent guess for the end of the period of the Judges
900 B.C.E.	End of Iron Age I and beginning of Iron Age II

Chapter Outline

I. Moving into the Promised Land
II. Continuing the Story of Occupation
III. Proposed Models for the Israelite Occupation of Canaan

CHAPTER OVERVIEW

The book of Deuteronomy ended with the Israelites in Moab while Moses spent his last moments on a mountain gazing at the Promised Land. By the beginning of the book of 1 Samuel, the Israelites will appear to be reasonably settled in their land, ready to make some important political and national decisions. The books of Joshua and Judges attempt to portray the process that connects these two positions, but it is not an easy portrait. A vast array of images are presented of a people moving into a land, attempting to take control of it, and trying to find a way to exist in this new place. The book of Joshua will primarily present a picture of a military campaign that carves out a place where the Israelites can settle, although plenty of difficulties with a straightforward process of invasion will emerge. The book of Judges will portray a people struggling to stay free of the powers and influences that surround them, while looking for sustainable patterns of organization and leadership.

MOVING INTO THE PROMISED LAND

In many places, the books of the Pentateuch present the idea that Israel is to go to the land of Canaan, displace or exterminate the people living in the region, and take control of the land that God had promised them since the days of Abraham and Sarah. This course of action presents obvious moral problems, of course, and there are also enormous practical difficulties associated with such an effort. The writers of the books of Joshua and Judges, who tell the stories of this part of Israel's experience, are well aware that Israel's attempt to conquer the Promised Land was a complicated process that had mixed results. These two books are often understood as two opposing views of how the conquest worked, and many efforts have been made to use the material in Joshua and Judges, along with archaeological evidence, to reconstruct an account of "what really happened" in Canaan in the early centuries of the **Iron Age.** The results of these attempts have varied widely and have proved to be problematic, indicating that the evidence from the Bible and other sources of information are not sufficient for such a reconstruction. Description of the literary structure of the books of Joshua and Judges will appear in this chapter and will demonstrate that each of these books has a literary and theological purpose that determines its contents and shape in a way that makes them unsuitable for such historical reconstruction. We know that a political, ethnic, and territorial entity called Israel eventually existed in the land that had been known as Canaan, although the nature and extent of this entity varied significantly over time. How it came into existence is a process that we cannot explain with any precision.

The International Scene

Conditions in Palestine in the period 1300 to 1100 B.C.E. had changed considerably from those of previous centuries. Canaan, later known as Palestine, had been dominated by the Egyptians for a long time. By the time of Joshua's entry into the land, however, Egypt and the Hittites of Asia Minor, the two contenders for control of the vital land bridge between Asia and Africa, had fought an exhausting war. Egypt was possibly the winner, but it was left weakened. This was during the reign of Ramses II, around 1285 B.C.E. The Exodus may have taken place about that time.

Another problem facing Egypt was an invasion by the "Sea Peoples," invaders who seem to have come from the area of modern Greece. Merneptah (1224–1211 B.C.E.), the son of Ramses II, succeeded in driving the invaders off, but after his death, the Egyptian Empire went into a rapid decline. As noted earlier, Merneptah mentions the Israelites in a monument for a battle fought in 1220 B.C.E.

The Sea Peoples, driven out of Egypt, settled on the southern coast of Canaan and became known as the Philistines. It was from them that Canaan got the name Palestine. Israel's major problem was to fight the people of the land, because the Egyptians, the Hittites of Asia Minor, and the Assyrians of the Mesopotamian region were too weak to interfere in Canaan in the twelfth century B.C.E.

POLITICAL TRANSFORMATION. Historical and archaeological information about the period in which Israel came into existence as a political and territorial entity is scarce, but there is enough evidence to draw a broad, general picture of the time and place in which this happened.

The Literary Structure of Joshua

The book of Joshua tends to fall fairly naturally into two halves, with the first half dominated by narrative material and the second half by nonnarrative. Such a structure is reminiscent of the book of Exodus, and this may be no accident. The story of the crossing of the Jordan in Joshua 3 recalls the crossing of the sea in Exodus 14–15. Other elements in the early part of Joshua, such as the sending of spies into Jericho, serve to portray Joshua as a character similar to Moses. The conquest of the Promised Land in Joshua 1–12, therefore, has much in common with Exodus 1–18, which tells the story of Moses' triumph over the Pharaoh and the departure of the Israelites from Egypt. The somewhat tedious apportionment of the land in Joshua 13–21 resembles the legal material that fills most of Exodus 19–40.

Two stories, the Battle of Jericho (Ch. 6) and the Battle of Ai (Chs. 7–8), form the center of the first half of the book of Joshua and function as ideal models of victory and defeat. Stories of specific battles continue in Joshua 9, but they generally diminish in length and detail until Joshua 12 presents simply a list of defeated kings. This list is bounded by two remarkable statements in 11:23 and 13:1. The first of these statements, in 11:23 says, "Joshua took all of the land, according to all which YHWH spoke unto Moses, and Joshua gave it for an inheritance to Israel according to their tribes, by their allotments. Then the land rested from war." The second statement, in 13:1b, says, "And very much of the land remains to take." A discerning reader will want to ask which of these two statements is true. Their contradictory nature, however, reveals much about the purpose of the book of Joshua. The book of Judges, which follows Joshua, will reveal that the second statement portrays the actual situation in Israel's story. The taking of the land is an ongoing struggle that will never fully end.

The second half of the book of Joshua is filled with descriptions of the allotment of land, and this reveals the purpose of the statement in Joshua 11:23. In order for Joshua to allot the land to the tribes, it must be at least imagined as fully possessed by Israel. This statement then serves as an act of imagination that allows the land allotment to proceed. One by one the tribes receive their share and the boundaries are delineated. This portion of the book stands in some tension to the first half. Joshua 12:16–23 states that the land was fully conquered by Joshua and that a time of peace was achieved. Joshua 13:1–7, on the other hand, acknowledges that the conquest was far from complete and much land remained to be taken.

The book of Joshua concludes with stories of Joshua's farewell address (Ch. 23) and a covenant renewal ceremony (Ch. 24). These grand scenes reflect the book of Deuteronomy and reinforce the Moses-like portrayal of Joshua as his life comes to an end. The end of the book of Joshua performs one more literary function in relation to the Pentateuch. In Joshua 24:32, the bones of Joseph are buried, concluding a theme that began in Genesis 50:24–26 when Joseph made his brothers promise to bury him in the Promised Land and continued as the Israelites carried Joseph's bones throughout their journey in the wilderness (Exodus 13:19). Thus the Book of Joshua is the end of the story of how the Israelites came to be a people living in the land of Canaan.

At the beginning of the Iron Age in 1200 B.C.E., the land of Canaan was occupied and controlled by a collection of **city-states.** The portrait presented indirectly in the book of Joshua, of a fairly large number of walled cities, each with its own "king" (see the list in Joshua 12), fits the evidence from other sources. Likewise, the portrait of this region two or three centuries later, presented in the biblical books of 1 and 2 Kings, of a smaller number of comparatively large territorial kingdoms, such as Israel, Syria, Moab, and Ammon, seems to match the general picture provided by information from outside the Bible. The emergence of Israel as a political and territorial kingdom took place within this larger matrix of transformation, but the precise process of Israel's emergence and of the region's general political transformation is largely beyond our ability to know.

The Invasion of Canaan

PREPARATIONS FOR THE INVASION (JOSH. 1–2:24). Israel's new leader was no newcomer to responsibility. As a soldier, Joshua had proven his ability as a leader in the battle against the Amalekites (Exod. 17:8–16). As one of the twelve spies, he had already gotten a firsthand look at the territory to be invaded. He had come away firmly convinced that it could be conquered, despite the fact that only one other of the twelve (Caleb) agreed with him (Num. 13:1–33). Assured of the LORD's presence and leadership (1:1–18), he began the preparations for the invasion.

First, he ordered the people who were to cross the Jordan to prepare themselves. Then, he placed them under strict orders of obedience to his authority (1:10–18). Next, he sent two spies to Jericho to bring back information about the enemy. To provide a cover-up, they went to the house of a prostitute named Rahab. The ruse did not work, because the king of Jericho sent men to Rahab's house to try to find them. She had hidden them, however, and was able to convince the king's men that they were not in the house. Because her house was located on the city wall, she was able to let them down by a rope on the outside of the wall. Returning to Joshua, the spies gave their report (2:1–14).

THE WATERS PART AGAIN (JOSH. 3:1–5:1). There followed another of the remarkable series of timely events that Israel saw as the "wonder" of God. Several miles above Jericho stood the city of Adam, or Adamah. At the site, the Jordan follows its twisting path between high clay banks. At times, the river undercuts the banks so that they fall into it, forming a natural dam that holds it in check for several hours. When Israel needed it to happen, it did. As the biblical writer describes it:

> When the people set out from their tents to cross the Jordan, the priests bearing the ark of the covenant were in front of the people. Now the Jordan overflows all its banks throughout the time of harvest. So when those who bore the ark had come to the Jordan, and the feet of the priests bearing the ark were dipped in the edge of the water, the waters flowing down from above stood still, rising up in a single heap far off at Adam, the city that is beside Zarethan, while those flowing toward the sea of the Arabah, the Dead Sea, were wholly cut off. Then the people crossed over opposite Jericho. (3:14–16)

The Ark of the Covenant, the symbol of the LORD's presence with the Israelites, was carried to the midst of the riverbed to remind them that it was the LORD's doing that was enabling them to cross the flooded river (3:17).

The passage through the Jordan was commemorated by a pile of stones set up as a memorial to the event to serve as a teaching aid, so that when children of future generations asked, "What do these stones mean?" the elders would tell them of the LORD God's deliverance of the people (4:1–5:1).

AND THE WALLS CAME TUMBLING DOWN (JOSH. 5:2–6:27). After crossing the Jordan, all the men and boys underwent circumcision as an act of consecration to the LORD (5:2–12). When they had recovered, preparations got underway for the attack on Jericho. In a vision, Joshua saw "the commander of the army of the LORD." There are elements here that parallel Moses' vision on the mountain (Exod. 3). Joshua was assured of divine leadership in the days ahead (5:13–6:7).

Jericho, the first major target of the Israelites after they crossed the Jordan, is one of the world's oldest continuously existing cities. Located just north of the Dead Sea, this well-watered oasis was settled at least as early as 7000 B.C.E. Much archaeological effort has been spent in excavating Jericho, and interpretations of the results have run the gamut. An early excavator, John Garstang, interpreted the evidence as supporting the biblical account. Then Dame Kathleen Kenyon concluded that Jericho was not even a city when Joshua was supposed to have conquered it. Now a new assessment of Kenyon's excavations by Bryant Wood, an American archaeologist, has led him to conclude that Jericho was indeed conquered in the manner described in the book of Joshua, aided by an earthquake. The major problem arises in relating this to Joshua's conquest. Wood dates this fall at 1400 B.C.E., too early for Joshua by most estimates. The whole question of the nature of the Exodus and the conquest is in such a state of flux, however, that it is difficult to reach any firm conclusions at this time.[1]

In the description of the fall of the city, there are some significant features. For one thing, the religious nature of Israelite warfare can be seen in the act of carrying the Ark of the Covenant around the walls of the besieged city, accompanied by the raucous blaring of the ram's horn trumpets (Heb. *Shopharim*) (6:1–11). In the second place, the prominent role that the number 7 plays in the story shows the importance of numerology in Hebrew thought. In addition to 7, the numbers 1, 3, 4, 10, and 12 and their multiples had significance other than their numerical value—7 symbolized completeness, 10 perfection, and 12 Israel (6:12–16).

Of great significance is that this was a **holy war.** Everything was to be destroyed as an act of dedication to God. Only the prostitute, Rahab, who had helped the spies, was to be spared (6:17–25). Finally, when the city was conquered, a curse was pronounced on it to prevent its rebuilding (6:26–27). These reports of holy wars are troubling to many modern readers. It is important to notice that the ancient writers may have shared some of this uneasiness. Careful readers will notice that the battle of Jericho is actually described three times in Joshua 6. The first description is in God's instructions to Joshua in 6:2–5. The second and third descriptions, in Joshua's instructions to the Israelites and the actual narration of the event, are intertwined in 6:6–27. Each successive description becomes more detailed and more violent. At the same time, the presence of God becomes more removed in this progression. God is first present as a speaking character, giving Joshua instruction. As the scene progresses, God is represented symbolically by the Ark, which is carried around the city. Once the Israelites enter Jericho to slaughter the inhabitants, even the symbolic representation of the Ark is not mentioned. The writer of this story seems to want to keep God at a distance from the actual bloodshed. Although these observations do not negate the assertion that God commanded the destruction of Jericho, they may indicate a sense of discomfort concerning God's involvement in brutality that extends back into ancient times.[2]

TROUBLE IN THE CAMP (JOSH. 7:1–26). As harsh as the requirements of the holy war were, an incident involving an Israelite would make them seem even more harsh. Strict rules governed the disposal of goods captured in the holy war. A violation of the **ban** on the taking of spoils for personal use was punishable by death to the offender. In the battle for Ai, a stronghold in the hill country west of Jericho, the Israelites were driven back. Unknown to Joshua, Achan, one of the warriors, had taken certain banned objects at Jericho (7:1): a beautiful robe, a large number of silver coins, and a bar of gold. Unfortunately for Achan, the word of his crime was—in modern parlance—"leaked" to Joshua, although at first the name of the culprit was not revealed. Knowledge that someone had gotten by with violating the ban seems to have had a divisive effect on the army, resulting in a stinging defeat at Ai (7:2–5).

Joshua was perplexed, feeling that the LORD had let him down (7:6–9). Then Joshua became aware that this was not the case: rather, someone had violated the ban (7:10–15). An investigation revealed Achan as the culprit, and in due course, he confessed his sin (7:16–26).

By our standards of justice, what followed would seem to be unjust, for the text says:

> And Joshua and all Israel took Achan . . . with the silver, the mantle, and the bar of gold, with his sons and daughters, with his oxen, donkeys, and sheep, and his tent and all that he had . . . and all Israel stoned him to death; they burned them with fire, cast stones on them. (7:24–25)

Why did his family have to suffer the consequences of his sin? Because of a view that is best described by the term *corporate personality.* In this view, a person was not seen as an individual, but as part of a larger unit—the family, the tribe, or the clan. Our society emphasizes the importance of the individual. Early Israelite society emphasized the importance of the group. Because of this, whatever action a person took was thought to affect not only himself, but the group as a whole, either positively or negatively. For this reason, Achan's guilt had to be shared by the group of which he was a part. It affected not only those related to him, but also whatever he possessed. The destruction of Achan, his family, and his possessions was looked upon as the only way to clear the larger group, the people as a whole, of Achan's sin. When the punishment was carried out, the battle was renewed and was won (8:1–29). There follows an account of building an altar on Mount Ebal in the Shechem area. It may possibly belong with Joshua 23–24, in which an account of a covenant ceremony is given. It will be discussed later (8:30–35).[3]

THOSE TRICKY GIBEONITES (JOSH. 9:1–27). Gibeon, some six to seven miles northeast of the present city of Jerusalem, was typical of the small Canaanite villages of the time. Having heard of the brutal Israelite conquest of the nearby towns, the Gibeonites decided that they would rather not have to face such a fate. They put on their most ragged clothes and worn-out sandals, took stale bread and wineskins that were brittle with age, and set out for the Israelite camp. When they arrived, they told the Israelites a fanciful tale, designed to appeal to the Israelite ego, about how they had heard of the greatness of the Israelites, but more especially of the greatness of their God (9:3–10). As a result, they said they had set out to find these people who worshiped the LORD to make a covenant with them.

The Israelites were completely taken in by their story. Without any investigation, they made a covenant with the Gibeonites. They confirmed the covenant with a covenant meal and by taking a solemn oath. Under the terms of the covenant, the Gibeonites were to be spared and thus would become part of Israel (9:11–15).

After the covenant was made, the truth came out. Their word having been given, the Israelites could not change the terms, except to make the Gibeonites "hewers of wood and drawers of water for the congregation and for the altar of the LORD" (9:27). This is one of the few breaks in the idealized picture of the conquest, and it reveals an important fact—namely, that many of the people who later became part of Israel never came from Egypt and were joined to Israel by covenant in the worship of the LORD.

THE FIVE KINGS OF THE SOUTH (JOSH. 10:1–27). The local kings, more like self-appointed rulers of small towns of a few hundred people, became alarmed over the Israelite successes. Five of them joined forces, including the kings of Jerusalem, Hebron, Eglon, Lachish, and Jarmuth (10:3). The battle took place in the Valley of Aijalon, one of the few routes from the coastal plain up into the southern section of the central hill country. The attack, which probably came at dawn, was aided by a violent hailstorm that lasted into the day. The great hailstones killed many of the enemy and caused the Israelite minstrels to sing a song about the sun standing still at Gibeon (10:1–14).

The kings were captured, and a symbolic ceremony was conducted in which the Israelite leaders placed their feet on the kings' necks. As they did, Joshua charged the leaders to be strong. He promised that the LORD would lead them to be just as successful against all of Israel's enemies if they remained faithful to the LORD (10:15–27).

SUMMARY OF JOSHUA'S CONQUESTS (JOSH. 10:28–12:24). Although the first twelve chapters of the book of Joshua may give the impression of a rapid march through the land of Canaan and a fairly thorough destruction or defeat of its major cities, this simple picture will just as quickly be qualified by the negative assessment in 13:1. The book of Joshua is determined to present a fulfillment of the great work of Moses under the leadership of Joshua. Joshua 11:20, among other verses, provides echoes of the earlier stories of the Exodus and Moses' leadership. A careful examination of the summation of Joshua's "conquests" in 10:28–43 and 11:16–12:24 reveals that this activity is limited to a fairly small region often known as the *central hill country.*

A few moments of reflection are enough to show that the complete extermination or displacement of hundreds of thousands of people from an area the size of Canaan is not feasible, regardless of how we understand the divine assistance the Israelites received. Even the most brutal genocides in human history have all fallen short of their ultimate goal. Nevertheless, the military reports of Joshua 1–12 provide an adequate introduction to the land apportionment in the second half of the book. The book of Judges will continue exploring the complexities of Israel's existence in the midst of the other inhabitants of Canaan.

Dividing the Land and Renewing the Covenant

THE DIVIDING OF THE LAND (JOSH. 13:1–21:45). Joshua speaks as though the land is already conquered, but the boundaries described in 13–21, in reality, represented the territory that each tribe was responsible for conquering, not what it had already captured.

Of special interest are the cities assigned to the Levites (21:1–42). They had no territorial boundaries, but the Levites were to receive cities within each of the territories, centrally located to provide (1) accessible worship centers and (2) centers for the administration of justice, including refuge centers where an accused killer could stay until some disposition could be made of the case. Otherwise, the killer would be at the mercy of the *avenger of blood,* a member of the family against whom the crime had been committed. Under the family law of custom, the avenger was judge, jury, and executioner when there was no ruling state to carry out punishment for a crime against a family member.

THE ALTAR THAT WAS NOT AN ALTAR. An insight into how the early Israelites dealt with problems that arose between tribes can be seen in the story of an altar built by the tribes east of the Jordan. When word came back to the tribes in the west, an alarm was raised. Such an altar would seem to violate a ban on worshiping anywhere except at one central shrine, which in those days probably was Shechem or Shiloh (22:12). In a tribal assembly, it was decided to send Phineas, a priest, accompanied by ten tribal representatives, to investigate the situation. When they inquired of the Reubenites, the Gadites, and the half-tribe of Manasseh, they were told that the altar was a memorial, "a witness between us and you . . . that we do perform the service of the LORD in his presence with our burnt offerings and sacrifices and offerings of well-being" (22:27). Satisfied about the purpose of the altar, the tribal representatives returned, and the planned attack was averted (22:30–34).

JOSHUA'S FAREWELL AND A COVENANT-RENEWAL CEREMONY (JOSH. 23:1–24:28; SEE ALSO JOSH. 8:30–35 AND DEUT. 27:1–26). A recognition that Joshua's conquest was not complete appears in Joshua's farewell address to the Israelite leaders. The LORD God had given them the land from the Jordan to the "Great Sea in the west," and he would enable them to conquer the people who still occupied the land, provided that Israel was faithful to God's law as given to Moses (23:1–13). Unfaithfulness would lead to loss of life and land (23:14–16).

The climax of Joshua's story is the covenant-renewal ceremony described in Joshua 24:1–28. The site of the ceremony was Shechem, an ancient religious center (Gen. 34) located at the head of a pass between Mount Gerizim and Mount Ebal in the central section of the hill country. Shechem is not mentioned among the cities conquered by Joshua, possibly because the natives of the area were somehow related to the Israelites and had joined Israel by a covenant in which they agreed to worship the LORD.

Deuteronomy 27:1–8 contains a command for the people to set up a memorial on Mount Ebal when they entered the land. Joshua 8:30–35 describes the fulfillment of this command and goes on to describe briefly a covenant-renewal ceremony. An altar was built, sacrifices were offered, a copy of the law was written and read to the people, and a ceremony of blessing and cursing was carried out, with half of the Levites standing on Mount Gerizim and the other half standing on Mount Ebal (Josh. 8:33; but see Deut. 27:12–13, in which all the tribes are mentioned, with Levi as a secular tribe).

Shechem, then, obviously had strong traditions connecting it to the early days of Israel's history. The covenant-renewal ceremony at Shechem described in Joshua 24 has many of the same elements as the suzerainty (superior–inferior) treaty. The important men of Israel gathered at the sanctuary (24:1). Joshua recounted the LORD's call to the patriarchs, and how the people were brought out of Egypt under the leadership of Moses and Aaron and into the land of Canaan (24:2–13). After reminding them of the LORD's blessing, Joshua called on them to accept the obligations of the covenant. Joshua 24:14–15 indicates that not all the people present were descendants of those who came out of Egypt, for he spoke of those who were worshiping "the gods your ancestors served . . . beyond the River or the gods of the Amorites in whose land you dwell." A careful reading of this passage suggests that at least four groups were present: (1) the Joshua-led Israelites; (2) Israelites who had filtered into the land apart from those led by Joshua; (3) Semitic peoples who had never been to Egypt but who shared the patriarchal traditions of Israel; and (4) non-Semitic peoples who joined Israel by covenant. The most numerous among these undoubtedly were the Canaanites.

THE INFLUENCE OF CANAANITE RELIGION. That Canaanite religious practices were much more influential in the development of Israelite religion than was formerly thought is becoming more widely recognized today. This is because (1) the number of people entering Palestine from the outside is now believed to have been much fewer than once was thought, and consequently (2) the Canaanite population was much larger than was earlier thought, especially because the views of the nature of the conquest have changed substantially. Among those elements adapted from Canaanite religion by the Israelites would have been the divine name *El* as the equivalent to *YHWH* and three festivals that originally were agricultural in nature—Tabernacles, Weeks, and Unleavened Bread. Outside the religious sphere, Israel's adoption of the kingship undoubtedly was influenced by the Canaanites (1 Sam. 8:20; Psa. 110:4).[4]

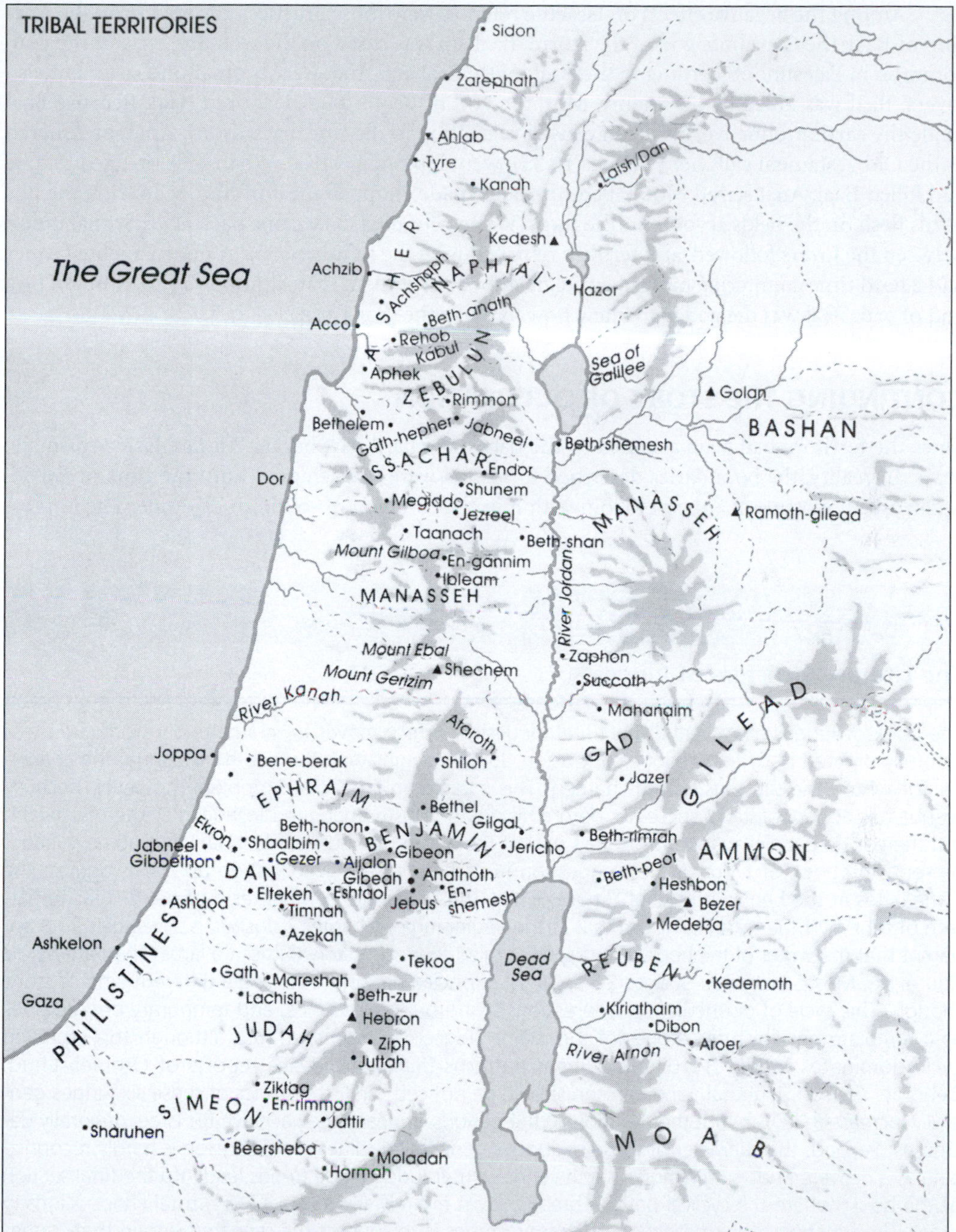

FIGURE 5–1 The division of the land (Josh. 13:1–19:51). Artwork by Margaret Jordan Brown, from *Mercer Dictionary of the Bible.* © 1990, courtesy of Mercer University Press.

Among the negative effects on Israelite religion were those practices adopted from the worship of Baal, the Canaanite god of the storm. Baalism was based on the wet–dry cycle of the year, common in Palestine. According to the Baal myth, Baal and Anat were brother and sister but also lovers. Baal was killed by his enemy, Mot, the god of death. Mot devoured Baal. Because Baal made the earth productive, his death caused vegetation to die (the dry season). Anat, or Asherah as the Old Testament calls her (1 Kings 16:33), went looking for Baal. When Mot bragged that he had killed Baal, Anat seized Mot, killed him, and made chopped meat of him, scattering the bits of his flesh on the fields as food for the birds. When Mot died, Baal came back alive. Sexual union between the lovers followed, and fertility returned with the rainy season.[5] A poor Israelite farmer had a hard time countering his Canaanite neighbor's argument that, although YHWH might be a god of war, Baal was the god who knew how to make the crops grow.

CONTINUING THE STORY OF OCCUPATION

Once the territory had been assigned to the tribes, the hard part began. Warfare lasted for many years. In reality, the boundaries described in Joshua were not achieved until the time of David. Judah asked the tribe of Simeon to join with it in the conquest of southern Palestine. The impres-

The Literary Structure of Judges

The book of Judges has a very distinct literary design, which moves from a halting introduction to a carefully ordered body to a chaotic conclusion. Judges begins with the death of Joshua, the character for whom the previous book is named. This creates an immediate problem, however, because Joshua has not appointed a successor before his death. Moses appointed Joshua in Deuteronomy 34, but there is no parallel action on Joshua's part at the end of the book of Joshua. With no new leader present, the book of Judges poses a question in its first verse: "Who will go up for us against the Canaanites at the beginning to fight them in it?" The remainder of Chapter 1 presents a failed pattern of tribe-by-tribe warfare. Notice that at the beginning of Chapter 2, Joshua is alive again. It is apparent that the writer of the book of Judges struggled to write a story without a larger-than-life heroic figure, like Moses or Joshua. Judges 2:11–23 establishes a pattern for telling a different kind of story, though. This cycle of disobedience, oppression, crying out, deliverance, and temporary peace serves as a template on which the stories of the major judges can be placed. But although this repeated cycle dominates Judges 3–16, some linear patterns in the successive reports of Othniel, Ehud, Deborah, Gideon, Jephthah, and Samson should be noticed. First, the stories of these six judges generally increase in length, but the duration of the periods of peace they achieve for Israel generally decreases. Second, the character of these six judges generally declines, until Samson is hardly recognizable as a deliverer, but is little more than a vengeful marauder. These trends lead into the final section of the book, where the cyclical pattern breaks down entirely. In Judges 17–21, total chaos reigns in Israel. The function of this collection of chaotic stories is to support the repeated refrain that frames them in 17:6, 18:1, 19:1, and 21:25. "In those days there was no king in Israel; all the people did what was right in their own eyes." This statement might appear to be neutral by itself, but the horrifying nature of the stories it surrounds points in a negative direction. Israel is out of control, and the book of Judges ends by promoting the monarchy as the solution to this problem.

sion is given (1:8) that they conquered Jerusalem, but in a later account, David is named as its conqueror. There is also the mention of the capture of three cities of the Philistines: Gaza, Ashkelon, and Ekron. The LXX, however, specifically says that these cities were not captured. As a whole, this section is a record of the failure of the majority of the tribes to conquer the territory assigned to them. For the biblical historian, the military failure was brought on by the failure to keep the LORD's Covenant. Failure would continue to haunt them as long as they were unfaithful to the Covenant.

Establishing a Pattern for the Judges (Judg. 2:6–3:6)

After a description of the death and burial of Joshua comes a verse reminiscent of Exodus 1:1: "Now a new king arose . . . who did not know Joseph." Judges 2:10 says in part, "Another generation grew up after them, who did not know the LORD or the work he had done for Israel."

The basic pattern of the book of Judges starts with this theme and is based on a four-part sermon, a concise form of which is found in Judges 3:7–11: (1) "The Israelites did what was evil in the sight of the LORD" (3:7); (2) "the anger of the LORD was kindled against Israel" and an enemy oppressed them (3:8); (3) "when the Israelites cried out to the LORD, (4) the LORD raised up a deliverer for the Israelites" (3:9).

First of all, the theme of sin–punishment–repentance–deliverance is the Deuteronomic theme. It is so named because scholars believe that the books beginning with Joshua and extending through 2 Kings (with the exception of Ruth) were put in their present form during the Babylonian Exile by Jewish historians who had been influenced by the book of Deuteronomy. In 621 B.C.E., during the reign of Josiah, a major portion of Deuteronomy, with its strong emphasis upon the necessity of Israel's faithfulness to the Covenant, had been found during a major repair of the Jerusalem Temple. Its discovery had led to a strong religious revival for a time, but after Josiah's death, the revival quickly died. A few years later, the Babylonians invaded and carried many of the Israelites into captivity. The historians of Israel concluded that their troubles stemmed from the failure to be faithful to the Covenant. Furthermore, the whole history of the people from the time of their entry into the land had been marred by this same unfaithfulness to the Covenant. Thus, the historians' version of the history of Israel was interpreted in the light of this conviction.

In the second place, it is in this section of the book that the judges are first mentioned. From the description in 2:16, "Then the LORD raised up judges who delivered them out of the power of those who plundered them," one can discover the major function of the judges of the book of Judges, namely, that they were military leaders. They have been described as "charismatic military leaders," meaning that they were persons who had qualities that inspired others to follow wherever they led.

Because Israel was composed of twelve tribes, however, not one of the judges was able to get all the people to follow his or her leadership. At this time, the tribe was more important than the people as a whole. There was little, if any, national unity. It was not until the monarchy of David that tribal feeling began to take second place to national feeling. Even then, tribal feelings were not completely dead.

The Major Judges

OTHNIEL. The first specific example of a judge is a man named Othniel. The brief story of this judge repeats the basic steps in the cycle demonstrated above, with a minimum of added detail. The "evil in the sight of the LORD" is described as "serving the Baals and the Asherahs," Canaanite divinities; the king who oppresses them is named Cushan-Rishathaim of Aram; the oppression from which the Israelites cry out lasts for eight years; and Othniel's deliverance of the Israelites leads to forty years of peace before he dies.

EHUD (JUDG. 3:12–30). The oppressor was Eglon, king of Moab. Ehud, of the tribe of Benjamin, was chosen to take an annual payment to Eglon to keep him from attacking the Israelites. In preparation for his visit, Ehud strapped a short sword to the inside of his right thigh. After the money had been paid, he sought a private conference with the king. When they were alone, Ehud drew his sword and stabbed Eglon in the belly:

> the hilt also went in after the blade, and the fat closed over the blade, for he did not draw the sword out of his belly; and the dirt came out. (3:22)

Ehud's bold assassination of Eglon rallied the Ephraimites around him, and the Moabite oppression was ended (3:26–30).

DEBORAH (JUDG. 4:1–5:31). Much has been written about the low status of women in ancient times, but the story of **Deborah** is an indication that outstanding women had a way of making their mark. Two versions are given of Deborah's story: a later prose version appears in Judges 4:1–24, and the original poetic version is found in 5:1–31.

The two accounts differ somewhat. The prose story speaks of Jabin, the king of Hazor, as Israel's oppressor (4:2). According to Joshua 11, Joshua defeated Jabin and destroyed Hazor some years earlier. The poetic account does not name Jabin, nor does it mention Hazor. Only Sisera, a general, is mentioned.

Deborah, described as a prophetess (4:4), was judging Israel near Bethel in the hill country of Ephraim (4:5). She seems to have functioned as an adviser on personal matters and in settling disputes between contending parties. The oppression was so bad that

> In the days of Shamgar son of Anath,
> in the days of Jael, caravans ceased
> and travelers kept to the byways.
> The peasantry prospered in Israel,
> they grew fat on plunder,
> because you arose, Deborah,
> arose as a mother in Israel. (5:6–7)

Deborah's role was to rally the people to fight against the enemy. Barak served as her general, but he refused to go unless she went with him. She agreed, but she told him that a woman would get the glory for winning the battle (4:6–10).

The poetic version calls the roll of the tribes who joined in the battle fought on Mount Tabor, located at the apex of the triangular plain of Megiddo or Esdralon. After speaking of Ephraim, Benjamin, Machir, Zebulun, and Issachar as tribes that contributed soldiers to the cause, the poet speaks of those who refused to join:

> Among the clans of Reuben
> there were great searchings of heart.
> Why did you tarry among the sheepfolds,
> to hear the piping for the flocks?
> . . .
> Gilead stayed beyond the Jordan;
> and Dan, why did he abide with the ships?
> Asher sat still at the coast of the sea,
> settling down by his landings. (5:15d–17).[6]

FIGURE 5-2 In Judges 4:6, Deborah sends Barak to prepare his army on Mount Tabor. This photograph shows Mount Tabor today.

The Canaanites, equipped with heavy war chariots (4:3), were drawn up on the level plain, while the ill-equipped Israelites were on the slopes of Mount Tabor. A heavy storm broke. The Kishon River, usually no more than a trickle of water, became a raging torrent. It flooded the plain and turned it into a muddy swamp. The heavy iron chariots, so fearsome on solid ground, became liabilities instead of assets. The Israelites rushed down the mountain and cut the enemy to pieces (4:13–16; 5:19–21).

When he saw how the battle tide had turned, Sisera decided to take care of the most important person he knew—himself. He fled on foot from the battlefield. After some time, he came to the tent of a Kenite named Heber. Jael, Heber's wife, was at home. When Sisera asked for refuge in her tent, Jael, true to the law of custom, invited him in and gave him refreshments. While he was eating and drinking, she killed him by driving a tent peg through his skull. Like the gunfighter in the western movie,

> He sank, he fell,
> he lay still at her feet,
> at her feet, he sank, he fell;
> where he sank, there he fell dead. (5:27)

The poetic version ends with a picture of Sisera's mother looking for him, not knowing that he is dead. The closing line is

> So perish all your enemies, O LORD (5:31)

GIDEON (JUDG. 6:1–8:35). More stories are told about **Gideon** than about any other judge except Samson. The oppressors were the Midianites, who were aided by the hated Amalekites and "the people from the East" (6:3). In their raids, they (like the locusts) destroyed crops, bringing famine on the land (6:1–6).

The people cried to the LORD, who reminded them through a prophet that they had been unfaithful to Him (6:7–10).

Deliverance began when Gideon, a member of the tribe of Manasseh, received a divine visitor who told him that he was chosen to lead the war against the Midianites (6:11–24).

The first thing Gideon did was destroy his own father's altar to Baal, the chief deity of the Canaanite fertility cult. In its place, he built an altar to the LORD and made a sacrifice on it (6:25–32).

Next, he prepared to attack the Midianites. First, he sent messengers through the country calling for volunteers to fight. Then he asked God for a sign to show that He approved of what Gideon was doing. When the sign was positive, Gideon prepared his forces for battle (6:33–40).

Because there were too many volunteers, Gideon gave them a series of tests to reduce the number. Only 300 were left when the testing was over (7:1–8). These 300 men gathered in the hills surrounding the main Midianite camp, located in a valley. Gideon divided his small army into three parts, giving each soldier a torch, a pitcher to cover it with, and a ram's horn trumpet (7:9–18).

He stationed his men at strategic places, where they waited until the Midianites were asleep. When the signal was given, they raced down from the hills, waving their torches and yelling, "A sword for the LORD and for Gideon" (7:20). The Midianites, awakened from their sleep, probably thought all the Israelites in the world were attacking them. They fled in terror and confusion. Gideon's men were then joined by the others in pursuit of the disorganized Midianites (7:19–8:3).

As the battle ended, Gideon captured two Midianite chieftains, Zeba and Zalmunna, who had killed two of his brothers. Gideon tried to disgrace them by telling his teenage son to kill them. This deeply offended Zeba and Zalmunna. They said to Gideon, "You come and kill us; for as a man is, so is his strength" (8:21). What this meant was, "Kill us yourself. A man has a right to be killed by one who is his equal." This sense of rank and honor was common in ancient societies and is still strong in many Eastern societies today. The fear of disgrace was greater than the fear of death (8:4–21).

Returning home from the defeat of the Midianites, Gideon was so popular that the people tried to make him king. He refused; but he made a religious image, called an **ephod,** possibly to commemorate the victory, and urged the people to follow the LORD. Instead, the image he made became an idol that the people worshiped. He died, shunned by the people he had rescued (8:22–35).

ABIMELECH (JUDG. 9:1–25). Abimelech, Gideon's son by a slave wife, was his father's opposite, a "mock judge." Although Gideon did not seek power, Abimelech did; God called Gideon, but Abimelech called himself; Gideon acted with honor; Abimelech died in disgrace.[7] After skillfully manipulating the leaders of Shechem into supporting him financially and otherwise, he hired a group of thugs and slaughtered all his brothers except one. Then he had himself proclaimed king (9:1–6).

The brother who had escaped Abimelech's thugs was Jotham, Gideon's youngest son. Climbing to the top of Mount Ebal, Jotham shouted down to the Shechemites and told them "The **Fable** of the Trees." The moral was this: When good men fail to act, evil men will act with evil results. Their response to Gideon's leadership had been to choose the worst of his sons to rule over them simply because he was related to them. Jotham further warned that the results of their foolishness would soon be obvious (9:7–21).

Rebellion, led by Gaal, the son of Ebed, was not long in coming. Gaal stirred up the Shechemites against Abimelech, but Abimelech's supporters in the city betrayed Gaal, causing his defeat (9:22–41). Abimelech then burned the city of Shechem, including a large number of people who had taken refuge in the Tower of Shechem (9:42–49). Abimelech's victory was short-lived, however. In his attempt to capture a tower at Thebez, a woman dropped a millstone on his head. To avoid the disgrace of being killed by a woman, he asked his armor bearer to kill him, which he did (9:50–57).[8]

JEPHTHAH (JUDG. 10:6–12:7). Two minor judges, Tola (10:1–2) and Jair (10:3–5), are mentioned before Jephthah is introduced. Israel had been unfaithful again, and Gilead, a Transjordan tribe, had fallen under the heel of the Ammonites, who also crossed the Jordan to raid southern Palestine (10:6–9).

Repenting of their unfaithfulness, the people pleaded for deliverance, promising to support anyone who would lead them (10:10–18). For a leader, they chose an unlikely prospect. Jephthah was the son of a harlot, cast out by his half-brothers because of his illegitimate birth. He became an outlaw, probably raiding caravans on the King's Highway (11:1–3).

The Gileadites, desperate for someone to lead them, went to Jephthah and pleaded with him to become their leader. He agreed on the condition that, should he succeed, he would become the permanent head of the tribe. This done, Jephthah rallied the people around him and prepared for war. Before he began the battle, he vowed that if he were successful, he would sacrifice to the LORD the first thing he saw when he returned from the battle.

He was successful. When he returned, the first thing he saw was his daughter. He kept his **vow,** thus giving the only clear example in the Old Testament of an Israelite practicing human sacrifice to the LORD (11:29–40). This practice was strongly denounced by all the great prophets of Israel.

Not all battles were fought against non-Israelites. The Ephraimites again became jealous (as they did in the case of Gideon) because they had not shared in the glory of Jephthah's victory. They decided, therefore, to attack Jephthah and the Gileadites—but they got the worst of the battle. As the fugitives from the battle tried to slip back across the Jordan, the Gileadites, who controlled the crossing places, made each person prove where he was from by giving a password. If he said "Shibboleth," he was released, for he was not an Ephraimite. If, however, he said "Sibboleth," he

The Daughter of Jephthah

Jephthah is the fifth of the six characters often designated as *major judges* in the book of Judges. According to Judges 11:1–3, Jephthah is the son of a prostitute who is driven away from his father's house by his half-brothers and given no inheritance. When the Ammonites begin to oppress the Israelites, the elders of Gilead go to Jephthah to request his help in fighting them. Jephthah demands that he be made the head of the Gileadites if he leads them to victory. The deal is made and Jephthah becomes their leader. After some communication with the Ammonite king, Jephthah takes his army to fight the Ammonites. It is not clear here to what extent all of the Israelite tribes are involved in this action.

When the time of the battle comes, Judges 11:30–31 reports that Jephthah makes a vow to God. He promises that if he is victorious, he will sacrifice the first person who comes out of his house when he returns home. Some interpreters attempt to dodge the difficulty of this text by insisting that Jephthah's intent is to sacrifice an animal, but the clear sense of the text is that a person is intended. It is not clear, however, who Jephthah thinks this might be. After the victory Jephthah returns home and is greeted by his daughter, his only child, running from the house. Even though this seems unexpected, Jephthah is determined to complete the vow. He tells his daughter about it, and she agrees to participate if she is allowed two months to go to the mountains with her friends to grieve because she has no children to maintain her memory. It is tragic that the biblical text neglects to tell us the name of this young woman, yet Judges 11:39–40 reports that a tradition of remembering her each year developed among young women in Israel. Jephthah completes his vow and kills his daughter. The book of Judges makes no evaluation of his action, even though human sacrifice was forbidden in Israel. No angel descends to stop Jephthah, as the angel did to stop Abraham from sacrificing Isaac in Genesis 22. Other places in the Bible, like Hebrew 11:32, remember Jephthah as a faithful hero. This reveals a typical pattern in the Bible, and in religion generally, in which women and children suffer so that men may be considered faithful.

was seized and killed, for only those who spoke the Ephraimite dialect pronounced the Hebrew *sh* sound as an *s* (12:1–7).

SAMSON (JUDG. 13:1–16:31). Three other minor judges—Ibzan (12:8–10), Elon (12:11–12), and Abdon (12:13–15)—are mentioned before Samson is introduced. The most important thing about any of them was the large size of their families.

The **Samson** stories are introduced with a familiar theme: "The Israelites again did what was evil in the sight of the LORD." Oppression came from the Philistines, who would be Israel's mortal enemies until David conquered them.

The Philistines controlled the southern Palestinian coast from five strong cities: Gaza, Ashdod, Ashkelon, Ekron, and Gath. They came to Palestine around 1200 B.C.E. and, religion aside, theirs was a much more highly developed society than that of the Israelites. Their pottery was a buff-colored, white-slipped decorated ware that has been found in a number of Philistine archaeological sites. In contrast, Israelite pottery from the same period (the early Iron Age) was very crude and rough. More importantly, the Philistines possessed the secret of smelting iron, giving them weapons for war far superior to the stone and bronze weapons of the Israelites. Israel did not possess such weapons—at least not until after the time of David.

The pressure begun in Samson's time would mount until it did what none of the judges had been able to do—namely, to drive the twelve stubbornly independent Israelite tribes to unite under a single leader. Samson had a flair for the dramatic. This trait might have made him a leader, but unfortunately, he possessed neither the will nor the character to be one.

The story of Samson has the familiar theme of the barren wife, who, after many years, bears a son. Because of the pledge made by his mother before his birth, Samson was a Nazirite. The Nazirite vow required that a person (1) not cut his hair, (2) not drink wine, and (3) not touch a dead body (13:1–25).

Samson's home was in the foothill country, bordering on the Philistine territory. His mother's pledge that he would be a **Nazirite** did not keep him from growing up as a domineering and arrogant young man, one who was accustomed to having what he wanted. The first thing he wanted was to marry a Philistine woman, an unthinkable thing for a well-brought-up young Israelite man. But Samson knew what he wanted, so his browbeaten parents gave in. The Israelite storyteller interpreted it as the LORD's way of providing an excuse for Samson to strike a blow at the Philistines (14:1–4).

On the way to see the girl, a young lion attacked Samson. Samson killed the lion and left the carcass by the roadside. Later, as he came back, he found a swarm of bees in the body of the lion. When the wedding festivities were taking place, Samson made a bet with the Philistine men that he could give them a riddle they could not solve. If they solved it within the seven-day period of the feast, he would give them thirty linen garments and thirty festal garments. The riddle was:

> Out of the eater came something to eat,
> Out of the strong came something sweet. (14:14)

Unsuccessful at first, the young men threatened Samson's bride, telling her that they would kill her if she did not get the answer from Samson and tell them. She used a number of ways to try to get the answer. Finally she used the ultimate weapon—tears—and he told her.

When the Philistines gave Samson the correct answer, he immediately knew his wife had told them.

> Then the Spirit of the LORD rushed on him, and he went down to Ashkelon. He killed thirty men of the town, took their spoil, and gave the festal garments to those who explained the riddle.

Note that Samson's great strength is said to have existed because "the Spirit of the LORD rushed on him," in keeping with the idea that all things were from the LORD (14:5–20).

Thus began a series of conflicts between Samson and the Philistines. His wife was given to another man, causing Samson to gain vengeance by setting the grain fields on fire by tying torches to foxes' tails and loosing them in the fields. (Today, a fox with a torch tied to its tail is the Israeli roadside warning against carelessness with fire.) In revenge, the Philistines burned his ex-wife and her father to death (15:1–8).

Next, they put pressure on the men of Judah to capture Samson for them; otherwise, they would make war against Judah. Samson allowed himself to be captured, only once he was handed over to the Philistines, he broke the ropes that bound him. Seizing the jawbone of an ass, he cut a deadly swath with it, leaving dead Philistines in his path (15:9–20).

His passions kept getting him in trouble. A harlot in Gaza almost caused him to be captured (16:1–3). Then came Delilah, a woman from the Vale of Sorek, who would finally lay him low.

Completely under Philistine control, she set out to lead Samson to his downfall. Some lines from the book of Proverbs describe his response:

> With much seductive speech she persuades him;
> with her smooth talk she compels him.
> Right away he follows her,
> and goes like an ox to the slaughter,
> or bounds like a stag toward a trap
> until an arrow pierces its entrails.
> He is like a bird rushing into a snare,
> not knowing it will cost him his life. (Prov. 7:21–23)

She began a campaign to find the secret of his strength. He played along with her, giving her misleading answers each time. Each failure on her part frustrated her even more. Finally, her tears flowed and the secret was told—his strength lay in his hair. All that was left was for her to tell the Philistines and then lull Samson to sleep so that she could cut his hair (16:4–19).

The magic was gone for Samson. When he awoke, the Spirit of the LORD was gone. He had abused the power, and he had lost it. He was blinded and put to doing menial work in a prison (16:20–22).

Finally, Samson was ready to die. When he was brought out to entertain Philistine notables in the shrine of the Philistine god Dagon, his strength returned long enough for him to pull the temple down on himself and the worshipers (16:23–31). His epitaph could well have been "So those he killed at his death were more than those he had killed during his life" (16:30c).

The Minor Judges

The six *major* judges in the book of Judges are properly labeled this way for two reasons. First, there is a large amount of material about them, although the size of their stories varies tremendously from the five verses dedicated to Othniel to four chapters about Samson. More importantly, the stories about them follow the plot line established in Judges 2:11–23 and display all of its major elements. Six other judges are mentioned by name in the book for whom there are not complete stories following this plotline. Therefore, they are often called the *minor* judges. Shamgar appears alone in a single verse in 3:31. The others appear in two groups: Tola and Jair in 10:1–5 and Ibzan, Elon, and Abdon in 12:8–15. These six characters participate in the general movement of the book of Judges in at least two ways. First, their increasing number, from one to two to three, contributes to the general sense of growing disorder in the book; second, the shorter periods of time for which they rule are part of the general decline in these numbers.

There Was No King in Israel: Three Stories

MICAH AND THE LEVITE (JUDG. 17:1–13). The final chapters of Judges illustrate the troubled and confused times preceding the establishment of the monarchy. Religious confusion is illustrated by the story of a man named Micah, who confessed to his mother that he had stolen 1100 silver coins from her. When he confessed, she gave the coins to him. He, in turn, had an idol made to worship (17:1–6). A traveling Levite passed through, and Micah hired him to be his priest on the assumption that a Levite would make his worship legitimate (17:7–13).

THE MOVE OF THE TRIBE OF DAN (JUDG. 18:1–31). The pressure exerted by the Philistines is illustrated by Judges 18. The tribe of Dan had been assigned a territory lying between those of Judah and Ephraim, Israel's two most powerful tribes, and the dreaded Philistines. They sent out spies to locate a new place to settle. Eventually, they came to a place in northern Palestine, where the sources of the Jordan River arose at the base of Mount Hermon. On their return, they discovered Micah, the Levite, and his idol. When the tribe moved north, they took Micah's idol and his priest and set up a shrine in the new territory that they captured (18:1–31).

THE LEVITE AND THE SIN OF BENJAMIN (JUDG. 19:1–21:25). A strange but fascinating story closes the book of Judges. A Levite living in the territory of Ephraim had to bring back his slave wife after she ran away to her father's home (19:1–9). On the way back, they thought of stopping at Jebus (Jerusalem) for the night but decided against it, because it was not an Israelite city. Instead, they went on to Gibeah, a Benjaminite city near Jerusalem. They were invited into the home of an elderly Ephraimite who lived in Gibeah after no Benjaminite extended hospitality to them (19:10–22).

During the night, some local men demanded that their host give up the Levite so that they could have sex with him. This was a *nabalah,* the vilest offense imaginable (19:23). When they threatened violence, the Levite finally gave them his slave wife, whom they raped repeatedly. The next morning, her dead body was found at the door (19:22–28).

Taking her body home, he cut it into twelve pieces and sent one piece to each tribe (19:29–30). This seems to have been the signal for an emergency meeting for all the tribes. Saul, in later years, cut up a team of oxen to call the people to war against the Ammonites (1 Sam. 11:7).

The tribal leaders, along with their soldiers, assembled at Mizpah. The Levite told them what had happened. A decision was made to attack Gibeah to punish its people for allowing such a crime to happen there (20:1–11). First, however, they gave the tribe of Benjamin (in whose territory Gibeah was located) a chance to surrender the men who had committed the crime. Instead, the Benjaminites took up arms against the other tribes in defense of Gibeah (20:12–17).

At first, the battle favored the Benjaminites (20:18–28). Finally, however, they were soundly defeated, and their towns were burned to the ground (20:29–48).

The victory turned to ashes when the other tribes realized that they had practically wiped out one of the twelve tribes. Another assembly was called at Bethel to deal with the situation. What was needed were wives for the surviving Benjaminite men so that they could raise families. Yet a vow had been taken that none of the other tribes would permit their women to marry a Benjaminite.

What could be done? A two-part solution was advanced. First, the city of Jabesh–Gilead in Transjordan had not supported the war against Benjamin. Because of this, the city was attacked and 400 young girls were taken and given to the Benjaminites for wives (21:1–15).

When this did not fill the need, a second solution was put into effect. Each year at Shiloh there was a dance for the grape harvest. The men who needed wives were told to hide in the vineyards so that when the young girls came dancing through them, each man could grab a girl and carry her away. This solved the problem, allowing Benjamin to survive as a tribe of Israel (21:16–24).

Summary of the Book of Judges

The book of Judges is summarized quite well by its final verse: "In those days there was no king in Israel; all the people did what was right in their own eyes" (21:25).

The final chapters illustrate that theme, but they also say some important things about the times and the ways in which the tribes functioned in emergencies. It was a time of developing crisis, as the Philistines began to exert more pressure on the Israelite territories. The Israelites were poorly organized and were not really prepared to respond to the Philistine threat.

Yet, as the story of the Levite and his concubine shows, there seems to have been a kind of organization among the tribes. The term *amphictyony*, referring to a league of tribes in Greece, has been used to describe it. That such a league existed in Israel before the time of the monarchy has been increasingly questioned. If so, its purpose would have been twofold: (1) to bring the tribes together for major religious ceremonies, such as the covenant-renewal ceremony (Josh. 24), and (2) to call the tribes together for war when a situation arose that demanded it. In this latter sense, the chief priest functioned like one of the judges, because war was also a matter of religion. The opening chapters of 1 Samuel show two such priest-judges in action—Eli and Samuel. Just as in our present world, religion was used to justify violence. Such claims ought to be questioned and resisted.

PROPOSED MODELS FOR THE ISRAELITE OCCUPATION OF CANAAN

The conquest of Palestine (Canaan) is one of the most widely discussed subjects in biblical studies. As has already been seen, Joshua and Judges seem to give two different views of the Palestinian conquest. Added to this, the archaeological evidence, like most archaeological data, suffers from two major limitations: (1) Most excavations cover only a small fraction of the total area of any given site, thus limiting what we can know about the site, and (2) most of what is found is nonverbal (that is, pottery,

The Judges and the Length of Their Rule

Othniel	Forty years
Ehud	Eighty years
Shamgar	No number provided
Deborah	Forty years
Gideon	Forty years
Tola	Twenty-three years
Jair	Twenty-two years
Jephthah	Six years
Ibzan	Seven years
Elon	Ten years
Abdon	Eight years
Samson	Twenty years
Eli (recorded in 1 Samuel)	Forty years

If added together, these numbers total 336 years. When combined with the periods attributed to the rule of Eli and Samuel, the period of Joshua, and the forty years in the wilderness, and placed before the traditional date of the beginning of the monarchy at about 1000 B.C.E., such a scheme would push the Exodus and the entry into the Promised Land back into the fifteenth and fourteenth centuries (see the discussion of the date of the Exodus in Chapter 4). On the other hand, many of these numbers appear to be figurative, particularly in their relationship to the metaphorical value of forty, and the characters named as judges often appear to be merely regional figures whose periods of rule could have overlapped. Therefore, these numbers are not very useful in attempting to reconstruct a precise chronology of Israelite history.

wall and house foundations, animal bones, the village garbage, etc.) and must be interpreted. As a result, different scholars take much the same evidence and reach widely differing conclusions from it. Nowhere is this more evident than in views of the conquest. They follow at least four major models.

AN INVASION. There are those who see the evidence as basically supporting the biblical picture in Joshua, with a violent attack on the land from the eastern desert region. They point out Lachish, Bethel, and Hazor as cities destroyed in the second half of the thirteenth century B.C.E.[9]

A PEACEFUL INFILTRATION. Others propose that the Israelites were clans or clan groups of sheep and goat herders who moved into the cultivated areas, especially in the central hill country, when vegetation was too scarce on the desert fringes. Gradually, they began to settle in unoccupied areas and became farmers. It was only later, when they came into conflict with the Canaanites, that they captured the larger cities.[10]

A PEASANTS' REVOLT. Others theorize that most of the Israelites were Canaanite peasant farmers for whom herding was a secondary occupation. Mixed in with them were a few people of desert origin who had the Exodus–wilderness stories as part of their tradition. These lower-class people gained power by revolting against their Canaanite overlords. In addition, they used treaties, intermarriage, settlement on unoccupied land, and a commitment to Yahwism to unite them and give them identity. This theory sees the lower-class people moving from the cities on the coast into the scarcely populated hill country.[11]

CANAANITES TURNED ISRAELITES. Although, in a sense, this is a variation of the peasants' revolt, it rests on seemingly sounder archaeological foundations. Based on surveys in Transjordan and the central hill country indicating that there was an east-to-west movement in the development believed to be the first Israelite settlements, it has been proposed that the Israelites really were Canaanite farmers who, centuries earlier, were forced by changing social and economic conditions to become herdsmen living on the desert fringe in Transjordan and southern Palestine. Then, around 1250 B.C.E., the Palestinian coastal cities declined, depriving the herdsmen of their markets. They then gradually moved back into the hill country, established villages, and became farmers, becoming what we know as Israelites. Because this proposal only deals with the economic and social aspects of the settlement, the question of religious development is left open.[12]

Yet, for the biblical interpreter, the religious question is the crucial question. The questions concerning the nature of the conquest probably never will be resolved to everyone's satisfaction. It certainly was more complicated than a superficial reading of Joshua and Judges suggests. Elements of all the major theories may have actually been present. That question aside, the religion of Israel started somewhere, somehow, and under the leadership of someone. No nonbiblical evidence can cancel the imprint of Moses on the people who became known as the Israelites.

Key Terms and Names

Study Questions

1. Why does a careful reading of both Joshua and Judges provide a more balanced view of the conquest?
2. Who were the Sea Peoples, and what role did they play in the story of Israel?
3. How do the stories of Jericho, Achan, and Ai illustrate the religious aspects of the Israelite understanding of war?
4. How does the story of the Gibeonites illustrate the importance of a covenant?
5. What kind of leaders were the judges?
6. What does the story of the covenant-renewal ceremony at Shechem tell us about the makeup of the people of Israel?
7. What was the value of covenant-renewal ceremonies?
8. What elements of Israel's religion may have been borrowed from the Canaanites? Was all such borrowing necessarily bad?
9. What is the Deuteronomic theme, and why is it so named?
10. What is meant by saying that the judges were "charismatic leaders"?
11. What role did women play in the defeat of Sisera?
12. What was the basis of Gideon's strategy against the Midianites?
13. What is the meaning of Jotham's fable (Judges 9:7–15)?
14. In light of the story in Genesis 22, how do you interpret Jephthah's vow that resulted in the sacrifice of his daughter?
15. How does Samson's activity compare to that of the other leaders portrayed in the book of Judges?
16. What set of circumstances finally served to unite the Israelite tribes?
17. In the current debate over the nature of the Exodus and the Palestinian conquest, identify and summarize the major theories.

Endnotes

1. Bryant G. Wood, "Did the Israelites Conquer Jericho? A New Look at the Evidence," *BAR,* XVI, 2 (March–April 1990), 44–57. For another view of the Joshua conquest stories, see Yigael Yadin, "Is the Biblical Account of the Israelite Conquest Historically Reliable?" BAR, VIII, 2 (March–April 1982), 22.
2. See the discussion of this literary pattern in Mark McEntire, *The Blood of Abel: The Violent Plot in the Hebrew Bible* (Macon, GA: Mercer University Press, 1999), 64–74.
3. J. W. Rogerson, "Corporate Personality," *ABD,* I, 1156–1157.
4. John Day, "Canaan, Religion of," *ABD,* I, 831–837.
5. Along with many other stories about Baal, this is part of the Ugaritic materials from the fourteenth century B.C.E. Translations may be found in Pritchard, *ANE,* 92–118.
6. Lawrence E. Stager, "The Song of Deborah: Why Some Tribes Answered the Call and Others Did Not," BAR, XV, 1 (January–February 1989), 51–64, points out that the tribes that followed Deborah were farmers, while those that did not were seafarers whose living depended upon a good relationship with the Canaanites.
7. This insight into the story of Abimelech is from Wesley A. Kort, *Story, Text and Scripture* (University Park: Pennsylvania State University Press, 1988), 32.
8. For a look at archaeological evidence from Shechem during the period of the judges, see Gaalyah Cornfeld and David Noel Freedman, eds., *Archaeology of the Bible: Book by Book* (New York: Harper and Row, 1976), 77–79.
9. Strong advocates of this view were Yadin, "Is the Biblical Account of the Israelite Conquest Reliable?" 16–23, and Abraham Malamat, "How Inferior Israelite Forces Conquered Fortified Canaanite Cities," *BAR,* VIII, 2 (March–April 1982), 24f.
10. First proposed by Albrecht Alt, it is summarized by Manfred Weippert, *The Settlement of the Tribes in Palestine: A Summary of Recent Scholarly Debate,* trans. James D. Martin (Napierville, IL: Alec R. Allenson, 1970).
11. Advocated by Norman K. Gottwald, *The Tribes of Yahweh* (Maryknoll, NY: Orbis, 1979).
12. First propounded by Israel Finkelstein, the most recent expression of this theory is by Neil Asher Silberman, "Who Were the Israelites?" *ARCH,* 45, 2 (March–April 1992, 22–30. He also gives a summary of the other positions.

CHAPTER

6

The Beginning of the Monarchy

Samuel, Saul, and David

Timeline

1200 B.C.E.	Frequent guess for the beginning of the period of the judges
1050 B.C.E.	Approximate time of the fall of Shiloh
1020 B.C.E.	Approximate time of Samuel and Saul and the end of the judges
1000 B.C.E.	Approximate time of the beginning of David's reign

Chapter Outline

CHAPTER OVERVIEW

The book of Judges ends on an ominous note, indicating the failure of the existing pattern of leadership and pointing toward monarchy as a new form of government for Israel. So, it is a little surprising when 1 Samuel opens with the miraculous birth and rise of a new judge. The surprise does not last long, however, as Samuel turns out to be a transitional figure who helps bring about kingship in Israel. The books called 1 and 2 Samuel will tell the story of the emergence of the Israelite monarchy. The story is dominated by three great characters: Samuel, Saul, and David. These books begin with the birth of Samuel, and conclude with David's reign approaching its end. Their stories are made complex by the rapidly changing world around Israel and the ongoing struggle of Israel to determine what it means for them to be God's people.

THE SOURCES FOR THE STORY OF THE ISRAELITE KINGDOMS

The four books traditionally called Joshua, Judges, Samuel, and Kings form the collection Jewish tradition refers to as the Former Prophets. The Christian canons all divide Samuel and Kings into two books each. The resulting six books form a story of Israel from the entry into the Promised Land until the Babylonian Exile, which is typically referred to as the **Deuteronomistic History** in academic contexts. The books called 1 and 2 Samuel are dominated by Samuel, Saul, and David, while 1 and 2 Kings proved the story of a long succession of monarchs.

The Deuteronomistic History is the final product of al long process of writing, which utilized a wide variety of sources. 2 Kings 25:27–30 tells of the release of King Jehoiachin from a Babylonian prison in 560 B.C.E., so this is the earliest date at which the final composition could have taken place. This means that the full sweep of these books covers about seven centuries.

Some of the sources are mentioned directly: The Book of Jashar (2 Samuel 1:18), The Book of the Acts of Solomon (1 Kings 11:41), the Book of the Annals of the Kings of Israel (1 Kings 14:19), and the Book of the Annals of the Kings of Judah (1 Kings 22:45). In addition to these sources from which materials were taken to write the biblical books of Samuel and Kings, readers have also tried to identify earlier stages in the composition. One such possible source is found in 2 Samuel 9–20 and 1 Kings 1–2, a sequence that some have called the *Court History of David* or the *Succession Narrative*, an intimate inner look at the palace with all of its plots and intrigues, which is quite different from the other parts of these books. One of the remarkable things about the books of Samuel and Kings is that the final composition presents such a variety of perspectives on the story of Israel's **monarchy,** both positive and negative.

There is another version of the history that is different from the version found in 1,2 Samuel and 1,2 Kings. This version is found in 1,2 Chronicles, a history of Israel written sometime after the Babylonian Exile. Many passages in Chronicles are lifted word for word from the Samuel to Kings history, yet there are important differences. David's weaknesses are glossed over in Chronicles, as are the weaknesses of other Judean kings, such as Manasseh. Much attention is given to genealogies and to the activities of the priests and of other Temple officials. There is also a different theological viewpoint. Whereas 2 Samuel 24:1 says, "the LORD caused David to number the people," 1 Chronicles 21:1 says, "Satan" caused David to number them. Even with these differences, 1,2 Chronicles preserves valuable supplemental information about Israel's history. The presence of the books of Chronicles in the canon indicates that there was more than one version of Israel's story. These parallel histories present alternative visions of Israel's story and identity, and they should help the reader to realize that history is always told from a particular point of view.

THE STORY OF SAMUEL

Birth and Dedication (1 Sam. 1:1–2:10)

Hannah, the favorite wife of Elkanah (an Ephraimite), bore one of the heaviest burdens an Israelite woman could bear—she was childless. Peninah, the other wife, was fruitful and lorded her success in childbearing over Hannah. It was a bitter pill for Hannah to swallow (1:1–8).

On an annual trip to **Shiloh** for one of the major festivals, Hannah was so distraught and earnest in prayer that **Eli,** the head of the shrine, thought she was drunk. When he started to scold her for her supposed drunkenness, Hannah told him of her distress. Eli, in turn, assured her that her prayer would be answered (1:9–18).

Eli must have known something, for Hannah was soon pregnant. In due time, the promised son was born. Hannah did not go to the festival until **Samuel** was able to eat solid foods. Then she took him, offered a sacrifice, and dedicated him to serve the LORD at the Shiloh shrine (1:19–28). As part of the description of that service, there is a beautiful psalm of thanksgiving called the *Song of Hannah.* Later, parts of this poem are quoted in the Song of Mary in Luke 1:46–55 (2:1–10), in which Mary expresses her joy at the promise of the birth of Jesus.

As the book called 1 Samuel opens, Israel's archenemy, the **Philistines,** has already been introduced in the previous book. The charismatic military leaders called *judges* had not been successful in overthrowing this enemy. The opening of 1 Samuel ignores this national story line for a while and focuses instead on a single family and the birth of a child. As soon as Samuel is raised to adulthood, however, in the first few chapters, the Philistine army reappears with a vengeance and routs the Israelites, even going so far as to capture the Ark of the Covenant in 1 Samuel 4. This defeat convinces the Israelites that they can no longer compete in Canaan with amateur leadership and leads to their demand to be ruled by a king "like the other nations." Samuel becomes the transitional figure who reluctantly brokers this political transition, becoming the last of the judges and the first prophet in Israel to anoint a king.

Training and Call to Service (1 Sam. 2:11–4:1)

Samuel was left with Eli, who was to train him for the priesthood (2:11). Unfortunately, Eli's sons, who served as priests at the shrine, were poor examples. The Hebrew text calls them the *sons of Belial,* a term of cursing and condemnation (2:12). They were greedy, irreverent, and immoral (2:13–17, 22). Because of this situation, a prophet (a man of God) came to Eli and told him that his family would lose the privilege of serving at the shrine because his sons had abused their offices as priests and leaders (2:22–36). Despite the bad examples before him, Samuel grew "both in stature and in favor with the LORD and with the people" (2:26).

The corruption at the Shiloh shrine was a symptom of the times. "The word of the LORD was rare in those days; visions were not widespread" (3:1). The Deuteronomic historian saw the lack of moral integrity in the family of Eli, Israel's most important leader, as contributing to a state of religious apathy throughout the country. Few people were in a spiritual condition to receive a revelation from God.

Then came Samuel's call from the LORD. He was still a young boy when he heard the LORD speak to him in the night. Thinking Eli was calling him, he awakened the old man to ask what he wanted. Eli told him that he had not called. Samuel heard the voice once again, and once more went to Eli with the same result. The third time, Eli told him that the LORD must have been calling. Then Samuel answered and was told that he eventually would replace Eli. Eli's family, furthermore, would meet with disaster (3:2–14).

The Literary Structure of Samuel

How one perceives the literary structure of Samuel depends a great deal upon certain initial assumptions. Samuel appears originally to have been a single book that was later divided into 1 Samuel and 2 Samuel, as they now appear in most Bibles. Should this division influence our understanding of the literary design of the book? The book of Samuel is connected to other books in the Bible. It is part of the Genesis–Kings complex, often referred to as the *Primary History*, which tells the grand story of Israel from creation to the Exile. Was Samuel originally an independent work that was later integrated into this larger work, or was there a grand, undivided epic that has now been pulled apart into nine (or eleven) separate books? Samuel is also part of the set of books from Joshua through Kings called the *Deuteronomistic History*. What is Samuel's relationship to this set of books, and how is it complicated by the observation that David lives through the end of 2 Samuel and dies in 1 Kings? The answers to these questions determine the extent to which we understand the present boundaries of the book or books of Samuel as beginnings and endings of stories. This discussion will treat Samuel as one book and attempt to balance the influences that the canon imposes on it. Samuel is a distinct book that is also part of a cohesive sequence of books.

The book of Samuel is generally considered the most artfully composed piece of narrative literature in the Old Testament. When we gaze upon its story from a distance, it is impossible to miss the imposing figures of its three major characters. The lives of Samuel, Saul, and David, and the relationships between them, form the contours of the book. The end of the book of Judges clearly points toward the monarchy, and the birth of the Davidic **dynasty** is the primary subject matter of the book of Samuel.

These three major characters are not just treated sequentially. Their lives are intimately intertwined. Samuel is the main character in 1 Samuel 1–8 as the story moves inevitably toward the establishment of the monarchy. Once Samuel anoints Saul in 1 Samuel 9, Saul becomes the main character, but Samuel remains an important presence. The story becomes significantly more complicated when Samuel anoints David in 1 Samuel 16. A struggle for power then ensues in the narrative between Saul and David, with Samuel in the background. The death of Samuel in 1 Samuel 25 and the death of Saul in 1 Samuel 31 clear the way for David to become the sole focus of the story. Those who divided the book of Samuel into two books at some point chose the death of Saul as a significant dividing line. Still, Saul does not disappear from the narrative, as his sons continue to vie for the throne in the early chapters of 2 Samuel. In fact, Saul's presence is not fully put to rest until David kills his remaining heirs in 2 Samuel 20. The final chapters of 2 Samuel constitute an appendix with a variety of materials. Although David is not quite dead at the end of the book, his story is finished. The foundation is established for the story of the House of David in the book of Kings, beginning with Solomon. Solomon is not prominent in the book of Samuel, but the conflict in the House of David, which begins with the Bathsheba affair and culminates in the deaths of Amnon and Absalom, seems to be preparing his path to the throne.

The picture of the book of Samuel presented here is that of a grand, sweeping story carried along by interlocking characters. Through the development of this story, this book answers important questions. How did Israel get to be a monarchy and why? How did the monarchy become the Davidic dynasty and why?

When Samuel arose in the morning, he tried to avoid telling Eli what had happened. When Eli insisted on being told, however, Samuel related his vision. Gradually, the word spread that Samuel was a prophet in Israel (3:15–4:1a). As a prophet, he was looked upon as one who had direct access to God and who acted as God's earthly spokesman. For this reason, the prophets introduced their messages not with "I say" but rather "Thus says the LORD." A fuller discussion of prophets and prophecy will come later.

The Battle of Ebenezer (1 Sam. 4:1–22)

Israel's internal confusion, coupled with the increasing Philistine strength, finally led to a full-scale attack by the Philistines. The Philistine army massed at Aphek, where the great international trade road was forced inland by the swamps caused by the slow-flowing Yarkon River. From Aphek, the hill country was only a short distance away. The Israelites were camped at Ebenezer on the edge of the hills.

The Philistine war plan was to cut the country in half by driving through the mountains to the Jordan. Because the Philistines had iron weapons that were far superior to anything the Israelites had, the prospects for Israel looked bleak.

The first day's battle ended with heavy losses for the Israelites. In desperation, they decided to invoke the memories of the holy war the next day by carrying the Ark of the Covenant before them into battle. But as the holy object was borne by Eli's two unholy sons, Hophni and Phineas, even the Ark could not change the tide of the battle (4:1–5).

The result was a disaster for Israel. The Philistines were inspired to fight harder. Not only did they defeat the Israelites, but they killed Hophni and Phineas and captured the Ark (4:6–11).

FIGURE 6–1 "[The Israelites] encamped at Ebenezer, and the Philistines encamped at Aphek" (1 Sam. 4:1d). Aphek was a strategic point on the great coastal highway. The remains of a sixteenth-century Turkish fort now occupy much of the site.

When a messenger took the word to Eli, the shock was so great that it killed him also (4:12–18). Last of all, the wife of Phineas died as she gave birth to a son. Before she died, she gave him the name Ichabod, symbolic of the disastrous day. The child's name meant "the glory (the presence of God) has departed" (4:19–22).

That Troublesome Ark (1 Sam. 5:1–6:21)

The Philistines carried the Ark, symbol of the presence of Israel's God, home in triumph. Before long, however, they wished they had never seen it. First, they put it in the temple of their chief deity, Dagon, as a symbol of Dagon's superiority to the LORD. The next morning, Dagon's image was found lying facedown on the floor (5:1–5).

Next, a plague struck Ashdod. People began to develop skin tumors. The people of Ashdod decided that the people of Gath had a right to keep the battle prize for a while, so they sent the Ark there. The Gathites, too, broke out in sores. They decided that the people of Ekron would surely want to see the famous Ark. The disaster was repeated. Panic mounted in the Philistine towns (5:6–12).

They then decided that the Ark was bad luck and that the only thing to do was to send it back where it belonged. Because no one volunteered to carry it back home, they decided on a plan. They hitched two cows to a cart, placed the Ark on the cart, put an offering of gold with the Ark to appease the Israelite God, and turned the cows loose, heading them toward Beth–Shemesh in Israelite territory (6:1–13).

When the Ark was found by the Israelites, the cart was broken up and the cattle were sacrificed. A number of Israelites died, however, perhaps because the holy Ark was not handled properly. Ancient people feared holy things so much that such fear could actually cause death. A similar thing happens today among people who believe in voodoo, macumba, or similar rites of black magic (6:14–20).

The text is silent about the matter, but Shiloh must have fallen while the Ark was held by the Philistines. The Ark was taken to a private home in Kiriath–Jearim after being returned to the Israelites (6:21–7:2). It was to remain there until David became king and had it moved to Jerusalem (2 Sam. 6:2; 1 Chron. 15:1–29).

The Roles Samuel Played

The career of Samuel, as presented to us in the Old Testament, embodies the powerful changes taking place in the life of Israel at this point in the story. In one way, it is odd that the books we most often refer to as 1 and 2 Samuel carry his name, because he essentially vanishes from the story after 1 Samuel 16. Samuel reappears briefly in a passive role in 1 Samuel 18:19–24, his death is noted in 25:1, and his ghost is conjured up in a séance in 28:3–28, but his name never even appears in the book we now call 2 Samuel. Still, the rapidly developing national institutions in place in Israel by the time of the great Davidic–Solomonic Kingdom all flow out of this profound figure.

SAMUEL, THE JUDGE (1 SAM. 7:3–17). Samuel was a judge with a difference. He was, first of all, a spiritual leader who reminded the people of their obligation to live by the Covenant (7:3–4). 1 Samuel 7:12–14 describes significant military success during the time of Samuel, but there is no description of any direct participation of Samuel in these military efforts. He was a judge in the modern sense of the term. He is portrayed traveling a circuit of four cities (Bethel, Gilgal, Mizpah, and Ramah) adjudicating legal cases (7:15–17).

SAMUEL, THE PROPHET (1 SAM. 8:1–9:14). In ancient Israel, one of the tasks of a **prophet** was to speak the word of God to the people, warning them of the consequences of their decisions and of the responsibilities that came when decisions were made. Chapter 8 reflects the strong resistance that existed among some in Israel to the idea of the kingship. This feeling continued to exist long after the monarchy was established. In some ways, certain of the prophets reflected this attitude with their condemnation of the reigning monarch.[1] Thus, 1 Samuel 8:4–22 has Samuel telling the people of the dangers that they would face if they had a king. The people did not listen, but insisted that a king be chosen for them. Finally, the LORD and Samuel gave in (8:22).

It was in his role as prophet that Samuel first met Saul, the son of Kish. Like the hero in a romantic movie, Saul was tall and charismatic. He was the kind of person who stood out in a crowd:

> There was not a man among the people of Israel more handsome than he; he stood head and shoulders above everyone else. (9:2)

Saul was sent out by his father to find some donkeys that had strayed. After searching for some time without success, Saul, at his servant's suggestion, went to consult the famous prophet Samuel at his home in Ramah.

Samuel seemingly had what is called *second sight*, or the power of clairvoyance. Hence, he was called *the seer* (9:9), a term used to describe many of the early prophets, who functioned more as fortune-tellers than as critics on the moral issues of the time. As a prophet, Samuel seemed to function in both roles: (1) as a moral critics and (2) as a clairvoyant who could help find lost objects. It was, then, as a clairvoyant that Samuel first met Saul (9:3–14).

SAMUEL, THE KING MAKER (1 SAM. 9:15–10:27). **Saul** was so impressive on first sight that Samuel was convinced that he was the LORD's choice to be the king. Saul's journey to find his father's donkeys, then, brought a rather shocking result. Samuel told Saul that the donkeys were already at home. Then he invited Saul to a banquet at the shrine. When Saul arrived, thirty persons were present. He, an obscure young man from one of Israel's smallest and weakest tribes, was given the seat of honor and was served the choicest portion of the meat (9:15–24).

Undoubtedly, Saul was mystified by all this. But the greatest surprise was yet to come. After spending the night in Ramah as Samuel's guest, Saul prepared to return home. Samuel, going with him to the outskirts of the village, asked Saul to send his servant on ahead so that the two of them could be alone. When the servant had gone, Samuel took a vial of olive oil, poured it on Saul's head, and told him he was to be Israel's first king (9:25–10:1).

The Meaning of Anointing

Samuel's act of **anointing** Saul marked the king as God's choice. It was an act separate and apart from the actual installation of the king, especially in the early monarchy. Saul was not crowned for a week after he was anointed (10:8). David, who succeeded Saul, was anointed by Samuel several years before he actually became king. Later on, anointing was probably a part of the coronation of the king; at most, it came only a short time earlier.

When Israel had no king, the terms *to anoint* and *the anointed one*[2] took on a new meaning. Israel looked back at its days of glory. David, its greatest king, became the example of the kind of king Israel wanted in a future time of glory, which it believed the LORD would bring. Because of that hope the term *mashiach,* "the anointed one," was used to speak of a hoped-for king. When *mashiach* was translated into Greek, it became *Messias,* which, in turn, became *Messiah* in English. Furthermore, when *mashiach* was translated into Greek by Christian writers, it became

Christos, which becomes *Christ* in English. Thus, the title *the Christ,* which was applied to Jesus of Nazareth by early Christians, came to mean "God's chosen one" or "God's anointed one."

After Samuel had anointed Saul, he told him to return home for seven days. On the way, certain signs would be given to him that he was the LORD's choice as king. One of them would be that he would meet a group of ecstatic prophets. When he did, he would be overwhelmed by the "Spirit of the LORD," which would cause him to prophesy with them. These prophets represented another kind of prophet—one who went around in groups and whose prophesying was accompanied by various expressions of extreme emotionalism, such as trances, mass hysteria, and emotional frenzy (10:2–8).

When things happened as Samuel had said, some people began ridiculing Saul. The question "Is Saul also among the prophets?" (10:11) was asked in a mocking tone rather than a tone of approval (10:9–13). When his uncle asked him where he had been, Saul told of his visit to Samuel, but said nothing about being anointed to be king (10:14–16). This basic shyness would be a major problem for Saul throughout his life.

Even when Samuel called the tribal league together at Mizpah to approve his selection of Saul as king, Saul showed the same kind of shyness. When he finally was confirmed and certified by Samuel as the LORD's choice, the people had to search for him. He was found hiding among the baggage, an act that certainly caused many to be slow in following him as king. Others, however, gave him their wholehearted support (10:17–27).

THE ESTABLISHMENT OF SAUL'S KINGSHIP (1020–1000 B.C.E.)[3]

Transition from Samuel to Saul

Saul made no move to exert his authority as king, even though he had been crowned in a public ceremony. Instead, he went on leading the life of an Israelite farmer until circumstances forced him to take action. Jabesh–Gilead, a town located just east of the Jordan River and about twenty-five miles south of the Lake of Chinnereth (Sea of Galilee), came under attack by the Ammonites, led by King Nahash (the "Snake").[4] Finding themselves in dire straits, the men of Jabesh–Gilead asked for terms of peace to avoid wholesale slaughter by the superior Ammonite forces. The Ammonites agreed, but only on the condition that they could gouge out the right eyes of all the men of the town.[5] After asking for seven days to consider the proposition, the elders managed to send messengers to Saul at Gibeah to seek his help (11:1–4).

On hearing their predicament, Saul reacted strongly, for "the Spirit of God came upon Saul in power" (11:6). Taking the team of oxen with which he had been plowing, he killed them, cut them into twelve parts, and sent one piece to the leaders of each of the tribes. This was the signal to mobilize for war. Men responded quickly to his call, especially from the tribe of Judah (11:8; cf. Judg. 19:29). Dividing his forces into three groups, Saul attacked the Ammonites early in the morning and routed them. His successful troops, inspired by his leadership, were ready to turn their wrath upon those Israelites who had refused to support Saul, but he would not let them do so. Saul was confirmed as king in a service of celebration (11:5–15).

The version of Samuel's farewell address in 1 Samuel 12:1–25 contains familiar themes. First, the sense of honor and honesty characteristic of the themes of Israel's great prophets can be seen in Samuel's demand for the people to testify against him if they knew of an act of fraud or dishonesty that he had committed (12:1–5).

A second theme that appears throughout the Old Testament is a recounting of the wonderful works the LORD had done on Israel's behalf in the Exodus and the conquest; in the exploits of the judges [note that Samuel is mentioned in the past tense (12:1), which suggests the influence of a later hand]; and Saul's victory over the Ammonites (12:6–12). Woven into this account is the Deuteronomic theme—sin, punishment, repentance, and deliverance (12:9–11). The qualms about the kingship are reflected in the warning that no king could lead the Israelites to success if they were not faithful to the LORD (12:13–17).

A thunderstorm added emphasis to Samuel's warning and gave occasion to repeat the warning that "righteousness brings blessing—sin brings punishment" (12:18–25). This idea, commonly called *retribution theology*, underlies much of the Old Testament. Other parts of the Old Testament, such as Job and Eulesiastes, will call it into question.

The Nature of Saul's Kingship

Saul was not a king in the usual sense of the word. He might be described as a more powerful judge, who, because of the circumstances, was able to gain the majority support of the people. More important, he seems to have gained at least the qualified support of the establishment—tribal chieftains, chief priests, and prophets.[6] Part of that support grew out of the fact that Saul was an impressive man physically, and obviously he had certain personality traits that, on first impression, caused people to follow him. Still, he remained a man of the people who never became arrogant. The fact that he was from a small tribe and not from one of the two dominant tribes, Ephraim or Judah, may have added to his support from all the other tribes.

His residence, the remains of which have been uncovered at Gibeah (Tell en-Nashbeh), was not elaborate. It was a rough stone fortress designed not for luxury, but as a stronghold for defense against an enemy attack.

This fear of an attack from the Philistines was itself a major element in Saul's support. The Israelites faced the real possibility of being destroyed by the Philistines unless they united, and, at that time, Saul offered the best hope for rescue from the Philistine danger.

But an even more important factor than Saul's abilities or the Philistine threat was the influence of Samuel. He was old, but he was still a man of great influence, and Saul was pliable enough for Samuel to manipulate to his own ends. Samuel had been influential enough to put an obscure Benjaminite on the throne of Israel, but in the long run, he was not able to make Saul successful because of Saul's personal flaws, which hindered him from the beginning. The withdrawal of Samuel's support, the increasing popularity of his son-in-law David (encouraged by Jonathan), and his deep sense of insecurity growing out of his family background would eventually destroy Saul. Some see him as a tragic figure; others agree with the assessment that he was "a bungler from the beginning."[7]

The length of Saul's reign is uncertain, because a number is missing in the Hebrew text, which simply says, "he reigned . . . and two years over Israel" (13:1). Most scholars would say that he ruled about twenty-two years. If one takes the biblical evidence, twelve years might be more logical. The Ark was captured by the Philistines some time before Saul began to reign. According to 1 Samuel 7:2, it was kept in Kirath–Jearim "some twenty years." It was taken to Jerusalem in the early part of David's reign (2 Sam. 6:1–15), but David reigned for over seven years at Hebron before Jerusalem was captured (2 Sam. 5:5). If this twenty years is to be taken literally or even as meaning around twenty years, it would seem to limit Saul's reign to no more than twelve years.

Saul's Kingship Undermined

Saul gained some support through some early victories over the Philistines. Much of his success came from the courage and skilled leadership of his son Jonathan, who led the army to victory at

Geba (located about five miles northeast of Gibeah). The reference to the battle for Geba shows how the Philistines had penetrated the central hill country as part of their strategy to cut the country in two (13:2–4).

Samuel's support of Saul began to erode rather quickly. Like an elderly person who insists that someone should take his place and then resents it when someone does, Samuel had made his farewell speech, but he was not about to give up all his power. He insisted, as chief religious official of the kingdom, that no battle should take place without the proper religious ceremonies.

Things came to a head when Saul gathered his army at Gilgal for an attack on the Philistines. He was impatient to get started. But although Saul waited seven days for Samuel to come, Samuel did not appear. With his troops scattering, Saul decided to take matters into his own hands. He offered the burnt offering himself, only to have Samuel appear just as he finished (13:5–10).

When Samuel asked Saul why he had not waited, Saul said that the people were getting impatient. Samuel rebuked him, saying that he had disobeyed God and, as a result, his kingdom would not continue (13:11–15a).

Saul had only 600 soldiers at Gilgal (near Jericho) to face the large Philistine force encamped at Michmash, about ten to twelve miles west. The problem was compounded by the fact that the Philistines had far superior weapons, because only Saul and Jonathan among the Israelites had iron swords (13:22). The narrative makes the problem more vivid by telling how any Israelite who had an iron tool or weapon had to take it to the Philistines to have it sharpened. Imagine what would happen if an Israelite went to the Philistines and said, "I want to start a war with you tomorrow. Would you sharpen my sword?" (13:15b–23).

Courage and ingenuity saved the day for Israel. Jonathan and his armor bearer crept up a narrow pass overlooking the Philistine camp, then stood up, and called to the Philistines to get their attention. They had already agreed that if the Philistines came up to challenge them, it would be a sign that the LORD would give them victory. They fought the Philistines in the narrow pass, so that they had only to fight a few at a time. Jonathan would knock them down, and his servant would finish them off. The Philistines became so demoralized by Jonathan's success that they fled in fear. An earth tremor added to the Philistine panic (14:1–15).

Word got back to the camp about the uproar Jonathan was causing among the Philistines. Although Saul started to consult the priest, so many of his men were rushing to join the battle that he went on without the required religious ceremony being performed. Before he went, however, he did a rash thing by ordering that no one was to eat anything until the Philistines were defeated. To do so would bring death by execution (14:16–24).

Jonathan, unaware of the order, came upon some honey in the forest. After he had eaten some of it, one of the men following him told him of Saul's oath to kill anyone who ate before the battle was won. Jonathan openly criticized his father for taking a foolish oath, because the people were weak with exhaustion. As a result of their hunger, when the battle was over, they seized cattle and killed them, eating blood with the meat (14:25–32). This was in direct violation of an ancient taboo among the Israelites. Leviticus 17:14 says:

> For the life of every creature—its blood is its life; therefore I have said to the people of Israel: You shall not eat the blood of any creature, for the life of every creature is its blood; whoever eats it shall be cut off.

This principle led to the development of rules in Israel and, later, in Judaism about the proper way to kill animals for food. Such rules are still observed by many Jews today.

Saul ordered the people to stop what they were doing. He took it upon himself to make an altar to offer a sacrifice for them. He also saw to it that they were fed properly (14:33–35).

Afterward, Saul wanted to continue the battle on into the night, but the priest suggested that he ask for a sign from God. When no sign was forthcoming, Saul took it to mean that someone had violated the oath. To find the culprit, he consulted the Urim and Thummim. These probably were two marked stones thrown to get "yes" or "no" answers to questions. In our day, this would be considered a game of chance, but it was not thought to be such in Saul's time. The LORD controlled the way the holy stones fell, and in this manner God's will was revealed. The first question was "Did some of the people violate the oath?" The Urim and Thummim signaled "No." When the question related to Saul and Jonathan, the answer pointed to Jonathan (14:36–42).

Saul would have killed Jonathan had the people not overruled him. Jonathan was a hero to them, and it was unthinkable that he should be killed for his father's foolish vow. Either an animal was sacrificed in his place or someone may have volunteered to die for him. Either way, Saul lost the people's confidence because of his bad judgment (14:43–46).

After a summary statement about Saul's military activities (14:47–52), the story of Saul's final break with Samuel is told. Samuel brought a message from the LORD telling Saul to wage a holy war against the Amalekites. He was to "utterly destroy all that they have; do not spare them, but kill both man and woman, child and infant, ox and sheep, camel and donkey" (15:3).

The Amalekites, who lived in the Negev and the upper Sinai, had attacked the Israelites when Israel came out of Egypt. As a result, there seems to have been a long-standing hatred between the two groups. On the other hand, the Kenites, who had been friendly to Israel and lived in this same territory, were given warning of the attack so that they could move out of the area of the battle (15:1–6).

When the attack took place, Saul did not keep all of the holy war provisions. For one thing, he did not kill Agag, the Amalekite king. Nor did he destroy the Amalekite herds. Instead, he took them as spoils of war (15:7–9).

When Samuel found out about Saul's disobedience, he rebuked Saul. Saul argued that he had only taken the best of the animals for a sacrifice to the LORD. Saul's motive may have been to win the favor of his soldiers, whose faith in him was already badly shaken. Sacrifices other than the whole burnt offering allowed the offerers the rare chance to eat all the meat they wanted. Sacrifice days literally were feast days, and they were anticipated with delight by the average person. Samuel's rebuke, however, was based on the principle that Israel was to live in total commitment to the LORD, including carrying out the rules of the holy war (15:10–20).

Saul tried to excuse himself by saying that the people had taken the animals to offer a sacrifice. Samuel's reply was perhaps the best-remembered statement in the Saul stories:

> Has the LORD as great delight in burnt offerings and sacrifices,
>   as in obeying the voice of the LORD?
> Surely, to obey is better than sacrifice,
>   and to heed than the fat of rams.

The questioning of the meaning of sacrifice without the proper attitude was to be repeated with even stronger emphasis by Israel's great prophets. Some would even go so far as to question the need for sacrifice[8] (15:21–23).

The Old Testament provides a conflicted portrait of King Saul. The book of 1 Samuel begins with the birth story of Samuel, the judge/prophet/priest, but elements of Saul's birth story seem to be embedded within it at 1:27–28 and 2:10. It is clear from the beginning that the idea of kingship does not have Samuel's support, and although he appears to warm to Saul in the beginning, he quickly returns to his antimonarchy position. Stories of Saul's early victories over the Ammonites and the Philistines look promising, but this wave of success fades in the face of the events portrayed as Saul's sins. When examined more closely, these mistakes look relatively minor or even appear to be set up by Samuel, like the story of Saul's improper sacrifice in 13:1–15. Even Saul's pursuit of and attempts to kill David look mild in comparison to the brutal purge of potential rivals carried out by David and Solomon at later points. The essence of this ambivalence about Saul is captured in the strange little interaction between God and Samuel in 15:34–16:1. The problems involved in translating and interpreting this text make it difficult to determine exactly why God and Samuel are angry and grieving, but the outcome is the decision to anoint David as the next king, even though David is apparently still young and King Saul is far from dead.

THE APPEARANCE OF DAVID

Early Encounters of David with Samuel and Saul

Samuel's work was not done. Having told Saul that he would be the last of his family to rule Israel, he set out to find the LORD's next choice to be king.

This time he went to Bethlehem in Judah to find the future king. He was led to the family of Jesse, a sheepherder. Here, Samuel called for Jesse to parade all his sons before him so that he could select the one the LORD had chosen. Several young men appeared before him, but he did not feel that any of them was the correct choice. He asked if there were others and was told that only the youngest, who was watching the sheep, was missing. When David was brought, Samuel knew that he was the one and proceeded to anoint him (16:1–13).

The damage to Saul's ego inflicted by Samuel's rejection was too much for his weak personality. He was thrown into a deep depression, caused by an "evil spirit from the LORD." His servants thought that music might help him, so they suggested that someone be found to play the harp for him. David's reputation as a musician had reached Saul's court, with the result that David was brought in to play for Saul (16:14–23).

The story of David and Goliath is well known, but it has problems.[9] One of the chief ones is that 2 Samuel 21:19 says:

> Elhanan, the son of Jaareoregim, the Bethlehemite, slew Goliath the Gittite, the shaft of whose spear was like a weaver's beam.

The passage in which this verse appears (2 Sam. 21:18–22), however, may suggest a possible solution, because it speaks of four giant Philistine soldiers. Thus, the most logical solution is that both Elhanan and David slew giants but that the name of one of them has been lost from the Samuel tradition. Furthermore, 1 Chronicles 20:5 tries to deal with the inconsistency by saying that Elhanan slew "Lahmi the brother of Goliath the Gittite."

Another problem seen by scholars is that the passage 17:55–58 seems to suggest that Saul did not know David. One explanation given is that the story of David's playing the harp for Saul is based on a different tradition from that of the Goliath story and that there were two different versions of how David met Saul. Another possible explanation is that Saul's unbalanced mental state would account for his failure to recognize David as the one who played for him.

The story itself is a familiar one. Things were going badly for Israel in a battle with the Philistines in the Valley of Elah. This valley was located in southern Judah and was one of four such valleys that provided access to the hill country from the coastal plain. Without the access these valleys provided, going from the coast to the hills would have been virtually impossible. The control of the valleys, then, was essential to the defense of the Israelite positions in the hills.

The two armies had taken up positions opposite each other with the Valley of Elah in between. The Philistines challenged the Israelites to send someone to fight their champion, the giant Goliath, who was said to be ten feet tall. No one from Israel dared to take up the challenge, even though Saul had offered his daughter in marriage to anyone who would fight Goliath and win (17:1–10, 25).

David, who had come to the battlefield to bring supplies to his brothers who were serving in the army, was astounded to find that no Israelite was willing to risk his life for the honor of his people (17:11–27). As a result, David, despite the sneering of his brother Eliab (17:28–30), volunteered to fight Goliath.

Saul, relieved to have someone to meet Goliath's challenge, offered David his armor. David refused, however, choosing not to sacrifice his mobility for whatever protection Saul's armor might offer. After all, a ten-foot-tall giant would be considerably less agile than the much smaller David (17:31–39). Instead, he chose to use his favorite weapon, the sling, to fell his victim (17:40).

The sling consisted of a leather pouch to which two leather strings were attached. A stone weighing several ounces was placed in the pouch. The strings were held in such a way that when the slinger whirled the sling rapidly, he could turn loose one string and send the rock toward the target. One practiced in the use of the sling could be quite accurate and deadly. Ancient armies regularly used the sling as a weapon.

David's well-aimed rock hit the giant between the eyes, knocking him to the ground unconscious. It was then a simple matter to take Goliath's sword and finish the job by beheading him. David's success led to an Israelite rout of the Philistines (17:41–58).

When David entered the king's court, things changed radically for the Bethlehem shepherd boy. First, he gained a friend. Jonathan, Saul's son and general, was instantly attracted to David (18:1–5). David's success as a warrior preceded him, for the women of the village were dancing in the streets and singing his praises. Saul, insecure as he was, became jealous of David. Slipping again into a period of mental disturbance, he attempted to kill David while David was playing music for him (18:6–11).

Saul then attempted to get rid of David by putting him in charge of an army squadron, hoping David would be killed in battle. Instead, this gave David further opportunity to add to his exploits and to gain more admiration from the people (18:12–16).

After reneging on the promise to give David his older daughter's hand in marriage, Saul then proposed that David marry Michal, his younger daughter. To earn this right, however, he had to kill 100 Philistines and bring their foreskins as proof of what he had done. David believed in doing the job right: he brought back 200 foreskins (18:20–30)!

After a while, David began to feel Saul's rejection of him, especially after Jonathan told him of Saul's order that he be killed (19:1–7). Continued attempts were made on David's life (19:8–17), causing him finally to flee to Samuel at Ramah. When Saul sent messengers to capture David, the awesome sense of God's presence with Samuel made them unable to carry out Saul's orders. Finally, Saul himself went. But he, too, was overcome, just as he had been after his anointing by Samuel (19:18–24).

Finally, David saw that the situation was impossible and decided to separate himself from Saul's household. Jonathan agreed to tell Saul that David had gone to Bethlehem for a feast day (20:1–6). Jonathan, furthermore, was to note Saul's reaction to David's absence and then give David a signal indicating whether it was safe for David to return. When David remained absent, Saul became violent, showing Jonathan that it was unsafe for David to return. By a prearranged signal, therefore, Jonathan let David know that Saul was determined to kill him (20:7–42).

In his flight from Saul, David came to Nob, just east of Jerusalem. Pretending he was on a mission for the king, he persuaded the priest Ahimelech to give him some of the leftover holy bread, usually only eaten by the priests. He also persuaded Ahimelech to give him the sword of Goliath that was kept at the shrine. Leaving Nob, he went to Philistine territory, but he was recognized there. To avoid being killed, he pretended to be a madman (21:1–15).

David, the Outlaw

The years following his escape from Saul saw David in the rather questionable position of being an ally to the Philistines while, at the same time, proclaiming his loyalty to his own people. His power base was Judah, whose rough terrain furnished an abundance of hiding places for his forces, which were continually being reinforced by people who were becoming disillusioned with Saul.

Word that David had broken with Saul brought many discontented men to David's side (22:1–2). As a precaution against an attack on his family, David took his father and mother to the king of Moab and asked him to protect them (22:3–5).

In the meantime, Saul was intensifying his efforts to kill David. Unfortunately, he heard that the priests at Nob had aided David. As a result, he ordered their deaths. But he did not stop with the priests. He also ordered that Nob be treated as an enemy city in the holy war; it was to be

Michal and David

Once David is secretly anointed by Samuel as the next king, he quickly attaches himself to Saul's family in a number of ways. In 1 Samuel 16, David is brought into the royal court to play the lyre to drive away the evil spirit that torments Saul. David quickly becomes a close friend of Saul's son, Jonathan, and 1 Samuel 18:20 reports that Saul's daughter, Michal, falls in love with David. At first, Saul decides to give his oldest daughter, Merab, to David as a wife, but then Saul withdraws this offer and gives her to another man. Then Saul gives Michal to David, and David becomes the son-in-law of the king. Michal, in 1 Samuel 19:8–17, helps save David's life when Saul plots to kill him. Michal is not mentioned again until 1 Samuel 25:44, when she is given to another man in marriage, even though David has circumcised 200 Philistines and brought their foreskins to Saul as a bride price for Michal.

Michal becomes a point of contention between the houses of David and Saul. David, in 2 Samuel 3:12–16, gets Michal back in a deal he makes with Abner, Saul's former military commander. In 2 Samuel 6:20–23, Michal objects to David's behavior during the procession that brings the Ark of the Covenant to Jerusalem. The final verse in this text reports that Michal never had any children. It does not state specifically that this is a punishment for her opposition to David, but this idea may be implied. A child who would have been heir to both the dynasty of Saul and the dynasty of David would have been a powerful figure and would have further complicated this story. Mysteriously, 2 Samuel 21:8 reports that Michal had five sons. Most biblical translations understand this as a mistake and replace Michal's name with Merab, her older sister, whom she originally replaced as David's wife in 1 Samuel 18. Michal stands out as a striking figure who dares to stand up to David. The Old Testament reports her life in a fragmented way, making it difficult to piece together. This is one more aspect of the immensely complicated relationship between Israel's first two kings.

completely wiped out. When the Israelite soldiers refused, he hired mercenaries led by Doeg, an Edomite, to do the dirty work. The only survivor, Abiathar, a priest, escaped to tell David what had happened (22:6–23).

David and his men attacked the Philistines, who were about to seize Keilah, a Judean village. Instead of being grateful for David's help, however, the villagers were ready to surrender him to Saul's wrath (23:1–14).

David fled, with Saul in pursuit, to the area south of Hebron. There, Jonathan found David, but assured him that he would keep David's whereabouts a secret from Saul. They reaffirmed their personal friendship by a covenant (23:15–18). In the meantime, spies brought word of David's hiding place, causing Saul to set out after him. Just as he was closing in on David in the rough, hilly country of the Arabah, word came of a Philistine attack, drawing Saul away (23:19–29).

Next, Saul heard that David was at Engedi, an oasis on the western side of the Dead Sea. While he pursued David, Saul stopped in a cave "to relieve himself" (24:3), not knowing that David was hiding there. When Saul was there, David crept up and cut off a piece of the robe that Saul probably had taken off. He resisted the temptation to kill Saul, however.

When Saul left the cave, David called to him and told him that he had not taken the opportunity to kill him. Saul was so shaken by the event that he admitted he had wronged David. Saul exacted a promise from David not to kill his family after David became king (24:1–22).

If one translated a description of David's activity into our modern idiom, it could be said that he was president and chairman of the board of the South Judah Protection Agency. He protected the Judean villages and the more nomadic Israelites of the area from raids by the Amalekits and other non-Israelite groups who also traveled about in the area. For this service he expected gratitude in the form of food and other provisions for his rather sizable personal army. Some contributed willingly, if not cheerfully; others were more difficult to convince of their need for David's services. One such attempt to collect eventually ended rather surprisingly.

That the biblical storytellers had a great sense of humor is often reflected in the names they give certain characters. Like our nicknames, such as "Slim" or "Stone Face," the names they used were part of the meaning they wished to convey in the story. Such a name was given to a sheepherder from Carmel in the Judean wilderness near the Dead Sea. The narrator calls him Nabal, meaning "vile thing." Although this could have been his name, it is more likely that it is just a term used to describe his nasty personality.

Nabal had large herds of sheep and goats—3000 sheep and 1000 goats—that David had protected from raiders. When he sent word to Nabal that he would appreciate a nice gift in gratitude for his services, all he got was an insulting message that Nabal had nothing to give a renegade who had broken away from his master (25:1–13).

David, proud and hot tempered, immediately set out to pay back the insult with a show of force. At this point in the story, Nabal's wife, Abigail, a woman of intelligence as well as beauty (25:3), decided that something had to be done to head off David. She was wise enough to realize that David's request was reasonable and that he would not stand such an insult without retaliation (25:14–17).

Unknown to her husband, who probably was busy counting his sheep, Abigail prepared a generous gift of food and drink and set out with her servants to head off David before he descended in fury upon their camp.

Abigail had figured correctly. When she met David, she used an unbeatable combination of flattery, food, and an appeal to his religious instincts. She convinced David that what he was about to do was foolish. Because he had received the supplies he had originally sought, he returned to his headquarters (25:18–35).

When Abigail returned, she found Nabal on a drinking binge. The next morning, when his hangover was upon him, she told him what had happened. The shock caused a sudden attack in the form of a paralytic stroke. The text says, "He became like a stone" (25:37). He died ten days later (25:36–38).

When David heard of Nabal's death, he thanked the LORD for keeping him from a foolish attack on a fellow Judean. Such a thing would have given his detractors a weapon and would have alienated others who looked upon him as a hero.

Abigail, now a widow with 3000 sheep and 1000 goats, was so attractive that David felt he must marry her to show his gratitude for her thoughtful action on his behalf. Abigail was willing, so the marriage was carried out. David also married Abinoam from Jezreel but lost Saul's daughter Michal, whom Saul had given to another man when David fled. This was an act designed to insult David, because to invade a man's harem could cost one his life.[10] At the time, David could do little about the insult (25:39–44).

This story has many parallels to the one in 24:1–22, but it differs in important details. David and two of his men slipped into Saul's camp and took Saul's spear and water jug. As in the previous story, David refused to kill Saul. David went to the top of a nearby mountain and shouted down to Abner, Saul's general, accusing him of being careless in protecting Saul. Saul answered and admitted that he had wronged David.

This story, telling of David's alliance with the king of Gath, takes care to put David's action in as good a light as possible. It shows how David walked a fine line in claiming to have the interest of his people at heart while acting as the bodyguard for the Philistine king. In addition, it did keep him safe from Saul.

The End of Saul's Reign

Saul was desperate. The Philistines had moved from Aphek, in the central coastal plain, to Shunem, near Mount Gilboa, where Saul's troops were assembled. There was an air of doom about Saul as the Philistine army gathered for the battle that would come the next day. Samuel was dead, David was in the camp of the enemy, and Saul was overwhelmed by his lifelong sense of inadequacy. When he tried to get some sort of leadership from the religious officials, no word came. He could not dream up a solution, the Urim and Thummim would not fall right, and his prophets claimed that the LORD had nothing to say (28:3–6).

Saul sought a **medium** (or witch) who supposedly could call up the dead. Finding a medium was difficult, because most of them had been banished by Saul's own order (28:3). Finally, a medium was found in the nearby village of Endor. He sought her out at night and asked her to call up Samuel for him. She claimed to be in contact with Samuel, but the message she gave Saul was one of doom. He was reminded of his failures as a king and was told that he and his sons would die the next day (28:7–19).[11] Saul was terrified and fell to the ground. Finally, the woman persuaded him to eat. After resting for a time, he left (28:20–25).

Instead of proceeding immediately to the story of the battle for Mount Gilboa, the narrative switches back to David, probably to make it clear that he had no part in the death of Saul. David had been asked by Achish, the king of Gath, to go with him to fight Saul. David had consented. The other Philistine kings, knowing of David's background and his popularity among the Judeans, objected vigorously. As a result, David and his forces were sent back to their base.

While David was away, there was an Amalekite raid on his camp at Ziklag in the Judean foothills (30:1–6). David set out to pursue the raiders. When he returned from a successful attack

FIGURE 6–2 "They put [Saul's] armor in the temple of Astarte, and they fastened his body to the wall of Beth-Shan" (1 Sam. 31:10). Tell Beth-Shan, in the valley of Jezreel, was the site of an ancient city that guarded an important crossing of the Jordan.

on them, some of his men did not want to share any of the spoils of battle with those who had stayed behind to guard the camp. David ruled that every man should receive an equal share. Furthermore, he shared the spoils with the elders of Judah (30:7–31).

Saul and his sons died in the battle on Mount Gilboa. Saul, mortally wounded, committed suicide. The Philistines hanged the bodies of Saul and some of his sons on the wall of Beth-Shan. The people of Jabesh–Gilead stole the bodies during the night and disposed of them properly.

SAMUEL, SAUL, AND DAVID: A SUMMARY

The book of 1 Samuel presents three enormous and fascinating personalities in Samuel, Saul, and David. The transformation of Israel from a loosely knit band of clans and tribes, beset by their surrounding enemies and often at war among themselves, into a unified nation, ruled by a king and defended by a professional army, is no easy process. Samuel and Saul are necessary figures in this drama. Samuel brings the old traditions of judge, prophet, and deliverer, which date back to Moses, and hands them to a new kind of leader, a king. Israel's reluctance to have a king is on full display in 1 Samuel, but Saul, as the first king, serves to carry away most of that negativity. Both Samuel and Saul pave the way and clear the stage for David to emerge as a heroic, fresh-faced force of nature. The transformation of Israel into a nation that can develop into a regional power is not yet complete, but all of the background work is accomplished, and David is prepared to be the great, ideal king who can take credit for this national transformation.

DAVID: KING OVER JUDAH

David Responds to Saul's Death and Assumes Control of Judah (2 Sam. 1:1–2:11)

David was at Ziklag when the news of Saul's death on Mount Gilboa arrived. The messenger told David that he had found Saul still alive, but that he had killed Saul as Saul had asked him to do. He had brought Saul's crown and armband as proof that Saul was dead.

David's reaction to the story was severe. He ordered the messenger's death because he had claimed to have killed Saul, the "LORD's anointed" (1:14). The messenger was not helped by the fact that he was an Amalekite. In view of the different story told in 1 Samuel 31, it would seem that this story either (1) is from another tradition or (2) that the Amalekite made up his role in Saul's death to gain David's reward for eliminating the last barrier to David's becoming king (1:1–16).

David's **lament** over Saul and Jonathan came from the Book of Jashar (quoted in Joshua 10:13). This book, which now is lost, seems to have been a collection of traditional songs used by biblical writers. The lament speaks of both Saul and Jonathan, but the feeling expressed for Jonathan was in keeping with the accounts of their strong bond of friendship (1:17–27).

By popular consent, David was anointed king of Judah at Hebron (2:1–4a). David commended the people of Jabesh–Gilead for their bravery in stealing the bodies of Saul and Jonathan from Beth Shan and giving them an honorable burial (2:4b–7).

In the meantime, Abner (Saul's general) had placed Saul's son, Ishbaal (1 Chr. 8:33), on the throne. The Israelite narrators, however, changed Ishbaal's name to Ishbosheth to show their contempt for him, because Ishbaal ("Baal's man") was a Baal worshiper. Because of this, they called him "man of shame" (Ishbosheth). He ruled from Transjordan over the northern tribes (2:8–11).

Civil War between Judah and Israel (2 Sam. 2:12–4:12)

Before long, a civil war broke out at the "pool of Gibeon." The battle started when the forces of Abner and of Joab, David's general, met there. A wrestling match was proposed for twelve men from each side, but it turned deadly when swords were used instead. Asahel, Joab's brother, ran after Abner as he fled from the scene. Abner warned Asahel to stop, but when he failed to do so, Abner killed him. Joab pursued Abner's forces until they took a stand, causing Joab to withdraw (2:12–32).

Abner soon became disillusioned with Ishbosheth, who had committed treason by taking a woman from Saul's harem as his slave wife. Ishbosheth, who by custom had inherited his father's harem, was too weak to do anything about it (3:1–11). Abner went to David and offered to surrender the rest of the country to him. He wanted to make a covenant with David, but David first demanded that Michal, his former wife, be given back to him. Abner did this, and the covenant was made (3:12–21).

As Abner was leaving the meeting with David, Joab met him. Calling him aside as if to have a conversation, Joab stabbed and killed Abner. His justification was that Abner had killed his brother and he was acting as Asahel's avenger. This was a violation of customary law, however, because killing in war was not subject to the rule of blood vengeance. Abner and David had a covenant that made David responsible for avenging Abner's murder. Although he lamented Abner, David's excuse was that Joab and his brother were too strong to fight. It may well be that he also felt that he needed their support to accomplish his goals (3:39).

With Abner dead, Ishbosheth's kingdom fell apart. Two men murdered him as he slept. They cut off his head and carried their gory trophy to David at Hebron. David reacted as he had to the report of Saul's death—he had the murderers executed.

DAVID: KING OVER ALL ISRAEL

David Consolidates His Kingdom in Jerusalem (2 Sam. 5:1–7:29)

David ruled for another five and one-half years from Hebron (5:1–5) before he captured Jerusalem. This heavily fortified Jebusite city, according to tradition, was built on the site where Abraham attempted to sacrifice Isaac (Gen. 22). The invaders got into the city by entering a tunnel that carried the waters of a spring under its walls. A shaft was cut down to the tunnel so that people could reach the water without going outside the walls. David's men got inside the city and then opened the gate so that others could enter.

The choice of Jerusalem was one of a number of shrewd political moves that David made. While he was still a fugitive from Saul, David drew people to him who were unhappy with Saul. He also was careful to present himself as champion and protector of the common folk of Judah. In addition, he wooed the village chiefs with presents when he took spoils in battle (1 Sam. 30:26–31).

David never raised his hand against Saul. Even when opportunists tried to gain his favor by claiming to have killed Saul and Ishbosheth, David had acted correctly—he had put the admitted murderers to death.

The choice of Jerusalem as the capital was a good move because it was a neutral site. It had never been held permanently by Israel and thus belonged to no tribe. To have made Hebron, a city of Judah, the permanent capital would have stirred up considerable resentment, especially from the Ephraim, Judah's rival for first place among the tribes.

More importantly, David appeared as a man of integrity, whose dedication to the LORD, the God of Israel, was without question. His leadership fulfilled the ideal of the possession of the land promised to the patriarchs. David's success was so impressive that it caused the covenant at Sinai to fade into the background. It was replaced with the concept of the covenant with David, which said that David's descendants would sit on the throne of Israel during the ages to come.

After mentioning (1) David's alliance with Hiram, king of Tyre, who furnished builders and materials for David's projects (5:11–12), and (2) David's wives and children (5:13–16), the narrator of Samuel turns to the Philistine threat, the first major problem that faced David when he became king. How he dealt with the Philistines would determine his success as king over all of Israel. Saul's lack of success against the Philistines had been his chief failure.

The Philistines did not wait long to test David. Twice they attacked Israel in the Rephaim Valley, and David, after consulting the LORD, defeated them both times (5:17–25).

The Ark, the sacred symbol of the LORD's presence with Israel, had been kept in a private home for over twenty years. David was determined to bring it to Jerusalem. The first attempt ended in tragedy when Uzzah, one of the men who was moving it by cart, died when he touched the Ark. The text says, "and God smote him because he reached out his hand to the ark" (6:7). Awe of the holy object caused an immediate halt to David's plan for three months (6:1–11).

During the three-month period, Obed-edom (in whose house the Ark was kept) had evidence of God's blessing on him. David concluded that it would be safe to try again to move the Ark. This time, a sacrifice was made after the Ark was moved only six steps. David played the role of priest, wearing the priestly garment and dancing before the Ark as it was brought into the city (6:12–17).

Michal, who had been returned against her will to David's harem as a condition of the covenant with Abner (3:13), watched the events from her window. The next time she saw David, she told him that he had acted like a dirty old man. David argued that he was dancing to honor the LORD. Because of her criticism (6:16–23), she was demoted in the harem.

After David's palace was complete, the question arose about building a temple to the LORD in which the Ark could be housed permanently. At first, Nathan the prophet, who functioned as

David's spiritual advisor, encouraged him. Later, however, he told David that he had had a vision in which (1) the LORD had always dwelt in the Tabernacle from the Exodus until the present time (7:4–7), (2) the LORD had made David what he was (7:8–11), and (3) future rulers of Israel would be David's descendants (7:12–17). David praised the LORD and prayed that the promise spoken by Nathan would be fulfilled (7:18–29).

David's Military Success (2 Sam. 8:1–18)

Israel controlled more territory during David's reign than at any other time in its history. Beginning with the defeat of the Philistines, David led his armies to conquer the territory east of the Jordan (8:2, 12–14); north to the upper reaches of the Euphrates River, including all of Syria (8:3–11); and south to the borders of Egypt (8:15–18).

He ruled his kingdom well. One reason for this may have been that, when he captured Jerusalem, he captured people who had been trained in Egypt to run the government. Instead of killing them, he put them to work organizing and running his empire.[12]

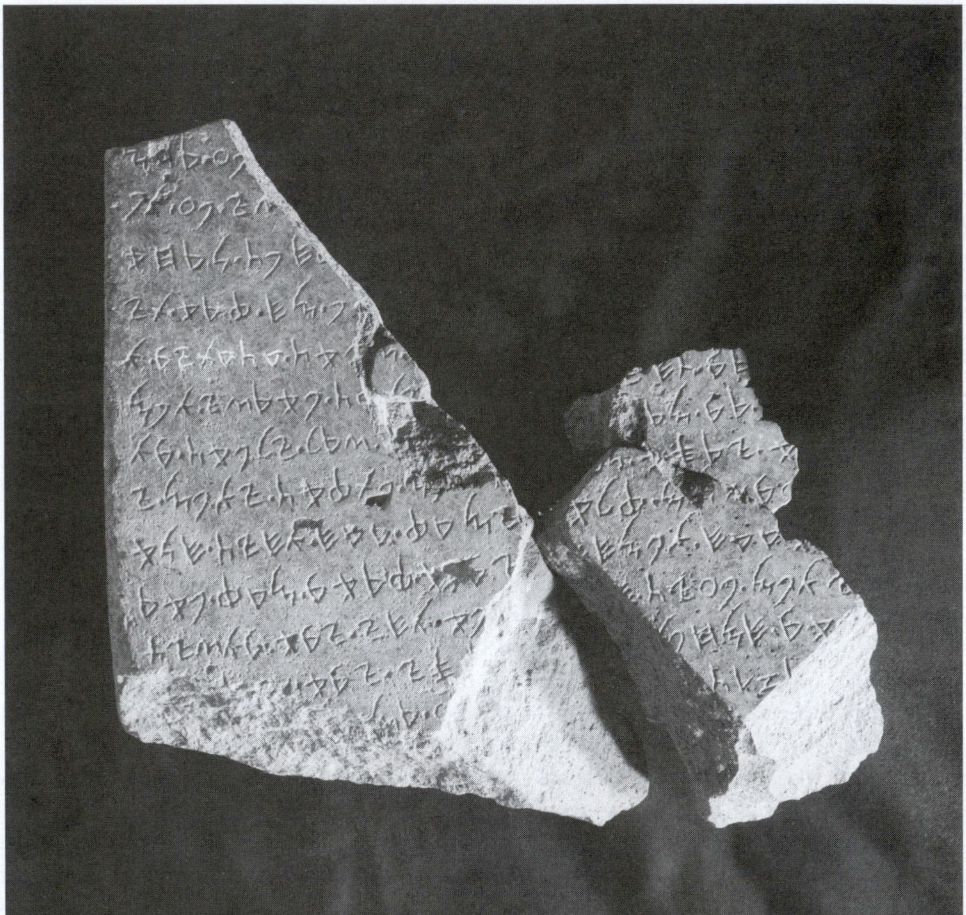

FIGURE 6–3 This inscription, found at Tell Dan in northern Israel, was part of a victory stele or column erected by an Aramean (Syrian) ruler to brag about his success in a battle against the house of David.

THE COURT HISTORY OF DAVID

A Brief Period of Calm (2 Sam. 9–10)

The book of 2 Samuel provides a fairly continuous narrative of David's reign as king of Israel, but the list of David's administrative officers at 8:15–18 brings the period of intense consolidation to an end, and the surprising question asked by David in 9:1 opens a different kind of scene. Irony abounds when David asks, "Is there still anyone left from the house of Saul, that I might act with kindness to him in the passing of Jonathan?" David, of course, had killed or ordered the deaths of all of the male descendants of Saul to eliminate rivals for the throne. The only remaining male heir of Saul is Jonathan's son, Mephibosheth, whom the text describes as "crippled." Whatever this physical disability was, it must have been the reason he was not considered a threat to David and was not killed. When David brings Mephibosheth into his own house, along with all of the inheritance of Saul's family, the matter of **succession** to the throne is fully settled. In 2 Samuel 10, David can then go out on the military exploits befitting a great king, and his bold activity in these accounts serves as a pointed contrast to the troubling sequence of stories to come.

The Bathsheba Affair and Its Repercussions (2 Sam. 11:1–15:6)

During the Ammonite wars, David stopped going to battle with his men. There may have been two reasons for this: (1) With the enlarged kingdom, David probably felt that he had to pay more attention to matters of government, and (2) his advisors may have insisted that he no longer go to battle with them because, had he been killed, it would have been an irreplaceable loss to the kingdom. In any case, he stayed home (11:1).

During this time, as he was taking a stroll on his roof in the evening, he saw a beautiful woman taking a bath. Shortly thereafter, **Bathsheba** made a command appearance in the palace, with the result that she became pregnant with David's child (11:2–5).

What followed is a vivid example of how a deeply religious man can be so concerned with protecting his image that he can forget his religious principles. First, David tried by various means to make it possible for Bathsheba's husband, Uriah, to believe that he was the father-to-be. But Uriah, a loyal soldier in David's army, would not cooperate. He felt it was unpatriotic to enjoy the pleasures of wife and home while his friends were still fighting. Finally, in desperation, David sent Uriah back to the battle, carrying a secret order to Joab to put him in the front lines so that he would be killed (11:6–21). Soon, the word came back that Uriah was indeed dead. After a proper period of mourning, Bathsheba entered the king's harem (11:22–27).

David must have breathed a sigh of relief, but it was not for long. Nathan, prophet and spiritual advisor to the king, confronted David with what he had done. In that confrontation, some of the character of the king was revealed. Instead of banishing or even killing Nathan for his audacity, David faced his guilt and admitted his wrong (12:1–15).

From the time of its birth, the baby was ill and David mourned. When told of the baby's death, David, having prayed for the child to live, ceased mourning (12:16–23). Not long afterward, a second child, Solomon, was born (12:24–25). After Solomon's birth, David returned to battle against the Ammonites and defeated them (12:26–31).

David's moral failures, coupled with his failure to control his children, brought a bitter harvest. **Absalom** and Tamar were the children of one of David's wives, while Amnon was the son of another wife. Amnon fell in love with Tamar, his beautiful half-sister, but there seemed to be no

Tamar, Amnon, and Absalom

After David's affair with Bathsheba, he is punished in two ways. First, the illegitimate child produced by the affair dies in 2 Samuel 12:15–19. The prophet Nathan also declares to David in 2 Samuel 12:11 that God will "raise up trouble against you from within your own house." This prediction begins to be fulfilled in 2 Samuel 13 when a strange story unfolds among David's children. It is interesting to note that David's "punishments" always involve the suffering of people other than himself.

David's oldest son, Amnon, is smitten with Tamar, his half-sister. Tamar is the daughter of David by a different wife. Amnon concocts a ruse in order to be alone with Tamar and he rapes her; then he sends Tamar away in shame despite her offer to be married to him. This story contains a number of fascinating connections to the story of David and Bathsheba, and raises further questions about whether that earlier story is best understood as a romantic affair or a sexual assault. Conflict arises from this incident as David takes no action, while Tamar's full brother, Absalom, quietly plots revenge. Absalom demonstrates amazing patience as he waits two years, carefully plotting the assassination of Amnon. Once he has committed the act, however, he flees from the land for three years while David and his remaining sons mourn the loss of Amnon. It is easy to think that Absalom's motives may have been mixed, though. Although he is justly angry over the attack on his sister, the killing of Amnon removes David's apparent firstborn from the line of succession to the throne and opens the way for Absalom himself.

Absalom's royal ambitions emerge when he returns to Jerusalem and is forgiven and accepted by David. 2 Samuel 15–18 tells the story of Absalom's rebellion. The prince gains enormous popularity, drives his father out of Jerusalem, and assumes the position of king in the palace. Nathan's statement to David in 2 Samuel 12:11, that God would "take your wives before your eyes, and give them to your neighbor, and he shall lie with your wives in the sight of this very sun," is fulfilled in 2 Samuel 16:21–22 when Absalom has sexual relations with David's concubines on the roof of the palace. Eventually, David's army recovers and defeats the forces of Absalom. Absalom is killed in a bizarre scene in which his hair gets caught in a tree while he is riding a mule, and he is left hanging where he can be easily murdered. Despite his son's rebellion, David mourns the loss of Absalom bitterly. David regains the throne, but he seems a weak and pathetic figure for the remainder of his life. Many layers of irony are revealed as all of this trouble in David's family, which is portrayed as punishment for his actions toward Bathsheba, prepares the way for Bathsheba's son, Solomon, to assume the throne after the death of David.

way he could marry her. At the suggestion of a cousin, the lovesick Amnon persuaded David to send Tamar to his house to cook for him while he pretended to be ill. While she was there, he raped her and then refused to marry her (13:1–19). This meant that Tamar would never be able to marry, because virginity was considered essential for marriage. David took no action against Amnon for his abuse of Tamar.

Two years later, after all seemed to be forgotten, Absalom invited Amnon to a party. Under orders from Absalom, his servants waited until Amnon was drunk and then stabbed him to death. Absalom, with Joab's help, fled to his mother's homeland of Geshur (13:38), where he stayed for two years.[13]

Joab, knowing that David wanted an excuse to let Absalom return home, took an old woman from Tekoa to David. She told him a sad story of her two sons. According to this story, one of the widow's sons had murdered the other. Her relatives were ready to kill the surviving son to avenge the death of the dead son. Because this would leave no living male to carry on the family name, she was appealing to the king for protection for the murderer. David ruled that the need for an heir to carry his father's name was more important than punishing a murderer.[14]

When David had so ruled, the grieving mother suddenly turned and rebuked him for not allowing Absalom to come home. David immediately suspected that Joab had planned the performance of the "widow." Even so, he commanded Joab to bring Absalom home, but on the condition that he not be allowed to see David (14:18–24).

Absalom was not content with being allowed to return to Jerusalem. He asked Joab to see him, but twice Joab refused. To get Joab's attention, he set Joab's barley field on fire. Joab then agreed to persuade David to allow Absalom to return to court. David agreed (14:25–33).

Then Absalom began a systematic campaign to undermine his father. He would stand at the palace gate, and when a man came to bring a problem before the king, Absalom would call him aside and tell him that it was a waste of time to try to see the king, even though his complaint was a just one. Absalom would then assure the man that should *he* be king, he would give justice. He would allow no man to give the traditional bow of respect, but would warmly embrace him like a brother.

> Thus Absalom did to every Israelite who came to the king for judgment; so Absalom stole the hearts of the people of Israel. (15:6)

Absalom's Rebellion (2 Sam. 15:7–19:8)

After four years, Absalom made his move. He sent word to his supporters to gather at Hebron, David's first capital. He told David that he was going to celebrate a feast and received David's blessing on the trip. Once there, however, he had himself proclaimed king. Among those who joined him was Ahithophel, one of David's court advisors (15:7–12).

On hearing the news, David chose to run away rather than fight his own son. He made plans to leave Jerusalem. He instructed ten of his wives to stay behind to take care of his house, but all of his servants and his personal bodyguards went with him. Most of them were foreigners who were more loyal to David than to the nation of Israel. Typical of this was the servant Ittai, a Philistine from Gath (15:13–23).

David was not without eyes and ears in Jerusalem, however. Zadok and Abiathar started to take the Ark of the Covenant with David, but he sent them back and told them to stay in Jerusalem. Hushai, one of David's counselors, also agreed to be a spy in Absalom's camp. Among the three of them, they managed to keep David informed of Absalom's moves (15:24–37).

Leaving Jerusalem, David went across the Kidron Valley, which separates the eastern boundary of the city from the Mount of Olives (15:30). As he crossed the mountain, he was joined by Ziba, the servant of Mephibosheth (Jonathan's son), who brought an offering of food and drink, as well as donkeys for David and his household to ride. Mephibosheth had gone over to Absalom's side (16:1–4).

Further on, David was roundly cursed and stoned by Shimei, a supporter of Saul's family. When one of his men offered to kill Shimei, David prevented him. Instead, he continued on toward the Jordan River (16:5–14).

Meanwhile, Absalom entered Jerusalem. Hushai greeted Absalom and convinced him that he had deserted David. One of Absalom's first acts was to have sexual relations with one of David's concubines in full view of the people. This was meant to show that he had taken over his father's kingdom (16:15–23).

Conflicting advice was given to Absalom by Hushai and Ahithophel. Ahithophel advised immediate pursuit of David, but Hushai suggested that they wait. He stated, furthermore, that

Absalom could prove his leadership ability to the people by personally leading the pursuit (17:1–14). Absalom took Hushai's advice. When he did so, Hushai got word to Zadok and Abiathar, who, after some difficulty, managed to inform David (17:15–22). In the meantime, when Ahithophel saw that Absalom would no longer listen to him, he committed suicide (17:23).

David stopped when he reached Mahanaim in Transjordan. Mahanaim was located near Penuel, where Jacob was said to have wrestled with the angel (Gen. 32:22–23). Loyal followers in the area brought necessary supplies (17:24–29).

In preparation for the battle, David split his army into three parts, appointing a commander over each. David wanted to lead, but his commanders refused to let him go. As they left, David asked that they "deal gently" with Absalom (18:1–5).

The battle raged in the forest of Ephraim. A patrol spotted Absalom and gave chase. As Absalom's mule ran under an oak, Absalom was caught by the head in a tree branch and left hanging. When Joab heard, he ordered his men to kill Absalom. When they refused, Joab personally killed him, had his body thrown into a pit, and covered it with stones (18:6–18).

When the messengers brought the news to David, he wept loudly, lamenting Absalom's death (18:19–23). When the people heard him lamenting, their shouts over the hard-won victory turned to shamed silence. Joab's power over David was never more vividly illustrated than when he told David that if he wanted the support of those who had saved his life, he should stop crying and praise the people for what they had done. "For," Joab said,

> you have made it clear today that commanders and officers are nothing to you; for I perceive that if Absalom were alive and all of us were dead today, then you would be pleased. (19–6)

David arose and did as he was told to do (19:1–8b).

Repairing the Nation (2 Sam. 19:8c–43)

As David returned to Jerusalem, those who had supported Absalom either fled or tried to get back into David's good graces. Shimei, for example, who had cursed David as he left, met him and begged forgiveness. David promised not to kill Shimei, but he did not promise that someone else might not do it (19:8c–23).

Mephibosheth, Jonathan's son, came begging; but David divided his property, giving half of it to Ziba, Mephibosheth's servant, who had brought food to David's men (19:24–40). David offered a place of honor to Brazilli, the Gileadite who had also brought supplies to him. Brazilli asked David to give it to his servant instead (19:31–40).

When David arrived in Jerusalem, the elders of the northern tribes and the elders of Judah got into a dispute over who had the right to bring him back to the city. The Judeans claimed it was their right by kingship, while the northerners claimed it was their right by majority rule. The Judeans seem to have won (19:41–43).

Taking advantage of the friction between the northern tribes and the Judeans, Sheba started another revolt against David, which gained a number of followers. David put Amasa in charge of the army, replacing Joab after he killed Absalom. Amasa was given orders to put down the rebellion. Before he could get organized, Amasa was murdered by Joab (20:1–10c). Joab took over the army and soon had the rebellion under control (20:10d–26). The ultimate effect of this rebellion would be to allow **Solomon** to establish the Israelite monarchy more on the order of the other eastern kings. In other words, Solomon was a more autocratic ruler than either Saul or David had been.[15]

An Odd Collection of Materials Concerning David's Reign (Sam. 21–24:25)

The last three chapters of 2 Samuel do not fit into the story of the ins and outs of David's court. First, there is the story of a famine that lasted for three years. Through prayer, David became convinced that an atrocity that Saul had committed against the Gibeonites (Josh. 9) had not been forgiven by the LORD. He went to the Gibeonites and asked them if there was anything he could do to make things right with them for the harm Saul had done. They replied that the only thing he could do was to turn over to them seven of Saul's sons. He did as they asked, and the Gibeonites hanged the men. Rizpah, the mother of two of the victims, kept their bodies from being attacked by birds of prey until only the bones were left. Then David had Saul's and Jonathan's bones returned to Jerusalem from Jabesh–Gilead and buried Saul and his sons together.

The point of this story is that the ancient Israelites believed that murder (in this case, Saul's unjust killing of the Gibeonites) had to be punished by the death of the murderer. Because Saul was dead already, his sons had to bear the blame. When justice was not done, the whole land suffered. One way that suffering came was through such natural disasters as drought and famine. The only way to bring such natural disasters to an end was to see that justice was done (21:10–14).

The next block of material mentioned the giants who might be described as the heavyweight champions among the Philistines. The Israelites who defeated them are listed (21:15–22).

Chapters 22 and 23:1–7 are what are known as *orphan psalms*—that is, psalms found outside the book of Psalms. Both are said to have come from David, and both are hymns of praise. Following the psalms is a series of episodes describing exploits of David's mighty men, his personal bodyguards, who were fiercely loyal to him. As a matter of fact, David's army was largely a private army, recruited and paid by him (28:8–38).

Chapter 24 describes a census by David, probably for the purpose of taxation. Then, as now, the power to tax was the power to control. The LORD was said to have told David to take the census. The story in 1 Chronicles 21:1 provides a different understanding of this event, saying that "Satan" caused David to take the census. A plague came. To ease the plague, David bought Araunah's threshing floor on top of the mountain overlooking Jerusalem. Later, the Temple was built there. The large rock that formed the threshing floor would become a sacred spot for three great religions—Judaism, Christianity, and Islam. When David bought the site and made sacrifices, the plague was lifted (24:1–25).

An Evaluation of David

David's accomplishments as king caused him to be ranked with Moses in importance in Israelite tradition. It is true that there were no major challenges to David's rule from Egypt, Asia Minor, or Mesopotamia, but the fact that he could take a rather disorganized and divided people and achieve what he did in the short span of forty years marked the man as a genius in military organization and administrative skill. Although Solomon's kingdom would be more spectacular in its display of wealth and power, it was only because David's conquests were complete. Solomon had a period of peace in which to develop the kingdom economically.

Beyond the period of the united monarchy, David's influence was felt in three areas. First, in his choice of Jerusalem as his capital, he gave the world its most revered city. To Jew and Christian alike, it would become the earthly version of God's heavenly city. That is why the writer of the New Testament book of Revelation spoke of the ideal age as beginning when "the holy city, the new Jerusalem," would come down from heaven to earth (Rev. 21:2). Because the Dome of the

Rock supposedly is built over the site from which Mohammed ascended to heaven on his white horse, for Muslims it ranks second only to Mecca in importance.

Now, some 3000 years later, Jews, Christians, and Muslims make their way to a city whose influence far outweighs any importance it should have. Many cities are larger, more influential economically, and have more to offer in culture, education, and the arts, but none have the special quality and drawing power of Jerusalem.

Secondly, the monarchy, referred to biblically as the *house of David*, was established. Until recent years, no known contemporary references to the Davidic monarchy had been discovered by archaeologists. As a result, some scholars have argued from this silence that the Davidic rule was a figment of the biblical writer's imagination. Now the phrase *house of David* has been discovered in an **inscription** at Tell Dan in northern Israel.[16]

The Davidic monarchy would last for more than 400 years, but its influence would extend even further. Part of its longevity lay in the conviction that the LORD made a covenant with David, saying that his descendants would rule Israel. That covenant replaced the Sinai covenant in the thinking of the average Israelite, especially the Judeans. Essentially, a covenant based on moral demands was replaced by one that primarily emphasized family continuity in the monarchy. Following David's time, when the covenant was mentioned, it was assumed that the reference was to the covenant with David.

When the monarchy ended with the Babylonian Exile, the hope for its restoration lived on, especially as it was and had been proclaimed by the great prophets (Isa. 9, 11; Mic. 5:2–4). In the midst of the post-Exilic period, the hope for the ideal king who exemplified the best qualities of David grew into the doctrine of God's Anointed One, the Messiah. Jesus' disciples saw him as the fulfillment of that ideal, while Jewish interpreters continued to look for the new David who would rescue his persecuted people.

In the third place, David left his mark on the poetic literature of Israel. How many of the psalms he actually wrote is subject to vigorous debate. That he wrote some of them seems certain enough for him to be looked upon as the father of Israelite hymns. The psalms are different from other biblical literature because they are people's deepest emotions addressed to God. Because David is represented as a deeply emotional man, it is fitting that he was connected with the most emotional literary form in the Old Testament.

Overall, Israelite kingship differed from that of other Near Eastern societies. Both in Egypt and in Babylonia, the king was regarded as divine, although somewhat more so in Egypt, where the king was worshiped as a god. In Israel, there was a strong belief that the LORD was king, while the earthly king was the LORD's representative but was still human. This is why, especially during the early monarchy, the prophets dared to call the kings to account if they did not follow the LORD's will (cf. Nathan and David, Elijah and Ahab). It also is illustrated by the fact that Samuel, in his role as prophet, could choose David as king and have him accepted by the people.[17]

Key Terms and Names

Absalom, *137*
Anoint, *123*
Bathsheba, *137*
Deuteronomistic History, *118*
Dynasty, *120*
Eli, *119*
Hannah, *119*
Medium, *132*
Monarchy, *118*
Philistines, *119*
Prophet, *123*
Samuel, *119*
Saul, *123*
Shiloh, *119*
Solomon, *140*
Succession, *137*

Study Questions

1. What attitudes toward the monarchy are present in the books of Samuel and Kings?
2. What was the Court History of David? How did it differ from usual accounts of the reigns of ancient kings?
3. In what ways are the birth stories of Samuel (1 Sam. 1:1–2:11) and Isaac (Gen. 18:9–11; 21:1–8) similar?
4. Why was Samuel turned over to Eli at such an early age?
5. In what ways did Samuel act as judge, prophet, and priest?
6. What series of events caused Israel to unite and eventually choose a king?
7. What was the significance of the ceremony of anointing?
8. Why should Samuel be described as a *king maker* and a *king breaker*?
9. Why was Saul chosen as king over Israel?
10. What were Saul's strengths and weaknesses as a king?
11. Why did Samuel turn against Saul?
12. How many times was David anointed, and when did he actually become king?
13. What are the two different versions of how Saul and David met? What does this seem to say about the sources used in writing the Deuteronomistic History?
14. What was David's relationship to Saul and his family?
15. Why did David not kill Saul and take over the kingdom?
16. What does the story of David and Abigail indicate about David's relations to the people during his outlaw period?
17. Why did David join forces with the Philistines?
18. How did David react to the deaths of Saul and Jonathan, and what motivations may have caused his behavior?
19. How did David eventually become king over all of Israel?
20. In the process of becoming king over all of Israel, what did David do to allay the suspicions of the supporters of Saul and his family?
21. What made Jerusalem the logical choice for the capital?
22. What were the long-term effects of David's affair with Bathsheba?
23. What events led to Absalom's estrangement from David?
24. What seemed to be Nathan's role in David's court?
25. How did Absalom undermine David, and what were the results of his rebellion?

Endnotes

1. See Jeremiah 22:10–30; see also Amos 6:1–14, in which criticism is directed toward the ruling class.
2. One of the earliest uses of this title was to refer to King Cyrus of Persia (Isaiah 45:1, LXX). For a description of anointing the king, see Sigmund Mowinckel, *He That Cometh* (Nashville, TN: Abingdon Press, 1954), 63f.
3. This date, as well as the dates for David and Solomon, is approximate and may vary as much as ten years in the different chronologies. Dates are more accurate for later kings.
4. Because the term is insulting, this probably was given to him by the Israelites. See Larry G. Herr, "Whatever Happened to the Ammonites?" *BAR*, XIX, 6 (November–December 1993), 28.
5. For an explanation of such mutilation, see Victor H. Matthews, *Manners and Customs in the Bible* (Peabody, MA: Hendrickson Publishers, 1988), 66.
6. Richard Eliott Friedman, *Who Wrote the Bible?* (New York: Harper & Row, 1987), 37, points out that Israel's kingship was dependent upon the consent of these three groups.
7. Kenneth I. Cohen, "King Saul: A Bungler from the Beginning," *BAR*, X, 5 (October 1994), 34–39, 52, argues that not only Saul's personality but also his background condemned him from the start.
8. Isaiah 1:12–17.
9. On these stories, see Emanuel Tov, "The David and Goliath Saga," *BR*, II, 4 (Winter 1986), 34–41.
10. See Solomon's treatment of his brother Adonijah when Adonijah asked permission to marry Abishag, David's wife, who became part of Solomon's harem (1 Kings 2:19–25).
11. For a discussion of Israelite views of the afterlife, see Bernhard Lang, "Afterlife," *BR*, V, 1 (February 1988), 12–23.
12. For an elaboration of this theory, see George E. Mendenhall, "The Monarchy," *INT*, XXIX, 2 (April 1975), 155–170.

13. On the location of Geshur, see Moshe Kochavi et al., "Rediscovered! The Land of Geshur," *BAR*, XVIII, 4 (July–August 1992), 30–44, 84.

14. For a fuller discussion, see John H. Tullock, *Blood Vengeance Among the Israelites in the Light of Its Near Eastern Background* (Ann Arbor, MI: University Microfilms, 1966), 44.

15. So argues Rainer Albertz, *A History of Israelite Religion* (Louisville, KY: Westminster–John Knox Press, 1994), I, 123.

16. "David Found at Dan," *BAR*, XX, 2 (March–April 1994), 26–39. The Tell Dan inscription seems to commemorate a victory over the kings of both Israel and Judah. See also André Lamaire, "House of David Restored in Moabite Inscription," *BAR*, XX, 3 (May–June 1994), 30–37, who suggests that the Moabite Stone also refers to the house of David.

17. Carol Stuart Grizzard and Marvin E. Tate, "Kingship," *MDB*, 1990, 490–491.

CHAPTER 7

The Division of the Monarchy I

The Reign of Solomon and the Story of the Northern Kingdom

Timeline

960 B.C.E. Approximate death of David and beginning of the reign of Solomon

922 B.C.E. Common estimate of the death of Solomon and division of the kingdom

900 B.C.E. End of Iron Age I and beginning of Iron Age II

876 B.C.E. Beginning of the reign of Omri and the Omride dynasty in the Northern Kingdom

869 B.C.E. Beginning of the reign of Ahab

745 B.C.E. Approximate date of the beginning of Hosea's prophetic career

722 B.C.E. Fall of Samaria to the Assyrian Empire

Chapter Outline

I. The Reign of Solomon
II. Approaching the Divided-Kingdom Story
III. The Division of the Kingdom
IV. The Dynasty of Omri
V. Elijah's Confrontation with Ahab and Jezebel
VI. Jehu to Jereboam II (842–746 B.C.E.)
VII. The Destruction of the Northern Kingdom

CHAPTER OVERVIEW

The book called 1 Kings opens with David on his deathbed, while the members of his family and his officials struggle to determine who will succeed him on the throne of Israel. Solomon won this struggle and began an ambitious reign, which included the development of foreign alliances and massive building projects. Once Solomon died, however, the Israelite monarchy was no longer able to hold itself together. This chapter includes the story of Solomon, the division of the kingdom after his death, and the line of kings who ruled over the northern nation after the division, until this northern kingdom was conquered and dispersed by the Assyrian Empire. The story of the Northern Kingdom of Israel in 2 Kings also includes an increasingly prominent and shifting role for prophetic figures, particularly Elijah and Elisha. A parallel account of the period of the Israelite monarchy is presented in 1 and 2 Chronicles. This account places more emphasis on the reigns of Solomon and David, often omitting material that reflects negatively on them, and it omits the story of the Northern Kingdom almost entirely.

THE REIGN OF SOLOMON

If Saul was a judge who tried to be king and David was an empire builder, then Solomon introduced Israel to the rule of a typical oriental despot.

Getting Rid of Potential Rivals

Solomon moved quickly to consolidate his power. Whereas David had nothing directly to do with the elimination of anyone who might have been his rival, Solomon had no qualms about dealing with his enemies. Adonijah was his first victim. When Adonijah asked Bathsheba to persuade Solomon to let him have Abishag, David's last concubine, for his wife, Solomon found the wickedness in Adonijah that he had been looking for as an excuse to kill him. The request Adonijah made actually was an insult. David's harem became Solomon's responsibility on David's death, even though the concubines probably were not viewed as Solomon's wives, because his own mother was in the group. Adonijah's request was his own death warrant (2:13–25).

Dealing with Abiathar was a more delicate matter. Not only was he a priest, but he had been David's chief northern priest in tandem with Zadok, the chief priest from Judah. His execution would certainly alienate the northern tribes at a time when Solomon could ill afford to lose their support. By exiling Abiathar to Anathoth, Solomon still offended the northerners somewhat, but not to the extent of losing their support. The prophet Jeremiah probably was a descendant of Abiathar (2:26–27).[1]

Solomon probably considered Joab his most dangerous rival. Even though he was old, Joab was a cunning and ruthless man who had managed to hold power in the army even when David tried to get rid of him. But his luck had run out. Solomon was just as ruthless as Joab, or more so. He ordered Joab's execution. When Joab fled to the sanctuary for refuge and refused to come out, Solomon defied the taboo against killing anyone in the sanctuary. He ordered Joab killed even as he held onto the horns of the sacred **altar.** His executioner, Benaiah, the son of Jehoida, took Joab's place as general over the armies of Israel (2:28–35).

The last to be dealt with was Shimei, who was placed under a form of house arrest that forbade him to leave the city of Jerusalem. Shimei observed the rules for three years, but when one of his slaves ran away, Shimei went after him. Solomon had not forgotten—Shimei died (2:36–46).

FIGURE 7–1 "Joab fled to the tent of the LORD and grasped the horns of the altar" (1 Kings 2:28). The "horns of the altar," as illustrated by this tenth century B.C.E. limestone altar from Megiddo, were supposed to keep a fugitive safe as long as he clung to them. This did not happen in Joab's case. Courtesy of the Israel Antiquities Authority.

Solomon, the Wise One (1 Kings 3:1–28; 4:29–34)

The Israelite historian, in his evaluation of Solomon as a religious man, could not be quite as complimentary as he was about David. Perhaps he was hinting at one of the obstacles to Solomon's devotion to the LORD when he mentions his Egyptian wife. She and other of his wives influenced him to worship pagan gods.

In describing a prayer offered by Solomon, the narrator tells of the LORD appearing in a dream and telling him to ask what he should be given. Instead of asking for great riches, Solomon asked for wisdom to govern his people. The LORD, in turn, promised both wisdom and riches (3:1–15).

An illustration of Solomon's wisdom is the famous story of the two women who claimed the same child. After the women argued before him, Solomon ordered the child cut into two pieces, one piece to be given to each woman. One woman agreed, but the other asked Solomon to spare the child and give it to the other woman. The assumption of the story, and of King Solomon in the story, was that the woman who objected to killing the child was the true mother, and so Solomon awarded the child to her (3:16–28).

A summary statement concerning Solomon's wisdom describes Solomon as wiser than all the eastern wise men. He was a speaker and collector of proverbs, a zoologist and a biologist, and a marvel to all who heard him (4:29–34). The queen of Sheba came from North Africa (Ethiopia) to marvel at his wisdom. Ethiopian tradition has it that she carried away more than wisdom, since later Ethiopian rulers were called in part, "the Lion of Judah" (1 Kings 10:1–10). According to legend, the first emperor of Ethiopia, Menilik, was the son of Solomon and the queen of Sheba, and he took the Ark of the Covenant to Ethiopia, where many believe it still resides.[2]

Solomon, the Organizer (1 Kings 4:1–28)

In organizing the kingdom, Solomon seems to have had two purposes in mind: (1) to divide the land as evenly as possible to provide for the systematic support of his elaborate court and for other taxation purposes and (2) to break down the old tribal distinctions by paying little or no attention to tribal lines when dividing the country into tax districts. In his first purpose, he succeeded; in the second, he failed.

Solomon, the Builder

David built an empire by conquest, but Solomon covered it with buildings. Of all the building projects carried on by Solomon, the **Temple** at Jerusalem ranked first in importance for the Israelite historian.

THE BUILDING OF THE TEMPLE (1 KINGS 5:1–38; 7:15–51). To build as Solomon was said to have done takes skilled workmen and quality materials, neither of which was abundant in Israel. The one thing that Israel had in abundance was stone, but it lacked the forests to supply the needed wood.

To provide the needed materials and skilled workmen, Solomon turned to David's ally, Hiram, king of Tyre and Phoenicia. Hiram agreed to supply cedar and cypress wood, as well as skilled workmen, to carry out the building of the Temple and the palace complex in Jerusalem. In turn, Solomon agreed to supply food to Hiram. Solomon also furnished Israelites to do the labor of cutting the wood and quarrying the stone in Israel. Israelite men had to work without pay for the state, one month out of every three.

Like Jerusalem itself, the Temple—first built by Solomon, then destroyed, then rebuilt again in the post-Exilic period, and built a third time by Herod the Great—has managed to seize the imaginations of countless people for nearly 3000 years. Its remains, except for portions of the wall that supported the platform on which it was built, under an area containing two Islamic mosques—the Dome of the Rock and the Al-Asqa Mosque. As a result, archaeological work on the Temple Mount is forbidden.

By taking the biblical description, however, and comparing it with similar temples found in Israel and Phoenicia, a fairly accurate idea of the Temple's appearance can be gained. One such building was a Canaanite temple found at Hazor in northern Israel. It had the three-room plan used in the Jerusalem Temple. A later temple, from the period of the Israelite monarchy, was found at Arad, south of Jerusalem. In addition, a horned altar, like the one mentioned in the Old Testament, was found at Beersheba (1 Kings 1:50–2:28).

In 1 Kings 6:1, it says that the Temple was built 480 years after Israel left Egypt. This poses a problem in chronology, because it does not agree with other evidence for the date of the Exodus. One possible explanation is that the figure 480 represents twelve generations. Biblical writers figured a generation as 40 years, while today, 25 years equals a generation. If this were the case, twelve times 25 equals 300 years, which would place the Exodus at about 1300 B.C.E.

According to all descriptions, both biblical and archaeological, the Temple was divided into three parts: (1) a porch or vestibule, 15 feet deep and 30 feet wide; (2) the Holy Place, 60 feet long

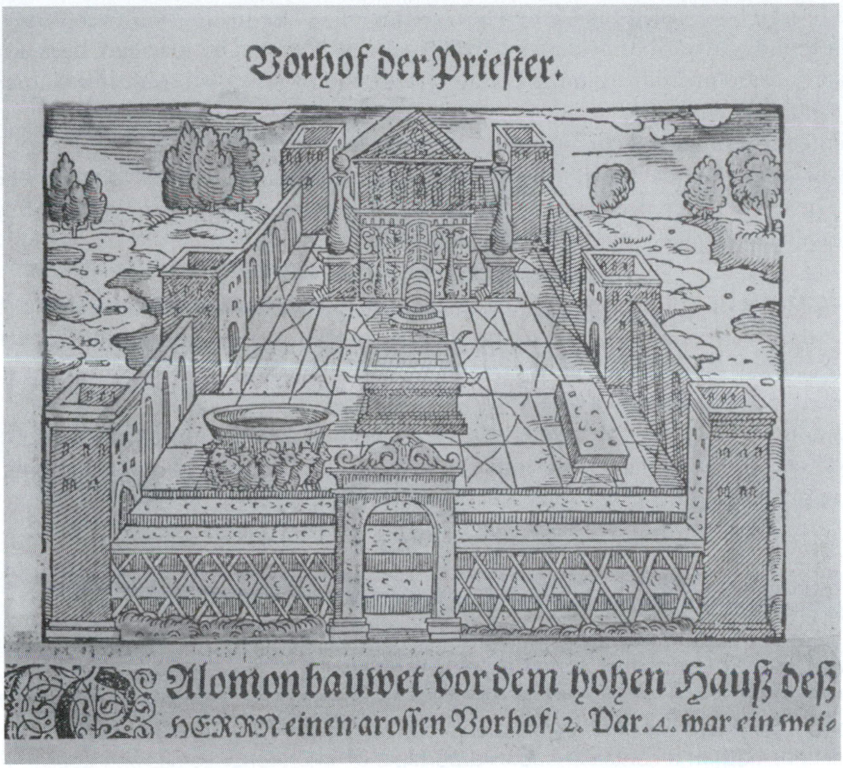
Vorhof der Priester.
Salomon bauwet vor dem hohen Hauß deß
HERRN einen grossen Vorhof/ 2. Par. 4. war ein

FIGURE 7–2 A sixteenth-century engraving depicts Solomon's temple with the horned altar in the center and the Holy of Holies beyond it.

and 30 feet wide; and (3) the Holy of Holies, which was a perfect cube—30 feet long, 30 feet wide, and 30 feet high. The interior height of the rest of the building was 45 feet. Along the outside of the building were three levels of rooms, used for storage and other purposes. The interior of the building was decorated with elaborate carved woodwork. Gold also was used extensively in decorating the interior (6:1–36).

The Holy Place contained three principal items: the altar for incense, the seven-branched lamp stand, and the table for the sacred bread (shew bread, or bread of the presence). In later times, the lamp stand became a seven-branched candlestick called a *menorah.*

The Holy of Holies originally contained the sacred box, the Ark of the Covenant. At either end stood a winged creature 15 feet high. It was carved from olive wood and plated with gold. It probably had both human and animal features, designed to represent all living creatures giving praise to the LORD, whose dwelling place was the Holy of Holies. Once a year, on the solemn Day of Atonement (*Yom Kippur*), the High Priest would enter the Holy of Holies. Even he had to undergo an elaborate ceremony of cleansing before he could enter the room. His purpose was to bring before the LORD the sins of the people so that they might be forgiven. Thus, the Holy of Holies represented for Israel the meeting place between God and humankind.

In the Temple courtyard stood the great altar made of uncut stones upon which the sacrifices were made. Two huge bronze columns, named Jachin and Boaz, stood to the north and south of the entrance of the Temple. Their meaning and purpose are unknown (7:15–22). An elaborate bronze bowl called the **Molten Sea,** resting on a base made from twelve bronze bulls, also stood in the courtyard. It held about 10,000 gallons of water and may have been a reminder of the watery chaos mentioned in the Creation story and of how God overcame it to create the world (7:23–26).

All the furnishings and equipment for the Temple were made by the Phoenicians. It should not be surprising, then, that the descriptions given in the Bible match things found in Phoenician temples. The major difference seems to be that Israel's Temple contained no image of the Deity, while Phoenician temples contained many such images (7:27–51).[3]

THE DEDICATION OF THE TEMPLE (1 KINGS 8:1–66). After years of labor, the Temple was finished. The first act of Solomon was to have the Ark of the Covenant moved into its permanent home, the Holy of Holies. It was moved with elaborate precautions and with many sacrifices being offered (8:1–13).

The address and prayer of Solomon (8:14–53) emphasized the importance of the covenant with David and the building of the Temple as carrying out Solomon's responsibility in light of that covenant (8:14–26).

The Ark of the Covenant in the Old Testament

The Ark of the Covenant has often been an object of fascination for a variety of reasons. This object, which functions both as a container and as a portable Divine throne, comes and goes in the Bible. Below is a book-by-book list and description of how it appears.

Exodus—the ark is mentioned about twenty times in Exodus 25–40, which contains both God's instructions to Moses about how to make it and a description of its construction.

Leviticus—the Ark is mentioned only once, in the description of the Day of Atonement rituals in Leviticus 16.

Numbers—the Ark is mentioned six times in descriptions of its care and movement by the priests, but it is not mentioned after Numbers 14:44.

Deuteronomy—the Ark is mentioned eight times, all in Chapter 10, where Moses is recalling the making and purpose of the Ark in a speech, and in Chapter 31, when Moses and the Levites produce a "book of the law" and place it in the Ark.

Joshua—after its construction in Exodus, the Ark remains in the background for the next several books, but it becomes much more prominent in the book of Joshua, where it is mentioned more than twenty-five times, all in Joshua 3–8, as the Israelites cross the Jordan and begin conquering cities in the Promised Land.

Judges—the Ark is mentioned only once, in Judges 20:27, as an oracular object residing in Shiloh.

1 Samuel—the Ark is mentioned more than thirty times but only once after 1 Samuel 4–7, a passage sometimes called the *Ark Narrative*. 1 Samuel 14:18 is the only time Saul makes use of it.

2 Samuel—the Ark is mentioned about twenty times, more than half of these concentrated in 2 Samuel 6, where David brings the Ark to Jerusalem.

1 Kings—the Ark is mentioned about a dozen times, all in the first eight chapters, where Solomon is established as king, builds the Temple, and places the Ark in it.

1 and 2 Chronicles—of approximately forty remaining references to the Ark in the Old Testament, all but two are in 1 and 2 Chronicles, mostly in passages that parallel those in Samuel and Kings.

The last two references to the Ark in the Old Testament are in Psalm 132:8 and Jeremiah 3:16 as it seems to disappear into distant memory.

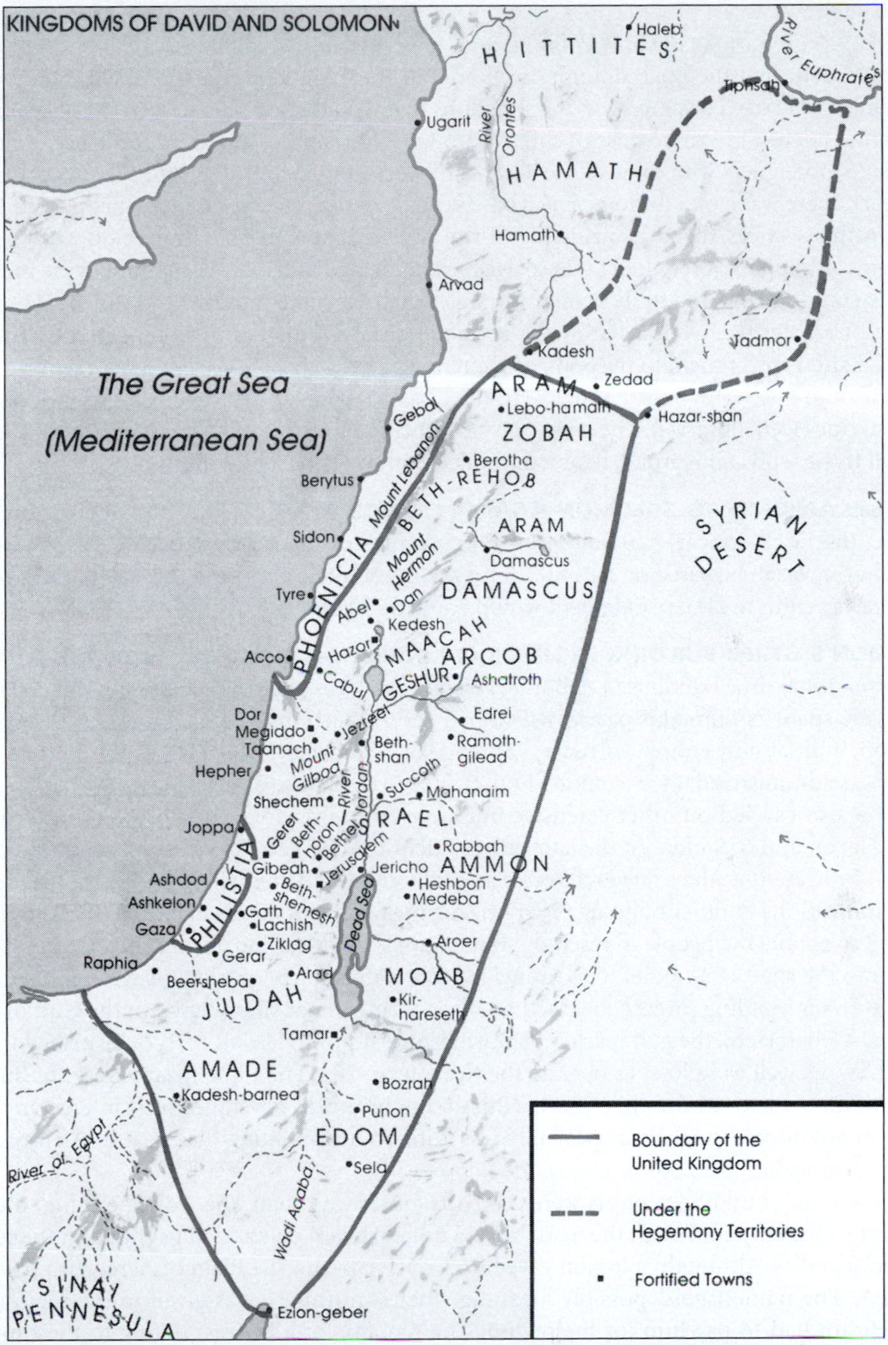

FIGURE 7–3 David's kingdom and the united monarchy. Artwork by Margaret Jordan Brown, from *Mercer Dictionary of the Bible.* © 1990, courtesy of Mercer University.

The prayer was a plea for the LORD to keep the Divine side of the covenant. The story in 1 Kings 8:27–30 is particularly important because it emphasizes what many Israelites forgot in later years—namely, that the LORD did not dwell only in the Temple in Jerusalem. No mere building could hold the LORD. The prayer lists the situations that would give rise to prayer: (1) sin against one another; (2) defeat in war because of sin; (3) drought; (4) famine caused by pestilence, mildew, or locusts; (5) foreigners who came to the Temple to worship; (6) holy war; and (7) sin against God. With each there was a plea for forgiveness based on the choice of Israel as God's people (8:31–53).

In this section, then, the principle of the covenant was in operation. God, who gave the covenant, although not required to do so, was self-obligated to Israel because of Divine mercy. An Israelite could call on God to show mercy on his behalf when he came to God in repentance. One could not expect forgiveness without a proper attitude. This theme is repeated by the great prophets and is prominent in the book of Deuteronomy.

After the people were led in praise to the LORD, to conclude the dedicatory services, elaborate festivities were observed. The seven-day feast, held at the time of the feast of Tabernacles, sent away all those who came proud, happy, and filled with roast beef and mutton (8:54–66).

THE LORD APPEARS TO SOLOMON AGAIN (1 KINGS 9:1–9). After the dedication of the Temple, the LORD appeared to Solomon. The promise of the continuance of David's line was made, but it was to be based on faithfulness to the LORD If Solomon and those who followed him turned away from the LORD, judgment would come upon Israel.

SOLOMON'S OTHER BUILDING PROJECTS (1 KINGS 7:1–12; 9:10–28; 10:14–29). Solomon spent even more time building an elaborate system of palaces and government buildings. Thirteen years were spent building his palace, which had several sections: (1) the House of the Forest of Lebanon, built almost entirely of cedar; (2) the Hall of Pillars; (3) the Hall of the Throne, where justice was administered; (4) Solomon's house; and (5) the house of his Egyptian wife.

He also carried on other extensive building programs, including projects in Jerusalem, Gezer, Hazor, and Megiddo. At the latter three, identical city gates have been found. This would seem to indicate that the same architect planned and constructed all three. Each of these cities shows indications of other building programs during Solomon's time. Elaborate shafts were constructed to enable the people to reach the water supply. At Megiddo, for instance, stone steps led down into the shaft to a tunnel. This tunnel led to a water source outside the city wall.[4]

Another building project consisted of a fleet of merchant ships, based in the Gulf of Aqaba at Ezion–Geber. Here, the gulf reaches its northernmost point. Hiram of Tyre furnished the vital know-how, as well as sailors, to operate the fleet (9:26–28). The Phoenicians were the supreme sailors of the ancient world, while Israel, with no suitable ports, developed little interest in the sea, except in Solomon's time. Trade probably was with countries along the coast of Africa and the Arabian Peninsula.

Solomon's building projects were costly in more ways than one. For one thing, they cost him part of his empire. For all the work he had done, Hiram demanded payment in the form of territorial grants. Although Solomon gave him twelve cities in the Plain of Acre, Hiram was still unhappy. The name *Cabul,* possibly meaning "that is nothing," was given to the region. Even then, Hiram had to pay him for the region. The remains of a fortress dating to the time have been found. It seems to have served as the administrative center for the area, whose local products—wine, olive oil, and cereals—were collected and stored. That these cities belonged to the northern tribes probably did nothing to increase Solomon's popularity there (9:10–14).[5]

The monetary cost was also great. Solomon got money from various sources, the most obvious of which was taxation. But that was not enough. He would also have collected tariffs from caravans that used the international highways, the Via Maris, and the King's Highway. Another source of income was international trade. Among other things, Solomon traded horses and chariots. He seems to have been the middleman in the trade between Egypt and the Asian and Mesopotamian states. An elaborate description of Solomon's luxuries (10:14–29) helps us to understand why so much money was needed in addition to the money for his building programs.[6]

The Seeds of Division (1 Kings 9:15–23; 11:1–43)

The greatest cost of maintaining Solomon's elaborate kingship was in human freedom. That cost eventually would destroy the united monarchy. Slavery made the building projects possible. It is said that "Solomon conscripted forced labor out of all Israel" (5:13) and that the non-Israelite population was enslaved to carry on the building projects (9:15, 20–23). In so doing, Solomon sowed the seeds of social unrest that eventually would erupt in rebellion. It is said that the Israelites were "the soldiers, . . . his officials, his commanders, his captains, and the commanders of his chariotry and cavalry" (9:22). Although it says that "of the Israelites Solomon made no slaves," they did have to give one month out of every three in free labor for the state.[7]

Another divisive force was Solomon's large harem. Composed of more than 1000 women, the harem functioned primarily as a status symbol. Just as a wealthy man today may collect expensive automobiles as a way of showing off his wealth, so some kings collected beautiful women. With the women, many of whom were married to Solomon to symbolize a covenant relationship with a foreign ruler, came the various deities they worshiped. Solomon's tolerance of foreign gods did not sit well with devout Israelites, especially when he built altars for these gods and even participated in worshiping them in defiance of the LORD's commands (11:1–13).

Solomon's last years saw the seeds of destruction begin to take root and grow. People on the fringes of his empire began to rebel and break away. First, it was Edom, led by Hadad, a member of its royal house who had escaped to Egypt when David conquered his country (11:14–22). Soon, Rezon, a Syrian leader, took control of Damascus (11:23–25).

More serious than either of these events were stirrings of rebellion within Israel itself. The old rivalry between Ephraim and Judah had been suppressed during David's and Solomon's time, but it still survived. Surviving with it was the belief that the LORD through a prophet should designate a leader, not a dying king who passed on the kingdom to his son. Solomon, on the other hand, seems not to have had a prophetic advisor in his court, such as Nathan had been to David. Solomon most certainly would have encouraged the idea that the LORD's covenant with David was more important than the idea that a prophet should choose the future king.

The charismatic figure around whom the dissidents rallied was Jeroboam, an Ephraimite who had been in charge of all of Solomon's forced labor. A prophet who also was a northerner, Ahijah the Shilonite, met Jeroboam one day. Taking a cloak, Ahijah tore it into twelve pieces to symbolize that an emergency existed. Ten of the pieces he gave to Jeroboam, telling him he was chosen to be leader over ten tribes, leaving only two to Solomon's house. Ahijah said that the LORD was bringing judgment upon Solomon for following foreign gods (11:26–40). Ahijah was the first independent prophet who participated in an attempt to overthrow an existing ruler who had become intolerable to the people.[8]

Word came to Solomon of Jeroboam's disloyalty. Fortunately for Jeroboam, he was able to escape to Egypt before Solomon could have him arrested, where he found refuge. Shishak, the new Pharaoh of Egypt, seems to have encouraged and protected Jeroboam, as he had other rebels and fugitives from Solomon (11:40).

The Literary Structure of Chronicles

The book of Chronicles is perhaps the most neglected book in the Old Testament. It is a story of Israel that lives in the shadow of that other story of Israel told in the books of Genesis–Kings, the Primary History. It is true that more than half of the contents of Chronicles appears in Samuel and Kings, which invites readers to look at them in parallel fashion and compare the way certain stories are told and used in each. Chronicles was almost certainly written after Samuel and Kings, so it can be assumed that the writer of Chronicles used the earlier history as a source, and that much can be learned of this writer's thinking and purpose by closely examining the differences. The result of these patterns of study is that the book of Chronicles is rarely read as a unified work of literature in its own right. Originally a single book, Chronicles is now typically divided into 1 Chronicles and 2 Chronicles. These designations will be used when necessary for references below.

The book of Chronicles opens in a surprising way. The first word in the book is *Adam*. The second word is *Seth*. The first nine chapters of 1 Chronicles are almost entirely genealogical in nature. The part of Israel's story from creation through the beginning of the monarchy is covered in a very rapid manner through this genealogical material. The story slows down slightly to tell about Saul and his family in Chapter 10, but it is David who finally receives full attention beginning in Chapter 11. As the story of David moves toward its conclusion, the attention of Chronicles turns to the temple in 1 Chronicles 22–29. Brief attention is given to priestly offices in 1 Chronicles 9, so that the rise of David and the monarchy is surrounded by issues of worship. 1 Chronicles ends with the death of David. Solomon has been anointed king and is fully prepared to begin construction on the Temple. The building of the Temple occupies the first seven chapters of 2 Chronicles. The report of the construction of this dwelling place for God matches the creation of the world and the development of Israel in the first part of 1 Chronicles. It is followed in 2 Chronicles 8–9 by the report on the remainder of Solomon's career and his death.

Second, Chronicles 10–36 describes the reigns of the rest of the kings of Judah after Solomon. Chronicles is even less interested in the northern kingdom of Israel than are Samuel and Kings. The pattern is one of general decline until the destruction of the Temple in Chapter 36. The exceptions to this pattern of decline are the reforms mounted by certain kings, such as Jehoshaphat, Hezekiah, and Josiah, which receive extended attention. The resulting story in the book of Chronicles thus highlights the establishment of institutions, the Israelite monarchy and the Jerusalem Temple, and the lives of the two great kings, David and Solomon, in alternating fashion. The story of the decline of these institutions then offers a paradigm for their reestablishment.

Finally, considerations of Chronicles as a literary work are complicated by its relationship to Ezra–Nehemiah. The last few verses of Chronicles present the Decree of Cyrus, which released the Israelites from captivity and authorized them to return to Judah. The opening verses of Ezra are a somewhat different version of this decree. The overlap connects these books in a way that is difficult to determine. The books of Chronicles and Ezra–Nehemiah are sometimes referred to collectively as the **Chronistic History.** The Hebrew canon places Chronicles at the very end, with Ezra–Nehemiah actually preceding it, a decidedly nonchronistic move. The Christian canon reverses the order of these books and moves them to the middle of the canon, immediately following Kings. This emphasizes the notion that Chronicles is secondary to Samuel and Kings, a perception from which Chronicles continues to suffer.

The End of Solomon's Reign (1 Kings 11:41–43)

After forty years of magnificence, Solomon died. He had acquired wealth, built buildings, and gained fame for his wisdom. It was during Solomon's time, furthermore, that Israelite literature began to flourish. Wisdom literature undoubtedly was rooted in Solomon's reign, making him the patron saint of Israelite wisdom. The long period of peace possibly saw the first attempts to write down Israel's history. A good example of such an attempt may have been the Court History of David. Others have conjectured that the stories of the Egyptian oppression took form then because of Solomon's oppression.[9]

But Solomon also lit the fuse for the bombs that would soon blow the kingdom apart. Excessive taxation, denial of human freedom, and religious apostasy were but a few of the problems left for Solomon's egotistical son and successor, Rehoboam, to solve. Rehoboam, unfortunately, was so self-centered that he did not even realize that any problems existed.

APPROACHING THE DIVIDED-KINGDOM STORY

Northern and Southern Perspectives

One problem in studying the divided monarchy is how to organize it. The books of 1 and 2 Kings combine the histories of the two kingdoms in order to compare the beginning of one king's reign with that of his counterpart in the other kingdom. Because this is somewhat confusing to the reader, in this discussion their histories will be divided as follows: This chapter will discuss the history of the Northern Kingdom (Israel) from the breakup of the united monarchy to the fall of Samaria in 721 B.C.E. Chapter 8 will deal with the history of the Southern Kingdom (Judah) from the breakup through the fall of Jerusalem to the Babylonians (586 B.C.E.).[10]

As the previous chapter described, the Bible contains two great historical narratives that run parallel to one another, the *Primary History* in Genesis–2 Kings and the *Chronistic History* in 1 and 2 Chronicles. The two accounts of Israel's story run in particularly close parallel beginning with David's reign. For example, the story of the division of Israel into the Northern and Southern Kingdoms, which will be the starting point for this chapter, is reported in identical fashion in 1 Kings 12:1–19 and 2 Chronicles 10:1–19. The most significant difference between the accounts of the divided kingdom in 1 Kings 12–2 Kings 24 and 2 Chronicles 10–36 is that the latter will give no attention to the Northern Kingdom, unless its activities have a direct impact on the story of the Southern Kingdom.

Chapter 6 reported on what is often called the *united monarchy*, as opposed to the *divided monarchy* after the death of Solomon. It is important to acknowledge that even within the biblical account of this story, the kingdom is never fully united. Hints of the fracture between north and south run throughout the accounts of the "unified" reigns of Saul, David, and Solomon in texts like 1 Samuel 11, 2 Samuel 2, and 1 Kings 11.

The Problem of Chronology

If one reads several books about the Old Testament, one may find different dates for the same person or event. The reason for this is that biblical calendars, unlike modern calendars, followed no universally accepted starting point. Today, the calendars of the Western world use the a medieval approximation of the date of the birth of Jesus as the starting point, a hypothetical "year one." In the ancient world, every nation had a different way of figuring dates. For the Israelites, time was figured from the beginning of a king's reign. Thus, a given event was said to have occurred "in the eighth year of King Hezekiah." How do we know when the eighth year of King Hezekiah was by our way of reckoning time?

It is necessary to pinpoint a few key dates in the history of Israel and calculate from them. Fortunately, the Assyrians and Babylonians kept accurate calendars based on the rule of their kings, which always began on the first day of the new year. Their method was to name each year after a different court official to keep it separate. In addition, important events were recorded for each year. For scholars, the most important events used for dating are eclipses, the mention of contacts with the Israelite kingdoms, and the mention of specific Israelite rulers. As a result, at least two key dates, 853 B.C.E. and 605 B.C.E., can be established. The first was the battle of Qarqar, involving the troops of Ahab, king of Israel. The mention of an eclipse within a few years of this battle is important because, if one knows where it occurred, an eclipse can be dated with precision. Qarqar is not mentioned in the Old Testament but Ahab is, so the time of his reign can be pinpointed. The same is true of the battle of Carchemish in 605 B.C.E. The records mention Jehoiakim, king of Judah. An eclipse again was the vital clue to the date.

This does not solve all the problems, but it helps. The Israelites were not always arithmetically precise in recording the length of a king's reign. For instance, Uzziah was said to have reigned for fifty-two years. Yet, when he developed leprosy, his son Jotham came to the throne as his coregent and reigned for sixteen years. In reality, the total time was somewhere between fifty-two and fifty-six years, depending on the date of Uzziah's death. This creates difficulties for one working on chronologies and is the major reason why dates vary from one scholar's scheme to another. Most authors pick what seems to be the best chronology and stay with it.

THE DIVISION OF THE KINGDOM

Rehoboam's Choice (1 Kings 12:1–19)

After the deat of Solomon, internal strife was not long in coming. Solomon was powerful enough to keep things under control as long as he lived; but his successor, Rehoboam, lacked the sound judgment needed to deal with the problems he inherited from his father.

After his coronation in Jerusalem, Rehoboam went to the old northern shrine at Shechem for another coronation by the northern tribes. The people appeared before him and asked for relief from the harsh requirements laid on them by Solomon. Rehoboam, instead of taking the advice of his senior counselors to lighten their burdens, listened to his younger friends. His arrogant answer was that if they thought things had been harsh under Solomon, they had not seen anything harsh yet (12:1–11).

The northern tribes, led by Jeroboam, revolted. Rehoboam tried to put down the rebellion by sending his labor foreman to threaten the people. They killed him by stoning, and Rehoboam barely escaped in his chariot. Thereafter, the kingdoms would be known as *Israel* and *Judah*. (From this point on, when discussing the two kingdoms, kings of Israel will be identified with [I], while kings of Judah will be identified with [J].)

Jeroboam's Reign (1 Kings 12:20–14:20)

Jeroboam was installed as king of the northern tribes, leaving only the tribe of Judah and perhaps the tribe of Benjamin under Rehoboam's control (12:20). Rehoboam raised an army to take back the northern territory, but a prophet named Shemaiah warned that such an attempt would be futile.

Jeroboam got the better part of the kingdom by almost any standard. Israel, stronger economically, had a larger population, controlled the major roads, and had the best and most productive

FIGURE 7–4 The excavated ruins of the ancient city of Bethel where, according to 1 Kings 12:28–29, King Jereboam set up two golden cows as a worship site for the Northern Kingdom of Israel.

land. Its greatest weakness was the instability of its government. No consistent way had developed for making the transition from the rule of one king to another. Israel's material assets also made it more attractive to outside powers, to which Israel was accessible by its roads. Judah, on the other hand, had the poorest land and a smaller population. It was isolated, which made it less attractive to invaders. Its greatest assets were Jerusalem, with its already rich traditions, and the Davidic monarchy, which assured stability in government.

While reading the history of the divided kingdom, one must be aware of certain things. First, the writers were from Judah, and they admired David. Because Israel opposed the Davidic monarchy and the Davidic covenant, the historians had negative feelings about anything connected with the Northern Kingdom. Second, Jerusalem (to the Deuteronomic historians) was the only place where true worship could be performed. When Jeroboam led the revolt and set up worship centers at Dan and Bethel, he chose golden calves to replace the Ark of the Covenant as the symbol of the LORD's throne. For this reason, Jeroboam was considered a worshiper of false gods by the religious leaders of Judah, and all who followed Jeroboam were put in the same category.

By choosing calves as symbols of the throne of God, Jeroboam chose the symbol of Hadad, the chief god of the **Baal** religion (12:25–33). This brought down on him the wrath of the prophets. A Judean prophet came to Bethel and pronounced the LORD's judgment upon it (13:1–3). Jeroboam tried to punish the prophet, but paralysis struck him and caused him to back down. Then, he offered to pay the prophet, but the prophet refused (13:4–10).

On his way back to Judah, the prophet was stopped by another prophet who invited him in for a meal. The Judean refused, saying that the LORD had told him not to eat in Israel. The Israelite persuaded him to do so by telling him that he had a message from the LORD that he should eat.

While they were eating, the Israelite told the Judean that he would be killed for disobeying the LORD. When the prophet was killed by a lion, the Israelite buried him and commanded that he, too, should be buried in the same tomb (13:11–32).

As further evidence of the LORD's displeasure with Jeroboam, the prophet Ahijah told Jeroboam's wife that their son Abijah would die. He said, furthermore, that Jeroboam's dynasty would be replaced. All this is an indication of the important roles that prophets played in relation to the kings of both Israel and Judah. When Jeroboam died, he was succeeded by Nadab, another of his sons (13:33–14:20).

The Succession of Kings in Israel after Jereboam (1 Kings 15:25–16:20)

After the death of Jeroboam, Israelite kings came and went with surprising rapidity. The biblical text contains no description of a selection process or anointing ceremony, and provides little detail about the reigns of these kings. This passage functions much like some of the geneologies in Genesis, as a literary "fast-forward" mechanism for the author to get to a more significant part of the story. The following is a summary of this turbulent time:

King	*Period of Reign*	*Fate*
Nadab	(901–900 B.C.E.)	Murdered by Baasha
Baasha	(900–877 B.C.E.)	Died naturally
Elah	(877–876 B.C.E.)	Murdered by Zimri
Zimri	(876 B.C.E. [7 days])	Suicide provoked by Omri
Omri	(876–864 B.C.E.)	Succeeded by his son

THE DYNASTY OF OMRI

Israel and Its Neighbors

Israel and Judah had been fortunate to survive the first fifty years following the collapse of the united monarchy in 922 B.C.E. The key to their survival came from the outside, because Egypt was powerless and no one state had achieved dominance in Mesopotamia. For a brief time, it seemed that the quiet period would end when Assyria, led by Asshur-nasirpal (884–860 B.C.E.), rose to power and pushed all the way to the Mediterranean. His conquests probably did not reach as far south as Israel, nor were they permanent. He set a standard for cruel treatment of captives that other Assyrian rulers tried to emulate. In one inscription, he said of his captives,

> I flayed as many nobles as had rebelled against me [and] draped their skins over the pile [of corpses]; . . . some I erected on stakes on the pile. . . . I flayed many right through my land [and] draped their skins over the walls.[11]

Because of such cruelties, the Assyrians were the most dreaded conquerors in the ancient Near East.

The more immediate problem for Israel was its relationship with Syria (called *Aram* in the Hebrew text). Ben-Hadad, whose reign extended from about 884 to 842 B.C.E., was strong enough to be a constant problem to Omri and his son Ahab. As a result, the two small countries alternated between being at war and being allies. When no one else threatened them, they fought each other. But whenever a threat arose from Assyria, they joined forces for mutual protection.

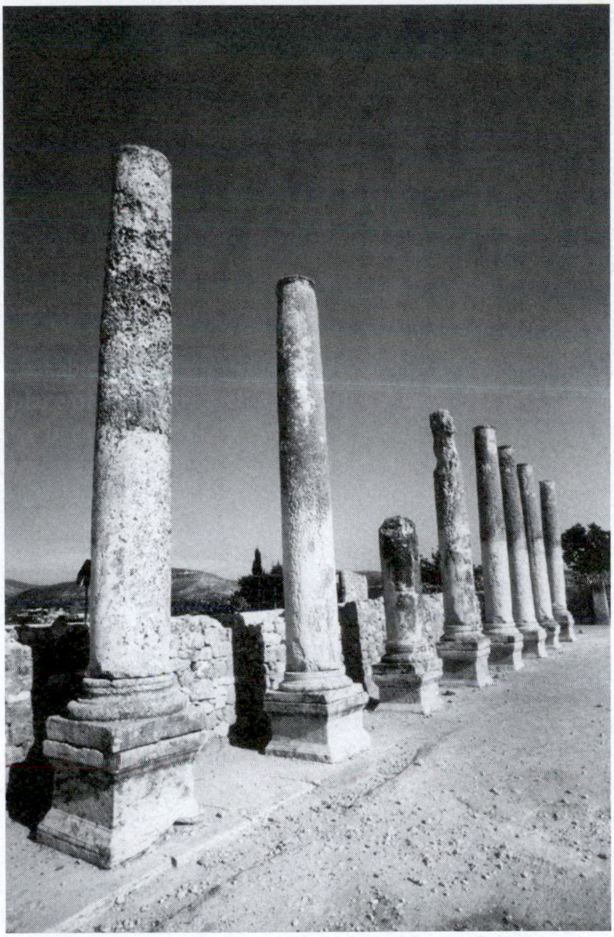

FIGURE 7–5 King Omri of the Northen Kingdom of Israel established his capital city at Samaria according to 1 Kings 16:24. This photograph shows the ruins of the palace likely used there by Omri and Ahab.

Omri also renewed with Phoenicia the old alliance that had been so profitable for both David and Solomon. To seal the covenant, Omri's son Ahab was married to Jezebel, the daughter of the king of Tyre. This marriage would have far-reaching effects upon Israelite society and religion.

Israel's relations with Judah changed for the better during the Omrid dynasty. The two kingdoms became allies, with Israel being the dominant party. To symbolize the union between the two kingdoms, Athaliah, who probably was Ahab's daughter (2 Kings 8:18, 26), was married to Jehoram of Judah.

The Influence of Omri (1 Kings 16:21–28)

Omri (I, 876–869 B.C.E.), after overcoming brief opposition from another contender named Tibni, moved quickly to organize his kingdom along the lines of the Davidic and Solomonic kingdoms. He renewed old alliances, began building programs (which Ahab extended), and moved the capital from Tirzah to the hill of Samaria.

This last accomplishment (1 Kings 16:23–24) showed something of Omri's sense of judgment. From a military standpoint, the hill of Shemer, on which Omri and Ahab built Samaria, was an excellent city site. A century later, it would take the Assyrian army several years to capture it.

By Omri's time, water was no longer the problem it had been because the Israelites had developed the cistern in the tenth century. A cistern was an underground jug dug into the rock and plastered with lime to keep it from leaking. During the rainy season, runoff water was channeled into the cisterns to be stored for the dry months.

The ruins of Omri's and Ahab's palace have been found at Samaria. The exceptionally fine masonry work enclosed an area 582 feet long by 424 feet wide. The palace, which Ahab built for Jezebel, was 89 by 79 feet. In this palace were found many ivory pieces fitting the description in 1 Kings 22:39 as "the ivory house that he built." During the Omri–Ahab years, extensive building programs were carried out in other cities, including Megiddo.[12] Omri's power and influence can also be seen in the fact that, many years after his death, Israel was known in Assyrian records as "the land of Omri." The Moabite Stone (found in 1868) also gives an account of how Moab was conquered by Omri and lists the annual tribute or bribe the Moabites had to pay to Israel. Mesha, the king of Moab who erected the stone, threw off Israelite control during Ahab's wars with Syria.[13]

Despite Omri's achievements, the biblical writer only mentions that he built Samaria and that "he did more evil than all who were before him" (1 Kings 16:25–28).

The Reign of Ahab (I, 869–850 B.C.E.) (1 Kings 16:29–22:4)

As far as the biblical writer was concerned, the news about **Ahab** was bad—first, last, and always. He was worse than his father, Omri (16:30). He married **Jezebel,** an ardent worshiper of the Canaanite god Baal, and he worshiped her gods. He also built altars to Baal and made an idol to represent Asherah, Baal's mistress. The implication is that he gave approval to human sacrifice as part of worship (16:31–34).

Aside from the Bible, Ahab, in purely secular terms, was a much more impressive ruler. As excavations at Megiddo, at Samaria, and now at Dor on the coastal plain attest, Ahab was a prodigious builder, "the greatest of the builder kings between Solomon and Herod." What once were thought to be Solomon's stables at Megiddo are now credited to Ahab. In the military realm, Ahab was able to supply 2000 war chariots for the western alliance against Shalmaneser III at the battle of Qarqar.[14]

Elijah Among the Prophets

Elijah was not the first **prophet**, but he significantly expanded the role of the prophetic figure, andin later Jewish tradition, he became the symbol of the ideal prophet, as Moses was the symbol of the ideal lawgiver (Luke 9:30, 33). Before examining Elijah, it may be helpful to look at the whole idea of prophecy as it was practiced in Israel and Judah in the time of the monarchy. (In this discussion, the term *Israel* will apply to all the people, north and south, not just those of the Northern Kingdom.)

Israel was not alone in having prophets. Balaam (Num. 22:1–24:25) was not an Israelite, as both the Bible and a recently found inscription show.[15] Mari, a city in northern Mesopotamia, had prophets who gave oracles (sayings) in much the same manner as the Israelite prophets.[16,17] Furthermore, as later discussions will show, not all Israelite prophets were admirable men. Some simply were "yes men" to the kings. But the true prophets of Israel were in a class by themselves.

Canaanite Fertility Religion

One of Israel's major problems from the day it entered Palestine was what to do about the Canaanite culture and religion. The harsh demands for a holy war were one attempt to deal with the problem. Israel's leaders were intelligent enough to know that the sexually oriented religion of the Canaanites would make the more demanding requirements of the worship of the LORD harder to live by. For this reason, the uncompromising demands of the holy war, if carried out, would eliminate not only the religious shrines, but all who taught the religion.

But although holy war may have been practiced occasionally, it was not on a large scale. Israel failed to conquer the land completely. Instead, the Canaanites were absorbed into the population, even when Canaanite lands were taken. With the Canaanites came their culture and religion.

Imagine what it would be like to be Sam Israelite, who comes from the desert fringe, where his principal occupation has been that of a shepherd. Suddenly, he finds himself in possession of a house and land of his own. He is now a farmer. He plants his crops, but they fail. He has a Canaanite neighbor who plants his crops and they produce abundantly.

He goes to his neighbor, Joe Canaanite, and says, "Say, Joe, how is it that your barley looks so much better than mine?"

Joe answers, "Why, Sam, the problem with your crops is that you worship the wrong god. Your god was okay when it came to warfare, but he is just not experienced at growing crops. Come with me tomorrow to the shrine of Hadad. We are having our spring fertility dance and, man, are those temple girls beauties. After all, Baal really knows how to make that barley grow!" It is not hard to imagine what many Israelite men would have done in that case.

It was this religion that Jezebel was so ardently promoting in Israel. She also donated money to it. In the court alone, there were 450 prophets of Baal and 400 prophets of Asherah (1 Kings 18:19). Baalism threatened to sweep over the land, but one man—the prophet Elijah—stemmed the tide.

Three Hebrew terms are used to describe the prophets. Two of them, *ro'eh* and *hozeh*, are often translated as "seer." The third word is *navi'*, which probably meant "one who speaks for another." Thus, Aaron was the *navi'* for Moses, because he was the one who spoke for Moses (Exod. 7:1). Moses, of course, was also desgnated as a *navi'*, because he spoke for God (Deut. 34:10). *Seer* was a term used earlier to describe the prophets, but by the time of the great prophets in the eighth to sixth centuries B.C.E., it was more of a derogatory term.

Two other related terms used to talk about prophets and prophecy in the ancient Near East were *ecstatic* and *diviner*. Ecstatics were prophets whose prophecy came as part of an altered physical state, such as a trance or a frenzy. This was what was meant when Saul was described as being among the prophets (1 Sam. 10:10–13). Ecstatic prophets did strange things and had strange experiences. Diviners, on the other hand, read the signs of nature, such as the patterns of the clouds or the patterns of the internal organs of animals, somewhat like the reading of palms or tea leaves today. None of the great prophets were diviners in this sense of the word, but a number of them (especially Ezekiel) did have some characteristics of the ecstatics.

Up until the time of Elijah, most of the prophets mentioned in the story of the Israelite monarchy held official positions as royal advisors. Samuel, Gad, and Nathan often provided divine counsel for Israel's early kings. At a later point, Isaiah also functioned in this role. Of course, their work could include confronting the king about disobedient behavior, such as Samuel did with Saul (1 Sam. 13:8–15) and Nathan did with David (2 Sam. 12:1–15). Elijah, however, is portrayed as a prophet entirely outside of the palace. His interactions with royal leaders were only confrontational, and they did not seek his advice. Thus, Elijah separates the institutions of palace and prophecy, and creates a distinct and independent role for prophets in the story of Israel.

These characteristics marked Israel's prophets:

1. They claimed to speak for God, often introducing their sayings with formulas like "Thus says the LORD."
2. They were courageous persons, unafraid to deliver their message, regardless of the personal danger involved.
3. They were moral persons who preached a message that demanded the highest moral living from their hearers.
4. They were compassionate persons, sensitive to the difficulties of the poor and the oppressed.
5. They were sensitive persons, aware of what was happening in the world around them and convinced that the LORD was in control of events.

Two other common misunderstandings of Old Testament prophets need to be mentioned. First, the prophets were primarily concerned with their own time and what was about to happen to their people. The desire to turn their messages into elaborate and esoteric predictions about the distant future can often obscure the meaning of what they were saying. Their message has meaning for later generations, including ours today, because they were applying divine principles to the human problems they saw right in front of them. This is still the task of religion. Second, time was the sure test of the validity of a prophet's message. Readers often look back on these situations in the Old Testament and wonder how the audiences of the prophets ignored or misunderstood such obvious messages, but many times it was very difficult to distinguish between the contradictory messages of two prophets. Naturally, the people often preferred the word of the prophet with the more positive message. The same problem is with us today.

ELIJAH'S CONFRONTATIONS WITH AHAB AND JEZEBEL

Although there is no book in the Bible that bears Elijah's name, he is given more space in the Deuteronomistic History than any other prophet, including Isaiah and Jeremiah.

Elijah was a mysterious person. He would appear, give an oracle (pronouncement), and disappear. He was a prophet of doom and a man who could be both courageous and cowardly. His first confrontation was with Ahab. He appeared before Ahab to tell him that there would be a three-year drought in Israel. The point was that Baal, whom worshipers claimed could bring rain, was to be challenged at his own game (17:1). Elijah finished his immediate task and returned to the eastern side of the Jordan, where he was in familiar territory and safe from Ahab's clutches (17:2–5). When the drought began to devastate the Transjordan, Elijah, at the LORD's command, went to Phoenicia, where he stayed with a widow and her son. The presence of the man of God in her home brought prosperity to her and restored her son to life after he died (17:8–24).

Things were bad in Israel—so bad, in fact, that the king himself went out looking for water for the royal animals. Accompanying Ahab was Obadiah. Unknown to Ahab and Jezebel, during a purge by Jezebel, Obadiah had been responsible for saving one hundred prophets of the LORD (18:1–6).

When Obadiah and Ahab separated to increase their chances of finding water, Obadiah met Elijah. Elijah asked Obadiah to tell Ahab that he wanted to see him. Obadiah was afraid that if he did, Elijah would disappear again. Finally, Obadiah was convinced and agreed to do as Elijah asked (18:7–16).

FIGURE 7–6 "Ahab took as his wife Jezebel . . . and went and served Baal, and worshiped him" (1 Kings 16:31). Baal was the god of the storm, and thus the god of fertility, since water was essential for the growth of crops. This stele (stone monument) of Baal, which is from the nineteenth or eighteenth century B.C.E., is from Ras Shamra. It shows the god holding a bolt of lightning.

King and prophet confronted each other, each accusing the other of being a "troubler of Israel." Then Elijah issued a challenge: Bring the people and all the Baal prophets to Mount Carmel for a test of strength (18:17–19).

Ahab took up the challenge and did as Elijah proposed. Mount Carmel was an ancient worship site, a mountain that juts out into the Mediterranean Sea on Palestine's northern coast. Its height causes clouds blowing in from the sea to release their moisture, so that the vegetation stays green longer there than in any other place in Israel. The sure sign of severe drought was when the vegetation on top of Mount Carmel withered (Amos 1:2). Thus, it was a favorite shrine for Baal worshipers. Like Moses' challenge to Pharaoh by the Nile, Elijah was issuing a challenge from the LORD to play the contest on Baal's home court (18:20).

The people gathered. Elijah challenged them to follow either Baal or the LORD. Then he challenged the 450 Baal prophets to prepare a sacrifice. They were to call on Baal to ignite the fire, as he was the god of storm and fire (lightning). Elijah would do the same thing and would call on the LORD. The god who answered by fire would be the winner. The people agreed and pledged to follow the god whose power was revealed (18:21–24).

The Baalites prepared their sacrifice and began a day-long ritual designed to evoke Baal's response. Doing a sort of limping dance, they circled the altar crying, "O Baal, answer us!" Noon came, but there was no response from Baal. Elijah made sarcastic remarks and suggested that they were not crying loud enough, that Baal was meditating, relieving himself, traveling, or perhaps just sleeping. The frenzy among the prophets increased. They cut themselves, hoping that the flow of blood would cause rain to fall. "But there was no voice, no answer, no response" (18:25–29). The rain did not come. Baal had failed.

When evening came, the exhausted Baalites gave up their futile efforts. Elijah went into action. He built an altar, prepared the sacrificial bull (which, ironically, was the symbol of Baal), and then soaked everything thoroughly with water. Elijah's prayer was simple:

> "O LORD, God of Abraham, Isaac, and Israel, let it be known this day that you are the God in Israel, that I am your servant, and that I have done all these things at your bidding. Answer me, O LORD, answer me, so that this people may know that you, O LORD, are God, and that you have turned their hearts back." Then the fire of the LORD fell. (18:36–38)

What happened on Mount Carmel? Some say that lightning appeared; others say that the water contained petroleum or gas. What happened really defies explanation, but it was a vital moment in the history of a people. The LORD had beaten Baal at his own game by bringing rain when Baal could not. Elijah took a practical approach to limiting the power of Baalism. He called upon the people, who seized the Baal prophets and killed them, even as Jezebel had killed the prophets of the LORD. Elijah did not stop Baalism completely, but he dealt it such a severe setback that it, at least, did not envelop Judah as much as it had Israel (18:30–40).

When the rains came, Ahab had to ride furiously to get down the mountain. Elijah showed his ability as a distance runner by outrunning Ahab's chariot to Jezreel, some seventeen miles away. It was just a warm-up for his encounter with Jezebel (18:41–46).

Courageous Elijah soon became cowardly Elijah when Jezebel heard what he had done to her prophets. She sent him word that when she got her hands on him, it would be the end of him. Elijah decided that it was time for him to beat a hasty retreat.

Being an experienced runner, he lost no time in putting distance between himself and Jezebel. His servant could not keep up, so Elijah left him at Beersheba and continued south toward Sinai. In the wilderness, where he stopped to rest, he prayed to the LORD to take his life. Instead, he awoke to find food. After eating, he continued his journey (19:1–8).

Arriving at Horeb (Sinai), Elijah rested in a cave. While he was there, the LORD appeared (theophany) with an accusing question: "What are you doing here, Elijah?" (19:9). Instead of answering the question, Elijah complained that he was the only faithful servant of the LORD left. Told to go stand on the mountain, he experienced wind, earthquake, and fire, but the LORD did not appear in any of the natural phenomena. Instead, in the quietness following the tumult, a still, small voice asked the same accusing question: "What are you doing here, Elijah?" (19:13). Elijah gave the same whining excuse (19:14). The answer came back: "Get up and get busy. There are seven thousand people in Israel who are still faithful" (19:9–18). On his return, he found a new disciple named Elisha (19:19–21).

The most dangerous enemy Ahab had was Ben-hadad of Syria. Warfare between the two kingdoms was frequent, each side winning some and losing some. Ben-hadad laid siege to Samaria and took tribute, as well as Ahab's wives and children. Ahab, on the advice of an unknown prophet, launched a surprise attack and routed the Syrians. Later, in a battle at Aphek in Transjordan near the Sea of Galilee, Israel defeated Syria and took Ben-hadad prisoner. He pleaded for his life and agreed to grant Ahab business concessions in Damascus. Ahab agreed to let Ben-hadad go. The unknown prophet rebuked the king for freeing Ben-hadad to fight again. The prophet had seen the war as a holy war in which Ben-hadad should have been killed (20:1–43).

Naboth's story illustrates the changes that were taking place in Israel. On the surface Ahab's offer to buy his land seems fair, but Naboth's refusal to sell illustrates the strong sense of responsibility that Naboth had to preserve the family inheritance for his children. It was a legacy to be passed on from generation to generation.

When Naboth refused, Ahab went home and sulked. Jezebel found out the cause of his unhappiness and set out to get Ahab what he wanted (21:1–7).

Skillfully using the law to the advantage of the royal house, Jezebel bribed the village elders to call a meeting of the group, of which Naboth probably was a member. Then she hired two of the most dishonest witnesses that money could buy to swear that they had heard Naboth curse God and the king. Two witnesses were required by the law to prove any charge (Deut. 17:6). The penalty for blasphemy (cursing God) was death by stoning. After Naboth was accused, tried, and convicted, the sentence was carried out (21:8–14). To compound the tragedy, Naboth's supposed crime also made his sons liable to the death penalty, thus effectively eliminating any heirs for the property within his family (2 Kings 9:26).

The story of Naboth's land illustrates two important matters: (1) the role of the prophet as the conscience of the nation and (2) the transition of Israelite society from a nation of small, independent landowners to one in which most of the land was owned by a few wealthy men. This left the rest of the population more or less at the mercy of the rich.

With the last obstacle out of the way, Ahab took over Naboth's land. When he went to inspect it, however, the first person he saw was Elijah. Elijah pronounced the LORD's judgment upon Ahab and his family, and more specifically upon Jezebel. He said she would be eaten by dogs. This was the most disgraceful thing that could happen to a person. Ahab repented, but it stayed the execution for only a little while (21:15–29).

More Stories of Kings and Prophets

Before the incident described here, an important historical event had taken place. In 853 B.C.E., at Qarqar on the Orontes River in northwestern Syria, Shalmaneser III of Assyria fought against an alliance of western kings, including Ahab of Israel and Ben-hadad of Syria. They, along with other small kingdoms, patched up their differences long enough to face a common enemy. A measure of Ahab's prosperity can be seen in the fact that he furnished 2000 war chariots, half of the total number of chariots used by the western alliance. The importance of this battle lies in the fact that it can be dated precisely and thus is an invaluable aid in dating events in the Old Testament.[18]

Three years later (850 B.C.E.), Ahab and Ben-hadad were ready to go at it again. The bone of contention was Ramoth–Gilead, a border city in Transjordan. Ahab (I) called on Jehoshaphat (J) to go to battle with him to recapture Ramoth–Gilead (22:1–4).

After assembling his troops and making it obvious what he was about to do, Ahab took Jehoshaphat's advice and consulted his 400 court prophets. They saw what the king wanted to do and, because he fed and clothed them, they were not about to contradict his wishes. So, with one accord, the 400 told Ahab to go into battle and the LORD would give him victory. Jehoshaphat could not accept that much agreement and asked if there was another prophet. Ahab replied that there was one, Micaiah ben Imlah, but that he was a negative thinker who was always predicting doom (25:5–12).

At Jehoshaphat's urging, Micaiah was called. When he seemed to agree with the 400, Ahab was suspicious. Then Micaiah gave an oracle predicting the death of the king. He told of being in the heavenly council (a way of emphasizing that the message was the LORD's, not his) and hearing the LORD say that he would cause Ahab's prophets to lie to him (22:13–23).[19]

Ahab accepted the advice he wanted to accept and went to war. He left orders for Micaiah to be jailed and fed bread and water until he returned. Micaiah's last word was that if Ahab returned, the LORD had not spoken by him (22:24–28).

Ahab died in the battle, bleeding to death from a chance shot by a Syrian archer. When they returned his body to Samaria, harlots washed themselves in the water made bloody from washing his chariot. The water presumably gave them special appeal. The fate of Micaiah is unknown (22:29–40).

The only reason Ahaziah rated any notice was that he was consulting a pagan god about an injury he had received. When Elijah heard of it, he sent word to Ahaziah that he would die. When Ahaziah sent soldiers to arrest Elijah, they met with disaster. Finally, he pleaded for Elijah to come. When Elijah went, he simply repeated his judgment—that Ahaziah would die because he consulted a pagan god (2 Kings 1:1–18).

Shortly afterward, **Elisha,** Elijah's assistant, was told by a group of prophets that Elijah was going to be taken away in a whirlwind. Elisha did not want to accept this prophecy. When it happened, Elijah's **mantle** was left for Elisha, symbolizing his role as Elijah's successor. Other prophets saw Elisha as Elijah's successor and joined with him, making him their mentor. Unlike Elijah, who was a very private person, Elisha was more of a public figure and a political activist. As a result, many miracle stories were told about him (2:1–25).

The relation of Mesha of Moab to Israel was that of vassal, described in the Moabite Stone. During the Israelite–Syrian wars, he broke away. Jehoram (I) and Jehoshaphat (J) went on an expedition against Mesha. When they saw him sacrifice his son to his pagan god, they were horrified and turned back.

Stories about Elisha (2 Kings 4:1–9:14)

Numerous stories grew out of Elisha's ministry. Like Elijah, he was said to have helped a poor widow (4:1–7). His prayer to the LORD was credited with making fruitful a barren woman who had befriended him. Later, he restored her child to life when it died (4:8–37). He was said to have made poisonous stew safe to eat and to have multiplied loaves of bread (4:38–44).

One of the most famous stories is about the healing of Naaman, a Syrian army commander, of **leprosy.** Naaman had heard of Elisha through an Israelite slave girl. When

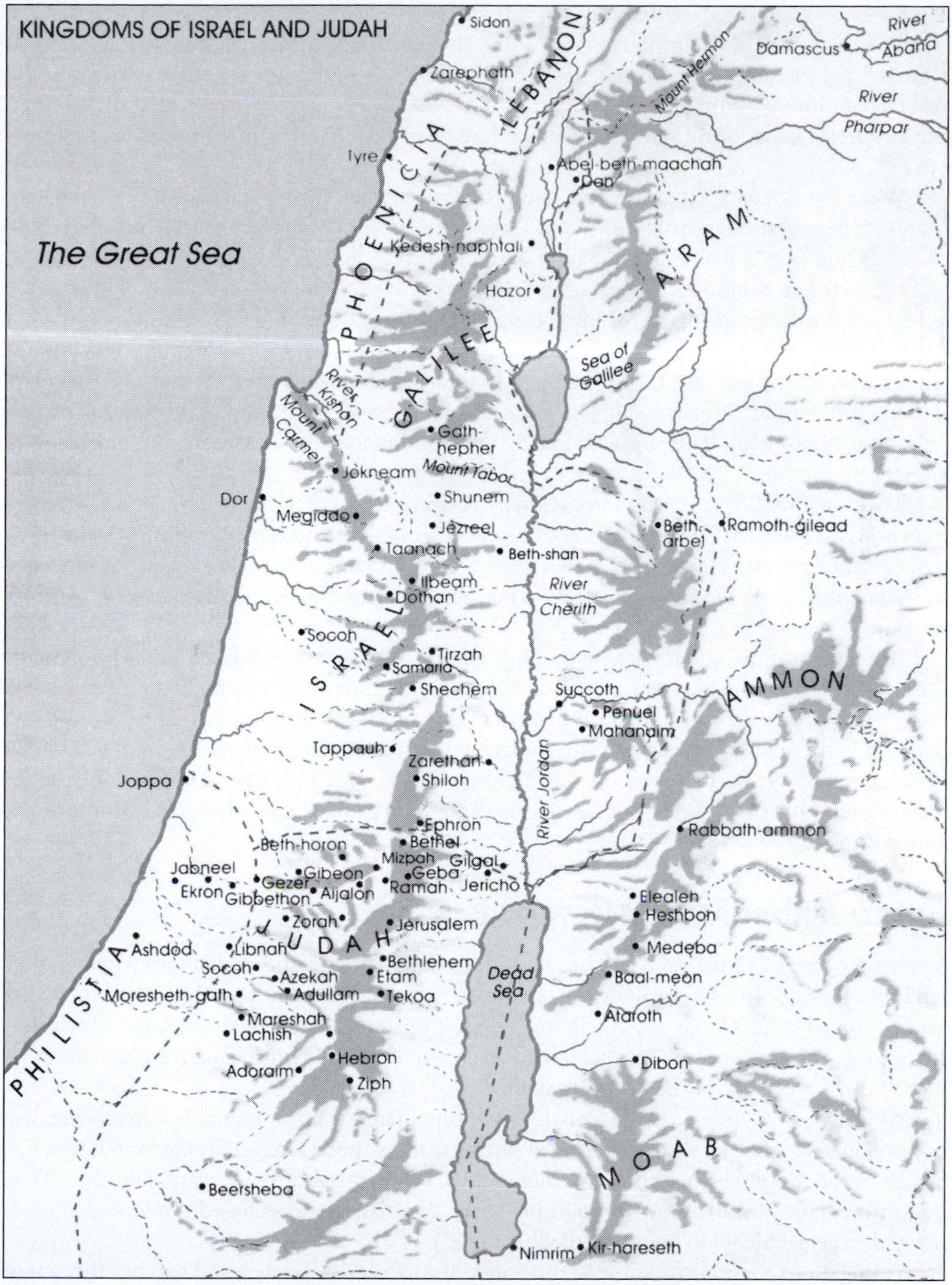

FIGURE 7–7 Israel and Judah—850 B.C.E. Artwork by Margaret Jordan Brown, from Mercer Dictionary of the Bible. © 1990, courtesy of Mercer University Press.

Naaman came to Elisha, he offered to pay for the cure. Elisha refused but instructed Naaman to wash seven times in the Jordan River. When the leprosy disappeared, he tried again to pay Elisha, but the payment was refused. Then Gehazi, Elisha's servant, saw a chance for some easy money. He followed Naaman and, telling him that Elisha had changed his mind, took Naaman's money. When Elisha found out what Gehazi had done, he cursed him with Naaman's leprosy (5:1–27).

When Ben-hadad, king of Syria, tried to attack Israel, Elisha warned the Israelites and frustrated Ben-hadad's plans. Ben-hadad gave orders for Elisha's capture, but they failed (6:8–23). Then Ben-hadad attacked Samaria and laid siege to it. Food became so scarce that the people resorted to cannibalism. Because Elisha had provoked the king (probably Jehoram), he was blamed for the problems in Samaria, causing Jehoram to seek to arrest him. When the men came to Elisha's house, he told them that food would be plentiful by the next day. Having been frightened by noises of what they thought was an army about to attack them, the Syrian army fled during the night. Four Israelite lepers found their abandoned camp and brought the news to the city (6:24–7:20). The supplies left by the Syrians fell to the Samaritans, fulfilling the prophet's prediction.

The final mention of Elisha shows him as a political activist. Called by the ill Ben-hadad of Syria to predict whether he would die, Elisha confirmed that he would, sending word by the messenger Hazael and telling him that Hazael would be king in his place. Hazael returned to Ben-hadad and made Elisha's prediction come true—he smothered Ben-hadad and seized the throne (8:7–15).

In the meantime, Judah also had a king named Jehoram (849–842 B.C.E.), who managed to lose control of Edom. He married Athaliah, Ahab's daughter. When he died, their son Ahaziah (J, 842 B.C.E.) succeeded him. Ahaziah died that year (8:16–29). Jehoram of Israel (Joram) was killed in a battle that same year by Jehu, a chariot commander in his army. Jehoram's death and Ahaziah's death were the direct result of an action of Elisha. He chose Jehu to be king of Israel and commissioned him to destroy the family of Ahab. Jehu's army unit supported him and proclaimed him king (9:1–13).

JEHU TO JEROBOAM II (842–746 B.C.E.)

The century from 842 to 746 B.C.E. began with a violent purge and ended with the Northern Kingdom's most glorious days, under Jeroboam II. Although the Assyrians flourished for a short time and forced Israel's kings to pay tribute, their last serious threat came from Adad-nirari II. He destroyed Syrian power in 802 B.C.E., but he was unable to follow up his advantage. Syria and Assyria both were weak for the next fifty years.[20]

After Jehu was anointed king (9:1–13), he immediately set out to establish his power. King Jehoram (Joram) of Israel was recovering at Jezreel from wounds received in the Syrian war. King Ahaziah of Judah was visiting him. Jehu met the two kings at Naboth's vineyard. Jehoram (I) was killed immediately by an arrow through his heart. Ahaziah (J) was chased down and shot. He managed to get to Megiddo before he died (9:14–29).

Going on to Jezreel, Jehu came to the house of Ahab's wife, Jezebel, and had her thrown out of a second-story window into the street. When soldiers came by later to pick up the body, all but her hands had been eaten by dogs (9:30–37). Then Jehu systematically slaughtered all the relatives of Ahab, as well as his close advisers. Ironically, if the reference to Jehu as "the son of Omri" on the Black Obelisk of Shalmaneser III of Assyria is correct, Jehu was killing members of his own family![21] In addition, he killed relatives of the Judean king who had come north to visit

(10:1–17). Pretending he was a Baal worshiper, he called a meeting of Baal worshipers. When they gathered together, they too were slaughtered (10:18–31).

What Jehu did was the equivalent of a new president's taking office and having all members of the former president's family, all his advisers, and all government workers killed. It also had the same effects that such a purge would have on the government of the United States—Jehu's new government was very unskilled. Later on, Hosea, an eighth-century prophet of Israel, would condemn the bloodthirstiness of Jehu. Jehu lost territory to Syria (10:32–36) and paid tribute to Shalmaneser III of Assyria in 841 B.C.E.

The next two Israelite kings were not particularly distinguished. Jehoahaz (I, 815–801 B.C.E.) was reduced by the Syrians to a military weakling. His successor, Jehoash (I, 801–786 B.C.E.), had a bit more success than his father, because the Assyrians had virtually destroyed Syria in 801 B.C.E. It was during his reign that Elisha died (13:1–25).

Israel's last burst of prosperity came during the reign of Jeroboam II, who combined with Uzziah of Judah (J, 783–742 B.C.E.) to extend the limits of the Hebrew kingdoms to those achieved during the days of David and Solomon. Such prosperity was made possible by two things: (1) Assyria's defeat of Syria in 801 B.C.E., combined with Assyria's own fifty-year weakness after that event, and (2) the talents of Jeroboam as a military leader and civil administrator. Uzziah of Judah seems to have been equally talented. While condemning his religious failures, the narrator speaks volumes in one verse about Jeroboam:

> He restored the border of Israel from Lebo-hamath as far as the sea of the Arabah, according to the word of the LORD, the God of Israel, which he spoke by his servant Jonah son of Amatti, the prophet, who was from Gath-hepher. (14:25)

Even the Syrian capital of Damascus came under Israelite control.

Another quick succession of kings in Israel (2 Kings 15:8–31). After Jeroboam's death, if one became king in Israel, it was almost a guarantee that he would be murdered. Had there been an insurance company to insure the lives of kings, it almost certainly would have been bankrupted.

FIGURE 7–8 "The time that Jehu reigned over Israel in Samaria was twenty-eight years" (2 Kings 10:36). Jehu's reign began with a bloodbath and ended in submission. "Jehu, son of Omri," is shown in an artist's representation of a panel of the Black Obelisk on display in the British Museum. He is paying tribute to Shalmaneser III of Assyria. Courtesy of The British Museum. Drawn by Buford Winfrey.

The following table lists the four kings of Israel immediately following Jeroboam, the length of their reign, and the fate of each:

King	*Period of Reign*	*Fate*
Zechariah	(746–745 B.C.E.)	Murdered by Shallum
Shallum	(745 B.C.E.[1 month])	Murdered by Menahem
Menahem	(745–738 B.C.E.)	Became Assyrian vassal
Pekahiah	(738–737 B.C.E.)	Murdered by Pekah

Pekah (I), Jotham (J), Ahaz (J), and the Syro–Ephraimitic War (2 Kings 15:27–16:20; see also Isa. 7:1–25). As the threat from the Assyrian **Empire** approached, the story of the two kingdoms becomes entangled, and it is difficult to keep them separate as they dealt with this common threat. At the beginning of the reign of Pekah (I, 737–732 B.C.E.), the Assyrians struck against the northern region of Israel (later known as *Galilee*). Pekah probably had failed to pay the required money into the Assyrian treasury. At the same time, Jotham (J, 742?–735 B.C.E.) was ruling in Judah, having been coregent with Uzziah for many years. A coregent was one who carried out the king's duties when the king was unable to perform them.

Jotham was succeeded by Ahaz (J, 735–715 B.C.E.), his son. Pekah, smarting under Assyrian rule, tried to stir up a rebellion against Assyria. In that action, he was supported by Rezin, king of Syria. When Ahaz refused to join, Pekah and Rezin threatened to invade Judah and put their own man on the throne.

Israel and Syria did attack Judah in 734 B.C.E., but the attack was unsuccessful, just as the prophet Isaiah had told King Ahaz (Isa. 7:1–25). Ahaz, however, put more trust in Assyria's armed might than he did in the prophet's promises. He carried a huge bribe to Tiglath-pileser to buy his favor. Ahaz went out of his way to prove his loyalty to Tiglath, even to the extent of setting up a bronze altar to the chief Assyrian deity in the Temple court. In addition, he commanded that regular sacrifices be made to the deity (16:1–20).

Meanwhile, back in Israel, disaster was developing. Tiglath probably needed no encouragement from Ahaz to invade. In 734 B.C.E., he followed the international highway south, knocking out Philistine cities that were also involved in the rebellion. Then, he reduced Israel to a few square miles of territory in the central hill country surrounding Samaria. In 732 B.C.E., he destroyed Damascus, killed Rezin, and added Syria to his empire (16:9).

With the fall of Samaria, the kingdom of Israel disappeared, never to rise again. The biblical writers saw the LORD at work in its downfall, just as Amos and Hosea saw its inevitable ruin. The narrators named Jeroboam I as the chief culprit. He had brought about the division of the kingdom and had introduced the golden calves as objects of worship (17:7–23).

Assyria's policy of switching populations among its vassal states was continued in the Northern Kingdom by Shalmaneser and Sargon II. That action would produce a mixed race of people known in later times as the *Samaritans.* That result came about when the new inhabitants intermarried with the poor people who had been left in the land. The mixing of cultures included a mixing of religions. This mixed religion would be looked down upon with contempt by later Jews because they felt the true worship of the LORD had been corrupted (17:24–41).

THE DESTRUCTION OF THE NORTHERN KINGDOM

Hoshea (I, 732–722/21 B.C.E.), Israel's last king (2 Kings 17:1–41). Hoshea, like most of his immediate predecessors, became king by murder. Pekah became his victim in 732 B.C.E. Hoshea played the role of the obedient servant to Assyria for a time, but when Tiglath-pileser died in

727 B.C.E., Hoshea got ideas about rebellion. The change of kings always was a time of testing, because major empires, like Assyria, also had those who coveted the kingship enough to murder for it. The vassal states hoped for a power struggle, thus giving them an opportunity to regain their freedom from the overlords, who were beset with internal problems.

Hoshea had chosen an inadequate ally when he appealed to Egypt for help. Egypt was like an aged man who had been living on a starvation diet. It could hardly support itself, much less offer help in a rebellion against Assyria. Shalmaneser V of Assyria (726–722 B.C.E.) struck Samaria in 725 B.C.E. and besieged the city. That siege showed that Omri had chosen well when he moved the capital to Samaria. It took the armies of Assyria three years to capture it in 722/722 B.C.E. (17:1–6).

When the Assyrians, led by Sargon II, finally were able to break down Israel's last remaining stronghold, Samaria, in 722/721 B.C.E., the Northern Kingdom died. Although some think Sargon's brother, Shalmaneser, actually was the one who did it (2 Kings 17:1–6; 18:9–12), Sargon took the credit and boasted that he removed 27,290 captives to other locations and, in turn, repopulated the city with captives from other territories that he had captured.

Apparently the Assyrian notion of how to run an empire involved forced removal and resettlement of peoples. The Bible itself provides very little information about the Northern Kingdom after this event, but this would explain the apparent end of the northern tribes as an identifiable political or social entity. Judah was able to avoid destruction by the Assyrian Empire, although it is unclear exactly how. King Ahaz of Judah did not join in the alliance against Assyria with Israel and Syria, but seems to have made an arrangement with Assyria that likely involved the payment of tribute. Assyria threatened Judah again during the reign of Hezekiah. 2 Kings 19 reports the mysterious death of nearly 200,000 Assyrian soldiers who were on the brink of an invasion of Judah. This part of the story will be addressed more fully in the next chapter.

Key Terms and Names

Study Questions

1. How was Solomon's reign more like that of other Eastern kings rather than like his father's reign?
2. How did David's reign pave the way for Solomon's success?
3. What were Solomon's strengths and weaknesses as a king?
4. What were the major sections of Solomon's Temple and the function of each?
5. How did Solomon pay for his building projects?
6. What two dates are pivotal for the development of chronologies for the Old Testament, and how are they determined?
7. What factors contributed to the negative reaction of the northern tribes to Rehoboam?
8. What advantages and disadvantages did Jeroboam have as he began his rule over the Northern Kingdom (Israel)?
9. Why was Israel called the *land of Omri* for many years after that king's short reign?
10. Why was Omri able to make Samaria his capital, and what were its advantages?
11. Why did the worship of Baal appeal to the Israelites so strongly?
12. How were the messages of the great prophets related to the future?

13. What were the issues in Elijah's contest with Baal's prophets on Mount Carmel?
14. Why did Ahab handle Elijah differently from the way Jezebel dealt with him?
15. What changes in Israelite society does the story of Naboth reflect?
16. Who was Miciah ben Imlah? What is his significance in the story of Ahab?
17. How are the portrayals of Elijah and Elisha alike, and how do they differ?
18. In what ways did Jehu's purge of the house of Omri contribute to the instability of Israel?
19. What international conditions made it possible for Israel and Judah to flourish during the reigns of Jeroboam II and Uzziah?
20. How might Jeroboam's reign be evaluated from a purely political perspective?

Endnotes

1. Richard Elliott Friedman, *Who Wrote the Bible?* (Upper Saddle River, NJ: Prentice Hall, 1987), 44.
2. For a different view on the location of Sheba, see Stephen D. Ricks, "Sheba, Queen of," *ABD*, V, 1170–1171.
3. For what is known about Solomon's Temple, see Victor Hurowitz, "Inside Solomon's Temple," *BR*, X, 2 (April 1994), 24–37, 50.
4. G. Ernest Wright, *Biblical Archaeology*, 2nd ed. (Philadelphia: Westminster Press, 1960), 129ff. On the city gate and the Hazor water system, see Yigael Yadin, *Hazor* (Oxford: Oxford University Press, 1992), 187–247. It has excellent drawings plus black-and-white photographs.
5. Zvi Gal, "Cabul: A Royal Gift Found," *BAR*, XIX, 2 (March–April 1993), 39–44, 84.
6. Alan R. Millard, "Does the Bible Exaggerate Solomon's Golden Wealth?" *BAR*, XV, 3 (May–June 1989), 20–24.
7. Rainer Albertz, *A History of Israelite Religion*, I, 140f.
8. Ibid., 141.
9. Ibid., 141f.
10. To help students keep the kings and their countries straight, (I) will follow the names of Israel's kings and (J) will follow the names of Judah's where there might be confusion.
11. Albert Kirk Grayson, *Assyrian Royal Inscriptions, Part 2* (Wiesbaden, Germany: Otto Harrassowitz, 1976), 124, quoted by Erika Bleibtreu, "Grisly Assyrian Record of Torture and Death," *BAR*, XVII, 1 (January–February 1991), 57.
12. Gaalyah Cornfeld and David Noel Freedman, eds., *Archaeology of the Bible: Book by Book* (New York: Harper & Row, 1976), 119–121. See also Martin Noth, *The History of Israel*, 2nd ed. (New York: Harper & Row, 1960), 231.
13. J. B. Pritchard, ed., *ANE*, 209.
14. Ephraim Stern, "The Masters of Dor—Part 2: How Bad Was Ahab?" *BAR*, XIX, 2 (March–April 1993), 18–29. See also Rainer Albertz, *A History of Israelite Religion*, I, trans. John Bowden (Louisville, KY: Westminster–John Knox Press, 1994), 149.
15. Jo Ann Hackett, "Deir Alla, Tell: Texts," *ABD*, 129–130, is an up-to-date discussion of this important discovery.
16. Jean-Marie Durand (Jennifer L. Davis, trans.), "Mari (Texts)," *ABD*, IV, 529–538.
17. On the threat of Syria to the Israelite kingdoms, see Noth, *The History of Israel*, 240–241.
18. Yohanan Aharoni and Michael Avi-Yonah, *MBA*, rev. ed. (New York: MacMillan USA, 1977), 81.
19. Walter Brueggemann, *Theology of the Old Testament: Testimony, Dispute, Advocacy* (Minneapolis: Fortress Press, 1987), 628–632, gives an extended discussion on the "heavenly council" and the idea of authoritative utterance.
20. Albertz, *History of Israelite Religion*, 159–163.
21. Tammi Schneider, "Did King Jehu Kill His Own Family?" *BAR*, XXI, 1 (January–February 1995), 26–33, 80, presents a sound argument for such an interpretation.

CHAPTER

8

The Division of the Monarchy II

The Story of the Southern Kingdom

Timeline

922 B.C.E.	Division of the united monarchy into the Northern and Southern Kingdoms and beginning of the reign of Rehoboam in Judah
735 B.C.E.	Beginning of the reign of Ahaz and the Syro–Ephraimitic crisis
715 B.C.E.	Beginning of the reign of Hezekiah
701 B.C.E.	Sannacherib's invasion
700 B.C.E.	Approximate beginning of the rise of the Babylonian Empire
640 B.C.E.	Beginning of the reign of Josiah
612 B.C.E.	Fall of Nineveh
605 B.C.E.	Beginning of the reign of Nebuchadnezzar in Babylon
597 B.C.E.	First Deportation of Judahites to Babylon
586 B.C.E.	Destruction of Jerusalem by the Babylonians

Chapter Outline

CHAPTER OVERVIEW

While the story of the Northern Kingdom of Israel continued for about two centuries, as recorded in the previous chapter, the kingdom of Judah made its own way in the south under the rule of the Davidic dynasty. This chapter will describe the three and a half centuries of the kingdom of Judah after the division of the monarchy. The kings of Judah will be labeled with a J, and the same estimated dates used in Chapter 7 will be used to provide approximate time frames for their reigns. In most cases, the stories of these kings in the books of 1 and 2 Kings will be supplemented by parallel texts in 2 Chronicles, which provides information only about the Southern Kingdom. Chapter 7 described the appearance of prophets in the Northern Kingdom, Those who were only narrative characters, like Elijah and Elisha, were described more fully, while those we know primarily from books that have their names on them will be discussed in later chapters. This chapter will follow the same pattern, with the exception of Isaiah, the only prophet to appear prominently in the books of I and 2 Kings and to have a separate book named for him.

JUDAH AFTER THE DIVISION

Rehoboam's Reign (1 Kings 14:21–31)

Rehoboam (J, 922–915 B.C.E.) had a notably unsuccessful reign. Not only did he have to deal with the revolt of the northern tribes, but he also had a war on his southern border. Shishak of Egypt had dreams of reviving the glory of the Egyptian Empire. To do that, he had to control Palestine and its vital highways. He attacked in the south, penetrating the hill country and the coastal plain. He extended his conquests all the way north to Megiddo, as both Egyptian records and an inscription found at Megiddo attest. Jerusalem, as well as a number of cities in the hill country, came under attack, forcing Rehoboam to pay an enormous bribe to keep Shishak from destroying the city (14:21–28).[1] At his death, Rehoboam was succeeded by his son Abijam (14:29–31).

Abijam and Asa of Judah (1 Kings 15:1–24)

The reports on the reigns of Abijam (J, 915–913 B.C.E.) and Asa (J, 913–873 B.C.E.) are confusing for a number of reasons. They are identified in 1 Kings 15:8 as father and son, but 15:2 and 15:10 identify the same mother for both of them, "Maacah, daughter of Abishalom." Maacah is given an official designation in 15:16, using the rare Hebrew word, *geviyrah*, which is most often translated as "Queen-mother." This word appears only fifteen times in the Hebrew Bible and has a variety of meanings, seeming to be the only case in which it is specifically used to designate a woman within an Israelite royal family. In fact, this verse reports that Asa removed Maacah from this position because she worshipped the goddess Asherah. Both Abijam and Asa are reported to have continued the war with Jereboam of Israel. Abijam's reign was quite short, while Asa's was extremely long, and the latter is credited with significant religious reforms. The parallel account in 2 Chronicles alters the story significantly. It alters Abijam's name to Abijah and changes the name of his mother, to clear up the problem of he and Asa having the same mother in 1 Kings. It also credits Abijah with significant military success against Jereboam and the Northern Kingdom, even in his short reign. He captured Bethel, Jeshanah, and Ephron. This pushed Israel's front lines back some six to eight miles in places (2 Chron. 13:1–22; 1 Kings 15:1–8).

The war with Israel continued during Asa's reign. Baasha of Israel was able to move within five miles of Jerusalem, where he fortified Ramah, a town on the main road through the hills. In desperation, Asa sent an expensive bribe to Ben-hadad, the king of Syria, to persuade him to attack

Israel. Ben-hadad obliged, invading the northern and eastern territories of Israel and capturing a number of cities, including Dan and Hazor. This forced Baasha (I) to retreat. Asa took advantage of the retreat to use the materials in the fortifications at Ramah to strengthen Mizpeh and Geba. In recent years, evidence of the fortifications has been found by archaeologists (15:9–24).[2] In 2 Chronicles 14:9–15, there is a story of another military attack on Judah by Zerah the Egyptian, but Asa was successful in defeating his armies. Both 1 Kings and 2 Chronicles evaluate Asa positively, more because of his religious reforms than his military successes. This report is the beginning of an interest in religious reform that will intensify as the story of Judah continues.

Jehoshaphat (J, 873–849 B.C.E.), a Good King (1 Kings 22:41–50)

With the coming of Ahab to the throne of Israel, relations between the two states took a more positive turn. Jehoshaphat and Ahab formed an alliance, confirming it with the marriage of Jehoshaphat's son Jehoram and Ahab's daughter Athaliah (2 Kings 8:18, 26). They united to fight their old nemesis, Syria. The disastrous results of this war were foretold by Micaiah ben Imlah (1 Kings 22).[3]

After the incident involving Micaiah, Jehoshaphat's reign is summarized briefly. For the most part, his was a positive rule that rooted out corrupt religious practices, made peace with Israel, took control of Edom, and tried to reestablish sea trade through Ezion-geber. He was succeeded by Jehoram (J, 849–842 B.C.E.).

Jehoram (J, 849–842 B.C.E.) and Ahaziah (J, 842 B.C.E.) (2 Kings 9:16–29; 10:1–17)

From 849 to 842 B.C.E., both states had kings named Jehoram, although Israel's king is sometimes called Joram. Neither king was notable. Judah's king Jehoram escaped the Jehu uprising, described in Chapter 8 of this book, dying before it took place, but his son and successor, Ahaziah, was not so fortunate. Both he and Jehoram (Joram) of Israel were Jehu's victims (2 Kings 9:16–29). In addition, those of Ahaziah's relatives who were so unfortunate as to be in Israel during the uprising also became Jehu's victims (2 Kings 10:1–17).

Athaliah (J, 842–837 B.C.E.) (2 Kings 11:1–21)

The only woman to rule either kingdom was Athaliah of Judah, the mother of Ahaziah, whom Jehu had killed. She seized power and started a purge of her own but failed to kill prince Joash, a small boy who was hidden in the Temple for six years by his aunt, Jehosheba. Eventually, Jehoiada, the chief priest, led a coup that overthrew Athaliah and put seven-year-old Joash on the throne.[4]

Joash (J, 837–800 B.C.E.), the Boy King (2 Kings 12:1–21)

Joash's long reign was peaceful except for an attack by Syria led by Hazael. Hazael was bribed to withdraw, using monies that Joash had collected to repair the Temple, along with any other money he could find.

Amaziah (J, 800–783 B.C.E.) (2 Kings 14:1–22)

Amaziah came to the throne after his father, Joash, was assassinated. This in itself was a testimony to the stability of Judah's government, because the succession to the throne of the Davidic line could survive even attempted coups. Warfare between Israel and Judah broke out once more, resulting in Amaziah's (J) capture by the army of Jehoash (I).

FIGURE 8–1 "[Hezekiah] rebelled against the king of Assyria and would not serve him" (2 Kings 18:7). Hezekiah had this tunnel, which brought water from the Gibon Spring into Jerusalem, dug as a defensive measure. Courtesy of the Israeli Antiquities Authority.

Uzziah (J, 783–742? B.C.E.) (2 Kings 15:1–7; 2 Chron. 26:1–23)

Uzziah is given no more notice in 2 Kings than Jeroboam (I). Yet he also brought to his kingdom unparalleled prosperity. In the Chronicler's history, his accomplishments are more fully told: (1) He conquered the Philistine territory and reestablished Judah's control of the vital coastal highway; (2) he pushed back the Ammonites and the Arabs of Transjordan and in the Negev to the traditional borders of Egypt; (3) he fortified Jerusalem and cities in the Negev, as well as in the foothills of Judah and the coastal plain; (4) he promoted agriculture; and (5) he modernized his army, equipping it with the latest weapons (2 Chron. 26:1–15).

During his reign, he became a leper. The Chronicler blamed the disease on Uzziah's pride, which caused him to try to assume the priestly role. When he became angry because of the priests' opposition, "a leprous disease broke out on his forehead, in the presence of the priests in the house of the LORD" (2 Chron. 26:19). A leper was segregated from all public contact. This meant that even though Uzziah was still called the king, his son Jotham, as coregent, carried on his duties as king until Uzziah died in 742 B.C.E. Some, however, would date his death to 735 B.C.E., the same year Jotham died.

Judah during Israel's Last Days

When Tiglath-pileser III came to the throne in **Assyria,** Judah had ideas of rebellion, but soon decided that this was not the wisest course of action. In 743 B.C.E., Judah under Uzziah had led a coalition of western states in opposition to Assyria, but it was unsuccessful in its attempts to stop Tiglath-pileser III. When Ahaz (J, 735–715 B.C.E.) came to the throne, he faced a more immediate threat from Israel, led by Pekah, and Syria, whose king was Rezin. These two kings tried to persuade

Ahaz to join them in opposing Tiglath-pileser III. Unlike his grandfather Uzziah, however, he chose to join Assyria rather than to fight it. He therefore appealed to Assyria to help against the threats by his neighbors. Tiglath-pileser III readily obliged, taking tribute from Ahaz and quickly subduing Syria and Israel.

JUDAH AFTER THE DESTRUCTION OF ISRAEL

Isaiah and the Kings of Judah

Soon after the destruction of Israel, Judah was blessed with **Hezekiah** (715–687/686 B.C.E.), one of its best kings, according to the evaluations of the writers of both Kings and Chronicles. This evaluation was based primarily on Hezekiah's efforts to reform religious practices in Judah. This is a place where multiple books of the Bible intersect. Isaiah, the prophet, appears in the story of Hezekiah, and much of I Kings 18–20 is copied in the book of Isaiah (ch. 36–39). II Chronicles 29–32 gives even greater attention to Hezekiah's religious reforms, but removes almost all of the references to Isaiah. The prophet Isaiah served as counselor to Ahaz in the midst of the Assyrian crisis.

ISAIAH AND AHAZ (ISAIAH 7). Previously, Isaiah had advised Hezekiah's father, **Ahaz,** but Ahaz did not welcome Isaiah's advice. Ahaz was troubled by the threat of **Syria** and Israel. Isaiah gave him a message from the LORD to ignore the threats. Instead, he counseled, "Take heed, be quiet, do not fear," for the little tyrants threatening him would soon vanish. The prophet showed his contempt for King Pekah (I) by referring to him only as the "son of Remaliah" (7:5–9).

Ahaz ignored the warnings, even though Isaiah continued to issue them. Isaiah gave another son the ominous name Maher-shalal-hash-baz. (Someone suggested that he was nicknamed "Hash" because his name was so long!) The name means "Quick loot, fast plunder" (TEV) and describes the greed and destructiveness of the Assyrians. Isaiah told Ahaz that if he refused the LORD's peaceful waters, he would find himself floundering in the Assyrian flood (8:1–15). The reference to the waters of Shiloah ("peaceful waters") probably referred to the waters of an irrigation stream that ran along the edge of the Kidron Valley, while "the River" was the Tigris–Euphrates and, by extension, the Assyrians who came from that region (8:5–8).

Finally, because the people would not listen to him, a frustrated Isaiah told his disciples to record what he had said. If the people were more interested in listening to fortune-tellers than to the word of the LORD, then that was their responsibility (8:16–21).

ISAIAH AND HEZEKIAH (2 KINGS 18:1–20:21; ISA. 20:1–6; ISA. 36:1–39:8). Isaiah found a more receptive listener in Hezekiah (715–687/686 B.C.E.), who succeeded his father, Ahaz. Isaiah was Hezekiah's friend and counselor in at least two major crises during his reign—the Ashdod rebellion and Sennacherib's invasion.

Hezekiah came to the throne when Assyria's attention was diverted from the western states. Given a bit of breathing room, he set out to reform the religious practices in Judah. He moved vigorously to destroy the pagan altars built by his father and destroyed shrines where Baal worship still persisted. One such place where an altar probably was destroyed was at Arad, south of Jerusalem in the Negev region, where a temple had existed since early in Judah's history. The altar was destroyed either in Hezekiah's reform or in a later reform by Josiah. Similarly, the remains of an altar were found at Beersheba, where the stone was reused as building material.[5] Hezekiah even destroyed the bronze serpent made by Moses that was kept in the Temple as a reminder of

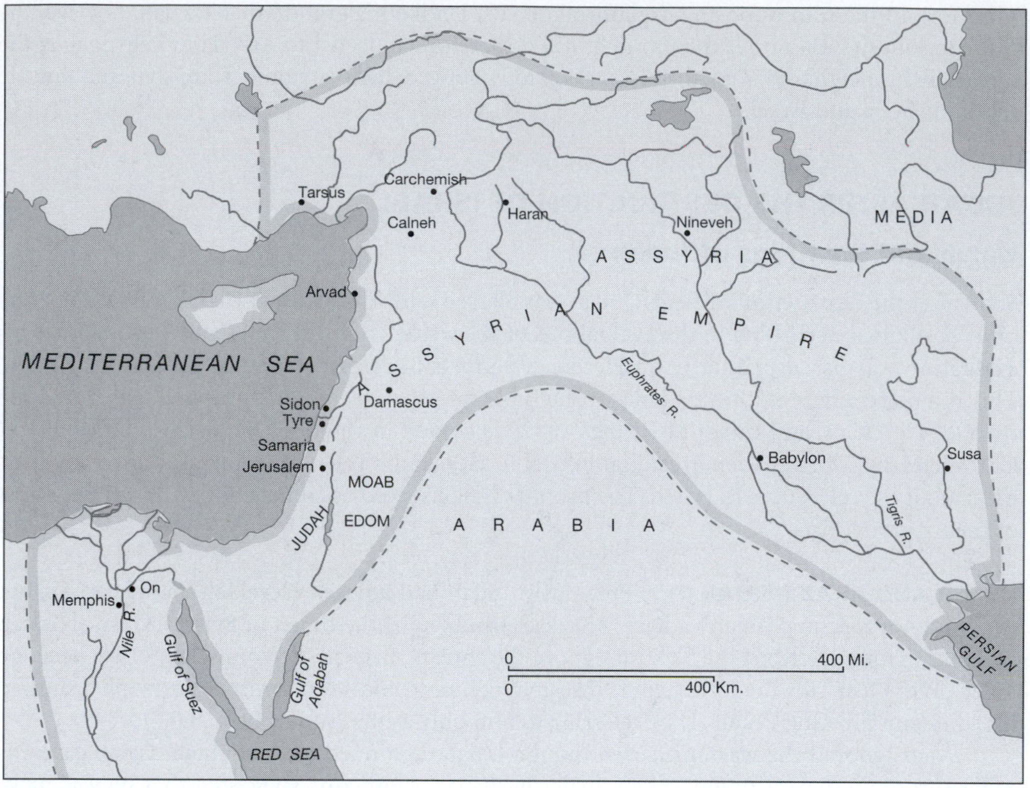

FIGURE 8–2 The Assyrian Empire.

Israel's days in the wilderness. It had become an object of worship, with people burning incense to it as if it were divine. The evaluation of Hezekiah was that

> He trusted in the LORD, the God of Israel; so that there was no one like him among all the kings of Judah after him, or among all the kings of Judah before him. (2 Kings 18:5)

He slightly enlarged his kingdom, especially at the expense of the Philistines. For a short period of time, he also refused to pay **tribute** to the Assyrians (18:1–12).

Soon, Assyria was advancing in the direction of Judah again. In 714 B.C.E., the people of Ashdod, a Philistine city, tried to lead a rebellion against the Assyrians. Egypt, which, for a change, had a strong king, encouraged the rebellion because the Assyrian power was too close to its borders. Hezekiah was invited to join the leaders of the other small western states.

Isaiah advised Hezekiah to steer clear of the fight. To emphasize the gravity of what he said, Isaiah walked about Jerusalem naked and barefoot for three years. This was to stress what could happen to Judah if Hezekiah was foolish enough to oppose the Assyrians. Although such an action would seem strange to us today, Isaiah was portraying an all-too-familiar sight to the Judeans—naked captives of war being paraded through the streets (Isa. 20:1–6).

Hezekiah seems to have stayed out of the rebellion that was crushed in 711 B.C.E. But trouble would not stay away for long. Near the end of Sargon's life, revolt flared again in the Assyrian Empire. Babylon, under Merodoach-baladan, led the revolt. Egypt stirred up the western states,

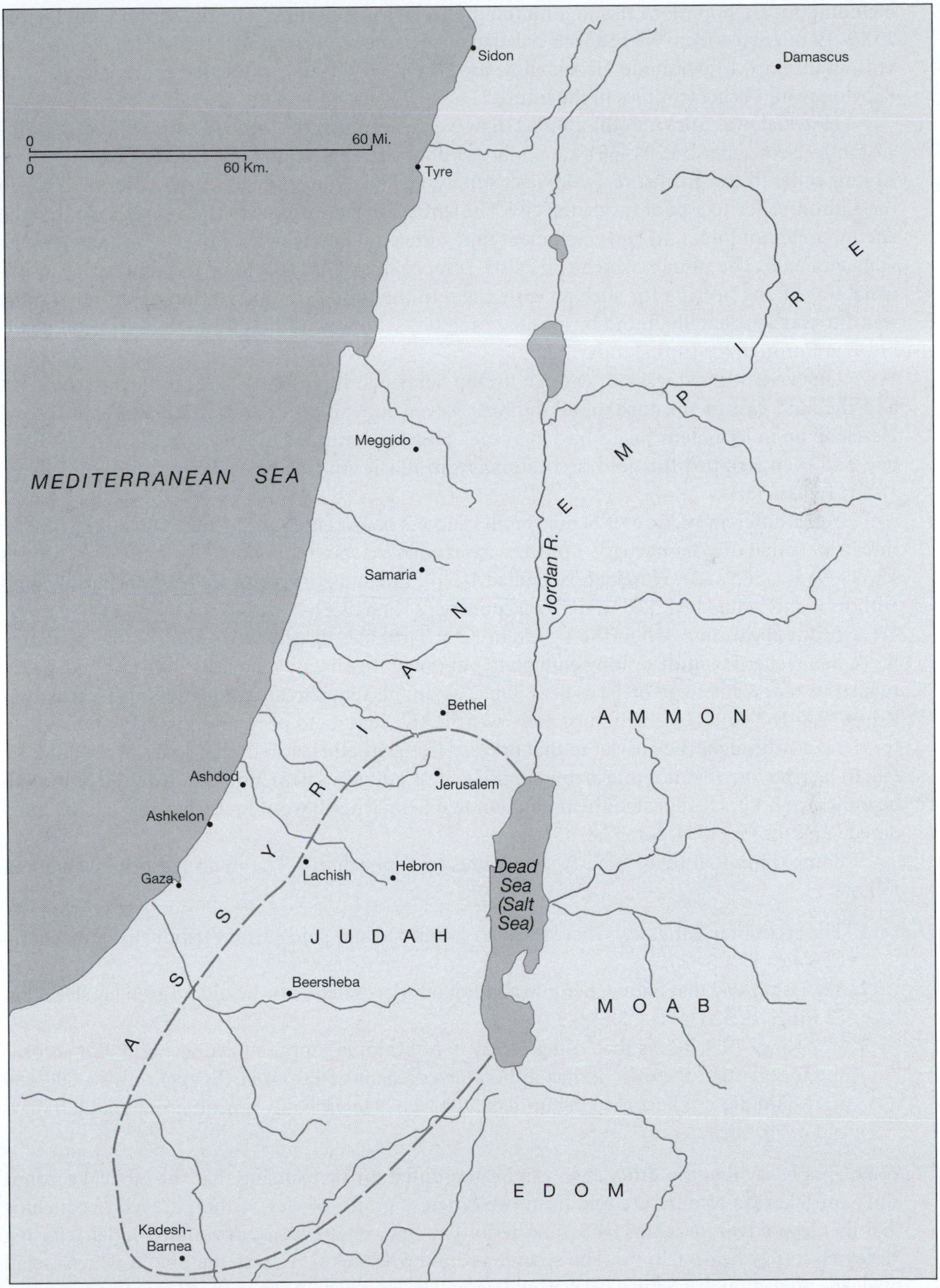

FIGURE 8–3 The kingdom of Judah—seventh century B.C.E.

including Judah, hoping to regain a foothold for itself in Palestine. The descriptions in 2 Kings 20:12–19 of envoys from Merodoach-baladan, who came to Hezekiah from Babylon, may represent an attempt to persuade Hezekiah to join the revolt. Isaiah protested that dealings with Babylon would bring troubles in the future.[6]

Hezekiah was drawn to the conflict, however, with much the same results. Expecting an invasion by Sennacherib (704–681 B.C.E.), he set about strengthening the defenses of Jerusalem. Among other things, to ensure a safe water supply, he had a tunnel dug from the Gihon Spring in the Kidron Valley to a pool inside the city. The source of the spring was then covered so that the enemy could not find it. In New Testament times, the pool into which it flowed was known as the *Pool of Siloam.* The tunnel, which still exists, is more than 1700 feet long and represents an unusual feat of engineering for such an early time. In the tunnel, an inscription describing how it was dug was accidentally found by a young Arab boy who was wading through it. It is still possible to go through the tunnel today.[7]

One water tunnel was not enough to stop Sennacherib. In 701 B.C.E., he attacked the coast and the land east of the Jordan, taking forty-seven Judean cities and, in his words, shutting Hezekiah up in Jerusalem "like a bird in a cage." Hezekiah emptied his treasury, the Temple treasury, and even stripped the gold decorations from the Temple to pay off Sennacherib (2 Kings 18:13–16; Isa. 36:1).

Yet, a different picture of Sennacherib's success is presented in 2 Kings 18:17–19:37. After threats were made by Sennacherib's officers about what the Assyrians would do to the city (2 Kings 18:17–37; Isa. 36:2–22), Hezekiah consulted Isaiah. Isaiah assured him that Sennacherib would withdraw and would be killed in his own country (2 Kings 19:1–7; Isa. 37:1–7).

In the meantime, when the Egyptian King Tirhakah threatened Sennacherib's southern flank, Sennacherib withdrew long enough to put down the threat. When that was finished, he returned to renew his seige of Jerusalem. Once again, he sent threatening letters to Hezekiah (2 Kings 19:8–13). And Hezekiah once more went to the Temple to pray, and Isaiah, as spokesman for the LORD, brought the answer to that prayer. He reassured Hezekiah that Jerusalem would not fall. In fact, he said that not one arrow would be shot into Jerusalem, nor would any siege mound be built around it. He repeated the prediction that Sennacherib would return home and be murdered (2 Kings 19:14–34; Isa. 37:8–35).

Some think that there were two invasions by Sennacherib. The main reasons given are as follows:

1. The account in Kings says that Hezekiah submitted and paid a heavy tribute to Sennacherib (2 Kings 19:13–16).
2. Yet, Isaiah said that Sennacherib would not take Jerusalem, nor would he even lay siege to it (2 Kings 19:32–34; Isa. 37:33–35).
3. In 2 Kings 19:9, it says that "King Tirhakah of Ethiopia" opposed Sennacherib. But according to Egyptian records, Tirhakah became coregent of Ethiopia (Egypt) only in 690/689 B.C.E. and did not become king until 685/84 B.C.E. He probably was no more than ten years old in 701 B.C.E.

Some simply say that the differences can be accounted for by realizing that the biblical account and Sennacherib's account are told from two different points of view. Others are led to conclude that there were two invasions by Sennacherib. The first, in 701 B.C.E., devastated Judah, causing Hezekiah to pay heavy tribute. The second, around 690/689 B.C.E., was the one in which Isaiah made the prediction that Sennacherib would never take Jerusalem. 2 Kings 18–19 contains a description of that invasion. Sennacherib started to attack Jerusalem, only to be drawn away by

Hezekiah's Illness

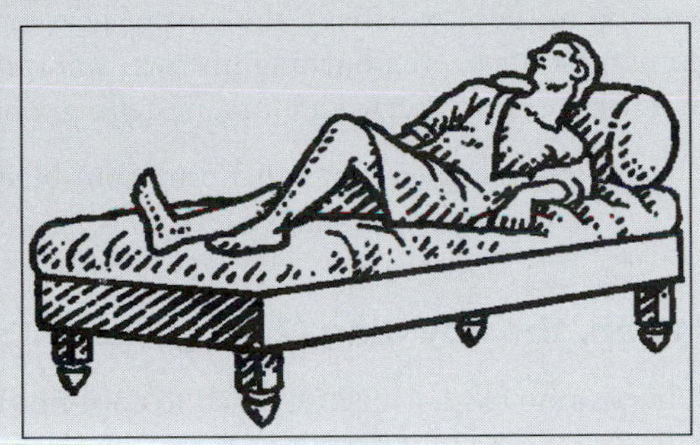

Hezekiah was the king of Judah during the late eighth century B.C.E. Stories of his reign, particularly those related to the invasion of the Assyrian Empire, are recorded in 2 Kings 18–21. A parallel account of these episodes in Hezekiah's life appears in Isaiah 36–39. One of these stories reports that Hezekiah became ill after God miraculously repelled the Assyrian invasion. This illness is the occasion of one of Hezekiah's encounters with the prophet Isaiah. In 2 Kings 20:1, Isaiah tells Hezekiah's that he is about to die from his illness. This report is followed by Hezekiah's prayer. Isaiah is commanded by God to go back to Hezekiah and tell him that his prayer has been granted and that he will live for fifteen more years. Isaiah's command in 20:7 to have a compress of figs applied to Hezekiah's boil is somewhat puzzling. Is the boil the potentially fatal illness? Does God heal Hezekiah or does the treatment prescribed by Isaiah?

Isaiah also gives Hezekiah a sign that he will be cured, and Isaiah describes a strange event involving something called the *dial* or *steps* of Ahaz. Apparently, this was some type of device or structure with divisions over which a shadow moved as the day passed. The sign of Hezekiah's healing will be the backward movement of this shadow. Isaiah 38 reports these events, leaving out the fig compress and adding a lengthy prayer by Hezekiah after he has recovered.

Both 2 Kings 21 and Isaiah 39 use the occasion of Hezekiah's recovery to report the visit of Babylonian envoys. These envoys come bringing a gift from the Babylonian king, who had heard about Hezekiah's illness and recovery. In a strange turn, these envoys are given a tour of Ahaz's palace and all of his belongings. Ahaz reports the visit of the envoys to Isaiah, who makes predictions about the future. In the book of Isaiah particularly, this visit of the Babylonian envoys seems to be an oblique way of reporting the Babylonian invasion and destruction of Jerusalem.

Tirhakah's threat. After taking care of that, he came back, only to meet disaster in the form of a devastating plague that struck his army. As the historian writes:

> That very night the angel of the LORD set out and struck down one hundred eighty-five thousand in the camp of the Assyrians; when morning dawned, they were all dead bodies. (19:35; Isa. 37:36)

Later, Sennacherib was murdered by his own sons (19:36–37; Isa. 37:37–38).[8]

One other narrative (other than the visit by the Babylonian representatives, which probably preceded the Sennacherib invasion) concerns Isaiah and Hezekiah. Hezekiah was ill. The prophet came and told him he would die. Hezekiah prayed, requesting that he be permitted to live longer. Isaiah then returned and said that Hezekiah would live another fifteen years. As a sign that he would recover, the shadow of the sundial was to go back ten steps (Isa. 38:1–8).

Bad Days under Manasseh (2 Kings 21:1–18; 2 Chron. 33:1–20)

Israel's historians had little good to say about Manasseh. Both the Bible and Assyrian records indicate that he was a puppet king. 2 Chronicles 33:11–13 reports that he once was bound with chains and taken before an Assyrian king in Babylon.[9]

His reign saw a rebirth of Baal worship in Judah. He rebuilt the **high places** where he set up altars to the Canaanite fertility gods and goddesses. He also built altars in the Temple area for the worship of the star deities ("the host of heaven"), also showing Assyrian influence. He practiced human sacrifice, even burning his own son on an altar to a pagan god; and he encouraged the practices of black magic and fortune-telling. Those who opposed him were severely persecuted:

> Manasseh shed very much innocent blood, until he had filled Jerusalem from one end to another. (2 Kings 21:16)

Josiah, the Boy King (2 Kings 22:1–23:30)

When Amon (642–640 B.C.E.) tried to continue the policies of his father, Manasseh, he signed his own death warrant. After ruling for two years, he was assassinated. His eight-year-old son, **Josiah,** was put on the throne in his place.

Josiah (640–609 B.C.E.) came to the throne at a time when Assyria was fading as a world power. Egypt was still weak, and Babylon had not yet become a threat to the western states. Because he was only eight years old, the government actually was controlled by the High Priest, who was the chief religious official of the kingdom (2 Kings 22:1–2).

Hilkiah, the High Priest, influenced Josiah to take strong action early in his reign to destroy the pagan religions that Manasseh had so ardently promoted. This activity extended even into the cities of the old Northern Kingdom. This seems to have begun in 627 B.C.E., the year that Asshurbanapal, the last strong Assyrian king, died.[10]

Changes under Josiah (2 Kings 22:3–23:27)[11]

Finding the scroll (2 Kings 22:3–20). If the High Priest hoped to shape the young king's thinking to cause a return to the basic religious foundations of the nation, he did a good job. Efforts at reform may have begun as early as 630 B.C.E. and gained intensity over the years.

In 622 B.C.E., an important event took place. On instructions from Josiah, a major cleansing of the Temple began under the direction of Hilkiah, the High Priest (22:3–7). In the process of cleaning out the building, a scroll containing a version of the Law of Moses was found. The manuscript was taken to the king's secretary, Shaphan, who in turn reported its discovery to the king (22:8–10).

When the scroll was read to Josiah, he was greatly upset and tore his clothes in despair. He immediately gave orders that Huldah, a prophetess, should be consulted about the course of action that should be taken (22:11–13). The oracle that Huldah gave spoke of the LORD's displeasure at idol worship in Judah, but it promised that Josiah would prosper because of his penitent attitude (22:14–20).[12]

Covenant renewal and religious reform (2 Kings 23:1–17). When Josiah received word of Huldah's oracle, he led the people in a ceremony of covenant renewal (23:1–3). But he went further than just pledging to keep the law of the LORD; he applied the law in practical ways to the situation. Josiah's actions, based on the law that had been discovered, have led scholars to conclude that the scroll was the major part of what is known today as the *Book of Deuteronomy.* Thus, they refer to Josiah's reform as the *Deuteronomic reformation.*

His first major step was an attempt to rid the land of **pagan** cults and the high places, which were sites of unauthorized worship. In Jerusalem, many altars to pagan deities had been erected in Manasseh's time. These were destroyed, along with various images that were part of the worship. Extending the purge further, orders were given that not only were the altars in Judah to be destroyed, but also the altars in northern cities, such as Bethel. To rid the land of their influence, those who were priests at the pagan shrines were slain.

Next, Josiah ordered the celebration of a great Passover, reminding the people of the LORD's mighty acts in bringing them out of the land of Egypt (23:21–23). This reminder of the LORD's covenant with Moses was a call for revival of the old-time religion that for the most part had been forgotten, replaced by the emphasis on the covenant with David. So impressive were the Passover services that the historian said of them:

> No such passover had been kept since the days of the judges who judged Israel, or during the days of the kings of Israel or the kings of Judah. (23:22)

A most important aspect of the reform was the gathering of all the priests of the LORD in Jerusalem for the purpose of centralizing all the worship services in the Jerusalem Temple. This was done to ensure that the worship would be kept pure, not mixed with elements of pagan worship. This was a noble idea, but one major result of the action would prove fatal to the whole reform. Out of the centralization of worship developed the ideas that (1) the Temple was the LORD's dwelling place; (2) the LORD would never permit his dwelling to be destroyed; and (3) because the Temple was located in Jerusalem and the LORD lived in the Temple, Jerusalem would never be destroyed. The conclusion that Jerusalem was safe from all attack, furthermore, seemed to be supported by Isaiah's words, spoken during the days of Sennacherib's invasions, to the effect that Jerusalem was protected by the LORD (Isa. 37:33–35; 2 Kings 19:32–34).

MEANWHILE, IN THE REST OF THE WORLD. Josiah had been able to operate so freely because Assyria was so weak that it was on the verge of being completely eliminated from the international scene. The beginning of the end came when the Babylonians gained their independence and joined the Medes in an attack on Assyria. The Egyptians came to the aid of Assyria, but it was a case of too little, too late. In 614 B.C.E., the Medes captured Asshur, Assyria's early capital. In 612 B.C.E., the combined forces of the Medes and Babylonians captured and destroyed Nineveh. The final blows came with the fall of Haran and the failure of an attempt by the Assyrians to recapture it. The giant was dead.[13]

THE DEATH OF JOSIAH (2 KINGS 23:28–30; 2 CHRON. 35:2–27). Josiah, the most capable of the Judean kings, died a tragic death on the famous battlefield of **Megiddo.** Pharaoh Neco of Egypt was pushing north along the coastal highway to try to stop the advance of the Medo-Babylonian armies at Carchemish. For some unknown reason, Josiah chose to try to stop Neco, but he only succeeded in getting himself killed. The year was 609 B.C.E. His death would set in motion a chain of events that would lead to the death of the nation itself.[14]

The Reigns of Jehoiakim and Jehoiachin (2 Kings 23:31–24:17)

Josiah's death brought radical changes in Judah. The reign of his son Jehoahaz (609 B.C.E.), who had succeeded him, was cut short by Pharaoh Neco of Egypt. Once more, Judah was put under a foreign overlord. Jehoahaz was imprisoned and died in Egypt (23:31–34).

In his place, the Egyptians made his brother, Eliakim, king. When Eliakim became king, his name was changed to Jehoiakim (23:24). Among some peoples, the king always took a new name when he became ruler. Such may have been the case in Israel, but this is the only direct evidence of it.

Jehoiakim (609–597 B.C.E.) paid heavy tribute to the Egyptians for the first few years of his reign. That did not keep him from spending rather extravagantly for his own comfort, however.

FIGURE 8–4 "King Josiah went to meet him; but when Pharaoh Neco met him at Megiddo, he killed him" (2 Kings 23:29). Josiah lost his life on this famous battlefield, called the Plain of Megiddo or Esdralon, when he tried to block Egypt's invasion of the Babylonian Empire.

At Beth-kerem, just south of Jerusalem, he had an elaborate palace built, which was to draw the fire of the prophet Jeremiah:

> Woe to him who builds his house by unrighteousness,
> and his upper rooms by injustice;
> who makes his neighbors work for nothing,
> and does not give them their wages;
> who says, "I will build myself a spacious house
> with large upper rooms,"
> and who cuts out windows for it,
> paneling it with cedar,
> and painting it with vermilion.
> Are you a king because you compete in cedar? (Jer. 22:13–15a)

The remains of his palace have been found, and some of the stones still have traces of the bright red paint.[15]

Jehoiakim's loyalties changed in 605 B.C.E. when the Babylonian army defeated Egypt at the battle of Carchemish in northern Mesopotamia. The only thing that kept the Babylonians from sweeping south through Palestine was the death of Nabopolassar, the ruler of **Babylon.** He was succeeded by Nebuchadnezzar, who demanded and got Jehoiakim's submission, with the resulting money payment.

The Destruction of Jerusalem

The Babylonian Empire destroyed the Assyrian Empire in the late seventh century B.C.E. and became the dominant force in the ancient Near Eastern world. The westward movement of the Babylonian army followed the standard path out of Mesopotamia, along the Fertile Crescent, and down the Mediterranean coast. This meant that the nation of Judah and its capital, Jerusalem, were in the path of Nebuchadnezzar's mighty army. Jerusalem had managed to survive as the capital of a united Israel and then Judah for about four centuries, according to the Old Testament, but even its own prophets were now predicting its doom.

Information about the Babylonian attack is not presented in a comprehensive report in any one place in the Old Testament. A portrait of the invasion can be put together with information from a number of texts. 2 Kings 25 reports a siege of the city of Jerusalem lasting well over a year. This siege led to a famine, and eventually a breach was made in the wall. The Babylonian army burned the Temple and the palace and tore down the wall around Jerusalem. Many valuable items were carried off to Babylon. Jeremiah 52, the final chapter of this large prophetic scroll, is a reproduction of 2 Kings 24:18–25:30, with some minor alterations. 2 Chronicles reports all of this destruction and looting and adds a much more graphic picture of the slaughter of many of the residents of Jerusalem, most strikingly the killing of young people in the Temple.

Many members of the royalty, the priesthood, and the upper social class of Jerusalem were carried off to Babylon; some escaped and fled to Egypt. Most of the ordinary people seem to have been left behind to continue to work the land. The beleaguered condition of these people is perhaps best portrayed in the description of the Babylonian siege and its aftermath in Lamentations 1–2:

> My eyes are spent with weeping; my stomach churns;
> My bile is poured out on the ground because of the destruction of my people,
> Because infants and babes faint in the streets of the city.

Jehoiakim struggled to find a way to save Judah and protect his own reign over it. By 601 B.C.E., he had switched his loyalties back to Egypt. The Babylonians, having seized control of the coastal plain by 602 B.C.E., fought a battle with Pharaoh Neco's forces in 601 B.C.E. Both sides suffered heavy losses, causing Nebuchadnezzar to withdraw from Palestine for a time to recover and reorganize his army. Jehoiakim quickly switched his allegiance to Egypt, which was a fatal mistake. In 598 B.C.E., the Babylonians invaded Judah with force. It was a convenient time for Jehoiakim to die, and he did—either from natural causes or by assassination (2 Kings 24:1–6). His son Jehoiachin (597 B.C.E.) succeeded him, coming to the throne just in time to be captured when the city fell in 597 B.C.E. Several thousand people—including the king, his mother, and many of Jerusalem's leading citizens—and an enormous amount of booty were taken to Babylon. Most of the people, among them a priest named Ezekiel, were settled in villages along a large irrigation canal called the *River Chebar* (Ezek. 1:1). Babylonian records describe the event and speak of the spoils of the victory. Jehoiachin would remain a captive until 560 B.C.E., when he was released and made a ward of the Babylonian royal court (2 Kings 25:27–30).

Key Terms

Ahaz, *177*
Assyria, *176*
Babylon, *184*
Hezekiah, *177*
High Places, *182*
Josiah, *182*
Megiddo, *183*
Pagan, *182*
Rehoboam, *174*
Syria, *177*
Tribute, *178*

Study Questions

1. What kept Rehoboam from enforcing his will over the northern tribes?
2. What happened to bring an end to the hostilities between Israel and Judah?
3. Who was Athaliah? Why is she a significant figure in Israel's story?
4. What were Uzziah's major accomplishments as king of Judah?
5. What role did Ahaz play in the eventual downfall of Israel?
6. How did Judah manage to survive the Assyrian invasions that destroyed Israel and Syria in the later eighth century (745–721 B.C.E.)?
7. What was Isaiah's relationship to Ahaz? to Hezekiah?
8. How did Hezekiah prepare for a possible invasion by the Assyrians during Sennacherib's reign?
9. What possible physical evidence has been found to confirm Hezekiah's reform?
10. Why do some interpreters think Sennacherib may have invaded Judah twice?

Endnotes

1. See J. Maxwell Miller and John H. Hayes, *A History of Ancient Israel and Judah* (Philadelphia: Westminster Press, 1986), 245–246, on Shishak's invasion.
2. On the military movements of Israel and Judah, see Johanan Aharoni and Michael Avi-Yonah, *MBA*, 122–123. For a description of the fortress, see G. Ernest Wright, *Biblical Archaeology,* 2nd ed. (Philadelphia: Westminster Press, 1974), 151ff.
3. See Wright, *Biblical Archaeology*, 181f.
4. On Athaliah's role as queen mother, see Susan Ackerman, "Warrior, Dancer, Seductress, Queen: Women in Judges and Biblical Israel," *ABRL* (1998), 137–138.
5. Ze'ev Herzog, Miriam Aharoni, and Anson F. Rainey, "Arad—An Ancient Israelite Fortress with a Temple to Yahweh," *BAR* (March–April 1987), reprinted in "The Best of *BAR*," I, edited by Hershel Shanks and Dan P. Cole (Washington, DC: Biblical Archaelogy Society, 1990), 203–224. See also Rainer Albertz, *The History of Israelite Religion,* trans. John Bowden (Louisville, KY: Westminster–John Knox Press, 1994), 180ff.
6. On Hezekiah's role in the rebellion against Sennacherib, see Martin Noth, *The History of Israel,* 2nd ed. (New York: Harper & Row, 1960), 265–267.
7. Dan Gill, "How They Met," *BAR,* XX, 4 (July–August 1994), 22–33. In the same issue of *BAR,* see also Simon B. Parker, "Siloam Inscription Memorializes Engineering Achievement," 36–38.
8. For a balanced evaluation of the debate over this sequence of events, see A. Kirk Grayson, "Sennacherib," in *ABD*, vol. 5, 1992, 1088–1089.
9. For a more thorough discussion of the relationship between Menasseh and the Assyrians, see Carl D. Evans, "Manasseh, King of Judah," *ABD*, vol. 4, 1992, 496–499.
10. For a survey of the history of the Late Assyrian Empire and its decline, see A. Kirk Grayson, "Mesopotamia, History of (Assyria)," in *ABD*, vol. 4, 1992, 744–747.
11. The traditional date for the beginning of the prophet Jeremiah's ministry is 626 B.C.E. However, because the major portion of his ministry followed the reign of Josiah, discussion will be reserved for the reigns of Jehoiakim, Jehoiachin, and Zedekiah.
12. On Huldah's role as a prophet, see Susan Ackermann, "Warrior, Dancer, Seductress, Queen: Women in Judges and Biblical Israel," *ABRL*, 107–108.
13. For details, Grayson, "Mesopotamia, History of (Assyria)," 746–747.
14. Noth, *The History of Israel,* 278, discusses possible reasons for Josiah's challenge to Neco.
15. See Gaalyah Cornfeld and David Noel Freedman, eds., *Archaeology of the Bible: Book by Book* (New York: Harper & Row, 1976), 171ff.

CHAPTER 9

The Exile and Restoration

Redefining Israel

Timeline

586 B.C.E.	Destruction of Jerusalem and second deportation of Judahites
573 B.C.E.	Approximate end of Ezekiel's prophetic career
550 B.C.E.	Rise of the Persian Empire
539 B.C.E.	Cyrus II conquers Babylon
538 B.C.E.	Decree of Cyrus releases Israelites to return to Jerusalem
522 B.C.E.	Beginning of reign of Darius I in Persia
520 B.C.E.	Second return of Judahites to Judah
515 B.C.E.	Completion of the Second Temple
458 B.C.E.	One estimate of the return of Ezra to Jerusalem
445 B.C.E.	Beginning of Nehemiah's term as governor of Judah

Chapter Outline

I. After the Fall of Jerusalem
II. The Lives of the Survivors
III. The Changing International Situation (538–486 B.C.E.)
IV. The Restored Community
V. Ezra and Nehemiah

CHAPTER OVERVIEW

The destruction of Jerusalem and its Temple and the deportation of many of the leading citizens of Judah was a traumatic event in the life of Israel. This kind of disruption required a reformulation of Israel's past story and its religious practice. The Exile would become a formative event for Judaism. The beginnings of this theological reformulation are found in prophetic books like Ezekiel and Isaiah 40–66. The Temple would be rebuilt after the Exile, and worship would eventually be established again in Jerusalem. At the same time, the dispersion of Israel would lead to the development of Jewish communities in places like Babylon and Egypt. Many religious and cultural innovations appear to have taken place in the wake of the Exile, including the initial movements toward a literary canon that could replace Temple and land as a religious center for these communities. The traumatic experience of dispersion and the shift toward literature as a central element of religious life likely caused revisions of many biblical books that had already been developed significantly before the Exile and the production of new books that represented an even greater variety of sacred writings. What little we know about the Exilic period and the Restoration that followed it typically has to be inferred from this literature.

AFTER THE FALL OF JERUSALEM

The land lay in ruins. Cities that once had been alive with people were now blackened piles of rubble. Fields that once had produced abundant crops of life-sustaining foods now lay idle, overgrown with weeds. Jerusalem, the once proud capital city of David and Solomon, was wrecked. Its houses,

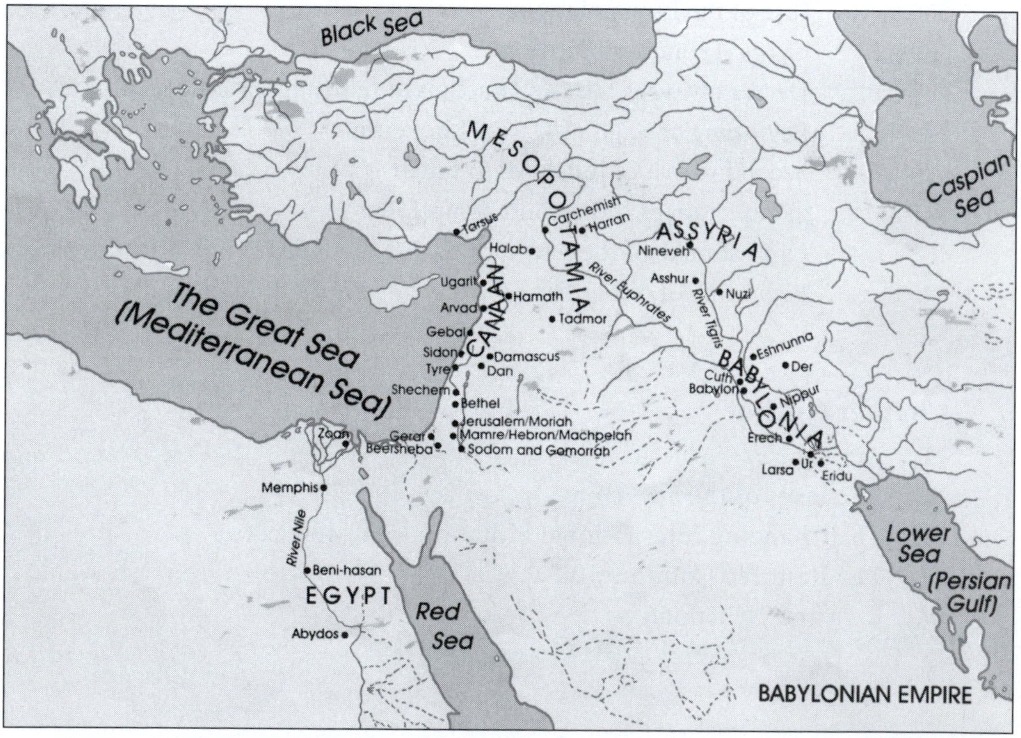

FIGURE 9–1 The Babylonian Empire—sixth century B.C.E. Artwork by Margaret Jordan Brown, from *Mercer Dictionary of the Bible*. © 1990, courtesy of Mercer University Press.

The Principles of Hebrew Poetry

There is no obvious place in a textbook like this to put an introduction to Hebrew poetry. Poetic texts appear in the Bible almost from the very beginning. The common assumption that poetry and prose form discrete categories of literature proves to be untrue as soon as we start trying to put real texts into these categories. Many English versions of the Bible print Genesis 1:27, 2:23, and 3;14–19 in a way that makes them look like poetry. More careful consideration reveals that all of Genesis 1 has some of the characteristics we would identify in poetry. It is certainly not the same kind of prose as a newspaper article or chemistry textbook. The designation of literature as prose or poetry is somewhat artificial, but it matters because readers make assumptions about the meaning of texts based upon such designations, even when they are unaware that they are making them. As always, our purpose is not to eliminate assumptions, but to raise them to a level of conscious awareness, so that we can evaluate them carefully, then decide which ones to retain.

For the purposes of reading the Bible, it may be better to think of poetry and prose as two ends of a continuum, rather than two discrete categories. The book of Lamentations lies very near the poetry end of the spectrum, while the book of Ezra is near the prose end. Other biblical books contain a mixture of literature that may be placed at various places along the continuum. A passage like Genesis 1 perhaps lies near the middle of the spectrum, combining qualities we would use to identify each of the poles. Beginning here with the book of Lamentations, the next several chapters will address biblical books made up largely, or entirely, of texts that fall close to the poetry end of the continuum. It will be helpful, therefore, to look at some of the characteristics that most often appear in these kinds of texts.

Parallelism

If asked to name the characteristics that most often define English poetry, many readers will respond by identifying rhyme and rhythm. Hebrew poetry, unlike English poetry, was less concerned with rhyme and rhythm than with the balancing of ideas within a line. Each line of Hebrew poetry had at least two parts, but rarely were there more than three. As a general rule, when a line of Hebrew poetry is translated into English, each part forms a separate line in English. Each part contains an idea. The other parts of the line either repeat it in a slightly different manner, state a contrary or opposite idea, or add to the original idea. This way of relating ideas to each other is called **parallelism.** Although there are many types of parallelism, three basic types discovered by Bishop Robert Lowth will be discussed here.

Synonymous Parallelism

In synonymous parallelism, the idea in the first part of the line is more or less duplicated in the second part, using different language. Some examples are:

> A good name is to be chosen rather than great riches, and favor is better than silver or gold. (Prov. 22:1)
> For the righteous will never be moved; they will be remembered forever. (Ps. 112:6)
> He raises the poor from the dust, and lifts the needy from the ash heap. (Ps. 113:7)

Antithetical Parallelism

In antithetical parallelism, the idea in the second part of the line is the opposite of the idea in the first part. Proverbs 10–14 contain many examples of antithetical parallelism:

A wise child loves discipline, but a scoffer does not listen to rebuke. (Prov. 13:1)
The righteous know the needs of their animals, but the mercy of the wicked is cruel. (Prov. 12:10)

Formal or Synthetic Parallelism

Formal parallelism actually is not parallel at all; the second part of the line adds to the idea of the first part.

Come and hear, all of you who fear God, and I will tell you what he has done for me. (Ps. 66:16)
So I looked upon you in the sanctuary, beholding your power and glory. (Ps. 63:2)

Growing out of Lowth's work, other types of parallelism—such as emblematic, which involves comparisons; stairlike, in which the second part repeats part of the first idea and adds to it; and introverted, which extends over several lines—can also be found. They will not be discussed in detail here, however.

Lowth's conclusions have been modified over the years, especially in the recent past. Now, the emphasis in the second or third part is seen as intensifying or elaborating on the idea expressed in the first part. As one scholar puts it, "If something is broken in the first verset [part], it is smashed or shattered in the second verset."[1]

Meter

Meter has to do with the rhythm of poetry. There is significant debate about whether Hebrew poetry has meter, and even those experts who argue that it does often disagree about how it works. The best text of the Hebrew Bible available to us has a system of accent marks, which some readers understand as an indication of a kind of meter. Each part of the line has either two or three strong accents or beats, and on rare occasions four. If the line has two parts and each part has three strong beats, the rhythm is 3:3. This is the most common rhythm. If the poet wanted to express quickness, he often used two strong beats for each part of the line. The meter then would be 2:2. Sadness was expressed by an uneven number of beats—three in the first part and two in the second part. This meter is called *qinah,* which means "dirge" or "sad song." The Book of Lamentations was written almost exclusively in this meter. Finally, if there are three-part lines, the meter could be 3:3:3 or 2:2:2.

Meter, like rhyme, is a literary feature that does not easily translation into another language, unless the translator makes deliberate choices to force the retention of these features. Therefore, it may not be helpful to give a lot of attention to this feature. The two qualities that Hebrew poetry clearly possesses in abundance are the use of parallel lines and the use of figurative language. Fortunately, both of these characteristics easily survive translation into another language, so they will be the ones to which we will pay most attention in our discussion of poetic texts.

from the hovels of the poor to the palaces of its kings, were burned to the ground; its massive walls were filled with gaping holes; and the Temple, the building that popular religion was sure would be the magic charm to protect the city, was just another heap of rubble. And the people who had given life to the city were gone. Many were dead in the city's ruins; others were exiles in neighboring lands. Most members of the upper echelons of society who had survived had been carried to Babylon as prisoners of war. This forced removal can be referred to as *exile* or **deportation.** Most of those left behind were poor farmers and shepherds, people unlikely to lead any kind of revolt against the powerful armies of Babylon. The fall of Jerusalem was a shattering blow to the people, who were convinced that the presence of the Temple would protect the city. The confidence in a permanent existence for Judah and Jerusalem, expressed just a few decades before, was replaced by gloom and despair. Nowhere was that spirit reflected more starkly than in the book of Lamentations.

Lamentations: Funeral Songs for a Dead City

In the Christian canon, the book of Lamentations is placed after Jeremiah as something of an appendix. The last chapter of Jeremiah is a slightly modified version of 2 Kings 25 that reports the siege and invasion of Jerusalem by the Babylonian army in 586 B.C.E. Lamentations appears to be a poetic response to this tragic event. In the Hebrew canon, Lamentations is one of the five festival scrolls or *Megilloth*, each of which is read in the synagogue service to commemorate a particular holiday. Lamentations is read on the *Ninth of Av*, which specifically recalls the destruction of Herod's temple by the Romans in 70 C.E. Although the narrative accounts of the Babylonian invasion in 2 Kings 25, 2 Chronicles 36, and the parabolic report in Isaiah 39 seem impersonal, and even evasive, Lamentations presents an inside-the-city view of the event that is filled with raw pain and grotesque imagery.

CHARACTERISTICS OF THE BOOK. There are two distinct characteristics to the poems. First, they are all in what is called *qinah*, or dirge, rhythm. To understand this, one must recall what was mentioned about Hebrew poetry. Hebrew was based on the principle of parallelism. To have parallelism, each line of poetry had to have at least two parts. What was said in the first part of the line was more or less answered or intensified in the second part of the line. Generally speaking, in English translation, a line in English is one part of a line in Hebrew. For instance, Lamentations 5:20 says:

> Why have you forgotten us completely?
>   Why have you forsaken us these many days?

What was said in the first part of the line was repeated in the second part of the line (the second line in English).

Rhythm also was vital in Hebrew poetry. Each part of the line had certain stresses or strong words. As a general rule, no part of the line had fewer than two or more than three stresses. In *qinah*, there were three stresses in the first part of the line and two stresses in the second part, creating a 3:2 rhythm. This 3:2 *qinah* rhythm was used for dirges (funeral songs) or laments over calamities that had occurred.

CONTENTS OF THE BOOK. The mood of the book is set by a cry of anguish in the first word. The English *how* translates a Hebrew expression of woe:

> *How* lonely sits the city
>   that once was full of people!
> How like a widow she has become,
>   she that was great among the nations!
> She that was a princess among the provinces
>   has become a vassal.

Jerusalem, the abandoned widow (1:1–22). Jerusalem was like a widow, weeping bitterly, because she had been deserted by all who loved her (1:2). Her people carried away (1:3–6), all she had left were her memories of past glory. The victim of her enemies, she was filthy and soiled (1:7–10). Hunger stalked the land. Because of her sins, the LORD's blessing had been withdrawn from her (1:11–13).

The Literary Structure of Lamentations

Many aspects of the structure of this book are discussed in the main body of the text. The question pursued here is the shape of the whole and how the parts contribute to that shape. There is a strong consensus that Lamentations consists of five poems. These are marked off by acrostic patterns in the Hebrew text and are accurately separated by the chapter divisions in the present form of Lamentations. **Acrostic** means that successive sections of the poem begin with successive letters of the Hebrew alphabet. Notice that because the Hebrew alphabet has twenty-two letters, Chapters 1, 2, 4, and 5 of Lamentations each have twenty-two verses. Because the acrostic pattern in Chapter 3 uses groups of three verses, there are sixty-six verses (3 × 22) in this chapter.

The first two poems, Chapters 1 and 2, are similar in structure and content. Both speak primarily of Jerusalem and its devastation. Both end with a plea to God to change the present situation. The central poem is by far the longest and deserves to be the center of attention. Aside from its length, its most noticeable feature is the change of voice. It is written in the first person. One way of understanding this is that expressed in the main body of this textbook: that the poet speaks of his or her personal experience. This past experience is analogous to the present experience of Jerusalem. Another possibility is that in this central poem Jerusalem itself speaks in a literary technique called **personification**. The former possibility perhaps invites the reader to consider her or his own personal experience in introspective fashion. The latter view provides a more dramatic scene, as the city that has been addressed in the first two poems steps forward to speak. Like the first two poems, the third ends with a plea to God for deliverance.

The fourth and fifth poems return to third-person address and also match the first two in length. The third poem ends on a more positive note. It speaks of trusting God and the hope for rescue from enemies. The fourth and fifth poems are unable to sustain this momentum. Suffering and despair are central in them, just as in the first two. The third poem stands apart at the center. The final poem ends with a dramatic question that highlights the tension of Jerusalem's present condition. God reigns forever and is capable of restoring Jerusalem, but God may have forsaken and rejected the holy city. In daring fashion, the book of Lamentations leaves this question open. Because the last verse is so negative, the practice of reading the book of Lamentations aloud in the Jewish tradition includes the repetition of the penultimate verse (5:21) again at the end.

Adele Berlin has argued that the five poems of Lamentations view the destruction of Jerusalem from five perspectives. Chapter 1 looks directly at the destroyed city of Jerusalem and its mournful shame. Chapter 2 moves back to portray the actual destructive event. Chapter 3, narrated by a man, describes "the process of exile" and its accompanying emotions. Chapter 4 focuses directly on the people who suffered through the siege and destruction of Jerusalem. Finally, Chapter 5 presents the desperate prayer of those who remain after the destruction.[2]

Those sins had become a yoke on Jerusalem's neck. Its best soldiers had been helpless before the power of the invader. Mocked and despised by its neighbors and with no comforters, Jerusalem wept (1:14–17). Yet the LORD had been just because Jerusalem had been disobedient. Its allies had refused its pleas for help. Only now, with death and destruction everywhere, was there sorrow for sins committed. Its enemies taunted it because of its condition. The poem ends with a plea for the enemy to be punished in the same measure that Jerusalem has suffered (1:18–22).

The punishment of Jerusalem (Lam. 2:1–22). The second lament falls more easily into natural divisions. Lamentations 2:1–9 describes the destruction of the land and city; 2:10–12 describes the emotional and physical effects of the **siege**; 2:13–19 is an address to Jerusalem reminding it of the causes of its condition; and 2:20–22 is a prayer to the LORD to be aware of what was happening to the city.

1. ***The destruction of the land (2:1–9).*** The Temple, the LORD's dwelling place, was abandoned. The LORD had gone through the land destroying without mercy both villages and cities. Forts and palaces alike were in ruins. The Temple was smashed—the services were ended. The strong walls that protected Jerusalem were broken down. The gates where justice was dispensed and where the ebb and flow of humanity was seen as people entered the city were buried in the rubble of the walls.

2. ***The effect on the people (2:10–12).*** Old men sat in an unbelieving daze, while young girls bowed to the ground in sorrow. The author had wept until he could weep no more. Famine stalked the city so that hungry children fell like wounded men, while others died in their mothers' arms.

3. ***O Jerusalem, how can I comfort you? (2:13–19).*** Jerusalem's condition was hopeless. It had let itself be deceived by lying prophets. Now, people passed by and poked fun at its condition. Its enemies sneered at it. The LORD's patience had run its course, and destruction had come. The poet called for Jerusalem's walls to cry out to the LORD for mercy for its children, who were "starving to death on every street corner" (2:19 TEV).

4. ***LORD, look what you are doing (2:20–22).*** The poet pleaded with the LORD to look at the suffering. Mothers were becoming cannibals, eating their own children. Priest and prophet, young and old, were being slaughtered everywhere. Jerusalem's enemies were having a "carnival of terror" (2:22 TEV) at its expense.

A personal lament, advice about God's righteousness and mercy, and a prayer for help against the enemy (3:1–66). This poem is two things. First, it is actually a combination of three poems, each with a different purpose. Second, the poems appear here as one triple alphabetic acrostic; that is, instead of each line starting with a different letter of the alphabet, each set of three lines starts with a different letter.

1. ***A lament about life (3:1–24).*** The poet had known suffering. He had been quite ill or injured and had come close to death (3:1–5). He had cried to God, but there seemed to be no answer. Instead, like Job, because God's arrows had pierced his body, he felt that God had used him for target practice. He had been pushed down into the dirt so many times that he had lost hope (3:6–18).

Yet, in the depth of his bitterness, he remembered an important thing:

> The steadfast love of the LORD never ceases,
> his mercies never come to an end;
> they are new every morning;
> great is your faithfulness.
> "The LORD is my portion," says my soul,
> "therefore I will hope in him." (3:22–24)

2. ***The importance of trusting God (3:25–51).*** As if to answer, and to add to the positive note found in the last stanza of the previous psalm, this poem speaks of the importance of patience. That it was a different poem can be seen in the shift from the singular to the plural in the use of personal pronouns.

The goodness of the LORD was to all who trusted Him. Patience should be practiced, therefore, in whatever situation life brought. The LORD might permit sorrow and pain, but He took no pleasure in doing so. He was aware of what was happening to everyone. His will would be carried out. The people should admit their sin. The calamities that had come upon them caused the poet sorrow, especially for what had happened to the women of the city.

3. *Rescued from my enemies (3:52–66).* This was a combination of a lament and a thanksgiving. The poet spoke of his treatment by his enemies. He cried to the LORD and was assured that he would be rescued. The LORD's word came true. The poet then prayed for punishment of the enemy.

Conditions during the siege of Jerusalem (4:1–22). The horrors of the siege of Jerusalem are nowhere more vividly portrayed than in this chapter. The holy objects of the Temple were scattered in the streets, and people were smashed like clay pots. Those who survived lost all sense of humanity in their wild urge to live. Children starved to death because adults would not share food with them. The upper classes, always the healthier members of the population because of their better diet, starved like the poor. Those who died by the sword were the fortunate ones. Things were so bad that mothers boiled and ate their own children (4:1–10).

The LORD's wrath rained down on the city with such violence that Jerusalem's neighbors were shocked. None of them believed that Jerusalem could be conquered. Prophets and priests who had misled the people were now shunned as though they were lepers. The city's leaders were ignored instead of being honored (4:11–16).

The survivors kept looking for help, but none came. It was not safe to walk in the streets; if a person fell, he could be eaten (4:17–19)!

The end came. Those who tried to flee were chased down. The king, trying to escape the city, was captured. The Edomites, Judah's neighbors to the southeast, taunted the victims, increasing the natural hatred the two peoples had for each other. Judah's punishment was complete (4:20–22).

Restore us, O LORD (5:1–22). The people were under the oppressor's heel. Taken from their land, they were like motherless children. Everything they got had a price, even the water they drank. The punishment for their sin was upon them. The famine produced diseases that brought raging fevers; their women were abused physically by the invading soldiers; oppression was the rule and not the exception. Joy had turned into mourning (5:1–18).

The LORD was their only hope. The only question was whether or not they had been completely rejected (5:19–22).

THE LIVES OF THE SURVIVORS

It has been common within Old Testament scholarship to talk about "the Exile" as if this term describes the experience of most of the citizens of Judah. Recent studies indicate that this was clearly not the case. This situation has been summarized well by Jill Middlemas, who has responded by offering a new term, "The Templeless Age," to replace the use of "the Exile," because the one factor that all of the resulting communities had in common in this era was coping with the absence of the Temple.[3] What developed during this period were three different population centers: (1) Those who remained in Judah, under some degree of Babylonian control, (2) those who were taken to Babylon in three deportations (597, 587, and 582 B.C.E.), and (3) those who moved to Egypt at various times and for various reasons. Describing these groups is difficult for two reasons. First, there is very little information about them outside of the Bible itself. Second, the material that is in the Bible was probably produced by members of the third group listed above, so we have only their perception of the situation, and of the other two groups.

Those Who Remained in Judah

The biblical tradition tends to diminish or ignore this remaining population. In 2 Kings 25:12, they are the "poorest people of the land," left behind by the Babylonians to be "vinedressers and tillers of the soil." The focus is placed on those taken into exile as the true remnant of Israel. Ezra 1–6 provides glimpses of some later conflict between the returnees and those who remained, along with attempts to incorporate some of them into the group that considered themselves returnees.

Some recent studies have indicated that this may have been a larger and more active group as was once thought.[4] Archaeological evidence indicates severe damage and destruction to Jerusalem and surrounding cities in the southern region of Judah, but the northern part of the region may have been spared much of this. Thus, although the population of Judah was not nearly what it had been during the seventh century, the land was by no means empty, and in some places life likely continued much as it had before. Jerusalem and its temple were essentially gone, but it is difficult to say whether these had ever played a significant role in the daily lives of these people. The various practices involving religious pilgrimages, particularly at festival times, would have been disrupted or significantly changed.

Those Who Moved to Egypt

As had been noted previously, a number of people, including Jeremiah, were left in the land under the governorship of Gedaliah. When Gedaliah was murdered in 582 B.C.E., those who were his supporters fled to Egypt, thinking they would be blamed for the murder. They, and others who went to Egypt from time to time, would develop into a significant Jewish community in later centuries, especially in and around Alexandria. This group appears to have been the one most open to adapting to new ideas and contexts. It is not clear exactly who was involved in the process of translating the Hebrew Scriptures into Greek, the body of texts eventually known as the Septuagint, but it is commonly accepted that the process began in the third century B.C.E. and was generated by this Alexandrian Jewish community.

Those in Captivity in Babylon

The people who went into exile in Babylon survived not only as individuals, but also as an identifiable group of people. Their religion, although tested in the fires of war and surrender, also survived. But some important changes took place. While in captivity, most of these people seem to have shifted their everyday language from Hebrew to **Aramaic**, the language of the Babylonians. Aramaic was the most widely spoken language in the Near East. It was similar to Hebrew, so that the change was not difficult to make. Hebrew continued to be used to some extent, especially in religious services.[5] The bilingual nature of their existence is reflected in the two bilingual books of the Old Testament, Ezra and Daniel, both of which contain significant amounts of Aramaic, mixed with Biblical Hebrew.

Exile and destruction disrupted the work of the Temple and its system of sacrifices, but the communities in Judah, Egypt, and Babylon found new ways to think about, speak about, and engage the presence of God, even in very different contexts. Whether the practice of synagogue study and worship was founded in the period from 586 to 538 B.C.E. cannot be determined with

FIGURE 9–2 This illustration shows the Ishtar Gate, the entrance to the ancient city of Babylon.

certainty. Undoubtedly, the conditions that led to its founding were present, especially for those in a foreign land. Services of prayer, praise, and reading of sacred writings surely must have been carried on. From the worship services, it was only a short step to the formal structure that made up synagogue worship. Even after the Judahites were permitted to leave Babylon and return to the land of Judah, many remained there and a vibrant Jewish community continued to develop, one whose remnants can be seen even in modern times in the Jewish communities of Iraq and Iran.

New Directions in Theological Thinking

The Exile brought the threat of the loss of the sacred traditions of Israel. Because many of them were unwritten, it was a matter of urgency that they be committed to writing before those who knew them died. Many of those who remembered such traditions had already perished in the siege of Jerusalem. The Exile must have been a time of unusual literary activity. That at least the final materials were added to Israel's history that had been preserved in 1,2 Samuel and 1,2 Kings (the Deuteronomistic History) can be seen from the account of the release of King Jehoiachin from prison in 560 B.C.E. (2 Kings 25:27–30). The priests who had been deported to Babylon likely participated in the work of writing and editing sacred texts, and they may have been the primary force behind this process, which would continue for many years.[6]

The scriptures edited and produced during the period of the Babylonian captivity overwhelmingly present the idea that this was God's punishment for Israel's unfaithfulness, particularly the worship of other gods. Worship of Israel's God in other locations and places, outside of the control of the central priesthood in Jerusalem, was also often understood as unfaithfulness. It is not surprising, therefore, that an approach to religion developed during this period that was more strictly monotheistic and more closely tied to central institutions. The development of religious views in this direction would set up a situation of conflict when the returnees from Babylon encountered those who were already in the land of Israel when they returned. The group who had been taken into captivity in Babylon referred to itself as the *"Golah"* group, a word that literally means something like "the exposed ones." This sense of identity would become the one that all of the restored community would be required to accept for itself, whether they had actually been captive in Babylon or not.

THE CHANGING INTERNATIONAL SITUATION (538–486 B.C.E.)

The Collapse of Babylon

The Babylonian (Chaldean) Empire reached its peak and collapsed within a relatively brief period of time. When Nebuchadnezzar died in 562 B.C.E., Babylon began to die. His successor, Evil-Merodach (562–560 B.C.E.), released King Jehoiachin of Judah from prison (2 Kings 25:27–30), but Evil-Merodach died in the same year. Other kings came to the throne, Nabonidus (556–539 B.C.E.) being the final one. He aroused great antagonism by trying to make major changes in the national religion. Nabonidus was interested in excavating and exploring ruins and abandoned temples—a sixth-century B.C.E. archaeologist! He left the running of the kingdom to his son Belshazzar. He even refused to come to Babylon for the New Year's Festival, the chief religious festival of the year and one in which the king played a leading role. This brought major unrest among the people just as a new power was rising in the East.

Babylon's most dangerous rival was Media. When a revolt led by the Persian king, Cyrus, broke out in the Median Empire, Nabonidus may have supported it. But Cyrus rapidly became a dangerous rival to be reckoned with. By 550 B.C.E., Media was under his control. He defeated an

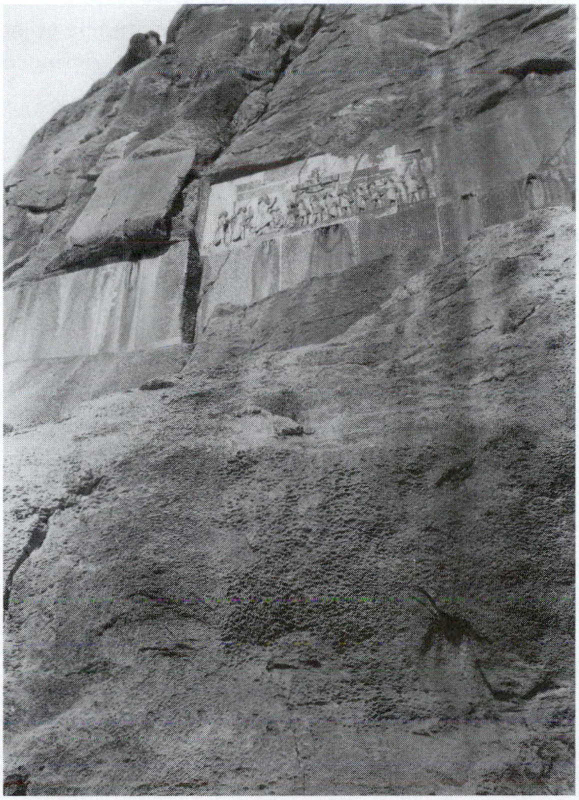

FIGURE 9–3 This ancient relief, carved on a mountain in what is now southern Iran, illustrates the grandeur of Darius I, the king of Persia mentioned in Ezra 5–6. The relief includes parallel inscriptions in three different ancient languages, which helped archaeologists decipher these languages.

alliance of Egypt, Babylon, and Lydia by conquering Lydia in 546 B.C.E. and Babylon in 539 B.C.E. and penetrating all the way to the Egyptian frontier by 538 B.C.E.[7]

The final Babylonian emperor, Nabonidus, was apparently ineffective in many ways. The Persians, under the capable leadership of Cyrus, were able to take advantage of this situation in the middle of the sixth century and establish their own empire in the region, from the western parts of India to the eastern edges of Egypt. In 539 B.C.E., the armies of Cyrus entered Babylonia itself and met no resistance, because Nabonidus had already fled. The starkly different imperial policies of Persia would bring about the release of the Israelites from captivity by the following year. The Babylonian captivity had lasted for about sixty ears, a relatively small portion of Israel's long story, and it is uncertain what percentage of Israel's population had actually been involved, but this experience had a powerful formative effect upon the Israelite people. Although the Israelite homeland would be reestablished to some extent, the rest of Israel's story would always involve a significantly dispersed population. In the words of Rainer Albertz, "The Babylonian exile became the prototype for Israel's life in the Diaspora."[8]

The Persian Empire (538–486 B.C.E.)

Cyrus died in 530 B.C.E. and was followed as emperor by his son, Cambyses, who extended the Persian Empire further into Egypt by 525 B.C.E. During a period of rebellion in the empire, Cambyses apparently killed himself, and the Persian throne was seized by Darius, one of his military officers. After a period of widespread revolt in the wake of these events, Darius was able to stabilize the empire and solidify his position as emperor; his reign continued for over thirty years.

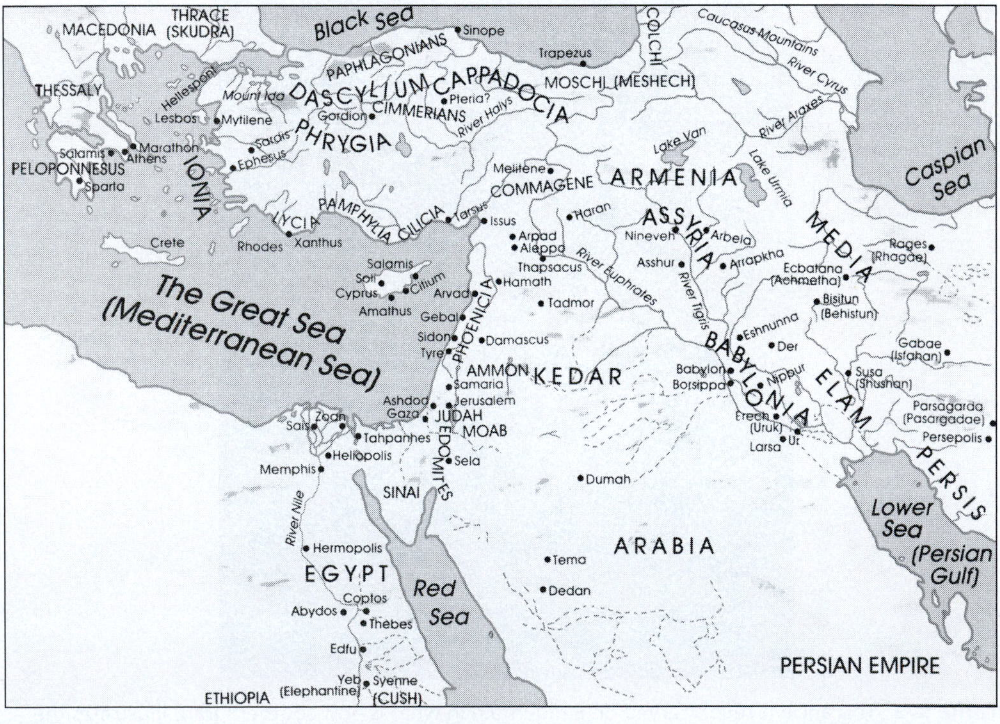

FIGURE 9–4 The Persian Empire. Artwork by Margaret Jordan Brown, from Mercer Dictionary of the Bible, © 1990, courtesy of Mercer University Press.

The Persian Empire itself continued to rule the entire region for about two centuries until the rise of the Greeks under Alexander the Great. The imperial policies of Persia, including the promotion of local culture, religion, and economy and the appointment of governors, would have a great influence on the restored land of Judah during this time period.[9] What is typically called the "Persian Period" in the story of Israel would last until the rise of the Greek Empire under Alexander the Great two centuries later. What is portrayed in the Bible as the **restoration** of Jerusalem and Judah took place under the control and sponsorship of Persia, so it would be heavily influenced by the policies and culture of this empire.

THE RESTORED COMMUNITY

The day that many in the community held captive in Babylon had probably dreamed about came in 538 B.C.E. The captives were permitted to return to Palestine and to rebuild their Temple, which had lain in ruins for over forty years. In II Chronicles 36:21 this period is explained as a forced rest for the land enacted by God as a response to Israel's failure to observe the policies of Land Sabbath prescribed in Leviticus 25. The length of time provided there, seventy years, is probably somewhat figurative, but might roughly correspond to the period between the destruction of Solomon's temple in 586 and the completion of the second temple in about 520.

The Decree of Cyrus (Ezra 1:1–4)

The restoration was the result of the policies of Cyrus the Great. He reversed the policies of the previous kings who had dominated the Near East. Whereas they had deported people to help defuse rebellion, Cyrus permitted all exiles who wanted to return to their original homes. Whereas previous kings had tried to destroy such religious shrines as the Temple, Cyrus encouraged subject peoples to rebuild their shrines. He even provided financial and other resources to assist in the construction.

In 538 B.C.E., Cyrus issued a decree that permitted exiled persons to return to their homelands.[10] One version of this decree is found in 1 Chronicles 36:22–23. Another version is found in Ezra 1:2–4. In it, Cyrus declared that the LORD had given him the responsibility of ensuring that the Temple was rebuilt. The returning exiles were to be given help in "silver and gold, with goods and with animals, besides freewill offerings" (1:4). The biblical version of this decree gives the impression that only the Judahites were given such help. It seems, however, that Cyrus did this for peoples of all locations and religions who were released from captivity. Cyrus is also mentioned in Isaiah 45, where he is given the status of "anointed one (messiah)" because of his deliverance of the Israelites from their captivity in Babylon.

The Returners (Ezra 1:5–2:70)[11]

In the years after 538 B.C.E., several groups of Jews returned to Palestine. The first group was led by Sheshbazzar, "the prince of Judah," who was the son of Jehoiachin. They carried with them some of the Temple treasures Nebuchadnezzar had taken away. All Sheshbazzar was able to accomplish was to lay the foundations of the new Temple (Ezra 3:10–13), then a pause in the recovery took place. This condition had several major causes: (1) the harsh realities of coming into a land still bearing many of the marks of the Babylonian conquest; (2) conflict with the people who had remained in the land, who felt it was theirs by virtue of the fact that they had lived there undisturbed for more than forty years; and (3) conflict with the people of the old northern territories, who considered themselves as still faithful to the religion of Israel. The returnees, on the other hand, looked down upon them and their religious practices as impure.

The Literary Structure of Ezra–Nehemiah

Ezra and Nehemiah are two books that, in their final forms, belong together. Both books take a large variety of materials concerning the post-Exilic period in Israel and attempt to mold them into a coherent story. A number of factors tie these two books together. First, Ezra appears as a character at the middle and end of both books. Second, both books include the long list of those who returned to Judah from Babylon. This list appears in Ezra 2 and Nehemiah 7. Third, both books contain first-person narrative written from the point of view of the title character. These sections are sometimes referred to as the *Ezra* **Memoir** and the *Nehemiah Memoir*. Fourth, both books report the process of expelling foreign wives from Israel. In both cases, this takes place at the end of the book, in Ezra 10 and Nehemiah 13.

All of these connections lead to the realization that the books of Ezra and Nehemiah have a parallel structure. Ezra 1–6 tells the story of the building of the **Second Temple** in Jerusalem. Nehemiah 1–7 tells the story of the rebuilding of the wall around Jerusalem. Ezra 7–10 reports the program of reform initiated by Ezra after his return to Jerusalem. Nehemiah 10–13 records the story of another program of reform led by Ezra and Nehemiah. The climax of the two books is the public reading of the law by Ezra in Nehemiah 8. What these two books accomplish together is to present a picture of Israelite religion centered on the Temple and the law. This religion is practiced by a purified people in a city surrounded by a wall and under God's protection.

There are costs to pay for such a well-ordered picture. A real cost in the story is the destruction of numerous families when the women are sent away because they are foreign. The literary costs are a number of narrative inconsistencies that must be tolerated or ignored. The most obvious of these is Ezra's acknowledgment of the presence of the wall in Ezra 9:9 before Nehemiah builds it in Nehemiah 1–7. The writer of these stories is willing to pay such costs, however, because of the ideological tasks that these books perform so well.

Multiple points of view are held together in Ezra–Nehemiah by a careful weaving together of the books' components. There is a great temptation to separate these components into small pieces of text so that they do not contradict each other, but when this is done the complexity of the story is largely lost. This book tells a story filled with conflict. This narrative of conflict is adequately matched by the conflict present in the literary texture of the book.

Because there seem to have been less than ideal agricultural conditions in those early years, making a living turned out to be difficult. By contrast, Babylon, with its well-irrigated fields and busy cities, offered money and food in abundance. Because of its prosperity, conditions were so attractive that many Jews chose to remain there. Babylonian records indicate that some Jews became prominent bankers, businessmen, and high government officials. Some of those who returned to Palestine probably wished at times that they had not done so.

The ultimate fate of Sheshbazzar is uncertain. He is mentioned only in scattered references. He may have died or been replaced as leader by Zerubbabel, who probably returned with another group of exiles in 520 B.C.E. The spiritual leader was Joshua, who was High Priest. Some additional clues about the continuing work of restoration are present in the prophetic books of Haggai and Zechariah, which will be examined in Chapter 12.

These prophets, along with Zerubbabel and Joshua, inspired the people to return to rebuilding the Temple with vigor. Trouble would not be long in coming, however. The ruler of the province of which Jerusalem was a part sent someone to investigate what was going on. He found out who was responsible and sent someone to the Persian capital to see if the work had indeed been authorized by Cyrus, as the Jews claimed. When the answer came back, not only was the right to rebuild the Temple confirmed, but also the governor, Tattenai, was instructed to pay the building costs out of royal revenues. The building was finished and dedicated with joyful ceremonies in 515 B.C.E.

With the completion of the Temple, a curtain was drawn over events in Palestine for more than fifty years. What happened, no one knows. Zerubbabel's hopes of creating the messianic kingdom was certainly not fulfilled. In fact, his hopes and the efforts of the prophets to promote him as the Jewish ruler may well have had fatal results. The Persians, while remarkably tolerant in their policy toward conquered peoples, were so highly organized that revolt was kept at a minimum. It could be that Zerubbabel was removed because of the hope that he would be the promised messiah.

EZRA AND NEHEMIAH[12]

With the fading away of Zerubbabel, the hope of reestablishing the Davidic monarchy also faded. When the Jews once more became visible on the stage of history, there was no mention of a king. Instead, the dominant figure in Jewish life was the priest. In the hands of the High Priest would come to rest both the chief religious and political powers of the Jewish people.

Ezra the Priest and Scribe

In the person of Ezra, we meet perhaps the most influential person in the post-Exilic community. His activities have sometimes earned him the title "Father of Judaism." The work of Ezra and the religious traditions he helped to establish the point at which it is most appropriate to begin using terms like *Jews*, *Jewish*, and *Judaism* to distinguish the identity of these people and their religion from that of the ancient Israelites.

Ezra led a group of immigrants from Babylonia to Jerusalem "in the seventh year of Artaxerxes the king" (Ezra 7:7). Given the dates of Artaxerxes I (465–424 B.C.E.), it would seem simple to conclude that Ezra arrived in Jerusalem in 458 B.C.E. But things are not quite that simple; there were two kings named Artaxerxes. Artaxerxes II ruled from 404 to 358 B.C.E. Ezra could have arrived in Jerusalem in 397 instead of 458 B.C.E. A third date that has been suggested is 428 B.C.E., based on the belief that Ezra came in the thirty-seventh year of Artaxerxes I. This would assume that the word *thirty* has fallen out of the biblical text. There is little evidence to support such an assumption.

Recent evidence has given new support to the first date, 458 B.C.E. One of the major arguments against that date is that Ezra started some important reforms, of which Nehemiah found little evidence when he arrived in 445 B.C.E. As one scholar has pointed out, however, reformers in biblical history were not noted for their long-lasting success. Good examples were King Hezekiah and King Josiah, both of whom had reforms that died quickly.[13] It is assumed here, therefore, that Ezra returned in 458 B.C.E., the seventh year of the reign of King Artaxerxes I.

The Work of Ezra (Ezra 7:1–10:44; Neh. 8:1–9:37)

THE RETURN TO JERUSALEM (EZRA 7:1–8:36). The picture given of Ezra is that he, like many Jews, had achieved a position of some respect in the Persian kingdom. This was shown by the fact that not only did King Artaxerxes permit him to gather a group of immigrants to return to Jerusalem, but he also gave a generous amount of money to subsidize them (7:1–24). Ezra, furthermore, was to "appoint magistrates and judges, who may judge all the people in the province Beyond the River" (7:25).

In Ezra 7:27, the narrative switches to a first-person account of what happened on Ezra's trip to Jerusalem in 458 B.C.E. (7:7–9). First, there was a prayer of thanksgiving for the undertaking

(7:27–28), then, in true priestly fashion, there was a listing of those who made the trip (8:1–4). Finding that there were not sufficient priests, Ezra sent some eloquent and influential men to the Levites to persuade some of them to go along on the trip (8:15–20).

They were successful, and after Ezra gave a selected group of the priests responsibility for looking after the money and sacred vessels given for use in the Temple, the pilgrims set out on the long trip to Jerusalem. When they arrived safely, the money and vessels were turned over to the Temple officials for safekeeping, and the proper calls of respect were paid to the local Persian officials, who were given letters of instruction from Artaxerxes concerning their part in aiding Ezra (8:21–36).

Ezra's reforms (Ezra 9:1–10:44). Ezra lost no time making his presence felt in the community of Jerusalem.

1. ***The problem of foreign wives (Ezra 9:1–10:44).*** Discovering that many of the Jews, including priests, had married non-Jewish women, Ezra tore his clothes, pulled his hair, and went into mourning (9:1–5).

At the time of the evening sacrifice, he prayed an eloquent prayer of confession about this condition, which for him represented a great sin by the people (9:6–15). By the time his prayer was ended, he was joined by many others who also were confessing that they had sinned by marrying non-Jewish women. In the emotion of the moment, they made a covenant to divorce all non-Jewish wives. Ezra required all the Levites and others present to swear to do as they had promised (10:1–5).

After a night of prayer and fasting, Ezra called a meeting of all Jews in Jerusalem within three days. To impress on the people the importance of being present, he said that any person who failed to appear would lose his property. Needless to say, a large crowd gathered, even though a heavy rain was falling. It was decided that a council of leading men would be set up to deal with the matter. The council was formed, and those who had married non-Jewish women divorced them and sent them away, along with any children born to them (10:6–44).

2. ***The renewing of the covenant (Neh. 8:1–9:38).*** Again, Ezra called the people together. The purpose was a ceremony of covenant renewal, recalling an ancient custom going back to the years following Israel's covenant at Sinai (Josh. 24). First, Ezra read the law aloud. It is uncertain what this reading included, but a reasonable guess is that it was a version of the book of Deuteronomy very similar to what we have today. As Ezra read this law, it had to be translated into the language of the people, which was now Aramaic, not Hebrew. This, then, was the first recorded attempt to paraphrase the scriptures (8:1–8), and the origin of the translation of the Hebrew Scriptures into Aramaic, a practice that took place over several centuries. Various Aramaic versions in later years were known as the **Targumim**. These are often loose paraphrases of the Hebrew text with considerable added commentary.

While the Law was read, it was discovered that the seventh month (when this was taking place) was also the time for the celebration of the Feast of Tabernacles or Booths (**Sukkoth** Hebrew). The people went into the hills, cut tree limbs, and built shelters. They lived in the shelters for seven days to remind them of Israel's wilderness years. During those days, they spent their time studying the Law (8:9–18).

The festival was followed by a great day of repentance and confession. Some suggest that this may have come before the celebration of the Feast of Tabernacles.[14] The Jews separated themselves from all foreigners and confessed not only their own sins, but also those of their ancestors (9:2). They alternated hearing the Law read with confession of sin. The solemn day was climaxed by Ezra's prayer of confession. In it, in a style common to the Old Testament, he first praised God. Then, the reason for the praise was stated by retelling the story of the LORD's mighty act of delivering the people from Egyptian bondage and His mercy toward them, even though they had sinned so gravely against Him (9:1–31).

Finally, Ezra confessed the sins of the generation then present. Like their fathers, they, too, had sinned. As a token of their repentance, they entered into a solemn covenant, signed by the princes, Levites, and priests (9:32–38). This was the last mention of the work of Ezra.

Nehemiah, the Builder (Neh. 1:1–7:73; 13:1–31)

The time of Nehemiah's return is less debated than that of Ezra. He said in his memoirs that he returned to Jerusalem in the twentieth year of Artaxerxes. There is general agreement that Artaxerxes I (465–424 B.C.E.) is meant, thus dating Nehemiah's return to 445 B.C.E.

Nehemiah, a devout Jewish layman, was cupbearer to the Persian king. The cupbearer's position was one of great honor, as it involved great trust on the part of the king for the person who held the job.[15] Messengers came from Jerusalem, reporting that the walls and gates of the city were in ruins. Either they had never been rebuilt since the Babylonian invasion, or they had been destroyed by the Persians for some unknown reason. Nehemiah began a period of fasting and prayer when he heard the news (1:1–11).

The Night Ride of Nehemiah

The book of Nehemiah reports the work of Nehemiah, who returned to Palestine from Babylon during the Persian period and led much of the rebuilding and reestablishment of Jerusalem. He eventually became governor of the Persian province of Yehud. About half of the book of Nehemiah consists of first-person accounts told from the perspective of Nehemiah, and these passages are commonly called the *Nehemiah Memoir*. Nehemiah's central feat was the rebuilding of the walls around Jerusalem, which had been destroyed during the Babylonian invasion about a century and a half earlier. The poor condition of the walls meant that Jerusalem lay exposed, unable to defend itself. While still living in the Persian city of Susa, Nehemiah heard about the condition of Jerusalem and its walls. He wept and decided to return to Jerusalem to rebuild the city. He attained permission and sponsorship from the Persian Empire and journeyed back to Israel.

Soon after arriving in Jerusalem, Nehemiah awoke in the middle of the night and rode a donkey around the perimeter of the ruined city to inspect its condition. Nehemiah 2:11–16 reports Nehemiah's observations during this journey. Gate by gate, the broken condition of the wall and the burned condition of the gates are described in this passage. The text does not say why Nehemiah chose to perform this task at night, but when the rebuilding project begins in Nehemiah 3, the Jews face tremendous opposition from other people around them. They have to work on the walls with their weapons at hand, ready to defend themselves. Nehemiah's night ride may have been done secretly so that his enemies would not attack him and would not be aware that planning for the building project was beginning. Nehemiah 6:15–19 reports that the rebuilding of the walls was finished fifty-two days after it was begun and that the other groups of people living around the Israelites now lived in fear of them.

Several months passed. One day while Nehemiah was performing his duties as cupbearer, the king noticed his haggard looks and questioned him about it. When Nehemiah told him the reason, the king made Nehemiah **governor** of the province of **Yehud**, which included Jerusalem, and gave him money and materials to repair the city walls (2:1–8). Nehemiah was not welcomed by everyone. Sanballat, the governor of Samaria, who had dominated Judah for some time; Tobiah, the governor of Ammon in Transjordan; and Geshem (Gasmu), an Arab king, immediately took exception to Nehemiah's presence. They would cause much trouble in the days ahead (2:9–10, 19).[16]

Nehemiah's first action was to make a nighttime survey of the broken walls. Afterwards, he called the Jewish leaders together and told them of his plan to rebuild them. He received an enthusiastic response from them. The response from Sanballat, Tobiah, and Geshem, however, was to suggest that he actually was trying to stir up rebellion against the emperor (2:11–20). Organizing the people into construction gangs, Nehemiah proceeded with his plans (3:1–32). When Sanballat and Tobiah heard that construction was in progress, they immediately began to make threats. Nehemiah responded by dividing the Jews into two groups—one to stand guard against an attack and another to carry on construction (4:1–23).

Then, problems arose within the Jewish community. Many of the Jews had abandoned their villages and farms to aid construction and had borrowed from their rich fellow Jews to provide food for their families. When they could not pay their debts because of their contributions to the project, those to whom they owed money began to foreclose on them. Some even had to give their children as slaves to pay their debts. Nehemiah called the leaders together and told them that such practices must stop immediately. Anyone who was a slave must be freed. He threatened to call the wrath of God down on them if they did not do as he ordered. They believed him and obeyed (5:1–13). To show that he would not ask the people to do what he would not do himself, never in his first twelve-year term as governor did Nehemiah take a salary paid by tax money. Instead, he supported himself and 150 others out of his own resources (5:14–19).

Sanballat and Tobiah kept trying to undermine Nehemiah. They invited him to several meetings outside Jerusalem to discuss matters. Each time, Nehemiah refused to go. In an open letter to Nehemiah, Sanballat suggested that the wall was being built because the Jews intended to revolt and Nehemiah planned to have himself declared king by some of the prophets. Sanballat threatened to tell Artaxerxes what was going on. Nehemiah denied all the charges and continued his work. He also refused to take any special precautions for his safety (6:1–14). After fifty-two days, the construction was finished. Tobiah's sympathizers started a campaign to convince Nehemiah that Tobiah was a nice fellow after all. He had a Jewish father-in-law and a Jewish daughter-in-law. Nehemiah was still unconvinced. He posted trustworthy guards on the city gates with strict instructions about opening and closing hours (6:15–7:4).

When the building was completed, dedicatory services were held, the central feature being a service of sacrifice after a march around the walls. The march ended in the Temple area, where the service of thanksgiving was held (12:27–43).

> They offered great sacrifices that day and rejoiced, for God had made them rejoice with great joy; the women and children also rejoiced. The joy of Jerusalem was heard far away. (12:43)

To complete his work, Nehemiah made arrangements for regular services to be performed by people who were paid by the offerings given, as had been the practice in the time of the great kings. Because provisions were made for the regular collection of Temple revenues, the priests could attend to the services instead of working at other jobs for a living (12:44–47).

These were the major accomplishments of Nehemiah's first term as governor, which covered twelve years (445–433 B.C.E.). In the thirty-second year of Artaxerxes, Nehemiah returned to Persia (13:6).

Nehemiah returned to Jerusalem to find some rather disturbing developments. His old nemesis, Tobiah, had been given a room in the Temple itself. That an Ammonite would even be permitted within the Temple precincts was a shock to Nehemiah. The Deuteronomic Code contained a law that no Ammonite or Moabite would ever be allowed to become a part of Israel, because those peoples had opposed Israel's peaceful passage through their territory in the Exodus (Deut. 23:3–5). By the time of Nehemiah, the **Torah** was already the written law (13:1–3). When Nehemiah discovered that the High Priest Eliashib had allowed Tobiah a room in the Temple, he ordered Tobiah thrown out, along with his furniture. A special cleansing of the room took place, and it was then restored to its normal use (13:4–9).

Second, Nehemiah found that because the offerings had fallen off, the pay for the Levites to conduct the services in the Temple had ceased. The Levites had to return to farming for a living. Nehemiah immediately began collecting the tithes again for the support of Temple worship (13:10–14).

A third situation that confronted him in his second term was that many people were no longer observing the Sabbath. Instead, they were working on the Sabbath as though it was just another day. He ordered the city gates closed on the Sabbath so that foreign traders and farmers could not bring their goods to sell on that day. He issued a warning that anyone who violated the Sabbath would be punished (13:15–22).

Finally, he dealt severely with the still troublesome problem of mixed marriage. He beat Jews who were married to foreign wives, including the son of the High Priest Eliashib. He issued a decree that no such marriages would be permitted and rooted out foreign influences from Jewish life (13:23–31).

When the community was about to be swallowed up by its neighbors, Ezra and Nehemiah had played a vital role in preserving the religious life and culture of the Jews who had returned from exile. The zeal they inspired would be carried over into the period that, in Jewish historical records, is almost blank. Around 200 B.C.E., the curtain would be lifted again, when Palestine once again became the battleground between two powers trying to gain control of its territory.

Evaluating Crisis Leadership

Retrospective evaluation of leadership during times of crisis is very difficult. Recent examples in the history of the United States are illustrative of the problem. Attempts to assess Abraham Lincoln's declaration of martial law in 1863 and Franklin Roosevelt's establishment of internment camps for Japanese-Americans in 1942 may be the clearest examples. The latter was more obviously a mistake because it combined racial bias with a fear-driven suspension of constitutional rights. The expulsion of foreign wives in the stories of both Ezra and Nehemiah may generate this same kind of revulsion and a response such as "How could we have acted that way?" Perhaps we can find a way to recognize that such behavior in the midst of a crisis is understandable but not excusable. The restoration crisis brought out both the best and the worst in Ezra and Nehemiah as leaders, and the Bible makes no attempt to hide this reality. Within the full canon of the Old Testament, the story of Ruth, the Moabite great-grandmother of David; Rahab, the Canaanite woman who assists the Israelites in Jericho; and others serve to balance this tendency to blame our difficulties on those we consider outsiders or foreigners. This impulse is alive and well in all human hearts, and these stories may cause us to hesitate long enough to bring our irrational fears into the light of careful and compassionate reflection.

Key Terms

Acrostic, *192*
Aramaic, *195*
Deportation, *190*
Exile, *195*
Governor, *204*
Memoir, *200*
Personification, *192*
Restoration, *199*
Siege, *193*
Second Temple, *200*
Sukkoth, *202*
Targumin, *202*
Torah, *205*
Yehud, *204*

Study Questions

1. What is distinctive about the literary design of the book of Lamentations?
2. What does Lamentations tell us about conditions in Jerusalem during the Babylonian siege?
3. What changes did Israel experience as the result of the Babylonian Exile?
4. What were the three major groups of Israelites that formed in the wake of the Babylonian destruction, and how were they related to each other?
5. What caused the decline of the Babylonian Empire?
6. How did Cyrus' conquest of the Babylonians affect the Jews in exile?
7. What happened to the first group of Jews who returned from exile to Palestine?
8. Why is it difficult to date Ezra's return from exile? What evidence supports the various choices?
9. Assess the relative significance of Ezra and Nehemiah to the Jerusalem community.
10. What was the significance of the reading of the Law described in Nehemiah 8?
11. What were Nehemiah's accomplishments as governor?
12. How did Ezra and Nehemiah address the issue of foreign wives? Why?

Endnotes

1. Robert Alter, "The Characteristics of Ancient Hebrew Poetry," in *The Literary Guide to the Bible,* edited by Robert Alter and Frank Kermode (Cambridge, MA: Belknap Press, 1987), 615. See also an excellent brief discussion of the characteristics of Hebrew poetry in *NOAB* in *NRSV* (New York: Oxford University Press, 1991), 392–400, in the supplementary section on "Modern Approaches to the Bible."
2. See Adele Berlin, *Lamentations: A Commentary* (Louisville, KY: Westmінter–John Knox Press, 2002), 7.
3. Jill Middlemas, *The Templeless Age: An Introduction to the History, Literature, and Theology of the "Exile"* (Louisville, KY: Westminster Press, 2007), 1–27.
4. See Hugh G. M. Williamson, "Laments at the Destroyed Temple," *BR,* VI, 4 (August 1990), 12, who discusses recent discoveries that seem to indicate that a number of wealthy Jewish families lived in Jerusalem during the Exile.
5. On the history and sources of the Aramaic language, see Scott C. Layton, "Old Aramaic Inscriptions," Dennis Pardee, ed. *BA,* 51, 3 (September 1988), 172–189.
6. Noth, *The History of Israel,* 292, argues that the Deuteronomistic History was written in Palestine, while Richard Elliott Friedman, *Who Wrote the Bible?* (New York: Harper & Row, 1987), 146–149, believes that Jeremiah and Baruch were the author-editors of the work.
7. For further details, see Bright, *A History of Israel,* 354–355, 361–362, and Noth, *The History of Israel,* 300–302.
8. Rainer Albertz, *Israel in Exile: The History and Literature of the Sixth Century* B.C.E., translated by David Green (Atlanta: Society of Biblical Literature, 2003), 22. See also the description of "the emergence of a diasporic theology" in Daniel L. Smith-Christopher, *A Biblical Theology of Exile* (Minneapolis: Fortress Press, 2002), 6–15.
9. For more background and discussion of the Persian impact on post-Exilic Judah, see James M. Miller and John H. Hayes, *A History of Israel and Judah,* 2nd ed. (Louisville, KY: Westminster Press, 2006), 508–511.

10. The Persian version can be found in Pritchard, *ANE,* 206–208.
11. Unlike previous books, in which an attempt has been made to follow the order of the material as closely as possible, the order of Ezra and Nehemiah is somewhat confusing. References will be made to the material in chronological order as closely as possible.
12. For a more extended discussion, see Jacob M. Myers, "Ezra–Nehemiah," *AB,* 14 (Garden City, NY: Doubleday, 1965), 50–54.
13. Frank M. Cross, "A Reconstruction of the Judean Restoration," *INT,* XXIX, 2 (April 1975), 198. The article has a good summary of the arguments for the three basic dates.
14. Myers, "Ezra–Nehemiah," 165.
15. Myers, op. cit., discusses the location of Susa and the role of the cupbearer.
16. Cross, "A Reconstruction," 200.

CHAPTER

10 The Prophetic Literature I

An Introduction to Prophetic Literature and the Book of Isaiah

Timeline

735 B.C.E. Beginning of the reign of Ahaz and the Syro-Ephraimitic crisis
715 B.C.E. Beginning of the reign of Hezekiah
701 B.C.E. Sannacherib's invasion
700 B.C.E. Approximate beginning of the rise of the Babylonian Empire
640 B.C.E. Beginning of the reign of Josiah
612 B.C.E. Fall of Ninevah
605 B.C.E. Beginning of the reign of Nebuchadnezzar in Babylon
597 B.C.E. First Deportation of Judahites to Babylon
586 B.C.E. Destruction of Jerusalem by the Babylonians

Chapter Outline

CHAPTER OVERVIEW

This chapter begins the discussion of a new kind of literature, so it opens with an introduction to Prophetic Literature, dealing with what it is, where it came from, and how it is related to the persons we refer to as *prophets.* A general introduction to the first prophetic book in the canon, Isaiah, will identify issues specifically related to this example of prophetic literature. This introduction is followed by a more detailed survey of the contents of this sixty-six chapter book. The survey will describe the individual components of the book and attempt to evaluate how they fit into the whole book. The position taken here is that the book of Isaiah is the product of many writers over a period of two to three centuries. This is part of what provides the book such a complex nature. At the same time, there is a sense that the finished form of the book of Isaiah as we have received it is about something, and we will search for the answer to the question, "What is the book of Isaiah about?" even if our answers to this question can only be partial and provisional.

AN INTRODUCTION TO PROPHETIC LITERATURE

Definition

Judaism uses the terms *Prophets* to designate the entire second division of the canon. The eight books in this section are then divided into the Former Prophets (Joshua, Judges, Samuel, and Kings) and the Later Prophets (Isaiah, Jeremiah, Ezekiel, and the Book of the Twelve). For those accustomed to reading the Bible within the Christian tradition, these designations can cause some confusion. Although books like Samuel and Kings have characters designated as prophets within them, Christianity has more often referred to the "Prophetic Literature" as the books that have the names of specific prophets attached to them, beginning with the book of Isaiah, and continuing through the book of Malachi. The Christian Old Testament also places two books that are not prophetic literature, Lamentations and Daniel, within this sequence of books. This chapter and the next two in this book will examine the fifteen books that fit into this category because they have the name of a prophetic figure attached to them and they are composed primarily of the work and words that emerged from the traditions surrounding these prophetic figures.

Historical Context

These books designated as the Prophetic Literature were generated during a period of about three hundred years, from the middle of the eighth century to the middle of the fifth century B.C.E. This time period is framed by what are often understood as the three major crises in Israel's story. Previous chapters have dealt with these crises as they appear within the narrative accounts of books like Samuel, Kings, Chronicles, Ezra, and Nehemiah. The Prophetic Literature might best be understood as a particular kind of response to this part of Israel's story. Although these books are complete literary works in their own right, knowing the historical background that gave rise to them will assist our understanding.

The three major crises can all be portrayed as periods of several decades surrounding a focal event. Here is one scheme for doing that:

> ***The Assyrian Crisis***—approximately 740–710 B.C.E. with the Assyrian destruction of the Northern Kingdom in 722 as its focal point.
>
> ***The Babylonian Crisis***—approximately 610–550 B.C.E. with the Babylonian destruction of Judah in 586 as its focal point.

The Restoration Crisis—approximately 530–450 B.C.E. with the rebuilding of the temple in 520 as its focal point.

All of the books that fall into the category of prophetic literature are responses to one or more of these crises. A few of the persons whose names are attached to them, like Isaiah, Jeremiah, Haggai, and Zechariah, appear as characters in the narratives we have been examining as the story of Israel, while others we know only from the books that have their names.

Prophetic Figures and Prophetic Scrolls

The prophetic books have been handed down in tradition to us in four large, complex scrolls, each of which contains many different types of literary units. The primary type is the prophetic speech or utterance most often called an **oracle**. These fall into two primary types, salvation oracles and judgment oracles, but there are others that do not fit easily into these categories. Some of the prophetic books present only these speeches, but others include various amounts of narrative material about the prophets themselves. One common type is the **call narrative**, which, usually in first-person address, tells about the prophet's initial experience in which God assigned him with a task and a message. There are also narratives about prophets performing symbolic actions, rather than speaking in oracles, and stories about the prophets interacting with their audiences.

Because of this mixture of literary types, the relationships between the prophets as people and the books that have their names on them varies, and can be the source of confusion. When we say "Isaiah," for example, are we talking about the person named Isaiah or the book called Isaiah? Isaiah appears as a character only in a few places within the book that shares his name, in Chapters 6–8, 20, and 36–39. Jeremiah, on the other hand, appears as a character frequently throughout almost the entire book of Jeremiah. The book of Joel consists entirely of poetic oracles, and there is no character named Joel present at all in it. This is not the only way that the prophetic books extend beyond the persons with the same name. Many of these books show signs of continued development long past the physical life of the person they are named for. The book of Isaiah, for example, seems to have been written over a period of nearly three centuries. Parts of the book relate to all three of the Israelite crises listed above. Thus, the person named Isaiah, who lived in Jerusalem in the eighth century, is the beginning point of this great scroll and its tradition rather than the author of the finished product.[1] Isaiah 8:16 indicates that Isaiah had disciples who preserved and continued his work, likely continuing to edit and expand the book of Isaiah for a long time until it reached the form in which we have it. The book of Jeremiah is now present in two quite different forms, indicating that perhaps two separate groups continued to develop and expand this scroll after the person called Jeremiah was gone.

INTRODUCTION TO THE BOOK OF ISAIAH

The Scope of the Book

The book of Isaiah is a massive scroll, consisting of sixty-six chapters as they are now numbered. The composite nature of this work is evident in many ways. Isaiah 36–39 is an adapted edition of II Kings 18–20. In Isaiah 6, the prophet reports in first-person language about a divine encounter, a **theophany**, in which he was called to be a prophet, while Isaiah 7 is a story about a meeting between Isaiah and King Ahaz in the eighth century, and it refers to the prophet in the third-person. The person named Isaiah is never mentioned again after Chapter 39, and Isaiah 45 speaks about Cyrus, the king of Persia in the sixth century. These observations, among many others, lead most scholars to the conclusion that the book of Isaiah was produced by many people over a period of about three centuries. The greatest challenge may be how to read this book in its finished form as a unified work of literature.

It has been common practice to divide the book of Isaiah into three parts. Some interpreters go as far as to call these parts First Isaiah (ch. 1–39), Second Isaiah (ch. 40–55), and Third Isaiah (ch. 56–66). The focus here will be on reading Isaiah as a unified work, but the observations that have led to these divisions can still prove helpful. Much of Isaiah 1–39 seems to have the Assyrian Crisis of the eighth century as its background, and the prophet named Isaiah, who lived in the eighth century, appears as a character in this part of the book. The experience of the Babylonian Exile in the sixth century seems to be the background for most of Isaiah 40–55, in which Cyrus, the Persian king who released the Israelites from this captivity, appears. Finally, the restoration of worship in the second temple during the fifth century seems to be the most likely background for the final section of the book. The simplistic idea of three separate sections of the book from different time periods laid end to end does not work well, however. Chapters 13, 20, and 33–34 seem more closely associated with the middle section of 40–55, and Chapters 1–2 and 24–27 have strong connections to 56–66. This situation is better explained by the proposal that an original core of material closely associated with the prophet Isaiah underwent a series of major and minor revisions over a long period of time, resulting in the massive work we now have. The

Summary of Arguments on Authorship of Isaiah

Single Author

1. The oldest form of the book, the Dead Sea Scrolls manuscript, has the entire sixty-six chapters, much as it stands today.
2. The primary emphasis in prophecy was on prediction. God enabled the prophets to see what would happen hundreds of years in the future.
3. The author of the whole book, therefore, was Isaiah of Jerusalem in the eighth century B.C.E.

Multiple Authors

1. The prophets primarily spoke for their own time. The future they were most concerned with was the immediate future.[2]
2. Isaiah 1–39 and 40–66 are different in a number of ways:
   a. They differ in historical background: 1–39 was set in an eighth-century background, while 40–66 was set in the sixth and fifth centuries.
   b. They differ in style: 1–39 is narrative and constitutes typical prophetic oracles, while 40–66 is very elaborate poetry.
   c. They differ in their view of God: 1–39 speaks of the holiness of God, while 40–66 speaks of God as Creator.
   d. They differ in speaking of God's representative: 1–39 speaks of the Messiah, while 40–66 speaks of the Suffering Servant.
3. Isaiah 45:1 specifically mentions Cyrus, who was the king of Persia in the sixth century B.C.E.
4. The most obvious explanation for these observations is that the book was produced by multiple people over a long period of time.

best strategy for reading the book of Isaiah includes the awareness that it is a composite work, the pieces of which have different historical contexts, but that the finished book is a deliberate work of literary art, which also has a context and a purpose. An additional benefit of this approach is that every generation needs to do the work of examining this prophetic tradition and using it to engage the critical issues of our own context.

Some Major Components of the Book

The book of Isaiah begins with a **superscription** in 1:1 that introduces the prophet and places him in Jerusalem during the eighth century. A second, briefer superscription appears in 2:1, raising questions about whether the original superscription, which speaks of the "**vision** of Isaiah," applies to the entire book or just the first chapter. Isaiah's **call narrative** appears in chapter 6, an odd placement, considering that call narratives in other prophetic books tend to appear at the very beginning. There are two sets of stories about Isaiah's interactions with two of Judah's kings in Isaiah 7 (Ahaz) and Isaiah 36–39 (Hezekiah). Isaiah 2–5 and 9–12 contain numerous **judgment oracles**, but oracles that seem to speak of salvation are also present. Isaiah 13–23 is a large collection of judgment oracles directed at other countries, such as Assyria, Egypt, Babylon, Moab, and Ammon, a collection often called the **Oracles against the Nations**. In Isaiah 24–27 the language and perspective of the book change significantly, prompting many interpreters to refer to this section as the **Isaian Apocalypse**. The voice of the book shifts significantly in Isaiah 40 and the chapters following this are dominated by **salvation oracles**. Mixed in with these oracles about the salvation or redemption of Israel is a set of poems that refer to an unnamed figure as God's servant. These **Servant Songs** are typically identified at 42:1–4, 39:1–6, 50:4–9, and 52:13–53:12.

Once again, observations about these diverse components of the book highlight its composite nature, but they should also prompt us to ask, "What is the book of Isaiah about?" A more extensive survey of the book's contents may enable us to return to this question at the end of the chapter.

A SURVEY OF THE CONTENTS OF THE BOOK OF ISAIAH

Isaiah 1–12

Chapters 1–12 of Isaiah reflect the changing historical situations and the prophet's reactions to those changes. There seems to be no pattern by which they are arranged, except for certain catchwords that sometimes cause two oracles to be thrown together. For instance, Isaiah 1:9 mentions Sodom and Gomorrah, using those cities to show the devastation that has come to the cities of Judah because of the sins of the people. The oracle, which begins in 1:2, is an oracle lamenting Israel's unfaithfulness:

> Your country lies desolate,
> your cities are burned with fire;
> in your very presence
> aliens devour your land;
> it is desolate, as overthrown by foreigners. (1:7)

Such a description fits well into the context of Sennacherib's invasion of Judah in 701 B.C.E., when he captured city after city and laid siege to Jerusalem. The prophet's only consolation is that

> if the LORD of hosts
> had not left us a few survivors,
> we should have been like Sodom,
> and become like Gomorrah. (1:9)

The Literary Structure of Isaiah

The unity of the book of Isaiah is a much-debated issue. As the treatment of Isaiah in this book indicates, it falls rather easily into two sections, based upon the historical contexts assumed. Chapters 1–39 address the eighth century and the Assyrian crisis, and these chapters involve the personal activity of Isaiah himself. Chapters 40–66 seem to address the sixth and fifth centuries in Israel, which were dominated by the Babylonian crisis and the crisis of Restoration that followed the Exile. Thus, these sections have sometimes been labeled as *First Isaiah* and *Second Isaiah*. Some analyses further separate Isaiah 56–66 from the rest of the book and label it *Third Isaiah*.

The argument that the book of Isaiah is the product of a process of composition lasting two or three centuries and involving a large number of individuals is almost certainly correct, but in recent years more attention has been given to the final form of the book of Isaiah. This approach has raised, and attempted to answer, questions about the literary design of the whole book, regardless of the process of composition that produced it. This work is still in progress, but some preliminary results are beginning to emerge. The gap between Chapters 39 and 40 is still significant, but rather than using this realization to divide Isaiah into two books, it may be appropriate to ask how and why this material has been arranged in this way. Isaiah 36–39 becomes an important point of transition rather than a conclusion to the original book of Isaiah. The stories of Hezekiah's obedience and God's deliverance in those chapters point back to the reluctance and disobedience of his father, Ahaz, in Isaiah 7–8. They also point forward to the deliverance of the exiles in Isaiah 40–55, and further still to a future deliverance of Jerusalem that reflects its experience of salvation in the past.[3]

The character named Isaiah does not appear often in the book, but the narratives that portray this individual in Chapters 6–8, 20, and 37–39 serve as important cohesive elements in the first half of the book. Likewise, the character that the book of Isaiah refers to as the *servant*, who appears in four poems in 42:1–4, 49:1–6, 50:4–11, and 52:13–53:12, helps hold together the central section of the book in Chapters 40–55. An oracle against Babylon in Chapter 13 begins the long section of Oracles against the Nations in Chapters 13–23 and points forward to the defeat of Babylon highlighted in the poem about Cyrus in 45:1–8. Many other features of the book of Isaiah serve to hold together this seemingly disparate collection of material.

Like several other large books in the Old Testament, Isaiah demonstrates a sense of polarity. The majority of the first half of the book is negative in tone. Its contents are dominated by oracles of judgment, yet words of salvation are present. In the same way, the second half of the book is dominated by positive oracles of salvation, with words of judgment playing a minor role. Thus, the overall movement of the book is from a negative to a positive tone. It is disturbing, in light of this general observation, that the final verse of the book of Isaiah (66:24) is so harsh. The Jewish tradition of reading of this text copes with this harshness by repeating the penultimate verse (66:23) after the conclusion of Chapter 66, so the book ends on a more positive note.

Some interpreters see the final form of the book of Isaiah as a context for the reading of older traditions that come from Isaiah the prophet. Edgar W. Conrad has identified Isaiah 6–39 as the "vision of Isaiah," which was "bound up and sealed" (according to Isaiah 8:16–20) until a later point when it could become a coherent prophetic message. The book of Isaiah forms the context for this coherence. Isaiah 40:6 commands that this new reading of the old vision take place in a new social context.[4]

Thus, the book of Isaiah is a large prophetic complex that tells a continuous story. This story is about Israel's past, present, and future. Each of these facets influences the others. The past provides a program for the present and a vision for the future. The needs of the present and the future shape the presentation of the past. The book of Isaiah moves through all of these parts of Israel's story, offering a message of judgment, destruction, salvation, and hope.

The oracle that follows this one also mentions Sodom and Gomorrah, yet the historical situation is radically different. The people are so prosperous that they bring "multitudes of sacrifices" (1:11). Their worship is not lacking in quantity; instead, it is woefully lacking in quality. In this case, Sodom and Gomorrah are examples of decadence, not destruction. Hands spread in prayerful supplication condemn the worshiper because "your hands are full of blood" (1:15).

Another vivid oracle deals with the humiliation of the upper-class women of Jerusalem who

walk with outstretched necks,
    glancing wantonly with their eyes,
    . . .
Instead of perfume there will be a stench
    . . .
    instead of beauty, shame. (3:16, 24)

A series of judgment oracles in 5:8–23 catalogs the sins of a prosperous society: covetousness (5:8–10); drunkenness (5:11–12); failure to know the LORD (5:13–17); cynicism (5:18–19); glorifying evil instead of right (5:20); conceit (5:21); and judges who accept bribes (5:22–23).

One of the most unusual oracles is the Song of the Vineyard (5:1–7). It is in the form of a wedding song, but Isaiah used it to develop an allegory about Israel and Judah. A farmer plants the finest grapes after carefully preparing the soil. But, to his despair and disgust, what he thought were fine grapes actually were wild sour grapes, worthless for his purposes. In anger, he destroys the vineyard. The meaning of the allegory is then explained:

For the vineyard of the LORD of hosts
    is the house of Israel,
and the people of Judah
    are his pleasant planting;
he expected justice,
    but saw bloodshed;
righteousness,
    but heard a cry! (5:7)

Isaiah did not view the situation as hopeless. The people must turn to the LORD in true repentance by ceasing to do evil and learning to do good, meaning, specifically:

seek justice,
    rescue the oppressed,
defend the fatherless,
    plead for the widow. (1:17)
    . . .
    if you are willing and obedient,
you shall eat the good of the land;
    but if you refuse and rebel,
you shall be devoured by the sword;
    for the mouth of the LORD has spoken. (1:19–20)

Or again:

Zion shall be redeemed by justice,
    and those in her who repent by righteousness.

But rebels and sinners shall be destroyed together,
 and those who forsake the LORD shall be consumed. (1:27–28)

Christian tradition, beginning with the New Testament, has often made extensive use of passages from this part of Isaiah in constructing understandings of the identity of Jesus. Two such passages are oracles that seem to depict an ideal king figure. The first of these (9:2–7) would fit well into the early years of Isaiah's ministry. The Assyrian hordes had overrun the Northern Kingdom, while making Ahaz pay a terrible price for the safety of his kingdom. Such a time would have made anyone long for the blessings of peace. The occasion for the oracle may have been the birth of a royal child.[5] Ahaz's rejection of Isaiah's advice on other occasions gave no basis for hope for a sensible response from Ahaz this time. Thus, Isaiah had reasons to yearn for a leader who would be called "Wonderful Counselor, Mighty God, Everlasting Father, Prince of Peace," whose kingdom would be one in which justice and righteousness would be the hallmarks. When no contemporary king arose who fulfilled this dream, its projection to a future time was not difficult.

The other oracle in this category is found in 11:1–9. Some would argue that, because reference is made to "a shoot . . . from the stump of Jesse" (11:1), this oracle comes from a later time when the monarchy no longer existed. Although this is a significant argument for such a view, the figure of the stump also appeared in the call narrative (6:13). As the figure of speech is not strange to Isaiah, this oracle could well be from him. Whatever the case, whether from Isaiah or a later disciple, the ideal ruler will be one who will possess

the spirit of wisdom and understanding,
 the spirit of counsel and might,
the spirit of knowledge and the fear of the LORD. (11:2)

A substantial block of mostly narrative material sits in the middle of this section, occupying most of Isaiah 6–8. It begins with Isaiah's own account of his prophetic calling. Isaiah was a citizen of Jerusalem, perhaps from the upper classes of society. Some have even suggested that he might have been related to the royal family. He had access to the royal court and functioned as an advisor to at least two of the kings of Judah. The book of Isaiah identifies two of his sons by name, Shear-jashub in 7:3 and Maher-shalal-hash-baz in 8:3. The mother of this second son is referred to as the *prophetess.* This person is never mentioned again in the book of Isaiah, so her identity and function are uncertain. She is often presumed to be Isaiah's wife, but this is only an assumption based on the report that they had one child together. Her designation here raises the possibility that the group of prophetic disciples around Isaiah included female members. In what way this specific person may have functioned as a prophet is not mentioned.

Isaiah's call came in the year of King Uzziah's death. The young Isaiah was in the Temple, possibly watching the pomp and pageantry surrounding the coronation of Jotham, Uzziah's son. The king was supposed to be God's representative on earth. But Isaiah saw more than the earthly representative of God; it was the LORD sitting on the throne. In his **vision,** the LORD was flanked by two bright six-winged creatures called *seraphs* (NRSV) or *flaming creatures* (Today's English Version), who called out,

Holy, holy, holy is the Lord of hosts;
 the whole earth is full of his glory. (6:3)

The formula "Holy, holy, holy" was the Hebrew way of saying, "the most holy" or "holiest of all," because repeating the adjective took the place of the comparative and superlative degrees (holy, holier, holiest). This was not a reference to the Trinity (Father, Son, and Holy Spirit), as such an idea was unknown in Isaiah's day (6:1–3).

The Temple foundations shook under Isaiah's feet, and smoke rising from the altar gave an eerie appearance. The vision of the holy God overwhelmed the young man with a sense of sin and guilt. In his spiritual agony, he cried out in a confession of sins: "Woe is me! I am lost" (6:4–5). In his vision, Isaiah saw one of the flying creatures take a fiery coal from the altar and touch his lips, symbolic of the cleansing power of the LORD in forgiveness. Then he heard a call, "Whom shall I send and who will go for us?" Isaiah's response was "Here am I; send me!" (6:6–8). Then Isaiah was given a strange commission: He was told to go preach to people who would pay no attention to him. When he questioned how long he was to preach, he was told to preach until the land lay desolate, stripped of its inhabitants. Only a remnant would remain. In short, Isaiah was called to be faithful, not successful (6:9–13).

Chapter 6 contains two unique features of Isaiah's preaching. Like the other prophets, before and afterward, he would be a prophet of judgment and doom. But among the things that were different about his preaching were the ideas concerning the holiness of God and the righteous remnant of Israel.[6] The importance and meaning of these ideas will be discussed later.

The first appearance of Isaiah as a prophet is described in Chapter 7. Isaiah and his son Shear-jashub met Ahaz in Jerusalem. The son was taken along because his name represented a part of his father's message. The name was symbolic of Isaiah's doctrine of the remnant. It meant "A remnant shall return." As such, it reflected a hopeful theme in Isaiah's preaching (7:1–4). Ahaz was troubled by the threat of Syria and Israel. Isaiah gave him a message from the LORD to ignore the threats. Instead, he counseled, "Take heed, be quiet, do not fear," for the little tyrants threatening him would soon vanish. The prophet showed his contempt for King Pekah (I) by referring to him only as the "son of Remaliah" (7:5–9). Isaiah challenged Ahaz to ask for a sign from the LORD that what he was saying was true (7:11). Ahaz refused to do so (7:12). Isaiah then said that the LORD would give a sign anyway. That sign was that a young woman would have a child whose name would be Immanuel, a name that meant "God with us" (7:14). It was in keeping with the earlier promise to Ahaz that what he needed to do was to trust in the LORD, not in Assyria.

Ways of Reading Isaiah 7:14

Isaiah 7:14 is a verse that illustrates some of the difficulties and controversies involved in interpreting texts from the prophetic literature. In the Christian tradition, the problems with this verse stem from its use in the New Testament in Matthew 1:22–23. The writer of this gospel claims that in some way the birth of Jesus "fulfills" the statement in Isaiah 7:14. Understanding this issue should begin with an examination of translation problems. The New Revised Standard Version of Isaiah 7:14 says:

> Therefore the LORD himself will give you a sign. Look, the young woman is with child and shall bear a son, and shall name him Immanuel.

This seems significantly different from the King James Version, with which many readers are more familiar:

> Therefore the LORD himself shall give you a sign; Behold, a virgin shall conceive, and bear a son, and shall call his name Immanuel.

The major differences that affect the interpretation of this verse are the translation of the word "*Look/Behold*," the tense of the verb in "is with child/shall conceive," and the translation of the words *young woman/virgin*.

There are three basic understandings of this verse in Isaiah:

1. Isaiah is pointing to a pregnant woman in the presence of Ahaz and indicating that the child she will give birth to is a sign of God's presence with Ahaz and Israel in the eighth century B.C.E. Most likely, it refers to Ahaz's son Hezekiah, who succeeded him as king of Judah.

2. Isaiah is stating that at some time in the future, a miraculously conceived child will be born and this child will represent the presence of God. Many Christian interpreters understand this predicted child to be Jesus specifically and therefore the "virgin" is Mary.
3. The statement of Isaiah functions on two levels, one that addresses the situation in the eighth century B.C.E. and a child who was born then, and another that addresses the future, perhaps including the birth of Jesus in the first century C.E.

The first interpretation fits better with the *NRSV* translation and the second with the KJV translation. This is a good example of how translation and interpretation are necessarily linked.

The situation is complicated further by the ancient translation of the Hebrew scriptures into Greek. The Hebrew word in Isaiah 7:14 is clearly a general word for *young woman*. There is another Hebrew word that specifically means *virgin*, which is used elsewhere in Isaiah but not in this case. The oldest existing copies of the Greek translation of Isaiah, however, contain a word that specifically means *virgin,* and it is the same word that appears in the Greek New Testament in Matthew 1:23. These best copies, however, are from the fourth and fifth centuries C.E. and are Christian documents, so nobody can say for certain what word was present in the original Greek translation produced by Jews six or seven centuries earlier.

Those who argue for the first interpretation above insist that Isaiah's statement to Ahaz must be meaningful within the context of the Syro-Ephraimitic War of the eighth century B.C.E. and the threat it posed to Judah. A statement about a child to be born 800 years later would have no meaning in that context. Some of these interpreters would also argue that when the gospel of Matthew says that the birth of Jesus "fulfills" this text, it means something other than that Isaiah 7:14 was a specific prediction about a future event and that the birth of Jesus is this future event. Those who argue for the second interpretation seem most often to be interested in some kind of tangible proof that Jesus is the Messiah. The third interpretation is attractive to many readers because it seems to resolve the dilemma posed by the first two, but others respond that this is not a resolution at all but an evasion of the difficulties of this passage and the tough choices they require.

Who was the original child? Some believe that it was Ahaz's son, Hezekiah, who would become one of Judah's most devout and able kings. Another possibility was that the child was Isaiah's own son. This conclusion is supported by the fact that the two other children mentioned in this passage (7:1–8:15) are Isaiah's children.[7]

Isaiah 13–23

A feature common to all of the prophetic scrolls in the Old Testament is a collection of judgment oracles against other nations. These oracles were directed against those nations that in one way or another offended the prophet's sense of justice, particularly regarding that nation's attitude toward Israel.

In the book of Isaiah, there is a greater variety of oracles than in other books. Other materials have been introduced, which, at first glance, would seem to be out of place. For example, in Isaiah 20 is the story of Isaiah's symbolic action to protest Hezekiah's possible involvement in the Ashdod rebellion. Because Egypt was one of the instigators of this rebellion, this probably explains its inclusion here.

Less easy to understand is an oracle directed against an individual, Shebna, an official in Hezekiah's court. There, the answer may lie in the suggestion that he may have been a promoter of the same rebellion, an action that Isaiah strongly opposed.

Oracles against Foreign Nations (Isa. 13:1–23:18)

1. Against Babylon (13:1–14:23)
2. Against Assyria (14:24–27)
3. Against Philistia (14:28–32)
4. Against Moab (15:1–16:14)
5. Against Damascus (Syria) and Israel (Ephraim) (17:1–6)
6. Against idols (17:7–14)
7. Against Egypt (18:1–20:6)
8. Against Babylon again (21:1–10)
9. Against Dumah (Edom) (21:11–12)
10. Against Arabia (21:13–17)
11. Against Jerusalem (22:1–14)
12. Against Shebna (22:15–25)
13. Against Tyre and Sidon (23:1–18)

The two oracles against Babylon (13:1–14:23) may well be from Isaiah's later disciples. One's view of the relationship of Isaiah and such disciples is the crucial point in this conclusion. If one takes what seem to be clear historical references—the overall assumption that Babylon is the dominant world power; the reference to the rise of the Medes (13:17); and the mention of the oracle against the king of Babylon (14:3–23)—the conclusion could be reached that these oracles came from the sixth century B.C.E. If, on the other hand, one assumes that the prophet's primary function was long-range prediction, a different conclusion would be reached as to the source of these two oracles.

The oracle against the king of Babylon (14:3–23) is a good example of a biblical passage that often is misinterpreted. This is a dirge directed against a tyrant who has exalted himself against God (14:13–14). Now he will be brought down to the "depths of the pit" (death) and his power will vanish (14:15). That such tyrants are satanic in their abuse of power does not justify interpreting this passage as describing the fall of Satan. To do so is to *eisegete* (read a meaning into a passage) rather than to *exegete* (let the passage say what it says).

Not all these oracles were *against* foreign nations. In the Moab oracle (15:1–16:14), the prophet urges the people to give refuge to fugitives from Moab, even though he does regard Moab's troubles as a just punishment (16:5–7).

Egypt was a major object in Isaiah's foreign oracles (18:1–20:6). It was pressuring Hezekiah to rebel against the Assyrians. The prophet constantly warned the king to avoid such entanglements, advice that Hezekiah heeded in 714–711 B.C.E. (the Ashdod rebellion). Later, however, Hezekiah would not be so wise, thus provoking Sennacherib's 701 B.C.E. invasion.

Isaiah 24–27

Isaiah 24–27 is often called **apocalyptic** literature because these chapters share some characteristics with such books as Daniel and Revelation. Apocalyptic literature differed from prophetic literature in a number of ways, which are summarized in the box below. These chapters in Isaiah do not represent as clear an example of apocalyptic literature as later books both inside and outside of the Bible, but they may represent a transition between prophetic and apocalyptic literature.

Characteristics of Apocalyptic Literature

1. It aimed at encouraging the faithful of the LORD's people in a time of trouble instead of telling sinners among the LORD's people that judgment was coming.
2. It usually was written first and read later instead of being spoken first and written later.
3. It used unusual imagery and numbers to create a coded language. The readers for whom it was intended understood this language, but outsiders could not understand it.
4. It spoke of God being directly involved in conflict with the earthly enemy. This differed from the common Old Testament idea of God working through human and natural means.
5. It was concerned with the triumph of God over the forces of evil in the universe. This was a cosmic struggle.
6. The author usually was anonymous, because he did the work under the name of a famous person.

Like apocalyptic literature, they speak of the earth and the universe being in turmoil, while they alternate prophetic words of judgment with apocalyptic words of comfort for the faithful. The LORD is at work in the universe to bring deliverance to the faithful.

The authorship of this material usually is assigned to a later time. The first oracle depicts the earth in turmoil:

> The earth lies polluted
> under its inhabitants;
> . . .
> Therefore a curse devours the earth
> and its inhabitants suffer for their guilt. (24:5, 6)

Yet, the words of judgment are balanced by words of praise (24:14–16a) and promise (25:1–5). The righteous will be preserved in the midst of judgment (26:1–19). This section closes with the promise of a return of the exiles (27:12–13).

Isaiah 28–35

The final group of oracles from Isaiah 1–39, those found in chapters 28–35, is varied in time and context. For example, Isaiah 28:14–22 blasts cynical leaders who have "made a covenant with death" (28:15b) and thus expect it to pass them by. Instead, they will find that they are not immune to God's wrath (28:17–22). The prophet's indignation over Hezekiah's flirtation with the Egyptians likely created friction between him and the king (30:8–11). His feelings were aptly expressed in a scathing oracle in 30:1–7. He points out that

> Egypt's help is worthless and empty,
> therefore I have called her,
> "Rahab who sits still." (30:7)

Instead, Hezekiah is admonished to remember that

> In returning and rest you shall be saved;
> in quietness and trust shall be your strength. (30:15)

Failure to give heed will result in Judah being left

like a flagstaff on top of a mountain,
  like a signal on a hill. (30:17)

On the other hand, because they have themes that sound like Isaiah 40–66, the oracles in chapters 34 and 35 usually are assigned to the period of the Exile. The subject of 34:1–17 is the LORD's warfare against the nations that oppose Him. The LORD is spoken of as a dread warrior whose sword "is sated with blood . . . is gorged with fat" (34:6). The expression "the day of the LORD's vengeance" (34:8) was used in primitive justice and meant "the day when the LORD sets things right." *Vengeance,* in the biblical sense, meant "bringing back to even keel things that were uneven" or "balancing what was unbalanced" (34:1–8).

Edom was used as an example of those nations that opposed the LORD and thus opposed Judah. There seems to have been a particularly strong hatred between the Edomites and Israel, because Edom took every opportunity to strike at Israel when it was weak. Thus, the LORD's enemies will be left as desolate as Edom (34:9–17).

The other side of the LORD's judgment upon the nations would be the restoration and prosperity of Israel in the land. This is why vengeance and salvation are mentioned together in 35:4:

Say to those who are of a fearful heart,
  . . .
Here is your God,
  He will come with vengeance,
  with terrible recompense.
He will come and save you.

As a result,

the ransomed of the LORD shall return,
  and come to Zion with singing;
everlasting joy shall be upon their heads;
  they shall obtain joy and gladness,
and sorrow and sighing shall flee away. (35:10)

Isaiah 36–39

The **royal narrative** reporting Isaiah's interaction with King Hezekiah was already described in chapter 8 of this book, because it is such a close parallel to II Kings 18–20. Two comments may be important, however, about the salient role these texts play in the book of Isaiah. First, because only the book of Isaiah reports on Isaiah's interactions with Ahaz, the father of Hezekiah, it may be important to compare the two. Most significantly, although Ahaz resists receiving a sign of God's deliverance from Isaiah in 7:12, Hezekiah requested such a sign himself in 38:22. Hezekiah may be perceived as a more humble and faithful leader than his father. Second, the brief and puzzling Chapter 39 is placed at an important boundary in the book of Isaiah. Chapters 36–38 report Judah's survival of the Assyrian Crisis, and 40–55 rejoice over the end of the Babylonian captivity. The only thing filling this 150-year gap is the strange little story of the Babylonian envoys coming to Jerusalem and taking a tour of city. This is Isaiah's veiled view of the horrors of the Babylonian invasion.

Comfort to Israel (Isa. 40–55)

The prophet's call (40:1–11). It is quite possible to read the opening verse of Isaiah 40 as a second call narrative in the book, but neither the prophet nor the narrator provide an identity for this person. This is why interpreters who want to speak clearly of an individual behind the prophetic voice in this section often use the name "Second-Isaiah," a name that others use just to identify this section of the book. The keynote of Isaiah 40–55 was reassurance to a nation that had been trampled underfoot by Babylon, reviled and scoffed at by its neighbors, and exiled in a distant land. Rebuke enough had been flung at them. The LORD, through the prophet, sent a word of comfort:

> Speak tenderly to Jerusalem,
> and cry to her
> that she has served her term,
> that her penalty is paid,
> that she has received from the LORD's hand
> double for all her sins. (40:2)

Such a condition could have existed only after the fall of Jerusalem. Only then could it be said, "She has received from the LORD's hand double (punishment) for all her sins" (40:2).

A dialogue follows the opening lines. It seems to be the prophet's unique way of describing the LORD's call to him. He was told to be like a king's herald, going through the land announcing the king's imminent appearance. He was to see that the bumps in the road were smoothed down and the holes filled in. The LORD's overpowering presence was about to make itself known in the midst of the people as they would be led in a new exodus back to Palestine (40:3–5). A command came to "cry" or preach. When the prophet-to-be asked what the nature of His message would be, he was told to proclaim that, like the grass and the flower, everything would pass away except the enduring word of God (40:6–8). He was to herald the good tidings to Jerusalem from the high mountains that the LORD was about to return to rule the land with strength, justice, and compassion:

> He will feed his flock like a shepherd;
> he will gather the lambs in his arms,
> and carry them in his bosom,
> and gently lead the mother sheep. (40:11)

In Praise of the LORD, the Creator (40:12–32). The prophet's job was not an easy one. He faced the questions of the cynics who said, "My way is hidden from the LORD, and my right is disregarded by my God" (40:27). They could understand punishment for their sins, but what had happened to them seemed to have gone beyond the punishment they deserved. The prophet's answer was a magnificent poem on the LORD as Creator.

The poem consisted largely of rhetorical questions—that is, questions whose answers were already known both to the one asking and to the one of whom they were asked. By those questions, he pointed out that the LORD had created the universe (the waters, the heavens, and the earth). The LORD consulted no one, for the nations were as nothing to Him (40:12–17). The LORD could not be compared to idols, for they were only wooden gods created by a puny man:

> Have you not known? Have you not heard?
> Has it not been told you from the beginning?

Have you not understood from the foundations of the earth?
It is he who sits above the circle of the earth,
and its inhabitants are like grasshoppers;
who stretches out the heavens like a curtain,
and spreads them like a tent to live in;
who brings princes to naught,
and makes the rulers of the earth as nothing. (40:21–23)

A king scarcely was seated on his throne before he passed away, and his place was taken by another (40:24).

There was no one to whom the LORD could be compared; He had created the universe, giving each heavenly body its name and placing it in the created order (40:25–26). His people, therefore, had no reason to question His concern for them, for

The LORD is the everlasting God,
the Creator of the ends of the earth.
He does not faint or grow weary;
his understanding is unsearchable. (40:28bcde)

The LORD gives power to persons of every age:

those who wait for the LORD
shall renew their strength,
they shall mount up with wings like eagles,
they shall run and not be weary,
they shall walk and not faint. (40:31)

The message is that young children can reach their full potential ("mount up like eagles"); young people can still reach high goals ("run and not be weary"); and the elderly can still have a meaningful life ("walk and not faint") (40:29–31).

The Nations on Trial (41:1–29). The LORD was calling the nations to judgment, when they would have a chance to defend themselves (41:1). Although Cyrus was not named, the prophet described the rapid advances he was making. But Cyrus was the LORD's agent:

Who has performed and done this,
calling the generations from the beginning?
I, the LORD, am first,
and will be with the last. (41:4)

The nations were trembling at the news of the Persian advances. The idol makers were trying to encourage one another, hoping their idols would save them. But the LORD had taken Israel from the ends of the earth. Israel was the LORD's servant and could be assured of the LORD's presence and help (42:2–10). Israel's enemies would be put to shame, for the LORD would help Israel triumph over them (41:11–16). The desert, furthermore, would bloom for Israel as evidence that "the hand of the LORD has done this" (41:17–21).

The false gods were challenged, therefore, to submit evidence of their ability to produce results. They could not, of course, as they were nothing. Only the LORD had the power to move nations and men at His command. The coming of Cyrus (still not named) had been announced to Israel. When one looked to the idols for any help, one found nothing (41:22–29).

The Servant Songs

INTRODUCTION. One of the unique features of Second Isaiah is the *Servant Songs.* There are four poems (42:1–4; 49:1–6; 50:4–11; and 52:13–53:12). They are called the Servant Songs because they introduce a figure referred to as the **Suffering Servant.** Each poem adds more information about the Servant, with the climax coming in 52:13–53:12, where the Servant's trial and death are described.

Numerous questions are raised about the poems, especially in two major areas: (1) What is their relationship to the rest of 40–55? Did they originate separately from 40–55 or as a part of it? (2) Who was the Servant?

As for the first question, whether they originated separately or not, they are so skillfully blended into the rest of the material that they do not seriously interrupt it. The first poem, for example, climaxes the section on the LORD's judgment of the nations. The Servant is portrayed as the instrument of that judgment. These four poems serve as a literary thread that ties together 40–55 the way the occasional presence of Isaiah, son of Amoz, tied together 1–39.

The question of the Servant's identity will be left until the last poem is discussed.

THE FIRST SERVANT SONG: THE SERVANT'S MISSION (42:1–4). In this poem, the LORD describes the mission of the Servant, who would "bring justice to the nations" (42:1). Unlike military conquerors, he would do his work quietly, but his gentle manner would not deter him in his object:

> He will not faint or be crushed
> until he has established justice in the earth;
> and the coastlands wait for his teaching. (42:4)

I AM THE LORD YOUR GOD (42:5–46:13). Oracles in these chapters constantly return to a single theme: "I am the LORD your God." Like the theme notes of a symphony, they recur time and time again. Different subjects are discussed—idols and idol makers, Cyrus, the restoration of Israel—but all come back to the foregoing theme. God created heaven and earth with all of its inhabitants. His Servant had been given to bring light to the people. He alone would do it, for no idol could share his glory (42:5–9). The prophet broke out in a hymn of praise, calling on the whole of creation to praise God for His fight against His foes (42:10–13). In the battle, the people would be helped, even though they were blind to what God was doing for them. Even so, the LORD would keep His promises (42:14–17).

Unfortunately, all that Israel had seen was meaningless to the people. The LORD had wanted to save them, but they had been led from the land. They had been given over to the enemy because they had sinned against the LORD. They had learned nothing from their experience (42:18–25).

Yet, the LORD would rescue His people, because they were His.

> When you pass through the waters I will be with you;
> and through the rivers, they shall not overwhelm you;
> when you walk through the fire you shall not be burned,
> and the flame shall not consume you.
> For I am the LORD your God,
> the Holy One of Israel, your Savior. (43:2–3ab)

Others would be given in exchange for Israel. A new exodus would take place, bringing the people back to the land; they were the LORD's people, created for His glory (43:1–7).

In using the figure of a trial again, the prophet portrayed God as summoning the nations to demonstrate that He was God above all others. No god was formed before Him; none would be formed after Him. They were witnesses to that fact. The LORD had saved Israel before any other God came along. He alone could deliver them now (43:8–13). To prove His power, He was sending an army to conquer Babylon. Many years before, the LORD had led the nation in the first exodus from Egypt. Now a new thing was about to happen—a new exodus was about to take place (43:14–21).

Israel had sinned against God by failing to worship properly. Yet, He would not hold their sins against them. They were challenged to bring witnesses to court to prove that God had wronged them (43:22–28). He had created Israel. Israel was His servant, the people whom He loved. He would bless them so that they would thrive like plants that had plenty of water. Gradually they would come to recognize that He was the first, the last, the only God (44:1–8). In a scathing satire on idols (44:9–20), the prophet concludes that both idols and idol makers are nothing. After all, a man chooses a tree or metal and fashions it with his hand to make it look like himself. The maker of wooden idols took a tree, burned part of it to cook his food and to warm himself, and then used the other part to make a god to worship. Such a person was stupid. "He feeds on ashes; a deluded mind has led him astray, and he cannot deliver himself and say, 'Is not this thing in my right hand a fraud?'" (44:20).

The LORD had swept away Israel's "transgressions like a cloud" (44:21–22). The prophet broke out in song at the prospect of the LORD's redemption of the people. He who was doing this had created heaven and earth, had confounded the wisdom of men, and had promised that Jerusalem would be rebuilt. He was the One, furthermore, who raised up Cyrus the Persian to be His servant who would rebuild Jerusalem (44:31–28). In an address to Cyrus (45:1–7), the LORD promised to go before him and prepare the way for his conquests. What Cyrus was about to do was for the sake of the LORD's people. He had been chosen as the LORD's servant.

> I call you [Cyrus] by your name,
>   I surname you, though you do not know me.
> I am the LORD, and there is no other;
>   besides me there is no god.
> I arm you, though you do not know me,
>   . . .
> I form light and create darkness,
>   I make weal and create woe;
> I the LORD do all these things. (45:4b–5, 7)

Using a figure from Jeremiah, the prophet pronounces woe on one who strives against his maker, like a pot against the potter (Jer. 18). The created ones cannot question the Creator's actions. The man Cyrus was created to do the LORD's work in freeing Israel. The nations would acknowledge that Israel's God was supreme. He was the Creator, and He spoke the truth. No idol could take His place. The judicial decision must be made, therefore. Who was the Creator? Who is the only true God? Who could save the people? The LORD, the God of Israel. In Him alone is salvation, for to Him, "every knee shall bow, and every tongue shall swear" (45:8–25).

Look at the gods of Babylon. They had to be carried on donkeys' backs, because they could not go from place to place, much less create anything. They were dependent on their makers to move them. They could even be captured and carried away. Yet, the LORD had cared for Jacob from the beginning, and He would be with them to the end. Could the LORD be compared, then, to a god made of gold by a human craftsman? An idol that had to be carried on men's shoulders? Absolutely not! He was the One who would soon deliver Israel (46:1–13).

> for I am God, and there is no other;
>   I am God, and there is no one like me,
> declaring the end from the beginning
>   and from ancient times things not yet done. (46:9–10)

Sing a Sad Song for Babylon (47:1–15). The prophet sang a lament for Babylon. It would be reduced to slavery. Even though the LORD had permitted it to take Israel into exile, it had been proud. It thought it would rule forever, but its end would come (47:1–7). Although it thought it would never be like a childless widow, it would be (47:8–9). It thought it could do evil and no one would notice, but ruin would come quickly (47:10–11). Its sorcerers and wise men, who claimed they could save it, were like stubble and would fail because they could not deliver it (47:12–15).

You Have Heard, Now See All This (48:1–22). The prophet sums up in this chapter what he had said in Chapters 40–47. Chapter 48 marks the dividing point within chapters 40–55. In it, the LORD reminded the people that He had revealed the past to them long ago. Now, He was about to reveal new things to them—things they did not know. These things had been kept from Israel because of its previous inclination toward unfaithfulness. Because of that record, what the LORD was about to do was for His own sake. He would not give His glory to anyone else. It was the LORD who had created the heavens and the earth (48:1–13).

No one would have predicted that Cyrus would have attacked Babylon; yet the LORD had been behind the success of Cyrus. The prophet adds a note of reminder to his audience: "And now the LORD God has sent me and his spirit" (48:16). If the people had followed the LORD,

> Then your prosperity would have been like a river,
> . . .
> your offspring would have been like the sand,
> and your descendants like its grains;
> their name would never be cut off
> or destroyed from before me. (48:18–19)

The oracle ends with the prophet urging the people to begin the new exodus, to shout it to the ends of the earth: "The LORD has redeemed His servant Jacob." The LORD would lead them through the desert, making water flow from the rocks (48:14–22).

THE SECOND SERVANT SONG: THE SERVANT'S RESPONSIBILITY (49:1–6). The second Servant Song goes further than the first in describing the Servant and his role in the world. Notice that it is linked to the first Servant Song by the word *coastlands* in 49:1, which also appears in 42:4. Instead of being written in the third person, this poem was written in the first person. In it, the Servant described his call from God. Like Jeremiah, he felt that from birth he had been chosen by the LORD for his role. The LORD spoke of him as being like a secret weapon (49:1–2).

The first suggestion of the Servant's identity is in this oracle: "He said to me, 'You are my servant, Israel, in whom I will be glorified'" (49:3). The Servant protested that he had worked, but his strength was wasted. He realized that the LORD had his reward (49:3–4). After the identification in verse 3, verses 5 and 6 take away some of the certainty. After restating that he was "formed from the womb to be his servant," the LORD went on to state that one of the Servant's responsibilities would be to bring Jacob and Israel back to the LORD. But that was not a big enough job. The Servant was also given the responsibility of being "a light to the nations" so that the LORD's salvation might "reach to the ends of the earth" (49:4–6). Because verse 7 also refers to "the servant (*slave* NRSV) of rulers," some take it also to be a part of the second Servant Song. According to verse 7, the roles would be reversed, the kings serving those who had once been their servants.

The Return of the People (49:7–13). This seems, with verse 7, to be a response to the second Servant Song. The reference to "you" seems to refer to the Servant, who has been helped by the LORD and given "as a covenant to the people." They were called upon to come forth, as the LORD would lead them from exile, seeing to their physical needs along the way (49:8–12). The prophet interrupted to sing a song of praise because the LORD comforted the people (49:13).

Zion Shall Be Comforted (49:14–50:3). This is the first of what are sometimes called the *Zion poems*, which make up much of chapters 50–55. They deal with the restoration of Jerusalem, frequently called *Zion* in the Old Testament. This poem begins as a charge by Zion (as though it was a person), claiming that she had been forgotten by the LORD. The response was that the LORD could no more forget Zion than a mother could forget her suckling child (49:15). Indeed, His plans were for her rebuilding, her enemies becoming as ornaments for a bridal dress (49:14–18).

The time would come when the land would not hold the people. Then the people would have to live in other kingdoms simply because there would not be enough room in Palestine. No power, however, could keep the LORD's people captive; the LORD would take the side of Israel in court and win the case. The opponent would be punished by death (49:19–25).

Then all flesh shall know
  that I am the LORD your Savior,
and your Redeemer, the Mighty
  One of Jacob. (49:26)

Some would think that because the LORD had divorced His bride (Israel), this meant that He could not redeem her again. Such was Israel's law of divorce (Deut. 24:1–4). But He was God, not man. He could forgive sin, and He could redeem what had been put away. After all, Creation did His bidding (50:1–3).

THE THIRD SERVANT SONG: THE SERVANT'S SUBMISSION (50:4–11). The Servant again spoke, as in the second Song. He spoke of his God-given ability to comfort and encourage the weary and downtrodden. He was also open to the teaching that the LORD gave him day by day. But his work aroused opposition. He faced it with courage (50:4–5).

I gave my back to those who struck me,
  and my cheeks to those who pulled my beard;
I did not hide my face
  from insult and spitting. (50:6)

With God's help, he had not been discouraged by the insults and persecution. He depended upon God, who would stand up for him in court. No one could bring a charge against him when the Supreme Judge of all the universe was on his side. His opponents would wear out before they would be successful (50:7–9).

He urged all who feared God to keep up their courage. Those who were trying to plot against others ("lighters of firebrands") would answer to the LORD in the end (50:10–11).

Joy for Jerusalem and Beyond (51:1–52:12). Those who wanted the LORD's salvation only had to be reminded of how Abraham had been blessed. When it seemed that there was no hope, Isaac, his son and heir, was born. The LORD would bring joy and gladness to Jerusalem. It would become a new Garden of Eden (51:1–3). But that would not be all. The LORD would extend His teaching and His rule to the nations. The heavens would disappear, but the LORD's deliverance would last forever. Thus, the one who was in the right should endure taunts and insults because the LORD's deliverance would be everlasting (51:4–8). Verses 9–11 call for the LORD to wake up and deliver His people as He had done in the Exodus from Egypt. If He would do so, those who were traveling back to Jerusalem would reach it with singing and everlasting joy.

The LORD responded by assuring them that He was the same one who had created the heavens and the earth. Yet, they lived in constant fear of the Babylonians, from whom they had been freed. He was the Creator and Jerusalem's inhabitants were His people, whom He would teach and protect (51:12–16). Jerusalem was called upon to awaken. Its punishment was over, for it had experienced the double disaster of war and hunger. The anguish of the last days of Jerusalem would now be visited upon those who had caused it (51:17–23). Because Jerusalem's days of sadness and oppression were over, it was time to put on its most beautiful garments, for

How beautiful upon the mountains,
are the feet of the messenger who announces peace,
who announces salvation,
who says to Zion, "Your God reigns." (52:7)

Watchmen, who usually raised their voices in alarm, were to "sing for joy" as they watched "the return of the LORD to Zion" (52:8). Even the waste places would break forth in singing, for the LORD had redeemed His people. Then the ends of the earth would see the LORD's salvation. In preparation for the return, the people were to purify themselves. They did not have to leave Babylon in a hurry. They were not fugitives; instead, they were a people led and guarded by the LORD (52:1–12).

THE FOURTH SERVANT SONG: THE SERVANT'S TRIAL AND DEATH (52:13–53:12). With this poem, the Servant Songs reach their climax. Unlike poem 1, in which the LORD was the speaker; poem 2, in which the Servant describes his call from the LORD; and poem 3, in which the Servant talks of his initial suffering, poem 4 has at least two different speakers: God and a narrator. Nevertheless, the final poem speaks of the Servant in the third person, matching the first poem and bracketing the first-person speech of the Servant in the middle two poems.

The poem is divided into five stanzas of three verses each: 52:13–15; 53:1–3; 53:4–6; 53:7–9; and 53:10–12. In stanza 1, the LORD speaks about the Servant, while in stanzas 2–5, another speaks about the Servant.

1. ***The appearance of the Servant (52:13–15).*** The LORD introduced the Servant as one who had been given a high place, yet his physical appearance was shocking because he had been disfigured. When the kings of the earth saw him, they were astonished. Somehow, all of this seems to tie in to the Servant's commission to "be a light to the nations" (49:6).

2. ***The rejection of the Servant (53:1–3).*** The things reported about the Servant were unbelievable, especially as the LORD's power was said to have been revealed through him. He was like a dried-up, scrubby desert plant.[8] People were not attracted to him, for he was not compelling in his manner. In fact, he was hated and shunned—a lonely man who knew great sorrow.

3. ***The Servant suffering for others (52:4–6).*** The narrator became personally involved as he described the Servant's suffering for "us." This kind of suffering, in which an innocent person suffers for another, is called *vicarious* suffering. In this section, the personal pronouns *we*, *us*, and *our* are used ten times to emphasize that the Servant suffered for the narrator and those with him.

All we like sheep have gone astray;
we have all turned to our own way,
and the LORD has laid on him
the iniquity of us all. (53:6)

4. *The death and burial of the Servant (53:7–9).* The Servant was like a lamb about to be slaughtered or a sheep about to be sheared. The sheep is not noted for its intelligence. It will stand still and mute as it is being killed. So, the Servant offered no defense as he was unjustly condemned to death. He was "cut off from the land of the living." When he died, he was buried along with the wicked (which he was not) and the rich (which he was not).

5. *The vindication of the Servant 20 (53:10–12).*[9] The LORD had permitted the Servant's suffering on behalf of the sins of others. The Servant would see his reward because his action would lead to many being counted as righteous. Instead of physical children, he would have children of righteousness—those who owed their right relationship to God to him. Then an astonishing thing would happen. Because of the unselfish act he had done for others, the one who was despised and rejected would be classed with the great and the strong.

Israel Is Assured (54:1–17). This song of assurance reminds one of the picture of the "lonely widow" of Lamentations 1, who had lost her children but who now was assured that she would have more children than others who were married. It was a time to make plans for enlargement, for prosperity was just around the corner (54:1–3).

Who Was the Servant?[10]

This is a problem that has intrigued interpreters for centuries. The answers can be divided into two groups: (1) those who identify the Servant in a group or collective sense and (2) those who identify the Servant as an individual.

Those who argue for the first option point out that the Old Testament frequently spoke of a group as an individual. Throughout Second Isaiah, as well as the books of the other prophets, all the people of Israel were spoken of as Israel, Jacob, Jerusalem, or Zion. Israel (the nation), furthermore, is identified as the Servant in 49:3, as well as in several other places in Second Isaiah (41:9, 43:10, 44:1). Both Jewish and non-Jewish interpreters argue for Israel as the Servant. But, even among these interpreters, there is a distinction between those who see the reference to Israel as a whole and others who argue that the remnant (or ideal) Israel is meant. The Servant would not be Israel as it was but Israel as it ought to be.

Many are convinced that the fourth song indicates that the servant had to be an individual. A number of historical persons have been suggested—Jeremiah, or King Jehoiachin, or even Moses, because the prophet speaks of a new exodus.[11]

Just as there are those who identify the Servant with the ideal Israel, there are those who identify with an ideal person. Such a person would show Israel the revolutionary idea that, through suffering, the guilty could repent and enjoy the LORD's salvation.[12]

Christian interpreters, beginning with the early church, have looked upon the Servant as Jesus Christ. There can be little doubt that Jesus interpreted his own life in terms of the Servant, more than he did in terms of the kingly Messiah of Isaiah 9 and 11. When one does this, however, one must realize that, as a Christian, one is looking at the Servant Songs through Christian eyes. If such a person had been in the position of Second Isaiah, would that person have been so positive in his or her identification? Perhaps the safer estimate is that found in the following statement: "The Servant is the climactic figure in the prophetic line, who will proclaim the way of salvation and be himself the medium of salvation."[13]

The prophet goes back to the familiar husband–wife figure to speak of how the LORD had gone away from Israel for a while because of her unfaithfulness. But now, she had been taken back because of the LORD's great love for her (54:4–8).

It was like Noah's time, when God had destroyed the earth. Just as Noah was promised that the earth would not be destroyed again, a covenant was made with Israel that "shall not be removed" (54:9–10).

The new Jerusalem would be built, many sons would be born, and enemies would be defeated. Because the LORD made the weapon makers, He would see that no weapon would be made that could destroy Israel (54:11–17).

The Great Invitation (55:1–13). The climax of Isaiah 40–55 comes in an invitation for all to come and accept the LORD's free banquet. The LORD would make an everlasting covenant, for this banquet would be a covenant-making meal. Israel would call nations that did not know the LORD. They would come to "the LORD your God . . . the Holy One of Israel" (55:1–5). The invitation was to

Seek the LORD while he may be found,
    call upon him while he is near,
let the wicked forsake their way,
    and the unrighteous their thoughts;
let them return to the LORD, that
    he may have mercy on them,
and to our God, for he will abundantly pardon. (55:6–7)

Because God's ways of thinking and doing things are far superior to those of people, His word would accomplish its purpose when it was sent out. Thus, Israel would "go out in joy" and "be led back in peace" (55:12). As a sign of the LORD's doings, trees would grow where once only thorns grew (55:8–13).

ORACLES OF A RESTORED PEOPLE (56:1–57:24). These oracles no longer had the unbroken note of comfort found in Isaiah 40–55. Instead, there were mingled notes of comfort and rebuke, suggesting that the ideal conditions and conduct anticipated by the prophet had given way to the harsh realities of living once more in the land. When the exiles returned, they were confronted by at least two major problems: (1) Most of them were not prepared for the barrenness of the land compared to the lush, well-watered valleys along the Tigris and Euphrates Rivers; and (2) they encountered the people who had remained (or who had moved in), who (a) looked upon the land as theirs by right of possession and (b) looked upon themselves as still being true followers of the God of Israel. The returning exiles were not willing to agree on either point, thus setting up a troublesome conflict that would continue for a long time. It is likely that the conflict was intensified by priests from families who stayed behind in Palestine and still saw themselves as authentic representatives of the LORD, clashing with priests of the Zadokite line who accompanied the returning exiles. Growing out of this conflict would be a rival Temple that eventually would be built on Mount Gilboa in the territory of the old Northern Kingdom. In the post-Exilic period, the Zadokite priests gained control in Jerusalem.

Was There a Third Prophet? The source of this material is in question. Some argue for a third prophet, designated as *Trito-Isaiah*,[14] while others see these oracles as coming from the same person who was responsible for writing chapters 40–55. It has been suggested that the differences arise from the fact that chapters 40–55 are a unified composition, while chapters 56–66 consist of spoken oracles that were collected and written down later.[15] The changed circumstances of the returnees and language similarities also would seem to be sufficient to attribute these oracles to Deutero-Isaiah. An outline of the oracles follows:

1. The LORD's salvation is for all (56:1–8).
2. The beast and bad leaders (56:9–12).
3. The idol worshipers are back (57:1–13).
4. Peace to all but the wicked (57:14–21).
5. Holy day religion (58:1–14).
6. A call to repentance (59:1–21).
7. Poems about Zion (60:1–62:12).
   a. Jerusalem's glorious future (60:1–22).
   b. Good tidings to the lowly of Zion (61:1–11).
   c. New days and new names for Jerusalem (62:1–12).
8. The day of the LORD's vengeance (63:1–6).
9. A prayer and its answer (63:7–65:25).
10. The final words (66:1–24).

The LORD's Salvation Is for All (56:1–8). In the light of a later movement in Judaism known as *particularism*, which rigidly held that the Jews were the only people of the LORD, and in keeping with Isaiah 40–55, this oracle that extended the LORD's salvation and deliverance to such outcasts as eunuchs and foreigners showed a universal spirit. The eunuch, a man who had been castrated and thus had lost his ability to function sexually, was forbidden by law to ever be a part of the congregation of Israel. The book of Deuteronomy required kind treatment for foreigners, but it did not include them in the congregation of Israel. The prophet foresaw, however, a time when even the most extreme outcasts would be received by the LORD on the basis of their faithfulness to Him.

Holy Day Religion (58:1–14). The LORD could not fault the people for their Temple attendance. They were conscientious in keeping the law, sacrificing, and fasting. But it did not affect their relations with their workers or their neighbors. Kindness and justice did not increase when worship increased. The hungry were still just as hungry, and the naked still had no clothes. When the worship was translated into action, then the presence of the LORD would be near (58:1–9). Only then would God's blessing flow like a spring of cold water and the cities be rebuilt. Worship and service were twins—one must accompany the other (58:10–14).

A Call to Repentance (59:1–21). This oracle complains about a lack of justice in the land. For this reason, a wall separated God and the people. It was not the LORD's ability to save that had created the situation; rather, it was the people's sin (59:1–13).

> Justice is turned back,
>   and righteousness stands at a distance;
> for truth stumbles in the public square,
>   and uprightness cannot enter. (59:14)

God would give justice, both to the just and to the unjust. He would subdue the enemy and redeem His people. His spirit would come upon them and upon their children to follow them (59:15–21).

Poems about Zion (60:1–62:12)

1. ***Jerusalem's glorious future (60:1–22).*** Jerusalem had been in darkness for many years, but now the light of the LORD would once more shine in it as His presence was felt. Its people would return, along with the nations bringing gifts to the LORD from the desert countries and from the Mediterranean countries. Jerusalem would be open to all nations as the Temple would arise in new splendor.

> The sun shall no longer be your light by day,
> nor for brightness shall the moon
> give light to you by night,
> but the LORD will be your everlasting light,
> and your God will be your glory. (60:19)

2. *Good tidings to the lowly of Zion (61:1–11).* This oracle, made even more famous by Luke's account of Jesus' sermon at Nazareth (Luke 4:16–39), originally was a word of assurance to the poor and oppressed of the land of Palestine. The poor rarely had a champion, one who would protect their rights. The reference to "the day of vengeance of our God" meant the day when God would right those things that were wrong. The mourners would become rejoicers. The nation that had been poor and oppressed would be restored. Those who had mistreated the people would know the sting of justice, while Zion would know the joy of justice. This would come because the LORD loved justice and hated wrong (61:1–9). The oracle ends with a call to praise God (61:10–11).

3. *New days and new names for Jerusalem (62:1–12).* Jerusalem's restoration would not only bring a new day, but also new names for its changed condition. Before, it had been called "Forsaken" and "Desolate" (62:4); but now it would be called Hephzibah ("my delight is in her") and Beulah ("married"). It would be like a newly married woman.

The responsibility of the city's watchmen would be to remind the LORD of the LORD's obligations to Jerusalem until all that was promised was done. Among those promises was that hunger would no longer be a problem (62:6–9).

Jerusalem was also under an obligation to prepare the way for the returning exiles. They, too, would share in the new names, being called "The Holy People, The Redeemed of the LORD," "Sought Out, A City Not Forsaken" (62:10–12).

A Prayer and Its Answer (63:7–65:25). As a sort of prologue to the prayer that follows, the prophet reminded the people of the LORD's past blessings as opposed to the people's failures. They were reminded once again how the LORD had led the patriarchs in their wanderings and the Hebrews in the Exodus (63:7–14).

The prophet then prayed, addressing the LORD as "our father; our Redeemer from of old" (63:16). He asked for help to keep from erring. He prayed that the LORD would give aid against Israel's enemies. He was unlike any God man had seen. He helped the good and punished evil men. Israel had come to Him polluted, and He had hidden His face from them (63:15–64:7).

He pleaded that the LORD not be angry, for He was their Father. Their land was a wilderness, their Temple was burned, and the beautiful places were ruined (64:8–12).

In reply, the LORD said He was ready to answer prayer, but no one sought him. While He waited, they had rebelled against Him by sacrificing to pagan gods. They pretended to be so holy that others could not touch them, but the One who was really holy was angry at their lack of holiness. They would be punished as they deserved. They would not be destroyed, however, for the tribe of Judah would be chosen to receive the LORD's blessings. As examples of these blessings, the Plain of Sharon, formerly unusable to Israel because it was covered with forests, would become a pasture for sheep. The Valley of Achor, symbol of everything bad because of the incident involving Achan (Josh. 7), would be a place of rest for flocks (65:1–11).

Because of the evil they had done, those who were rebellious would be destined for the sword—nothing would turn out right for them. In contrast, the LORD's servants would prosper in everything. The rebellious would be under the curse, while the chosen would know the blessing of the LORD (65:12–16).

An ideal age with a new heaven and a new earth would come to be (this is an apocalyptic idea). Jerusalem and its inhabitants would prosper with long, good lives filled with prosperity and peace (65:17–25).

The wolf and the lamb shall feed together,
 the lion shall eat straw with the ox;
 but the serpent—its food shall be dust!
They shall not hurt or destroy
 on all my holy mountain, says the LORD. (65:25)

The Final Words (66:1–24). The LORD, who had His throne in heaven and earth as His footstool, had no need of a house built by people. What the LORD looked for were people who were "humble and contrite in spirit" and who trembled at the LORD's will. Sacrifices made by people who did not do the LORD's will were an insult. Such false religion would be punished (66:1–6).

Even though it did not seem possible, Jerusalem would be reborn because the LORD would do it. Those who loved it could rejoice with it. They could be nourished by it as a mother cared for and fed her children (66:7–12). It would carry them around like a baby on its hip. They would be comforted by the LORD and would prosper like grass in a rainy time.

However, the LORD would come in judgment upon those who defiled the land with idol worship. The survivors would be scattered to the nations of the world. They would carry the message of what the LORD had done. The people of Israel would be gathered, coming to Jerusalem by every means of transportation. As the new heaven and the new earth would remain, so the people of Israel would remain before the LORD, while the rebels would die (66:13–24).

SUMMARY OF ISAIAH

A book as long and complex as Isaiah resists a simple, synthetic description at the end. This book retells and responds to a long portion of the story of Judah and Jerusalem, and it does so using a wide variety of literary materials. Some interpreters have likened it more to a work of art than a historical document, comparing it to an oratorio or a mural. The book of Isaiah expresses trust in YHWH's compassion for Israel, but it struggles to hold that conviction together with the horrifying experience of suffering that Israel has endured. It blends examples from the past of obedience and disobedience, punishment and forgiveness, blessing and curse, and justice and injustice to help the Judah of the future chart a path toward redemption. The "new heavens and new earth" in 66:22 may be a final acknowledgment that Isaiah's vision cannot be fully realized in the midst of this creation.

Key Terms

Apocalyptic, *218*
Call Narrative, *210*
Isaian Apocalypse, *212*
Judgment Oracles, *212*
Oracle, *210*
Oracles against the Nations, *212*
Royal Narrative, *220*
Salvation Oracles, *212*
Servant Songs, *212*
Suffering Servant, *223*
Theophany, *210*
Vision, *212*

Study Questions

1. Why is it difficult to describe the relationship between individuals who were prophets and prophetic books that are named for them?
2. What were the three major crises in Israel that the prophetic literature responds to?
3. What was the nature of Isaiah's call to be a prophet?
4. What was Isaiah's relationship to Ahaz? to Hezekiah?
5. Do you think Isaiah's advice to Ahaz in the Syro-Ephraimitic crisis was sound? Explain your answer.
6. What was the significance of the names Isaiah and his wife gave their children?
7. Why do you think Isaiah advised Hezekiah as he did concerning the Ashdod rebellion?
8. How did Hezekiah prepare for a possible invasion by the Assyrians during Sennacherib's reign?
9. What possible physical evidence has been found to confirm Hezekiah's reform?
10. Why do some interpreters think Sennacherib may have invaded Judah twice?
11. What are the arguments supporting the single- and multiple-authorship views of the book of Isaiah?
12. What are the five major sections into which Isaiah 1–39 can be divided, and what is the central idea in each part?
13. How is Isaiah 40–66 related to Isaiah 1–39?
14. What are the major themes of Isaiah 40–55?
15. What are the Servant Songs?
16. How has the Suffering Servant been identified?
17. How do the oracles in Isaiah 56–66 differ from those in 40–55?

Endnotes

1. David L. Petersen has summarized well the various ways of understanding the relationship between the prophets as individual persons and the prophetic books that have their names on them. He has proposed the "generative answer" as the best way to think about this problem. The traditions found in these books grew out of the work of these prophets, although the books typically reached their final forms long after the lives of these individuals. See David L. Petersen, *The Prophetic Literature: An Introduction* (Louisville, KY: Westminster–John Knox Press, 2002), 1–4.
2. As far as the writer of this text is concerned, the point at issue in this statement for either view is not God's ability to do what He willed with the prophet. The central question was "What *did* God do?" not "What *could* God do?" I believe that the prophets spoke primarily about their own times and circumstances.
3. This understanding has been developed in the work of Christopher Seitz, *Zion's Final Destiny: The Development of the Book of Isaiah* (Minneapolis: Fortress Press, 1991), 193–208.
4. See Edgar W. Conrad, *Reading Isaiah* (Minneapolis: Fortress Press, 1991), 155–156.
5. For a discussion of this possibility, see Sigmund Mowinckel, *He That Cometh* (Nashville: Abingdon Press, 1954), 104f. For a differing interpretation, see John H. Hayes and Stuart A. Irvine, *Isaiah: The Eighth-Century Prophet: His Time and His Preaching* (Nashville: Abingdon Press, 1980), 180ff.
6. From now on, *Israel* will be used in the older sense of all the Hebrew people, not just those of the northern portion of the country.
7. For a fuller discussion of the proposed identities of both mother and child, see John H. Hayes and Stuart A. Irvine, *Isaiah: The Eighth-Century Prophet, His Times and His Teaching* (Nashville: Abingdon Press, 1987), 135f.
8. John L. McKenzie, "Second Isaiah," *AB* 20 (Garden City, NY: Doubleday, 1968), 131.
9. I owe the basic idea for this outline to J. Leo Green, Professor of Old Testament, Southeastern Baptist Theological Seminary.
10. An excellent discussion of this problem can be found in McKenzie, "Second Isaiah," xxxviii–lv.
11. Ibid., xlvii.
12. Ibid., liv–lv.
13. Ibid., lv.
14. George A. F. Knight, "Isaiah 56–66: The New Israel," *ITC*, xi–xvii, argues for such a view.
15. James D. Smart, *History and Theology in Second Isaiah: A Commentary on Isaiah 35, 40–66* (London: Epworth, 1970), 231, makes this argument.

CHAPTER

11

The Prophetic Literature II

The Scrolls of Jeremiah and Ezekiel

Timeline

640 B.C.E.	Beginning of the reign of Josiah
612 B.C.E.	Fall of Ninevah
605 B.C.E.	Beginning of the reign of Nebuchadnezzar in Babylon
597 B.C.E.	First deportation of Judahites to Babylon
586 B.C.E.	Destruction of Jerusalem by the Babylonians
586 B.C.E.	Destruction of Jerusalem and second deportation of Judahites
573 B.C.E.	Approximate end of Ezekiel's prophetic career
538 B.C.E.	Decree of Cyrus releases Israelites to return to Jerusalem

Chapter Outline

I. Introduction to the Book of Jeremiah
II. Survey of the Book of Jeremiah
III. Introduction to the Book of Ezekiel
IV. Survey of the Book of Ezekiel

CHAPTER OVERVIEW

There are two more large prophetic scrolls following Isaiah that are also designated with the name of a single prophet, Jeremiah and Ezekiel. These two prophets both lived and worked during the Babylonian crisis, which included the experience of exile, and these books are primarily concerned with understanding the destruction of Judah and finding a new way forward in the aftermath of this tragedy. This chapter will examine both of these books, seeking to describe individual texts within each of them and construct a portrait of the whole book. Attention will be given to observations that point to how, when, and why these scrolls developed, but the final form of each book, which we possess, will be the primary emphasis. These books share many features in common with Isaiah and with each other, so their distinctive features will be highlighted. The most distinctive feature of Jeremiah is a series of poems within Jeremiah 11–20 in which the prophet confesses and laments his personal struggles related to his work as a prophet. The book of Ezekiel stands out from other prophetic literature because the book is framed by reports of four elaborate visions that the prophet describes in intricate detail.

INTRODUCTION TO THE BOOK OF JEREMIAH

The book of Jeremiah is much more than a record of the prophetic ministry of the person named Jeremiah, but there is a greater coherence in this case than with Isaiah and his book. The book of Jeremiah begins with the passage that is typically identified as his call narrative. Whereas Isaiah appeared only sporadically in his book, Jeremiah appears frequently as a character. Jeremiah's name appears 131 times in the book, compared to only 16 uses of Isaiah's name in the book of Isaiah. The book of Jeremiah does not specifically report the death of the prophet, but chapter 43 does tell of his departure from Judah to Egypt, where tradition holds that he died.

The book of Jeremiah, like Isaiah, appears to be the product of a long and complex development of traditions generated by the prophet named Jeremiah. In this case, one of the disciples of Jeremiah who played a significant role in writing down and preserving some of the oracles and sermons of Jeremiah and stories about him is identified and named. The character called **Baruch** son of Neriah is first mentioned in Jeremiah 32:12, and 36:4 specifically reports that he wrote the words of Jeremiah on a scroll. This would have happened in the early part of the sixth century B.C.E., and such an event may represent the beginning of the production of the book of Jeremiah, but the entire process likely lasted another century, long past the lives and Jeremiah and Baruch.

The book of Jeremiah is unique among prophetic books because it exists in two significantly different forms. The book of Jeremiah that is in all English versions of the Bible is a translation of the form that is in the standard Hebrew text of the Bible, the Masoretic Text represented in the Leningrad Codex. The Greek version of the Old Testament, commonly referred to as the Septuagint, contains a book of Jeremiah that is about twelve percent shorter than the Hebrew version and has the chapters in a different order. The "Oracles against the Nations" that appear in Jeremiah 45–51 in the Hebrew version of the book are in Chapters 25–31 in the Greek version. When the Dead Sea Scrolls were discovered in the 1940s and 1950s, scholars were very excited to find among them two substantial scrolls of the book of Jeremiah. Because these scrolls are 400 years older than our oldest complete text of the Greek Bible, and 1000 years older than our oldest complete text of the Hebrew Bible, the expectation was that these scrolls would reveal which version of the book of Jeremiah was more like the original. To their astonishment, when the archaeologists unrolled these scrolls, a long a painstaking process, they discovered that one matched each of the two versions of Jeremiah. The existence of two different ways to present the Jeremiah tradition went back at least 2000 years, and it is possible that there never was a single authoritative way to produce this prophetic book, although the majority of opinion among scholars today is that the shorter text represented by the current Greek version was translated from a Hebrew version of the book that was closer to the "original" text.

Another indicator of a complex process of development is the presence of "doublets," occurrences of the same text in two different places, sometimes in slightly different form and sometimes identical. Jeremiah 10:12–16 and 51:15–19 is a good example of this phenomenon.[1] In other cases, two different kinds of accounts of the same event may be present in the book. For example, Jeremiah 7 provides the text of Jeremiah's famous "**Temple Sermon**," while the story in Jeremiah 26 seems to be the public reaction to the sermon, and the sermon is only summarized there.

The final form of the book of Jeremiah has a sense of movement similar to what was demonstrated in the book of Isaiah in the previous chapter. The first half of the book is largely negative, focusing on Jeremiah's proclamation of God's impending judgment on Judah and Jerusalem. A shift in tone takes place around the middle of the book. In a dramatic letter to the captives in Babylon, Jeremiah explains that the destruction of Judah and Jerusalem must be completed and that they must serve the seventy years of their punishment (29:10), but the letter assures them that this will come to an end and that YHWH will eventually restore Judah. From this point on the book is much more positive, speaking more often of comfort and redemption than of punishment and destruction.

SURVEY OF THE BOOK OF JEREMIAH

Jeremiah's Context and Call (Jer. 1:1–19)

Jeremiah was from a priestly family that lived in Anathoth. This was the village to which Abiathar, David's friend, who supported Adonijah as David's successor, had been exiled. Jeremiah may have been a descendant of Abiathar, but even if he was not a direct descendent, this "outsider" tradition was likely an important component of his identity. The superscription in 1:1–3 places Jeremiah's prophetic activity in the reigns of Josiah, Jehoiakim, and Zedekiah, and it continued until he was taken to Egypt by a group of rebels in 582 B.C.E., where traditions outside of the Bible report that he died.

The traditional date for the call of Jeremiah as a prophet is 626 B.C.E. This is based on the superscription in Jeremiah 1:2, which says, "To whom the word of the LORD came in the days of Josiah . . . in the thirteenth year of his reign." This date is problematic, however, because of the reference to the threat of a northern enemy against Palestine (1:13–19). Strict supporters of the 626 B.C.E. date argue that Jeremiah's "foe from the north" was the Scythian army. Little is known of the Scythians, a group of people from east of the Persian Gulf who gave Assyria increasing problems as its empire declined. If they did invade as far west as Palestine, as the Greek historian Herodotus says, it would have been about the time that Jeremiah was called. There is little hard evidence, however, that such an invasion took place, or that this is the group to which Jeremiah refers.[2]

The more realistic threat from the north was the Babylonians. For this reason, some interpreters date Jeremiah's call experience a decade later, in 616 B.C.E. These interpreters argue that the Babylonians were the real "foe from the north," an identification that fits much better with the primary concerns of the entire book. The chronological note that places the beginning of Jeremiah's ministry in "the thirteenth year of Josiah" can be explained as a scribal mistake that should read "the twenty-third year of Josiah." This concern of modern interpreters with

The Literary Structure of Jeremiah

Like the first large book within the prophetic literature, Isaiah, the book of Jeremiah shows evidence of a process of collection of materials and growth of traditions around a particular prophet and his followers over a long period of time, although the time period for the production of Jeremiah is probably closer to one century than to two or three. One place to look for help in understanding the structure of Jeremiah is the book of Isaiah. This observation proves to be quite instructive, because, like Isaiah, Jeremiah focuses on the tension between judgment and salvation, with a significant turn away from the former and toward the latter as the book progresses. Nevertheless, such comparisons should probably be kept at a very general level, and the book of Jeremiah should be allowed to demonstrate its own sense of literary development. A discussion of the structure of Jeremiah must acknowledge an awareness that the Greek version of the book presents the material in a different order. The Oracles against the Nations found at the end of Jeremiah in the Hebrew text tradition are found nearer the middle of the Greek text. Therefore, even in ancient times, Jeremiah had more than one literary structure. It appears likely that the middle of the book, as in the Greek text, is the earlier location, and that the Hebrew text has moved these oracles, perhaps to place the promise of the destruction of Babylon near the end of the book and adjacent to the story of the destruction of Jerusalem.

The book of Jeremiah is engaged in two key tasks—telling the story of Jeremiah's ministry as a prophet and reporting the words of Jeremiah's prophecies. Jeremiah is a much more prominent narrative character than Isaiah. The oracles of Jeremiah are the primary content of the first twenty-five chapters of the book, and most of the narrative material about his life is found in Jeremiah 26–45, then chapters 46–51 return to primarily oracular material. Thus, the life of Jeremiah is essentially framed by his words.

A number of interpreters have noticed an important set of phrases that is repeated at two key points in the book of Jeremiah.[3] In 1:16 God says to Jeremiah:

> See, today, I appoint you over nations and over kingdoms,
> to pluck up and to pull down,
> to destroy and to overthrow,
> to build and to plant.

The first half of the book of Jeremiah focuses upon the negative aspects of this saying and its realization in the Babylonian destruction of Judah. In Jeremiah 31:28, these words are revised in a saying of God through Jeremiah:

> And just as I have watched over them to pluck up and break down, to overthrow, destroy, and bring evil, so I will watch over them to build and to plant, says the LORD.

The focus turns to God's salvation for Israel in this portion of the book, which tells the story of Jeremiah and holds him up as a model of faithfulness to God. Those in exile who choose to see the situation as Jeremiah did are offered hope for deliverance.

Perhaps the most distinctive feature of the book of Jeremiah is the sequence of poems spread throughout chapters 11–20, and commonly known as either the "Confessions" or "Laments" of Jeremiah. These poetic expressions of the prophet's difficulty, typically expressed to God, offer an intimate, internal view of his life and thought that is unusual within the prophetic literature. The conversations between God and Jonah in Jonah 2 and 4 offer the closest parallels to these texts.

The Oracles against the Nations are presented in Jeremiah 46–51 as an aspect of God's deliverance of Israel. This section ends with a lengthy condemnation of Babylon. In the final chapter, the story of the destruction of Jerusalem is remembered, but appended to it in the closing verses is the story of the release of King Jehoiachin from prison in Babylon. The first step toward release from captivity is taken. It is up to those who read Jeremiah to choose to be part of this process of salvation.

chronological precision may not have been a concern of those who constructed the book of Jeremiah.

Jeremiah's career is comparable to Isaiah's in length, especially if his call came in 626 B.C.E. It extended over part or all of the reigns of five kings, as well as the rule of Gedeliah, the governor of the Babylonian province that included Judah. His influence, both positive and negative, extended across all lines of society and even across national boundaries. In the call of Jeremiah, several interesting features appear:

1. He felt that the LORD had destined him to be a prophet even before he was born (1:5ab).
2. He was called to minister beyond national boundaries (1:5c).
3. He was still quite young when he became conscious of his call (1:6).
4. The LORD assured Jeremiah that He would be with him and take care of him (1:7–8).
5. Jeremiah was called to be a prophet to the nations. His message, while one of judgment, would lead to a positive result (1:9–10).

Two visions were part of the **Call Narrative** of Jeremiah: the vision of the almond tree and the vision of the boiling pot. Jeremiah's visions involved ordinary things that took on much greater significance in the midst of his social and political context. These are not elaborate visions like we will encounter with Ezekiel later in this chapter. It is possible to understand them in a way that is not supernatural at all. The vision of the almond tree (1:11–12) involves a **wordplay**, using the noun *shaqed*, which in Hebrew meant "almond tree," while the verb "to watch" was *shoqed*. Jeremiah said, "I see a rod of almond (*shaqed*)." The LORD answered:

> "You have seen well, for I am watching (*shoqed*) over my word to perform it." (1:12)

The point was that the LORD would perform as promised, and the almond tree would remind Jeremiah of that assurance.

What did Jeremiah think of the reform under Josiah? This is one of the mysteries surrounding the book of Jeremiah. Whether Jeremiah preached at all during Josiah's reign is uncertain. His positive evaluation of Josiah appears in 22:15–16, which compares Josiah and Jehoiakim:

> Are you a king because you compete in cedar?
> Did not your father eat and drink
>   and do justice and righteousness?
> Then it was well with him.
> He judged the cause of the poor and needy;
>   then it was well.
> Is not this to know me?
>   says the LORD.[4]

The scroll of Jeremiah, however, was composed well after the ultimate collapse of Josiah's reform movement, so any enthusiasm the prophet may have had initially would have been reevaluated and reformulated by then.

The book of Jeremiah likely continued to grow and develop after the death of Jeremiah himself, as the prophetic tradition he began was continued by others who would have understood themselves to be his followers. More about the literary features and design of the book appears in the box titled "The Literary Structure of Jeremiah." The discussion below attempts to follow the prose sections of the book chronologically, based on the dates reported in them. The poetic, oracular portions of the book do not have such dates and will be discussed after the prose sections.

Jeremiah and the Final Leaders of Judah

If Jeremiah admired Josiah, his admiration did not carry over to his son, Jehoiakim. From the beginning of Jehoiakim's reign, he and Jeremiah were in conflict, and Jeremiah's prophetic work would face opposition from royal and religious power.

THE TEMPLE SERMON (JER. 7:1–15; 26:1–24). In 609 B.C.E., Jehoiakim was placed on the throne of Judah by Pharaoh Neco of Egypt. In that same year, Jeremiah appeared in the Temple during a festival to preach a scathing sermon. Its theme was as follows:

> Amend your ways and your doings, and let me dwell with you in this place. Do not trust in these deceptive words: "This is the temple of the LORD, the temple of the LORD, the temple of the LORD." (7:3–4)

Versions of this sermon appear in both Jeremiah 7 and 26. Chapter 7 contains a fuller version of the sermon. It attacked the popular notion that the LORD would not permit Jerusalem to be destroyed because the Temple was located there. Instead, the people's only hope was a return to the great moral principles of the Sinai covenant. If the people did not change their ways, Jerusalem's fate would be the same as Shiloh's, one of Israel's earliest shrines. It had been destroyed by the Philistines in 1050 B.C.E. (7:5–15; 26:2–6).

If Jeremiah hoped to move the people to action, he was not disappointed. The action, however, was directed toward him. He was seized and threatened with death (26:7–9). Word got to the community leaders about the commotion in the Temple. Jeremiah was saved from lynching, but he was put on trial for his life on the charge of blasphemy—that is, cursing the Temple, which was the LORD's dwelling place. This meant that he was cursing the LORD.

A formal trial followed. First, the evidence against Jeremiah was presented (26:10–11). Then, Jeremiah spoke in his own defense. He admitted saying what he had said and even repeated the essentials of his sermon (26:12–13). Having done that, he threw himself on the mercy of the court, but not without warning that if he were put to death, an innocent man would die (26:14–15). When the verdict came, Jeremiah was declared "not guilty." The judges cited Micah 3:12, in which Micah had also predicted Jerusalem's destruction. They pointed out that Hezekiah did not put Micah to death; therefore, Jeremiah should be freed (26:16–19).

Another prophet, Uriah, who made a similar prophecy, was not so fortunate. He fled to Egypt, but Jehoiakim brought him back and put him to death (26:20–23). Jeremiah still had powerful friends who protected him (26:24).

JEREMIAH'S CONFLICT WITH JEHOIAKIM. By 605 B.C.E., Jeremiah was in trouble with **Jehoiakim.** In a symbolic action that involved burying a linen waistcloth on the banks of the Euphrates River, he criticized Jehoiakim for submitting to the Babylonians. When he dug it up later, it was soiled. Judah's relations to Babylon would cause it to be as soiled and useless as the waistcloth (13:1–11).

Another action that aroused Jehoiakim's ire came when Jeremiah and a group of his supporters went to the Valley of Hinnom. There, Jehoiakim had set up altars to Baal and had practiced child sacrifice. Jeremiah condemned the pagan cults. He smashed a flask to symbolize how the LORD would smash Jerusalem and its inhabitants for following false gods (19:1–15).

Jeremiah was arrested by Pashhur, a Temple official. He was beaten and placed in the stocks for public ridicule. When he was released the next day, Jeremiah denounced Pashhur and repeated his warning, with a private word of judgment for Pashhur (20:1–6). This may have been the action that resulted in Jeremiah's being barred from the Temple. This would have occurred at the time when Baruch became his secretary and wrote what may have been the first edition of his book.

Finally, Jeremiah warned Jehoiakim that Babylon would destroy Judah. This warning may have come after the battle of Carchemish in 605 B.C.E. or it could have been a warning that preceded the Babylonian invasion of 598 B.C.E., which led to the first fall of Jerusalem. In any case, Jeremiah saw it as the certain judgment on Jerusalem for the people's failure to follow the law of the LORD (25:1–14).

JEREMIAH AND JEHOIACHIN. **Jehoiachin's** reign (598–597 B.C.E.) was so brief that Jeremiah said little about him. In an oracle in 22:24–30, he spoke of Jehoiachin (whom he called *Coniah*) as being like "a despised broken pot." He was to be considered childless, because none of his children would ever succeed him as king of Judah (22:30).

JEREMIAH AND ZEDEKIAH. Jeremiah's and **Zedekiah's** relationship was most unusual. When Jerusalem fell in 597 B.C.E., Zedekiah was put on the throne by the Babylonians. He was the son of Josiah and thus the uncle of the previous king. The Babylonians seem not to have deported all the leadership in 597 B.C.E. but rather to have left those they thought would be loyal to them. Their loyalty was short-lived. Soon a powerful group was pressuring Zedekiah to declare his independence from Babylon or to switch his loyalties to Egypt. A group of "righteous ones," probably led by some of the prophets, kept insisting that the LORD had permitted the Exile only as a temporary punishment. It would end in a year or so with a dramatic deliverance of the people. Zedekiah seems to have responded to whichever group was exerting the most pressure. He respected Jeremiah enough to ask him for advice, but he was too weak to carry out the advice he received.

Jeremiah's opinion of the **Exiles,** compared with those left in the land, is shown by the vision of the figs. To steal some lines from a nursery rhyme, the figs could be described as follows:

> The basket that was good was very, very good,
> but the one that was bad was horrid.

For Jeremiah, the good figs represented those taken into exile; the bad figs were those who had been left behind.

Pressure began to mount on Zedekiah to break away from Babylon as soon as **Nebuchadnezzar,** the Babylonian king, lessened the pressure on Jerusalem after its capture. Two things had led to this situation: (1) a revolt in Babylon involving some of Nebuchadnezzar's army—some of the Jews who were in exile may also have been involved; (2) the ascension of a new king, Psammethicus II (594–589 B.C.E.), to the throne of Egypt. He and his successor, Hophra (589–570 B.C.E.), both encouraged rebellion against Babylon.[5] The court prophets encouraged Judah to join the revolt, preaching that the LORD was about to deliver the exiles and bring them home. Those who opposed them were branded as traitors and unbelievers.

Jeremiah aroused the ire of the "superpatriots" by consistently insisting that Judah's only hope of survival lay in being loyal subjects of Nebuchadnezzar. To emphasize his point, he made a wooden yoke like that used to hitch oxen to a plow and wore it on his neck. This object lesson was to emphasize the wisdom of Judah's wearing the yoke of Babylon (27:1–22).

Hananiah, a leader of the superpatriots and a prophet from Gibeon, grabbed Jeremiah's wooden yoke and broke it. The LORD, he said, had broken Babylon's yoke and would return the exiles to the land in two years. Jeconiah (Jehoiachin), furthermore, would be restored to his rightful place as king (28:1–4; 10–11).

Jeremiah replied that he hoped Hananiah was right, but that the real proof would be whether his words came true (28:5–9). Later, Jeremiah came back with yoke bars made of iron. He told Hananiah that not only would Babylon's yoke not be broken, but that Hananiah himself would die (28:12–16). In that same year, in the seventh month, Hananiah died (28:17).

About 593 B.C.E., to help defuse the situation in Babylon and to help the exiles achieve a stronger hold on reality, Jeremiah wrote a letter. He made four major points:

1. Live as normally as possible. Do those things that would be done if you were at home and the country were at peace (29:4–6).
2. Be good citizens. What is good for Babylon is good for the exiles, for "in its welfare you will find your welfare" (29:7).
3. Pay no attention to the superpatriots and false prophets. They are just trying to deceive you. The LORD did not send them (29:8–9).
4. When the time is right, the LORD will bring you home (29:10–14). This is the meaning of the phrase *when seventy years are completed for Babylon.* In the same connection, Ezekiel would use forty years as his symbol for a complete period (Ezek. 4:6).

Jeremiah specifically named two prophets who were stirring up trouble—Ahab and Zedekiah. Nebuchadnezzar would soon snuff out their lives, for they were nothing but liars and deceivers (29:15–23). He had a further word for Shemaiah, who had written to Zephaniah, a Jerusalem priest, telling him to arrest Jeremiah and put him in the stocks. Zephaniah was Jeremiah's friend, however, and shared the letter with him. When he heard it, Jeremiah predicted the doom of Shemaiah (29:24–32).

Zedekiah's rebellion brought disaster. Jeremiah warned him that his only hope for a peaceful death with a proper burial was to surrender to Nebuchadnezzar, the king of Babylonia. By early 588 B.C.E., all the cities of Judah had fallen, except Jerusalem, Lachish, and Azekah (34:1–7). The Lachish letters, found in the ruins of that city a few years ago, describe the desperate situation. As a significant passage from one of the letters says:

> We are watching for the signals of Lachish, according to all the indications which my LORD has given, for we cannot see Azekah.[6]

This letter, written to the commander of the garrison at Lachish, indicated that Azekah had fallen and it would only be a matter of time until Jerusalem and Lachish also fell. There may also be a reference to Uriah, the prophet mentioned in Jeremiah 26:20–24, or a reference to Jeremiah himself in the letters, but this is uncertain.

The situation became so desperate in Jerusalem that Zedekiah was willing to do almost anything to improve it. One of the things he did was to persuade the people to free all their Israelite slaves. Such people usually were slaves because they were unable to pay debts they owed. The law provided, however, that they would never be held in bondage for more than six years against their will (Exod. 21:1–6; Deut. 15:12–18). It seems that by Jeremiah's time, this law was largely ignored. Thus, Zedekiah was reviving an ancient religious practice, thereby invoking divine favor. From a practical standpoint, the freed slaves would be more likely to fight for the city. Then, too, their owners would no longer be responsible for feeding them at a time when food was becoming increasingly scarce.

Scarcely had the action been taken when it was withdrawn and the freed people were once more enslaved. The probable cause of this reversal was the lifting of the siege of Jerusalem when the Egyptians marched out to oppose the Babylonians. Feeling that the threat was removed from the city, the wealthy men seized their former slaves and enslaved them again. Jeremiah warned that because of the dishonesty of the wealthy, the LORD would grant a release to them of "liberty to the sword, to pestilence and to famine" (34:17). The destruction of the city and its leaders was a foregone conclusion (34:11–22).

Jeremiah warned Zedekiah that the Babylonian withdrawal was temporary (37:6–10). Although the siege was lifted, Jeremiah sought to leave the city for a trip to Anathoth to inspect some property. Thinking that he was deserting to the Babylonians, an overzealous guard arrested him and brought him before the city leaders. They had him beaten and thrown into the dungeon (37:11–15).

Finally, Zedekiah ordered that Jeremiah be brought out secretly so that he could consult with him. When he asked Jeremiah if there was any word from the LORD, Jeremiah told him that there was—the same word of judgment that he had pronounced before. Then Jeremiah, weakened by the prison experience, begged Zedekiah not to return him to the dungeon. Zedekiah protected him for a time and saw that he got whatever food was available (37:16–21). This probably is the time when Jeremiah bought some ancestral property from his cousin Hanamel, as both 32:2 and 37:21 speak of Jeremiah being imprisoned in the "court of the guard."

The LORD told Jeremiah that his cousin Hanamel wanted to sell a field at Anathoth to him and that he was to buy it. Hanamel was following the law of redemption of property. That law provided that if any property was for sale, it had to be offered to one's nearest kin—brothers, uncles, and then cousins, in that order (Lev. 25:25–28).

When Hanamel came, Jeremiah bought the property and received a proper deed for it. The deed consisted of two copies, one that was kept sealed and another that could be opened for public inspection (32:1–15).[7] Hanamel's purpose in selling the field was to get money, which could be more easily held if the city fell. On the other hand, Jeremiah purchased the field to show his confidence that the people would survive the coming exile and would once more live in the land (32:16–44). In that sense, his purchase was carrying out the positive aspect of his call "to build and to plant." It illustrates quite vividly the prophetic view of judgment as redemptive and cleansing rather than annihilating—completely wiping out the people.

Meanwhile, the siege tightened and, as the food supply sank lower and lower, other conditions within the city worsened. Lamentations 4 describes in gruesome detail the effects of the food shortage: the dry, shriveled skin of people who once were sleek and healthy (Lam. 4:8); mothers resorting to cannibalism, eating their own children (Lam. 4:10); and the danger of walking in the streets for fear of being killed for food (Lam. 4:18).

Jeremiah's enemies were persistent, to say the least. When they found that Zedekiah had rescued Jeremiah from the dungeon, they pressured Zedekiah to turn the prophet over to them. Again, Zedekiah yielded, and once more, Jeremiah was in the hands of his enemies.

The next place where Jeremiah found himself was in a cistern. Cisterns are underground containers for water hewn out of the rock. They varied in size from those that held a few thousand gallons of water to others that held tremendous amounts. Jeremiah was thrown into a small cistern partially filled with mud that had been washed in. He sank into the mire, and had he not been rescued by one of Zedekiah's servants, he probably would have died there (38:1–13).

Once again, Jeremiah came before Zedekiah. Once again, Zedekiah asked the prophet if there was any message for him from the LORD. Once again, Jeremiah told Zedekiah that his only hope was to surrender to the Babylonians. Otherwise, death and destruction awaited him and the inhabitants of Jerusalem (38:14–23). But in contrast to their previous meeting, when Jeremiah pleaded for his life (37:20), Zedekiah was now pleading with Jeremiah not to let the leaders know Zedekiah had consulted him. If he did so, the leaders would kill Jeremiah. He assured Zedekiah that he would only tell them that he was pleading for his life. In exchange, Zedekiah kept him in prison in the royal quarters (38:24–28).

Famine, pestilence, and the Babylonian army finally prevailed. Jerusalem fell, probably in the year 587 B.C.E., although some date the fall to 586 B.C.E. Ancient armies won more battles by patiently waiting for their enemy to starve than they did by direct assault. For almost two years, Nebuchadnezzar's army had cut off the inhabitants of Jerusalem from any source of food other than what had been stored in the city. Because there was no room within the city walls to grow food, the people inevitably faced the choice of surrender or starvation if the siege could not be lifted by other means. The Babylonians had battering rams to break down the walls, but Jerusalem had strong fortifications that enabled it to hold out until starvation and disease took their toll on the defenders of the city (39:1–2).

Zedekiah, realizing that further resistance was futile, fled the city at night. He was captured near Jericho, however, and carried before Nebuchadnezzar at Riblah of Hamath in northern Syria. He was condemned to watch the slaughter of his sons and his chief officials. Then his own eyes were punched out, and he was taken to Babylon as a prisoner (39:3–7).

Meanwhile, Jerusalem was burned—including the palace complex and the Temple. The walls were broken down, and most of the talented inhabitants were taken to Babylon. The Babylonians sought to ensure the loyalty of the poor people by giving them land (39:8–10).

Jeremiah, still in prison as a result of his problems during the siege, was brought out and released. At first, it seems that he had been included among those to be taken to Babylon. Later, when given the choice of remaining in the land, he chose to do so. He was put into the custody of Gedaliah, an official of Zedekiah's court who had been appointed governor by the Babylonians.

After the Fall of Jerusalem (Jer. 40:7–44:30)

THE MURDER OF GEDALIAH (2 KINGS 25:22–26; JER. 40:7–41:18). The land was in ruins. The dream of independence was shattered, and the people were left beaten and disillusioned. The Babylonians appointed Gedaliah as governor over the Babylonian province of which Judah was now a part. The seat of government was moved to Mizpah, as Jerusalem was only a heap of blackened rubble (Jer. 40:7–8).

Gedaliah urged the people to serve the Babylonians (Chaldeans) and to gather what food they could from the vines and trees. People who had fled to Transjordan returned to their homes when they heard that the land was once more at peace. Fortunately for them, the fruit crops were abundant (40:9–12). Unfortunately, at the urging of the Ammonite king named Baalis,[8] Ishmael, who claimed descent from David, plotted against Gedaliah. Although warned of the plot, Gedaliah ignored it, to his own downfall. In 582 B.C.E., Ishmael killed not only Gedaliah but also a large number of Jews and a contingent of Chaldean soldiers. Among those he attacked were eighty men from Shechem, Shiloh, and Samaria who seemingly had come to the site of the ruined Temple to offer a sacrifice on that sacred spot. This would indicate that even though the Temple was destroyed, worship of a sort was still carried on there. Ishmael killed all but ten of the worshipers, who bought their lives with promises of food for Ishmael and his men. Ishmael also took captive the remaining inhabitants of Mizpah (41:1–10).

Johanan, a leader who had supported Gedaliah, soon raised a force to fight Ishmael. When the fight came, many of the people from Mizpah whom Ishmael had taken captive fled to join Johanan. Ishmael beat a hasty retreat to the other side of the Jordan (41:11–18).

THE FLIGHT TO EGYPT. Johanan, fearing that he would be blamed for Gedaliah's death, fled to Egypt. Jeremiah tried to persuade him not to do it, but Johanan did not heed Jeremiah's advice. Instead, Jeremiah was forced to go along (42:1–43:7). The last words of Jeremiah were predictions of doom for Egypt and for those who had fled to it for protection. Only Baruch, Jeremiah's faithful disciple, would escape with his life (43:8–45:5). As far as is known, Jeremiah died in Egypt.

The Oracles of Jeremiah[9]

The oracles of Jeremiah are scattered throughout the book. Those found in chapters 2–6, 8–20, 30–31, and 46–52 will be examined, emphasizing prominent themes found in them.

EARLY AND MIXED ORACLES

Early oracles (Jer. 2:1–6:30)

1. Remembering better days (2:1–3).
2. Israel has been unfaithful (2:4–37).
3. Repent, O Israel (3:1–4:4).
4. Beware the foe from the north (4:5–31).
5. Judah is hopelessly immoral (5:1–6:30).

Mixed oracles (Jer. 8:4–10:25)

1. The people have shown incredible stupidity (8:4–17).
2. The heartsick prophet (8:18–9:1).
3. Beware of your neighbor's tongue (9:2–9).
4. Cry for Zion (9:10–22).
5. The glory in serving the LORD (9:23–26).
6. Idols and those who make them (10:1–25).

These two groups of oracles are discussed together because they share some common themes.

Israel, the Unfaithful Wife. In the oracles of Jeremiah, one hears echoes of earlier prophets, especially Hosea. In 2:2–3. Jeremiah introduces the bride figure:

> I remember the devotion of your youth,
>   your love as a bride,
> how you followed in the wilderness,
>   in a land not sown. (2:2)

He continues this theme in an oracle found in 3:1, where he asks whether a woman, once divorced and remarried, can return to her original husband. Israel has known many lovers and wants to return to the LORD (3:1), but she has so polluted herself with Baalism that the land is filled "with your vile harlotry" (3:2). Still the LORD pleads for the people to return (3:12, 14, 22; 4:1).

The Worship of Idols. The prophet was perplexed over the people's fascination with idols. Idols, as such, were not seen as actual gods; rather, the deity was thought to be present in an image that was properly clothed and cared for.[10] How the people could be drawn away from the living LORD mystified the prophet:

> What wrong did your ancestors find in me
>   that they went far from me
> and went after worthless things,
>   and became worthless themselves? (2:5)
>   . . .
> Has a nation changed its gods,
>   even though they are not gods? (2:11)
>   . . .

for my people have committed two evils;
    they have forsaken me,
the fountain of living waters,
    and dug out cisterns for themselves,
    cracked cisterns
that can hold no water. (2:13)

Jeremiah's most extended polemic against idols is found in 10:1–25. He observes:

Their idols are like scarecrows in a
    cucumber field,
and they cannot speak;
they have to be carried
    for they cannot walk.
Do not be afraid of them,
    for they cannot do evil,
    nor is it in them to do good. (10:5)

The Foe from the North. A much-discussed theme from Jeremiah deals with oracles about a "foe from the north." In addition to the initial vision of the boiling pot (1:13–19), the prophet takes up the subject in other oracles. A series of such oracles is to be found in Jeremiah 4:5–31. Some of the prophet's most vivid language is used to describe this threat:

Blow the trumpet through the land;
    shout aloud and say,
"Gather together, and let us go
    into the fortified cities!"
    . . .
for I am bringing evil from the north,
    and a great destruction. (4:5, 6)

Later in the chapter, the devastation is described:

I looked on the earth, and lo, it was
    waste and void:
and to the heavens, and they
    had no light.
I looked on the mountains, and lo
    they were quaking,
and all the hills moved to and fro.
    . . .
I looked, and lo, the fruitful land
    was a desert,
and all its cities were laid in ruins
    before the LORD, before his fierce anger. (4:23–26)

The Prophet's Responsibility. Jeremiah, like other prophets, was particularly disturbed by those religious leaders, both priest and prophet, whose main concern was to curry favor with the rich and powerful. He speaks of those who

have treated the wound of my people
    carelessly,

saying, "Peace, peace,"
  when there is no peace.
They acted shamefully, they
  committed abomination;
yet they are not ashamed,
they did not know how to blush. (6:14–15; 8:11–12)

The responsible prophet would warn the people of the dangers they faced (28:8). Jeremiah was a realist who tested the people the way an assayer would test ore to determine its metal content (6:27–30).

THE CONFESSIONS AND OTHER ORACLES (JER. 11:1–20:18)

1. The broken covenant (11:1–17).
2. The first confession: Save me from those who would kill me, O LORD!
3. The LORD's lament (12:7–13).
4. The fate of Judah's neighbors (12:14–17).
5. The spoiled loincloth (13:1–11).
6. The wine jar (13:12–14).
7. The fate of Judah and the shame of Jerusalem (13:15–17).
8. Oracles during a drought (14:1–16).
9. The certainty of calamity (14:17–15:9).
10. The second confession: Why do you treat me this way, LORD? (15:10–21).
11. No wife for Jeremiah (16:1–9).
12. Mixed oracles (16:10–17:4).
13. The proverbs of Jeremiah (17:5–13).
14. The third confession: Heal me, O LORD (17:14–18).
15. A trip to the potter's house (18:1–17).
16. The fourth confession: Let them have it, LORD! (18:18–23).
17. The message of the shattered flask (19:1–20:6).
18. The fifth confession: You have made a fool of me, LORD (20:7–13).
19. The sixth confession: Why was I ever born, LORD? (20:14–18).

The Prophet's Frustrations: The Denial of Family Life. The primary personal aim of every normal Israelite male was to marry and to have children. In pre-Exilic times, a doctrine of life after death had not developed. As a result, a man thought of living beyond his life in terms of living through his children. If he did not marry, then he could not legitimately fulfill this basic desire. Or, if his marriage produced no children, the desire was frustrated. This was why barren women were portrayed in the Old Testament as being persons who made great efforts to become pregnant. That the man might be the one who was to blame seems never to have entered their thinking.

Jeremiah was told not to marry because to do so would only bring tragedy to him. He was better off without any family rather than seeing his family destroyed by the war (16:1–4).

In addition, he was to avoid the normal social functions. These included funerals, parties, and weddings—three of the chief social functions of his day (16:5–9).

The Prophet's Frustrations: The Confessions. One of the unique features of the book of Jeremiah is a series of oracles called the ***confessions** of Jeremiah.* They are found in 11:18–12:6, 15:10–21, 17:14–18, 18:18–23, 20:1–13, and 20:14–18. These confessions give us a window on Jeremiah's inner struggles as he tries to carry out his prophetic ministry. Because of their importance, they will be discussed individually.

The First Confession: Save Me from Those Who Would Kill Me, O Lord! (11:18–12:6). The first **confession** follows a sermon in which Jeremiah spoke of being told to pronounce judgment upon those who refused to follow the covenant. He was even told not to pray for them because of the vileness of their sins (11:1–17).

Such sermons did not earn Jeremiah the "Favorite Prophet of the Year" award from the board of trustees of the Jerusalem Temple. Instead of repentance, their reaction took the form of threats of violence. When Jeremiah heard of their threats, he did not say, "O Lord, forgive them." Instead, he asked the Lord to protect him from those who would kill him (11:18–20).

To make matters worse, Jeremiah was told that the leaders among the plotters were his own kinfolk, "the men of Anathoth" (11:21). Again, he pleaded for the Lord to come to his rescue. He could not understand how such wicked men could prosper (12:1–4).

The answer was not encouraging. The Lord said, in effect, "Jeremiah, if you think things are bad now, cheer up—they will get much worse!" (12:5–6).

The Second Confession: Why Do You Treat Me This Way, Lord? (15:10–21). Following another oracle that continues the theme of Judah's doom, Jeremiah's second confession begins. In words that echo Job's lament (Job 3:1–10), Jeremiah bemoaned his fate. Nothing he did pleased men, even though he had pleaded with the Lord on their behalf. The assurance came to him that the doom of the sinners was certain (15:10–14). Jeremiah recalled the circumstances of his call to be a prophet:

> Your words were found and I ate them,
> and your words became to me a joy
> and the delight of my heart;
> for I am called by your name,
> O Lord, God of hosts. (15:16)

He had shunned the society of others, especially places of merrymaking, because he was so moved by indignation over the conditions in the country. But that had only brought him pain. Like a wet-weather spring that promised water all year long but dried up when the rains ceased, the Lord had deceived him (15:15–18).

After that outburst, a word of assurance came to Jeremiah. If he faithfully preached the Lord's words he would still have enemies, but they would not overcome him. The Lord would be with him to deliver him out of the hands of those who would harm him (15:19–21).

The Third Confession: Heal Me, O Lord (17:14–18). This confession was a prayer for healing and salvation. Jeremiah's enemies were cynics who would not believe him. He declared that he had not prayed for disaster for his enemies. If he had not before, he did then. He called for them to be destroyed with "double destruction!" (17:18).

The Fourth Confession: Let Them Have It, Lord! (18:18–23). This confession is introduced by a report of the plots against Jeremiah. What is of particular interest is the mention of the three major classes of religious leaders—the priests, the wise men, and the prophets. This is one of the few places where the wise men are classed with the priests and prophets as leaders of the religious community. The wise men were particularly concerned with the practical matters of how to get along in human society. They were the "school men" or teachers of the young. Their major interest was the day-to-day existence of humanity (18:18).

Jeremiah's enemies ganged up to counteract anything he said about them. They decided to "bring charges against him." In desperation, the prophet turned to the Lord to plead his case once again. Reminding the LORD how he had pleaded for those who were abusing him, Jeremiah appealed for justice for himself. In a scathing tirade against his enemies, he asked that the worst of calamities befall them and their families because of their plots against him (18:19–23).

The Fifth Confession: You Have Made a Fool of Me, LORD (20:7–13). This confession reflects the prophet's increasing sense of frustration as he tried to minister to the people of Jerusalem. The LORD had deceived him into being a prophet with promises of His presence. But the life of a prophet, even with the LORD's presence, was more than Jeremiah had bargained for. He got so tired of preaching about violence and destruction that he decided to quit. Instead, the urge from the LORD was so strong that he found himself preaching again in spite of his resolutions not to do so. Because even his closest friends were trying to destroy him, he did not need enemies (20:1–10).

Suddenly, his mood shifted. As he realized that the LORD would take care of his enemies, his complaints changed to praise (20:11–13).

The Sixth Confession: Why Was I Ever Born, LORD? (20:14–18). The final confession probes the depths of the prophet's misery. Like Job (Job 3), he curses the day he was born: "Why did I come forth from the womb to see toil and sorrow and spend my days in shame?" (20:18).

The Significance of Jeremiah's Confessions. In the confessions, the agony of Jeremiah's inner struggles is revealed. Here was an honest man whose faith in the justice of God led him to put aside all pretense in his prayers. He survived those horrible times because he was able to purge himself of his inner conflicts through prayer to the One whom he experienced as the personal LORD.

The Prophet's Image of Hope: The Parable of the Potter (18:1–7). Although this incident ends with a rather negative conclusion, it does have a positive premise, namely, that at the time the prophet spoke, the situation of Judah was not hopeless. Were the people willing to submit to the LORD's direction, salvation was still possible. Their stubbornness, however, negated that hope.

The Prophet's Words of Hope: The Oracles of Consolation (30:1–32:40). These oracles expressed the positive side of Jeremiah's call to prophesy. Judgment on Judah was not the final act of God. It was a cleansing fire designed to burn away the impurities. The LORD would restore the purified people to the land (30:1–3). Although there are **salvation** oracles that emphasize the Restoration, the most noted passage in this section is 31:23–40 and the incident involving the purchase of the field. As the LORD had watched over the people (1:12) to "pluck up and break down, to overthrow, destroy, and bring evil" (31:28; see also 1:10), so the LORD would now "watch over them to build and to plant" (31:28).

In earlier times, the emphasis had been on how the sins of one affected his whole family, so much so that a common proverb said, "The parents have eaten sour grapes and the children's teeth are set on edge" (31:29). This would no longer be so. The responsibility for acts of sin rested upon the one who committed them. This concept of individual responsibility introduced by Jeremiah was one of his distinct contributions to biblical theology. Ezekiel would take this idea and expand on it (Ezek. 18, 33).

An idea growing out of Jeremiah's teaching about individual responsibility was that of the new covenant (31:31–34). The old covenant had been written on stone tablets and, more often than not, had failed to make the transition from written principle to living practice. The principles had not become personal guidelines for life. Jeremiah looked for a day when the LORD's law would be the normal way of life. Each person would "know the LORD" and live by that knowledge. Jeremiah illustrated the LORD's relationship to Israel by comparing it to the fixed order of nature (31:35–37). Jerusalem would be rebuilt and become the LORD's sacred city again (31:38–40).

ORACLES AGAINST FOREIGN NATIONS (JER. 46:1–51:64). The Oracles against Foreign Nations was standard for many of the prophets.[11] Many of Jeremiah's oracles were dated to a specific time and situation, whereas other prophets' oracles had less specific dates.

1. Against Egypt (46:2–28)
2. Against Philistia (47:1–7)
3. Against Moab (48:1–47)
4. Against Ammon (49:1–6)
5. Against Edom (49:7–22)
6. Against Syria (49:23–27)
7. Against Kedar and Hazor (49:28–33)
8. Against Elam (49:34–39)
9. Against Babylon (50:1–51:64)

Sign-Acts in the Prophetic Books

Along with their oracles (prophetic speeches), the prophets of Israel sometimes performed symbolic actions to communicate a message. Such acts are performed by several prophets, but Ezekiel is the most prolific performer. Below is a list of **sign-acts** in the prophetic literature.

Text	Action
Isaiah 8:1–3	Isaiah writes a cryptic message on a tablet and then visits a "prophetess." They conceive a child and give him a name related to this message.
Isaiah 20:1–4	Isaiah walks naked for three years, symbolizing the taking of captives.
Jeremiah 13:1–7	Jeremiah buys a new waistcloth, wears it, buries it by the Euphrates River, returns later to dig it up, and finds it ruined.
Jeremiah 16:1–5	Jeremiah remains celibate, not marrying or having children.
Jeremiah 19:1–13	Jeremiah smashes a clay jug as part of a prophetic speech.
Jeremiah 27–28	Jeremiah wears a wooden yoke symbolizing captivity. The yoke is smashed by another prophet, Hananiah, so Jeremiah replaces it with an iron yoke.
Ezekiel 4:1–3	Ezekiel builds a mode of Jerusalem and the Babylonian equipment that will be used in the siege of the city.
Ezekiel 4:4–8	Ezekiel lies on his right side for 390 days and his left side for 40 days to symbolize the length of Israel's punishment.
Ezekiel 4:9–5	Ezekiel is commanded by God to eat bread baked over a fire made from human dung. When he protests, God allows him to use cow dung.
Ezekiel 5	Ezekiel shave all the hair off his body and divides it into thirds. He then burns a third, chops a third with a sword, and scatters a third in the wind to symbolize what will happen to Israel.
Ezekiel 12	Ezekiel packs luggage and departs Jerusalem through a hole he digs in the wall, symbolizing Judah going into exile.
Hosea 1:2–8	Hosea marries a prostitute, has three children with her, and gives them names symbolizing Israel's future punishment.
Hosea 3:1–5	Hosea purchases a woman who is an "adulteress."

It is rarely clear who the audience of such actions is and whether they understand the meaning of the performance. At this point, these sign-acts exist as written descriptions that are part of prophetic books, so they have literary contexts, which are quite different from the historical context of the events described.

Four of these oracles will be discussed.

Against Egypt (46:2–28). These two oracles, the first of which is dated to 605 B.C.E., taunted Egypt because of its defeat at Carchemish in northern Mesopotamia by the armies of Nebuchadnezzar of Babylon. Jeremiah saw it as a day when the LORD brought a well-deserved punishment to Egypt. No amount of medicine would heal its wounds (46:2–12).

The second oracle referred to one of the times when Babylon met Egypt on its own territory. This was either in 605 or 601 B.C.E., when Jehoiakim switched his loyalties to Egypt after the two armies fought each other to a standstill. Jeremiah foresaw the eventual destruction of Egypt by the Mesopotamian power (46:13–26). The LORD's people would survive, even though they had to face judgment for their sins (46:27–28).

Against Philistia (47:1–7). This brief oracle describes the march of invading armies down the coast, isolating the Phoenician cities of Tyre and Sidon, then moving down the coastal highway to knock out the main Philistine cities of Gaza and Ashkelon.

Against Moab (48:1–47). To read the oracle against Moab with real understanding, one needs a Bible atlas with detailed maps. It was a travelogue of Moabite territory, listing most, if not all, of its major cities. Although it speaks of Moab's destruction, it ends with a promise of restoration of Moab "in the latter days." This reflected the fact that the Moabites and Israelites were not so antagonistic toward each other as Israel had been toward others of its neighbors. The story of Ruth, told to support the claim that David had a Moabite grandmother, gave an indication of the relatively friendly relations between the two peoples.

Against Babylon (50:1–51:64). The oracles of Jeremiah conclude with a series of oracles against Babylon, as it was Israel's chief foreign enemy. There was a constant shifting of persons spoken of in these oracles. The oracles began with the LORD announcing to the nations that Babylon has been taken (5:2–3). The people of Judah would return to the LORD, asking the way to Zion (50:4–5). They had been like lost sheep attacked by wild animals (50:6–7).

The LORD addressed the people and told them to flee from the land of the Chaldeans (Babylon), for invaders were coming who would destroy everything in their path (50:8–10). Babylon was told that its doom was sure. It would be hissed at by all who passed it (50:11–13). Its enemies were invited to attack it, for they would be carrying out the LORD's vengeance against it (50:14–16).

Attention then shifted to Israel, which was compared to a sheep hunted by lions. Assyria, then Babylon, had attacked Israel. Now the tables would be turned. Israel would be restored as Babylon was destroyed (50:17–20).

There follows a series of oracles describing the destruction of Babylon. The hammer that had broken many was now broken (50:21–28). The archers were summoned to bend their bows at it. Fire would burn its cities (50:29–32); the LORD would redeem Israel, but the sword would devour Babylon (50:33–38); unrest would upset its inhabitants (50:39–40). As it had come from the north to devastate Palestine, so a northern foe would devastate it. Its king would be helpless, for the enemy would be like a lion in a sheepfold (50:41–46).

Jeremiah 51 continues the theme of Babylon's destruction. It would be winnowed as a farmer winnowed grain (51:1–7), and no balm could heal its great wounds (51:8–10). The enemy was summoned to prepare its weapons and to mount an assault against the city, for the LORD had promised victory (51:11–14).

FIGURE 11-1 "Nebuchadnezzar, king of Babylon and all his army came against Jerusalem and besieged it; in the eleventh year of Zedekiah, in the fourth month, on the ninth day of the month, a breach was made in the city" (Jer. 39:1–2). These are the ruins of a seventh-century B.C.E. wall that was destroyed by the Babylonian invaders.

In the midst of the oracles of doom, there is a hymn-like section describing the LORD's power in nature. In contrast to that power, the idol was the powerless product of stupid men. It could not compare to the God of Jacob (51:15–19). In 51:20–23, there is the oracle of the hammer. Babylon had been a hammer by which the LORD had meted out punishment to those who had sinned against Him. Now, however, the destroyer would be destroyed. The LORD summoned the nations to make war against it, to make it a land of desolation and waste (51:24–33). What Nebuchadnezzar had done to Jerusalem would be done to Babylon (51:34–37). It would be like a land awash with the waves of the sea (51:38–44). Judah was warned to flee, for the LORD's wrath would be poured out on the land (51:45–46). Babylon's fall would come because of what it had done to Israel (51:47–51). The LORD, the God of Justice, would see to it that Babylon was laid waste (51:52–58).

According to 51:50–64, Jeremiah wrote on a scroll all the oracles against Babylon. He sent it to Babylon by Seraiah, the quartermaster of Zedekiah's court. Seraiah was told to read the oracles in Babylon. Having done that, he was to tie a stone to the scroll and throw it into the Euphrates. Just as the scroll would sink in the river, so Babylon would sink—to rise no more.

THE IMPORTANCE OF JEREMIAH 52. This chapter, which briefly summarizes Zedekiah's reign (52:1–3a), is concerned mainly with the details of Jerusalem's capture by the Babylonians. After duplicating 39:1–12, it gives additional details. That the Babylonians took some of the poor people as captives is unusual, because such people usually were passed over (52:15). The final note about King Jehoiachin (52:31–34), found also in 2 Kings 25:27–30, indicates that the book of

Jeremiah did not reach its final form until some time after 560 B.C.E., the year that Jehoiachin was released from prison. Actual records of the allowances given for the king and his family have been found among Babylonian archives.

INTRODUCTION TO THE BOOK OF EZEKIEL

Jeremiah had done his part to prepare the people for the Exile, as well as to help those who were in exile to take a realistic view of their situation. Even so, religiously, the Exile was a shock, as the book of Lamentations so vividly illustrates. The inevitable question "Why did it happen to us?" must have been asked of the religious leaders in the Exilic community. Some wanted to believe the predictions of the false prophets that the Exile would end soon, when the LORD would bring about a miraculous overthrow of the Babylonians. In line with that belief, indications are that a number of people plotted to overthrow the Babylonian government and were executed. It was to counter such false optimism that Jeremiah's letter to the exiles had been written (Jer. 29). Others in the community were not willing to accept any explanations and gave up any idea of God. For a third group, two prophetic traditions made sense and enabled them to survive the Exile with a faith grounded in a deeper understanding of the presence of the LORD, the God of Israel. The book of Ezekiel presents one of these traditions, while the other is found in the second half of the book of Isaiah.

The Character Named Ezekiel

Ezekiel 1:1 reports that Ezekiel was a priest before he became a prophet, and that his father was Buzi, who is not mentioned anywhere else in the Bible. We know Ezekiel was married, because Ezekiel 24:15–18 tells of the death of his wife. From the first chapter of his book, it is evident that he was a most unusual man, who had fabulous visionary experiences, acted out many of his messages to the people instead of delivering them orally, and had a mathematician's delight in precise detail. Ezekiel had been taken to Babylon in the deportation of 597 B.C.E., when he was still a priest. In 593 B.C.E., he experienced a call of the LORD to be a prophet, and for the next twenty years or so, he performed that role.

All his ministry was among the exiles, doing in Babylon what Jeremiah was trying to do in Jerusalem—that is, (1) trying to prepare the people for the inevitable fall of Jerusalem and (2) trying to put a damper on the false hopes for an immediate return to Palestine, which some of the prophets were promoting. Once Jerusalem fell in 587/586 B.C.E., however, Ezekiel became a prophet of hope, trying to prepare the people for their return to the land. He laid out a blueprint for a restored Temple and worship system.

The Book

The book of Ezekiel is much more closely connected to the person it is named for than the book of Isaiah. The books of Isaiah and Jeremiah both contained some material reported in first-person speech, but the book of Ezekiel is composed entirely of first-person reporting, so it is the voice of the prophet speaking to the reader throughout the book. Ezekiel's name appears rarely in the book, because he refers to himself using the first-person pronoun, and God consistently refers to Ezekiel using the enigmatic designation, *ben-adam*. This phrase literally means "son of a human being." One common contemporary translation, is "mortal," which understands this not a name or title, but a constant reminder of Ezekiel's humanness.

The book of Ezekiel has the most precisely dated oracles of any of the large prophetic scrolls, but they are not always presented in chronological order. This reflects a general sense in which chronology does not function as the book's organizational principle. Two features of the book provide its macrostructure. First, it falls naturally into three major divisions: Chapters 1–24, oracles against Jerusalem; Chapters 25–32, oracles against foreign nations; and Chapters 33–48, oracles of restoration. The resulting movement from negative to positive is similar to that found in Isaiah and Jeremiah. The unique structural feature is the presence of four great visions that form a framework for the whole book. Unlike the simple visions or sights in Jeremiah, however, these visions of Ezekiel are clearly supernatural and they serve as a reminder that although the person named Ezekiel is physically located in Babylon, the setting of his prophetic activity is not limited to that place.

The Literary Structure of Ezekiel

Ezekiel is the third of the large prophetic scrolls in the Old Testament. It is difficult to read this book without Isaiah and Jeremiah forming part of our frame of reference. The book of Ezekiel contains familiar types of material: call narrative, judgment oracles, visions, stories about the prophet. It also manifests the familiar sense of movement from a focus on judgment at the beginning to a focus on deliverance and salvation at the end. In Isaiah and Jeremiah, first-person reporting by the central prophetic character was rare, but in Ezekiel it is present throughout the book.

Certain features point to possible ways of thinking about the structure of the book of Ezekiel. The most striking of these is the sequence of four grand **visions** that are spread throughout the book. The beginning of each of these visions is signaled by the statement that the Hand of YHWH was on the prophet (1:3, 8:1, 37:1, and 40:1). Ezekiel's first vision fills Chapters 1–3. In this first-person account, the prophet records his initial encounter with God while living by the river Chebar in Babylon. This vision serves as Ezekiel's call narrative and presents him with his task.

The second vision is in Ezekiel 8–11. This experience places Ezekiel in Jerusalem, where he witnesses a sequence of events culminating in the departure of God's glory from the Temple. This vision is presented in the midst of a long sequence of judgment oracles against Judah in Ezekiel 4–24 and dramatically portrays the ultimate result of Judah's disobedience. God's departure makes way for the destruction of Jerusalem and the Temple.

The third vision is the best known of the four. The "valley of the dry bones" in Ezekiel 37 depicts the skeletons of Israel's defeated army. Ezekiel sees the army restored. At the end of the vision, the soldiers stand up, ready to fight. The vision stands in the midst of a collection of prophetic messages in Ezekiel 33–39 that focus on the restoration of Israel. These predominantly positive chapters are the turning point of the book of Ezekiel. Like Isaiah, Jeremiah, and the Book of the Twelve, the book of Ezekiel moves from a mostly negative tone in the first half of the book to a mostly positive tone in the second half.

The final vision in the book of Ezekiel is the prophet's preview of the reconstructed Temple after the end of the Exile in Chapters 40–48. This vision frames the book at the end and ties together themes from the other visions. Ezekiel has completed his prophetic task, the temple is restored, and God's glory returns to dwell in the reconstructed temple in Jerusalem.

SURVEY OF THE BOOK OF EZEKIEL

Oracles against Jerusalem (Ezek. 1–24)

1. ***The call of Ezekiel (1:1–3:27).*** The call of Ezekiel was similar to that of earlier prophets, such as Isaiah and Jeremiah, in that visions were associated with it. It was different in the nature and extent of the visions.

a. ***The prophet called (1:1–28).*** Ezekiel was by the river Chebar, which actually was a major irrigation canal on the Euphrates River (1:1).[12] The young priest probably was in a meditative mood when the dark clouds of an approaching thunderstorm caught his attention (1:4). The mention of "brightness around it," "fire flashing forth continually," and the reference to "gleaming amber" (1:4) all suggest a particularly violent thunderstorm, with much lightning and possible hail associated with it. Up to that point, Ezekiel's description would fit any violent summer storm.

From then on, the storm forms the backdrop for an astounding vision, which, for Ezekiel, seems to be normal. Unlike Amos, who saw messages from the LORD in ordinary events, Ezekiel saw extraordinary sights that became bearers of the Divine message.

First, there were the creatures of the vision. They had four faces, four wings, and the legs of bovine animals with hooves like calves (1:5–7). Under the wings were human arms and hands. The faces were those of an eagle, an ox, a lion, and a man. The eagle suggested mobility, the ox suggested strength, the lion suggested lordliness, and the human face suggested intelligence. The number 4 denotes that the power of God stretches to the four corners of the earth.[13] Their wings permitted them to fly in any direction without turning around. Fire (lightning?) was in the midst of the creatures, symbolic of the cleansing power of the LORD (1:11–14).

The creatures were accompanied by wheels arranged somewhat like a gyroscope. In other words, there were two wheels, one of which was arranged at a 90° angle from the other. Or they were like a ball with quarter sections cut out, except for a small band of material. This permitted them to roll in any of the four major directions (1:15–17). The eyes that decorated the rims were suggestive of the all-knowingness, or *omniscience*, of God. Wherever the living creatures went, so did the wheels (1:18–21).

Above the creatures—symbols of all living creation at the service of the LORD—and the wheels, Ezekiel saw a vision of the LORD sitting on a throne, just as Isaiah did (Isa. 6). The creatures covered their bodies with two wings in the LORD's presence (1:22–23; see Isa. 6:2). As they flew, the sound of the wings was like the thunder of the storm. When they came into the LORD's presence, they stopped flying (1:24–25).

The prophet-to-be saw the LORD from the waist down. The upper part of the body was obscured by fire, the brightness of which reminded him of the rainbow that followed the Flood (1:26–28). "This was the appearance of the glory of the LORD" (1:28). The word *glory* as used here might also be translated as the "overwhelming presence" of the LORD.

What the first chapter describes is basically the same thing Isaiah describes—that is, a theophany or appearance of the LORD to the one who was being called. Behind all of the elaborate symbolism was the prophet's basic conviction that the LORD who had called him to be a prophet was master of the universe and not just master of a narrow little strip of land called Palestine. As such, the LORD could be anywhere, even among the forlorn exiles by the river Chebar in Babylon.

b. ***The prophet commissioned (2:1–3:27).*** Ezekiel, who had fallen on his face when he realized he was in the LORD's presence, was commanded to stand. He was addressed as "son of man" ("O mortal," NRSV), which, for Ezekiel, emphasized the difference between himself and the exalted LORD (2:1–3). "I am sending you" expresses a standard formula that appeared in prophetic calls (cf. Jer. 1:7).[14] He was given a fivefold commission:

1. ***As a prophet to a rebellious people (2:1–3:3).*** They were an "impudent and stubborn" people (2:4), but he was not to let that stop him from doing his job. In an action symbolizing the receiving of the LORD's message of lamentation, mourning, and woe, Ezekiel ate a papyrus scroll that tasted as sweet as honey. He would enjoy speaking the LORD's message.
2. ***As a prophet to a stubborn people (3:4–9).*** Although the word was sweet to Ezekiel, it would be distasteful to those to whom it would be preached. Their failure to understand would not be because of a language difference, but because of a lack of willingness to hear.
3. ***As a prophet to the exiles (3:10–15).*** Ezekiel's mission was directed to the people who were in exile, more specifically to the exiles at Tel-abib (from which the modern Israeli city of Tel Aviv derives its name) on the Chebar canal. Ezekiel went there and sat silently in the midst of the community for seven days.
4. ***As a watchman for the house of Israel (3:16–21).*** The emphasis in this commission laid the responsibility upon Ezekiel to carry out his call as a prophet. Like Isaiah, he was called to be faithful whether or not he was successful (Isa. 6:11–13).
5. ***As a portrayer of the LORD's judgment (3:22–27).*** Ezekiel, more than any other prophet, was the master of symbolic action. By such pantomimes, he acted out what was about to happen rather than describing with words the Lord's impending judgment. As part of this phase of his ministry, he was to remain silent until the Lord told him to speak.

2. ***The prophet in action (4:1–5:17).*** Almost immediately, it seems, Ezekiel began to prophesy by pantomime. The symbolic performances of Ezekiel are often called *sign-acts*.

a. ***Let's play war (4:1–3).*** First, he played war. Using a large sun-dried brick as a symbol for Jerusalem, he set up miniature camps and siege lines around it, built dirt ramps up to it, and made miniature battering rams as if to knock down the imaginary walls. He took a small piece of iron to make a movable shield like those used by attacking armies as they tried to get near city walls to attack them. Then, he enthusiastically played war.

b. ***The long rest (4:4–8).*** Next, Ezekiel was commanded to lie on his side for 390 days as a sign of the length of Israel's punishment. For Judah's punishment, he was to lie on his side for forty days. While each day was to indicate a year's exile, the significance of the numbers is not explained further. The period of 390 years may simply indicate that Israel's exile would go on indefinitely; forty years would seem to indicate for Ezekiel what seventy years represented for Jeremiah—a symbol of the completion of the LORD's time. When things were right, the exiles would return.

c. ***Food is scarce (4:9–17).*** A third action involved the mixing of various grains, beans, and peas to make flour for bread. Under ordinary circumstances, such a thing was not done; but when a siege was on, one ate anything available. The command to cook the food over dried human manure was too much for Ezekiel's priestly instincts. When he pleaded for an exception, the LORD permitted the use of dried cow manure for the cooking fires. All this demonstrated the extreme conditions that existed during the siege of Jerusalem.

d. ***The prophet's haircut (5:1–17).*** A man's hair was his pride. The prophet got a lesson in humility when he was told to cut his hair like a captive of war. Then he took the hair from his shorn head and divided it into three parts. One-third was burned, one-third was chopped to pieces with the sword, and one-third was scattered to the wind. A few hairs left clinging to his garments were divided in the same manner. In the explanations that followed, the symbolism of this action was explained. Like the prophet's hair, the inhabitants of Jerusalem would be divided:

> One-third of you shall die of pestilence or be consumed by famine among you; one-third shall fall by the sword around you; and one-third I will scatter to every wind and I will unsheathe the sword after them. (5:12)

Although the LORD had made Jerusalem the center of the universe, it was doomed (5:5).

3. ***The prophet preaching (6:1–7:27).*** A spoken sermon follows the descriptions of the pantomimed sermons. Its title might be "Judgment on the Mountains." The sermon was directed against the mountains on which the Baal cults had their worship centers. The sermon had four

The Bizarre Behavior of Ezekiel

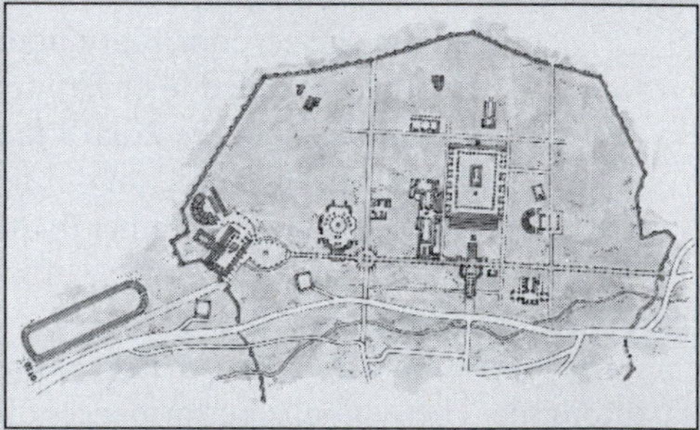

Prophets encountered in the Bible before Ezekiel sometimes performed actions that were intended to communicate a message. These *sign-acts* sometimes involved standard elements of their lives, such as Hosea's marriage and naming of children in Hosea 1 or Jeremiah's purchase of a field in Jeremiah 32. Other sign-acts were symbolic performances, such as Isaiah walking around naked in Isaiah 20 or Jeremiah walking into town wearing a yoke in Jeremiah 27.

Ezekiel took the performance of sign-acts to a new level. In Ezekiel 4:1–3 he builds a small model of Jerusalem and an invading army laying siege to the city. This is intended to portray the coming invasion of Jerusalem by the Babylonian army. In 4:4–8, he lies on his left side for 390 days and then on his right side for forty days to symbolize the length of punishment for Israel and Judah. God commands Ezekiel in 4:9–15 to eat bread baked over a fire made with human dung. At this point, the prophet protests because this method of cooking would render the food unclean. God gives in and allows Ezekiel to use cow dung to build his cooking fire. This unusual means of cooking is also meant to portray the desperate condition Judah will find itself in when it is invaded. Ezekiel 5 describes an elaborate performance in which Ezekiel shaves all the hair off of his body and then carefully separates it into three equal measures. He burns one-third of his hair, hacks another third with a sword, and scatters the final third in the wind. He retains only a small amount of his hair, which he sews into the hem of his robe. The different bunches of hair are meant to represent the fate of different groups of Judahites. Some would be killed by the sword during the attack, others would be killed in the ensuing fire, and those left alive would be scattered. Only a small remnant would be saved, like the hairs in the hem of Ezekiel's robe.

In Ezekiel 12, the prophet symbolically enacts the Exile itself. He packs and prepares baggage like someone who is being exiled and carries it out of Jerusalem. He exits the city by digging a hole in the wall to portray a desperate, secret escape from the invading army. The book of Ezekiel typically presents these sign-acts in the words of God's commands to Ezekiel. The actual performance of the acts is not described. Thus, we do not know if many people watched the performances or if the prophet explained his actions in words, or whether the people were left to interpret them on their own. Did the people of Jerusalem recognize Ezekiel as a prophet and his actions as a portrayal of their own fate, or did he appear to be a deranged lunatic?

parts, each closed by the refrain "I am the LORD." The first division was spoken to the mountains as if they were living persons, describing how the pagan altars, designed to celebrate life and fertility, would be the scene of death and barrenness (6:1–7).

The second part spoke of the scattering of the people into foreign lands. They would remember how they had grieved the LORD and would realize that His threats had not been in vain (6:8–10).

The third division called for mourning to take place because men would die of pestilence and famine. When corpses were found on the altars, the high hills, and every place they worshiped god, when the land was made desolate, then "they shall know that I am the LORD" (6:11–14). The sermon closes with oracles of doom for the land (7:1–27).

4. *Heresy in the Temple (8:1–11:25)*

a. *Those abominable idols (8:1–18; 11:1–21).* Pages have been written about the visions of Ezekiel found in Chapters 8–11. One of the major questions relates to whether they were really visions or whether Ezekiel actually was present in Jerusalem to witness the things he described. Travel back and forth to Jerusalem from Babylon was not unknown. Ezekiel's intimate knowledge of the Temple, growing out of his training as a priest, however, would explain his detailed descriptions. His powers of discernment and previous visionary experiences, furthermore, would seem to argue for these being visions on the order of extrasensory perception.

As Ezekiel described it, he was transported to Jerusalem by a hand that held him by a lock of hair. He was brought in vision to the northern gateway of the inner court, where there seemed to be some sort of pagan image. Immediately, he was aware of the overpowering presence of the God of Israel (8:1–4).

After the pagan image and the ceremonies were pointed out to him (8:5–6), he was shown a hole in the wall. Following instructions, he dug into the hole and found a door. Entering the door, he saw seventy of Judah's leaders, led by a Temple official, worshiping pictures of animals drawn on the walls (8:7–13). They may have been evidence of the worship of Egyptian deities.[15]

Going to the north gate of the Temple, Ezekiel found women weeping for Tammuz, the Babylonian god of vegetation (8:14–15).[16] Next, he went to the east side of the Temple, where he found twenty-five men worshiping the rising sun. Thus, in the house in which the LORD alone was to be worshiped, all sorts of services to pagan gods were being carried out (8:16–18). Jerusalem's doom was certain:

> Therefore I will act in my wrath; my eye will not spare, nor will I have pity; and though they cry in my hearing with a loud voice, I will not listen to them. (8:18)

This passage seems to be continued in 11:1–21. There, specific people who were leaders in the worship of pagan deities are named. In his vision, Ezekiel saw one of them, Pelatiah, the son of Benaiah, die. The hope for a righteous remnant was mentioned, along with certain judgment for the sinners of Jerusalem.

b. *Marked for destruction (9:1–11).* The LORD called for the executioners to make ready. Six men, prepared to act as the LORD's executioners, stepped up with their weapons ready. A seventh man with a writing case was with them (9:1–2). The LORD instructed the seventh man to go through the city and put a mark on the foreheads of those who were disturbed by the abominations that were being practiced in the Temple. They were the righteous who would survive the siege. This was in keeping with a commonly held theological view that the righteous would enjoy blessings and a long life, while sinners would die young. Ezekiel would have said that those who died during the siege were sinners (9:3–4).

Once the righteous were marked, the executioners were ordered to do their job. As Ezekiel experienced this vision, he, like Amos, prayed to the LORD, asking Him if He was going to destroy all the people. The LORD answered that the guilty would not be spared. The scribe reported that he had done as the LORD had commanded him (9:5–11).

c. *No more glory in the Temple (10:1–22; 11:22–25).* When Ezekiel looked, he saw a repeat of the vision by the river Chebar with the LORD on His throne, the winged creatures (now called *cherubim*), and the wheels. The LORD commanded the scribe to take fire from among the cherubim, which was done. The fire was scattered over the city to burn it (10:1–8).

In 11:22–25, the glory of the LORD (the overpowering presence) left the Temple, accompanied by the cherubim and the wheels. This was Ezekiel's way of saying to the exiles that the Temple and Jerusalem could no longer claim the LORD's protective presence. Thus the vision ended. The time was 592 B.C.E., only five years before Jerusalem was destroyed.

5. *In action again (12:1–20).* In an activity closely related to this word about the withdrawal of the presence of the LORD from Jerusalem, Ezekiel acted out before the people what would happen to the survivors in Jerusalem. Like one who was going into exile, he gathered up his portable possessions. He dug through the mud wall of his house at night and crawled through the hole, taking his baggage with him (12:1–7). He was then instructed to tell the people that his action symbolized what King Zedekiah was attempting to do to escape from Jerusalem. Zedekiah would not be successful, however. He would be captured, blinded, and taken to Babylon as a captive (12:8–16).

Ezekiel then drank water and ate, quaking and trembling like one who was mortally afraid. This would be the condition of the people in Jerusalem as they awaited the fall of the land (12:8–16).

6. *Hard words for false prophets and unfaithful people (12:21–14:23)*

a. *The LORD will vindicate Ezekiel (12:21–28).* Some people made fun of Ezekiel, saying that he kept predicting doom but it never came. He was told to warn the people that judgment no longer would be delayed. His words were not for the sweet by-and-by; they were about a harsh here-and-now (12:21–28).

b. *The fate of false prophets (13:1–16).* The prophets of popular religion were not concerned with the LORD's message. Instead, they were busy thinking up messages that would soothe the people and cause them to react favorably to the messenger. Instead of building a wall of truth behind which Israel could be secure, they built a faulty wall. Then they covered their mistakes with whitewash. When the flood of judgment came, the whitewash would not hold the wall together. The prophets who kept on crying peace when war was unavoidable would be destroyed like the faulty wall.

c. *The fate of fickle women (13:17–23).* Ezekiel condemned women "who sew bands on all wrists, and make veils for all persons of every height" (13:18). This referred to some sort of witchcraft or magical practice that was condemned in Israel in the time of the early monarchy (1 Sam. 28:3). These women had led righteous people astray. As a consequence, the judgment upon them would be severe. Ezekiel closes the oracle with a favorite theme: "Then you will know that I am the LORD" (13:20–23).

d. *The fate of idol worshipers (14:1–23).* When certain leaders of the people came to Ezekiel, it was revealed to him that they were idol worshipers. The LORD would not permit such a person to receive a correct message from the prophet because of that person's false worship (14:1–5). The only hope for the idol worshiper was to repent and put away his idols. Idol worshipers would be cut off even if they tried to appear righteous by consulting a prophet. Both the idol worshiper and the prophet he consulted would be false and would face the LORD's judgment (14:6–11).

Such unfaithfulness would condemn the land. Even if Noah, Daniel, and Job still lived in the land, their righteousness would save them but not others (14:12–20). (This idea of individual responsibility was further discussed by Ezekiel in Chapters 18 and 33.) Jerusalem was about to face four severe acts of judgment—"sword, famine, wild animals, and pestilence, to cut off humans and animals from it!" (14:21). Any survivors would testify that the LORD's action was just (14:22–23).

7. ***The prophet and his allegories (15:1–17:24).*** Ezekiel was particularly fond of allegories—that is, stories in which an actual person or event is represented by a symbol.

a. ***Jerusalem, the grapevine (15:1–8).*** Here, Jerusalem is represented by a grapevine. The grapevine's main function is to act as a fruit-bearing plant. Because its wood was useless as lumber, it could only be burned. So, Jerusalem was like a dead grapevine, ready to be burned.

b. ***Jerusalem, the faithless wife (16:1–63).*** Next, Jerusalem was like an unfaithful wife. Ezekiel suggested that the racial background of the Jews was mixed: "Your father was an Amorite and your mother was a Hittite." The LORD found her (the people of Israel) when she had been abandoned to die at birth, and He brought her up. When she was a grown woman, He wooed her and won her as His bride. He gave her all the luxuries that a beautiful woman desired (16:1–14).

Unfortunately, she became a harlot, selling her favors to anyone who passed by. She gave to others the blessing the LORD (her husband) had given her. She even sacrificed her children to her lovers. Egypt and Assyria had been her lovers, but she had been so lustful that she had paid them to take her favors instead of them paying her (16:15–34).

Her days were numbered. She would be stripped naked before the world and held up to shame. Her land and possessions would be given to others. She would be cut to pieces by the swords of those who had patronized her (16:35–43). Samaria and Sodom had been her sisters. They had been bad, but not nearly so bad as Jerusalem. She had used Sodom as a byword in the days when things had been going well for her. Now Jerusalem would be like Sodom (16:44–58).

The LORD would restore Jerusalem. The very act of restoration would cause her to blush in shame when she remembered how she had acted in the past (16:59–63).

c. ***The great eagles (17:1–24).*** This **allegory** of the eagles concerned the royal house of Judah and its attempts to play one power off against another. The first eagle represented Babylon, which took Jehoiachin to Babylon and set Zedekiah in his place. But Zedekiah—instead of doing as the Babylonians wanted and, in so doing, preserving the lives of the people—sent envoys to Egypt (the second eagle). The result would be the destruction of the kingdom and Zedekiah's deportation. This allegory applied to the intrigues that led to the second Babylonian invasion of Palestine in 589 B.C.E.

8. ***The soul that sins shall die (18:1–32).*** One of the new features of Ezekiel's theology was his doctrine of individual responsibility. The dominant view in Israel was the idea of corporate responsibility. In this view, the emphasis was on the group rather than the individual. Out of it grew the concept that a child could suffer for the parent's sins or vice versa. This was expressed in

a common proverb: "The parents have eaten sour grapes, and the children's teeth are set on edge." It was also enshrined in the law in Exodus 20:5, where it says that the children would be punished "for the iniquity of the parents, to the third and the fourth generation." Now things had changed. The new rule was this: "The person who sins shall die" (18:1–4).

The remainder of the chapter was spent illustrating that basic point. A righteous man who kept the covenant provisions would live. If he had a son who broke every law in the book (of the covenant), the son would die for his sins but the father would be blameless (18:5–13).

The reverse of that situation was also true. The righteous son of a covenant-breaking father would live, but the unrighteous father would die for his own sins. If the sinner turned to righteousness or the righteous man turned to sin, he who turned to righteousness would gain life, while he who turned to wrong would lose it. Some were saying that the LORD was not doing right, but they were the ones who were wrong. The LORD was the judge, who preferred to give life rather than death. What they must do is turn from their sins so that the LORD could give them life (18:14–32).

9. *Two poetic allegories (19:1–14).* Reverting to the allegorical form again, Ezekiel combined it with the lament, or dirge, rhythm. The allegory was of a lion with two cubs that she raised in proper "lion fashion" to adulthood. One (Jehoahaz, Josiah's successor) was captured and taken to Egypt. The second was either Jehoiachin (598–597 B.C.E.) or Zedekiah (597–587/586 B.C.E.), both of whom were taken as prisoners to Babylon (19:9).

10. *Three sermons (20:1–22:31)*

a. *The will of God (20:1–49).* In 590 B.C.E., some of the community leaders came to Ezekiel to ask him what the LORD's will was for the people. Undoubtedly, this was a perplexing question, because they had been getting advice from the other prophets of the community. This contradicted the advice given them by Ezekiel and by Jeremiah in his letter to the exiles (Jer. 29). In answer to their questions, they were reminded of the long and sordid history of disobedience of their forefathers. Time after time, the LORD had affirmed and reaffirmed the covenant to be their God and to lead them to a good life on the condition that they put aside other gods and worship the LORD only. They had violated this covenant and gone after other gods in Egypt. Yet, the LORD had delivered them (20:1–9).

Both in the desert and in the land that the LORD had promised to give them, they had been given the LORD's laws and the sabbath as the sign of the covenant (20:10–30). Still, they turned to the worship of other gods. The LORD was disgusted with such behavior. The present generation was committing the same sins that its fathers had committed, in its desire to be like "the nations" (20:30–32).

The LORD was determined to weed out the sinners from among the people. Only the righteous would be allowed to return to Palestine. If they were going to serve idols, they had better do it while they could. This would not be allowed when the return came. They would worship the LORD only. The LORD was acting to protect His honor. For that reason, the people's wickedness would not be dealt with as severely as it deserved (20:33–44).

The sermon ends with a short oracle about a fire in the south. Judah (the Southern Kingdom) would be devoured by a northern fire. Instructed to deliver this warning, the prophet protested against having to speak in riddles (20:45–49).

b. *The sword of the LORD (21:1–32).* The sense of urgency that frequently appeared in Jeremiah's prophecies as Judah's end neared can also be seen in these oracles on the sword. As one of the common weapons of war, the sword symbolized death and destruction. The LORD is spoken of as drawing a sword to kill the people of Jerusalem (21:1–4). The prophet was told to groan and to cry out in despair. When the people asked why he was groaning, he was to tell them what was to happen. The news was about a sword, sharpened and polished for the battle, ready to slaughter whoever got in the way (21:5–13). The prophet was to act as a soldier, using his sword in battle to bring home the truth of his message (20:14–17).

The prophet then was told to draw a map of the roads from Mesopotamia to the west. There was a fork in the road—the west fork leading to Jerusalem and the east fork leading to Rabbah, the capital of Ammon. The king of Babylon was described as standing at the fork, consulting his gods about which city to strike. Taking a handful of arrows, he shook them and threw them down. He hoped that the pattern they made would indicate which road he should take. By means of divination or casting lots, he consulted his gods and examined an animal's liver, another mode of divination. The arrows pointed to Jerusalem (21:18–22).

This would shock the people of Jerusalem, who had made treaties with Babylon but had forgotten how they sinned against the LORD. They were guilty, and Babylon was the sword of the LORD's righteous anger. The rulers would be exiled, and the land would be given to the poor. Ruin! Ruin! This would be the fate of Jerusalem (21:23–27).

Although the Ammonites had been spared, they had no reason to gloat. Their day was coming. The sword and the fire would destroy them in their own land (21:28–32).

c. ***The sins of Jerusalem (22:1–13).*** This sermon contains a laundry list of the sins of Jerusalem. The commandment said, "You shall not murder," but they were murderers (22:1–4a). The commandment said, "You shall make no graven images," but they worshiped idols (22:36). The commandment said, "Honor your father and mother," but they dishonored their parents (22:7a). The commandment said, "You shall not steal," but they stole from foreigners, widows, and orphans (22:7b). The commandment said, "Remember the sabbath," but they did not keep the sabbath, and they desecrated holy things (22:8). The commandment said, "You shall not lie," but now they faced the death penalty for lying about one another (22:9a). The commandment said, "You shall not commit adultery." Not only had they committed adultery, they also had committed incest (22:9b–11). Beyond the Ten Commandments, they loaned money at interest and took bribes to murder. They had forgotten the LORD (22:1–12).

Those sinners would not go unpunished. They would be scattered among the nations as evidence that the LORD was the ruler (22:13–16). Ezekiel compared what would happen to the people to refining metal. The impure metal is put into a hot furnace, where the heat is used to separate the pure metal from the waste, or *slag*. The people of Jerusalem would be refined in the fires of the Exile as sinners would be separated out for destruction (22:17–22; cf. Jer. 6:27–30).

The major problem was the leaders of the land: the upper classes, the priests, and the prophets. They were like voracious animals, seizing by force things that were not theirs. The priests had become so materially minded that spiritual things were meaningless to them. The rulers had become thieves, while the prophets had become purveyors of false oracles. The people had followed the examples of their leaders. They were extortioners and robbers. The LORD had looked for someone to stem the tide of corruption, but he had found no one. Judgment was certain (22:23–31).

11. ***Those wild, wild sisters (23:1–49).*** In this allegory Samaria and Jerusalem are represented as two sisters, Oholah and Oholibah. Together, they represented all of the Israelite people, both north and south. They had already been guilty of sexual immorality in Egypt. Just as the prophet Hosea took Gomer as his wife, they, too, had become the LORD's wives, despite their previous record of sexual looseness. Children were born, but the sisters would not stay away from other men. First, it had been Egypt and Assyria. Oholah (Samaria) became a victim of Assyria, who had disgraced her and then killed her (23:1–10).

Oholibah (Jerusalem) was even wilder. She cavorted with Assyria and Babylon. She was especially attracted to the Babylonian officials. But, as was generally the rule, they abused her so much that she sought other lovers. She became even more immoral, offering herself to any who would take her (23:11–21).

Her former lovers, the Babylonians, would be her executioners. Their well-equipped armies would pour down the northern invasion routes and rape the land. She would be handed over to people who hated her. Soon her fate would be like that of her sister Oholah (Samaria) (23:22–35).

The oracles close with a restatement of what had been said previously, repeating the theme "You shall know that I am the LORD God" (23:36–39).

12. ***The rusty pot (24:1–14).*** The allegory of the rusty pot was dated to January 588 B.C.E. as Nebuchadnezzar's army laid siege to Jerusalem. Ezekiel was using this figure to say that Jerusalem's "goose was cooked"—that is, its fate was sealed. Because of the bloody atrocities they had committed that had gone unpunished, Jerusalem's inhabitants would be destroyed. The reference to blood poured out on a rock (24:7) comes from the idea that one's life was in the blood. If blood was shed, as in a murder, the victim usually was left unburied. The ancients believed that the spilled blood cried out to God for the murderer to be punished. Blood poured on a rock would be especially conspicuous, because it would stain the rock and thus would be hard to wash out. The rusty pot spoke of the filthiness of Israel's sin. The only way to get rid of it was to burn it out, so the destruction of Jerusalem was part of the cleansing process (24:1–14).

13. ***The prophet's wife dies (24:15–18; 33:21–22).*** Ezekiel's final oracle of doom was the most difficult of all. It was an acted oracle. He was told that his wife would die and that when she did, instead of following the usual customs of wailing, going without a turban, going barefoot, having the mouth covered, and eating only "the bread of mourners" (24:17), he was to act as if nothing had happened (24:15–18).

After his wife's death, the people asked the reason for his strange and unconventional behavior. He told them, as instructed, that the news of Jerusalem's fall would soon reach them. When it did, they were to take no special note of it. Instead, they were to go on with life as usual. As Ezekiel had done when his wife died, so they were to do when Jerusalem died (24:19–24).

Ezekiel was told that when a fugitive came to bring the news of Jerusalem's fall, a new phase of his ministry would begin (24:25–27). The sequel to this passage appears in Ezekiel 33:21–22. In January 586 B.C.E.,[17] a messenger arrived in Babylon, bringing news of Jerusalem's fall. Ezekiel had been silent since the evening before, but when the news came, he began to proclaim a new message.

Oracles against Foreign Nations (25:1–32:32)

As was standard, at least among the more prominent prophets, Ezekiel had a fairly long section on oracles against foreign nations. At times, his arrangement of oracles suggests the influence of the Amos traditions, about which Ezekiel undoubtedly knew. Ezekiel's oracles were confined to the nations immediately surrounding Israel and to Egypt. Notably absent were oracles against Babylon and Syria. Syria probably was omitted because it had long since ceased to be a threat to Judah.

1. A roll call of the neighbors (25:1–17).
2. Many words against Tyre and the Phoenicians (26:1–28:19).
3. A short word about Sidon (28:20–23).

4. Blessings on you, Israel (28:24–26).
5. The fall of Egypt (29:1–32:32).
   a. The Egyptian crocodile (29:1–16).
   b. Egypt is given to Nebuchadnezzar (29:17–21).
   c. Egypt is doomed (30:1–19).
   d. Oracles against the Pharaoh (30:20–32:32).

MANY WORDS AGAINST TYRE AND THE PHOENICIANS (26:1–28:19). Ezekiel had a multitude of oracles against Tyre. The Phoenicians, for whom Tyre was the most representative city, had played an important role in the history of the Israelite people. Although the fact is not mentioned in biblical history, the Phoenicians had a vital impact on the language and thought of the Hebrews. During the Israelite monarchy, furthermore, Tyre was an important ally of the Israelites. For David and Solomon, as well as for Omri and Ahab at a later time, the Phoenicians furnished building materials and expert help to carry out the huge building programs of those kings. They also provided a sea arm for those Israelite kingdoms. Because Israel had no suitable ports, their alliance with the Phoenicians served Israel well. Throughout most of their history, the Phoenician and Israelite kingdoms were united by covenants. There is no mention of any warfare between the two peoples.

Despite their previous history of peaceful relations, Ezekiel said that Tyre had tried to profit from Jerusalem's troubles. As a result, its people would feel the hand of judgment and "They will know that I am the LORD" (26:1–6). Nebuchadnezzar would besiege the city for thirteen years. Finally, its surrender to him would bring an end to Phoenician life. It would finally be joined to the mainland by a causeway built by Alexander the Great in his conquest of the city in 333 B.C.E. It continued to exist as an important city down to the New Testament era.[18]

Ezekiel saw the LORD's punishment for Tyre growing out of its gloating over Jerusalem's fall (26:2). He went on to describe in vivid detail what would happen to the city and especially to cities on the coast around Tyre. All this was to demonstrate the LORD's power (26:7–21).

Chapter 27 was a lament or funeral song for Tyre. A description of its ships—the vehicles of commerce that made it a great trading center—is found in 27:1–9. Its armies were mercenaries, soldiers hired from other nations (27:10–11). A directory of goods, services, and clients gives an insight into the wide range of Tyre's merchant ships (27:12–24). A funeral song would be sung, while shocked mourners would stare in disbelief at the fate of the great merchant city (27:25–36).

Ezekiel then turned his attention to the king of Tyre. The king was pictured as being puffed up with pride, ripe for the calamity that was about to befall him (28:1–10). No matter how rich and handsome he was, his evil conduct would be his undoing. He would be hurled to the ground and his city destroyed (28:11–19).

THE FALL OF EGYPT (29:1–32:32). These chapters contain a number of oracles about Egypt dating from 587 to 571 B.C.E.

1. ***The Egyptian crocodile (29:1–16).*** Egypt was like a giant crocodile, lying in the Nile River and waiting for a victim to come within its range. The LORD was going to take a large hook and catch the crocodile. Then it would be thrown, covered with fishes, into the desert to die (29:1–6a).

Israel had gone to Egypt for support, but it was attacked instead. The LORD was going to make Egypt a wasteland because of the way Israel had been treated. Its people would be scattered, and only a weak kingdom would continue to exist there (29:6b–16).

2. ***Egypt is given to Nebuchadnezzar (29:17–21).*** This oracle, dated 571 B.C.E., was the last dated oracle of the prophet Ezekiel. Nebuchadnezzar had laid siege to Tyre in 585 B.C.E. After thirteen years, Tyre surrendered; but it was a hollow victory for Nebuchadnezzar, as what he gained was not worth the cost.[19] Ezekiel, whose earlier oracles had spoken of the devastation that was coming upon Tyre at Nebuchadnezzar's hand (26:17–21), spoke this oracle that recognized the realities of the situation regarding Tyre. Nebuchadnezzar's army had fought hard, so much so that "every head was made bald and every shoulder was rubbed bare" (29:18). Because he had failed at Tyre, he was given Egypt as his pay for hard work against Tyre (29:20).

3. *Egypt is doomed (30:1–19).* Continuing the theme of Nebuchadnezzar's conquest of Egypt, Ezekiel compares it to the "day of the LORD" (Amos 5:18). Egypt and all its allies would fall (30:1–9). Nebuchadnezzar was about to carry off all of Egypt's wealth and devastate the land (30:10–12). Along with the other destruction would come the destruction of Egypt's idols. Its strong cities would no longer protect it. From one end of the land to the other, devastation would come (30:13–19).

4. *Oracles against the Pharaoh (30:20–32:32).* Turning from the land in general, the oracles were directed toward the ruler of Egypt, Pharaoh Apries, otherwise known as Hophra (589–570 B.C.E.). In 587 B.C.E., Ezekiel said that the LORD would weaken the king of Egypt ("break his arms," 30:22) and strengthen the king of Babylon (30:20–26).

In an allegory of the cedar tree, Pharaoh Hophra was compared to a cedar in Lebanon. In that country, cedars grew to magnificent size, making the country famous for that particular wood. In the allegory, one particular tree outgrew all the rest because it had more water (the Nile River). It was so big that it towered over the other trees. Even the trees of the Garden of Eden could not match it (31:1–9). But the woodcutter came (Babylon). The tree was cut down and left. Its valuable wood became nothing more than a brush pile in which the birds nested. That would be Pharaoh Hophra's fate. He would die and go to Sheol (the grave), where all men went. Hophra was assassinated in 570 B.C.E. (31:10–18).[20] A lament was sung for Pharaoh Hophra (32:1–16). He had been a lion among the nations, but God would throw a net over him and cast him to the ground. His body would become food for the birds. Babylon would come with the sword and make the land of Egypt desolate. The prophet pictured Egypt in the grave with the other nations that had perished—Assyria, Elam, Meshech and Tubal, Edom and the Sidonians. The Pharaoh might not like it, but that would be his end (32:17–32).

Hope for a Better Day (33:1–48:35)

From Chapter 33 on, the oracles of Ezekiel were directed toward encouraging the people to plan for the future, when they would be restored to the land of Palestine. Chapters 33–39 deal with oracles of **restoration,** while Chapters 40–48 deal with rebuilding the Temple and the restoration of worship.

Oracles of Restoration (33:1–39:29)

1. *The watchman's responsibility (33:1–20).* This oracle took a principle and illustrated it by a number of examples. The principle was that a watchman bore the responsibility to warn the community of danger. If he did his job well and the community failed to heed his warning, then the community as a whole bore the blame for whatever happened. If, however, the watchman failed to be alert and to warn the community of imminent danger, when they had to suffer because of his failure, the watchman also shared in the suffering (33:1–6).

So it was with people and their sins. If the prophet warned them, then only the people were responsible for their sins. If the prophet failed to warn them, then the prophet had to share the responsibility (33:7–20; see also Chapter 18).

2. ***Oracle against the inhabitants of the land (33:23–29).*** The people who had been left in the land had claimed the abandoned properties for themselves. But that would not be so, because they had sinned by continuing to act the way they had before the exiles had been taken away.

3. ***They don't believe you, Ezekiel (33:30–33).*** The people were listening to Ezekiel, but they took him no more seriously than they would an entertainer who sang songs to them.

4. ***The responsibility of shepherds (34:1–31).*** Shepherds who enjoyed all the benefits derived from their flocks but failed to take care of them soon would lose them. So it was with the spiritual shepherds of Israel. In looking out for themselves first, they had lost their flocks (34:1–10).

In contrast, the LORD would go out and search for the lost sheep until they were found. He would bring them back and care for them—caring for the sick, separating the good from the bad, and protecting the poor and mistreated from the strong who would oppress them. A Davidic king would be restored to the throne, and Jerusalem would prosper once more. By this they would know the LORD (34:11–31).

5. ***You are going to get it, Edom (35:1–15).*** This sounds like a misplaced oracle against a foreign nation. At the least, it indicates the depth of the antagonism between the Israelites and the Edomites. This was true especially after the Edomites seemed to have taken advantage of Judah during the Babylonian war. Edom was accused of saying that it would rule Judah and Israel (35:10), but the LORD would ensure that Edom was left desolate (35:15).

6. ***Blessings on you, Israel (36:1–38).*** This is a continuation of the oracle against Edom. The nations surrounding Israel had mocked it in its time of calamity. The situation was about to change, however. Israel would prosper, while they would be humiliated. Israel's cities would be rebuilt when the people returned to Palestine. The land had devoured them before, but that would no longer happen (36:1–15).

When the Israelites had lived in Palestine before the Exile, they had defiled it. They had disgraced the name of God. What the LORD was about to do, then, was for the sake of the Divine name and reputation. The implication was that this was an act of grace toward Israel, something it did not really deserve:

> A new heart I will give you, and a new spirit I will put within you; and I will remove from your body the heart of stone and give you a heart of flesh. I will put my spirit within you, and make you follow my statutes and be careful to observe my ordinances . . . you shall be my people and I will be your God. (36:26–28)

7. ***O dry bones, hear the word of the LORD (37:1–14).*** Perhaps the most famous of Ezekiel's visions was the vision of the dry bones. The prophet, either physically or in a vision, was taken to a battlefield. The corpses of the slain had been left to rot in the sun or to be devoured by animals. As a result, bones were scattered everywhere. The prophet was commanded to preach to the bleached bones. As he preached, the bones came together. When the bones were connected into a skeleton, the prophet was told:

Prophesy to the breath [ruach] . . . and say to the breath [ruach] . . . Come from the four winds [ruachoth], O breath [ruach], and breathe upon these slain. (37:9)

As can be seen by the words in brackets, there is a play on words (pun) here. The point of the whole oracle was to continue to express the idea that the Jews would be restored. The nation that was dead and scattered, like the bones, would be resurrected by the LORD's action.

8. ***The two shall be one (37:15–28).*** The prophet was told to take two sticks and to write the word *Judah* on one and *Israel* on the other. Then, he was to hold them in his hand as though they were one. His action would symbolize the reunion of the two parts of the nation under one king.

9. ***The LORD and Gog of Magog (38:1–39:29).*** With these oracles, Ezekiel moves into the realm of the apocalyptic. Instead of pronouncing judgment on Israel for its sins, the LORD promises to intervene from heaven to overthrow the forces of evil arrayed against Israel. Not all the apocalyptic elements are present here, but these oracles carry out the major theme of the triumph of the LORD over those who would destroy Israel.

Attempts have been made to identify Gog of Magog (38:2) with some ruler of Ezekiel's time. The best that can be said is that, with our present knowledge, no satisfactory identification is possible. This has led to numerous attempts over the centuries to identify Gog with rulers of various nations by those who see these oracles purely in a futuristic sense, with unfortunate results. Perhaps the best that can be said is that Gog was representative of those forces that have opposed, and will continue to oppose, the LORD's rule in the world. This would seem to be supported by the fact that the descriptions of Israel (which Gog was to invade) was an idealized description that had not existed before Ezekiel's time, nor has it since. Ezekiel expected it in the near future.

The invasion would be the signal for the LORD to intervene by unleashing the forces of nature against Gog—"Then they shall know that I am the LORD" (38:23). The devastation of the armies of Gog would be so great that Israel would be burning abandoned weapons (those with wooden handles) as firewood, thus saving its own trees (an early form of recycling?). As the Israelites attempt to clean up the land, it would take them seven months to bury all of Gog's dead soldiers (39:1–20). That Ezekiel was talking about something in the near future would seem to be indicated by the closing part of the oracle, in which once again he spoke of Israel's restoration to the land. This would be done to show the LORD's holiness—"Then they shall know that I am the LORD" (39:21–29).

THE RESTORATION OF THE TEMPLE (40:1–48:35). The remainder of the book of Ezekiel deals with the rebuilding of the Temple and its related buildings, along with the altar for sacrifices (40:1–43:27); the priests (44:1–31); the division of the country (45:1–8); the prince's lands and the rules of conduct (45:9–46:18); the priest's quarters (46:19–24); the Temple foundations (47:1–12); the division of the land (47:13–48:29); and the names of the gates of Jerusalem (48:30–35).

This interest in priestly things was in keeping with Ezekiel's interest in the priesthood. He of all the prophets would be the most likely to try to transform into practical activities the principles preached by the prophets. For him, this would include not only social action, but also worship activity. The Temple would continue to be the center of such worship activity in the restored community. Thus, the vision of the Temple, with details of its dimensions, would be of interest to Ezekiel. He, a former priest, would be receptive to such a vision (40:1–42:20). As he envisioned the overpowering presence of the LORD leave the Temple (11:22–25), so he envisioned its return to the restored community and the rebuilt Temple. It was to be a new day when the people with new hearts of flesh would be obedient to the LORD's commands (36:26), would be ashamed of their old ways, and would serve the LORD alone in faithfulness (43:1–12). The responsibility of priestly service would be limited to those priests who were the descendants of Zadok. All other Levites would serve as helpers, but because of their unfaithfulness, they would not be allowed to serve as priests (44:10–31).

Special lands were to be set aside for the LORD, including the area around the Temple (45:1–6). The ruler, now called the *prince* instead of the *king*, was also allotted certain territory, but he was given severe warnings about his conduct toward the people (45:7–9). Instructions were given about what the prince was to receive in offerings from the people. He, in turn, was to furnish animals and materials for national offerings during important festivals and other holy days (45:10–46:15).

Among the unusual features of this series of visions was the description of a stream of water flowing from the base of the Temple toward the Jordan Rift and the Dead Sea. The further it flowed, the deeper the stream was. When it reached the Dead Sea, the Dead Sea's stagnant waters came to life with all kinds of animals and fish. One of the features of the Garden of Eden was that it was well watered. To people who lived in a dry land, a stream of fresh water was priceless. For Ezekiel in his idealized vision of the restored land, the "LORD in his holy Temple" would be the source of life for a land and a people who had been to the grave of exile but had returned from the dead. Even the Dead Sea would come alive in that time (47:1–12).

Key Terms and Names

Allegory, *259*
Baruch, *235*
Call Narrative, *238*
Confessions, *246*
Exiles, *240*
Jehoiachin, *240*
Jehoiakim, *239*
Nebuchadnezzar, *240*
Sign Act, *249*
Temple Sermon, *236*
Vision, *253*
Wordplay, *238*
Zedekiah, *240*

Study Questions

1. What is unusual about Jeremiah's call to be a prophet?
2. What was the meaning of the two visions associated with Jeremiah's call?
3. How did Jeremiah compare Josiah and Jehoiakim?
4. What was the Temple Sermon, and what were its results?
5. Describe Jeremiah's dealing with King Zedekiah.
6. What advice did Jeremiah give the exiles, and why did he feel it necessary to give such advice?
7. What act of Jeremiah demonstrated his faith in the future of the nation?
8. Why was Jeremiah considered a traitor by many of the people of Jerusalem?
9. What happened to Jeremiah when Jerusalem fell?
10. Why is there disagreement about the identity of the "foe from the north?" What are the arguments for the differing positions?
11. What were some of the factors that created the sense of frustration that Jeremiah expresses in the confessions?
12. What are the points of connection between the work of Ezekiel in exile and the work of Jeremiah in Jerusalem?
13. What appears to be Ezekiel's understanding of his call experience?
14. What symbolic actions did Ezekiel perform, and what was their significance?
15. What symbolized for Ezekiel the inevitable doom of Jerusalem?
16. Compare Ezekiel's view of individual responsibility to that of Jeremiah.
17. Why did Ezekiel not mourn his wife's death?
18. Name four allegories that Ezekiel used.
19. What was the meaning of Ezekiel's vision in the valley of dry bones?
20. What was the basic message of the Gog of Magog oracles?
21. What is the overall theme of Ezekiel 40–48?
22. How are Ezekiel 11:22–25 and 43:1–4 related to the two divisions in which they appear, 1–24 and 33–48?

Endnotes

1. For a more complete list and discussion the occurrences of this phenomenon, see Rainer Albertz, *Israel in Exile*, 304–305.
2. See Karen S. Rubinson, "Scythians," in *ABD*, vol. 5, 1056–1057.
3. For example, see Walter Bruggemann, *To Pluck Up, to Tear Down: A Commentary on Jeremiah* (Grand Rapids, MI: Wm. C. Eerdman, 1988), 9–10.
4. On Jeremiah's evaluation of Josiah in this passage, see Walter Brueggemann, *Theology of the Old Testament: Testimony, Dispute, Advocacy* (Minneapolis: Fortress Press, 1997), 613.
5. Bustenay Oded, "Zedekiah," in *Encyclopedia Judaica*, vol. 21 (Farmington Hills, MI: Gale Cengage, 2006), 487–489.
6. J. B. Pritchard, *ANET*, 213.
7. Such deeds were found in recent years among the Bar Kochba letters. Yigael Yadin, *Bar Kochba: The Rediscovery of the Legendary Hero of the Second Jewish Revolt Against Rome* (New York: Random House, 1971), 229ff.
8. The official seal of "Milkom'ur, servant of Baalyasha (Baalis)" has been found, confirming the historicity of this Ammonite king. See Larry G. Herr, "Whatever Became of the Ammonites?" *BAR*, XIX, 6 (November–December, 1993), 33f.
9. For a look at the oracles of Jeremiah 1–20 in the light of rhetorical criticism, see Jack R. Lundbom, *Jeremiah 1–20: A New Translation with Introduction and Commentary*, *AB* 21A, particularly 68–85.
10. Philip J. King, "Jeremiah's Polemic Against Idols: What Archaeology Can Teach Us," *BR*, X, 6 (December 1994), 23–29.
11. See Amos 1–2; Isaiah 13–23; Ezekiel 25–32; Zephaniah 2:4–15.
12. Walter Eichrodt, "Ezekiel," *OTL* (London: SCM Press, 1970), 52.
13. Walther Zimmerli, *Ezekiel*, *HER* (Philadelphia: Fortress Press, 1979), 120.
14. Ibid., 132.
15. See note on Ezekiel 8:10, *NOAB, NRSV*.
16. Pritchard, *ANE*, 76–79.
17. According the *NOAB, NRSV* note on Ezekiel 33:21.
18. A. S. Kapelrud, "Tyre," *IDB*, IV, 721–723.
19. For a fascinating article on Tyre and Phoenicia, see S. W. Matthews, "The Phoenicians: Sea Lords of Antiquity," *National Geographic*, 146 (1978), 149–189.
20. Donald B. Redford, "Hophrah," in *ABD*, vol. 3, 286–287.

CHAPTER

12

The Prophetic Literature III

The Book of the Twelve and the Continuation of the Prophetic Tradition

Timeline

745 B.C.E.	Approximate date of the beginning of Hosea's prophetic career
722 B.C.E.	Fall of Samaria to the Assyrian Empire
700 B.C.E.	Approximate beginning of the rise of the Babylonian Empire
612 B.C.E.	Fall of Nineveh
597 B.C.E.	First deportation of Judahites to Babylon
586 B.C.E.	Destruction of Jerusalem by the Babylonians
550 B.C.E.	Rise of the Persian Empire
538 B.C.E.	Decree of Cyrus releases Israelites to return to Jerusalem
515 B.C.E.	Completion of the Second Temple

Chapter Outline

I. Introduction to the Book of the Twelve
II. The Opening Sequence: Hosea, Joel, and Amos
III. Jerusalem and Nineveh: Obadiah, Jonah, Micah, and Nahum
IV. Shifting the Focus to Babylon: Habakkuk and Zephaniah
V. The Prophets of the Restoration: Haggai, Zechariah, and Malachi
VI. The End of Prophecy?

CHAPTER OVERVIEW

The Book of the Twelve, like Isaiah, has a historical background that spans about three centuries. The historical background for this collection of prophetic literature is found in chapters 7, 8, and 9 of this book. This chapter will give primary attention to the contents of these books and will do so in two interdependent ways. Each of the smaller works within the Book of the Twelve has its own structure and content, but each one also participates in the larger scroll, both giving and receiving meaning. The components of the Twelve will be treated in four groups. The context, size, and significance of the books known as Amos and Hosea sets them, and the small book of Joel that lies between them, apart as an opening sequence. Continued emphasis on the Assyrian Empire and its effect on Israel makes it convenient to put the books called Obadiah, Jonah, Micah, and Nahum together. Habakkuk and Zephaniah are the two books in the collection that have the Babylonian crisis as their primary subject. Finally, the last three books, Haggai, Zechariah, and Malachi, close the collection and focus attention on the restoration of Judah, Jerusalem, and the Temple.

INTRODUCTION TO THE BOOK OF THE TWELVE

The collection of twelve prophetic "books" from Hosea to Malachi is placed at the end of all Christian canons, and they are typically considered individually by Christian readers. Jewish tradition more often views these small works together as "the Twelve," and there are important reasons to look at them collectively, while also allowing each of the twelve parts to have some individual identity as well.[1]

There is no simple reason why the Book of the Twelve is organized in the order in which we typically find it, but it is obvious that chronology was one important factor in its formation. Nine of the twelve books can be connected to one of the three major crises that shaped the life of Israel during the eighth to fifth centuries and generated the prophetic literature, as described in chapter 10 of this book. Hosea, Amos, Obadiah, Jonah, and Micah are related to Assyria in various ways, Habakkuk and Zephaniah to Babylon, and Haggai and Zechariah to the Restoration. This leaves Joel, Nahum, and Malachi without clear connections to the historical sequence. These observations do not mean that these respective time periods in the eight to fifth centuries are necessarily the time periods in which the books were written. Some, such as Amos, show internal signs of multiple revisions over a long period of time. The story of Jonah is closely connected to Nineveh, the capital of the Assyrian Empire, but its language and theological concerns likely place its writing much later than the eighth century. Still, the order of these books is shaped to some degree by this chronological sequence, and the chronological scope of the Twelve is roughly the same as that of the book of Isaiah.[2]

Another important feature that deserves attention at the beginning of the discussion is the development of the idea of "the **Day** of the YHWH" in the Book of the Twelve. This phrase has already appeared twice in Isaiah and twice in Ezekiel, but the highly concentrated four appearances in the little book of Joel are most striking and they make this idea the central theme of that book. Furthermore, it may explain why this little book with no discernable historical connections to any specific time period is commonly placed second within the Twelve. The full phrase appears five more times, and numerous, shortened uses of "the day" seem to address the same idea. Some interpreters consider this phrase a unifying theme for the entire Book of the Twelve.[3]

The Book of the Twelve contains all of the types of literary units that have been on display throughout the books of Isaiah, Jeremiah, and Ezekiel. There are oracles of salvation and judgment, call narratives, sign-acts, and visions. The books of Amos and Obadiah contain "oracles against the nations," and their placement within the Book of the Twelve puts this feature in a position similar to that found in Isaiah, Ezekiel, and the Greek version of Jeremiah. Some of the prophets in this collection, such as Hosea, Jonah, and Haggai, appear prominently as narrative characters, while others are completely absent. The relative concentrations of words of judgment and redemption give the Twelve the same kind of polarity and negative to positive movement seen in the other prophetic scrolls. When viewed in full, the Book of the Twelve looks a lot like the Book of Isaiah, although it is impossible to say whether one served as a model for the other. This sense of a "plot" in the book is perhaps the greatest benefit that comes from considering the Twelve as a somewhat unified work of literature.

THE OPENING SEQUENCE: HOSEA, JOEL, AND AMOS

Two of the prophets, Amos and Hosea, preached in the northern nation of Israel in its last days. Hosea revealed the heartbreak of an insider, who saw his beloved country sliding toward the brink of destruction, while Amos came up from the south to preach to Israel from an outsider's perspective. Between these two books sits the enigmatic Joel whose vivid references to locust plagues and severe weather have often fascinated readers.

Hosea: The Prophet with a Broken Heart

When Jeroboam died in 746 B.C.E., the government that had seen forty years of stability and progress fell apart like a sand castle before the ocean waves. The causes were both internal and external. Just as Amos had seen the internal rottenness, which had created a situation that made it impossible for the kingdom to last much longer, **Hosea** was the witness to the disintegration of the kingdom brought on by that rottenness. If that was not enough, the giant who had been sleeping between the Tigris and Euphrates Rivers woke up hungry and began to look in all directions for victims to gobble up. The nightmare the prophets had been talking about was on its way to becoming a frightening reality.

THE EXTERNAL HISTORICAL CONTEXT. Assyria, the Mesopotamian state, had overrun the small west Asian countries before, but had not been able to maintain its hold on them. Now it had a new and vigorous king, Tiglath-pileser III (745–727 B.C.E.). He had an empire as his goal, and he set out to get it. His armies went in all directions, conquering as they marched. He first conquered his neighbors, the Babylonians, and took the name Pulu (or Pul, as the Old Testament calls him). More important to this story, he moved westward in 743 B.C.E., invading the Syrian city-states. It seems that Uzziah of Judah led the opposition to Tiglath-pileser but was unable to deter him. By 738 B.C.E., the northern Syrian states were paying heavy tribute to him.

But money was not the only price Tiglath-pileser demanded of his victims. Determined to crush rebellion before it started, he had a policy of taking all the survivors in the upper levels of society, along with the skilled workers, and moving them to other parts of his empire. This was particularly true in Galilee, where resistance had been strong. There the land was left barren. In other areas, where resistance had been less severe, the land was repopulated by bringing in peoples from other captured lands. This policy was also followed by the next king, Sargon II, who even incorporated Israelite troops into his army. Of the original population, only the poor people, the elderly, and the sick were left behind—none of whom were able to provide leadership for a rebellion.[5]

The Literary Structure of the Book of the Twelve

The books most often designated as the *Minor Prophets* are often discussed independently, particularly by Christian interpreters. Explanations of their structure and content typically appear at the points where they fit within the story of Israel. Amos and Hosea seem to have been prophets in the northern nation of Israel in the eighth century; Micah was likely a prophet in Judah in the eighth century; Zephaniah, Habakkuk, and Nahum in the seventh century; Haggai and Zechariah in the sixth century; and Obadiah, Malachi, Zechariah (9–14), Jonah, and Joel are more difficult to place chronologically.

These books are more properly described, however, as the *Book of the Twelve*. They appear in both the Hebrew Bible and the Christian Old Testament in this order: Hosea, Joel, Amos, Obadiah, Jonah, Micah, Nahum, Habakkuk, Zephaniah, Haggai, Zechariah, and Malachi. Notice that this order is similar, but not identical, to the assumed historical order above. The work of the prophets can be understood as responses to crises in Israel's story. It is possible to identify three major crises—the Assyrian (eighth century) crisis, the Babylonian crisis (late seventh and early sixth centuries), and the crisis of the Restoration (late sixth and early fifth centuries) within this story. The general trend within the Book of the Twelve is for the books near the beginning to address the Assyrian crisis, those in the middle the Babylonian crisis, and those at the end the crisis of Restoration. That this is just a general trend and is not followed precisely indicates that this cannot be the only factor determining the order of the books. But this factor does begin to point to the possibility that the structure of the Book of the Twelve reflects that of the book of Isaiah, which also seems to address all three of these crises in the same order. This realization leads to the recognition that other possible factors related to the book of Isaiah may be in play in the organization of the Book of the Twelve.

The material in Isaiah 13–23 is often designated as the *Oracles against the Nations*. The other two big prophetic books, Jeremiah and Ezekiel, also have similar sections. Oracles against the Nations aptly describes much of the books of Joel, Amos, Nahum, and Obadiah, so the Book of the Twelve has material similar to Isaiah in a similar position. We noticed earlier that the character named Isaiah does not show up often in the book of Isaiah, but his appearances in chapters 6–8, 20, and 37–39 help to hold the first half of the book together. Likewise, there is relatively little narrative material presenting the prophets as characters in the Book of the Twelve. The most prominent places where these characters do appear are in the books of Hosea, Jonah, and Haggai—the first, fifth, and tenth books of the scroll. The use of prophetic characters in narratives in the Book of the Twelve at least resembles the situation in Isaiah. The latter half of the book of Isaiah focuses on salvation, God's universal concern for humanity, and the requirements of proper worship. These themes are also central to the books that come later in the Book of the Twelve, especially Jonah, Micah, Haggai, Zechariah, and Malachi. In Isaiah, Jeremiah, and Ezekiel, we observed a sense of polarity; that is, the first half of each of these books is dominated by judgment oracles with a primarily negative tone, while the second half of each is dominated by salvation oracles with an overall positive tone. Again, the Book of the Twelve displays a similar literary pattern. It seems quite possible that these twelve smaller prophetic books were formed into a single scroll with many of the same ideas that shaped the three large prophetic books, particularly Isaiah, serving as a model.

The second section of the Hebrew canon is called the *Prophets*, and it has traditionally been divided into two groups: the Former Prophets and the Latter Prophets. The Former Prophets contains four scrolls—Joshua, Judges, Samuel, and Kings. The Latter Prophets also contains four scrolls—Isaiah, Jeremiah, Ezekiel, and the Book of the Twelve. So, in addition to producing a large scroll that functions like the other prophetic scrolls, the combination of these twelve books also provides a sense of balance and symmetry to the middle portion of the canon. There may be some evidence within the Book of the Twelve itself of attempts to tie these books together. Scholars have noticed that the last poem in a book often contains a significant number of words that also appear in the first poem of the next book. For example, Micah 7:8–20 and Nahum 1:1–8 both include the words *anger*, *dust*, *enemy*, *darkness*, *day*, *river*, *mountain*, *inhabitants*, *Carmel*, and *Bashan*. The ability to observe this *catchword phenomenon* in English will depend on the translation you are using.[4] There are multiple explanations for these observations. It could be a coincidence, or the books may have been placed in order based on this common vocabulary at the beginnings and ends, or beginning and ending poems may have been added to each book by the person who actually compiled the twelve smaller books into one large one. It is impossible to prove whether all of these observations about the Book of the Twelve correspond to the intentions of those who designed the canon, but the attempt to perceive the Book of the Twelve as a unified literary work has been fruitful in understanding how the messages of these prophets were used within early Judaism. This approach to the Book of the Twelve will likely continue and deserves the attention of those who wish to read these books and understand them to their fullest extent.

THE CHARACTER NAMED HOSEA. Hosea was a native of the Northern Kingdom, whose judgments were severe, but they were spoken with a tone of tearful pleading instead of righteous indignation. The book of Hosea is one of the most difficult Old Testament books to translate from Hebrew. Some interpreters relate this to the highly emotional nature of the prophet. It is also apparent that the book has been poorly transmitted through the centuries, which may also be partly the result of its many theological tensions.

One important aspect that contributes to the emotionally charged nature of the book is the connection it makes between God's struggles with Israel and Hosea's own family. The use of marriage as a metaphor for the relationship between YHWH and Israel first came into clear view in Jeremiah 2. This image seems very useful in terms of grabbing the attention of the audience, but it creates two significant problems as well. First, the situations in which it is used always involve Israel's disloyalty to YHWH, so the wife in the metaphorical image is always portrayed as unfaithful, while the husband is always faithful. Second, this metaphor is used in conjunction with the theological idea that the destruction of Israel is God's punishment for Israel's disobedience. In the context of the marriage metaphor, this punishment is, therefore, portrayed as physical abuse of the wife by the husband, and, in these cases, the abuse is always portrayed as justified. In the case of Hosea, we are not quite sure how to understand the portrayal of his family. If Gomer was actually his wife, and Jezreel, Lo-ruhama, and Lo-ammi were really children, then these are actual human beings whose lives were more than mere object lessons for Hosea's audience. These are important issues for us to keep in mind as we explore the contents of the book of Hosea.

THE BOOK OF HOSEA

Setting, Marriage, and Family (Hos. 1:1–2:1). The introductory verse suggests that the time of Hosea was after 750 B.C.E. to the downfall of Israel in 722/722 B.C.E. This superscription looks very much like the one found at the beginning of the book of Isaiah. It is possible that this similarity is a factor contributing to the placement of Hosea in the first position in the Book of the Twelve. Very quickly, though, the book of Hosea moves in a different direction. The prophet as a character and the members of his family are in view from the beginning. On the LORD's command, Hosea married Gomer, the daughter of Diblaim:

> Go, take for yourself a wife of whoredom and have children of whoredom, for the land commits great whoredom by forsaking the LORD. (1:2)

Did the LORD actually command his prophet to marry a common prostitute? This question has been answered in several ways:

1. The LORD actually commanded Hosea to marry a prostitute, which he did.
2. Gomer was not a prostitute physically. Instead, she was a Baal worshiper and, as such, was spiritually unfaithful. Whether she was physically unfaithful is unimportant.
3. Gomer was a virgin when Hosea married her, but she became unfaithful after marriage. Later, when Hosea looked back upon the experience, he realized that she already had this tendency when he married her.
4. The whole story is an allegory, which has no real relationship to Gomer's morals.

Hosea and Gomer

The lives of the prophets and the messages they are commanded to communicate often become intertwined. Isaiah, for example, gives his children names that have symbolic meaning and, on at least one occasion, takes one of these children with him to perform a prophetic task (Isaiah 7:3). The most troubling instance of this kind of impingement upon the life of the prophet occurs in the book of Hosea. At the beginning of the book, Hosea is commanded to "take a wife of whoredom and have children of whoredom." The "whoredom" within Hosea's family is supposed to represent the idolatrous religious practices of Israel. As a result of God's command, Hosea marries a woman named Gomer and has children to whom he gives names that mean "God sows," "No mercy," and "Not my people." Hosea 1:3 introduces Gomer but says little about her other than her name and the name of her father. Gomer may have been a prostitute. Women in ancient Israel were typically forced into prostitution out of economic necessity. They may have been widows or those considered ineligible for marriage for a variety of reasons.

Although this marriage symbolizes something negative, the birth of many children also would have appeared to be a blessing. At the same time, we may raise serious questions about children being given negative names in order to make a point. Many interpreters deal with the troubling aspects of this story by supposing that it is just an allegory that has little or nothing to do with the actual lives of the prophet and his family. Others argue that such interpretation is just a way of evading difficult questions and that there is no reason not to take the biblical text at face value.

After a sequence of prophetic speeches in Hosea 2 that often draws upon the symbolism of Hosea's family, the prophet is commanded in 3:1 to "Go, love a woman who has a lover and is an adulteress." Hosea purchases this woman and takes her. The text does not say whether this is Gomer again or some other woman. Hosea's ownership of this woman and her commanded abstinence from sexual intercourse are presented as a symbol of Israel's political and religious situation. The remainder of the book of Hosea consists entirely of prophetic speech. The prophet and his family members do not enter the book as characters again, so their story is incomplete. Metaphors drawing on images of marriage and family do continue to appear frequently in the book of Hosea, however. There may have been a more complete story of Hosea and Gomer, but the book of Hosea has only revealed fragments of that story as a framework for its message.

The first three possibilities are the ones most often advanced. The fourth is usually rejected on the grounds that, if it were not true, no self-respecting prophet would tell such a story about his wife. If he did, he surely would have trouble at home!

Hosea's children not only had to bear the burden of their mother's disgraceful conduct, but their names became part of their father's sermon illustrations. The firstborn, Jezreel, or "God Sows," reflected Hosea's opinion of Jehu's bloody purge, which had been commissioned by the prophet Elisha. Because Jeroboam was of the Jehu dynasty, Hosea saw the LORD's judgment coming upon Israel because of Jehu's indiscriminate slaughter of people (1:3–5).

The second child was a daughter, Lo-ruhama, or "No mercy." This meant that judgment would come upon the sinful nation and no pity would be shown by the conquerors (1:6–7).

The third child's name may have a double meaning. It was a son named Lo-ammi, or "Not my people." Primarily, the name was meant to say that Israel could no longer claim to be a nation of the LORD's people. It may also reflect Hosea's suspicions about his wife's indiscretions by saying, "This one is not mine!" (1:8–9).

In 1:10–2:1, the prophet spoke a word of hope that the day would come when the message of the children's names would be changed. On that day, instead of the LORD saying to Israel, "You are not my people," they would be called "sons of the living God." Lack of pity would give way to pity, and Jezreel would be a place of joy, not destruction.

Unfaithful Wife—Unfaithful People (Hos. 2:2–23). In an oracle calling for his children to plead with their mother to change her ways, Hosea compared his relations with Gomer to the LORD's relations with Israel. Just as Gomer had followed her lovers and had been unfaithful to Hosea, so Israel had gone after the Baal cult and had forsaken the LORD. Israel praised Baal for making the land fruitful when, in reality, it was the LORD who had brought fertility to the land. The LORD would punish Israel, therefore, for its unfaithfulness (2:2–13).

But punishment was not all. Once Israel had been punished, it would be wooed by the LORD as it had been when it came from Egypt to the wilderness, in hopes of bringing back the love of its youthful days. Again, a play on the names of Hosea's children was used to emphasize the LORD's hope for his people (2:14–23). Recent interpreters have brought to light some significant problems with this metaphor. Along with these passages in Hosea 1–3, there are also prominent passages that use this metaphor in Jeremiah 2–3, Ezekiel 16 and 23, and other prophetic texts. Within this marriage metaphor, it is always the woman who is unfaithful and the violent response of the husband is often portrayed as an acceptable reaction. The accumulated weight of the uses of these metaphors of marriage, infidelity, and violent response raises troubling questions about the character of God. They also can be perceived as supportive of violent reactions to unfaithfulness and suspected unfaithfulness in human marriages.[6,7]

The Purchase (Hos. 3:1–5). Whereas chapter 1 tells Hosea's and Gomer's story in the third person, chapter 3 tells how the story ended in the words of the prophet himself. Few details are given, but it can be assumed that, because she had been abandoned by her lovers, Gomer probably was being sold as a slave. Hosea bought her for the price of a slave—fifteen shekels of silver and about ten bushels of barley. He did not restore her immediately to the place of a wife, however. She had to undergo a period of probation before that could happen. In like manner, the LORD would do the same for Israel. It, too, would be bought back, but not without penalty on its part (3:1–5).

1. *The LORD's lawsuit (Hos. 4:1–3).* The prophets often used the language of the court to give their message of judgment. This is usually indicated in English translations by the terms *controversy* or *contention.* This is not just an argument—it is a legal charge. Three key terms stand out in the accusation in 4:1: "There is no *faithfulness,* or *loyalty* or *knowledge of God* in the land." The lack of these three qualities was the basis for all the other failures of the people. Faithfulness meant carrying out the promises that were made. Loyalty had about it the sense of "steadfast love," because the Hebrew word used here is most often translated in that way. It included a sense of compassion that had depth and meaning. Knowledge referred to an intimate, personal kind of knowing, such as was shared by husband and wife, and the word was used for this kind of relationship. These terms recur frequently in the oracles of Hosea and are the key to understanding the book.

The lack of these qualities had caused

> Swearing, lying, and murder, and stealing and adultery break out;
> bloodshed follows bloodshed. (4:2)

2. *The guilt of the religious leaders (Hos. 4:4–10).* The first ones indicted in the LORD's lawsuit were corrupt priests and prophets. They were dispensers of the knowledge of God, so vital to the survival of the people. As a result of their failure, the people were being destroyed because of their lack of knowledge (4:4–6).

Religious prosperity had brought increased sin. More priests and prophets meant more leaders to lead the people astray, because the people followed their leaders. The LORD's priests had led the people to the worship of Baal (4:7–10).

3. *The harlotry of the people (Hos. 4:11–5:2).* Baalism had the people in its grip. They worshiped the wooden poles, phallic symbols of Baal. The young women of Israel, married and unmarried, became involved in the sexual rites at the shrines (4:11–13) with the knowledge and approval of the men of the family (4:14). As a result, worship at the traditional shrines was a mockery. They paid no attention to the LORD and stubbornly went their own way (4:15–19). False leaders had brought them to destruction and punishment (5:1–2).

4. *The result of idolatry (Hos. 5:3–7).* Israel had become so mired in the muck of Baal worship that the people could no longer find their way back to the LORD. Even though they might seek the LORD, it would be in vain. The LORD had withdrawn from them because of their sin.

5. *War on the horizon (Hos. 5:8–14).* Another device of the prophet was to speak of the approach of an invading army, announcing its progress from town to town (5:8). Judah and Ephraim, the two strongest tribes, symbolized for Hosea the two kingdoms. They sought the aid of the great powers when they were in trouble, but they ignored the LORD, who would turn from healer to destroyer. The only hope was that their suffering would bring them to their senses (5:9–14).

6. *False repentance (Hos. 5:15–7:2).* Even though Israel repented, it was a false repentance. It had no more permanence than a fog in the morning (5:15–6:4). The key verse in Hosea is as follows:

> For I desire steadfast love and not sacrifice,
> the knowledge of God, rather than burnt offerings. (6:6)

As was true of Amos, Hosea's understanding of the LORD's demands was that acts of worship alone were not enough to please Him. Sacrifice as an attempt to bribe the LORD was useless, for the LORD would not be bribed. Only a commitment of love whose endurance was based on knowing and doing what the LORD demanded was satisfactory.

Instead of steadfast love and the knowledge of God, Israel's worship was a flagrant violation of everything good. At every shrine, sin was multiplied. At Adam, the covenant was broken; at Gilead, there was bloodshed; even the priests at Shechem were murderers, and harlotry was accepted (6:7–10). Every time the LORD blessed Ephraim, there was more evidence of corruption uncovered (6:11–7:2).

7. *Anarchy in the country (Hos. 7:3–7).* This passage reflects the period when the kings came and went in rapid succession. There were plots and counterplots in the palace, and one king had hardly taken the throne when he was murdered and another took his place. Hosea compares the plotting to an oven filled with hot coals ready to burst into flame when they get sufficient oxygen (7:3–7).

8. *Ephraim is a half-baked cake (Hos. 7:8–16).* Here, Hosea shows his mastery of figures of speech. Bakers had to turn the flat, thin pieces of bread for them to cook properly. Israel was like a cake unfit to eat—left unturned, it burned on one side and was doughy on the other. Again, Israel was like a dove, a bird easily snared in a net. So Israel had fallen into the trap of its powerful enemies by trying to play the game of international politics. In religion, the people turned to Baal, even though the LORD was the one to whom they owed their blessings (7:8–16).

9. *False worship and false friends (Hos. 8:1–14).* The enemy was hovering over Israel like a bird of prey. The kings it had chosen were not the LORD's choice. The idols the people worshiped were false gods. They had sown "the wind and they [would] reap the whirlwind" (8:7). The friends they had tried to buy were false. The numerous altars they had built were for sinning, not for worshiping. They sacrificed so as to gorge themselves on meat, not to truly worship the LORD. Israel and Judah both faced the LORD's judgment (8:1–14).

10. *The judgment to come (Hos. 9:1–17).* Because Israel had forsaken its God and had been a harlot for Baal, Egypt and Assyria would destroy it (9:1–3). All worship would end and would be replaced by mourning. The days of punishment had arrived. Even the prophet, who was supposed to be the LORD's spokesman, was listened to no longer. The people called him a fool and tried to destroy him. But God would bring judgment upon them (9:4–9).

Israel had once been faithful. When it entered Canaan, however, it took up Baal worship. Now barrenness would afflict Israel. "No birth, no pregnancy, no conception" would be the rule (9:11). Baal could not make Israel fertile. Even when women did give birth, the children would die in infancy or be slaughtered by the invaders (9:10–17).

11. *Increased altars—increased sin (Hos. 10:1–8).* Like a grapevine heavy with grapes, Israel was filled with places of worship, but these would be destroyed (10:1–2). The people were liars, making covenants with no intention of keeping them. Their major concern was to preserve their licentious worship, but it would be destroyed by the armies of Assyria (10:3–6). There would be no place to hide when judgment came (10:7–8).

12. *Judgment must come (Hos. 10:9–15).* Hosea refers to the atrocity of the Benjaminites at Gibeah (Judg. 19) as the kind of sin that was still present in Israel. The LORD was pleading with them to sow good things—righteousness and steadfast love—and seek Him (10:9–12). Instead, they were sowing iniquity and reaping injustice. They were trusting in military power and not in the LORD. They would have war, but they would suffer destruction instead of enjoying victory (10:3–15).

13. *The LORD still loves Israel (Hos. 11:1–11).* Despite its sins, the Lord still loved Israel.

> When Israel was a child, I loved him
>   and out of Egypt I called my son.
> The more I called them,
>   the more they went from me;
>   . . .
> Yet it was I who taught Ephraim to walk,
>   I took them up in my arms;
> but they did not know that I healed them.
>   I drew them with cords of human kindness,
>   with bands of love. (11:1–4)

Despite the LORD's love, Israel turned away. Now, it faced judgment at the hand of Assyria. Those people who escaped Assyria's clutches would flee to Egypt (11:5–6). But this was not what the LORD wanted:

How can I give you up, O Ephraim?
  How can I hand you over, O Israel?
How can I make you like Admah?
  How can I treat you like Zeboiim?
My heart recoils within me,
  my compassion grows warm and tender.
I will not execute my fierce anger,
  I will not again destroy Ephraim:
for I am God and no mortal,
  the Holy One in your midst,
  and I will not come in wrath. (11:8–9)

Hosea had hope for the survival of the nation despite the fact that it had to go through judgment. This applied to the people as a whole, including Judah (11:10–12).

14. *Judgment must come (Hos. 12:1–13:16).* Judgment had to come. The people had sinned too much to avoid it. From Jacob's deception to the prophet's day, the record was one of sin and broken promises (12:1–6). There was cheating in the marketplace (12:7–9); there was no attention paid to the warnings of the prophets—they were all to no avail. Even though a prophet (Moses) brought them out of Egypt, the people turned away from God (12:10–14). Idols were made in abundance, and sin was piled on top of sin (13:1–2). Because of this, the nation would vanish like the morning mist or like the chaff of wheat before the wind (13:3).

The LORD, who wanted to be Israel's savior, had to be its destroyer instead. Like the beast of prey when it is provoked, he would destroy Israel. No king could save it, for kings, too, would be destroyed (13:4–11). Only the LORD had power to defeat even death and the power of Sheol (the grave). But, because of Ephraim's sin, it would not be done (13:12–16). The writer assumes that the destruction of Israel is God's direct judgment. The prevailing worldview of that day would probably not have permitted any other assumption.

15. *A plea to return (Hos. 14:1–8).* Hosea made one last plea to the people to put their trust in the LORD and not in Assyria. Only the LORD could heal them of their wickedness. Only the LORD would be to them like water to thirsty plants, like a tree under whose shade they could dwell.

16. *A wisdom saying (Hos. 14:9).* Hosea closes with a word of wisdom:

Those who are wise understand these things;
  those who are discerning know them.
For the ways of the LORD are right,
  and the upright walk in them,
  but transgressors stumble in them.

The Book of Joel

As the introduction to this chapter mentioned, the book of Joel does not have clear historical indicators. One benefit of this absence is that it makes the book and its message extremely flexible. Perhaps two aspects make the book stand out most. One is its powerful use of destructive images of nature. Earthquakes, locust swarms, fires, and storms all come into play in Joel. All of these forces contribute to a sense of destruction, which ultimately focuses on "the Day of YHWH," a phrase and concept that Joel introduces to the Book of the Twelve, and that will continue to be present throughout the collection.

The Locusts Are Coming! (Joel 1:1–2:27).[8] The prophet was "**Joel**, the son of Pethuel" (1:1). Beyond that, nothing personal is known about him. The outstanding feature of the book is its vivid description of one of the most frightening plagues known to ancient peoples—the locusts. Locusts are large, voracious grasshoppers, destructive beyond description (1:4). When they descended by the millions on an area, they literally devoured every living plant.

> It [the locust] has laid waste my vines,
> and splintered my fig trees;
> it has stripped off their bark and thrown it down;
> their branches have turned white. (1:7)

But the locust plague was only a way for Joel to introduce a bigger and more important idea—the day of the LORD (see Amos 5:18).

> Alas for the day!
> For the day of the LORD is near,
> and as destruction from the Almighty it comes.
> Is not the food cut off from your eyes,
> joy and gladness from the house of God? (1:15–16)

Using words that sounded as if they were borrowed directly from the prophet Amos, Joel spoke of the day of the LORD as a "day of darkness and gloom, a day of clouds and thick darkness" (2:2). The locusts, which were the LORD's agents for bringing in the great day of the LORD, were like a conquering army sweeping over the land:

> Like warriors they charge,
> like soldiers they scale the wall.
> Each one keeps to its own course,
> they do not swerve from their paths. (2:7)

The locusts were everywhere, even in the houses of the people.

The whole universe got involved. There was an earthquake, the sun and moon could not be seen, and the stars disappeared (2:10–11). The LORD called on the people to repent and return to him. As in times of calamity, a solemn fast was observed, during which all the people came together. The priest led the people in prayer for a lifting of the plague (2:12–17).

The LORD heard and would return his blessing to the land. Peace and prosperity would follow. Food would be plentiful, peace would prevail, and the LORD would rule the people (2:18–27).

THE GREAT DAY OF THE LORD (JOEL 2:28–3:21). Part of this passage (2:28–32) is well known to Christians because it is quoted in Peter's sermon at Pentecost (Acts 2:17–21). It shows the characteristics of apocalyptic judgment in its references to the darkening of the sun and the moon turning to blood as signs of its approach. Now the other nations would be subject to judgment, but Judah and Jerusalem would be restored to a place of glory. Tyre, Sidon, and Philistia were used as examples of cities that oppressed Judah. The reference to the Greeks (3:6) seems to give a hint about the time of the prophet's work. If so, it was sometime in the fifth or fourth centuries B.C.E. (3:1–8).

The nations would be called to judgment in the valley of Jehoshaphat, whose name meant "the LORD judges." Like a farmer harvesting grain, the nations would be cut down. It would be a time of decision with the multitudes gathered (3:9–15). The words of Amos were quoted:

> The LORD roars from Zion,
> and utters his voice from Jerusalem,
> and the heavens and the earth shake. (Amos 1:2)
> But the LORD is a refuge for his people,
> a stronghold for the people of Israel. (Amos 3:16)

For Judah and Jerusalem, the day of the LORD promised a time of unparalleled prosperity. For Egypt and Edom, which had long been thorns in Judah's side, the day would mean drought and desolation for crimes committed against Judah. The LORD would see that justice was done (3:17–21).

Amos

THE HISTORICAL CONTEXT OF AMOS. **Amos** preached in Israel after Jeroboam II had completed his wars of conquest. The nation was riding the crest of a superficial prosperity. There was a merchant class whose motto must have been "Buyer, beware!" Short-weight, shoddy merchandise and inflated prices were the rule and not the exception. The small farmer was cheated when the merchants bought his surplus grain. They used oversized measures when buying and weighed out the farmer's money on rigged scales. When they, in turn, sold grain to common people, they used a substandard measure and charged an inflated price. The grain, furthermore, was rotten and full of trash. The demand of the law, "Love your neighbor as yourself" (Lev. 19:18), was forgotten in their greed for gain.

Religion was very popular. The shrines were filled with worshipers, and feast days were numerous. The king had his personal shrine at Bethel. Sacrifices were offered in abundance, and many people even slept near the altar at night to demonstrate their devotion to the LORD. But all their religiosity had little effect on dealings in the marketplace.

Society was divided into the haves and the have-nots. The rich were getting richer, and the poor were becoming poorer. The rich cared nothing about the poor. Harsh debt laws not only permitted the rich to take a person's property if one could not pay the debt, but also allowed enslavement of members of one's family. If the poor starved to death, it would just decrease the surplus population.[9]

While things were tranquil on the domestic scene, they were beginning to change on the international front. Within a few years of the time Amos appeared at Bethel, Assyria would rouse itself and begin a westward march that would crush the small western kingdoms, including Israel.

THE CHARACTER NAMED AMOS. There has been much discussion about Amos. After all, he was the first prophet whose words became an Old Testament book. Nothing is known about his family or whether he even had one. He was a Judean, a native of Tekoa, a small village about twelve miles south of Jerusalem in the hill country.

Amos was a shepherd. Much of the debate about Amos is over the Hebrew term used to describe him, as it is not the usual word for shepherd. The only other time the word is used in the Hebrew Bible is in 2 Kings 3:4, where Mesha, king of Moab, was described as a "sheep breeder" (Amos 1:1). Amos also described himself as a "dresser of sycamore trees" (7:14). The sycamore was a kind of low-quality fig used for food for both cattle and poor people. To "dress a sycamore tree" seemed to involve pinching or puncturing its fruit to hasten its ripening. The sycamore did not grow at Tekoa, so Amos had to go either to Jericho or westward to the Shepelah (foothills) to do that job.

Opposite conclusions have been drawn from these known facts about Amos. Either (1) he was a poor man who had to have two jobs to make a living or (2) he owned flocks and lands that others looked after, freeing him to take wool from his flocks to Bethel and Samaria, where there were more traders and prices were better.

Whatever the truth was, he did go north, and what he saw provoked his imagination. He was a passionate believer in the LORD, the God of Israel. What he saw taking place in the cities of Israel did not agree with what he knew of the requirements of the covenant the LORD made with his people at Sinai. He went to preach not because he wanted to, but because he felt compelled by the LORD: "The LORD *took* me . . . and the LORD said to me, '*Go*, prophesy to my people Israel' " (7:15) [emphasis added].

THE BOOK OF AMOS. Although the book of Amos, as it stands, probably was put in its final form during the Babylonian Exile, many of the messages were likely spoken sometime in the middle of the eighth century B.C.E.

The Introduction (Amos 1:1–2). After an introduction that is somewhat standard for the prophets, the theme of the book, "the LORD roars from Zion," emphasizes the source of the prophet's message.

Look at What the Neighbors Are Doing (Amos 1:3–2:5). Amos' sermon started out by painting a lurid picture of the sins of Israel's neighbors. Syria had committed unspeakable atrocities in war by tearing captives to pieces under iron threshing sledges (1:3–5); the Philistines were slave traders (1:6–8); the Phoenicians also traded in slaves and were covenant breakers (1:9–11); Edom had maintained an undying hatred for Israel (1:11–12); the Ammonites had mercilessly ripped open the stomachs of pregnant women (1:13–15); Moab had desecrated the bones of the Edomite king (2:1–3); and Judah had rejected the law of the LORD (2:4–5). Each section opens with "For three transgressions of—and for four, I will not revoke the punishment" and ends with "I will send a fire. . . ."

You Are Even Worse, Israel (Amos 2:6–16). Amos charged Israel's neighbors with one major sin, but the charges against Israel were many. The rich enslaved the poor for the least of debts (2:6). They pushed the poor down at every opportunity (2:7a). Father and son patronized the same prostitute at the shrine where the LORD supposedly was worshiped (2:7b). In violation of Israelite law, they took a man's only garment and kept it overnight (Deut. 24:13), with the excuse that they needed it for religious purposes (2:8a). The priests and their friends used religious funds to buy wine for drinking parties (2:8b).

They did these things despite the LORD's blessing upon them (2:9–11). In fact, they went even further. They demanded that the prophets not prophesy and tried to get Nazirites to violate their vow not to drink wine (2:12). Because of these sins, judgment would be swift and certain (2:13–16).

Hear This Word (Amos 3:1–5:17). These chapters contain three sections, introduced by the phrase "Hear this word." In chapter 3, the theme is "privilege brings responsibility." The reason for the severity of Israel's punishment was that it had been blessed more than any other people by being chosen by the LORD (3:1–2). As a result, the LORD God was bringing a judgment that would destroy shrine and altar, winter house and summer house (3:3–15).

Chapter 4 was directed to the women of Samaria. Amos compared them to the fat, sleek cows of the pastures of Bashan. They, like their husbands, were greedy drunkards concerned only with their own desires. When the invader came, instead of being given an honorable burial, their dead bodies would be speared with hooks and dragged through the broken city walls to be cast out for the animals to devour (4:1–3).

Religion had become sin because it was false worship (4:4–5). The LORD had warned the people by famine (4:6), drought (4:7–8), blight and locusts (4:9), war (4:10), and natural catastrophe (4:11), but none of these had turned the people back to the LORD. Thus, judgment was certain (4:12). In 4:13, there is a hymn to the power of the LORD:

For lo, the one who forms the mountains, creates the wind,
reveals his thoughts to mortals,
makes the morning darkness, and treads on the heights
of the earth—
the LORD, the God of hosts, is his name.

The prophet set before Israel the alternatives in 5:1–17—death or life. He sang a funeral song in the limping, halting rhythm of the dirge:

Fallen no more to rise
is the maiden Israel;
forsaken on her land,
with no one to raise her up. (5:2)

Israel's only hope for life was to seek the LORD, for life could be found in Him (5:4, 6, 14). Otherwise, judgment would be so severe that farmers would have to be pressed into service as wailers, because there would not be enough professional wailers to meet the need (5:16–17).

The Day of the LORD Is Upon You (Amos 5:18–27). In some of the most vivid imagery found in prophetic literature, Amos described the day of the LORD. In popular thought, the day of the LORD was to be a day of triumph and celebration when the LORD would give Israel victory over its enemies (5:18). Not so, said Amos. It would be a day of

. . . darkness, not light;
as if someone fled from a lion,
and was met by a bear;
or went into the house and
rested a hand against the wall,
and was bitten by a snake.

The Israelites' religious services were such farces that they had no effect on the way people lived. The only thing that could satisfy the LORD was to

. . . let justice roll down like waters,
and righteousness like an ever-flowing stream. (5:24)

This verse sums up the major theme of the preaching of Amos—that a righteous God demanded right living to accompany sincere worship. Right living involved giving every man his due. When viewed from the standpoint of mercy, justice can have an almost negative quality; mercy means that personal merit does not come into consideration. So the rich men of Israel preferred mercy. The poor, however, looked at justice as a positive quality. They had never rated that high on the scale of human values. When a person suffering injustice achieves justice, it is a blessing.

Amos also raised the question of the value of sacrifice (5:25). What he seemed to say was that what was wrong with the system was not sacrifice so much as the sacrificer. A wrong attitude changes worship of any kind into blasphemy.

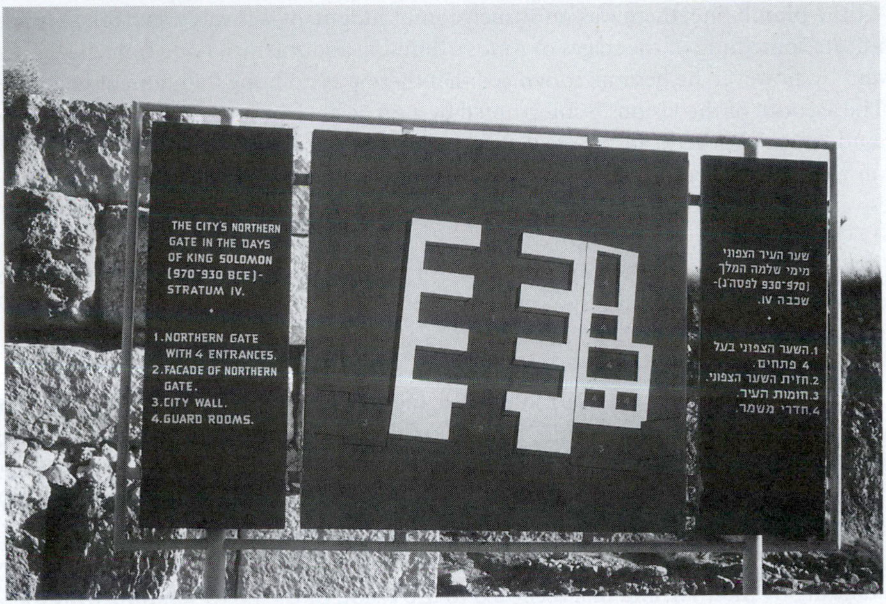

FIGURE 12–1 "Hate evil, and love good, and establish justice in the gate" (Amos 5:15). The city gate, shown in the plan of the gate at Megiddo, was the courthouse in ancient Israel. The city elders met in the alcoves to conduct the business of the city, which included trials.

Woe to the Wealthy (6:1–14). Amos saw pride and self-indulgence as major problems in Israel. Because of the nation's military successes, its leaders pictured themselves as the great leaders of the world. But the LORD had brought down other nations, so Israel should not think that it could not fall (6:1–3).

The upper classes spent time in drunken carousing, bragging about their greatness, and caring nothing for their fellow Israelites. The term Amos used to describe their rites, *marzeah*, may have involved ceremonies memorializing the dead and most likely included sexual orgies performed in the name of worship. They were celebrating while their ship was sinking, unaware of the danger around them (6:4–7). Because of their pride, judgment was inevitable.[10]

The Visions of Amos (7:1–9:14). The visions of the prophets were a major part of the prophetic experiences. Five visions are described in the book of Amos: (1) the locust plague, (2) the judgment by fire, (3) the plumb line, (4) the basket of summer fruit, and (5) the LORD by the altar.

What was the nature of these visions? The visions of Amos—as well as those of later prophets, especially Isaiah, Jeremiah, and Ezekiel—seemed to begin with some ordinary circumstance of the prophet's life. But in a particular situation, the ordinary event took on extraordinary meaning and significance for the prophet. He drew from it a lesson that had an application to the situation with which he was dealing. This could mean that the prophet never went through any trancelike state or extreme emotional condition, as the ecstatics did. Rather, it may well be that the vision was played out in a sort of glorified imagination. Ezekiel's visions by the River Chebar (Ezek. 1) would seem to be the exception. Even so, those visions, strange as they were, began when Ezekiel observed the approach of a thunderstorm (Ezek. 1:4).

The first two visions of Amos were different from the other three. They threatened judgment, but when the prophet pleaded for the people, judgment was suspended (7:1–6). With the vision of the plumb line, there was no suspension of judgment—it was inevitable. These visions may indicate something of the stages of Amos's thinking about Israel. For a time, he had hope. As time went by, however, he became convinced that there was no hope—judgment had to come.

The account of the visions is interrupted by a prose description of a confrontation between Amos and Amaziah, the head priest of the king's shrine at Bethel. Amos was told to go back to Judah and mind his own business. Amos replied, in effect, that he was minding the LORD's business and that Amaziah would not escape judgment, even though he was a religious leader (7:10–17).

The fourth vision (8:1–3) contains a pun or **wordplay.** Written Hebrew words contained only consonants. The consonants for "summer fruit" and "the end" are *qts,* though the two words, respectively, are *qayits* and *qets.* So when Amos was asked, "What do you see?" he replied, "A basket of *qayits* (summer fruit)." The LORD said, "The *qets* has come upon my people Israel." This word of judgment formed the text for a sermon of judgment on those who could not worship because they were thinking of how they could cheat their neighbors in the market when the religious holiday was over. For such people, judgment would include famine for those who were gluttons. There would be a famine, furthermore, of the word of the LORD when people wanted most to hear it (8:4–14).

The final vision spoke of judgment coming upon the religious shrine. Amos probably saw a priest standing by the altar, and that scene led to the vision of the LORD standing by the altar calling for judgment (9:1). No matter how men tried to escape, there would be, in the words of the spiritual, "No hiding place down here" (9:2–4). Following another hymn (9:5–6) comes one of the most remarkable statements in the book:

> "Are you not like the Ethiopians to me
> O people of Israel?" says the LORD.
> "Did I not bring Israel up from the land of Egypt,
> and the Philistines from Caphtor and the Arameans from Kir?" (9:7)

This question attacked a commonly held view among the Israelites—that the LORD was their God alone and was not concerned with any other people. Other people had their own gods. A conflict between two nations meant a conflict between the respective deities of those nations. But, both here and in the opening words of judgment on Israel's neighbors, Amos was saying that the LORD, the God of Israel, was God of all nations. Because of that, the LORD was concerned not only about the Israelites, but about other peoples as well.

A Better Day (Amos 9:11–15). The book of Amos ends with a hopeful note that may have been added by a Judean editor during the dark days of the Babylonian Exile (9:11–15). By that time, the judgments spoken of by Amos were a reality, and the role of the prophets had changed from pronouncing doom to holding out hope for the future. None of the earlier prophets, however, had seen God's judgment as the complete destruction of the people. Instead, they saw it as a means whereby the nation would be cleansed of its corruption and purified for a new and better day.

JERUSALEM AND NINEVEH: OBADIAH, JONAH, MICAH, AND NAHUM

The next sequence of books is not easy to characterize as a group. The strongest connections are the references to Assyria and the Assyrian crisis in the books of Jonah, Micah, and Nahum, but later events and issues are also in view. Regardless of time and context, these books bring the attention of the Twelve back to Jerusalem, and away from the northern focus present in Hosea and Amos.

Obadiah

Nothing is known about the author of this short book. The name means "the LORD's servant," which may not be a name, but just a title. Part of the book almost duplicates sections of Jeremiah (verses 1–9 are quite similar to Jer. 49:7–22).

The biblical stories of conflicts between Jacob and Esau found in Genesis 25–36 reflect a long-standing animosity between the Israelites and the Edomites. The time of these oracles could be almost any period of Israelite history, but recent archaeological findings indicate Edomite intrusions into Judah's Negev territory just before or after the fall of Jerusalem in 587 B.C.E.[11] This date would disrupt the chronological scheme of the Twelve, and make the placement of **Obadiah** somewhat puzzling. Perhaps the explicit reference to "the Day of YHWH" in 1:15 and the constant presence in the background of the entire poem help explain this placement.

The theme of the book was that **Edom** was doomed. Petra (or Sela), its capital, was so secure that the prophet compared it to an eagle's nest built on a lofty peak. But, nevertheless, the LORD would bring it down (1:1–4). Just as Edom had gloated over the rape and pillage of Jerusalem, the Jews would have the opportunity to gloat over the ruin of Edom. The day of the LORD would be directed toward the enemy, and these people would receive just punishment for their sins. When the LORD's kingdom was created, the Jews would be triumphant over such enemies as Edom and Philistia (1:5–21).

Jonah

The tragedy of the book of Jonah is that a great missionary plea is known largely as a fish tale. The fish was not a major character—it only played a supporting role!

The historical character **Jonah** was a fiercely nationalistic prophet who lived in the days of Jeroboam II (2 Kings 14:25). The book that bears his name is *about* Jonah, not by him. Unlike the other prophetic books that contain the oracles of the prophet, the book contains only one oracle of Jonah, which consists of only five Hebrew words.

The importance of this book did not lie in what the prophet said. Instead, the important thing was what the book said. Arguments about whether a man could survive for three days in the belly of a fish, while they may be interesting, miss the point. It is tragic that most people are so fascinated by the story of the fish that they never get to chapter 4, where the real purpose of the book unfolds.

1. ***Jonah, the stubborn prophet (1:1–17).*** There are interesting parallels between Jonah and Israel. In chapter 1, Jonah, called by God to go to Nineveh, was stubborn and rebellious. He decided to do things his way, so he went down to Joppa to board a ship to Tarshish (probably Spain), exactly the opposite direction from which Jonah was supposed to be going. The next thing he knew, a storm was tossing the ship. Jonah ended up being tossed into the sea, where a great fish swallowed him. As it was with Jonah, so it had been with Israel. Its prophets constantly had called on it to do the LORD's will, but Israel had been stubborn and rebellious. The Babylonians, to use Isaiah's figure of speech about the Assyrians (Isa. 8:7), had overflowed the land. Israel had been swallowed up in the Exile.
2. ***Jonah, the prophet in the depths (2:1–10).*** To symbolize Jonah's despair over his condition, a psalm of lament comprises Jonah 2. Such psalms undoubtedly were common in the Exile as the Israelites poured out their feelings of despair. These psalms often ended on a note of renewed commitment and praise to the LORD. As Jonah came out of the depths, so Israel came out of Babylon.
3. ***Jonah, the reluctant prophet (3:1–10).*** When Jonah finally decided to do what he was called to do, he achieved unusual success. The king ordered that even the animals should

wear sackcloth as a symbol of mourning and repentance. With high hopes, Israel had returned to the land. The people of the land offered to join with them to rebuild the Temple, but the particularistic Jews had rejected all such offers. They did not want to contaminate their faith, which had been purified by the Exile in Babylon.

4. ***Jonah, the angry prophet (4:1–11).*** God's failure to destroy Nineveh was frustrating to Jonah. He wanted his problem solved by the annihilation of Nineveh, not by its transformation by God. Many Israelites, like most other people, wanted their enemies wiped out rather than taken in by God's grace.

There was a stinging satire in the description of Jonah's vigil on the hill overlooking Nineveh as he waited for its hoped-for destruction. The LORD, who had already "provided a great fish to swallow up Jonah" (1:17), now "appointed a bush" to shade Jonah's head (4:6). Just as Jonah was beginning to relax in its shade, "God appointed a worm" that attacked the bush and caused it to wither (4:7). If that was not enough, God "prepared a sultry east wind," which combined with the sun beaming down on his head, adding to his exterior discomfort and his inner turmoil. Jonah begged to die so as to end his misery (4:8). In return, the LORD chided Jonah for being more concerned with plants than with people, even the hated Ninevehites.

Those favoring a more inclusive understanding of God's grace felt that the more exclusive Israelites were more concerned with their own "plants" than with people, the most important of God's living creatures. They could not be "a light to the nations" using Jonah's method. Instead, they had to be concerned enough about other people to gladly carry the word to them. In short, the book of Jonah was a missionary tract that proclaimed the views of post-Exilic Jews who believed that they had to provide active examples in a non-Jewish world.

Micah: An Anti-Establishment Prophet in Jerusalem

While Isaiah was counselor to the kings of Judah during the second half of the eighth century, a prophet from the country village of Moresheth-gath in the Philistine territory was also preaching the word of the LORD in Jerusalem. It is difficult not to wonder whether these two prophets were aware of each other and, if so, what they thought of each other's messages, which are not always in harmony.

The small book that bears Micah's name falls into four parts: oracles against Jerusalem (1:1–3:12), a new day for Israel (4:1–5:15), oracles against Israel (6:1–7:7), and Israel restored (7:8–20). This book is part of the Book of the Twelve.

Micah preached before the Northern Kingdom had fallen, so part of his preaching was directed toward Samaria and its sins. But the main use of Samaria and its sins was to say that Jerusalem was just like it. Just as the LORD's judgment was coming on Samaria, so it would come on Jerusalem (1:1–9).

Micah, like the other prophets, enjoyed using puns. In a series of puns in Hebrew, which are not easily translated into English, he described the destruction of the small cities in the path of the invaders (1:10–16).

Micah reserved his most scathing comments for the upper classes of society. He accused them of lying awake, plotting to steal from the common man (2:1–5). They tried to stop the prophets of the LORD from prophesying the truth, preferring that a prophet would

> go about uttering empty falsehoods,
> saying, "I will preach to you of wine and strong drink,"
> such a one would be the preacher for this people! (2:11)

The oracle was softened by a later addition that spoke of the righteous remnant (2:12–13).

Particularly biting was an oracle about the leaders of Judah. They hated good and loved evil. They were like cannibals,

> who tear the skin off my people,
> and the flesh off their bones;
> who eat the flesh of my people,
> flay their skin off them,
> break their bones in pieces,
> and chop them up like meat in a kettle,
> like flesh in a caldron. (3:2–3)

The LORD would not hear them on the Day of Judgment (3:1–4).

Prophets, too, felt the lash of Micah's tongue, especially those prophets who curried the favor of the rich. They would be disgraced, but the true prophet would be vindicated (3:5–7). Micah, of course, considered himself to be a true prophet:

> But as for me, I am filled with power,
> with the spirit of the LORD,
> and with justice and might,
> to declare to Jacob his transgression
> and to Israel his sin. (3:8)

Whereas Isaiah had said that Jerusalem would not fall to the armies of Sennacherib in 701 B.C.E., Micah had no such faith in the future. The sins of the city's leaders were sure to bring doom. He foresaw a day when Zion would "be plowed like a field" and Jerusalem's hills would be covered with trees instead of houses (3:9–12).

In startling contrast to chapters 1–3, this section of Micah speaks of restoration and a glorious future, leading many interpreters to say that another prophet of a later time was responsible for it. The first passage (4:1–3), in particular, has been questioned because it also appears in Isaiah 2:2–4. It speaks of a time of universal peace when all nations would come to worship the LORD, the God of Israel. It would be a time when weapons of war would be turned into instruments of peace and safety (4:1–5). The crippled and rejected peoples of the earth would receive special attention from the LORD (4:6–8). The next oracle speaks of the Babylonian Exile and how the LORD will rescue His people from it. Under the LORD's plans, Israel will triumph over its enemies and live by the LORD's will. The present condition, however, is an enemy siege (4:9–5:1).

One of Micah's most famous sayings was the Bethlehem oracle (5:2–6). Because the messianic concept was connected with the Davidic monarchy, it would be quite natural to expect the birth of the future king to be connected to David's city, Bethlehem. This was quoted in the New Testament as a messianic prophecy (Matt. 2:6). The remainder of chapter 5 deals with the defeat of the Assyrian army and the restoration of the remnant of Jacob, who will be scattered "like dew from the LORD." The remnant would be purified from its worship of idols (5:7–15).

If only one sermon from Micah had survived, Micah 6:1–8 would be sufficient to rank him among the great prophets of Israel. In this oracle, he managed to sum up the important point of the message of each of the three other eighth-century prophets. The oracle is a classic example of the use of court language by the prophet to present the LORD's case against Israel. The essentials of a trial are present:

1. ***The court is called to order (6:1–2).*** The LORD, who is judge, jury, and prosecuting attorney, calls on the mountains and hills to be spectators at the trial and announces that the court is in session.

2. ***The indictment and the evidence all presented (6:3–5).*** The indictment is presented in a series of questions (6:3) charging the people with being tired of the LORD. The LORD's past dealings with Israel are recalled to show that Israel has no right to complain.
3. ***The defense pleads its case (6:6–7).*** Protesting their innocence, the people ask, "What more can we do? Does the LORD require more offerings?" If so, they would be willing to sacrifice even their firstborn children.
4. ***The verdict is delivered (6:8).*** What the defense had said was that whatever bribe the LORD demanded, the people would pay. But that is the heart of the matter. Material offerings, even firstborn children, are meaningless when that is all that is offered.

He has told you, O mortal, what is good;
 and what does the LORD require of you
but to do justice, and to love kindness,
 and to walk humbly with your God? (6:8)

In this verse, Micah sets forth Amos's theme of justice, Hosea's theme of love (kindness), and Isaiah's theme of the quiet, confident walk with God.

Following this oracle, Micah spoke against cheating in the marketplace and oppression of the poor by the rich. These sins would bring the LORD's judgment in the form of famine and desolation (6:9–16). He lamented the fact that good men had perished and that the ungodly seemed to be everywhere, ready to murder at every opportunity. Bribery was rampant, no one could be trusted, and children were disobedient to their parents. In such an evil time, the only hope was to look to the LORD for salvation (7:1–7). Israel would not always be under the enemy's heel. The time would come when the LORD would deliver Israel, and the enemy would be destroyed (7:8–10). The nations that despised Israel would be drawn to it (7:11–13). Micah 7:14 is a prayer to the LORD as a shepherd to his flock; a response from the LORD follows in 7:15–17, promising a repeat of the marvels of the Exodus days. The nations will be subject to Israel instead of the reverse.

Finally, the book closes with a short psalm of praise to God:

He will again have compassion upon us;
 he will tread our iniquities under foot.
You will cast all our sins into the depths of the sea.
 You will show faithfulness to Jacob,
and unswerving loyalty to Abraham,
 as you have sworn to our ancestors
 from the days of old. (7:19–20)

Nahum: An Oracle against Nineveh

Almost nothing is known of **Nahum.** He is called *Nahum of Elkosh* in 1:1. Speculation about the location of Elkosh suggests that it was either in Judah, the Galilee region, or Mesopotamia. The name of the city of Capernaum, famous in the New Testament, literally means "village of Na(h)um." This probably is the basis of the belief that Elkosh was located in Galilee. The only thing that can be said with certainty about Nahum is that he hated the Assyrians. The book of Nahum dates from about 612 B.C.E. It mentions the plunder of Thebes (Nah. 3:8), which took place in 663 B.C.E. and thus could not be earlier than that date. Because **Nineveh** was destroyed in 612 B.C.E., that would seem to be the latest year to which one should date the book.

THE LORD IS A JEALOUS GOD (NAH. 1:1–11). The book starts with an ancient poem of the LORD as an avenging God. It is an acrostic—that is, different letters of the alphabet start each line. Because not all the letters of the Hebrew alphabet are used, it is an incomplete acrostic. The poem may be original with Nahum, or he may be quoting it from some other source.

The LORD punishes those who have set themselves against Him (1:2–3a), using the forces of nature to carry out the judgment (1:3b–5). No one can endure the wrath of the LORD, for

> He will make a full end to his adversaries,
> and will pursue his enemies into darkness.

Behind this concept of the LORD as the avenger is the basic idea that the LORD is the God of justice, the one who can set things right in the universe. The LORD's enemies are those who would destroy the principle of justice on earth, but things will be set right. The LORD's vengeance is directed toward punishing the guilty and righting things that have been made wrong.

YOU ARE DOOMED, NINEVEH (NAH. 1:12–3:19). In what is absolutely the most powerful poetry in the Bible, Nahum describes the fate of Nineveh, the capital of the hated Assyrian Empire. There is little that is positive in the poem, except the words of assurance to Judah in 1:12–13 and 1:15, in which Judah was told that it would be delivered from the Assyrian threats. Between these words of assurance were words of doom for Assyria (1:14).

In vivid language, Nahum described the fall of the doomed city. First came the warning of the approaching armies (2:1), followed by a description of the invaders. The scarlet-clad soldiers were accompanied by the gleaming metal war chariots that flashed like torches under the dazzling Mesopotamian sun (2:3–4). The defenders of the city were caught unprepared for the attack. They rushed about in confusion, trying to organize the defense, but it was all in vain (2:5). The invaders were already inside the city walls, even in the king's palace, carrying off the queen. To describe the fall of the city, the poet used the image of a dam breaking, releasing the waters of a pool (2:6–8). As a result,

> Devastation, desolation, and destruction!
> Hearts faint and knees tremble,
> all loins quake, all faces grow pale! (2:10)

In another powerful poem (3:1–19), one hears the sound of the pounding horse's hooves and the rumble of chariots on cobblestone streets (3:1–3). Nineveh was like a harlot who had lost her allure, who now would be stripped naked and assaulted with manure. She was now viewed with contempt (3:4–7). Nineveh was no better than other great cities that had fallen, such as Thebes, the ancient capital of Egypt. No matter how strong Nineveh's defenses might be or how large its population, it was doomed. Its unceasing evil would soon end, and it would be wiped from the face of the earth (3:18–19).

SHIFTING THE FOCUS TO BABYLON: HABAKKUK AND ZEPHANIAH

Habakkuk: The Philosopher Prophet

If philosophers are people who ask important questions, then **Habakkuk** must be called a philosopher. While most prophets said, "Thus says the LORD" or "Thus the LORD is about to do," Habakkuk asked, "Why, LORD, are you about to do what you are about to do?" Nothing personal is known about Habakkuk. Unlike other prophets, no mention is made of his family or birthplace. Other than a brief reference in a book of the Apocrypha, no other mention is made of him in any Jewish religious literature. What can be learned of him has to come from the way he approached his work as the LORD's spokesman. Living at a time when the Babylonians were threatening to overrun Judah, Habakkuk raised some searching questions about the meaning of God's activity in the events of his day, the period from about 609 to 597 B.C.E. The writers of the Dead Sea Scrolls interpreted the prophet's words as bearing directly on their own situation (165 B.C.E.–70 C.E.). A Scrolls commentary on Habakkuk 1–2 interprets the reference to the Chaldeans as meaning the Romans. The book falls naturally into three sections: 1:1–2:5, Habakkuk's questions; 2:6–20, woes; and 3:1–19, a psalm entitled *Habakkuk's prayer.* This book also is part of the Book of the Twelve.

HABAKKUK'S QUESTIONS (HAB. 1:1–2:5). The first question was this: "LORD, how long must this flouting of your will go on?" Who was flouting the LORD's will? Was it the people of Judah? Or was it the Babylonians? Habakkuk probably was referring to the situation in Judah that developed after Josiah's death.

The answer to the question came: The Chaldeans (Babylonians) were being sent to punish the Judeans for disobeying the will of the LORD (1:2–11).

That answer shocked Habakkuk and brought forth a second question: "LORD, how can you punish us with people who are more unrighteous than we are?" After all, the Babylonians were cruel and merciless pagans who were catching small nations in their nets as fishermen catch fish (1:12–17).

As the answer did not come immediately, the prophet mounted a watchtower to see what the LORD would do (2:1). Then the answer came: The LORD did things in His own good time. The person who would survive and live was the person who was faithful to the LORD. The great Christian apostle Paul quoted Habakkuk 2:4 in his letter to the Galatians (3:11): "The just shall live by faith." Later, in the sixteenth century C.E., this verse was instrumental in setting Martin Luther on his way to the beginning of the Protestant Reformation.

"WOE TO HIM" (HAB. 2:6–20). The woes, a common feature of prophetic oracles, are directed to five groups: (1) Woe to him whose greed drove him to plunder to get riches, (2) woe to the violent man, (3) woe to the bloody man, (4) woe to the drunkard, and (5) woe to the idol maker.

HABAKKUK'S PRAYER (HAB. 3:1–19). The psalm has the name of a tune by which it was to be sung, indicating that it was used in the worship services of the Temple. It was used to praise the LORD's mighty works (3:1–15). The Exodus events are described in highly figurative language:

> The mountain saw you, and writhed:
> a torrent of water swept by;
> . . .
> In fury you trod the earth,
> in anger you trampled nations.
> . . .
> You trampled the sea with your horses,
> churning the mighty waters. (3:10, 12, 15)

The psalmist was overcome by what he had seen of the LORD's activity and waited expectantly for what he would do to the invaders (3:16). This caused the psalmist to rejoice, even though all else failed around him, for

> God, the LORD, is my strength;
> he makes my feet like the feet of the deer,
> and makes me tread upon the heights. (3:19)

Zephaniah

HIS LIFE. Before Josiah's reform made too much headway, the prophet **Zephaniah** seems to have been active. Little is known about Zephaniah, except that his ancestry was traced back to Hezekiah. It probably is safe to assume that this was King Hezekiah. This would mean that Zephaniah was related to the royal family. Although he preached during Josiah's reign (1:1), the nature of his preaching would indicate that his ministry took in the early years of Josiah, perhaps from 640 to 630 B.C.E.

THE BOOK. The major idea in the book of Zephaniah is the day of the LORD, which indicates that the traditions about Amos had had significant influence on him. Many of the phrases in Zephaniah's description of the day of the LORD are almost direct quotes from Amos, especially Amos 5:18–20 and 8:9–14.

The LORD's Sweeping Judgment (Zeph. 1:2–6). The LORD's judgment would devastate land and sea. The special object of that judgment would be Judah's idols and those who worshiped them—the Baalites; the worshipers of the heavenly bodies; the followers of Milcom, an Ammonite deity; and any others who had turned from the LORD.

The High and the Mighty of Jerusalem (Zeph. 1:7–13). Judgment would begin at the top, where responsibility was greatest. It was Judah's leaders who had led the people astray, and judgment would reach even to the royal family itself. Among the pagan practices they observed was the custom of leaping over the threshold or doorsill because they believed a demon lived there. If one stepped on it, evil would result. The custom of carrying the bride over the threshold may have had its origin in a similar belief (1:7–9).

From the palace, the judgment would sweep on through the city, where the merchants hawked their wares. The LORD is pictured as going though the city with a lamp, searching every nook and cranny, trying to find the cynical men of Judah who had said that He would not do anything to them. These men were compared to wine that had become thick and useless because the lees—small sandlike particles—settled to the bottom of the wineskins as the wine aged (1:10–13).

The Great Day of the LORD (Zeph. 1:14–18). In tones like those of Amos, Zephaniah described the day of the LORD that was rapidly approaching. It would be a day of wrath,

a day of distress and anguish,
  a day of ruin and devastation,
a day of darkness and gloom,
  a day of clouds and thick darkness,
a day of trumpet blast and battle cry
  against the fortified cities
  and against the lofty battlements. (1:15–16)

Hope for the Righteous (Zeph. 2:1–3). Zephaniah did see hope for the humble people of the land, who would come to the LORD and "seek righteousness" and "seek humility."

Devastation on the Nations (Zeph. 2:4–15). As was common among the prophets, Zephaniah did not see the day of the LORD's judgment as being limited to Judah. Judgment would come as well on Judah's enemies, for they too were rebels against the LORD. The Philistines (2:4–7), Moab and Ammon (2:8–11), Ethiopia (Egypt) (2:12), and Assyria (2:13–15) would know the wrath of the LORD. Of Assyria he said:

Herds shall lie down in it,

  . . .

the owl shall hoot at the window,
    the raven croak on the threshold;
for its cedarwork will be laid bare.
. . .
What a desolation it has become,
    a lair for wild animals!
Everyone who passes by it
    hisses and shakes the fist. (2:14–15)

Woe to Jerusalem (Zeph. 3:1–7). Having pronounced the LORD's judgment on Judah's enemies, Zephaniah once more turned to Jerusalem and its officials. He compared its officials to beasts of prey (the lion and the wolf). Its prophets were immoral men, disgraces to the name of the One whom they claimed to represent. The LORD alone was concerned with justice; there was no responsible human representative to see that it was done.

A Better Day Is Coming (Zeph. 3:8–13). The net effect of the LORD's judgment would be to cleanse the earth. The defiled speech that began with man's rebellion at the Tower of Babel would be purified when the people were brought back to the land (3:8–10). Sins would be forgiven, and pride would be no more. In its place, the people would be humble and lowly, teachable and truthful (3:11–13).

Jerusalem Shall Be Restored (Zeph. 3:14–20). The climax of the new day would be the restoration of Jerusalem. Judgment would achieve its purpose of cleansing the nation. When the people were once more gathered in the land, days of mourning would become festival days.

THE PROPHETS OF RESTORATION: HAGGAI, ZECHARIAH, AND MALACHI

Haggai: Promoter of Temple Building

In four oracles dated to 520 B.C.E., **Haggai** challenged the people to get on with the job of rebuilding the Temple. This event places the book of Haggai in the Restoration period, along with Zechariah and Malachi. Together, these three books bring the Book of the Twelve to a close.

If You Expect The LORD's Blessings, Then Do the LORD's Will (1:1–15). In reaction to the people's excuse that the time had not "yet come to rebuild the LORD's house" (1:2), Haggai reminded them that they had not let anything stop them from building their own homes. Yet, despite all efforts to meet their own needs, they still were not prosperous. Their efforts in agriculture had brought little produce, and they never seemed to have enough to eat and drink. Inflation also had taken its toll. Haggai's picturesque way of saying it was that "you that earn wages earn wages to put them into a bag with holes" (1:6). They needed to rebuild the Temple if they expected the LORD to bless them. Otherwise, drought would continue to devastate their crops (1:1–15).

There Will Be a Greater Temple Than Solomon's (2:1–9). To encourage the builders, the prophet asked if there was anyone who remembered Solomon's Temple. As there must have been some who did, the prophet went on to assure them that, regardless of the unpromising beginnings of the second Temple, "the latter splendor of this house shall be greater than the former." This promise would be kept many centuries later, when Herod the Great rebuilt the Temple for the second time.

If the Temple Is Built, You Will Prosper (2:10–19). Haggai pointed out once more what their lot had been since they returned to Palestine. If they wanted to prosper, the Temple had to be completed.

Zerubbabel, You Are the Chosen One (2:20–23). The uproar in the Persian Empire undoubtedly caused Haggai's enthusiasm to outrun his judgment. In reference to the problems of Darius I, Haggai promised that this meant that Israel would be freed and Zerubbabel would be the Messiah.

Zechariah: Man of Visions

The book of Zechariah is a sudden surprise in the Book of the Twelve. As the scroll nears its end, the books seem to be getting short, then Zachariah appears with its fourteen chapters. This book is often treated in two separate sections. Zechariah 1–8, which opens with a sequence of visions and closes with oracles or restoration, is closely connected to the preceding book of Haggai. Zechariah 9–14 is a distinct set of oracles that some interpreters refer to as "Second Zechariah." This section seems more closely related the book of Malachi, which follows it. What most distinguishes the two parts is that Zechariah 1–8 seems to speak about the rebuilding of the temple as if it has not happened, or at least is not finished, yet. Zechariah 9–14 presumes a completed second temple. Still, there are unifying factors, and it seems likely that 9–14 was deliberately written to revise and reapply 1–8.

Zechariah was the second prophet who helped stir up the people to work on the Temple. His messages were different from those of Haggai, however. Haggai dealt with bread-and-butter issues; that is, he saw completing the Temple as a necessary condition for receiving the LORD's blessings in a practical form, such as food, clothing, and an improved standard of living. Only briefly did he mention the possibility of the coming of a messianic age.

Not so with Zechariah. First of all, the form of his messages was radically different. Instead of oracles like those of Haggai and most of the pre-Exilic prophets, he, like Ezekiel, experienced numerous visions. Second, those visions dealt almost exclusively with the coming of the messianic age. This means that Zechariah was as much an apocalyptist as he was a prophet. He delivered messages like a prophet; their content was apocalyptic. He preached to encourage the people as they tried to do a hard job in a difficult time. That he and Haggai succeeded in inspiring the people to rebuild their ruined house of worship is a tribute to their faith and perseverance. They were not among the greatest prophets of Israel, but they served a useful function in their own day.

The oracles in chapters 1–8 are to be dated from 520 to 518 B.C.E. Many interpreters believe these chapters contain the genuine materials from Zechariah. Chapters 9–14 are also apocalyptic, but the internal historical references indicate that they originated in the Greek period.

Return from Your Evil Ways (1:1–6). Like those of the earlier prophets, this first oracle was a call to repentance: "Return from your evil ways and from your evil deeds" (1:4). From this point on, however, Zechariah's visions, similar to Ezekiel's allegories, follow. The vision is presented and is then followed by an explanation, the meaning of which, unfortunately, is not always clear.

The First Vision: The Four Horsemen (1:7–17). In this vision, a man was seen riding a red horse, accompanied by three others riding red, sorrel, and white horses. They were sent out by the LORD to patrol the earth to check on conditions. The earth was at peace, but Jerusalem still lay in ruins. The LORD promised that the city and the Temple would be rebuilt.

The Second Vision: The Four Horns and the Four Smiths (1:18–21). The horn was used throughout the Old Testament as a symbol of strength and power. In this vision, the four horns stood for the four great powers that had great influence on the destiny of the Israelite peoples: Assyria, Media and its ally Babylon, plus the Persians. The smiths were metalworkers who made the weapons that gave the strong nations their power. Because they could give power, they could also take it away.

The Third Vision: The Man with the Measuring Line (2:1–5). In modern society, such a man would be called a surveyor. He was marking out property lines, a practice only appropriate for land that was about to be occupied. The vision meant that Jerusalem's population would increase so that it would spill over any walls built around the city.

A Call to Flee from Babylon (2:6–13). Many Jews remained in Babylon. The prophet said that the LORD would allow Babylon be plundered. Many nations would be drawn to the LORD and His people. Here was a prophet proclaiming the day of the LORD like the popular view in the time of Amos. Zechariah assumed that the Jews' day of judgment was over and their time of glory was about to begin.

The Fourth Vision: The Accuser and Joshua (3:1–10). In one of the three places (the others are 1 Chron. 21:1 and Job 1–2) in the Old Testament where most English translations use the proper noun *Satan*, this adversarial figure stood up at the right hand of God to make an accusation against Joshua, the High Priest.[12] Obviously, there were those who tried to discredit Joshua as High Priest, because he is pictured as wearing dirty clothes. In the prophet's mind, this was the work of Satan. The LORD knew the truth and changed Joshua's dirty clothes for clean clothes (3:1–5).

Joshua was promised that if he followed the LORD wholeheartedly, he would "rule my house and have charge of my courts" (3:6). The LORD, furthermore, would bring His servant "the Branch." This probably refers to Zerubbabel. When this happened, "You shall invite each other to come under your vine and your fig tree" (3:10).

The Fifth Vision: The Gold Lamp Stand and the Two Olive Trees (4:1–14). This vision of a gold lamp stand with branches for seven lamps represented the presence of God. The lamps were small clay lamps containing olive oil and a string that served as a wick. In later Judaism, the seven-branched lamp stand became a seven-branched candlestick. It is called a *menorah* and is still a common Jewish religious symbol. The light of the gold lamp stand and the number 7 all represented attributes of God (4:1–5; 10–14).

On either side were two olive trees representing Joshua as spiritual leader and Zerubbabel as the messiah figure. There followed a word of assurance to Zerubbabel that he would be successful in completing the Temple. It would happen "not by might or power, but by my Spirit, says the LORD" (4:6).

The Sixth Vision: The Flying Scroll (5:1–4). The flying scroll was a written curse that would afflict thieves and those who took false oaths. This reflects the commonly held belief that a curse had the power to destroy whatever or whoever it was directed toward. It was not a flying saucer!

The Seventh Vision: The Woman in an Ephah (5:5–11). The ephah was an object similar to a wicker basket. This particular basket had a lead cover on it so that the contents could not escape easily. A woman whose name was "Wickedness" was in the basket. Two winged women carried her off to Shinar (Babylon), the sin city of Zechariah's day. This wickedness was removed from the land in preparation for the messianic kingdom.

The Eighth Vision: The Four Chariots (6:1–8). The final vision was of four chariots pulled by red, black, white, and gray horses. They were sent out to the "four winds of heaven," although only three directions were mentioned (north, south, and west). The vision seems to be incomplete, because no explanation was given. It undoubtedly had something to do with the announcement of the coming of the messianic kingdom.

Concluding Oracles (7:1–8:23). Zechariah was approached by some northerners who had been observing a fast commemorating the fall of Jerusalem in 587 B.C.E. They asked if they should continue to observe such fasts. Zechariah gave a response raising questions about the purposes of fasting during times of mourning and celebrating feasts during times of prosperity. Like the earlier prophets, he called upon the people to

> Render true judgments, show kindness and mercy to one another, do not oppress the widow, the orphan, the alien, or the poor; and do not devise evil in your hearts against one another. (7:9–10)

Failure to live by these principles had brought on the Exile in the first place (7:1–14). In the closing oracle, Zechariah saw Jerusalem restored and prosperous, a city in which the elderly could live in peace and children could play in freedom. The exiles in every land would be returned, the Temple would be rebuilt, and the Jews would no longer be the doormats of their enemies (8:1–13).

Although the LORD had good purposes in mind for Jerusalem, the Jewish people were not to forget the basic rules of justice and love for one another. The fasts once had been for mourning; the fasts of Jerusalem would become feasts of joy and celebration. The nations of the world would be drawn to the Jews, whose LORD had blessed them (8:14–23).

The Apocalyptic Writers

Joel marked the transition from prophetic to apocalyptic oracles. Discouraging times produced such men, whose purpose was to give the people hope when the situation seemed hopeless.

ZECHARIAH 9–14. This part of the book of Zechariah differs radically in form from the rest of the work. While chapters 1–8 consist of a series of visionary experiences in which Zechariah plays a major role, no mention is made of him in these chapters. The mention of the Greeks, furthermore, suggests a later time than that of the prophet Zechariah. These matters have led to the conclusion that chapters 9–14 of this book were from someone other than Zechariah, sometime before the Greek or **Hellenistic** period of Judah's existence (332–63 B.C.E.), as Tyre was still not captured (9:3–4). Tyre fell to Alexander in 333 B.C.E. after a seven-month siege.

The Day of the LORD Means New Life for Israel (Zech. 9:1–11:17). With the boundaries of Israel in the days of David and Solomon in mind, the writer envisioned the triumph of the LORD over Israel's enemies. The restored kingdom would stretch from northern Syria to the southernmost borders of David's kingdom (9:1–8). Yet, its king would not be warlike. He would ride a small burro, the symbol of peace, instead of the prancing stallion of a warlord (9:9–10).

The Jews would be gathered from the ends of the earth. Judah would even be triumphant over powerful Greece (9:11–13). The reason for this turn of events would be the LORD's leadership:

> Then the LORD will appear over them,
> and his arrow go forth like lightning;
> the LORD God will sound the trumpet,
> and march forth in the whirlwinds of the south. (9:14)

The people would be saved and would prosper in a well-watered land. The idols, on the other hand, and their prophets would be powerless to deliver on their promises. God's anger would be directed toward such false leaders (9:6–10:5). But the LORD would raise up leaders for Judah:

> Out of them shall come the cornerstone,
> out of them the tent peg,
> out of them the battle bow,
> out of them every commander. (10:4)

Israel would be strong once again because the LORD would gather the people from among the nations to which they had scattered. Egypt and Assyria, representative of the nations that had scattered the LORD's people, would be burnt out like a fire raging in the forest (10:6–11:3).

As the shepherd had life-and-death control over his sheep, so the Jews' rulers had life-and-death control over them. The prophet, acting for the LORD, took the role of the shepherd of the people. Symbolizing their former condition as a united people (Israel and Judah), he took two shepherd's staffs and held them together as one. Three rulers (shepherds) came and went in rapid succession. To express the LORD's unhappiness at the situation, the staff named *Grace* was broken. As a wage, the prophet was given thirty shekels of silver for being the shepherd. These he gave to the Temple treasury. Then the second staff (*Union*) was broken, symbolizing the separation of Israel from Judah. The LORD was going to raise up a shepherd (leader) who did not care for the people (11:4–17).

The Day of the LORD and the Triumph of Jerusalem (Zech. 12:1–14:21). As part of the apocalyptic vision of the day of the LORD, Jerusalem and the cities of Judah would be attacked by their enemies. But they would fail, for Jerusalem would be like an immovable rock straining the back of anyone who tried to lift it. While Jerusalem's people stayed safely within the city, the tide of battle would turn, with Judah's clans destroying the enemy (12:1–6).

Because the descendants of David were among Jerusalem's citizens, Judah's warfare on their behalf ensured that all Judah, not just Jerusalem, would receive praise for their success. Any nation that tried to attack Jerusalem would be destroyed. Its defense would be led by the descendants of David. The Jerusalemites and David's descendants would also take on a new spirit of mercy and prayer. They would mourn someone whom they had stabbed to death, possibly because they realized too late that he did not deserve such severe punishment. It would be like Baal worshipers mourning during the annual fertility rites in Megiddo. All the Jerusalem families would be in mourning (12:7–14).

In the day of the LORD, idols would be banished and false prophets sent out to do useful work, such as farming. Even their former friends would attack them if they tried to prophesy again. To purify the land, the people who were false would be destroyed (13:1–9).

But Jerusalem's troubles would not be over. Its enemies would attack again, and Jerusalem would fall. Then the LORD Himself would intervene. He would stand on the Mount of Olives, east of the city. A great earthquake would cleave an east–west valley through the mountain. The LORD with His angels would come, bringing in the ideal age (14:1–5).

The age would bring marvelous changes. There would be ideal weather (twenty-four-hour sunshine) and perpetual rivers flowing east and west from Jerusalem to the Dead Sea and the Mediterranean. Over this, the LORD would reign in triumph (14:6–9).

To the south, the land would become a plain, with only Jerusalem on a hill, dominating the land. Jerusalem's enemies would suffer horrible diseases. Judah would loot its enemies, becoming immensely wealthy. The enemy would realize that the God of the Jews was to be the LORD of all and would come to worship Him in Jerusalem each year during the Feast of Booths or Tabernacles. Those who refused would be wiped out in an epidemic.

Everything would be dedicated to the LORD, even the harnesses of the horses. Jerusalem would become one big worship center, with every pot in town set apart for the services of sacrifice (14:10–21).

Malachi: The LORD Questions the Community

Because none of the Israelites' historical material mentions **Malachi,** nor does the book give any sort of biographical information, this prophet, like Obadiah, is anonymous. The name means "my messenger." Malachi 1:1 could be translated as "The oracle of the word of the LORD to Israel by my messenger." The content of the book suggests a time not far removed from that of Ezra and Nehemiah.

Many of the problems were the same concerns with which Ezra and Nehemiah had had to deal. It was a time when the hopes of the returned exiles had turned bitter. The people had become cynical and were careless in their acts of worship. The prophet was trying to arouse a disillusioned community grown cynical with the continued delay of the glorious future Deutero–Isaiah had talked about.

The nature of the book is that of a dialogue. The LORD, through the prophet, made a statement. The statement provoked a question that, in turn, was answered by the LORD:

1. THE STATEMENT: "I have loved you."
   THE QUESTION: "How have you loved us?"
   THE ANSWER: "I chose Jacob instead of Esau to be my people. The Edomites (Esau) will be punished" (1:1–5).

2. THE STATEMENT: "You have not shown proper respect for me."
   THE QUESTION: "How have we disrespected you?"
   THE ANSWER: "By offering blemished animals. The priests have failed in their responsibilities to see that proper kinds of sacrifices were made" (1:6–2:9).

3. THE STATEMENT: "The LORD no longer accepts your offerings."
   THE QUESTION: "Why does He not?"
   THE ANSWER: "Because you have been faithless to your wives, as you have been faithless to the LORD's covenant. The LORD hates divorce" (2:10–16).

4. THE STATEMENT: "You have wearied me with your words."
   THE QUESTION: "How have we wearied you?"
   THE ANSWER: "By saying that God is unjust. The LORD is coming in judgment upon such sinners" (2:17–3:5).

5. THE STATEMENT: "Return to me, and I will return to you."
   THE QUESTION: "How shall we return?"
   THE STATEMENT: "You are robbing me."
   THE QUESTION: "How are we robbing you?"
   THE ANSWER: "In tithes and offerings."

   [This series of questions and answers suggests something of the same kind of situation Nehemiah found at the beginning of his second term as governor of Judah (3:6–12).]

6. THE STATEMENT: "You have spoken harsh words against me."
   THE QUESTION: "How have we spoken against you?"
   THE ANSWER: "By saying, 'It is vain to serve God. Evildoers not only prosper, but when they put God to the test, they escape.' But the LORD keeps a record of the righteous and will reward them according to their righteous deeds. In the judgment, evildoers will be punished" (3:13–4:4).

The book closes with a promise to send the LORD's messenger before the day when the LORD comes to call people to repentance (4:5–6).

THE END OF PROPHECY?

It is not possible to date with much certainty the last prophetic books in the Old Testament. It is probably safe to say that they had all been produced by about 300 B.C.E., and that any editing that took place after that, as these books moved toward canonical status, was minor. Often it is assumed that because there were no more prophetic books produced that entered the canon after this time, prophecy came to an end in Israel. Such a conclusion is probably too dependent upon an argument from silence. Another possibility is that prophetic activity moved away from the production of such literature. A new kind of literature, called *apocalyptic,* appeared and grew in influence as the production of prophetic literature faded away. Both Judaism and Christianity, when it began to form its New Testament canon, seemed reluctant to canonize apocalyptic literature. Whether the prophetic tradition was directly adapted by apocalyptic literature is a matter of dispute. The presence of early forms of apocalyptic literature in parts of prophetic books like Isaiah, Ezekiel, and Zechariah provides some support for this argument, but apocalyptic literature also appears to be connected to the wisdom tradition in books like Daniel and The Testaments of the Twelve Patriarchs.[13] The tradition we identify as "wisdom" was in some ways a competitor to the prophetic tradition, but it also seems to have contributed something to the emerging apocalyptic tradition. The frequent identification of John the Baptist (Matt. 11:9) and Jesus (Mark 8:28) as prophets by people in the New Testament seems to indicate that at least some people believed prophets were still around. All we can say for sure is that the production of canonical prophetic literature stopped. Of course, the production of all canonical literature stopped at about that time, although some other literary forms were produced that gained "deutero-canonical" status.

Key Terms and Names

Study Questions

1. Why should Hosea's attitude toward Israel have differed from that of Amos?
2. What problems are raised by God's command to Hosea to marry a prostitute? How do different biblical interpreters address this problem?
3. How did Hosea relate his marriage and the naming of his children to his message for Israel?
4. What images of nature does Joel use to describe the God's judgment?
5. How did Hosea make use of legal terms and forms to present his case against Israel?
6. What conditions gave rise to the ministry of Amos?
7. What do the Oracles Against the Nations (Amos 1:3–2:5) say about Amos's doctrine of God?
8. What were the major themes in the preaching of Amos?
9. What were the five visions of Amos? Where do they appear in the book, and how are they presented?
10. Compare Isaiah's attitude toward Jerusalem with that of Micah.
11. What did Micah see as the evils of Israelite society?
12. How does Micah 6:1–8 reflect the procedures of an ancient law court?
13. How does the book of Zephaniah reflect the influence of Amos?
14. What elements of the story of Jonah cause some readers to view it as a type of literature other than a straightforward historical report?
15. What was the book of Jonah designed to say?
16. How does one deal with the attitude of vengeance expressed in the book of Nahum?
17. What is the source of Obadiah's intense hatred of the Edomites?
18. Why might Habakkuk be considered an early Jewish philosopher?

19. What did Haggai's ministry to the Palestinian post-Exilic Jewish community help to accomplish?
20. What was the purpose of Zechariah's visions? What role did the idea of a messianic age play in them?
21. How does Zechariah 9–14 differ from Zechariah 1–8? What are some possible explanations for these differences?
22. What is unique about the form of the book of Malachi?
23. What does the book of Malachi tell us about the conditions at the time of its formation?
24. How does the Book of Twelve function as a single book made up of twelve little books?

Endnotes

1. For a fuller discussion, see Mavin A. Sweeney, *The Twelve Prophets*, vol. 1 (Collegeville, MN: Liturgical Press, 2000), xv–xvi.
2. Sweeney provides a fuller discussion of the role of chronology in the determination of the order of the Twelve. Ibid., xvi–xix.
3. Ibid., xxix–xxxv.
4. This catchword idea has been developed most fully in James Nogalski, *Literary Precursors to the Book of the Twelve* (Berlin: de Gruyter, 1993). Its validity has been questioned by others. See David L. Petersen, *The Prophetic Literature: An Introduction* (Louisville, KY: Westminster–John Knox Press, 2002), 175.
5. On the attraction that the western lands had for the Mesopotamian rulers, see Noth, *The History of Israel*, 253–254, and on population deportations, see K. Lawson Younger, Jr., "The Deportations of the Israelites," *JBL*, 117, 2 (Summer 1998), 201–227.
6. This metaphor and the problems associated with it have received a great deal of attention. Two representative works are Renita J. Weems, *Battered Love: Marriage, Sex, and Violence in the Hebrew Prophets* (Minneapolis: Fortress Press, 1995), and Gerlinde Baumann, *Love and Violence: Marriage as Metaphor for the Relationship between YHWH and Israel in the Prophetic Books* (Collegeville, MN: Liturgical Press, 2003).
7. John C. H. Laughlin, "Sargon," *MDB*, 797.
8. For an excellent discussion of the implications of a locust plague, see Harold Brodsky, "An Enormous Horde Arrayed for Battle—Locusts in the Book of Joel," *BR*, VI, 4 (August 1990), 32–39.
9. Albertz, *A History of Israelite Religion*, 160.
10. Philip J. King, "Using Archaeology to Interpret a Biblical Text: The Marzeah Amos Denounces," *BAR*, XV, 4 (July–August 1988), 34–44. Also see Eleanor Ferris Beach, "The Samaria Ivories, Marzeah, and Biblical Text," *BA*, 56, 2 (June 1993), 96 (inset).
11. Itzhaq Biet-Arieh, "New Light on the Edomites," *Bar XIV*, 2 (March–April 1988), 41.
12. In this text and throughout Job 1–2, the Hebrew text includes a definite article on this word, which is not typically done with a proper noun. It probably would be more accurate to translate the phrase as "the Accuser" (*NRSV* footnote) or "the Adversary."
13. See the introduction to this literary genre and its setting in John J. Collins, *The Apocalyptic Imagination: An Introduction to Jewish Apocalyptic Literature* (Grand Rapids, MI: Wm. C. Eerdmans, 1998), 1–42.

CHAPTER

13

A Legacy of Israel

Wisdom Literature and Psalms

Timeline

950 B.C.E. Approximate date of the building of Solomon's Temple
586 B.C.E. Destruction of Solomon's Temple
515 B.C.E. Completion of the Second Temple
332 B.C.E. Alexander conquers Palestine and Greek influence floods the region
200 B.C.E. Wisdom books and the book of Psalms approach their final form

Chapter Outline

CHAPTER OVERVIEW

The books known as Psalms, Proverbs, Ecclesiastes, Job, and the Song of Songs do not fit easily into the Old Testament story. These poetic books offer another way to look at and proclaim faith, which is significantly different from the chronological storytelling that characterizes much of the Old Testament. The wisdom tradition often addresses issues of daily living, with little or no reference to the record of Israel's covenant with God in the past. The individual poems in the book of Psalms likely reflect a major component of Israel's worship tradition, but we find them now in a literary collection with little evidence of when, where, and how they were used in ancient times. Some of these books have enjoyed enormous popularity throughout Christian tradition, perhaps because of their apparently timeless quality.

THE WISDOM LITERATURE

Israel contributed many things to the world, and its modern descendants (the Jews) are still making invaluable contributions to human society. Of all of its literature, the most admired must be the words of its wise teachings and the songs of its singers. Its proverbs and metaphors spice the speech of many lands. Its greatest literary masterpiece, the book of Job, ponders some of life's deepest mysteries. Its psalms reflect the full range of human emotion, from abject misery to ecstatic praise. Its love songs, the explicitness of which challenges both Jewish and Christian interpreters alike, sing of the "way of a man with a maiden" (Prov. 30:19). Because all these literary types use poetry as the medium of expression, they will be studied together.

Wise Ones and Their Work[1]

Wisdom was a product of the people, rooted in the experiences of life and representing the distillation of those experiences. Two of its most important characteristics were that (1) it originated in and was nurtured by the family or tribe and (2) its earliest forms were oral. Its origins are lost in the mists of time, but logic would dictate that it began when leaders began to use their experiences in life to teach the young.

WISDOM IN THE ANCIENT NEAR EAST. Long before the inhabitants of Israel appeared in history as a separate people, there was a wisdom tradition among the people of the Fertile Crescent. Among the Sumerians, scribes used proverbs, in Sumerian and Akkadian, both as a teaching device and as a means of learning a second language. The theme of the righteous sufferer was known in the area long before the book of Job was written. A Babylonian work, *The Dialogue about Human Misery* (1000 B.C.E.), had echoes of ideas found in both Job and Ecclesiastes.

In Egypt, wisdom literature was commonly used to train young people in morals and to ensure competent work in the court of the king. Especially important is "The Instruction of Amen-em-opet," which many scholars believe influenced Proverbs 22:17–24:22. That Solomon had an Egyptian princess as his chief wife had led to the suggestion that Egyptian wisdom influence entered Israel through Solomon's court.

WISDOM IN ISRAEL. Israelite **wisdom** undoubtedly had its oral stage. Later, however, it seems to have taken on a more formal structure. References to the wisdom of Solomon (1 Kings 4:29–34) probably were reinforced by the fact that (1) following the tradition of the Egyptians, he established schools of wisdom and (2) because the Israelites viewed prosperity as evidence of God's blessing and with it, the evidence of wisdom, they equated great wealth with great wisdom.

As Solomon's prosperity was unquestioned, it would have enhanced any reputation he gained as a wise man. Further evidence of wisdom schools connected to the royal court might be deduced from the reference to the "men of Hezekiah" (Prov. 25:1), who were said to have collected "proverbs of Solomon." Generally, it is agreed that the earliest reference to the "wise" as officials of the religious establishment is found in Jeremiah 18:18. Two books whose English names are often confused, Ecclesiastes in the Hebrew Bible and Ecclesiasticus from the Alexandrian Canon, seem to have been schoolbooks. Both are classified as wisdom books.

But wisdom knows no political or national boundaries. This was true especially when those boundaries did not act as barriers to travel, as they do today. Israel's wisdom was part of the larger pool of wisdom of the Near East. The book of Proverbs is a good illustration of this fact. In addition to collections of Israelite wisdom, it contains other materials that had been brought to Israel from other countries. For example, Proverbs 22:17–24:22 has thirty sections similar to "The Instruction of Amen-em-opet." There are numerous parallels between the two texts, suggesting that the Hebrew writer knew the Egyptian text. This would not be unlikely, as Solomon had close relations with Egypt. His scholars, who were concerned with collecting and developing Israelite literature, were undoubtedly influenced by others.[2]

Other examples can be found in Proverbs 30–31. The former is said to have been "the words of Agur son of Jakeh of Massa" (30:1), while the chapter is attributed to "Lemuel, king of Massa" (31:1). Massa was not in Israelite territory but was located in northwestern Arabia (Gen. 25:14).

Wisdom teachings were of two types. Practical wisdom was concerned with the problems of everyday living. The form of this wisdom was such that much of it was easily taught. Easily remembered literary forms—such as proverbs, fables, and short poetic discourses on some human problem—could be committed to memory. The proverb was a short, easily remembered saying that contained one main point. It could take the form of a comparison or a contrast. The fable (such as Jotham's fable in Judg. 9:7–15) was a story that had a moral, usually giving human characteristics to plants or animals. The short poetic discourses actually were just longer proverbs, still designed to make one main point. This kind of wisdom took a simple and orthodox view of life.

In the post-Exilic period, the wise men became the schoolmen in Israel. Perhaps the most famous was Ben Sirach, whose teachings were collected in the apocryphal book of Ecclesiasticus or the Wisdom of Ben Sirach. Practical wisdom was the chief concern of the schoolmen.[3]

Wisdom of a different kind was found in Ecclesiastes (not to be confused with the Wisdom of Ben Sirach) and the book of Job. These books belong to the realm of philosophical, or speculative, wisdom. They were extended discussions involving many of the deepest questions that confront human beings as they try to live in the world. They challenged many of the most widely held ideas of the time. They questioned things that most people would never dare to question. For them, life was far from simple. Indeed, they posed many unanswerable questions and challenged many traditional values.

Proverbs

Proverbs contains a diverse collection of orthodox wisdom. Life was viewed in a very simple manner—the man who followed wisdom would prosper, while the man who ignored wisdom would fail. The first was wise; the second was the fool—there was no middle ground.[4]

THE PURPOSE OF WISDOM (PROV. 1:1–7). Solomon's place in the wisdom movement is indicated in Proverbs 1:1, in which the whole book was credited to him, even though later parts of the book clearly indicate that he was not the author of all the proverbs. Because Solomon was the most famous of all of Israel's wise men, he was looked upon as the father of Israelite wisdom.

The purpose of the book of Proverbs is stated in 1:2–6. Three groups of people are mentioned—those who needed "wisdom and instruction," those who needed "words of insight," and those who received "instruction in wise dealing, righteousness, justice, and equity" (1:2–3). The simple needed shrewdness, and youths needed "knowledge and prudence" (1:4). The wise person needed to "gain in learning" and to acquire skill to understand proverbs, figures of speech, and the words and riddles of the wise (1:5–6). The section ends with the following theme:

> The fear of the LORD is the beginning of knowledge;
> fools despise wisdom and instruction. (1:7)

1. ***Child, listen to your elders (Prov. 1:8–19).*** A father pleaded with his son to turn a deaf ear to bad companions. He warned him to avoid their ways. Because violence breeds violence, if he followed the way of robbery, violence, and bloodshed, he would be setting a trap for himself.

2. ***Wisdom's sermon to the simple (Prov. 1:20–33).*** Wisdom, pictured as a female, went into the busy places of the city in the role of a prophetess. Her sermon was addressed to the simple—those lacking wisdom. If the simple did not accept her leadership, when calamity came she would mock them. When judgment fell, she would ignore their pleas for help.

3. ***Child, listen to wisdom (Prov. 2:1–22).*** The father called on his son to actively seek wisdom, because it came from the LORD. Because the LORD was the source, wisdom had great benefits for those who lived by it. To follow the path of integrity and justice was to be led by the LORD. Increased understanding of righteousness and justice would result. The ability to make right decisions would help the wise son to avoid evil men and evil ways. Most of all, he would avoid immoral women who would lead him to the grave.

4. ***Child, let the LORD lead you (Prov. 3:1–35).*** Loyalty and faithfulness characterized the good life. Loyalty to the LORD was supreme. To trust and follow the LORD was the simplest and best way of life. The wise understood that the LORD's correction was motivated by love. This, in turn, made life pleasant and meaningful. Because the LORD's people were safe, regardless of the disaster, fear was removed from life.

One should live in peace with one's neighbors, doing whatever was promised promptly. One should not be contentious, nor should one be jealous of evil people. They would come to a bad end.

5. ***Child, get wisdom and insight (Prov. 4:1–27).*** The father's father had handed down to him the principle that the supreme aim of life was to develop wisdom. With it, one could have protection and great honor. Because with wisdom one learned to avoid the pitfalls of life, the wise person lived a long life. To follow the wicked was to be led astray. Thus, they should be avoided because doing wickedness was their passion.

The road the righteous traveled got lighter, but the road of the wicked led into darkness. The life lived with care and planning, and characterized by truth and honesty, could be lived without shame.

6. ***Child, beware of that wild woman (Prov. 5:1–23).*** One of the most vivid passages in Proverbs contains the warning against consorting with an adulteress. Her smooth and seductive speech sounded sweet, but it led to death. The best thing to do was to keep as far away as possible, as she could only bring ruin.

Instead, a man should "drink water" from his own well and love the wife of his youth. The LORD's eyes were on men, so the wicked man could not escape the consequences of his sin.

7. ***Child, remember four important things (Prov. 6:1–19).*** (1) A man should be careful about giving security for another person's debt (6:1–5). (2) The diligence of the ant in its work should be an example to the lazy man (6:6–11). (3) A man should beware of a wicked man's

The Literary Structure of Proverbs

The book of Proverbs has a somewhat unfortunate name, because this title describes only a portion of its contents. The first nine chapters of this book are not composed of proverbial sayings, but are a series of extended poems (for a summary of the contents of these poems, see the following pages). The poems are addressed to "my son," which is indicative of the patriarchal nature of ancient Israelite culture. Some recent translations have used the gender-neutral term *my child* in an attempt to make the book of Proverbs more relevant to a modern culture that values the education of all children, male and female. The purpose of these poems is to portray two ways of life, wisdom and folly. Eventually, these two ways coalesce into two personified female figures, Lady Wisdom and Lady Folly. Each of these women calls out to young men to follow her and to enter her house (Proverbs 9). Wisdom is portrayed as the foundational principle of creation in Proverbs 8 and as a noble teacher of humanity in Proverbs 9. Folly is portrayed as an immoral woman who entices young men with wicked temptations in Proverbs 9. This series of poems establishes the setting for the main body of the book.

Those who choose correctly and enter wisdom's house are prepared to hear the wise sayings that make up most of the remainder of the book in Proverbs 10–29. These proverbial sayings are presented in collections introduced by superscriptions in 10:1, 22:17, and 25:1. This literary design has encouraged some to suppose that the book of Proverbs might have formed a kind of curriculum for an ancient Israelite school system and that Lady Wisdom's house is the school itself.[5] There is not ample evidence to prove such a position, but this idea is consistent with the structure and character of the book of Proverbs.

The last two chapters of Proverbs are somewhat more difficult to characterize. They are composed of a mixture of poems and proverbial sayings taken from foreign sources. It is difficult to say much more than that they form an appendix to the collection and indicate that the Israelite wisdom tradition was in conversation with the wisdom traditions of other cultures. The poem to a "worthy woman" or "capable wife" in Proverbs 31:10–31 may be perceived as a fitting end to the book. The young man addressed as "my son" in Proverbs 1–9, who has learned the wisdom contained in Proverbs 10–29, is now prepared to move into responsible adult life, and finding a suitable mate is a vital next step. As a parent, this person would then return to the beginning of the book to address his own son.

The book of Proverbs is a good place to introduce the ancient Jewish practice called *gematria*. Because Hebrew does not have separate symbols for numerals, the letters of the alphabet are used as numeric symbols. The first letter stands for 1, the second for 2, and so on. Because combinations of letters can be used, the eleventh letter is the symbol for 20, the twelfth for 30, the nineteenth for 100, the twentieth for 200, and so on. When the values of the letters within any word are added, a numeric value for the word is attained. The names in the superscriptions of Proverbs may be playing with this system of numbers. The names Solomon, David, and Israel in 1:1 have a combined gematria value of 930. This appears to be the number of lines of poetry in the entire book. Likewise, the section of proverbial sayings in 10:1–22:16, which has only the name "Solomon" in the heading, seems to contain 375 lines of poetry, which is the gematria value for Solomon.[6] This sort of numerical pattern shows up in at least two other places in Proverbs, which makes the pattern look more than coincidental. A word of caution is in order here. This idea has nothing to do with the fraudulent "Bible Codes" phenomenon that became popular in the 1990s. Nor are these patterns any kind of mysterious proof of the Bible's divine origins. If these patterns exist, they would not have been difficult for the human compilers of the book to construct. What these patterns do demonstrate is a quantitative approach to constructing the book of Proverbs that matches its view of life as a fairly straightforward equation in which wisdom leads to blessing and success while foolishness leads to failure.

words and ways that are the recipe for disaster. (4) The final warning was a numbers proverb using seven examples of disgusting things that the LORD hated:

> haughty eyes, a lying tongue
> and hands that shed innocent blood,
> a heart that devises wicked plans,
> feet that hurry to run to evil,
> a lying witness who testifies falsely,
> and one who sows discord in a family. (6:17–19)

8. *Child, wisdom will keep you safe from wicked women (Prov. 6:20–35).* A man who listened to the wisdom of his parents would be able to avoid loose women. The adulteress was even more dangerous than a harlot, because a harlot would only take a man's money, while an adulteress could cause him to lose his life. A jealous husband would not take payment to soothe his anger. Instead, in his rage, he would take a man's life.

9. *Child, let's talk some more about wicked women (Prov. 7:1–27).* Wisdom could keep a man from trouble involving the wife of another. The father told of a personal observation. He saw a naive young man passing the house of an adulterous woman. She came up to him, kissed him boldly, and told him that she had plenty of delicious food, a waiting bed, and an absent husband:

> With much seductive speech she persuades him;
> with her smooth talk she compels him.
> Right away he follows her,
> and goes like an ox to the slaughter,
> or bounds like a stag toward the trap
> until an arrow pierces its entrails.
> He is like a bird rushing into the snare,
> not knowing it will cost him his life. (7:21–23)

10. *Wisdom's sermon to humanity (8:1–36).* Wisdom stood at the city gates addressing the passersby. She spoke of her value to humankind (8:1–11); the high position she held in the affairs of life (8:12–16); the rewards that came to those who sought her (8:17–21); and her role in Creation as the first created thing and the companion to God in Creation (8:22–31). The prudent person would eagerly seek wisdom (8:32–36).

11. *The two ways: The wise and the foolish (Prov. 9:1–18).* To the ancients, prosperity was a sign of the LORD's blessing. Wisdom thus was pictured as having a beautiful house, vast flocks from which to choose animals for sacrifice, and an overflowing table to which she could invite those who lacked her blessings (9:1–6). There follows verses that compare the most foolish of the foolish with the wise person. The prize for the most foolish of all went to the scoffer who thought he knew something but actually knew nothing. Rebuking a scoffer only made the situation worse, but rebuking a wise person only made him wiser. The wise knew that fear of the LORD was the real beginning of wisdom (9:7–12). Listening to the foolish woman led to death (9:13–18).

The "Proverbs of Solomon" (Prov. 10:1–22:16). This section entitled "**Proverbs** of Solomon" (10:1) is made up exclusively of what modern comedians call *one-liners*: not in the sense that they are jokes, but in the sense that their message is contained in one line of Hebrew (two lines in the English translation). These short, pointed sayings each contain a simple truth designed to tell any person who hears them some lesson about how to live in relation to others. They are strung together like beads, each one different; yet, each one is concerned with how to live a good life in human society.

Lady Wisdom

In the poems that begin the book of Proverbs, a parent is speaking to a child, often describing wisdom as something to be sought and prized. In Proverbs 8 and 9 a character named Wisdom suddenly appears and begins to speak in a feminine voice. After she describes herself in a way very much like what is found in the first seven chapters, in Proverbs 8:22, Wisdom claims to have been with God in the beginning, assisting God in the creation of the world. She is the first thing created by God and she places herself in the creative process, right down to the creation of human beings in 8:31. Beginning with 8:32, Wisdom speaks to human beings in a parental voice, urging them to listen and follow her instructions.

The poems in Proverbs 9 move in a somewhat different direction. The poem in 9:1–5 describes Wisdom as a woman who has built a house and invites young people to come in and dine with her and gain insight. This Lady Wisdom character stands in contrast to another woman who is portrayed in 9:13–18. Sometimes referred to as Lady Folly, this woman also invites young people into her house, but she is described in a way that likens her to a prostitute who entices those passing by her house to their destruction.

Theologians have debated how to understand this **Lady Wisdom.** Is she merely a metaphorical figure, a literary device used by the writers of these poems to portray wisdom as a virtue? Could she be a reflection of an Israelite goddess, who may have been understood as a consort of YHWH at one time? As Israelite religion moved toward a more strict monotheism, the appearance of such a goddess in the biblical text would have been suppressed so that only vestiges like Proverbs 8 and 9 might have remained.

The possibility of such a figure suggests an interesting way to look at other biblical passages, such as the first-person-plural speech of God in Genesis 1:26 and the presentation of "the Word" or *Logos* that was with God in the beginning, according to John 1 in the New Testament. Too little evidence remains to answer such questions with any certainty. Lady Wisdom will probably always remain an enigma within the Old Testament.

That these are called the "Proverbs of Solomon" did not necessarily mean that Solomon spoke all of them. They probably were from many lands and many sources. The belief that Solomon collected proverbs and was noted for his wisdom made it natural that his name would be attached to such collections.

Because it would have been difficult to do so, no attempt was made to put these proverbs in any logical order. Although antithetical **parallelism** is the dominant form, other forms were also used. Of those that are antithetical, some examples of the contrasts made are as follows:

THE WISE AND THE FOOLISH:

A wise child makes a glad father,
but a foolish child is a mother's grief. (10:1)

THE PROUD AND THE HUMBLE:

It is better to be of a lowly spirit among the poor
than to divide the spoil among the proud. (16:19)

THE RIGHTEOUS AND THE WICKED:

The righteous have enough to satisfy the appetite,
but the belly of the wicked is empty. (13:25)

GOOD WIVES AND BAD WIVES:

A good wife is the crown of her husband,
but she who brings shame is like rottenness in his bones. (12:4)

TRUTH AND FALSEHOOD:

A truthful witness saves lives,
but one who utters lies is a betrayer. (14:25)

Other proverbs are of a synonymous nature or used formal parallelism:

Honest balances and scales are the LORD's:
all the weights in the bag are his work (16:11).
In the light of the king's face there is life,
and his favor is like the clouds that bring the spring rain. (16:15)

The Book of Thirty Sayings (Prov. 22:17–24:22).[7] This probably was a teacher's book of instructions to a pupil about some of life's important relationships. By reading it, the pupil could learn what was "right and true." Then he could give a "true answer" to whomever questioned him (22:17–21). Although some of its admonitions follow the one-line pattern of the previous section, for the most part they cover several lines. For instance, there were instructions on eating with a ruler (23:1–3); how to discipline children (23:13–14); the inevitable warning about wicked women (23:26–28); a rather long warning about excessive wine drinking (23:29–35); and a warning to "fear the LORD and the king" (24:21–22). One piece of advice was repeated twice, the second time being somewhat longer than the first (22:28):

Do not remove the ancient landmark
or encroach on the fields of orphans,
for their redeemer is strong;
he will plead their cause against you. (23:10–11)

The sayings of the wise ended with an appendix that contained condemnation for showing favoritism in judgment (24:23–25); a word on getting ready for work (24:27); a warning against bearing false witness and acting with spite (24:28–29); and a description of the lazy man (24:30–34).

More "Proverbs of Solomon" (25:1–29:27). This section, like 10:1–22:16, was composed mostly of individual one-line (Hebrew) sayings. The title suggests that King Hezekiah's time was a time when the interest in wisdom was blossoming, because these were said to be Solomonic proverbs collected by "the men of Hezekiah" (25:1). After two longer sections on the power of the king (25:2–7) and one on conduct in court (25:8–10), there follows a mixture of proverbs using *comparison:*

Like clouds and wind without rain
is one who boasts of a gift never given. (25:14)

and *contrasts:*

Better to be poor and walk with integrity
than to be crooked in one's ways even though rich. (28:6)

as well as *other poetic forms:*

If the king judges the poor with equity,
his throne will be established forever. (29:14)

The Words of Agur (Prov. 30:1–33). This chapter is made up of two types of material. Verses 1–9 were presented as a conversation. "The man" (30:1), who may have been Agur, told two men named Ithiel and Ucal that he had seen no evidence of God (30:2–4). He, in turn, was told that God's every word was true and that God protects those "who take refuge in him" (30:5). In 30:6–9, a speaker considers life's highest gifts as being food and truth.

The second part of the chapter opens with a series of statements beginning "There are those who." These include those who cursed their fathers (30:11), who were "pure in their own eyes" (30:12), who were proud (30:13), and who were greedy (30:14).

There followed a series of "numbers proverbs" that sound like the formula in the oracles of the prophet Amos: "for three transgressions and for four" (Amos 1:3ff.). Most of them use the *three–four* formula, although one (30:15–16) uses two, three, and four, while another lists only four things that "are small but they are exceedingly wise" (30:24). Three shorter proverbs are mixed in with the numbers proverbs.

The Words of Lemuel (Prov. 31:1–31). This chapter contains a mother's advice to her son (31:1–9) and the Old Testament's highest tribute to a woman—the description of the good wife (31:10–31). The first part is about a queen's advice to her son on how to rule wisely. The tribute to the ideal wife pictured her as being of good reputation, diligent in her work, prudent in her decisions, concerned for her family, compassionate toward the needy, wise in speech, and honored by her family.

The book of Proverbs would be followed in later Judaism by other books that imitated it somewhat. The most famous of these were the Wisdom of Solomon and The Wisdom of Ben Sirach, or Ecclesiasticus. Proverbs was orthodox in theology and practical in its view of life.

Job: When Orthodoxy Fails

Job represents the struggle of a person who had accepted orthodox answers to all of life's questions but found them useless when the bottom fell out of his world. To compound his problem, his friends still gave him the same old answers, never hearing the entirely new set of questions Job was raising. Discussions of the theological problems raised by human suffering are sometimes called **theodicy**.

Who Wrote Job, and When Was It Written? The traditional interpreters of Job have viewed the book as the work of a single author, but in recent years the emphasis has been on the book as a composite work. The story of the suffering righteous man is found in other literatures, and, indeed, the story of Job may well have originated outside of Israel, possibly in Edom. That the story is an old one is shown by Ezekiel 14:14, 20, where he speaks of "Noah, Daniel, and Job" as great, righteous men of the past.

Those who see the book as a composite take one of three positions: (1) The author of the poetic section wrote the prose section also, using older traditions that were common in the Near East; (2) the poetic discourse is the older part, the narrative being added later; or (3) the older prose story of Job was used by the author to introduce his own struggles about one of life's most

The Literary Structure of Job

The book of Job and its structure are discussed at length in the main body of this chapter, so only a summary is necessary here. The first two chapters of the book of Job and the final eleven verses of the last chapter form a fairly simple narrative framework around a long, complex epic poem. Regardless of the possibility that these two elements might have had independent histories of development, they form a unified work in the canonical book of Job.[8]

The first two chapters of Job transport the reader to the scene of the heavenly council. The reader's observation of the two conversations between God and the Accuser provide knowledge that the participants in the story—Job, his wife, and his friends—do not have. The reader is aware of the heavenly wager that lurks in the background of this story and should inform every line of the poetic dialogue, but the characters see only Job's misery and their own assumptions about it.

There is a growing understanding within biblical scholarship that the form of a literary work and its content reflect each other. Job 3–27 is a series of poetic speech cycles that is almost painfully precise and methodical. Job and his three friends speak in turn: Job-Eliphaz-Job- Bildad-Job-Zophar-Job-Eliphaz-Job-Bildad-Job-Zophar-Job-Eliphaz-Job-Bildad-Job. The pattern breaks only with the missing third speech of Zophar. The worldview known as **Retribution Theology**, which Job's friends present in response to his complaint, is also painfully precise and methodical. This view perceives all human events as God's reward or punishment for human obedience or disobedience. This position is as impressively logical and coherent as the speeches of Job's friends. At the same time, it is as heavy and oppressive to a suffering human being as their endless speeches are to Job. But Job perseveres, and the book of Job breaks form just as Job breaks through the barrier of Retribution Theology to confront God in 29–31. The speech of the fourth friend, Elihu, in 32–37 may be understood in a couple of different ways. Is it the last gasp of Retribution Theology or a reverential way of introducing the direct speech of God? It may also be possible to accept that it is both of these.

The book of Job reaches its climax and then its resolution in the Divine speeches of 38–42. The carefully constructed piety of the friends is demolished. Job is both praised by God and put in his place. Finally, Job decides to leave behind his posture of mourning and continue his life in faithfulness. The report of the restoration of his family and possessions at the end of the book reflects the enumeration of these aspects of his life at the beginning. What seems to be at stake in the book of Job is the freedom of God. A God who rewards human obedience and punishes disobedience is merely a mechanistic responder to human behavior. God breaks free of this constraint in Job, but we are left with questions about whether such a free God is reliable or capricious.

perplexing problems, namely, the suffering of the righteous. This seems to be the most logical of the three positions outlined here.

What we seem to have is an ancient folk tale about a good and patient man named Job. Although it possibly originated in Edom at an early time, it became a part of Israelite tradition. Just before or during the Babylonian Exile, an Israelite wisdom writer used the old story to introduce a poetic masterpiece in which he examines the problem of a righteous man's relationship to God in the context of great physical and emotional suffering. Either the author of the poetic discourse or someone who wished to make the book seem more orthodox added the ending from the old folktale.

Chapter 28, a discourse on wisdom, and the Elihu speeches (Chapters 32–37) add little to the overall arguments of the book and thus seem not to have been part of the original work. The Elihu speeches could have been added later by the original author after further reflection on the problem.

Some Things One Needs to Know for Help in Understanding Job. Some basic ideas common in early Israel form the background of Job. Certain basic assumptions had been made in theology: (1) God was just and gave justice to humankind. (2) This life was all there was. When people died, they went to Sheol, the abode of the dead. There was no life after death with rewards and punishments. (3) If justice was to be done, it had to be done in this life.

These assumptions led to certain conclusions: (1) The good person prospered, while the wicked person failed. (2) Sickness was a sign that a person had sinned. It was a part of God's judgment on sinners. These views of orthodox religion formed the basis of the arguments in the book of Job.

THE BOOK

1. ***Job, the righteous man: The prose story (Job 1:1–2:13).*** According to the old tradition, Job was an extremely wealthy man from the land of Uz. No one really knows where Uz was, although it could have been in Edom. He had seven sons, three daughters, and vast herds of livestock. He was a faithful worshiper of God (Elohim) (1:1–5).

But such bliss was not to continue. **Satan** (as in Zech. 3:2, he is *the satan,* literally "the Adversary") challenged the LORD (YHWH) about Job, accusing him of giving Job special protection. The LORD agreed to let Satan do what he wanted to Job, but he was not to touch Job's body (1:6–12). Disaster after disaster struck Job, causing him to lose all his children, as well as his livestock. But through it all, Job did not criticize God in the least (1:13–22).

Satan appeared before the LORD again. The LORD proudly reminded him that Job was still faithful. Satan replied that every man had his limits, including Job. Satan argued that when the LORD permitted Job to be afflicted personally, Job would break under the pressure and would curse the LORD. The LORD took up the challenge. Satan was permitted to do anything to Job except kill him (2:1–6).

Job's troubles intensified. He was covered with painful sores from head to foot. He sat on an ash heap and used a piece of pottery to scrape the tops off his sores. His wife urged him to curse God and die in order to end his misery, but Job refused. Then, three friends came to see him. When they saw him, they began to wail and to mourn over his condition. Then they sat and looked at him for seven days without uttering a single word (2:7–13).

This prose version of the story of Job pictured Satan as having easy access to the heavenly realms. He came when the "sons of God came to present themselves before the LORD" (1:6). In later theology, Satan was in violent opposition to the LORD, not someone who could come to visit whenever he decided to do so.

Job's wife's advice to curse God and die revealed that there was no developed doctrine of life after death at that time. The dead all went to Sheol (the grave), so this life was the only life there was. There was a kind of existence after death, but the only thing that could disturb it was when (1) a body was not properly buried or (2) a person had been murdered and his death was unavenged.[9]

2. *Job, the frustrated sufferer: The poetic discourse (Job 3:1–42:6).* This section of Job was cast in the form of a dialogue between Job and his three friends Eliphaz, Bildad, and Zophar. There are three cycles or sets of speeches, except that the third cycle was incomplete.

a. *Job's complaint (3:1–26).* In contrast to Job's refusal to complain in the prose story, the poetic version began with Job cursing the day he was born. In an extended example of synonymous parallelism, Job piles up phrase after phrase to say what was said in 3:2:

> Let the day perish in which I was born
> and the night that said,
> "A man-child is conceived."

Had he died at birth, he would have gone to the grave, where he would "be lying down and quiet" (3:13). Sheol was where "the wicked cease from troubling" (3:17), for "the small and the great are there, and the slaves are free from their masters" (3:19). But God had hedged Job in so that he had trouble, not peace and quiet (3:26).

b. *The debate: Round one (Job 4:1–14:22)*

1. *Eliphaz:* The man who has visions (4:1–5:27). The core of the argument of Job's friends was found in the first Eliphaz speech:

> Think now, who that was innocent ever perished?
> Or where were the upright cut off?
> As I have seen, those who plow iniquity
> and sow trouble reap the same.
> By the breath of God they perish,
> and by the blast of his anger they are consumed. (4:7–9)

For his friends, Job's sickness was clear evidence of his sinfulness. Why else should he be suffering if he had not sinned? Eliphaz's authority for his opinion was that he had a vision in the night that told him that God did not even trust his angels, much less mortal man, who was "born to trouble as the sparks fly upward" (4:1–5:7).

What Job needed was to seek God and to commit himself to Him. Although God had afflicted Job, with the proper attitude Job could be healed. Then he would have the traditional blessings of peace, prosperity, a large family, and a long life (5:8–27).

Perhaps the most distinctive mark of the argument of Eliphaz was his view of God. God did not trust anyone, even the most devout worshipers. God was just waiting for one of his creatures to do wrong so that He could destroy the wrongdoer.

2. *Job to Eliphaz: Round one (6:1–7:21).* Ignoring Eliphaz's charges, Job complained that God had become his enemy, filling him with arrows and lining up all sorts of terrors against him. All Job wanted was for God to crush him so that he would be out of his misery (6:1–13).

As for his friends, they were like wet-weather springs that had promised cool water all yearlong but had dried up when the hot days of summer came. He had not asked any of them for money. If they could teach him anything, he was willing to listen. Instead of being honest, they were talking nonsense. They did not know the difference between right and wrong (6:14–30).

Because life for him was so trying and tedious, he decided that there was no need to be reluctant to say how he felt:

Therefore I will not restrain my mouth;
I will speak in the anguish of my spirit;
I will complain in the bitterness of my soul. (7:11)

When he sought comfort, he got terror. He had terrifying dreams. He was tired of living under such circumstances. But his God would not even leave him alone to swallow his spittle. God was using him for "target practice" (7:20, TEV). Soon he would die, and then God would not be able to find him because he would be in the grave (7:1–21).

3. ***Bildad, the traditionalist (8:1–22).*** Bildad vigorously defended the justice of God. He suggested that Job's suffering was caused by the sins of Job's children. All that Job had to do, if he were "pure and upright" (8:6), was to seek God and everything would be fine (8:1–7). Anyone who knew the teachings of the fathers (as Job surely did) would realize the truth of what Bildad was saying. The law of God was that the bad men were destroyed and the good men prospered. If Job followed that philosophy, happiness would be his (8:8–22).
4. ***Job to Bildad: Round one (9:10–10:22).*** Job would not argue about God's power and ability to do what He chose. No man could stand up against God and hope to win. Even if a man were innocent, God could take that man's words and condemn him. Job questioned a basic tenet of orthodox religion, because he had begun to doubt that God really was just:

It is all one; therefore I say,
he destroys both the blameless and the wicked.
. . .
The earth is given into the hand of the wicked;
he covers the eyes of its judges—
if it is not he, who then is it? (9:22, 24)

Job's days were passing swiftly. With them, his hope of receiving justice was also passing. He and God were in separate realms, and there was no mediator who could bridge the gap between them (9:1–35).

He was tired of living. Ignoring Bildad, he spoke to God. God had made him. Now was God going to destroy him? He was sure that God had a purpose in making him, but now life was so confusing. He could not win for losing. Because he had to live, he just wanted to be left alone so that he could possibly have a little comfort before he died (10:1–22).

5. ***Zophar, God's right-hand man (11:1–20).*** Zophar was tired of Job's nonsense. If Job would just listen, Zophar would give him God's point of view about his problems. God knew all things, but Job knew very little. Job just needed to get rid of his sin, and everything would be all right.
6. ***Job to Zophar: Round one (12:1–14:22).*** Job was tired of the advice of his friends:

No doubt you are the people,
and wisdom will die with you.
But I have understanding as well as you;
I am not inferior to you.
Who does not know such things as these? (12:2–3)

Anyone could see that his condition had been brought on by the LORD. Anyone knew that when God decided to do something, there was no way to stop Him (12:1–25). Their defense of God was self-serving. They lied for God, hoping that their sins would be overlooked. But that would not work. They could not deceive God by their actions (13:1–12).

Job therefore would speak his mind even if it cost him his life. He fully expected God to kill him for being so bold, but that would not stop him. He had prepared his case. He only wanted two concessions from God: (1) that God would hear him and (2) that God would not terrify him while he was speaking (13:13–22).

Job then presented his case to God. He wanted to know why God had ignored him and attacked him as though he were an enemy. As one's time on earth was brief, why was he not allowed to enjoy it? If a tree was cut down, it could sprout again. Not so with man. If man had a hope of life after death, it would make life's misery bearable. This yearning for life after death represented a reaching out for what later became accepted teaching in Judaism and Christianity. When life was seen to be unjust, the doctrine of the justice of God demanded a future life in which God's justice could be carried out fully. The only other choice was to declare God unjust, an idea both Judaism and Christianity rejected.

But even as Job reached out for the hope of a future life, he turned back in despair. The situation was hopeless. This life was all there was (13:23–14:22).

c. ***The debate: Round two (Job 15:1–21:34)***

1. ***Eliphaz speaks again (15:1–35).*** Job's failure to agree with his friends led to increasingly sharp words being flung at him. Eliphaz charged him with undermining religion by assuming that he knew more than his friends, the elders, and even God (15:1–14). Eliphaz returned to his theme of a God who did not trust anybody:

> God puts no trust even in his holy ones,
>   and the heavens are not clean in his sight;
> how much less one who is abominable and corrupt,
>   one who drinks iniquity like water! (15:15–16)

He then proceeded to tell Job what his fate as a wicked man would be. Because such a person had defied God Himself, he would suffer great pain and terror. His wealth would melt away, and destruction would come to him (15:17–35).

2. ***Job lambasts his friends and questions God (16:1–17:16).*** Job's patience with the carping of his friends wore out. They were "miserable comforters" who would sing a different tune if they were in Job's place. Everybody was against him, especially God. God had worn him out, dried him up, and "gnashed His teeth" at him. He was at ease before, yet God had attacked him, even though he had done violence to no one and had been innocent (16:1–17).

Job 16:18–17:2 represents one of the low places in the book of Job. The afflicted man cried out for the earth not to cover his blood when he died.[10] His unburied blood, which carried his life, would cry out to be avenged. This was a plea for justice to be done. God knew that Job deserved justice even though his friends scorned him. But death was closing in on him, and justice had not been done. His friends, so sure of their own wisdom, really did not have a wise man among them (17:3–14). Added to their insults was his lack of hope of recovery:

> Where then is my hope?
>   Who will see my hope?
> Will I go down to the bars of Sheol?
>   Shall we descend together into the dust? (17:15–16)

3. ***Bildad plays the same record again (18:1–21).*** Bildad added little to what had been said.
4. ***Job reaches the bottom (19:1–29).*** Continuing his rebuke of his friends, Job pointed out that even if he had sinned, it had been a personal fault, not a public one. God had put him "in the wrong" (19:6), stripped him of everything, and loosed the Divine troops against Job. As if that were not enough, even his closest friends and relatives now shunned him, including his wife. He pleaded with his friends:

> Have pity on me, have pity on me, O you my friends,
> for the hand of God has touched me!
> Why do you, like God, pursue me,
> never satisfied with my flesh? (19:21–22)

Job wanted his words to be written in a permanent record. He was confident that one would come who would prove him right. The "redeemer" of whom he spoke (19:25) would be the one who cleared his name. To biblical people, one's honor and reputation was of supreme importance. Job desired that his name be cleared above all, and somehow he believed God would see that justice was done. At the lowest point, there came a glimmer of hope, another instance of reaching out to the later doctrine of life after death.

5. ***Zophar knows the answer (20:1–29).*** Zophar was insulted by what Job had said. He knew how to reply, however, because he was one of those persons who always had an answer even if he did not know the question. He proceeded to lecture Job on the fate of the wicked according to traditional wisdom. No matter how he prospered, it would only be temporary. God would wash him away in the flood of Divine wrath.
6. ***Job replies to Zophar (21:1–34).*** Job replied that his quarrel was not with them. After all, look what had happened to him. Some of the evil men he knew were prospering, while he, a righteous man, was suffering. With this argument, Job went completely counter to traditional teaching. Just as his friends had overstated their case to prove him wrong, Job now overstated the case the other way. His so-called friends were just liars.

d. *The debate: Round three (Job 22:1–27:23).* The third cycle of speeches is incomplete. Perhaps the text was scrambled over the years. In part of one speech assigned to Job, he sounds like Zophar.

1. ***Eliphaz gets nasty (22:1–30).*** Eliphaz began to level wild charges against Job. According to him, there was no end to Job's sins. He had oppressed his brothers, starved the hungry, and oppressed widows and orphans. His only hope lay in turning to God before it was too late. He could only be delivered if his hands were clean.
2. ***Job searches for God (23:1–24:25).*** Ignoring Eliphaz's charges, Job complained of his inability to find God. He believed God would give him a fair hearing if he could only get a chance to lay his case before God. But no matter how much Job sought Him, God could not be found. The terrifying thing, however, was that God knew where Job was. He could do to Job whatever He chose, and no one could stop Him (23:1–17).

Job 24:18–25 sounds more like the arguments of Zophar than of Job, because it argued that the wicked were punished, in contrast to the arguments just stated, that sinners escaped their just punishment.

3. ***Bildad contrasts God and humanity (25:1–6).*** In a short speech, Bildad spoke of God's rule over "a mortal, who is a maggot, and a human being, who is a worm!" (25:6).
4. ***Job replies to Bildad (26:1–4).*** In an abbreviated reply, Job lambasted Bildad for his arrogant attitude toward him.
5. ***The continuation of Bildad's speech on God and humanity (26:5–14).*** This section was part of Bildad's third speech, as it continued to speak of God's rule over the universe. Its theme was God's mastery of the created order of things.
6. ***Job ends his part of the debate (27:1–12).*** To the end, Job defended his point of view, yielding nothing to his friends. He wished that those who opposed him would get the punishment they deserved.
7. ***Zophar again? (27:13–23).*** In another speech that sounded like Zophar's bombastic style, the debate was ended. He spoke as God's supposed authority on the fate of the wicked, which he described in loving detail.

e. ***The wisdom poem (Job 28:1–18).*** This poem, which separates the speech cycles from Job's final statement of his innocence, would fit well into the book of Proverbs. Its theme is the value of wisdom. Men dug deep into the earth for minerals and precious metals (28:1–11). Wisdom, however, could not be found in the depths of the earth, nor could it be bought with humankind's most precious material possessions. Nothing could compare with it in value. Only God knew where wisdom could be found. It was present in Creation; its worth had been tested and proven. God declared:

Truly the fear of the LORD, that is wisdom
  and to depart from evil is understanding. (28:28)

f. ***Job presents his case (Job 29:1–31:40).*** Job's final argument fell into three divisions: (1) his past prosperity, (2) his present problems, and (3) his code of conduct.

Looking back over his life, Job yearned for the good days he had enjoyed. His family had surrounded him, his flocks had prospered, and he had had an honored place in the community (29:1–10). He had been known in the community for his kindness and generosity toward the poor and oppressed. He had been praised by those around him. They had come to him for advice because he was a leader among those who knew him (29:11–25).

But things had changed. He was ridiculed by the people who formed the very lowest levels of society, people whom once he would not have trusted to care for his flocks. Now they spat on him, made him the butt of their ridicule, and harassed him at every turn. He was in pain—both in body and in spirit—for God had cast him down into the dirt (30:1–19).

Turning to God, Job charged God with treating him cruelly and refusing to listen to Job's pleas. Job's skin had turned black and fallen away. He mourned his fate (30:20–31).

As a climax to his speeches, Job set forth his code of conduct. It has been described as "the code of an Old Testament gentleman."[11] Except for the first, each common breach of conduct in society was introduced by the formula "If I have . . ." followed by a sort of self-curse: "Let {me} . . ." with the appropriate punishment. (1) He had not looked on a virgin with lust in his heart (31:1–4). (2) He had not lied, nor had he coveted the possessions of others (31:5–8). (3) He had not committed adultery (31:9–12). (4) He had been sensitive to the needs and rights of his servants (31:13–15). (5) He had seen to the needs of the less fortunate (31:16–23). (6) He had not put his trust in wealth, nor had he worshiped the sun or the moon (31:24–28). (7) He had not gloated over another man's ruin, failed to be kind to strangers, or sinned any secret sins (31:29–34). If an indictment against him were written down, he would carry it to God as a prince wore a crown (31:35–37). Finally, he had taken care of his land (31:38–40).

g. ***The Elihu speeches (32:1–37:24).*** A new character appears, Elihu by name, who makes four speeches. They reveal a brash young man who possesses more wind than wisdom. The speeches are ignored, both by the previous characters in the drama and by the LORD, who addresses Job following the Elihu speeches. This has led to suggestions that (1) these speeches are not a part of the original arguments and (2) Elihu is not a real person, but a disguise "adopted by Satan to press his case for the last time."[12] In any case, he plows ahead with such an outpouring of verbiage that Job and his friends could not answer even if they had wished to do so. Perhaps the passage that captures the flavor of Elihu's speech better than any other is 36:1–4, in which he concluded:

I have something to say on God's behalf.
    I bring my knowledge from far away,
and ascribe righteousness to my Maker.
    For truly my words are not false;
    one who is perfect in knowledge is with you.

h. ***The divine speeches (38:1–41:44).*** God spoke from the whirlwind, chiding Job for questioning divine wisdom. Then followed a series of divine test questions on the mysteries of nature. Beginning with Creation, they were concerned with various aspects of Creation and the natural order, but especially with water in nature (38:1–38). Then the questions turned to Job's knowledge of animal life, ranging from wild animals to domestic animals, such as the horse. The answer to all of the questions was "Only God knows these things." Job admitted his ignorance and vowed to speak no more (38:39–40:5).

God was not through with his speech, however. Job was challenged to use his power to bring down all the proud men of the earth. Then God would acknowledge Job's power and wisdom (40:6–14).

The Divine speeches were concluded by the description of two legendary animals—Behemoth, an exaggerated description of the hippopotamus, and Leviathan, a legendary creature of the sea and rivers that was modeled on the crocodile (40:15–41:34).

i. ***Job's final speech (42:1–6).*** Job has been powerfully affected by the Divine encounter in 38–41. The words of his final speech are the key to a proper understanding of the book, but they have often been translated in odd ways. One must keep in mind that both the beginning of the book of Job in 1:1 and the end in 42:8 have evaluated Job as upright and blameless. Whatever Job says must fit into that context. In 42:3 he says something like this:

Therefore I have declared and I have not understood,
    acts too wonderful for me and I did not know.

Job acknowledges his inability to understand the ways of God, and now he has to decide what to do next. What Job says in 42:5–6 is very difficult to render in English. A rough approximation is:

By hearing of an ear I have heard you,
    And now my eye has seen you.
Therefore, I reject and refuse
    concerning dust and ashes.

This text is often translated in a way that indicates that Job is repenting. But the book of Job makes it clear that Job has nothing for which to repent. As the translation above shows, what Job does decide is to turn away from or leave behind his posture of mourning in the dust, where he has been sitting since 2:8.

The Traditional Ending of the Story (42:7–17). The unorthodox ending of the poetic portions of Job was too much for the traditionalists. To bring it in line with orthodoxy, the ending of the older story was added. In it, Job's friends had to have him sacrifice for them because they had misrepresented God.

As for Job himself, his health and wealth were restored. His family, who had shunned him in his illness, now gathered to comfort him once the ordeal was over. He lived a long life, accumulated twice as many animals as before his illness, and once again had the perfect number of children: seven sons and three daughters.

Job: A Summary. Job has long been regarded as one of the great literary masterpieces of all time. The question with which it deals still intrigues and baffles thoughtful people of our age—the problem of human suffering, and, more specifically, the suffering of righteous or innocent people. The problem is crucial, especially in the context of the belief in a just and all-wise God. Job really did not solve the problem. Instead, Job's vision of God changed his focus from his own problems to faith in a personal God. The air of mystery surrounding Job and the problem with which the book deals remain. Perhaps that is part of the reason the book is still so fascinating.

Ecclesiastes: Skeptical Wisdom

Ecclesiastes illustrates how far some Jewish thinkers had strayed from orthodox theology in the post-Exilic period. Except for occasional orthodox corrections, the book voiced the skeptical, pessimistic feelings of a man who had tried everything but had found nothing satisfying or meaningful in which to invest his life. The main speaker in the book was "the Preacher, the son of David, King in Jerusalem" (1:1). "Preacher" is but one possible translation of the Hebrew title **Qoheleth.** It was used to refer to a schoolmaster, or one who was in charge of an assembly of people.

The reference to the son of David, King in Jerusalem, has led to Solomon's being identified as the author of Ecclesiastes. In reality, Solomon's relation to this book probably was the same as Ruth's relation to the book of Ruth—that is, he was the main character portrayed by the book rather than the author. The language and thought of the book suggest that it was post-Exilic in origin. Like Proverbs, it probably was used as a textbook.

Vanity of Vanities (Eccl. 1:1–2:26). "**Vanity** of vanities! All is vanity" (1:2). With these words, the writer of Ecclesiastes gives his opinion of the world and life in it. Nothing was lasting—nothing was of real value. Although he was not an atheist (one who denied the existence of God), he was a deist, one who believed in God but who thought that God had little or nothing to do with what went on in the world.

The Preacher had tried many things. He had tried work, but he concluded that it was for nothing. The world was going in circles. Life had no purpose.

> What has been is what will be,
> and what has been done is what will be done;
> there is nothing new under the sun. (1:9)

So, work did not satisfy him (1:2–11).

The Literary Structure of Ecclesiastes

Attempts to determine a sense of literary unity and coherence in the book of Ecclesiastes have been frustrating. Many readers have largely given up and declared it to be just a loose collection of wisdom materials. Ecclesiastes does contain a wide variety of literary units. There are stories, poems, proverbs, and more. Is there a way to look at the book as a whole?

Some readers have observed that Ecclesiastes has a deliberate prologue (1:1) and epilogue (12:9–14) that frame the rest of the book. This is a helpful starting point because it shows that Ecclesiastes is a self-consciously literary work. The prologue and epilogue are spoken by a narrator who introduces the character called the Teacher, who speaks the main body of the book. Just inside the prologue and epilogue, in 1:2 and 12:8, is the Teacher's most poignant and identifiable saying. The *NRSV* has followed the King James tradition in translating it as "Vanity of vanities, all is vanity." In contemporary English this saying has lost much of its force because we tend to associate *vanity* merely with pride in personal appearance and no longer with a lack of meaning. A translation like "Meaningless, meaningless, all is meaningless" is not as grammatically precise, but it may more accurately reflect the sense of the statement. The word that appears three times in this saying occurs about thirty times in Ecclesiastes out of only about seventy total occurrences in the entire Old Testament. Ecclesiastes is a desperate search for meaning. Thus, it should be no surprise that it runs here and there in this search, its parts linked together by this word and the purpose of the search.

Ecclesiastes 1:2 is the beginning of a long poem in 1:2–11 that poses the problem that the entire book addresses. Ecclesiastes then follows the life of the Teacher in a pattern of observation and conclusion. These conclusions typically return to the problem of lack of meaning (see 4:16, 6:9, etc.). In chapter 2 the Teacher talks about his early life and education, and in chapter 12 he reflects upon the end of his life. Although the Teacher never seems to discover the key to life's meaning, for which he searches throughout his life, it is important to recognize that he continues to search unfailingly until his death. The epilogue is actually an epitaph. This one who never relented in his quest for meaning is remembered and celebrated as a wise person (12:9).

Next, he tried wisdom. He acquired great wisdom, but it too was emptiness, for "he who increases knowledge increases sorrow" (1:2–18). Pleasure was tested without restraint, but it, too, proved to be worthless (2:1–11). When he considered wisdom and folly, he realized that both the wise man and the fool died with no lasting memory of their accomplishments or failures (2:12–16). When he realized that what a man gained in this life had to be left to someone else to enjoy, he was led to despair (2:17–23). So he concluded:

> There is nothing better for mortals than to eat and drink,
> and find enjoyment in their toil. . . .
> For to the one who pleases Him God gives wisdom and knowledge and joy. (2:24, 26)

The latter verse sounds more like the voice of orthodoxy speaking.

"For everything there is a season" (Eccl. 3:1–15). These famous lines, a setting out of opposites to stress the paradoxical nature of life, represented a view of history that was strange to the rest of the Old Testament. The general Old Testament view was that history had a beginning and it will have an end. It was moving toward a goal under the expert direction of God.

A philosophy of history that saturated the book of Ecclesiastes—history moving in circles, having no purpose or goal—was clearly expressed in 3:1–15. This view, held in common by the Greeks and a number of Eastern religions (Buddhism, Hinduism, etc.) is not a Hebrew conception of history. This seems to suggest that Ecclesiastes was influenced by the Hellenistic culture that saturated the Near East following the conquests of Alexander the Great (3:1–8).

Although God had given people a sense of time as past and future, they were not given the ability to look at life as a whole. Their hope lay in taking life as it came while doing their best (3:9–15).

The Question of Justice (Eccl. 3:16–4:4). As far as justice was concerned, it too was a matter of chance. Wickedness triumphed just as often as righteousness did. Humankind had no advantage over the animals. The oppressed cried out, but no one comforted them. Power was behind the oppressors. As a result, the dead were better off than the living. The unborn were even more fortunate, because they had not had to experience life.

The Futility of Working Alone (Eccl. 4:5–16). People worked out of a sense of rivalry with others. It was better to work with someone to have the protection that a partner could give. It was better to be young, poor, and wise than to be an old and foolish ruler. Being a hero was also just temporary, because heroes were soon forgotten.

Do Not Fool Around with God (Eccl. 5:1–7). The Preacher warned that a person should avoid calling God's attention to himself. God should be obeyed without question. If one could not keep a vow, it would be better not to make it. Silence was better than chatter that might make God angry.

Life Had Problems (Eccl. 5:8–6:12). If the government oppressed people, they had no hope for justice, because every official was protected by the one above him (5:8). Kings and the rich had money, but life was not a bed of roses for the rich. More riches meant that one was responsible for more people. The rich lost sleep worrying about money, while the laborer slept peacefully. If people saved money, they could lose it and leave the world as they came into it—with nothing. The best thing to do was to accept what God gave and not worry about it (5:10–20).

There was no justice in the Preacher's way of looking at life. People could be wealthy and lose it all. They could have large families and long lives and still be disgraced by not having a proper burial. If people could not be happy with the way they lived, they would have been better off not to have been born. The best thing to do was to take what one saw rather than to desire the unseen thing. Things were already predetermined, so there was no profit in arguing about it (6:1–12).

Thinking About Life (Eccl. 7:1–8:1). Life's end was more important than its beginning. Mourning was better than joy, and sorrow was better than laughter. Only a fool laughed. The wise rebuked the fool. Wisdom was the best guarantee that people would keep what they had. The key to life was moderation. Wisdom had shown the Preacher that "wickedness is folly and that foolishness is madness" (7:25). But the worst of all things was woman. A very few men could be trusted, but no woman was worthy of trust.

Watch Out for the Ruler (Eccl. 8:2–9). The only safe thing to do in regard to rulers was to stay out of their way. If people were wise enough, they could make the right choices about what to do and when to do it. Unfortunately, no one had that kind of wisdom.

There Is No Justice in Life (Eccl. 8:10–9:12). The wicked prospered as though they were righteous. There was no way the Preacher could understand the ways of God. Even those wise persons who claimed to know God's ways really did not know them. The Preacher had decided that the wise and righteous were controlled by God, however (8:10–9:1).

The righteous and the wicked suffered the same fate. A sinner was just as well off as a saint. Of course, where there was life, there was hope. While one was living, he should enjoy life with his wife. He should do what he did with diligence, for there would be no chance to do anything once he went to the grave. His time would end before he knew it (9:2–12).

Wisdom and Foolishness (Eccl. 9:13–10:20). This section contains a number of illustrations about wisdom and foolishness. According to the Preacher, a little wisdom would go a long way, but a little foolishness would cancel out the effects of a great deal of wisdom. Foolishness was especially bad when it infected those who had power.

The Actions of the Wise (Eccl. 11:1–6). A man wise in business spreads his investments around. One who always worried about the weather would never reap a crop. That was just the risk of living.

Advice to the Young (Eccl. 11:7–12:8). Long life should be appreciated, but such a life had dark days. A young man should relish his youth, but he should still remember that he had to account to God for it. For that reason, he should take God into account in his youth before the problems of age and death overtook him.

The End of It All (Eccl. 12:9–14). Another person summarized the Preacher's life. He had taught what he had discovered about life with honest conviction. A final word was given to students:

> Of making many books there is no end, and much study is a weariness to the flesh. (12:12)

A final orthodox word was added:

> Fear God, and keep his commandments; for that is the whole duty of everyone. (12:13)

What about Ecclesiastes? Ecclesiastes revealed that not all post-Exilic Jews were orthodox in their view of God. The writer of Ecclesiastes believed in God. For him, however, God was not actively involved in the everyday events of life—or, if He was, one could not discover how. The writer did not accept the orthodox view that righteousness was always rewarded with blessing and that sin was always punished.

PSALMS: ISRAEL SINGS ITS FAITH

Any complete discussion of Israel's poets and singers would involve every book in the Old Testament. A major portion of the materials in the books of the prophets was in poetic form. Jeremiah and Nahum, especially, excelled as poets. The historical works abound in poetic passages. Two notable examples of such passages are the Song of Deborah (Judg. 5) and David's lament over Jonathan and Saul (2 Sam. 1:19–27). As has been indicated previously, the wisdom materials made extensive use of poetic forms.

There was a reason for this extensive use of poetry. Poetry was much more easily remembered than prose. Putting words into a rhythmic pattern provided an additional device for aiding the memory of a people who had to depend on it as the most common method of preserving and passing along traditions they valued. The words plus the rhythm were easier to commit to memory, just as the words sung to a tune are easier to remember than words alone.

Two books in the Old Testament were devoted exclusively to preserving Israel's greatest poetry. One of them—the Song of Solomon, or Song of Songs—deals with what we would call a secular theme—human love—and, more specifically, love between a man and a woman.

It should be pointed out that, to the Israelite, this was not a secular theme. All of life and its relationships were the concern of the LORD of Israel, a biblical view that somehow has been lost over the centuries.

The second book, the Psalms, represented Israelite worship, both on the personal and on the community level. In it, all areas of life were touched on, from going to war to praising God. In it were placed poems expressing the full range of Israelite feelings, from their most violent expressions of hatred to their most joyous sense of praise for God's blessings.

The Song of Songs

This book has long been a source of uneasiness for Judaism and for the Christian church. It does not mention God anywhere. This failure has caused its place in the canon to be debated more than that of any other Old Testament book. Judaism and Christianity both solved the problem by interpreting it allegorically. For Jews, the "husband" was the LORD and Israel was his "bride." For Christians, Jesus was the "husband" and the church was the "bride." Song of Songs is one of the five "Festival Scrolls" in Jewish tradition, a collection discussed further in the next chapter. It is not easy to find a place for this book in a discussion of the Old Testament. Like the book of Psalms, its qualities as poetry seem to override any historical or thematic concerns.

THE NATURE OF THE BOOK. In reality, the book was a collection of love songs celebrating the joys of physical lovemaking. Its lesson was that sex was God's gift to humankind. Like all such gifts, it could be used properly or abused. But even though some abused it, this did not lessen its value or beauty.

The poems cover a wide span of years. They were brought together in their present arrangement in the post-Exilic period. Solomon was not only noted for his wisdom, but also seemed to enjoy a reputation for his way with women. He was reputed to have had 700 wives and 300 concubines (slave wives) (1 Kings 11:3). Thus, this book, like Proverbs, was attributed to him. The collector and arranger of the poems thought of Solomon as one of the main characters.

INTERPRETATIONS OF THE BOOK. There are two basic interpretations of the characters in the book. Some hold that there were two characters: Solomon and the maiden. Others argue that three characters were involved: Solomon, the maiden, and her hometown boyfriend. For the purpose of this discussion, it will be assumed that only two characters were involved.

A SURVEY OF THE BOOK

The Bride Is Prepared for Her Lover (Song 1:1–6). Before a bride was brought to her husband for the first time, she was carefully bathed and perfumed for the occasion. The poet has skillfully caught the thoughts of the bride as she approaches the time when she will first be brought to the groom. As she was anointed with oils, she anticipated his kisses. Her manner had charmed the maidens who waited on her (1:2–4).

She looked at herself. She was tanned by the sun. She wondered if this would make her less attractive. For this reason, she explained why she was so dark—she had been forced by her brothers to work in the vineyards.

The Bride and the Groom Together (Song 1:7–2:5). She asked where he was. He answered in a teasing manner that because she did not know, he was following the flock. He praised her beauty, comparing her to "a mare in Pharaoh's chariots!" (1:9). She in turn praised him. He was like "a

The Literary Structure of Song of Songs

Interpretation of the Song of Songs has gone in two very different directions, as the discussion in the main body of this textbook indicates. This choice can have significant influence on the understanding of the structure of the book. Although many readers decide to read the Song of Songs as an allegory, the book seems to be best understood as erotic poetry. Is it just a random collection of love poems, or is there a plot? Does the structure of the book relate to the subject matter? These are questions to keep at the center of a discussion of literary structure.[13]

The Song of Songs can be divided into seven sections. The differences between these divisions and those used in the main body of this textbook and in other schemes indicate the difficulty of determining a definite sense of structure in this book. Three of the seven sections proposed here—the first, second, and sixth—end with the repeated refrain in 2:7, 3:5, and 8:4, " . . . do not stir up or awaken love until it is ready." These seven parts of the Song are:

1:2–2:7	The initial encounter of the two lovers
2:8–3:5	The struggle of the two lovers to be together
3:6–4:5	The wedding procession and praise of the bride
4:6–5:16	The sexual union and praise of the groom
6:1–7:6	The woman and the man take on royal identity
7:7–8:4	The man and woman express their desire to be together
8:5–8:14	A closing encounter between the lovers

This structure proposes a sense of balance between corresponding parts from the outside in, first and last, second and sixth, and third and fifth. This type of literary structure is called a *chiasm*. Such a pattern highlights the central part of the book. Within this central part of the book, 4:6–5:16, the intensity of the sexual encounter is highlighted in 5:4–5, the central lines of the poem.

If the descriptions of each section above are accurate, then there seems to be a sense of development in the book. The individual love poems work together to tell a love story. The lack of any definite identity assigned to the lovers may invite an allegorical reading, as the history of interpretation of this book shows. It may also invite the association of these unnamed characters with those in other stories. In the Hebrew Bible, the Song of Songs has been placed just after the book of Ruth. This may be pure coincidence or the result of other forces, but it may show a desire on the part of some who shaped the canon to associate the lovers in the Song of Songs with Ruth and Boaz. Is the artful ambiguity of a work such as this intended to invite such playful reading?

cluster of henna blossoms in the vineyards of En-gedi" (1:14), an oasis on the Dead Sea. His next compliment was more appropriate for modern ears:

> Ah, you are beautiful, my love,
> ah, you are beautiful;
> your eyes are like doves.
> Ah, you are beautiful, my beloved,
> truly lovely. (1:15–16)

Compliments continued to pass back and forth between the lovers as he brought her to the banqueting house and fed her the finest delicacies (2:1–5).

The Bride's Memories of Love (Song 2:6–17). She remembered their lovemaking and longed for him to wake up from his sleep. She thought of how he had come to her and how he had used such beautiful words to woo her in that springtime season:

> Arise, my love, my fair one,
> and come away;
> for now the winter is past,
> the rain is over and gone.
> The flowers appear on the earth;
> the time of singing has come,
> and the voice of the turtledove
> is heard in our land. (2:10–12)

With these memories she rested, assured of his love for her.

The Bride Has a Bad Dream (Song 3:1–5). She dreamed that he had gone. She went out to search for him. She had just asked the watchman if he had seen her lover when she found him. She took him home so that he would be safe with her.

The King's Wedding Procession (Song 3:6–11). The king was borne to the wedding on the shoulders of servants in an elaborate litter or palanquin, preceded by sixty soldiers in battle dress as an honor guard.

The Groom Describes The Bride (Song 4:1–5:1). This was a twofold description: what the bride looked like to the groom (4:1–8) and how she had devastated his heart (4:9–15). Although the groom's description of the bride's features might not suit a modern maid, they were the highest compliments he could give a girl of his time. Her eyes were like doves (4:1); her hair was "like a flock of goats" (4:1); her neck was "like the tower of David" (4:4); her breasts were "like two fawns" of a gazelle (4:5). In short, there was no flaw in her (4:7). She had so captured him that she was like a garden of the most fragrant flowers and spices (4:9–15). The thoughts of her caused him to call her to him (4:16–5:1).

The Bride Has Another Dream (Song 5:2–6:3). In her dream, the bride heard her lover call at her door in the night. She ran to open it, but when she did he was gone. When she went to look for him, she was attacked by the city's watchmen (5:2–8).

Her dream changed. She was describing her lover to the women of Jerusalem. He was tall, dark, and rugged. They asked her where he had gone. She answered that he had "gone down to his garden, . . . to pasture his flock in the gardens, and to gather lilies" (6:2). The "garden" probably was an exaggerated description of the open pasture lands (5:9–6:3).

The Groom Describes the Bride (Song 6:4–10). Using many of the same terms found in 4:1–7, the groom described the bride. Of all his wives, she was the only perfect one. Even the other wives in the harem praised her beauty.

An Invitation to Dance (Song 6:11–7:9). She visited the garden where the fruit and nut trees blossomed. The next thing she knew, she was in her lover's chariot (6:11–12). Then she was invited to dance (6:13). Her dance evoked the poetry in the soul of her lover as once again he tried to describe her charms (7:1–9).

The Bride Invites the Groom to a Garden Meeting (Song 7:10–13). The bride invites the groom into the garden, where she will give herself to him. There grew the mandrake, a fruit believed to promote fertility (see Gen. 30:14–15).

A Poem in Anticipation of the Wedding (Song 8:1–4). This poem reflected the protected status of women. Strange men were not permitted to have any dealings with them. The bride-to-be wished that her lover was like a brother. Then he would have access to her in her tent as a member of the family.

Please Be Faithful to Me (Song 8:5–12). Here are some of the Song's most famous lines as she pleads for him to be faithful to her:

Set me as a seal upon your heart,
as a seal upon your arm;
for love is as strong as death,
passion fierce as the grave.
Its flashes are flashes of fire,
a raging flame.
Many waters cannot quench love,
neither can floods drown it.
If one offered for love
all the wealth of his house,
it would be utterly scorned. (8:6–7)

A Final Call (Song 8:13–14). The lovers call to each other as the book ends.

The Book of Psalms

No other book in the Old Testament is better known than Psalms, because no other Old Testament book mirrors human emotions better than Psalms. There are **psalms** for times of meditation, psalms for times of despair, psalms for times of worship, and psalms for times of joy. Unlike other Old Testament literature—that described what had happened to Israel, that contained messages to Israel from the LORD through the prophets, or that was the distilled wisdom of society—the psalms were Israel's expression of feelings to God. They were primarily messages *to* God, not messages *from* God. As a result, they run the gamut of human emotions.

WHO WROTE THE PSALMS, AND WHEN WERE THEY WRITTEN? There are no simple answers to these questions. David, called the *Psalmist* in Jewish and Christian traditions, undoubtedly wrote some of the psalms. But even the book itself—if the introductory comments found in some of the psalms are to be taken literally—indicates that David did not write all the psalms. Many names are attached to the psalms by the earliest commentators on psalms—those men who attached titles to individual psalms many years after they were written. Thus, the names of Asaph (Ps. 73–83), the sons of Korah (84, 85, 87), Heman the Ezrahite (88), Ethan the Ezrahite (89), and Moses (90) were attached to the psalms.[15] Many psalms have no one's name attached to them.

In reality, the book of Psalms was more like a modern church hymnal in that it was a collection of songs that came into existence over a long span of time. A church hymnal today may have hymns whose words date back to the early Christian centuries, while at the same time having hymns that were written especially for that edition of the hymnal. In the Psalms, for example,

The Literary Structure of Psalms

The tendency within both academic and general reading of the Psalms has been to look at them as individual poems. During the past couple of centuries, scholars have assigned individual psalms to categories, such as lament or hymn. They have then attempted to link each psalm with an original setting for its composition and performance. General readers have selected favorite psalms to use as a part of their prayer and their devotional lives. What both of these approaches have neglected is that Psalms is a book. Taking this idea seriously raises some important questions. Does the book of Psalms have an overall design? Does it do anything as a book beyond what the individual poems do? Perhaps more practically, when I read Psalm 22, should it matter that it sits between Psalms 21 and 23, or would Psalm 22 mean the same thing if it happened to be Psalm 100?

The book of Psalms is organized into five books. These books are marked off by the doxologies that appear at the ends of Psalms 41, 72, 89, and 106. This has led some readers to look for some parallel to the Torah. Although there appears to be no sense of detailed correspondence between the two, a common idea has emerged that the book of Psalms does reflect Israel's story. Book I (1–41) and Book II (42–72) focus on David and the great royal traditions of the Davidic dynasty. This section ends with the grand Psalm 72, whose title associates it with Solomon. It may be more appropriate to say that from a literary perspective it is Solomon's voice that speaks in Psalm 72 and brings the golden age of Israel to a close. Book III (73–89) appears to reflect the Exile. It begins with a psalm that contemplates the prosperity of the wicked and ends with one that laments inconsolably the collapse of Israel's monarchy. The end of the human monarchy is emphasized further by a sequence of psalms (93, 95–97, 99), which emphasize the phrase "YHWH is King." Book IV (90–106) and Book V (107–150) exemplify Israel's praise and worship of God and seem to be particularly associated with the Second Temple period. Toward the end of the book, the sequence of Songs of Ascents in 120–134 carries the reader up to Jerusalem. The "Hallelujah" Psalms become more frequent, building to a crescendo of praise in 146–150.

The overall movement of the book of Psalms seems to be from a concentration on lament psalms, which are most common in Books I and II, to hymns of praise, which are most prevalent in Books IV and V. Individual poems and small groups of poems, especially those found at the beginning and end of the five books, play a role in developing the overall plot of the book of Psalms.[14]

Psalm 29 was "a Yahwistic adaptation of an older Canaanite hymn to the storm god Baal"[16]—that is, the Israelites liked the hymn so much that they removed Baal's name and inserted the personal name of the God of Israel. Psalm 29 in its original form went back to at least the fourteenth century B.C.E. Similar adjustments are made in songs today when words to popular tunes are changed to give them a religious meaning. On the other hand, psalms such as Psalm 137 reflect an Exilic background, and some psalms probably even came from the post-Exilic period.

Within the book of Psalms, there is other evidence that the psalms come from different periods in Israel's history. The book, for example, had five divisions, corresponding to the five books of the Torah, or Law (1–41, 42–72, 73–89, 90–106, and 107–150). Each of the divisions has its own benediction. Psalm 1 serves as an introduction to the whole book and Psalm 150 serves as the benediction for the whole book. Book II (42–72) ends with the statement that "the prayers of David, the son of Jesse, are ended" (72:20). There are some psalms in other sections that are titled "a psalm of David," but it is generally agreed that most of the psalms that might have come from David are in Chapters 1–72 and most likely in Chapters 1–41.

The title "a psalm of David," furthermore, does not necessarily mean Davidic authorship. The Hebrew language allows it to be translated as "in the style of David," or "to David"—that is, "dedicated to David." These and similar titles indicate that there were several smaller sections of psalms before the final edition that we know as the book of Psalms.

Other evidence of such collections is duplications in the book of Psalms, the most notable of these being Psalms 14 and 53. They are identical for all practical purposes, except for their references to God. Psalm 14 refers to God as *Yahweh* (the LORD), while Psalm 53 uses *Elohim* (God). This must have been a popular psalm that was known in different parts of the country. Because the psalms were collected at local worship centers (shrines), this psalm got into two different collections. When the book was put together, the two collections were merged, ignoring the fact that they contained duplicate psalms. To conclude, David is called the Psalmist, but the psalms actually came from different periods of Israelite history. Before the present book of Psalms, there were a number of smaller collections. Sometime in the post-Exilic period, these were merged into the larger collection we call the book of Psalms.

THE STUDY OF PSALMS. Studies of the book of Psalms have changed much in the past seventy-five years. Archaeological discoveries, especially of Canaanite materials, have opened up new avenues of study. Whereas seventy-five years ago the tendency was to date the psalms late in Israelite history, now the trend is for a much earlier dating. Many words and phrases in the poems that once were obscure now have been clarified by the discoveries at Ugarit. It has become common in the study of the biblical psalms to look for these parallel words and ideas.

The most influential work in the recent study of the book of Psalms was that of Hermann Gunkel, a German scholar of the Old Testament. Before Gunkel's time, each psalm was studied individually. Scholars tried to discover its historical setting by connecting it to some person or event in Israelite history. Because the book of Psalms contains few historical references, scholars based their interpretations more on guesswork than on evidence. Gunkel, however, developed an important new methodological approach. He concluded that the psalms had to be looked at in the light of their association with Israelite worship services. By looking at the literary form of the individual psalms, he discovered that they could be separated into types. He concluded that there were five major types into which more than two-thirds of the psalms would fit. There were five other subtypes that would accommodate the rest of the psalms. Gunkel said that each psalm had a specific setting in life—that is, it was used in a particular form of worship service. Thus, when a person who had been ill and had recovered wanted to offer a sacrifice to show gratitude, he did not compose a psalm. There were already psalms for that purpose. Or, when a psalm such as a hymn was composed, it followed a rather fixed pattern, so all hymns shared certain basic characteristics.

Although there have been modifications of Gunkel's classifications, they still are accepted today as the basis for most modern studies of the psalms. For that reason—and because the length of the book of Psalms makes a comment on every psalm somewhat difficult—selected psalms following Gunkel's classes will be studied as examples of all the psalms.[17]

Hymns of Praise. The key word for the hymns was **Hallelujah**, which means "praise the LORD." It is one of the few Hebrew words that, when transliterated, comes into English virtually unchanged. **Hymns of Praise** usually had three basic parts: (1) a call to praise God, (2) the reason for praising God, and (3) a renewed call to praise God. Other than individual laments, the hymn of praise was the largest of Gunkel's classes.[18]

There were two subclasses of the hymn: Songs of Zion (46, 48, 76, 87), which were hymns praising Jerusalem; and Enthronement Psalms (47, 93, 97, 87), which were used in connection with the crowning of the king. This latter group was called *New Year's Psalms* by Sigmund Mowinckel, a Scandinavian scholar. Mowinckel argued that the Hebrews, in pre-Exilic times, had a New Year's festival in which the king portrayed the role of God in Creation. Psalms 47, 93, 95, 96, 97, 98, 99, and 100 were used, according to Mowinckel, as part of such a festival because they contain the phrase "the LORD reigns" (47:7).[19]

Communal Laments. These were prayers of petition to God to bring deliverance to the community in times of such disasters as war, famine, or epidemic. The **laments** usually contained (1) a cry to God for help, (2) a description of the situation that brought on the appeal, (3) a prayer for deliverance, and (4) sometimes an oracle from a prophet or an expression of confidence that the LORD would answer. Not all these elements were always present, nor did they necessarily follow the same order.[20]

Individual Laments. The laments of the individual had the same basic form as communal laments. They were used in services in which individuals asked God to deliver them from personal disaster. This was the largest class.[21]

Because laments contained an expression of confidence that the LORD would answer the plea of the sufferer, a subclass of the individual lament was the Psalms of Confidence. Psalms 4, 11, 16, 23, 27:1–6, 62, and 131 made up this subclass.

Individual Songs of Thanksgiving. These hymns were used by an individual to praise the LORD for deliverance from trouble. They had (1) an introduction; (2) a narration that told of his trouble, his cry to God, and his deliverance; (3) an acknowledgment of his deliverance; and (4) an announcement of an offering of thanks.[22]

The Royal Psalms. These psalms were used for special occasions in the religious services for the king. No major activity could be carried out by the king without the proper religious ceremony. Later, when Israel had no king, these psalms began to be interpreted as applying to God's anointed king of the future, the Messiah.[23]

The Other Psalms. Not all psalms could be fitted into the five major classes. There were five other classes: (1) Songs of Pilgrimage (84, 122); (2) Community Songs of Thanksgiving (67, 124); (3) Wisdom Poetry (1, 37, 49, 73, 112, 127, 128); (4) two types of liturgies—Torah Liturgies (15, 24, 121, 134) and Prophetic Liturgies (12, 14, 50, 53, 75, 81, 82, 85, 91, 95, 132); and (5) Mixed Poems, the largest group outside the major classes. These psalms often combined characteristics of the major classes (9–10, 36, 40, 77, 78, 89, 90, 94, 107, 108, 119, 123, 129, 137, 144).

A LOOK AT SELECTED PSALMS. Because of space limitations, only representative psalms from each category will be studied.

Psalm 1 (a Wisdom Psalm). This psalm seems to have been written to introduce the book of Psalms. Its theme is "the two ways." The psalm tells what the righteous man is (1:1), what he does (1:2), and what he is like (1:3). In contrast, the wicked are like wheat husks that can be blown away by the wind (1:4). They cannot endure the judgment (1:5), for

> the LORD watches over the way of the righteous,
>   but the way of the wicked will perish. (1:6)

Psalm 8 (a Hymn on the Glory of the LORD and the Dignity of Humanity). Although not opening with a call to praise as was typical of the hymns, Psalm 8 does open with praise to the LORD (8:1). The greatness of the LORD's presence can be seen in the heavenly bodies (8:2–3). They make the psalmist consider humankind, whom the LORD had made as the crown of Creation. Humankind had been given dominion or authority over all other creatures—whether the land animals, the birds of the air, or the sea creatures (8:4–8). The psalm closes with a repeat of the psalmist's praise of the LORD.

Psalm 117 (a Short Hymn). The shortest psalm is a classic example of a hymn. The call to praise begins with "Hallelujah," literally "praise to Yah(weh)." Verse 2 gives the reason for praising the LORD:

> For great is his steadfast love toward us;
> and the faithfulness of the LORD endures forever.

The renewed call to praise, "Hallelujah," ends the psalm.

Psalm 74 (a Communal Lament). The condition that gave rise to this psalm was an attack on the Temple. As a lament, it begins with a complaint to God. God had cast off His people. The congregation of Israel had been forgotten, because the Temple, God's dwelling place in Zion, was destroyed (74:1–3).

The psalmist described how the enemy destroyed the Temple woodwork and burned the Temple. There was no prophet to give a word from the LORD (74:4–9). He asked how long Israel had to endure the scoffing of the enemy (74:10–11).

It was not a lack of ability that had caused God not to deliver Israel from the enemy. God had created the heavens and the earth, had defeated the great sea monster Leviathan, had set the heavenly bodies in place, and had established the seasons (74:12–17).

God's honor needed to be defended:

> Rise up, O God, plead your cause;
> remember how the impious scoff at you all day long.
> Do not forget the clamor of your foes,
> the uproar of your adversaries that goes up continually. (74:22–23)

When God punished His foes for their scoffing, Israel's enemies would be destroyed. Thus, two needs could be met by one activity.

Psalm 22 (an Individual Lament). The largest class of the psalms was the individual lament. The opening words of this lament are familiar to Christians because, according to Matthew and Mark, they were quoted by Jesus on the cross (Matt. 27:46; Mark 15:34). The opening cry (22:1–2) is that God had forsaken the sufferer. Instead of an account of his own condition, the psalmist recalled God's activity on behalf of the fathers (22:3–5). He had a low opinion of himself, for he said, "I am a worm, and not human." Men mocked and scorned him. They also scoffed at God for not delivering him (22:6–8).

He recalled that he had depended on God from birth. For this reason, he still called on God. His enemies were like raging bulls. He was weak from illness, his strength was all gone, his mouth felt dry, and death seemed near. This encouraged his enemies to encircle him like a pack of vicious dogs, ready to snap and bite him, exposing his bones (22:9–18).

From the depths of despair, he moved upward toward assurance that God would hear him. He repeated his cry for help (22:19–21) and promised that he would praise God to his brethren. He exhorted those near him to stand in awe of the LORD. The LORD would hear the cry of the afflicted.

Addressing God again, he pledged to praise Him in the assembly (22:25–26). The remainder of the psalm was an expression of confidence in God. This type of ending, although not present in all laments, frequently did appear (22:27–31).

Psalm 23 (a Psalm of Confidence). The Psalms of Confidence grew out of the individual laments. This, the most famous of the psalms, is often referred to as the *Shepherd Psalm*. The figure of the shepherd does introduce the psalm, but there are two other figures in the psalm—the guide and the host.

The psalmist thought of the LORD as a shepherd to lead his flock to the best pastures, where there was tender grass and plenty of water (23:1–3a). The LORD was like a guide who led the traveler through the deep, dark ravines so common in the Palestinian hill country. There lurked thieves and wild animals ready to pounce on the unsuspecting traveler. The guide carried both a heavy stick and a weighted club to defend the one he was guiding. The traveler could proceed with assurance that the guide would protect him (23:3b–4).

The LORD was like a Bedouin sheik who took in a man fleeing from his enemies. The law of hospitality in the Near East, especially among the nomadic and seminomadic groups, was to take in a stranger, give him the best food, and protect him at the cost of the host's own life, if necessary.[24] The practice of anointing the guest's head with oil was an act of hospitality, as was the filling of the cup to overflowing. As the servants of the host would serve the stranger, so goodness and mercy followed the one blessed by the LORD throughout his days (23:5–6).

Psalm 51 (an Individual Lament). This is perhaps the most famous of the individual laments. Early Jewish interpreters connected it with David's seduction of Bathsheba and the child born from that act. Its appeal, however, like that of the psalms in general, is that it mirrors the inner conflict of any moral person who has committed a grievous sin of immorality. It contains a varied vocabulary to describe sin and repentance.

Verses 1 and 2 contain a plea for forgiveness based on God's "mercy," "steadfast love," and "abundant mercy." Sin was described in a threefold manner as "transgression" (or rebellion), "sin" (which basically means failing to come up to the accepted standard), and "iniquity" (meaning moral distortion). God's forgiveness also was described as a threefold action: blotting out or erasing; washing thoroughly; and cleansing in a ceremonial sense (52:1–2).

The psalmist had a deep sense of guilt. He felt that he had sinned against God and that the troubles he had been enduring were just punishment for his failures (51:3–5). He asked God to teach him wisdom. The cleansing he desired was both outward cleansing in a ceremonial act and inward cleansing through repentance and forgiveness. He wanted a sense of inner joy. This could only come with the assurance of sins forgiven (51:6–9).

He pleaded with God to create a clean heart within him, for God to keep him in His presence, and for God to restore him to the joy of the salvation that was God's (51:10–12). If these things were done, he promised to proclaim God's ways to sinners (51:13–14). Unlike other psalms in which animal sacrifices were offered, this one speaks of "a broken and a contrite heart" as the sacrifice most acceptable to God (51:15–17). A later addition by a priestly hand tried to bring it back to priestly orthodoxy by mentioning "burnt offerings and whole burnt offerings" (51:18–19).

Psalm 32 (an Individual Song of Thanksgiving). This psalm, like others of its class, was used in a service to offer thanks to the LORD when one had recovered from a serious illness. After speaking about the blessedness of being forgiven for his sins, the psalmist described how his sense of guilt made him physically ill, so that his "strength was dried up like the heat of summer" (32:3–4). But he had confessed his sins, and his happiness was restored (32:5). He would recommend that the godly pray to the LORD.

An oracle, probably spoken by a Temple prophet, interrupted the psalmist:

I will teach you and instruct you in the way you should go;
I will counsel you with my eye upon you. (32:8)

He was not to be like the horse or mule that had to be controlled with "bit and bridle" in order to obey (32:9).

The psalm closes with a call for joy because of the love that the LORD had given to those who trusted Him (32:10–11).

Psalm 116 (an Individual Song of Thanksgiving).[25] This psalm, more clearly than most, gives directions for worship. The individual had been healed of a devastating illness. He came to the Temple to make a sacrifice of thanksgiving. The service opened with an address to the other worshipers in which he described what had happened to him (116:1–4). Praise to the LORD followed because the LORD had delivered him from almost certain death (116:5–11).

Next, the offerings were made. They were introduced by the question, "What shall I return to the LORD for all His bounty to me?" Then followed the drink offering. The cup containing the wine was lifted to the LORD while he recited his vows and commitment (116:12–16). Then the animal sacrifice was made with the proper comments (116:17–19). The service ended with the shout, "Hallelujah!"

Psalm 45 (a Royal Psalm). This was a psalm for a royal wedding. It was sung by the court minstrel to celebrate the happy event that was about to take place. First, the singer addressed the king, using exaggerated language to describe him. In verses 6 and 7, especially, there appears the kind of language that led later interpreters to see this as a messianic psalm, particularly in those days when Israel had no king. The king was told that his "divine throne" would "endure forever and ever" (45:1–9).

Next, the queen-to-be was addressed. She was told how fortunate she was to be marrying the king of Israel. She was to forget her people and submit to the king as her lord (45:10–12). As though he were the writer of the bridal column in the Jerusalem *Gazette,* the psalmist described the queen's bridal attire as she was led by her escort to the wedding chamber (45:12–15).

The psalm ended with a forecast that the king would be succeeded by sons more famous than their forefathers. Because of the illustrious sons born to him and his queen, the king's name would be remembered for many generations (45:16–17).

Psalm 139 (an Individual Lament). This great psalm reflects a more developed theology than some of the earlier poems. It falls into four stanzas of six verses each. The first stanza speaks of God's knowledge of the psalmist's everyday activities and thoughts. The psalmist was awed by the intimate knowledge of him that the LORD possessed (139:1–6).

In the second stanza, he spoke of God's all-pervading presence in the universe. No matter where he might go in the future, God would be there, even in the grave. This was a new idea (139:7–12).

In the third stanza, he spoke of God's knowledge of him before he was even born. God had seen his creation in the womb. God knew what he would be before he existed. The thoughts of God were beyond his comprehension (139:13–18).

In the fourth stanza (139:19–24), he turned to his enemies, who were also God's enemies. Because he was powerless to overcome them, he called on God, who had the power to do so. Then the idea struck him that his thoughts might not be appropriate. He closed with a plea:

> Search me, O God, and know my heart;
> test me, and know my thoughts.
> See if there is any wicked way in me,
> and lead me in the way everlasting. (139:23–24)

Special Groups of Psalms. There are a number of psalm groupings and special psalms that need to be mentioned. One such group is Psalms 113–118. These psalms are still used today in the celebration of the Jewish feast of Passover. They are known as the *Egyptian Hallel.* Another such special group is Psalms 120–134. Each psalm in the group bears the title, *A Song of Ascents.* They were used in the great pilgrimage festivals. As devout Jews went up to Jerusalem, they sang these Songs of Ascents as they moved toward the Holy City.

Although they are not distinct groups, certain psalms have unique characteristics. Among these are the acrostics, the most famous of which is Psalm 119. It contains twenty-two sections or stanzas, each consisting of eight verses. All eight verses in a stanza begin with the same Hebrew letter, and all twenty-two stanzas begin with a different letter of the Hebrew alphabet in alphabetical order. Certain psalms were antiphonal. They were written so that a leader spoke lines that told a story while a choir or the people answered with a refrain. Thus, in Psalm 136, the speaker told the story of the Exodus while the congregation or choir responded with the refrain "For His steadfast love endures forever." When the refrain is removed, the words of the leader tell the story.

The Vengeance Psalms. One of the major problems that face interpreters of the psalms are those psalms that express violent hatred of the nation or of the psalmist, which are also called **imprecatory psalms.** Psalm 137 is an example of such attitudes. After lamenting the conditions that the exiles had to endure, the psalm turns to a violent denunciation of the Babylonians. It ends with the bitter words

> O daughter Babylon, you devastator!
> Happy shall they be who pay you back for what you have done to us!
> Happy shall they be who take your little ones
> and dash them against the rock! (137:8–9)

One must admit that this attitude was a far cry from that expressed by a great teacher of a later time who said, "Let the children come to me and do not hinder them, for to such belongs the kingdom of heaven" (Matt. 19:14). How does one deal with these psalms, and what value, if any, do they have? Certain things must be understood before these questions can be answered. In the background are certain ideas:

1. These psalms are grounded in ideas from the practice of blood vengeance. Blood vengeance was justice in its most primitive form. It arose at a time when there was no state to see that justice was done. Because of this lack of a neutral party to administer justice, the family or clan had that responsibility. The more specific responsibility fell upon the nearest kin of the person who had been wronged. Thus, if A^1 killed B^1, then A^1 could expect B^2 to try to avenge B^1. This avenger (or *redeemer*, as he was called) was judge, jury, and executioner. For example, see Gideon's revenge for the death of his brothers in Judges 8.
2. Closely allied with these ideas was the idea of corporate personality. The individual was so bound up with the group that whatever affected the individual affected the group.
3. The concept of covenant was also at work in these psalms. The LORD and Israel were bound together by a covenant. In that covenant relationship, the LORD became a part of Israel's "family," so to speak.
4. These psalms resound with belief in the justice of God. And the fact that justice had to come in this life led to the plea for God to destroy the enemy.

With these ideas in mind, the vengeance psalms reflect a condition in which Israel (or an individual) had been devastated by an enemy. There was no avenger who had survived the devastation or who had strength enough to see that justice was done. God, as Israel's covenant partner, was the only one left who could do this. Thus, basically, these rather brutal-sounding psalms really came from a people so brutalized that God was their only hope. So, in their primitive way, they cry for justice, just as oppressed groups still do today.

SUMMARY OF THE PSALMS. The psalms were the hymns of a people. They represent individual and group worship. For the most part, they reflect the kind of orthodox theology that the book of Proverbs and the friends of Job reflect: (1) God is just. (2) This life is all there is of real life. (3) Because God is just, the good will prosper and the wicked will suffer. Despite their simple view of life, the Psalms continue to speak to every generation, because they mirror the full range of human emotion.

Key Terms

Hallelujah, *326*
Hymns of Praise, *326*
Imprecatory Psalms, *331*
Lady Wisdom, *306*
Lament, *327*
Parallelism, *306*
Proverbs, *305*
Psalms, *324*
Qoheleth, *312*
Retribution Theology, *309*
Satan, *310*
Theodicy, *308*
Vanity, *317*
Wisdom, *301*

Study Questions

1. How was Israelite wisdom related to the wisdom of other countries?
2. How did the Egyptian "Instruction of Amenemopet" influence the Israelite book of Proverbs?
3. What was the primary theme of the book of Proverbs?
4. How do Proverbs 1–9 and 10–31 differ?
5. What does Proverbs 31:10–31 tell us about the status of women in ancient Israel?
6. What is the evidence that the book of Job is the work of more than one author?
7. What are some of the common assumptions and beliefs that form the background of the book of Job?
8. What is the role of Satan in Job 1 and 2?
9. How does Job in Chapters 1 and 2 differ from Job in 3:1–42:6?
10. Who are Job's friends, and what are their basic arguments to Job?
11. What are Job's arguments to his friends? To God?
12. What do the Elihu speeches add to the book?
13. Describe the form and content of God's response to Job.
14. What conclusion does Job reach about his suffering?
15. Why is Ecclesiastes called *skeptical wisdom*?
16. What sort of philosophy of life does Ecclesiastes advocate?
17. What does Ecclesiastes tell us about the theological views of at least some Jews in post-Exilic times?
18. What might have been the purpose of the Song of Songs?
19. How has the Song of Songs most often been interpreted, and why?
20. Who are the characters in the Song of Songs?
21. What difference in the nature of the psalms helps to explain some of the attitudes they express?
22. What evidence suggests that the book of Psalms is a collection of songs produced over a long period of time?
23. How is the book of Psalms arranged, and how might it function as a book rather than just as a collection of individual poems?
24. What might the expression *psalm of David* mean?
25. What did Hermann Gunkel contribute to our understanding of the book of Psalms?
26. What are Gunkel's five major classes of psalms?
27. What might the nature of some of the psalms indicate about Israelite worship practices?
28. What underlying factors might help us to understand the ideas expressed in the vengeance psalms?
29. What are the various ways readers might understand the designation *Qoheleth*?

Endnotes

1. For an excellent short introduction to wisdom literature, see Roland E. Murphy, "Wisdom Literature and Psalms," in *Interpreting Biblical Texts* (Nashville: Abingdon Press, 1983), 13–25. For a longer introduction, see James L. Crenshaw, *Old Testament Wisdom: An Introduction,* rev. and enl. (Louisville, KY: Westminster–John Knox Press, 1998).
2. Pritchard, *ANE,* 237–243.
3. An excellent work that thoroughly examines the development of schools both in Israel and in the rest of the Near East is James L. Crenshaw, *Education in Ancient Israel: Across the Deadening Silence* (New York: Doubleday, 1998). For a discussion of the law as "moral education," see Joseph Blenkinsopp, "Sage, Priest, and Prophet," in *Library of Ancient Israel* (Louisville, KY: Westminster–John Knox Press, 1995), 38ff.
4. For a superb introduction to and commentary on the first large section of the book of Proverbs, see Michael V. Fox, *Proverbs 1–9: A New Translation with Introduction and Commentary* (Garden City, NY: Doubleday, 2000). See particularly his description of the structure of this section as "ten lectures" (45–50).
5. See the discussion of this issue in James Crenshaw, *Education in Ancient Israel: Across the Deadening Silence* (New York: Doubleday, 1998).
6. See Roland E. Murphy, *Wisdom Literature: Job, Proverbs, Ruth, Canticles, Ecclesiastes and Esther* (Grand Rapids, MI: Wm. C. Eerdman, 1981), 50.
7. R. B. Y. Scott, *The Way of Wisdom* (New York: Macmillan, 1977), 24, suggests that this section was developed by an Egyptian-trained Hebrew scribe who copied what he remembered of "The Instruction of Amen-em-opet" and then supplemented it with other sayings to fill out the total of thirty.
8. Samuel Terrien, "The Book of Job: Introduction and Exegesis," *IB,* III, 877–902, is a comprehensive introduction to the book of Job.
9. John H. Tullock, *Blood Vengeance among the Israelites* (Ann Arbor, MI: University Microfilms, 1966), 141ff.
10. See Genesis 4:10; Ezekiel 24:7.
11. I am indebted to the late J. Philip Hyatt of Vanderbilt University for this phrase.
12. David Noel Freedman, "Is It Possible to Understand the Book of Job?" *BR,* IV, 2 (April 1988), 29.
13. This discussion is indebted to an unpublished paper by Loren F. Bliese, "Literary Structure and Theology in the Song of Songs."
14. For a more detailed development of this kind of idea, see Nancy L. deClaisse-Walford, *Reading from the Beginning: The Shaping of the Hebrew Psalter* (Macon, GA: Mercer University Press, 1997).
15. The sons of Korah and Asaph were professional singing guilds connected with the Temple (1 Chron. 25).
16. Mitchell Dahood, *Psalms I: Introduction, Translation, and Notes* (Garden City, NY: Doubleday, 1966), 175.
17. Gunkel's original work is now available in English translation. See Hermann Gunkel, *Introduction to Psalms: The Genres of the Religious Lyric of Israel,* trans. James D. Nogalski (Macon, GA: Mercer University Press, 1998). See especially his opening essay, "The Genres of the Psalms" (1–22).
18. It included Psalms 8, 19, 33, 65, 68, 96, 98, 100, 103, 104, 105, 111, 113, 114, 115, 117, 135, 136, and 145–150.
19. See Sigmund Mowinckel, *The Psalms in Israel's Worship,* 2 vols., trans. D. R. Ap-Thomas (Nashville: Abingdon Press, 1967), esp. ch. 3.
20. Among the communal laments are Psalms 44, 48, 60, 74, 79, 80, 83, 106, and 125.
21. It included Psalms 3, 5, 6, 7, 13, 17, 22, 25, 26, 27:7–14, 28, 31, 35, 38, 39, 42–43, 51, 52, 54, 55, 56, 57, 61, 63, 64, 69, 70, 71, 86, 88, 102, 109, 120, 130, 139, 140, 141, 142, and 143.
22. Psalm 18 (a Royal Psalm as well), 30, 32, 41, 66, 92, 116, and 138.
23. They include Psalms 2, 18, 20, 21, 45, 72, 101, 110, and 132.
24. See the story of Abraham and the two men (Gen. 18:1–33). Also see the story of Lot's attempt to protect the same men (Gen. 19:1–11).
25. The idea for what follows in the discussion of this psalm came from H. J. Flanders, R. W. Crapps, and D. A. Smith, *The People of the Covenant: An Introduction to the Old Testament,* 3rd ed. (New York: Oxford, 1988), 412f.

CHAPTER

14

The Time of Silence

Judah in Eclipse

Timeline

521 B.C.E.	Beginning of reign of Darius I in Persia
465 B.C.E.	Beginning of the reign of Artaxerxes I
332 B.C.E.	Alexander conquers most of the known world, including Palestine, and the Persian Empire comes to an end
323 B.C.E.	Alexander dies and Palestine comes under the control of Ptolemy and his descendants
198 B.C.E.	Antiochus III takes control of Palestine away from Ptolemy V
175 B.C.E.	Antiochus IV continues the Seleucid rule of Palestine
168 B.C.E.	Beginning of the Maccabean Revolt
63 B.C.E.	Roman Emperor Pompey conquers Jerusalem

Chapter Outline

I. The Historical Situation

II. The Festival Scrolls

III. The Maccabean Revolt

IV. Geographical and Canonical Boundaries and the Book of Daniel

CHAPTER SUMMARY

When we departed from the story line of Judah at the end of Chapter 9, it was a province on the eastern edge of the Persian Empire in the middle of the fifth century B.C.E. When the book of Nehemiah comes to an end, there are no internal sources for the continuation of this story. The chain of empires that ruled over Judah continued through the rise and fall of the Persian Empire and on to Greek rule over Palestine, which began with Alexander the Great and would prove to be the most influential in cultural terms. The historical records left behind by the Persian and Greek Empires offer evidence of only a general sense of the context within which Judah continued to develop. The emergence of new cultural forms and institutions in the second century B.C.E. allows only calculated guesses about what happened in this intervening period. Although events in Judah were important, most Jews at this time lived outside of Palestine, and "Diaspora" Judaism began to develop its own sense of identity. Many, if not most, of the biblical books went through their final stages of editing in this period, and may offer some indirect clues, but perhaps the most distinctive literary development was the emergence of stories about young people making their way in foreign contexts, such as Ruth, Esther, and Daniel. How to adjust to this way of being a people would prove to be a source of both great struggle and creativity.

THE HISTORICAL SITUATION

The Greek writer **Herodotus** is often given the title "The Father of History," and this title might be understood in two ways. His massive work that he wrote during the middle to late fifth century is often called "The Histories." This work provides a presentation of approximately the first century of the Persian Empire, through the middle of the reign of Xerxes I. Herodotus was Greek, so his reporting on the Persian Empire is immediately suspect, and there are many reasons why his work would not come close to meeting the standards of modern history writing. He was probably no more or less a historian than the writers of the biblical books of Samuel and Kings. This should not be understood as a failure on his part. His reasons for writing, like those of the writers of Samuel and Kings, were different from the reasons that modern historians write. So, the notion of the writings of Herodotus as the first history and Herodotus as its "father" is a misunderstanding. On the other hand, the idea of using sources to produce a narrative of a long period of time, reasonably comprehensive in scope and depth, was a bold and creative idea. Other writers in his time and earlier may have done similar work that was simply ignored or lost. In this second sense, then, Herodotus is an important ancestor of those who consider themselves historians today. Of course, Herodotus is fortunate that his work was preserved, even if in somewhat edited form.

Much of what we think we know about the Near East in the fifth century must be derived from Herodotus' writings, and it is probably correct to think about much of the fifth and fourth centuries as a slow collision between Persia in the east and the developing Greek nation and empire in the west. The beginnings of this conflict have been recently popularized in the film *300*, which is a heavily embellished retelling of the battle of Thermopylae in 480 B.C.E. These two powers would push back and forth against each other for more than another century, and Palestine would always be an important crossroad in struggles between eastern and western powers. Things happened in Palestine between 400 and 200 B.C.E., but our knowledge has to be based largely on inferences from what we know about the general context and from what we know about Jewish life when it emerged from the shadows in the second century B.C.E.

Persia's Last Days

The Persian Empire continued to control Palestine for the all of the fifth century and the first half of the fourth. Persia was not without its troubles, however. From the time of Nehemiah on, Persia faced constant problems—first from an Egyptian revolt, then from the Greeks, and finally from the rulers of the western part of the empire. Nevertheless, the four great Kings of Persia—Darius I, Xerxes I, Artaxerxes I, and Artaxerxes II—reigned for a collective 140 years, and their empire would provide an important context for the development of the Bible and some of the stories within it.

The greatest difficulty came for Persia, however, during the reign of Darius III (Condomannus) (336–331 B.C.E.), when Philip of Macedon (359–336 B.C.E.) rose to power, and Macedonia gained control of the Greek states in 338 B.C.E. When Philip was assassinated in 336 B.C.E., that tragedy was not to Persia's advantage because it put Alexander, his son, on the throne of Macedonia.[1]

The Campaigns of Alexander the Great

The young **Alexander** (356–323 B.C.E.) was a military genius. In 334 B.C.E., he invaded Asia Minor and quickly gained control of the entire area. At the battle of Issus (333 B.C.E.), he routed the main Persian army, even capturing Darius' wife and family. Moving down the Mediterranean coast, he quickly captured Phoenicia, except for Tyre and Palestine. He was well received by the Egyptians in 332 B.C.E., and from there he moved eastward until he reached the Indus River. In his wake, he left centers of Greek learning and culture, as he required his older soldiers to retire and live in the conquered lands. Because of the influence of Greek culture, over a period of several hundred years, the effects of Alexander's action changed the course of civilization. The province of Judah was caught up in this wave of cultural influence and would be permanently altered by it. The most significant artifact of this influence is the translation of the Hebrew Scriptures commonly known as the Septuagint.

Ptolemies and Seleucids in Palestine

When Alexander died in 323 B.C.E., his empire was divided among four of his generals. **Ptolemy**, Macedonian Greek and founder of the last Egyptian dynasty, was given control of Palestine, while Syria was given to Seleucus.[2] For a century, the Ptolemies dominated Palestine. During that time, Egypt gained a large Jewish population. It has been estimated that 1 million Jews lived in Alexandria in the first century B.C.E. But Egyptian domination of Palestine came under direct challenge from the Seleucids when Antiochus the Great (223–187 B.C.E.) came to the **Seleucid** throne. After a number of battles, Antiochus prevailed in the battle of Panium (Baniyas), where the later city of Caesarea Philippi (of New Testament fame) was to be located.[3]

Although Antiochus the Great was generally welcomed by the Jewish people—especially as he gave special favors to the priests and other leaders—the positive relations between Jews in Palestine and Seleucid rulers ended when Antiochus IV (Epiphanes) came to the throne in 175 B.C.E. Antiochus Epiphanes was determined that all of his subjects worship Greek gods, speak the Greek language, and follow Greek customs. He infuriated many of the Jewish people by his actions, especially when he interfered in the selection of the High Priest. He threw out Onias III, the ruling High Priest, and sold the office to Onias' brother Jason. Before long, Menelaus, a priest who did not belong to the high-priestly family, paid Antiochus a bigger sum of money, and Antiochus deposed Jason in favor of Menelaus.

The High Priest became the promoter of **Hellenization**—the adoption of Greek religion and culture. There followed a number of outrages by Antiochus against the Jewish people. Among other things, he forbade Jewish religious practices (including circumcision), set up an altar to the Greek god Zeus in the Temple, and sacrificed a hog on the altar. Those Jews who resisted him were slaughtered without mercy. When he ordered all Jews to sacrifice to Zeus, he provoked a revolt that would lead to Jewish independence for the first time in many centuries. What became known as the Maccabean Revolt will be described below, after an examination of some of the literature of the late Persian and early Greek periods.

THE FESTIVAL SCROLLS

The third section of the Hebrew canon, the Writings, contains a sequence of five small books known as the *Megillot*, or Festival Scrolls. The Masoretic tradition presents these five in the order: Ruth, Song of Songs, Ecclesiastes, Lamentations, and Esther. The three poetic books in this group were treated in earlier chapters of this book because their form and subject matter make them fit better in those discussions. The story of the book of Ruth is set in the period of the Judges, but the telling of the story seems to fit the issues and concerns of the Persian period in Palestine. The book of Esther is set in the Persian court and the multiple forms in which this book exists address the Persian and Greek periods of Israel's story. The formative period for Diaspora Judaism, the fifth to third centuries, was likely also to be the source of the idea of establishing set readings for the festivals. The inability of Diaspora Jews to make pilgrimages to Jerusalem created the need to celebrate these festivals in other ways.

The Book of Ruth

The setting for Ruth was the period of the Judges, which is probably the primary reason that the Christian tradition has placed it right after the book of Judges in all of its canons. A post-Exilic author composed a beautiful short story about Ruth, King David's great-grandmother, perhaps to confront the resistance to intermarriage expressed in other books, such as Ezra and Nehemiah. Ruth 4:7 reveals that the book was written at a time much later than its setting, when the writer must explain an obscure custom that was used "in former times."

The *Megilloth*

There is more than one festival calendar in the Bible and it seems to have taken some time before the list of festivals and the time of their celebration became fully standardized. Eventually, five major festivals were established and the five "Festival Scrolls" were assigned as synagogue readings for those dates.

Festival	Scroll
Shavuot (The Festival of Weeks, called Pentecost in Greek)	Ruth
Passover	Song of Songs
Sukkoth (The Festival of Booths)	Ecclesiastes
Ninth of *Ab*	Lamentations
Purim	Esther

An Israelite woman named Naomi had traveled with her husband, Elimelech, to live in Moab during a time of famine in Israel. The opening of this story should sound quite familiar to those aware of biblical traditions. The great ancestors of Israel often traveled into foreign territory because of famines. As an opening line to a story, "There was a famine in the land," creates many narrative possibilities, including movement, danger, and foreignness. Elimelech died in Moab, leaving Naomi with two sons, Mahlon and Chilion. Eventually, the sons married two Moabite women, Orphah and Ruth. Then the sons died, leaving the three widows with no way to preserve and continue their family line.

Naomi decided to return to Israel to live among her own people. The daughters-in-law were determined to go with her, but she tried to persuade them to return to their own people. Orphah did so, but Ruth insisted on going with Naomi:

> Do not press me to leave you
>   or turn back from following you!
> Where you go, I will go;
>   Where you lodge, I will lodge;
> your people shall be my people,
>   and your God, my God. (1:16)

These words, often used as a bride's vow to her husband in a wedding ceremony, were addressed to a mother-in-law in the book of Ruth (1:6–18).

At the time of the barley harvest, the women arrived in Bethlehem, where Naomi's husband had rights to ancestral property. As a widow, Naomi had no rights to the property, because in reality she was part of the property rather than owner of it. Whoever got the property had to assume responsibility for Naomi and Ruth (1:19–22). Elimelech's property was to go to his nearest male relative. Boaz, a wealthy landowner in Bethlehem, was a relative of Elimelech, but there was another who was more closely related than Boaz. Naomi sent Ruth to the barley fields to glean scattered heads of grain left by the reapers for the poor, and Ruth happened to be gleaning in Boaz's field when he noticed her. When told who she was, he ordered that extra grain be scattered where she could find it. Calling her to him, Boaz told her to follow his reapers closely so that she would be safe, and he invited her to drink from the vessels of water his workers had prepared. When Ruth asked why she was so favored, she was told that it was because of her kindness to her mother-in-law, Naomi (2:1–14). After Ruth ate the midday meal with Boaz, she gathered a large amount of grain because of his generosity. When Naomi saw this and heard Ruth's report, she was pleased with what Boaz had done (2:15–23).

Naomi continued her efforts to find a new life for Ruth and for herself. She told Ruth to bathe, put on perfume, and change into her best clothes. Then she told her to go down to the threshing floor where Boaz was threshing grain. When Boaz had finished eating and had lain down to sleep, Ruth was to go up and lie at his feet, pulling his cover over her (3:1–5). Ruth did everything just as Naomi told her. When Boaz awoke to find her lying at his feet, he was surprised, and he asked Ruth's identity. Once he discovered who she was, they continued their conversation, and Ruth made a request of Boaz that may be understood as a proposal of marriage. This seems like a bold move for a young woman in a foreign place, but Boaz responded favorably. The next morning, the story reports that Boaz gave Ruth a specific amount of grain to take back to her mother-in-law, an act that looks like a signal being sent from Boaz to Naomi. Naomi and Boaz never appear together or speak to each other in the book of Ruth, but this is one of many elements in the story that make it appear that they were communicating "off the stage" (3:6–18).

The Literary Structure of Ruth

The book of Ruth is perhaps the most carefully crafted single story in the Old Testament. It begins as a family story, in the form of a genealogy, but is quickly interrupted by death. Elimelech dies, and his two sons die before they can produce heirs. The family loses the possibility of continuing its heritage. The resolution of this story will require implementation of the **levirate marriage** custom. This custom is described in a legal text in Deuteronomy 25:5–10 and is worked out in the story of Judah and Tamar in Genesis 38. The book of Ruth appears to be closely related to both of these texts. The levirate custom, which requires a man to marry his brother's widow if his brother produced no heirs before his death, is complicated in Ruth because both brothers have died.

Over the past few decades, interpreters of the book of Ruth have emphasized the role of a literary device known as a **chiasm**.[4] In a chiasm, elements from the beginning of the story match elements at the end. Likewise, elements on one side of the middle match those on the other. The second half of the structure is, therefore, a mirror image of the first half. In this way, the fourth chapter of the book of Ruth matches the first. In Ruth 1 death interrupts a genealogy, while in Ruth 4 a birth repairs and continues it. In Ruth 1 the relationship between Ruth and Naomi is negotiated, while in Ruth 4 the relationship between Ruth and Boaz is negotiated.

In the same way, Ruth 2 and Ruth 3 mirror one another. In each chapter, Naomi sends Ruth out to encounter Boaz. In Ruth 2 they meet during the day in a field. In Ruth 3 they meet at night at a threshing floor. Together, these two stories determine Ruth's sense of identity. At the end of each story, Ruth returns to Naomi with food as a sign that the meetings have gone well. Many delicate literary features enrich this structure, although some are obscured by the translation. The description of Boaz as "worthy" in 2:1 is matched by the description of Ruth as "worthy" in 3:11. The coming of Ruth under God's "wings" in 2:12 is reflected by Ruth's request to Boaz to spread his "wing" over her in 3:9. The book of Ruth is thus a love story in the middle surrounded by the story of a family struggling for continuity.

The book of Ruth connects itself to the failed story of the levirate marriage custom in Genesis 38 by referring to Tamar and her son Perez in 4:12 and by beginning the genealogy with Perez in 4:18. Along with the repair of this family and its genealogy, the book of Ruth also redeems the levirate custom, which had failed in Genesis 38, with a story of how it can function well, so well that it makes the birth of Israel's greatest king possible. The appearance of *David* as the final word in the book of Ruth places an exclamation point on the story.

There were complications, however. Boaz was not the nearest relative, so he had to get the right to inherit the property. He found the nearest relative at the town gate, where all legal transactions took place, and told him about the property. The man said he would claim the right of inheritance, but when he found that the two women went with the property, he changed his mind. Because he would have to marry Ruth, the first son born to her would be credited to her first husband and thus would have the right to inherit Ruth's first husband's property.[5] Boaz then claimed the right of inheritance, as he was next in line. He married Ruth and she gave birth to a son named Obed. The law relating to levirate marriage in Deuteronomy 25:5–10 speaks only of the responsibility of a man when his brother dies, leaving behind a childless widow. That specific resolution is not possible in the book of Ruth because no brothers are left for Ruth to marry, but the story eventually finds another way to fix the genealogy that is interrupted by death in the first chapter. The genealogy at the end of the book continues to follow the line of Obed. He became the grandfather of David, which means that Ruth was the great-grandmother of Israel's greatest king. One of the apparent points of the story was that the Jewish people could not be an exclusive group, because the great-grandmother of their greatest king was a foreigner, and not just any foreigner, but a Moabite, an ethnic group that other texts, such as Deuteronomy 23:3, specifically banned from participation in the religious life of Israel.

The Book of Esther

This book, set against the background of the Persian Kingdom in the middle of the fifth century B.C.E., presents one of the worlds of Diaspora Judaism and raises important questions about the role of the Jewish people in the world and seriously ponders their prospects for survival. God is not mentioned in the book, leaving the divine role in this struggle for survival largely up to the reader to interpret. Another purpose of the book of Esther seems to be to explain the origin of the Jewish feast of Purim.

According to the story, Ahasuerus (Xerxes I, 485–464 B.C.E.), king of Persia, had a banquet for his friends. When he asked his queen, Vashti, to appear before his guests, she refused. In retaliation, Ahasuerus deposed her as queen and set up a national search for a replacement (1:1–2:4). At this point, Esther, the heroine of the story, was introduced. She was a beautiful, young Jewish woman who had been raised by her elderly cousin, Mordecai. The book reports that Mordecai sat "in the king's gate" (2:19, 21; 5:13; 6:10), which implies that he was a government official, as the gate was the site of the government offices. This would explain how he found out about a plot against the king and why he did not have to bow to Haman, the prime minister.[6]

When the rough equivalent of a national beauty contest was conducted, Esther, who concealed her ethnic background, was chosen as the new queen. Not long afterward, Mordecai heard of a plot against the king and, through Esther, was able to warn Ahasuerus. The conspirators were punished but Mordecai was not rewarded, although his action was noted in the king's chronicles (2:5–23).

The villain of the story was Haman the Agagite, prime minister to Ahasuerus. Mordecai refused to bow to Haman when he went out the palace gate, so Haman decided to get rid of Mordecai. Because Haman hated the Jewish people, he decided to get rid of all the other Jews as well (3:1–6). Casting lots (*purim*) to determine the best time for getting rid of the Jews, Haman finally felt that the time was right to approach the king. Using persuasion and an enormous bribe, Haman convinced the king to decree that on a certain day, all Jews were to be killed. The king, of course, did not realize that these were Esther's people (3:7–15). When the decree was published, Mordecai immediately went into mourning, and when word reached Esther that Mordecai was in mourning, she sent to ask him why. Because she stayed in the king's harem, she would not have known of the decree. Mordecai sent Esther a copy of the decree, asking her to go to the king and request that he lift the death sentence against the Jewish people. She was reluctant, but she finally agreed to do so, even though it meant risking her life (4:1–17). When she went to the king, he granted her the privilege of speaking to him. She asked him to invite Haman to a dinner for the three of them, and the king granted her wish. Haman, sure that his moment of glory had arrived, rejoiced, until he happened to see Mordecai at the palace gate. He went home and ordered carpenters to build a gallows in his garden so that he could personally hang Mordecai (5:1–14).

Meanwhile, the king was having a sleepless night. While reading through the official records of his royal court, he saw the report of how Mordecai had saved his life. The next morning, when Haman arrived, he was asked what would be a proper reward for a man whom the king wanted to honor. Thinking that he was the one the king intended to honor, Haman suggested that such a man should be clad in the king's robes, put on the king's own horse, led through the streets of the capital,

The Literary Structure of Esther

Like Ruth and Jonah, the book of Esther is probably best described as a short story. Unlike those other, shorter books, Esther does not exhibit a deliberate sense of overall design involving elements like chiasm and repeated motifs. One helpful way to understand a story is to look at the way the interactions between characters are presented, and Esther offers an excellent opportunity to examine this feature.

The primary scenes in the book of Esther involve interactions between the major characters, in pairs for most of the book and in groups of three at the end. These interactions are either in the form of conflict or collusion. The book opens with the portrayal of King Ahasuerus' banquet, which ends in conflict between the king and his wife, Queen Vashti. The next two major interactions are between Esther and the king. Esther has replaced Vashti. There are minor scenes in between these major interactions, which report briefly the meetings of Esther and of Mordecai, Esther's uncle, behind the scenes, in which Mordecai engineers Esther's entry into the palace and her revealing of the plot to assassinate the king. The next sequence introduces the character named Haman, and explains his conflict with Mordecai and the resulting interaction between Haman and the king, which produces the plan to annihilate the Jewish people. In the first three chapters, the narrator has introduced the major characters and, by reporting their interactions, has provided both the major conflict of the story and the means for its resolution.

The resolution is worked out in a sequence in Chapter 4 that pushes Mordecai further into the background while still allowing him to be a driving force in the story. Mordecai and Esther interact indirectly through a go-between. The focus of the story then shifts back to Esther's interaction with the king, which surrounds the discovery of Haman's plot to hang Mordecai. In the climactic sequence, Esther reveals Haman's plot to destroy the Jews in a scene involving the king, Haman, and Esther (7:1–10). A dramatic reversal takes place. As Haman replaces Mordecai on the gallows, Mordecai replaces Haman in the presence of Esther and the king (8:1–17).

The final two chapters of the book report the aftermath of the story and point toward the future, with the establishment of the festival of Purim as a celebration of the story. In the end, the story revolves around the revelation of evil plots. The plots to assassinate the king and to destroy the Jewish people are discovered by Mordecai, told to Esther by Mordecai, and revealed to the king by Esther. The gratitude of the king produced by the revelation of the first plot makes the demise of the second plot possible. The story has made its point: Courageous and honest behavior on the part of Jews living within a foreign empire will save them from destruction and even allow them to replace their enemies in positions of honor and prosperity.

The Hebrew text of the book of Esther described here is significantly different from the Greek version preserved in the Septuagint. The Greek version contains six additional elements. Aside from adding 150 verses to the book of Esther, these additions also contribute an increased religious tone to the book. Several of these elements are dreams or prayers. One of the oddities of the Hebrew version of Esther is that it never mentions God. This appears to have hampered, somewhat, Esther's inclusion in the Jewish canon. It seems reasonable to assume that the additions in the Greek story are a response to this concern. This situation reveals that the contents of some biblical books were still being negotiated even as the canon was being formed.

Esther

Esther is presented to the readers of the book bearing her name as a beautiful, young, Jewish woman living in the Persian Empire during the post-Exilic period. In the midst of a party, the Persian king, Ahasuerus, commanded his wife, Queen Vashti, to come and parade before his male friends so that they could observe her beauty. Vashti refused, so Ahasuerus removed her from the position of queen. To replace Vashti, the Persian royal court conducted a beauty contest. Esther won this contest and was made the new queen of Persia.

Esther's uncle, Mordecai, who had adopted her when her parents died, discovered a plot within the Persian court to assassinate King Ahasuerus. Mordecai informed Esther of the plot, and she told the king. As a result, the plot was thwarted, and the king was very grateful to Esther and Mordecai. Later, when Mordecai discovered another plot to exterminate the Jewish population of the empire, he again informed Esther. The villain of the story, Haman, also planned to execute Mordecai and had a large gallows built on which to hang him. Meanwhile, Esther was able to use her position of favor with the king to convince him of Haman's plot. The result was that Haman was exposed and was hanged on the gallows he had prepared for Mordecai. Eventually, all of those who were part of Haman's plan were killed.

Esther thus became a great hero in the Jewish tradition. The end of the book of Esther establishes a festival in honor of the memory of the deliverance of the Jews in Persia, thanks to Esther and Mordecai. The Festival of Purim is still celebrated within Jewish culture. The Hebrew version of the book of Esther does not mention God, and because of this there seems to have been some hesitation in accepting it within the canon. That the book provides the basis for this important festival and is read as part of the celebration was likely the major factor supporting its inclusion in the Hebrew canon.

and have it proclaimed that the man was being honored by the king. The king approved of this suggestion and, in an ironic turn, commanded Haman to have Mordecai honored in precisely this way. Haman followed the king's order, but went home dejected because of the failure of his plans (6:1–14).

The day of Haman's dinner with the king and queen came. Ahasuerus asked Esther what she wanted him to do. She revealed her background, and she pleaded for her own life, as well as for the lives of her people. When the king, who seemed to have problems with his memory, asked who had caused all the trouble, she pointed an accusing finger at Haman. In anger, the king left the room for the cool of the garden, while Haman fell at the queen's feet as she lay on the dining couch. When the king returned to the room, "Haman had thrown himself on the couch where Esther was reclining" (7:8), and the king interpreted what he saw as Haman's attempt to rape the queen. For his crimes, real and perceived, Haman was hanged on the gallows he had built for Mordecai (7:1–10).

FIGURE 14–1 The book of Esther and parts of the books of Daniel and Ezra tell stories set in the ancient kingdom of Persia. The capital of this empire was a city the Greeks called Persepolis, which is located in what is now the western part of Iran. These are the remains of a place called the Apanda, constructed in Persepolis by Kings Darius and Xerxes in the late sixth and early fifth centuries B.C.E.

Because he could not revoke his decree about the slaughter of the Jewish people, the king sent out another decree that gave them the right to defend themselves against anyone who might attack them (8:1–17). The Jewish people took it as an opportunity to rid themselves of their enemies throughout the kingdom. The tenth day of the month of Adar was designated the day for the celebration of the Feast of Purim, which would commemorate the event (9:1–32), and Mordecai replaced Haman as prime minister (10:1–3).

Judaism and the Gentile World

The Exile reoriented Israel in many different ways. In the post-Exilic period, most Jewish people continued to live outside of Palestine, even after the Persians allowed them to return. Diaspora Jews lived in many places and among many cultures in Mesopotamia, Egypt, Asia Minor, and eventually Europe.[7] Two different, but related, sets of questions typically arose in these situations. The first had to do with the openness of Judaism to people who were not from a Jewish ethnic background. Two opinions developed on that subject. One said that the responsibility of the Jewish people was to be separate and distinct from the world around them, to be exclusively the people of God. Such people undoubtedly would have argued that the nations would be drawn to Israel's God if Israel was faithful in its commitment. This view has been designated as *particularism.* Others believed that Judaism should be fully open to others, and even that it was the responsibility of the Jewish people to include others. This missionary outlook encompassed all people and, as such, is known as *universalism.* This debate between these contrasting viewpoints plays a significant role in books like Esther, Ruth, and Jonah.

This is not a debate only within Judaism, but one that arises within all religious communities at various times. It would remain an important debate among the Jewish people, and would arise again in later centuries, as indicated by the book of Daniel. Understanding what was probably the final book produced in the Old Testament will require a return to the continuing story of the Jewish people.

THE MACCABEAN REVOLT

Before continuing with this part of the story of the Jewish people, it should be acknowledged that our primary sources of information about this era are the two books called 1 and 2 Maccabees. These books are included in certain Christian canons, and they are written from a perspective very sympathetic to the Maccabeans. In the first century of the Common Era, the Jewish "historian," Josephus, wrote about these events, but his primary source of information also appears to have been 1 and 2 Maccabees. So, we do not possess an account of these events that meets modern historical standards of objectivity and neutrality, and we can do little more than paraphrase what is found in these sources that we do have.

In 168 B.C.E., a representative of Antiochus went to the village of Modein to enforce the Hellenization decree. He called on a village leader, the priest Mattathias, to set the example by sacrificing to Zeus. Instead, Mattathias killed the king's officer, as well as one of his own people who had offered to make the sacrifice. Having done that, he fled into the Judean wilderness with his five sons.

FIGURE 14–2 Alexander's empire. Artwork by Margaret Jordan Brown from *Mercer Dictionary of the Bible*. © 1990, courtesy of Mercer University Press.

Mattathias soon died, but his son Judas Maccabeus became the leader of the revolt started by his father. Judas and his brothers were joined by a group of separatist Jews called the ***Hasidim***. Their revolt, commonly called the **Maccabean Revolt**, was so successful that by 165 B.C.E., they had recaptured Jerusalem. In December 165 B.C.E., the Temple was cleansed and rededicated to the worship of the LORD, an event commemorated by the Jewish festival of Hanukkah. Later, Judas was killed, and his brother Jonathan succeeded him. Jonathan recognized the power of the office of High Priest and took that office for himself in 150 B.C.E. Eight years later, Simon, another brother, led the Jewish people to independence from the Seleucids and founded the **Hasmonean** dynasty, which ruled Palestine until the Roman conquest in 63 B.C.E. This period of political independence, which lasted for about one century, became an important symbol for the Jewish people. For at least the next two centuries, calls for rebellion against Rome and actual attempts to throw off Roman rule would look back on the Heroic Maccabeans for inspiration, but no other effort would succeed like this one did. In fact, the most concerted of these latter efforts, the Jewish war against Rome in 66–70 C.E., would lead to the brutal Roman suppression that included the destruction of the temple in Jerusalem.

GEOGRAPHICAL AND CANONICAL BOUNDARIES AND THE BOOK OF DANIEL

During the second century B.C.E., there were thriving Jewish communities in many places, including the one in Palestine from which the Maccabees emerged. In southern Egypt, the Persians established a Jewish military colony at Elephantine. This colony even had its own temple, in which regular sacrifices were offered. This group was somewhat unorthodox in its beliefs, assuming that God had a wife and including other gods in its worship practices. Even so, there seems to have been the observance of such traditional Jewish holidays as the Sabbath, Passover, and the Festival of Unleavened Bread, and contact was maintained with religious leaders in Jerusalem.[8] The Elephantine temple was destroyed by the Egyptians around 410 B.C.E., and the colony appealed to Jerusalem for help in rebuilding it. When no help came, they then appealed to Bagoas, the governor of Judah, and the sons of Sanballat, who ruled Samaria, and they got the help they requested. This colony was still in existence as late as 399 B.C.E.[9] The exiles who had stayed behind in Babylon also thrived, and their geographical location would become the setting for the book of Daniel.

In all of these places, questions constantly arose about how to live a faithful life as a Jewish person in the midst of other peoples and other cultures. We have seen such questions addressed in other books of the Old Testament, and the latest book in the whole collection, Daniel, continued to struggle with these issues.[10] This is the formative period for the various sects within Judaism, which are visible in the writings of Josephus and the New Testament, and exemplified by the Qumran community that produced and preserved the Dead Sea Scrolls.

The Book(s) of Daniel

The name Daniel was well known in the Ancient Near East. An ancient, heroic figure with this name appears in various places in Canaanite literature.[11] Ezekiel mentioned someone named Daniel, along with Noah and Job:

> Even if Noah, Daniel, and Job were in it [Palestine], says the LORD God, they would save neither son nor daughter; they would save only their own lives by their righteousness. (14:20)

It is uncertain whether this refers to the character Daniel who appears in the book of Daniel. Noah and Job are timeless, international figures, so it would make sense to understand Ezekiel's reference to Daniel as one to a similar kind of figure. It is more likely, therefore, that the book of Daniel takes this larger-than-life name for its hero. According to Daniel 1:1–7, Daniel was taken to Babylon by Nebuchadnezzar in 606 B.C.E. So he is a very specific character living in a very specific time and place. Still, for the writer and original readers of the book of Daniel, most likely living in the second century, Daniel was a hero of the distant past. Although the stories in the book were set against the background of the Babylonian Exile, as it stands now, evidence suggests that it was put in its present form during the persecution by Antiochus Epiphanes to encourage those who were under persecution. Just as the LORD delivered Daniel, he would deliver the righteous ones who were being persecuted by the tyrant Antiochus IV.

The book of Daniel was not included among the books of the prophets in the Jewish canon. Instead, it was placed within the Writings, the last group of books to be accepted as Scripture. At least eight fragmentary copies of the book of Daniel have been discovered among the Dead Sea Scrolls, and some of the nonbiblical writings among the scrolls make references to Daniel. The variety found among the manuscripts themselves and the references seem to indicate that, at the same time, the book of Daniel had taken on the status of scripture and was still a fluid body of tradition.[12]

The book of Daniel is dynamic in many ways. It exists in more than one format. Like Esther, the Greek versions of the book of Daniel contain additional material not present in the Hebrew version. So, it is apparent that different communities preserved and understood the book in different ways. Even the "Hebrew" version of the book is not all in the Hebrew language. Daniel 2:4–7:28 is in Aramaic, the language the Jewish adopted in Babylon. Ezra is the only other book in the Bible that contains a significant amount of Aramaic, and much of that material consists of official documents of the Persian court, which would have been written in Aramaic. The discussion below will focus on the shorter, Hebrew/Aramaic version of the book. The second half of the book is also the clearest example in the Old Testament of the emerging form called **apocalyptic literature**. Some of the characteristic features of this kind of writing were identified earlier, in Chapter 10 of this book, because of the book of Isaiah (e.g., Isaiah 24–27) look like a very early form of this kind of writing.

The Contents of the Book. The book has two major divisions: (1) stories about Daniel and (2) apocalyptic visions of a brighter future for those under persecution.

1. *Stories about Daniel (Dan. 1:1–6:28).* The first story (1:1–21) concerns the captivity of Daniel and his three friends of the Jerusalem nobility. Each of the friends was given a Babylonian name. Daniel was called *Belteshazzar*, while the three friends were called *Shadrach*, *Meshach*, and *Abednego*. The king ordered that they were to be educated for three years for court service. As such, they were to be fed from the king's table. "But Daniel resolved that he would not defile himself with royal rations of food and wine" (1:8). Thus, he and his friends were resolved to be faithful to the laws of their Jewish faith.

When the servant brought them the rich food, they asked instead for vegetables, because there was no danger of violating Jewish dietary laws if they ate no meat or milk products. When the three years were up, the Jewish youths were as healthy as any others and much more wise. This indicated to those whom Antiochus was trying to force to follow Hellenistic customs that they could prosper, just like Daniel and his friends, if they were faithful to the law.

As in the story of Joseph, in which the Pharaoh's dreams were so important, the second story about Daniel concerns a dream of King Nebuchadnezzar (2:1–49). Nebuchadnezzar had a

The Literary Structure of Daniel

The book of Daniel falls into two halves in terms of form, content, and language. The first half of the book tells a series of stories about Daniel and three other young men who live under foreign rule in the Babylonian Empire. Daniel 7–12 takes the form of a series of visions reported by Daniel in first-person language.

The stories in Daniel 1–6 have several purposes. First, they introduce Daniel as a person who is divinely gifted to interpret dreams. Second, they establish a setting in the time of the Babylonian Empire for the activity of Daniel. Third, the portrayals of Daniel and his friends in the face of threats to their lives provide a model of faithfulness for readers living under imperial rule. This last is certainly the most important function of the stories on their own. After the Exile, the Jewish people were always subject to imperial power from Persia, Greece, or Rome. Thus, illustrations of how to live faithfully and successfully in such a context would have been of great value.

It is easy to assume that the language shift in the book corresponds to the shift in setting and content, but these two factors do not coincide precisely. The first six chapters of the book are stories that take place in Babylon, where Aramaic was the official language of the royal court, but the book starts off in Hebrew and does not switch to Aramaic until 2:4. The visions of Daniel begin in Chapter 7 and the language remains Aramaic until the end of that chapter, only returning to Hebrew at 8:1.

The three purposes listed above also function together, however, to provide a narrative framework for the visions in the second half of the book. Faithful Daniel, who survives wicked schemes and interprets the dreams of foreign kings, looks into the future to talk about Israel's continuing life under foreign domination. The visions of the future connect the time of Daniel with the time of the intended audience of the book.

Of course, there is significant debate concerning the origins of book of Daniel. Some readers see it as an actual historical portrayal of a young man in the Babylonian era having visions about the future. Others believe the book of Daniel was written during the later Greek period to which the visions seem to refer. This latter group would understand the stories as a literary device designed to grant authority to a perspective on the book's own present in the second century B.C.E. The understanding of the stories as a model of behavior in captivity and a narrative framework for the visions probably works with either view. From both perspectives, Daniel 12 looks toward the future and the promise of God's deliverance in the end.

dream his wisest men could not interpret. Daniel told him the dream had to do with things that would come to pass "in the latter days" (2:28). This emphasis on the last days of history is known as *eschatology* (2:1–30).

In Nebuchadnezzar's dream, he had seen a great image with a head of gold, "breasts and arms of silver," belly and thighs of bronze, legs of iron, and feet "partly of iron and partly of clay" (2:33). The image was broken by a stone that became "a great mountain and filled the whole earth" (2:35). The image represented kingdoms that had dominated the Near East, beginning with that of Nebuchadnezzar. Others were the Medes, the Persians, and the empire of Alexander. But Alexander's kingdom, the one made of iron, was so divided that part of it was mixed with clay. It (the Seleucids and Ptolemies) would crumble. Then, the kingdom of God would emerge and replace all earthly kingdoms (2:31–45). Because of Daniel's success in interpreting the dream, he was given a place of honor in the king's court (2:46–49).

The third story concerned Daniel's companions Shadrach, Meshach, and Abednego. When the king set up an idol and demanded that everyone worship it, the three young men refused. Nothing was said about where Daniel was when all this was going on. When the news of the Jews' refusal to worship reached the king, they were ordered to be thrown into a fiery furnace. When the king arrived to see what had happened to them, he saw not three but four, one of whom was like "a son of the gods" (3:25 NIV). It was a vision of assurance to those who were undergoing the fiery trials of persecution by Antiochus Epiphanes (3:1–30).

Next came the story of another dream of the king. He dreamed of a mighty tree that covered the earth; but, on God's orders, a heavenly being descended and cut down the tree. When Daniel was asked to interpret the dream, he told the king that he (the king) was the tree. He would suffer temporary insanity, during which he would act like an animal because he exalted himself above God. When a year had passed, the king suffered as Daniel said. Then, the king acknowledged the power of the Most High God (4:1–37). In this story, the apocalyptist was saying what Deutero–Isaiah had said many years before:

By myself I have sworn,
from my mouth has gone forth in righteousness
a word that shall not return:
"To me every knee shall bow,
every tongue shall swear." (Isa. 45:23)

That even included the tyrant Antiochus, who called himself "God manifest" (Epiphanes). Chapter 5 tells the story of Belshazzar's feast. Belshazzar was the son and coregent of Nabonidus (he was called the son of Nebuchadnezzar in 5:2). Nabonidus was an amateur archaeologist who was more interested in old ruins than in the breakdown of his kingdom. While Belshazzar was having a wild drinking bout using sacred vessels from the Jerusalem Temple, he saw a message written on the wall: "MENE, MENE, TEKEL, PARSIN." Daniel, when called to interpret them, explained that they pronounced Belshazzar's doom. His days were numbered, for he had been found lacking in leadership qualities. Now, his kingdom would be divided among the Medes and the Persians. According to the book of Daniel, the kingdom was taken by "Darius the Mede." According to Persian records, it was Cyrus. Darius, the Persian ruler, came to the throne after Cambyses (530–522 B.C.E.) in 522 B.C.E. (5:1–30).

The final story of Daniel is the most famous. Exalted to the position of *satrap*, or governor, of a province of the Persian Empire, Daniel was still the faithful worshiper of the LORD. His fellow governors persuaded the king to pass a decree that no one could pray to any god for thirty days. Only the king could be petitioned. Daniel ignored the edict and continued to worship three times a day, as was his custom. As a result, he was thrown to the lions.

The king realized what a mistake he had made and worried all night about Daniel. But in the morning, Daniel walked out of the lion's den unharmed. Those who had set the trap for him were fed to the lions.

The object of all these stories was to tell the people who were suffering under persecution that, just as the LORD had delivered Daniel, Shadrach, Meshach, and Abednego, so they would be delivered. This was a common theme in apocalyptic literature—the delivery of the righteous from the fire of persecution and from the human animals who were trying to destroy them (6:1–28).

2. *Daniel's visions (Dan. 7:1–12:13).* In the visions recorded in Daniel, there was typical apocalypse. Unusual beasts, the use of numbers, and the view of the last days, including a messianic figure, were all common themes in such literature. Despite any persecution the saints might have been undergoing, the apocalyptic writer brought a message of hope whose theme was that God would win out over the forces of evil.

a. *The four beasts from the sea (Dan. 7:1–28).* In the first vision, four beasts arose out of the sea. For Jews, the sea was always a place of awe and mystery. It was a fearsome place, which had great monsters who swallowed up men who dared to venture out into it. It was not unusual for them to conceive of evil creatures coming from the sea. The beasts in the vision represented the strong empires of the time: the Babylonian; the Median, which lay east of the Mesopotamian region; the Persian; and finally, the Greek or Hellenistic empire of Alexander and his successors. The ten horns on the fourth beast represented the ten kings who followed Alexander. Because the horn was a symbol of power, the writer showed his contempt for Antiochus Epiphanes by referring to him as a little horn, a button with a big mouth "that spoke arrogantly" (7:20). But God ("the Ancient One," 7:22) would put an end to his persecution and his mouthings.

The kingship and dominion
    and the greatness of the kingdom under the whole heaven
shall be given to the people of the holy ones of the Most High;
    their kingdoms shall be an everlasting kingdom,
    and all dominion shall serve and obey them. (7:27)

b. *The ram and the he-goat (Dan. 8:1–27).* Daniel's next vision is that of a ram with ten horns that moved in every direction, defeating every beast it encountered. The ram was the Persian Empire, which owed much of its strength to an alliance with the Medes. Alexander (the he-goat) defeated the Medo–Persian Empire. At his death, four of his generals (the four horns) inherited his empire (8:22). Antiochus (a king of bold countenance, 8:23) persecuted the Jews. The 2300 "mornings and evenings" were three and one-half years of the period from the beginning of the Maccabean Revolt until the cleansing of the Temple in December 165 B.C.E.

c. *The seventy weeks (Dan. 9:1–27).* Numerology came into full play in this vision, along with the introduction of the angel Gabriel as the chief messenger for God. Daniel was pondering Jeremiah's prophecy of the seventy weeks "in the first year of Darius, the son of Ahasuerus . . . who became king over the realm of the Chaldeans" (9:1). This verse creates problems, as Persian records currently available show no knowledge of such a king. The Chaldeans, furthermore, were the Babylonians, not the Persians.

After a long prayer of repentance and confession, both of his sins and the sins of the people (9:3–19), Daniel was visited by the angel Gabriel. Gabriel's purpose was to reveal the meaning of the seventy weeks, which were explained as "seventy weeks of years," or 490 years. Unfortunately, the meaning of what was revealed to Daniel has not been passed on to us, either by written or oral tradition, making this passage one that has brought interpretations ranging from something less than sublime to the ridiculous. Seemingly, if the historical context is of any value, it referred to the period from the return (538 B.C.E.) to the Maccabean era (about 168 B.C.E.). It would end when one would come (the Messiah) who "desolates, until the decreed end is poured out on the desolator" (9:27). Again, this seems to refer to Antiochus Epiphanes, who profaned the altar by sacrificing a hog on it. That this interpretation is widely disputed can be readily admitted. One can find all sorts of contrary interpretations, including some current best sellers, applying this to some future event. History is full of such interpretations (9:20–27).

d. ***The last days (Dan. 10:1–12:13).*** A favorite theme of apocalyptists was the last days, when the LORD would bring an end to evil and usher in the Kingdom of God. It has always been tempting, especially in trying times, for Jewish and Christian interpreters to apply this passage to their own time. A notable example occurred in the 1840s, when a sincere preacher convinced thousands that the end would come in 1843. When it did not come, he changed the date to 1844. There were still many who believed him. But when the end still did not come, he died a disillusioned and broken man. This vision, like the others, seems best to be understood as referring to the events from 538 B.C.E. to the Maccabean period. References such as 11:31, "Forces from him (Antiochus Epiphanes) shall occupy and profane the temple and fortress. They shall abolish the regular burnt offering" seem to point to Antiochus and his atrocities against the Jews. For Daniel, this was the prelude to the coming of the Messiah who would deliver the righteous Jews. After a clear reference to a belief in life and death, with rewards and punishment (12:1–4), Daniel closed the veil, so that what came after was hidden from view.

Key Terms

Alexander, *336*
Apocalyptic Literature, *346*
Chiasm, *339*
Hasmoneans, *345*
Hellenistic, *337*
Herodotus, *335*
Levirate Marriage, *339*
Maccabean Revolt, *345*
Ptolemies, *336*
Seleucids, *336*

Study Questions

1. In what ways did the conquests of Alexander the Great influence subsequent history?
2. Identify Ptolemies, the Seleucids, Antiochus the Great, and Antiochus Epiphanes.
3. What were the causes of the Maccabean Revolt, who were its leaders, and what were its long-term effects on Jewish history?
4. Why was Elephantine an important location in Israelite history?
5. What position concerning Jewish ethnicity does the book of Esther support?
6. Why were the Greek additions to the book of Esther probably inserted into the book?
7. Why do some interpreters view the book of Ruth as a response the marriage policies in Ezra and Nehemiah?
8. What are the connections between the book of Ruth and the book of Judges?
9. What are the *Megilloth* and what is their purpose?
10. What were the viewpoints of the universalists and the particularists in post-Exilic Judaism? What conditions gave rise to these opposing views?
11. What are the most important purposes of the book of Daniel?
12. What are the two major divisions of the book of Daniel?
13. How is Antiochus Epiphanes symbolized in the book of Daniel?
14. Who were the Hasidim?

Endnotes

1. For a good description of the life of Philip of Macedon and his significance for the history of ancient Greece, see A. R. Burn, "Historical summary of Greece," in *Civilizations of the Ancient Mediterranean: Greece and Rome*, vol. 1, ed. Michael Grand and Rachel Kitzinger (New York: Charles Scriber's Sons, 1988), 30–34.

2. I am grateful to Professor Kathryn Larch of Pima County Community College for correcting my identification of Ptolemy.

3. For a concise survey of the Seleucid rule of Palestine, see Thomas Fischer, "Palestine, Administration of (Seleucid)," trans. Frederick H. Cryer, in *ABD*, vol. 5, 92–96.

4. See Stephen Bertman, "Symmetrical Design in the Book of Ruth," *JBL*, LXXXIV (1965), 165–168.

5. This was the law of the levirate marriage (Deut. 25:5–6).

6. Michael Heltzer, "Esther—Where Does Fiction Start and History End?" *BR*, VIII, I (February 1992), 29.

7. For a survey of these communities at the end of the Exilic period, see Albertz, *A History of Israelite Religion*, vol. 2, 370–375.

8. For an excellent short discussion of this community, see J. Maxwell Miller and John H. Hayes, *A History of Ancient Israel and Judah*, 2nd ed. (Louisville, KY: Westminster–John Knox Press, 2006), 496–497.

9. See Abraham Schalit and Lidia Matassa, "Elephantine" in *Encyclopedia Judaica*, vol. 6, 311–314.

10. The religious, political, and social dynamics of this period are extremely complex. An attempt to untangle all of the forces and movements, which reveals this complexity, is in Abertz, *A History of Israelite Religion*, vol. 2, 534–597.

11. See "*The Tale of Aqhat*" in James B. Pritchard, *ANET*, 118–132.

12. See the detailed description of the evidence related to Daniel in Martin Abegg, Jr., et al., *The Dead Sea Scrolls Bible: The Oldest Known Bible Translated for the First Time into English* (New York: HarperOne, 1999), 482–485.

CHAPTER 15

Epilogue

The Continuing Story

Timeline

63 B.C.E.	Romans conquered Jerusalem
66 C.E.	Beginning of the Jewish war against Rome and the approximate time the Dead Sea Scrolls were hidden
70 C.E.	Destruction of Jerusalem and the Temple
100 C.E.	Approximate time of the closing of the Hebrew canon

Chapter Outline

- **I.** Life in Jewish Communities
- **II.** The Development of Sectarian Judaism
- **III.** Literary Activity
- **IV.** Judaism's Oral Tradition
- **V.** A Closing Statement

CHAPTER OVERVIEW

By the first century B.C.E., all the books of the Hebrew canon and the Protestant Old Testament had reached their final form. Judaism was existing under the heavy political and economic influence of the Roman Empire and the continuing cultural influence of Greece. A great deal of literary activity was still occurring as existing books were being interpreted and translated into other languages. New books of great significance that did not make it into the narrower canon were being written. The process of shaping the canon was also taking place and continued into the first century C.E. Judaism thrived in Palestine, Babylon, Egypt, and other places. New groups formed within Judaism, including the early Christian movement. This sectarian environment would also influence the formation of the canon. In 70 C.E. the Romans attacked Jerusalem and destroyed the Temple. This crisis was probably the final force that drove Judaism toward a finished, closed canon by the end of the first century C.E.

LIFE IN JEWISH COMMUNITIES

The Old Testament story comes to its narrative conclusion at the end of the book of Nehemiah, and Daniel was probably the last book of the Protestant Old Testament to be written. There is some evidence that the number and order of the poems in the book of Psalms continued to vary into the first century B.C.E.[1] Despite what looks like the end of the production of the Bible from our vantage point, the persons living in Jewish communities at that time would not likely have perceived any kind of end. Jewish writers continued to produce works that followed in the lines of the sacred texts of the past. The great traditions of Israel's past—law, priesthood, monarchy, temple, prophecy, and wisdom—continued to survive in some ways, but they had adapted significantly and continued to evolve into new forms. The Maccabeans had put an end to the political and military influence of the Greek Empire, but its cultural influence would remain strong for centuries to come. The greatest impact can be seen in the production of a full Greek translation of the Hebrew scriptures and the use of Greek as the original language of the sacred texts of Christianity. At the end of the Maccabean period the political, military, and economic influence of Rome would help shape Judaism.

Except for the freedom they gained during the Maccabean revolt, Palestinian Jews, as well as those outside of Palestine, were subject to foreign rulers. Most Jewish people, in fact, did not live in Palestine. The Assyrian, Babylonian, Persian, and Greek conquests of Palestine had the effect of scattering Jews all over the Middle East. Babylonia and Egypt in particular had large Jewish communities. The **Diaspora** character of Judaism would become a permanent condition.

Although Israel was no longer a nation, it was still a people, spread from Babylon to Alexandria to Rome, yet bound together by devotion for God, dedication to the study of God's teaching (Torah), and a longing for God's city, Jerusalem. No matter how far one lived from Jerusalem, every faithful Jewish person vowed to go there to worship at least once in his or her life. This love for Jerusalem is expressed in the words of a lonely poet during the Babylonian Exile:

> How could we sing the LORD's song
>   in a foreign land?
> If I forget you, O Jerusalem,
>   let my right hand wither!
> Let my tongue cling to the roof of my mouth,
>   if I do not remember you,
> if I do not set Jerusalem
>   above my highest joy. (Ps. 137:4–6)

As a consequence of their loss of political independence, certain important changes took place in the Jewish community that had effects not only in Palestine, but also in the Jewish communities of the Diaspora. First, the High Priest increasingly assumed both religious and political roles in the Palestinian Jewish community, with his power in many ways extending to Jewish communities everywhere. An important step in this rise in political power came when Jonathan, the brother of Judas Maccabeus, combined the offices of political ruler and High Priest (circa 150 B.C.E.). Second, the oral traditions associated with prophecy and wisdom declined in significance as the written Torah gradually became the standard for both life and conduct. Because Torah basically means "teaching," the teacher or rabbi became a major force in Jewish life. More and more, the synagogue was where the teaching took place. While the Temple, located in Jerusalem, was Judaism's most sacred shrine, every Jewish community that had a minimum of ten Jewish men—a *minyan*—had a synagogue as the center of community life. Because the synagogue was an institution controlled by laypersons and the rabbi was a layperson rather than a priest the lay interpreters of the Torah became the most important influence in the lives of most Jewish people, wherever they lived. So, while the political power of the High Priest was increasing, the religious power of the priesthood as a group was decreasing.

Two important developments grew out of this situation. First, a tradition of identifying and elevating two great rabbis in each generation developed, and interpretations of Torah taught by these two took on great authority. These pairs, called *zugoth*, often embodied a typical conservative vs. progressive approach to addressing contemporary life using ancient laws. This tradition culminated in the two great rabbis of the first century, Hillel and Shammai. Second, oral tradition came to have equal status with the written Torah. This was based on the belief that (1) it, like the written Torah, had its origins in the time of Moses, and (2) it has been passed along over the centuries by word of mouth until it came to be entrusted to the *zugoth*, the pair of great rabbis whose word was law for that day.

THE DEVELOPMENT OF SECTARIAN JUDAISM

This period also saw the rise of numerous parties within Judaism that were to have major roles in its future. Before the Maccabean Revolt, the Samaritans, a group whose origins are uncertain, but who may have been descendants of the inhabitants of the territory of the Northern Kingdom that Assyria had conquered in 722/721 B.C.E., became a distinct group. Assyria had brought in foreign colonists who intermarried with the poor Israelites left in the land. In the Babylonian conquests, the poor also were left in the land, while most of those in the leadership classes were carried into exile. Open hostility developed between those who remained in the land and the Jews who returned after the Babylonian Exile. The people of the land still looked upon themselves as true followers of the God of Israel, but the Jews who returned felt that those who had stayed in the land had a corrupted faith and that their mixed heritage disqualified them from being a part of Judaism. Eventually, the **Samaritans**—so named because Samaria was their chief city—built a temple on Mount Gerizim, one of the mountains that overlooks the site of Shechem, the old Israelite capital. Later, John Hyrcanus, the Hasmonean ruler, forcefully converted the Samaritans to his version of Judaism, destroyed their temple, and earned their undying enmity both for himself and the type of Judaism centered in Jerusalem.[2] The Samaritans apparently accepted only the Torah as Scripture and their written tradition persists today in the manuscript tradition known as the **Samaritan Pentateuch**.

The extremely orthodox **Hasidim**, who had supported the Maccabean Revolt in its beginnings, became disenchanted when the revolt became more of an attempt to gain political power than a struggle for freedom. It is likely, although not proven, that two political groups important to later Judaism, the Pharisees and the Essenes, had roots in this movement. The Pharisees were made up predominantly of laymen who wanted to interpret the law so that its meaning was clear to each generation. The Pharisees were the party that emphasized oral tradition and produced the great rabbis who were to dominate later Judaism. The Pharisees accepted the Pentateuch (Torah), the prophets (*Nebi'im*), and the Writings (*Kethubim*) as authoritative. Although they would have strongly affirmed their religious orthodoxy, they were in fact the religious liberals of their day, introducing into Judaism such ideas as the belief in the resurrection of the dead and the belief in angels.

Josephus also mentions a **sect** he refers to as the **Essenes**, for whom he had great admiration because of their dedication to righteousness. There are very few references to this group elsewhere in ancient literature, and they provide very little information about the Essenes beyond what Josephus says. It is difficult to discuss this group without addressing the connections often made between them and the manuscripts called the Dead Sea Scrolls. The scrolls were clearly produced and preserved by a group that was not only dedicated to righteousness in the following of the law, but that also saw the religious establishment in Jerusalem as corrupt. The scrolls were discovered in caves near the northwestern corner of the Dead Sea, and archaeologists have also discovered near there the remains of a first-century settlement, known as **Qumran**. It is very common to connect these three pieces and to assume that the Essenes lived at Qumran and they produced and preserved the Dead Sea Scrolls. The case for this view is entirely circumstantial, but has been very influential.[3] Many interpreters believe the sect that produced the Dead Seas Scrolls withdrew from Jerusalem initially when Jonathan, the brother of Judas Maccabeus, seized the high priesthood (circa 150 B.C.E.). Frequent references are made in their literature to the "wicked priest." Whether or not this group corresponds to the Essenes, their literature provides important insight into the nature of sectarian groups, the conflicts among them, and the attitudes of some toward the institutionalized religion of Jerusalem. Their theology was similar to that of the Pharisees in many respects but had important differences. The Dead Sea Sect believed they were to prepare for the coming of the end of the age. Their literature was dominated by the idea that a great final struggle was approaching, a war between the "Sons of Light" (themselves) and the "Sons of Darkness" (all who opposed them). Everything they did was aimed at preparing for the day when God would intervene on their behalf and make them victorious over their enemies. Jonathan's attempt to combine the offices of High Priest and ruler was further carried out by the Hasmoneans, who ruled Palestine after the Maccabean Revolt gained freedom for the Jewish people in 142 B.C.E.

The priestly party, the Sadducees, dominated the political and economic life of Palestine the country but lost much of their religious influence over the common people. They were quite conservative religiously, accepting only the first five books of the Bible as Scripture—those books that describe the responsibilities of the priests. In contrast, because the prophets frequently attacked the priesthood, this would not have endeared them to the Sadducees. The Sadducees' political and economic power, as well as their religious views, led to a struggle between them and the Pharisees. This situation, in turn, led to severe persecution of the Pharisees during the days of Hasmonean rule.

Although there would be other parties and sectarian groups that would arise later within Judaism, these were the most important. Their existence illustrates that, as the Old Testament story closes, Judaism was not a unified religion in which everyone believed the same doctrines, nor did they interpret the scriptures or interact with the world in the same way. Instead, the Jewish people were composed of diverse groups, and their society and religion mirrored that diversity.

LITERARY ACTIVITY

As the period that produced the Old Testament came to a close, literary activity did not cease among religious people. Four major bodies of literature that extended the traditions of the Old Testament in various ways need to be examined briefly: the Apocrypha, the Pseudepigrapha, the Dead Sea Scrolls, and the oral tradition of the Jews that eventually produced the Talmud.

The Apocrypha

To speak of the **Apocrypha** as extrabiblical literature is not entirely accurate, because the Roman Catholic and Orthodox traditions accept these books as sacred Scripture. Because these books have been preserved only among Christian groups and within Christian manuscripts, it is often difficult to determine to what extent they had Jewish origins, and what their original language was. It is safe to say that all of the works included in the Apocrypha have Jewish origins that preceded Christianity, which will not be the case with the Pseudepigrapha. Books not included in the Jewish and Protestant canons, but that are in the Catholic and Orthodox canons, may be described in the following groups:

1. Additions to or extensions of biblical books

Apocryphal Book	*Related Biblical Book*
The Letter of Jeremiah	Jeremiah
The Prayer of Azariah and the Song of the Three Young Men	Daniel
Susanna	Daniel
Bel and the Dragon	Daniel
The Prayer of Manasseh	2 Chronicles
The additions to Esther	Esther

2. Apocalyptic literature—2 Esdras
3. Short stories or novellas focusing on Jewish piety—Tobit and Judith
4. Wisdom literature—The Wisdom of Solomon, Sirach, and Baruch
5. Historical/Narrative books—1 and 2 Maccabees, 1 Esdras

The books that are additions to extensions of biblical books are varied. Of the books listed in this category, many address issues related to living wisely and righteously within the Diaspora.[4] The three additions to Daniel are in the Greek version of the book and they add to or extend the narrative tales found in the first half of Daniel. The additions to Esther are also in the Greek manuscripts of that book, and consist mostly of prayers spoken by the characters, a feature that seems to seek to remedy the difficulty caused by the lack of any mention of God in the Hebrew version of the book. The Letter of Jeremiah is independent of the book of Jeremiah, but it seems to use the idea of Jeremiah writing a letter to the exiles, as he did in Jeremiah 29, as a starting point for writing to them warning against the dangers of idol worship.

Clearly, 2 Esdras differs drastically from 1 Esdras in that it is an apocalypse. The introduction and conclusion show evidence of being the work of Christian editors, while the core of the book is from a Jewish writer. Although it wrestles with the problem of how a just God can permit such an evil world (as do some of the wisdom books), its emphasis on revelations, angels, and the final judgment puts it in the category of the apocalyptic.

Tobit and Judith are contrasting stories that illustrate the variety of ways of relating to the world in post-Exilic times. Tobit is a man who is unusually sensitive to the hurts of his fellow

Jews. He even risks the wrath of the governing authorities because of his concern to see that the dead receive proper burial. After many reverses, including blindness, his faithful service to God is rewarded. Tobit's son, Tobias, carries out a mission for his father that secures the family's wealth, cures his father's blindness, and frees a beautiful woman from domination by a demon. The woman, Sarah, also becomes the wife of Tobias. The story of Judith, on the other hand, is not nearly so romantic. When her native city is surrounded by the Assyrian army, she follows God's guidance and uses her feminine wiles to cut off the head of the enemy general. The siege is lifted and the people are freed. Internal evidence within both books confirms that both Judith and Tobit are fictional characters.[5] The stories of these two characters have strong connections to the stories of Joseph, Daniel, and Esther. The question of how a faithful Jewish person should live in a complex world was still a difficult and important one.

The Wisdom of Solomon and Sirach are perhaps the most significant books in the Apocrypha. Had they come at an earlier time, they undoubtedly would have been included in the Hebrew canon. If handed portions from them to read, most modern Bible readers would likely assume they were biblical, perhaps from the book of Proverbs. The Wisdom of Solomon is from the Alexandrian Jewish community, probably from the first century B.C.E. It deals with the themes of the righteous and the wicked, immortality, the judgment of the wicked, and the importance of wisdom as the guide for life. In this book, wisdom takes on even more of the characteristics of a person than it does in earlier wisdom books. Chapters 10–12 illustrate how wisdom guided the great persons and events in Israel's history. The Wisdom of Jesus the Son of Sirach, is the work of a Jewish schoolmaster who lived around 200 B.C.E. It sets out rules for getting along in this world.

Tobias

The book of Tobit is found in the Apocrypha and tells the story of a Jewish family living in Assyria. Like Daniel and Esther, it is a story of faithful Jews in the Diaspora, which seems to assume the purpose of encouraging other Jews living in foreign settings. The story is told in the first-person voice of Tobit. He and his wife, Anna, live in Ninevah and their lives become difficult when Tobit becomes blind. The body of a murdered Jew had been discovered in the marketplace, and Tobit faithfully volunteers to bury him. Unclean from contact with a corpse, Tobit must sleep outdoors, where bird droppings fall into his eyes and destroy his eyesight.

Meanwhile, in another city, a young woman named Sarah is in a desperate situation because seven young men she had married had all died before her marriages to them were consummated. Like Tobit, Sarah prays for deliverance from her difficulties. God hears the prayers of both and sends the angel Raphael to help them.

Tobit sends his son, Tobias, on an errand to retrieve some money that he had left in trust in a distant city. Tobias undertakes this journey, with Raphael watching over him, and along the way he captures a large fish from the Tigris River. Raphael instructs him to keep some of the internal organs of the fish. While on the journey, Tobias also meets and marries Sarah. He then repels the demon who had killed Sarah's first seven husbands using the fish organs. Tobias eventually retrieves the money and returns home to his parents with Sarah, who is now his new wife. He again uses the fish organs, this time to heal his father's blindness. The angel Raphael is thus able to answer the prayers and solve the problems of two Jews in distant locations using the faithful action of young Tobias.

Unlike the book of Proverbs, in which sayings are not grouped according to subject matter, Ecclesiasticus tends to group material in a topical arrangement.

Of the two historical works, 1 Maccabees is the more valuable as history. It begins with the reign of Antiochus Epiphanes (175 B.C.E.) and ends with the beginning of the reign of John Hyrcanus, the first Hasmonean ruler (135 B.C.E.). Its major concern is the Maccabean Revolt. 2 Maccabees is not an extension of 1 Maccabees, but an overlapping version of much of the same time period. In 2 Maccabees, a shorter time period is covered, and it is concerned primarily with the exploits of Judas Maccabeus. Its writer has a strong bias against the Hasmonean rulers.

1 Esdras is essentially a duplicate of the biblical books of 2 Chronicles 35:1–36:23, all of Ezra, and the part of Nehemiah that tells of Ezra reading the Torah out loud in Jerusalem (7:38–8:12). The only original part of the books is a delightful story of three guards in the palace of the Persian king who compete for a prize by giving answers to the question, "What one thing is strongest?" (1 Esd. 3:5). One argues for wine; the second for the king himself; and the third, who is identified as Zerubbabel, wins the argument and the prize by praising women and truth. As his reward, he is allowed to return to Jerusalem to rebuild the Temple (1 Esd. 4:61–63).

The earliest books in the Apocrypha come from the late third century B.C.E., while the latest are dated as late as the first century B.C.E. They came from a time when many changes were taking place in the Near East and did their part to encourage the faithful during unsettled days.

The Pseudepigrapha

Pseudepigrapha literally means "writings with false superscriptions." This is an informal collection of literature works, many of which have certain characteristics in common: (1) they "are often attributed to ideal figures in Israel's past"; (2) the writers claim to be the bearer of God's message; (3) they usually use Old Testament ideas and narratives as a starting point; and (4) they usually are dated in the period 200 B.C.E. to 200 C.E. The number of known pseudepigraphical writings is now in the hundreds.[6] These texts have typically been preserved and transmitted by Christian communities. Some of them likely have Jewish origins, but these are very difficult to ascertain.

None of the writings classified as pseudepigraphical is found in either of the major canons of Scripture. This does not mean that they are of no value. As evidence of the regard in which some were held, the New Testament book of Jude quotes the Assumption of Moses (Jude 8) and Enoch (Jude 13–14). Another pseudepigraphical work, The Psalms of Solomon, was included in one of the most important collections of biblical manuscripts.[7] Some of the other prominently mentioned writings are The Letter of Aristeas, The Book of Jubilees, The Martyrdom of Isaiah, 4 Maccabees, the Sybylline Oracles, the book of Enoch, 4 Ezra, The Apocalypse of Baruch, The Testaments of the Twelve Patriarchs, The Life of Adam and Eve, and the Damascus Document. The major value of the Pseudepigrapha is that it shows the many currents of thought that were present at the end of the Old Testament era.

The Dead Sea Scrolls

In 1947, a young goat herder's curiosity led to one of the greatest archaeological discoveries of all time. A Bedouin boy threw a rock into a hole in a cliff that overlooks the Dead Sea. When he heard the sound of something breaking, he climbed up the cliff to investigate. Inside the caves were clay jars filled with manuscripts.

Most of these manuscripts eventually would fall into the hands of biblical scholars, who recognized their great value. This led to an investigation of a number of other caves in the area and the excavation of a nearby ruin. The result of these investigations was the finding of a large number of manuscripts and manuscript fragments from almost every Old Testament book, as well as manuscripts of numerous religious writings. The latter finds furnished a wealth of new information about the Dead Sea Sect itself, a Jewish group that existed in the early part of the Christian era and about whom little was known previously. Qumran, the settlement where many think the scrolls were produced, was located on the northwestern shore of the Dead Sea. It existed from Maccabean times off and on until the Roman conquest of Palestine around 70 C.E.

The most famous biblical manuscript found at Qumran is commonly known as the *Great Isaiah Scroll.* It is at least 1000 years older than any previously known manuscript of Isaiah, yet its discovery led to no radical changes in the translations of the book of Isaiah. Of the nonbiblical manuscripts, the best known is The Manual of Discipline, a rulebook for the conduct of the members of the sect; The Thanksgiving Scroll, which contains songs similar to those in the book of Psalms; and The War of the Sons of Light and the Sons of Darkness, a book describing a great battle to take place between the community members (the Sons of Light) and the Kittim or Romans (the Sons of Darkness). The latter work illustrates the apocalyptic nature of the community. Another major manuscript, the Temple Scroll, was published for the first time in 1978.[8]

The Dead Sea Scrolls and the people who produced them are just another illustration of the diverse character of Judaism as this period comes to a close.

JUDAISM'S ORAL TRADITION

The final body of literature we must mention is the growing oral tradition developed by the rabbinic interpreters of the Hebrew Scriptures. The aim of the great rabbis was to translate the principles in the Torah and the Prophets into rules for everyday living. Because of this felt need, a pair (*zugoth*) of outstanding rabbis, one representing the more orthodox or conservative viewpoint and one a more progressive approach, interpreted the Scriptures for the people of their day. As mentioned previously, they believed that this oral tradition extended all the way back to Moses, who, according to their view, received both an oral and a written Torah.

The time of the great rabbis began around 200 B.C.E. and would continue until 500 C.E. There were two types of oral literature: (1) *halakah,* or rules for living based on the interpretation of the legal portions of the Old Testament, and (2) *haggadah,* a more sermonic and illustrative kind of material that consisted of such things as fanciful expansions of the narrative parts of the Old Testament. It was designed to encourage the ordinary Jew to be diligent in observing *halakah.* By the end of the second century C.E., this material would be collected and organized into six divisions by the great rabbi Judah ha-Nasi. This was called **Mishnah**. Following this, a commentary on the Mishnah was developed that would be known as the *Gemara.* The Mishnah and the Gemara then joined to form the **Talmud**. There eventually were two Talmuds—a Palestinian and a Babylonian Talmud. One truly amazing thing about this was that each generation of rabbis memorized the interpretations of the previous generations, added their own interpretations, and passed them on to the succeeding generation. Nothing was preserved in writing until the fifth century C.E.! But these developments were only beginnings as the Old Testament story closes.

A CLOSING STATEMENT

This version of the Old Testament story comes to an end. Perhaps it has opened a few eyes to the treasures of the Old Testament. If so, the telling has been worth it. It may even inspire some to look again at the story and to try to make it theirs so that they can experience the thrill of walking in the steps of its characters; experiencing their joys, sorrows, and frustrations; tasting their foods; and savoring some of the smells of that world. If so, that is even better. But this version closes with the hope that even those who may never look at it again will in some way be a bit richer than before because they came this way to listen to the story.

Key Terms

Apocrypha, *356*
Diaspora, *353*
Essenes, *355*
Hasidim, *355*
Mishnah, *359*
Qumran, *355*
Pseudepigrapha, *358*
Samaritans, *354*
Samaritan Pentateuch, *355*
Sect, *355*
Talmud, *359*

Study Questions

1. How were religious and political power merged in Israel in the second century B.C.E.?
2. Why were laypersons increasingly influential in religious matters in post-Exilic Jewish communities?
3. How were the Samaritans related to Judaism?
4. What were the distinct beliefs of the Pharisees?
5. Why is the Dead Sea Scrolls set identified as an apocalyptic group?
6. What does the increasing understanding of sectarian movements indicate about Judaism at the turn of the eras?
7. Why is it not completely accurate to speak of the Apocrypha as extrabiblical literature?
8. Briefly state the nature of the following books of the Apocrypha: (a) 1 Esdras; (b) 2 Esdras; (c) Tobit; (d) The Wisdom of Solomon; (e) Ecclesiasticus, or the Wisdom of Jesus the Son of Sirach; (f) Maccabees.
9. Why does the Protestant Old Testament not include the books of the Apocrypha?
10. What illustrates the importance of the pseudepigraphical literature for Judaism and Christianity?
11. What do the Dead Sea Scrolls contribute to our knowledge of the Bible and first-century B.C.E. Judaism?
12. How did the Talmuds develop?
13. Define the terms *Diaspora, zugoth, Hasidim, Halakah, Haggadah, Mishna, Gemara, Talmud.*

Endnotes

1. See the discussion of the various psalm fragments found among the Dead Sea Scrolls, especially the psalm scroll found in Cave 11, and what they reveal about the continuing development of the book of Psalms in William L. Holladay, *The Psalms through Three Thousand Years: Prayerbook of a Cloud of Witnesses* (Minneapolis: Fortress, 1993), 100–102.
2. R. J. Coggins, *Samaritans and Jews,* rev. ed. (Garden City, NY: Doubleday, 1964), is a good up-to-date discussion of the Samaritans and their relationship to the Jews. The Samaritan temple was destroyed circa 128 B.C.E.
3. See the careful description of the "Essene Hypothesis" and its strengths and weaknesses in Michael Wise et al., *The Dead Sea Scrolls: A New Translation* (San Francisco: HarperSanFrancisco, 1996), 13–35.
4. See the discussion of these texts in George W. E. Nickelsburg, *Jewish Literature Between the Bible and the Mishnah: A Historical and Literary Introduction,* 2nd ed. (Minneapolis: Fortress, 2005), 17–40.
5. Carey A. Moore, "The Case of the Pious Killer," *BR,* VI, 1 (February 1990), 26–36, discusses the reasons why Judith was not in the canon of the Old Testament.
6. James H. Charlesworth, *The Old Testament Pseudepigrapha,* vols. 1 and 2 (Garden City, NY: Doubleday, 1983, 1985).
7. The Sinaiticus manuscripts.
8. Jacob Milgrom, "The Temple Scroll," *BA,* 41, 3 (1978), 105–120.

GLOSSARY

Below are definitions to all of the key terms highlighted in each chapter, with the exception of the names of important characters and places.

Acrostic An alphabetic pattern used in Hebrew poetry. Each line or group of lines in a poem begins with a successive letter of the alphabet. The entire book of Lamentations follows this pattern. Each of the four chapters is an acrostic poem.

Adultery Israelite law defines adultery differently for men and women. For a married woman, adultery is having sexual relations with anyone other than her husband. For a married man, adultery is having sexual relations with a woman who is married to another man. A married man may have sexual relations with an unmarried woman, as long as he then takes her as one of his wives (Exod. 22:16).

Akedah In Jewish tradition the story of Abraham nearly offering his son, Isaac, as a human sacrifice is called the *Akedah* story. This word is Hebrew for "binding," and is the word used for Abraham's binding of Isaac in Genesis 22:9.

Allegory An allegory is a complex story in which multiple imaginative elements represent real persons, places, or events. The story of the two sisters in Ezekiel 23 is a clear example of an allegory.

Altar In the early parts of the Bible, altars are open-air shrines where offerings are given to God. Eventually, the altar is the focal point in the Temple where the priests perform sacrificial rituals.

Annals Kings in the ancient Near East kept official records of their reigns. The Annals of the Kings of Israel and Annals of the Kings of Judah have not been preserved, but they are frequently mentioned by the books of 1,2 Kings as sources for these narratives.

Anoint As a symbolic action that identified a king in the ancient Near East, olive oil was poured on the king's head. This could be a private event or a public ceremony. The Bible describes Samuel's anointing of Saul and David.

Apocalypse The word *apocalypse* is derived from the Greek word for "reveal." An apocalypse is a literary work that typically reveals secrets about the future, often using highly charged imagery. This kind of literature typically assumes a dualistic understanding of good and evil that will culminate in a final battle between these two forces, which will lead to a new order. Isaiah 24–27 is sometimes labeled the *Isaian Apocalypse.*

Apocalyptic This adjective is often used to describe a particular worldview and the literature that arises from it. This worldview places great emphasis on the end of the age and a looming battle between good and evil in which God will achieve ultimate victory.

Apocalyptic Literature This is a type of literature dominated by apocalyptic elements, such as a strong sense of good versus evil dualism, coded language and bizarre imagery, secret knowledge, and a focus on a cataclysmic end of the world. In the Old Testament, Daniel 7–12 and Zechariah 9–14 are most often labeled apocalyptic literature. Isaiah 24–26 and the book of Joel may share some characteristics of apocalyptic literature, but they are more difficult to place in this category.

Apocrypha The Greek and subsequent Catholic canon both contain extra books not in the Hebrew and Protestant canons and additions to some of the books that are. This extra material, which includes books like 1 and 2 Maccabees and the Wisdom of Solomon and additions to the books of Daniel and Esther, is sometimes gathered together and printed at the end of Protestant Bibles and called the Apocrypha.

Apodictic Law Some laws in the Old Testament are given in short declarative statements, either positive or negative in form, with little or no explanation. Most of the Ten Commandments are apodictic laws.

Aramaic Aramaic is a northwest Semitic language closely related to Hebrew. It was the official language of empires like those of Babylon and Persia. Through the Exile and Restoration, it became the common language of Jews in Palestine. Portions of the books of Ezra and Daniel are written in this language. Eventually, all of the Hebrew Scriptures were translated into Aramaic.

Ark Although often pictured as a boat, the description sounds more like a large box. The Hebrew word that describes the vessel Noah built is not the same one that describes the container constructed by Moses called the *Ark of the Covenant.* The only other place this Hebrew word appears besides the Flood story is in the description of the container in which the baby Moses is placed in Exodus 2:4–5.

Ban In Joshua 6, as the battle of Jericho proceeds, Joshua instructs the Israelites not to keep materials, livestock, or people as spoils of war. All of the contents of the city are banned. Instructions for holy war that includes full destruction of a city and its contents appear in Deuteronomy 7:1–7.

Birthright In Genesis the oldest son in a family seems to have special status. When the father's property is divided, the oldest son receives an extra share. Esau trades away this extra share in Genesis 25. Joseph, the eleventh of Jacob's twelve sons, manages to acquire this extra share in Genesis 48.

Bronze Age Time periods in the ancient world are often divided according to the dominant metal used in making weapons and tools. There are no precise beginning and end points, but bronze replaced copper by about 3000 B.C.E. and was succeeded by iron by about 1200 B.C.E. The biblical matriarchs and patriarchs likely lived during the latter portion of this period.

Burnt Offering One type of offering described in Leviticus 1 is an animal that is burned on top of the altar by the priests. The intent is that the smoke goes up to God and provides a pleasing odor.

Call Narrative Many prophetic books provide an account of the prophet's initial experience. Some of them are brief reports identifying the prophet, while others are elaborate stories of a theophanic experience, like Isaiah 6.

Canon Any authoritative collection of literature can be given this designation. In relation to the Old Testament, the canon exists in three major forms: The scriptures Judaism known as the TANAK, the larger Old Testament canon of the Roman Catholic Church; and the Old Testament used by Protestant Churches, which matches the Jewish canon in content and the Catholic canon in order.

Casuistic Law As simple laws are applied in a variety of situations, a body of law grows and develops that answers the questions that arise. The case of the goring ox in Exodus 21:28–32 is an example of casuistic laws that develop as a simple law like "You shall not kill" is applied.

Census Twice in the book of Numbers the Israelites are counted. These counts seem to focus on the adult male population. Later, in 2 Samuel 24, David counts the Israelites, again only the adult males, and this act angers God.

Cherubim The cherubim appear to be winged angels or heavenly beings. They are depicted in some way on the ends of the mercy seat that covers the Ark of the Covenant and forms a throne for God. The cherubim guard the Garden of Eden after Adam and Eve are expelled, and they participate in the call experience of Isaiah in Isaiah 6.

Chiasm The writers of the Bible used a wide variety of literary forms and devices. A chiasm is a literary unit that uses matching elements at the beginning and end of the unit and works toward the center. The Greek letter *chi* is shaped like an X and can be used to demonstrate the shape of a literary unit that has a chiastic structure, so it was used to name this device.

Chronistic History The books commonly called 1 and 2 Chronicles tell the story of Israel from its creation to the Exile. This history, which parallels the one reported in the Bible's Primary History in Genesis–2 Kings, is sometimes called the *Chronistic History*. The books of Ezra and Nehemiah, which continue Israel's story after the Exile, are sometimes included in the Chronistic History.

Circumcision The act of cutting off the foreskin of the penis appears first in the Abraham stories in Genesis 17. The practice of circumcising Israelite males on the eighth day after birth is commanded in the law in Leviticus 12.

Cities of Refuge If a homicide was committed in ancient Israel, it was possible that the family of the person who was killed would take revenge before the case could be judged as deliberate or accidental. Texts like Exodus 21:12–14 and Deuteronomy 19:1–13 provide for places where the killer could flee and be protected until the case could be evaluated.

City-state When the Israelites arrived in the land of Canaan, likely around the end of the Bronze Age and the beginning of the Iron Age, it appears that walled cities and the area immediately around them were ruled individually. Over the next few centuries, this system was replaced by the kinds of territorial nations present during the Israelite monarchy.

Codex The term applied to manuscripts that are in what we understand as book form, with stacked pages of uniform size and some type of binding. Codices were developed around the beginning of the Common Era and gradually replaced scrolls over the next few centuries because of their ease of use and economy.

Concubine This English word typically designates a wife of secondary status, typically a slave or servant, in a polygamous culture. The Old Testament is not always clear in distinguishing such status. For example, Hagar is a servant of Sarah, but she is also Abraham's wife, and the Hebrew word typically translated as concubine, *pilegesh*, is not used in referring to her. Bilhah is called Jacob's *pilegesh* in Genesis 35:22.

Confessions A series of six or seven poems appears throughout Jeremiah 11–20, in which the prophet protests to God about his burdensome task and the way he is being treated. These poems are usually called either *Jeremiah's Laments* or *Jeremiah's Confessions.*

Covenant Code The Covenant Code is the name commonly given to the distinct set of laws that follow almost immediately after the Ten Commandments in the book of Exodus. The most common identification of its boundaries is 20:22–23:33. The code is dominated by casuistic laws and appears to be one of the oldest set of laws in the Pentateuch.

Cult In modern English this word is typically used in negative fashion to describe a closed, secretive religious group, usually one that is not considered orthodox. As a technical term in religious studies, it refers to any system of worship. Thus, the Old Testament laws concerning priests and ceremonies establish the ancient Israelite cult.

Cuneiform The earliest known form of writing, dating back to around 3000 B.C.E. It utilized a stylus with a pointed tip to make characteristically wedge-shaped markings on soft clay tablets, which were then hardened in ovens. Akkadian and Ugaritic are the two most significant languages that used this system, the latter of which is closely connected to Hebrew in terms of vocabulary and grammar.

Day of the LORD This is a phrase used frequently in The Book of the Twelve and may be its central theme. It can represent the coming of God either in judgment or salvation.

Decalogue This term, derived from the Greek words for "ten words," is often used to designate the collection of laws known as the "Ten Commandments." These laws are found in two slightly different forms in Exodus 20:2–17 and Deuteronomy 5:6–21. Neither passage makes any reference to the number ten, and the commands are enumerated in different ways by different traditions. The only reference to "ten words" in the Old Testament is in Exodus 34:28, and this seems most likely to be a reference to the law code immediately preceding it.

Deportation The carrying of many of the residents of Judah to Babylon happened in at least two acts of deportation. These deportations and the resulting captivity are collectively called the Exile.

Deuteronomistic History Modern biblical scholarship has arrived at a fairly unified position that the books immediately following Deuteronomy tell the story of Israel in the Promised Land from the same perspective that produced Deuteronomy. *Deuteronomistic History* is a contemporary academic term for Joshua, Judges, Samuel, and Kings.

Diaspora One result of the long succession of empires—Assyrian, Babylonian, Persian, Greek, and Roman—is that the Jewish people were scattered across most of the known world. Around the turn of the eras, there were Jewish communities in Egypt, Mesopotamia, Asia Minor, and Europe, as well as in Palestine. These Jewish people who lived outside Palestine are collectively called the *Diaspora.*

Dynasty A dynasty is a significant series of monarchs from the same family. In the Old Testament, Israel and then Judah were ruled by the Davidic dynasty for about four centuries.

Ephod In Exodus 25:7 the ephod is described as part of the priestly vestments in which stones are set. Elsewhere, it seems to be a garment worn during religious ceremonies by Samuel (1 Sam. 2:18) and David (2 Sam. 6:14). In Judges 8:27 Gideon makes a golden ephod that somehow becomes involved in idol worship.

Enuma Elish The name given to this ancient Babylonian creation narrative comes from the opening words in its text. This story, which appears to be much older than any of the creation stories in the Old Testament, tells of a conflict among the gods in which Marduk is victorious and which results in the creation of the earth and human beings. Many interpreters see Genesis 1 as a response to this Babylonian account of creation.

Ephraim Ephraim was the name of one of Joseph's sons in the book of Genesis and became the name of the most prominent Israelite tribe in the northern part of the nation. Because this tribe dominated the northern nation after the division of the kingdoms, it is sometimes used in the Old Testament as a synonym for the Northern Kingdom of Israel.

Exile Although *exile* can be used as a general term to describe the removal of a person or group of people from their land, the capitalized term is commonly used in the field of biblical studies to designate the period of captivity of the Israelites in Babylon.

Fable This term is used to describe various kinds of stories, including those about legendary persons of the past or those that include animal characters. The story told in Judges 9 by Jotham about trees negotiating about which tree will be their king is sometimes called *Jotham's Fable.*

Golden Calf This term typically refers to the story in Exodus 32, when the Israelites, confused about Moses' long absence from the camp at the foot of Mount Sinai, construct a golden image of a calf as a representation of YHWH. This event initiates a long and complex narrative in Exodus 32–34 that, among other things, elevates the status of the tribe of Levi, which will be rewarded with the position of priesthood for its assistance to Moses in quelling this revolt.

Governor Because Yehud remained a Persian province, the Israelite monarchy was not reestablished. It was ruled by a governor appointed by the Persian Empire. Nehemiah is the best known of these governors who ruled Yehud.

Hallelujah This word is a transliteration of a Hebrew phrase meaning "Praise Yah" or "Praise the Lord." The *hallelu* portion of the word is an imperative of the verb meaning "praise." The *jah* portion is a shortened form of God's unpronounceable name, YHWH. The shortened form apparently was pronounced. This phrase is especially prominent in many of the hymns of praise that appear near the end of the book of Psalms.

Hasidim The Hasidim were a sectarian group that arose during the second and first centuries B.C.E. within Judaism. This group was characterized by strict adherence to the Law and eventually separated from the Maccabeans because of the latter's overtly political activity.

Hasmoneans In the wake of the Maccabean Revolt, a succession of Jewish rulers, called *Hasmoneans*, ruled an independent Jewish state. Their dynasty lasted nearly a century, until the Romans conquered Palestine in 63 B.C.E.

Heavenly Court In two prominent places in Genesis, 1:26 and 11:7, God speaks in the first-person plural. The best explanation for this phenomenon is that Israelite tradition understood God to be accompanied by a large contingent of angels and other beings. This is portrayed in texts like Job 1 and Psalm 82.

Hellenistic This term is an adjective used to describe elements of Greek culture that spread throughout the ancient Near East with the military and political expansion of the Greek Empire beginning in the late fourth century B.C.E. Religions, literature, art, and philosophical systems are all commonly described using this adjective.

Hermeneutics The field of study that examines how interpretation works, particularly the interpretation of written texts. Modern hermeneutics is especially concerned with where and how meaning is determined.

High Places This is a pejorative term the Old Testament often uses for unauthorized worship sites. These may be places devoted to the worship of foreign gods, like Baal, or to Israel's God. The kings designated as reformers in Israel, like Hezekiah and Josiah, often destroyed these worship sites.

Holiness Code The material found in Leviticus 17–26 appears to be a distinctive set of laws that is particularly concerned with the purity of the people of Israel as a characteristic that sets them apart from other people. Scholars disagree concerning whether this code was a complete and distinct literary entity before being embedded within the book of Leviticus. This code addresses subjects such as the celebration of festivals and the treatment of slaves, which are addressed differently in other Old Testament law codes.

Hymn of Praise This common type of psalm is present throughout the book of Psalms but is more heavily concentrated in the second half. The sequence of *Hallelujah* psalms, Psalms 146–150, are prime examples of this type.

Imprecatory Psalms This is a term used to describe the psalms that are very negative, often violent in tone. They often ask God to take vengeance on the singer's enemies. These psalms are startlingly honest expressions of anger and hatred. Their presence in the book of Psalms presents interpretive problems for modern readers. Should we read the last verse of Psalm 137 in church?

Inscription This general term refers to ancient writings that were engraved in stone. Official inscriptions were typically commissioned by kings to record military exploits and building projects. The durability of such writings from the ancient world means that many of them are still being found in readable condition.

Iron Age The period beginning about 1200 B.C.E., when iron was the dominant metal used for making tools and weapons. The Israelites would have appeared in the land of Canaan around the beginning of this period.

Judgment Oracle An oracle is the form of prophetic speech we now find in literary form in the prophetic books of the Old Testament. A judgment oracle is one with a negative tone, which announces God's pending punishment of either Israel or its enemies.

Justice Justice is a frequent concern of the prophetic literature. The Hebrew words sometimes translated by this English word are words that can also be translated as "judgment" or "righteousness." The use of this term in books like Isaiah, Micah, and Amos has political, social, and economic dimensions.

Lament To lament means to complain about or mourn something. David's response to Saul's death, recorded in 2 Samuel 1, is described as a lament. This word is sometimes used to describe a category of poems. The song David sings in 2 Samuel 1:19–27 is an example of this type of poem. Lament psalms are the most common type found in the book of Psalms.

Leprosy In modern usage, this term designates a specific disease of the nervous system. The biblical words that are translated using this term likely referred to a variety of skin diseases that would have rendered a person unclean. Such diseases are mentioned frequently in Old Testament legal material, and one leper is healed by the prophet Elisha in 1 Kings 5.

Levant A French term designating the general area surrounding the eastern part of the Mediterranean Sea. Archaeologists and historians sometimes use this term as a nonpolitical designation for the land area that includes Israel.

Levirate Marriage Deuteronomy 25:5–10 is a legal text that requires a man to marry his brother's widow if his brother dies without having produced an heir. The first son produced by this levirate marriage is considered the son and heir of the dead brother. Genesis 38 and the book of Ruth tell stories in which this custom plays a role.

Maccabeans In the middle of the second century B.C.E., a group of Jewish warriors, led by Judas Maccabeus, rose up to overthrow Greek rule in Palestine. These warriors are often called *Maccabeans.*

Mantle This term is used in the Old Testament for various types of garments. Most significantly, it seems to be a garment that designates religious power and function. A mantle is worn by Samuel and by Ezra. The great prophet Elijah wore a mantle that, in 2 Kings 2:8, fell from him as he rode to heaven in a chariot at the end of his life and was picked up by his successor, Elisha.

Medium A medium is a person who performs supernatural acts, including communication with the dead. In 1 Samuel, Saul expels all the mediums from Israel, so he needs to travel to Endor to find a medium to conjure up the spirit of Samuel.

Megiddo This is the name of a large plain in the north central region of Israel. Because it is a vast, flat area, it has often been used throughout history as a battlefield. This is where Josiah confronted the Egyptians and was killed. This battlefield has taken on mythic proportions in the idea of a battle of Armageddon in which God will defeat the armies of evil.

Memoir This general term usually refers to a person's writings about the events of his life; thus, memoirs are typically written in first-person form. Most of the narrative in the Bible is written in third-person form by anonymous authors; however, Ezra–Nehemiah contains portions of first-person narrative from the perspectives of both Ezra and Nehemiah. These passages are often referred to as the *Ezra Memoir* (Ez. 7:27–9:15) and the *Nehemiah Memoir* (most of Neh. 1–7, 12:27–43, and 13:4–31).

Mercy Seat In Exodus 37:1–9 Moses supervises the building of the Ark of the Covenant by Bezalel. The cover of the Ark, which has cherubim at each end, is often called the *mercy seat.* In some descriptions the Ark appears to be at least a symbolic throne for God.

Merkabah The Hebrew word for "chariot" is often used to name the vision presented in the first chapter of the book of Ezekiel. This word does not appear in the text, but the description of "wheels" and movement has led many interpreters to understand this vision as a depiction of God's chariot.

Mesopotamia The general term for the land area in the southwest region of Asia, around the Tigris and Euphrates Rivers, which is the location of the modern nation of Iraq. This term itself is not used in the Bible, but this area was the home of empires such as those of Assyria and Babylon, which played a prominent role in Israel's story.

Middle Section of the Prophets This section consists of eight scrolls. The first four scrolls—Joshua, Judges, Samuel, and Kings—are designated the *Former Prophets.*

Mishnah Discussions and debates among great rabbis concerning the meaning of the Law were common within Judaism. During the early part of the Common Era, some of these debates were put in written form. Eventually an authoritative collection of rabbinic interpretation of the Torah, commonly called the *Mishnah,* was formulated and reached a fixed form in about 200 C.E. Versions of this collection are published as a single volume of about 1000 pages.

Molten Sea 1 Kings 7:23 reports that Solomon had a huge, round, bronze tank produced and placed in the Temple. This tank was filled with water and is commonly thought to have symbolized God's mastery over the sea.

Monarchy This term generally describes a form of government headed by a succession of leaders from a royal family. The Old Testament recognizes Saul as the first king of Israel. In Old Testament study the Monarchy refers to the period from Saul to the Exile when Israel was ruled by kings.

Mount Sinai After escaping from Egypt in Exodus 12, the Israelites are led by Moses through the wilderness until they arrive at a mountain in Exodus 19. The Bible most often calls this mountain Sinai, although there are biblical traditions that refer to it as *Horeb.* This is the traditional site of the giving of the Ten Commandments and the golden calf story. The actual location of Mount Sinai is uncertain, although the traditional site is a mountain called Jebel Musa near the southern tip of the Sinai Peninsula.

Nazirite Numbers 6 contains legal regulations for this special religious designation. Among other qualifications, Nazirites are not to cut their hair. Samson is dedicated as a Nazirite in Judges 13.

Nomad Many groups of people in the ancient world moved from place to place as different regions provided grazing plants for their livestock. Such wandering people are often called *nomads.* The early characters in the Bible are often described as *seminomads.* They would settle for significant periods of time but would move on when necessary.

Oracles In the Old Testament this term refers to prophetic speech. Oracles of various types appear in the prophetic books, typically as poetry, but sometimes in prose form. The relationship between the situation in which these oracles may have actually been spoken by the prophets and the literary contexts in which we now find them is uncertain.

Pagan This is a somewhat subjective term used to describe the practices and beliefs of other religions. From a Western Christian perspective, of course, *pagan* refers to any religious practice outside of the Jewish and Christian traditions. Within the study of the Old Testament, it refers to the religions of those around the Israelites, particularly the Canaanites.

Parallelism This is a literary device commonly used in Hebrew poetry, both in the prophetic books and in poetic books like Psalms and Proverbs. It consists of pairs, or sometimes triplets, of lines that are closely associated with one another. The relationship between the paired lines may vary from repetition of the same idea to posing of contrasting ideas.

Passover This word refers to the event recorded in Exodus 11–12, which involved the killing of the first-born of Egypt. It was this final plague that overcame Pharaoh's resistance to God's command to let the Israelites go. Passover also refers to the subsequent annual festival that commemorates this event. Instructions for this festival are first given in Exodus 12:1–21.

Pentateuch A word derived from the Greek used to designate the first five books of the Old Testament, the equivalent of what Jewish tradition sometimes calls the *Torah.* This term does not appear in the Bible, but is the most common designation among biblical scholars.

Personification Many times in the Bible, nonpersonal objects or abstract entities are portrayed as persons, or personified. Wisdom is personified in Proverbs 8–9, and the city of Jerusalem is personified in Lamentations and other places.

Philistines A group of people who occupied the coastal cities along the eastern and southeastern shores of the Mediterranean Sea in the Late Bronze through Early Iron ages. They were a persistent enemy of the Israelites; thus, the Bible paints them in a rather negative light. This led to the use of the word *philistine* as an adjective to describe a crude, unrefined person. Recent archaeological and anthropological studies have produced a more positive portrait of these ancient people.

Plague The biblical word that most precisely means plague, *magaphah,* appears only once in Exodus, in 9:14. Nevertheless, this English word appears more often in most English translations and is commonly used to designate all of the signs and wonders performed by God and Moses in Exodus 7–12.

Plenary Verbal Inspiration The belief that God spoke the actual words now present in the Bible to the human scribes who copied them onto the original scrolls of the Bible.

Prophet This term is used to describe a wide variety of individuals in the Old Testament. Samuel is one of the earliest. 1 Samuel 3:21–4:1 says that YHWH revealed himself to Samuel and that the word of Samuel came to all Israel. The task of speaking for God seems to be the primary factor that identifies a prophet.

Proverbs The Hebrew word *mashal* can refer to various types of sayings, including riddles, short stories, and wise sayings. The English word *proverb* usually refers to a short, easy-to-memorize saying. The Hebrew title of the book of Proverbs is *Mahalim,* and this book does contain a wide variety of literary material. The main body of the book, chapters 10–29, consists primarily of the kinds of sayings usually called proverbs.

Psalms The Hebrew title of the book of Psalms is *Tehillim,* which means "prayers." Psalm seems more closely related to the Hebrew word *mizmor,* which appears in the titles of many of the psalms and means "song." The word *psalm* itself comes from the Greek title of the book of Psalms, *Psalmi,* in the Septuagint.

Pseudepigraphical This word is derived from the Greek words that literally mean "false name." It became a common practice during the second and first centuries B.C.E. to write works of literature in the name of famous people from the past. Works like Enoch and the Testament of Adam are examples of pseudepigraphy. A large collection of Jewish writings that use this custom and other writings related to them are sometimes collectively called the *Pseudepigrapha.*

Ptolemies Ptolemy was a military commander under Alexander the Great. When Alexander died in 323 B.C.E., Ptolemy took control of a large part of the Greek Empire, centered in Egypt and sometimes including Palestine. The succession of leaders that followed him are sometimes called the *Ptolemies.*

Qoheleth This is the Hebrew name for the biblical book most often known in Christian tradition as Ecclesiastes. The word itself is used to designate the character who does most of the speaking in the book. It is a noun derived from the word for "gather." As a "person that gathers," this figure is most often referred to in English translations at "the Teacher" or "the Preacher."

Qumran Qumran is the name of a small settlement discovered by archaeologists near the Dead Sea. This settlement is very close to the caves where the Dead Sea Scrolls were found, so there has been a common assumption that the community that lived at Qumran produced, preserved, and hid the scrolls. These scrolls are even referred to sometimes as the *Qumran scrolls,* yet there is no direct evidence linking the two.

Restoration As a general term, *restoration* is used to describe numerous aspects of Israel's return to the land and rebuilding of its society after the Exile. More formally, *Restoration* designates the period in Israel's story beginning with the Decree of Cyrus and having an indefinite end point.

Retribution Theology Much of the Old Testament assumes a principle often called a *theology of retribution.* This may be simply expressed as the belief that the righteous who are obedient to God will be blessed, while the wicked who are disobedient will be cursed.

Sabbath The Torah defines the seventh day as the Sabbath day, which should be used for rest rather than work. Leviticus 26:34–39 also commands that the land be allowed to rest in the seventh, or Sabbath, year. Jeremiah claimed that the Exile was the result of Israel's failure to observe the land Sabbath.

Salvation Oracle The various forms of prophetic speech in the Old Testament are often labeled *oracles.* The oracles that have a mostly positive tone about how God will come to deliver Israel from its suffering and difficulties are called *Salvation Oracles.*

Samaritans By the time of the New Testament, this designation was used to a group of people of mixed heritage, including some Jewish background, but the origins of this group and this name given to them are uncertain. Some historians associate them with the disruption resulting from the Assyrian destruction of northern Israel in the eighth century B.C.E., but this is impossible to prove. The Samaritans appear to have had their own religious system and traditions, separate from the Second Temple system located in Jerusalem.

Samaritan Pentateuch The Samaritan people possessed a distinctive understanding of scripture, which included only the first five books of the Bible. The earliest manuscripts from this tradition come from the fifth or sixth centuries C.E., and they show some distinct differences from the Msoretic Text of the Hebrew Bible.

Satan This is a transliteration of a Hebrew word that first appears in the biblical tradition as a common noun meaning "adversary" or "accuser." Eventually, it became the proper name of a figure portrayed as God's archenemy in both Judaism and Christianity. There are no uses of this word in the Old Testament that clearly fit into this second category. In Job 1–2, the character with this designation is a member of the heavenly court, referred to as "the sons of God."

Second Temple This term distinguishes the rebuilt temple that replaced Solomon's temple. The Second Temple was completed by the restored Jerusalem community in about 515 B.C.E. It remained until it was replaced by Herod's temple five centuries later. The Jewish religion of this period is sometimes referred to as *Second Temple Judaism.*

Sect The term *sect* is usually applied to a smaller, well-defined group within a larger religion. Pharasism was a sect within Judaism, as was Christianity and the group that produced the Dead Sea Scrolls. At the turn of the eras, Judaism was characterized by a number of sectarian movements. Some might consider the Mormons or the Jehovah's Witnesses as sects within modern Christianity, but there is no consensus on the precise use of this word.

Seleucids Seleucus was a military commander under Alexander the Great. When Alexander died in 323 B.C.E., Seleucus took control of part of the Greek Empire, centered in Syria. The succession of rulers that followed him, including Antiochus the Great, are sometimes called *Seleucids.* The area they ruled sometimes included Palestine.

Siege A siege is a military strategy that was often used against walled cities in the ancient world. The attacking army would surround the city, not allowing anything or anybody to move in or out of it. Eventually, starvation and disease would weaken the inhabitants until they surrendered or were unable to defend themselves.

Septuagint This is the term most often used to designate the Greek translation of the Hebrew Scriptures into Greek, a process that likely began in the third century B.C.E. Aside from a few fragmentary documents among the Dead Sea Scrolls, this ancient version is only available in Christian manuscripts such as the Sinai Codex and the Vatican Codex.

Sign-Act Besides speaking the word of God, prophets in the Old Testament sometimes performed symbolic actions to communicate a message. Some of these actions, like Hosea's marriage to a prostitute, are integrated into the prophet's life. Others, like Ezekiel's lying on his side for hundreds of days, are more performance oriented.

Source Criticism The Bible itself acknowledges its use of prior sources, such as The Book of the Descendents of Adam (Gen. 5:1), The Book of the Wars of the LORD (Num. 21:14), and The Book of Jashar (Josh. 10:13). Source criticism is the attempt to identify and perhaps reconstruct some of these sources, particularly those used in the Pentateuch.

Succession The determination of the next ruler in a monarchy, the process called *succession,* is not always easy. In the Old Testament, kings are sometimes replaced by their oldest sons. This is called *dynastic succession.* At other times a king is chosen by a prophet, assumedly with Divine guidance.

Succession Narrative The Old Testament records a complex story of intrigue among those who wished to follow David on the throne. The account of these events in 2 Samuel 9–20 and 1 Kings 1–2 is often referred to as *The Succession Narrative.*

Suffering Servant The *Suffering Servant* is a term that has become a common designation for the servant figure or figures portrayed in the four Servant Songs in Isaiah. The second of these songs, in Isaiah 49, identifies the servant as Israel, but it is unclear whether this means the entire nation or certain representatives of it.

Sukkoth One of the festivals celebrated by Israel involved going out into the fields and living in small booths, or *sukkoth.* This was the festival of harvest ingathering celebrated at the end of the growing season. Instructions for this festival appear in several places, including Deuteronomy 16:13–15. This festival is celebrated by the restored community in Nehemiah 8.

Tabernacle In Exodus 25–31 God provides Moses with intricate instructions for constructing a tent and its contents to be used for worship. In Exodus 35–41 Moses and his helpers construct this tabernacle at the foot of Mount Sinai. The book of Leviticus typically refers to this object as the "Tent of Meeting." In the book of Numbers, the Israelites carry the tabernacle with them through the wilderness and set it up at each place they encamp. The tabernacle appears to be either a precursor to or a reverse projection of the temple in Jerusalem.

Talmud Additional rabbinic interpretations of the law, called the *Gemara,* were eventually added to the authoritative text of the *Mishnah.* There are two major versions of this huge collection, called the Talmud, which often fills about twenty large volumes.

TANAK The Hebrew canon is traditionally divided into three sections called *Torah* (Law), *Nebi'im* (Prophets), and *Kethubim* (Writings). The first letters of each of these sections are used to form an acronym that can be used to describe the Jewish Scriptures.

Targumim Because Aramaic replaced Hebrew as the common language of Jews living in Palestine during and after the Restoration, it eventually became necessary to translate the Jewish Scriptures into Aramaic. This unofficial body of Aramaic texts is called the *Targumim.*

Tell A flat-topped mound left behind by the accumulation of material from a long succession of human settlement at a particular location. Vertical trenches dug into these mounds reveal the layers left behind in different periods of settlement.

Textual Criticism The oldest documents related to the Old Testament exist as handwritten manuscripts far removed from their initial writing. The practice of comparing and contrasting all of the available manuscripts to understand the text and its transmission process is called textual criticism.

Theodicy Theodicy can be understood as an attempt to explain the existence of evil and suffering in the world, and particularly God's involvement in evil and suffering. This is perhaps the central theme of the book of Job, which appears to raise questions about Retribution Theology by portraying a righteous man who suffers severely.

Theophany *Theophany* refers to an appearance of God to a human being. God appeared to Abraham and Isaac, then later to Moses and the prophets. Sometimes these appearances seem to be in human form, while at other times they occur in phenomena like fire, smoke, or storms.

Torah This Hebrew word means "law" or "instruction." It eventually came to designate the first five books of the Hebrew Scriptures. Genesis—Deuteronomy, also called the *Pentateuch.* In Nehemiah 8:1, Ezra reads the book of the law of Moses to the gathered people of Israel. This may be the first time in the Bible that this word is used in a phrase that designates something like the form of the Pentateuch we have today.

Tribute Smaller nations often paid money and other materials to the kings of powerful empires to be left alone. Likewise, the subjects of a king would pay a portion of their produce or income for the benefit of his protection.

Vanity This English word is most commonly used to translate the Hebrew word *hebel* in the book of Ecclesiastes. *Hebel* can mean breath, something that is fleeting, or meaninglessness. When the King James Version used *vanity* to translate *hebel* in the seventeenth century, these words likely had very similar meanings. In modern English, vanity has come to mean primarily an obsession with surface appearances.

Vision The word *vision* is used to describe a variety of religious experiences in the prophetic literature. In Isaiah 1:1, the whole book of Isaiah, or a large part of it, is labeled a vision. Jeremiah (1:11–12) and Amos (8:1–2) have visions of fairly simple images that convey meaning through wordplay. Ezekiel has the most elaborate visions, such as the vision of God's glory in Ezekiel 1–2. It is not clear whether these are waking experiences that are different from dreams.

Vow Jacob makes the first biblical vow in Genesis 28:20. Leviticus 22 contains legal regulations concerning vows. In Judges 11, Jephthah makes a vow before a battle that results in the sacrifice of his daughter.

Whoredom Hosea was commanded by God to marry a wife of whoredom. It is not entirely clear whether this meant that she was a common prostitute, a cultic prostitute, or an unfaithful wife.

Wisdom As a technical term in Old Testament study, *wisdom* refers to a way of thinking and talking about the world embodied in the wisdom literature, which includes Proverbs, Ecclesiastes, Job, and the Wisdom Psalms. Whether wisdom ever became fully institutionalized in an Israelite school system is uncertain.

Wordplay The Hebrew prophets sometimes paired words that sounded alike to communicate a symbolic message. Amos, for example, reports seeing a vision of a basket of fruit (*qayits* in Amos 8:1–2). The accompanying message from God is that the end (*qets* in 8:2) is approaching for Israel.

Yehud After the Israelites were released from Babylonian captivity by the Persians, they returned to Judah but did not become a fully independent nation. Instead, their land became a province of the Persian Empire with limited autonomy. As a Persian province, the Jewish homeland was known as *Yehud.*

YHWH The name of God in the Hebrew text is not pronounceable because it has no vowels. God's personal name is represented by four consonants that are the equivalent of these four English consonants.

FOR FURTHER STUDY

CHAPTER 1

Biblical Archaeology Journals

Archaeology. A bimonthly magazine published by the Archaeological Institute of America that has occasional articles relating to biblical archaeology (*ARCH*).

Bible Review. A bimonthly magazine published by the Biblical Archaeology Society. It focuses on biblical interpretation using both archaeological and geographical information (*BR*).

Biblical Archaeologist (now *Near Eastern Archaeology*). A quarterly of the American Schools of Oriental Research. Its purpose is "to provide the general reader . . . with an interpretation of the meaning of new archaeological discoveries for the biblical heritage of the West" (*BA* or *NEA*).

Biblical Archaeology Review. A bimonthly magazine also published by the Biblical Archaeology Society. It has a popular magazine format and excellent photography (*BAR*).

Books on Archaeology

Avi-Yonah, Michael, and Ephraim Stern, eds. *Encyclopedia of Archaeological Excavations in the Holy Land,* 4 vols. (Englewood Cliffs, NJ: Prentice Hall, 1975–1978).

Coogan, Michael D., J. Cheryl Exum, and Lawrence E. Stager, eds. *Scripture and Other Artifacts: Essays in Honor of Philip J. King* (Louisville, KY: Westminster–John Knox Press, 1994).

Dever, William G. "Archaeology, Syro–Palestinian and Biblical," in *The Anchor Bible Dictionary* (hereafter, *ABD*), I. (Garden City, NY: Doubleday, 1992), 354–366.

Drinkard, Joel F., Gerald L. Mattingly, and J. Maxwell Miller, eds. *Benchmarks in Time and Culture: An Introduction to Palestinian Archaeology* (Atlanta: Scholars Press, 1988).

Hoerth, Alfred J. *Archaeology and the Old Testament* (Grand Rapids, MI: Baker, 1998).

Biblical Criticism

Alter, Robert. *The Art of Biblical Narrative* (New York: Basic Books, 1981).

Rofé, Alexander. *Introduction to the Composition of the Pentateuch* (Sheffield, UK: Sheffield Academic Press, 1999).

Tov, Emanuel. *Textual Criticism of the Hebrew Bible* (Minneapolis: Fortress Press, 1992).

Trible, Phyllis. *Rhetorical Criticism: Context, Method, and the Book of Jonah* (Minneapolis: Fortress Press, 1994).

Other Books and Articles on Old Testament Subjects

Harrelson, Walter. "The Hebrew Bible," in the *Mercer Commentary on the Bible* (hereafter, *MCB*) (Macon, GA: Mercer University Press, 1993), 13–22.

Harrington, Daniel J. "Introduction to the Canon," in *The New Interpreter's Bible* (hereafter, *NIB*), I (Nashville: Abingdon, 1994–2001), 7–13.

Matthews, Victor H. *Manners and Customs in the Bible: An Illustrated Guide to Daily Life in Bible Times* (Peabody, MA: Hendrickson, 1988).

Niditch, Susan. *Oral World and Written World: Ancient Israelite Literature* (Louisville, KY: Westminster, 1996).

Extrabiblical Texts

Abegg, Martin Jr., et al. *The Dead Sea Scrolls Bible: The Oldest Known Bible Translated for the First Time into English* (New York: HarperOne, 1999).

Hallo, William, and K. Lawson Younger, eds. *The Context of Scripture*, 3 vols. (Leiden: Brill, 1997–2002).

Martinez, Florentino, trans. *The Dead Sea Scrolls Translated: The Texts in English* (Leiden, The Netherlands: Brill, 1994).

Pritchard, James B. *Ancient Near Eastern Texts Relating to the Old Testament* (3rd ed. with supplements), 1969. (*ANET*).

————. *The Ancient Near East: An Anthology of Texts and Pictures,* 1958, and *Vol. II: A New Anthology of Texts and Pictures,* 1976.

CHAPTER 2

Aharoni, Yohanan, and Michael Avi-Yonah. *The MacMillan Bible Atlas,* rev. ed. (New York: Macmillan, 1977).

Aharoni, Yohanan. *The Land of the Bible,* trans. Anson P. Rainey (Louisville, KY: Westminster–John Knox Press, 1980).

Baly, Dennis. *The Geography of the Bible* (New York: Harper & Row, 1974).

Curtis, Adrian ed. *Oxford Bible Atlas,* 4th. ed. (New York: Oxford University Press, 2009).

Frank, Harry Thomas. *Discovering the Biblical World,* ed. James F. Strange (Maplewood, NJ: Hammond, 1988).

Hoerth, Alfred J., Gerald L. Mattingly, and Edwin M. Yamauchi, eds. *Peoples of the Old Testament World* (Grand Rapids, MI: Baker, 1994).

Pritchard, James B., ed. *The Harper's Bible Atlas* (New York: Harper & Row, 1987).

CHAPTER 3

Blenkinsopp, Joseph. *The Pentateuch: An Introduction to the First Five Books of the Bible* (New York: Doubleday, 1998).

Eskenazi, Tamara Cohn, and Andrea Weiss, eds. *The Torah: A Women's Commentary* (New York: URJ Press, 2007).

Freitheim, Terence E. "The Book of Genesis: Introduction, Commentary, and Reflections," *NIB*, I, 1994.

Humphreys, W. Lee. *The Character of God in the Book of Genesis* (Louisville, KY: Westminster, 2001).

Matthews, Victor H. *Manners and Customs in the Bible: An Illustrated Guide to Daily Life in Bible Times* (Peabody, MA: Hendrickson, 1988).

McEntire, Mark. *Struggling with God: An Introduction to the Pentateuch* (Macon, GA: Mercer University Press 2008).

Sarna, Nahum. *Genesis*, JPS Torah Commentary (Philadelphia: Jewish Publication Society, 1989).

Steinmetz, Devora. *From Father to Son: Kinship and Continuity in Genesis* (Louisville, KY: Westminster, 1991).

Turner, Laurence A. *Genesis* (Sheffield, UK: Sheffield Academic Press, 2000).

Urbock, William J. "Blessings and Curses," *ABD*, I, 755–761.

Westermann, Clauss. *Genesis: A Commentary*, 3 vols., trans. John J. Scullion (Minneapolis: Fortress Press, 1984–1986).

CHAPTER 4

Bellinger, W. H., Jr. *Leviticus, Numbers* (Peabody, MA: Hendrickson, 2001).

Brueggemann, Walter. "The Book of Exodus," *NIB*, I (Nashville: Abingdon Press, 1994).

Childs, Brevard. *The Book of Exodus*, Old Testament Library (hereafter, OTL) (Louisville, KY: Westminster–John Knox Press, 1974).

Durham, John I. "Exodus," *MCB*, 127-155.

Kaiser, Walter C., Jr. "The Book of Leviticus," *NIB*, I (Nashville: Abingdon Press, 1994).

Levine, Baruch A. *Numbers 1–20*, Anchor Bible (hereafter, AB), C4 (New Haven, CT: Yale University Press, 1993) and *Numbers 21–36*, AB, C4A, 2000.

Milgrom, Jacob. *Leviticus 1–16*, AB, C3, 1991, and *Leviticus 17-22*, AB, C3A, 2000, and *Leviticus 23-27*, AB, C3B, 2001.

Nelson, Richard. *Deuteronomy: A Commentary*, OTL, 2002.

Propp, William C. *Exodus 1–18*, AB, C2, 1999.

Sakenfeld, Katherine Doob. *Journeying With God: A Commentary on the Book of Numbers*, International Theological Commentary (hereafter, ITC) (Grand Rapids, MI: Eerdmans, 1995).

Sherwood, Stephen K. *Leviticus, Numbers, Deuteronomy* (Collegeville, MN: Liturgical Press, 2002).

Tullock, John H. "Deuteronomy," *MCB*, 201–226.

Weinfeld, Moshe. *Deuteronomy 1–11*, AB, C5, 1991.

CHAPTER 5

Ackerman, Susan. *Warrior, Dancer, Seductress, Queen: Women in Judges and Biblical Israel, ABRL*, 1998.

Gray, John. *Joshua, Judges, and Ruth*, NCBC, 1986.

Hamlin, E. John. *At Risk in the Promised Land*, ITC, 1990.

Nelson, Richard D. *Joshua: A Commentary,* OTL, 1997.

Schneider, Tammi J. *Judges.* Berit Olam (Minneapolis: Liturgical Press, 2000).

CHAPTER 6

Grizzard, Carol Stuart. "First and Second Samuel," *MCB*, 269–301.

McCarter, P. Kyle, Jr. *I Samuel*, AB, 8, 1980.

————. *II Samuel, AB,* 9, 1984.

Miller, J. Maxwell, and John H. Hayes. *A History of Ancient Israel and Judah,* vol. 20 (Louisville, KY: Westminster–John Knox, 2006).

Robinson, Gnana. *1 & 2 Samuel: Let Us Be Like the Nations*, ITC, 1993.

CHAPTERS 7 AND 8

Brueggeman, Walter. *1 & 2 Kings* (Macon, GA: Smyth & Helwys, 2001).

Cartledge, Tony. *1 & 2 Samuel* (Macon, GA: Smyth & Helwys, 2001).

Japhet, Sara. *I & II Chronicles: A Commentary*, OTL, 1993.

Smothers, Thomas M. "First and Second Kings," *MCB*, 303–322.

Williamson, H. G. M. *1 and 2 Chronicles*, New Century Bible commentary (hereafter, NCBC) (Grand Rapids, MI: Eerdmans, 1982).

CHAPTER 9

Ackroyd, Peter. *Exile and Restoration: A Study of Hebrew Thought of the Sixth Century* B.C.E. (Philadelphia: Westminster Press, 1968).

Albertz, Rainer. *Israel in Exile: The History and Literature of the Sixth Century* B.C.E., trans. David Green (Atlanta: Society of Biblical Literature, 2003).

Berlin, Adele. *Lamentations: A Commentary*, OTL, 2002.

Hillers, Delbert R. *Lamentations*, AB, 7A, 1972.

Holmgren Fredrick C. *Ezra–Nehemiah: Israel Alive Again*," ITC, 1987.

Middlemas, Jill. *The Templeless Age: An Introduction to the History, Literature, and Theology of the "Exile"* (Louisville, KY: Westminster, 2007).

Smith-Christopher, Daniel L. *A Biblical Theology of Exile* (Minneapolis: Fortress Press, 2002).

Williamson, H. G. M. *Ezra–Nehemiah* (Waco, TX: Word Publishing, 1985).

CHAPTER 10

Blenkinsopp, Joseph. *A History of Prophecy in Israel: From the Settlement of the Land to the Hellenistic Period* (Philadelphia: Westminster Press, 1983).

————. *Sage, Priest, and Prophet: Intellectual Leadership in Ancient Israel* (Louisville, KY: Westminster–John Knox Press, 1995).

————. *Isaiah*, 2 vols. The Anchor Bible (New York: Doubleday, 2000–2003).

Childs, Brevard. *Isaiah: A Commentary* (Louisville, KY: Westminster–John Knox Press, 2000).

Clements, Ronald E. *Isaiah 1–39*, NCBC, 1980.

Heschel, Abraham J. *The Prophets* (New York: Harper & Row, 1963).

Knight, George A. F. *Isaiah 40–55: Servant Theology*, ITC, 1983.

————. *Isaiah 56–66: The New Israel*, ITC, 1985.

Petersen, David L. *The Prophetic Literature* (Louisville, KY: Westminster–John Knox Press, 2002).

Seitz, Christopher, R. *Prophecy and Hermeneutics: Toward a New Introduction to the Prophets* (Grand Rapids, MI: Baker, 2007).

Whybray, R. N. *Isaiah 40–66*, NCBC, 1981.

CHAPTER 11

Brueggemann, Walter. *Jeremiah 1–25: To Pluck Up, to Tear Down*, ITC, 1988.

————. *Jeremiah 26–52: To Build, To Plant*, ITC, 1988.

————. *The Theology of the Book of Jeremiah* (Cambridge: Cambridge University Press, 2007).

Eichrodt, Walther. *Ezekiel*, trans. Crosslet Quin, OTL, 1980.

Greenburg, Moshe. *Ezekiel, 1–20*, AB, 22, 1983.

————. *Ezekiel, 21–37*, AB, 22A, 1997, 1995.

Holladay, William L. *Jeremiah 1*, Hermeneia (hereafter, HER) (Minneapolis: Fortress, 1986).

————. *Jeremiah 2*, HER, 1990.

Lundbom, Jack R. *Jeremiah 1–20*, AB, 21A, 1999.

Vawter, Bruce, and Leslie J. Hoppe. *Ezekiel: A New Heart*, ITC, 1991.

Zimmerli, Walther. *Ezekiel 1*, HER, 1979.

————. *Ezekiel 2*, HER, 1983.

CHAPTER 12

Andersen, Francis I., and David Noel Freedman. *Amos*, AB, 24A, 1989.

————. *Micah*, in *AB*, 24E, 2000.

Beeby, H. D. *Hosea: Grace Abounding*, ITC, 1989.

Berlin, Adele. *Zephaniah*, AB, 25A, 1994.

Crenshaw, James L. *Joel*, AB, 24C, 1995.

Hill, Andrew E. *Malachi*, AB, 25D, 1998.

Mays, James L. *Hosea*, OTL, 1969.

Meyers, Carol L., and Eric M. Meyers. *Haggai–Zechariah 1–8*, AB, 25B, 1998.

————. *Zechariah 9-14*, AB, 25C, 2004.

Paul, Shalom M. *Amos*, HER, 1995.

Rabbe, Paul R. *Obadiah*, AB, 24D, 1996.

Sasson, Jack M. *Jonah*, AB, 24B, 1995.

Steinmuller, Carroll. *Haggai and Zechariah: Rebuilding with Hope*, ITC, 1988.

Sweeney, Marvin. *The Book of the Twelve*, 2 vols. (Minneapolis: Liturgical Press, 2001).

CHAPTER 13

Anderson, Bernhard W. *Out of the Depths: The Psalms Speak to Us Today* (Louisville, KY: Westminster–John Knox Press, 1974).

Blenkinsopp, Joseph. *Wisdom and Law in the Old Testament* (London: Oxford University Press, 1983).

Clifford, Richard J. *Proverbs: A Commentary*, OTL, 1999.

Clines, David J. A. *Job*, 3 vols. (Waco, TX: Word Publishing, 1989–2006).

Craigie, Peter C., Marvin E. Tate, and Leslie C. Allen. *Psalms*, 3 vols. (Waco, TX: Word Publishing, 1983–1990).

Crenshaw, James L. *Ecclesiastes: A Commentary* (Louisville, KY: Westminster–John Knox Press, 1987).

————. *Old Testament Wisdom.* rev. and enl. ed. (Louisville, KY: Westminster–John Knox Press, 1998).

————. *Education in Ancient Israel: Across the Deadening Silence* (New York: Doubleday, 1998).

Exum, Cheryl E. *Song of Songs: A Commentary* (Louisville, KY: Westminster–John Knox Press, 2005).

Fox, Michael V. *Proverbs 1–9*, AB, 18A, 2000.

Gammie, John G., and Leo G. Perdue, eds. *The Sage in Israel and in the Ancient Near East* (Winona Lake, WI: Eisenbrauns, 1990).

Gunkel, Hermann. *The Psalms: A Form-critical Introduction*, trans. T. M. Horner (Louisville, KY: Westminster–John Knox Press, 1967). This is a Facet paperback giving the essentials of Gunkel's pioneering work in Psalms.

Holladay, William L. *The Psalms Through Three Thousand Years: Prayerbook of a Cloud of Witnesses* (Minneapolis: Fortress Press, 1993).

Janzen, J. Gerald. *Job: A Commentary for Teaching and Preaching* (Louisville, KY: Westminster, 1985).

Kugel, James L. *The Idea of Biblical Poetry: Parallelism and Its History* (New Haven, CT: Yale University Press, 1981).

McCann, J. Clinton. *A Theological Introduction to the Book of Psalms: The Psalms as Torah* (Nashville: Abingdon Press, 1993).

Mowinckel, Sigmund. *The Psalms in Israel's Worship*, 2 vols., trans. D. R. Ap-Thomas (Nashville: Abingdon Press, 1962). Mowinckel is second only to Gunkel in his influence on modern studies in the Psalms.

Murphy, Roland E. "Wisdom Literature: Job, Proverbs, Ruth, Canticles, Ecclesiastes, Esther," *FOTL*, XXVIII.

Perdue, Leo G., and W. Clark Gilpin. *The Voice from the Whirlwind: Interpreting the Book of Job* (Nashville: Abingdon Press, 1992).

Pope, Marvin H. *Job*, AB, 15, 1965.

————. *Song of Songs*, AB, 7C, 1995.

Rad, Gerhard von. *Wisdom in Israel*, trans. James D. Martin (Nashville: Abingdon Press, 1973).

Seow, Choon–Leong, *Ecclesiastes*, AB, 18C, 1997.

Westermann, Claus. *The Living Psalms* (Grand Rapids, MI: Wm. B. Eerdmans, 1989).

CHAPTER 14

————. *The Apocalyptic Imagination: An Introduction to Jewish Apocalyptic Literature* (Grand Rapids, MI: Wm. C. Eerdmans, 1998).

Campbell, Edward F. *Ruth*, AB, 7, 1975.

Collins, John J. "Early Jewish Apocalypticism," *ABD*, 282–288.

————. *Daniel*, HER, 1994.

Hanson, Paul D. *The Dawn of Apocalyptic: The Historical and Sociological Roots of Jewish Apocalyptic Eschatology* (Philadelphia: Fortress Press, 1979).

Lacoque, Andre. *The Book of Daniel* (Louisville, KY: Westminster–John Knox Press, 1979).

Moore, Carey. *Esther*, AB 7B, 1995.

Russell, D. S. *The Method and Message of Jewish Apocalyptic* (Louisville, KY: Westminster–John Knox Press, 1964).

Towner, Sibley. *Daniel: A Commentary for Teaching and Preaching*, (Louisville, KY: Westminster, 1984).

CHAPTER 15

Berquist, John L. *Judaism in Persia's Shadow: A Historical and Social Approach* (Minneapolis: Augsburg Fortress, 1995).

Brueggemann, Walter. *Theology of the Old Testament: Testimony, Advocacy, Dispute* (Minneapolis: Fortress Press, 1997).

Carmody, John, et al. *Exploring the Hebrew Bible* (Englewood Cliffs, NJ: Prentice Hall, 1988).

Charlesworth, James H., ed. *The Old Testament Pseudepigrapha*, Vols. 1 and 2 (New York: Doubleday, 1983, 1985).

Coggins, R. J. *Samaritans and Jews: The Origins of Samaritanism Reconsidered* (Louisville, KY: Westminster–John Knox Press, 1975).

Fishbane, Michael. *Biblical Interpretation in Ancient Israel* (Oxford: Oxford University Press, 1989).

Gottwald, Norman K. *The Hebrew Bible: A Socio–Literary Introduction* (Minneapolis: Augsburg Fortress, 1985).

Kugel, James. *The Bible as It Was* (Cambridge, MA: Belknap Press, 1997).

Levenson, Jon D. *Creation and the Persistence of Evil: The Jewish Drama of Divine Omnipotence* (San Francisco: Harper & Row, 1988).

Levison, John, and Priscilla Pope-Levison, eds. *Return to Babel: Global Perspectives on the Bible* (Louisville, KY: Westminster–John Knox Press, 1999).

Miles, Jack. *God: A Biography* (New York: Vintage Press, 1995).

Neusner, Jacob. *Rabbinic Judaism: Structure and System* (Minneapolis: Augsburg Fortress, 1995).

Nickelsburg, George W. E. *Jewish Literature between the Bible and the Mishnah*, 2nd ed. (Minneapolis: Fortress, 2005).

COMPREHENSIVE CHRONOLOGICAL CHART

ISRAELITE HISTORY		*THE LARGER WORLD*
EARLY BRONZE AGE 3000–2200 B.C.E.		
		First Sumerian Empire 2800–2350
		Egyptian Old Kingdom 2900–2300
		Akkadian Empire 2360–2180
		Ebla 2400–2250
MIDDLE BRONZE AGE 2200–1550 B.C.E.		
		Sumerian resurgence 2060–1950
		Amorites enter the Fertile Crescent
		Hammurabi c. 1728–1686
		The "Mari Age" 1750–1697
		Hyksos Rule in Egypt 1720–1570
LATE BRONZE AGE 1500–1200 B.C.E.		
		Hurrian kingdom (Mitanni)
The sojourn in Egypt		<u>Egypt</u>
		Amarna Age 1500–1370
		Amenhotep IV 1370–1353
		Nineteenth Egyptian Dynasty 1305–1200
		Seti 1305–1290
		Ramses II 1290–1224
The Exodus 1290–900 B.C.E.		
Wilderness wanderings 1290–1250 (?)		Merneptah invades Palestine 1224
Conquest and settlement 1250–1200 (?)		State of Merneptah 1220
IRON AGE I 1200–900 B.C.E.		
Period of the Judges 1200–1020 B.C.E.		Philistines settle in Palestine twelfth century
Fall of Shiloh 1050		
Samuel and Saul 1020–1000		
The United Kingdom 1000–922 B.C.E.		
David 1000–961		
Solomon 961–922		
Solomon dies–the kingdom divides 922		
THE DIVIDED KINGDOMS		
JUDAH	ISRAEL	
Rehoboam 922–915	Jeroboam 922–901	<u>Egypt</u>
Abijah 915–913		Shishak invades Palestine 918
IRON AGE II 900–600 B.C.E.		
		<u>Assyria</u>
Asa 913–873	Nadab 901–900	Assyrian power increases
	Baasha 900–877	
	Elah 877–876	
	Zimri (7 days) 876	
	Omri 876–869	

HEBREW HISTORY		*THE LARGER WORLD*
Jehoshaphat 873–849	Ahab 869–850 (Elijah)	Shalmaneser III 859–825 Battle of Qarqar 853
Jehoram 849–842	Jehoram 849–842 Jehu's rebellion 842	
(Athaliah 842–837) Joash 837–800 Amaziah 800–783 Uzziah (Azariah) 783–742	Jehu 842–815 Jehoahaz 815–801 Jehoash 801–786 Jeroboam II 786–746 (Amos)	
	Zechariah 746–745 (6 mo.) (Hosea) Shallum (1 mo.)	Tiglath–Pilesar III 745–727
Jotham 742–735 (Isaiah)	Menahem 745–738 Pekehiah 738–737	Israel pays tribute to Assyria
Ahaz 735–715 (Micah) Syro–Ephraimitic Crisis 735–732	Pekah 737–732	
	Hoshea 732–724 Samaria falls to Assyria 722–721	Shalmaneser V 727–722 Sargon II 722–705 Sennacherib 705–681
The Kingdom of Judah 722–587 Hezekiah 715–687/86 Sennacherib's invasion 701 Sennacherib's second invasion (?) 690		
Manasseh 687/86–642 Amon 642–640 Josiah 640–609		Rise of the Babylonian Empire
(Zephaniah, Nahum) (Habakkuk, Jeremiah)		Fall of Nineveh 612
Jehoahaz 609 Jehoiakim 609–598		Final defeat of Assyria at Haran 609 Nebuchadnezzar 605–562 Battle of Carchemish 605 Period of Babylonian dominance
Jehoiachin 598–597 Jerusalem falls–first deportation of the Jews 597 Zedekiah 597–587/86 Second fall of Jerusalem–second deportation 587/86 Governorship of Gedaliah 586–582 Third deportation 582		
IRON AGE III 600–? B.C.E.		
Babylonian Exile 587–538 (Ezekiel 593–573)		Nabonidus 556–538 (father of Belshazzar) Rise of Persia Cyrus II 550–530 conquers Media (550) and Lydia (546) and Babylon (539)
Deutero-Isaiah (540) Edict of Cyrus–First return of Jews (538) Second return (520)		Cambyses 530–522

HEBREW HISTORY	*THE LARGER WORLD*
Rebuilding of Temple 520–515–(Haggai and Zechariah)	Darius I 522–486
	Persia controls Egypt 525–401
(Malachi c. 500–450)	Xerxes (Ahasuerus) 486–465
[Ezra's mission 458 (?)]	Artaxerxes I (Longimanus) 465–424
Nehemiah's first governorship 445–433	
[Ezra's mission 428 (?)]	
Nehemiah's second governorship 430 (?)	Xerxes II 423
	Darius II 423–404
	Artaxerxes II (Mnemon) 404–358
(Ezra's mission 498 [?])	Artaxerxes III 358–336
	Darius III 336–331

EMPIRE OF ALEXANDER THE GREAT 336–323

At Alexander's death, his empire was divided among four of his generals. Of these, Ptolemy, who controlled Egypt, and Seleucus are important for Old Testament history and Jewish history.

Ptolemies and Seleucids

400–198 B.C.E. Palestine was controlled by Egypt and the Ptolemies. Antiochus III (223–187) wrested control of Palestine from Ptolemy V (203–181) in 198 B.C.E.

	<u>Seleucid Rulers</u>
	Antiochus III (the Great), 223–187
	Seleucus IV 187–175
Maccabean Revolt (168/67)	Antiochus IV (Epiphanes) 175–163
Judas (the Maccabee) 166–160	Antiochus V 163–162
Jonathan, 160–143	Demetrius 162–150
	Alexander Balas 150–145
Simon 143–134 (Jewish independence won)	Demetrius II 145–138
John Hyrcanus 134–104	

<u>63 B.C.E.–Pompey conquers Jerusalem, ending Jewish independence</u>

*Note: Names of kings are underlined to indicate a change in dynasty. Athaliah is parenthesized (1) because she was the only woman ruler and (2) she was the only non-Davidic ruler in Judah. Other parentheses indicate significant events during a king's reign.

CREDITS

Figure	Credit Line
1-2	Hershel Shanks/Zev Radovan
1-4	Laurence Pordes © Dorling Kindersley, Courtesy of The British Library
1-4	By permission of The British Library
2-3	Getty Images/Retrofile
2-4	Louis Goldman/Photo Researchers, Inc.
2-5	Erich Hartmann/Magnum Photos, Inc.
2-6	J. Allan Cash/Rapho/Photo Researchers, Inc.
2-7	Richard T. Nowitz/Richard Nowitz Photography
2-8	© Judith Miller/Dorling Kindersley/Richard Gardner Antiques
3-1	Used by permission of Broadman Films
3-Box	Alistair Duncan © Dorling Kindersley
4-1	Inge Morath/Magnum Photos, Inc.
4-2	John H. Tullock
4-3	Used by permission of Broadman Films
4-4	© MICHELE MOLINARI/DanitaDelimont.com
4-Box	Peter Dennis © Dorling Kindersley
5-2	Alistair Duncan/Dorling Kindersley Media Library
5-3	Peter Dennis © Dorling Kindersley
6-1 and 6-2	John H. Tullock
6-Box	Peter Dennis © Dorling Kindersley
7-1	© Z. Radovan, Jerusalem
7-3	© ANCIENT ART & ARCHITECTURE/DanitaDelimont.com
7-Box	Peter Dennis © Dorling Kindersley
8-1	Zev Radovan/Woodfin Camp & Associates, Inc.
8-2	Richard Nowitz Photography
8-3	Copyright Scala/Art Resource, NY
8-6	Richard T. Nowitz/Richard Nowitz Photography
8-7	John H. Tullock
8-8	Courtesy of the Library of Congress
8-Box	Peter Dance © Dorling Kindersley
9-2	Mercer University Press
9-3	Peter Dennis © Dorling Kindersley
10-1	Mercer University Press
10-2	John H. Tullock
10-3	David Rogers/Israel Office of Information
10-4	Peter Dennis © Dorling Kindersley
11-2	Nick Hewetson © Dorling Kindersley
11-Box	Chris Orr © Dorling Kindersley
12-2	Maynard Owen Williams/NGS Image Collection
12-3	Alistair Duncan © Dorling Kindersley
13-2	© Dorling Kindersley
14-Box	© Lebrecht Music and Arts Photo Library/Alamy
14-2	Corbis/Bettmann
14-3	Demetrio Carrasco © Dorling Kindersley
15-1	© Dorling Kindersley
COVER	Réunion des Musées Nationaux/Art Resource, NY

INDEX

E

F

G

I

J

K

N

O

Q

R

S

GREECE
30° Black
Sea
Istanbul
Troy
Aegean
Sea
Ankara
Bogaskoy
(Bogazkale)
TURKEY
Halys River
Kayseri
Konya
(Iconium)
Sardis
Barak
(Carchemish)
Tarsus
Til Barsi
35°
Alalakh
Halab
(Aleppo
Ra's Shamrah
(Ugarit)
CYPRUS
Hamath
Arvad
SYR
Mediterranean
Sea
Jubayl (Byblos)
Beirut
LEBANON
Sidon
Damascus
Tyre
Dan
Hazor
Meggido
Ramtha
Samaria
Beth-shan
Shechem
ISRAEL
Amman
Jerusalem
Jericho
Gaza
Hebron
Dead Sea
Alexandria
Beersheba
35°
30°
JORDAN
Suez
Canal
Cairo
Memphis
Elat
Al Aqabah
Gulf of Suez
Gulf of Aqaba
EGYPT
Tel el-Amarna
Nile River
Red Sea
Thebes
Western Thebes
(Karnak)
25°
Luxor
30°
35°

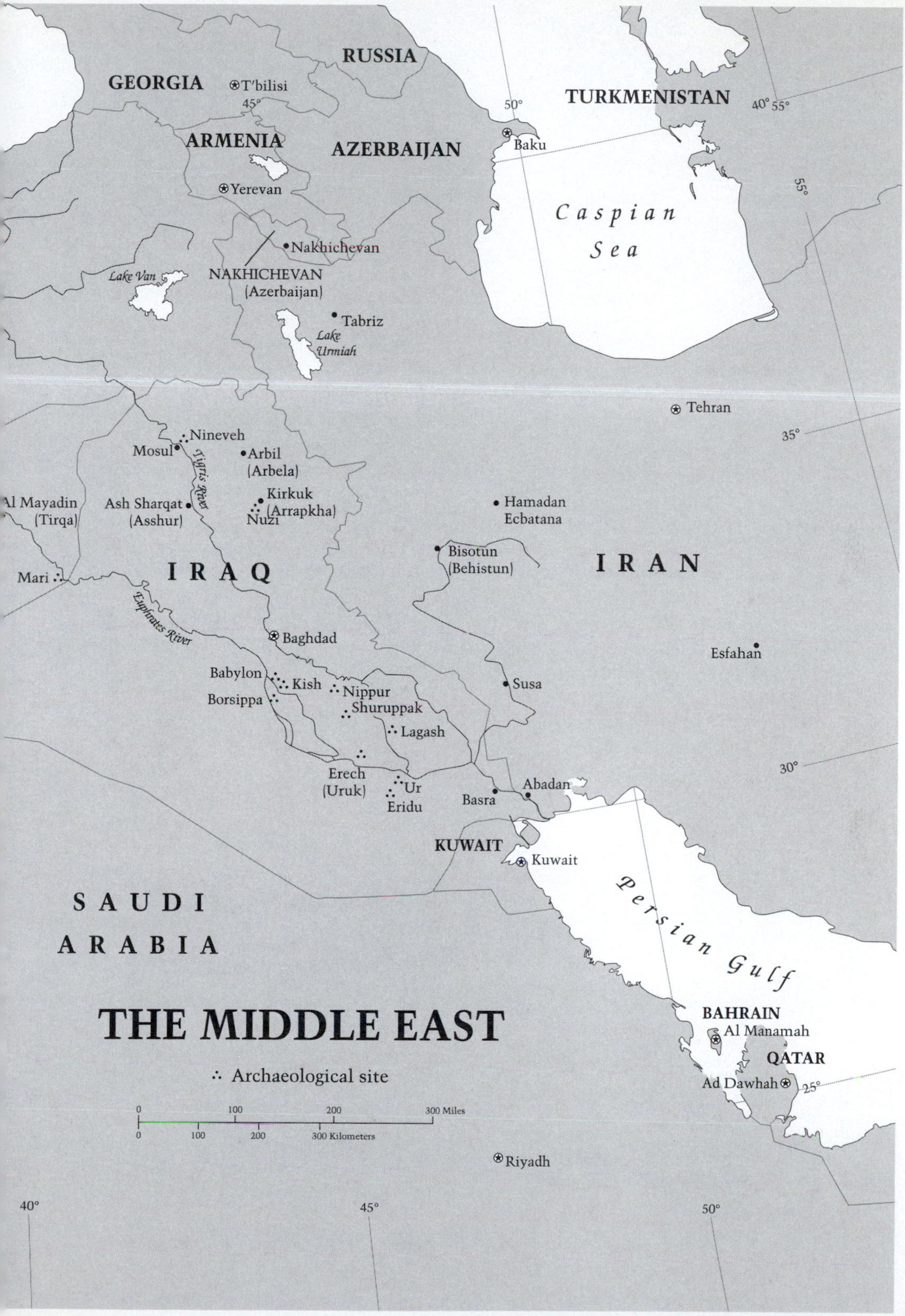

THE MIDDLE EAST
∴ Archaeological site
0 100 200 300 Miles
0 100 200 300 Kilometers
RUSSIA
GEORGIA
T'bilisi
ARMENIA
AZERBAIJAN
TURKMENISTAN
Baku
Yerevan
Caspian Sea
Nakhichevan
NAKHICHEVAN
(Azerbaijan)
Lake Van
Tabriz
Lake Urmiah
Tehran
Nineveh
Mosul
Arbil
(Arbela)
Tigris River
Al Mayadin
(Tirqa)
Ash Sharqat
(Asshur)
Kirkuk
(Arrapkha)
Nuzi
Hamadan
Ecbatana
Bisotun
(Behistun)
IRAQ
IRAN
Mari
Euphrates River
Baghdad
Esfahan
Babylon
Kish
Nippur
Borsippa
Shuruppak
Susa
Lagash
Erech
(Uruk)
Ur
Eridu
Basra
Abadan
KUWAIT
Kuwait
SAUDI
ARABIA
Persian Gulf
BAHRAIN
Al Manamah
QATAR
Ad Dawhah
Riyadh
40°
45°
50°
55°
35°
30°
25°